SELECTED PROSE OF

JOHN

HAMILTON

REYNOLDS

SELECTED PROSE OF

JOHN
HAMILTON
REYNOLDS

EDITED BY

LEONIDAS M. JONES

HARVARD UNIVERSITY PRESS

CAMBRIDGE, MASSACHUSETTS

1966

Distributed in Great Britain by Oxford University Press, London

Publication of this book has been aided by a
grant from the Hyder Edward Rollins Fund

Library of Congress Catalog Card Number: 66–15653

Made and printed in Great Britain by
William Clowes and Sons, Limited, London and Beccles

To the memory of
HYDER EDWARD ROLLINS
(1889–1958)
Scholar, Teacher, Friend

ACKNOWLEDGMENTS

It is my pleasant privilege to thank the following for assistance: Willard B. Pope of the University of Vermont, specifically for his catalogue of the Leigh-Browne Collection in the Keats Memorial House and generally for advice over a great many years; Walter Jackson Bate of Harvard University for initial encouragement of the project and helpful suggestions thereafter; William R. Maidment, Librarian of the London Borough of Camden and Curator of the Keats Memorial House, and the Libraries and Arts Committee of the London Borough of Camden for permission to reproduce as frontispiece a photograph of the miniature of Reynolds by Joseph Severn in the Keats Memorial Library, Hampstead, and to list the manuscript poems and letters by Reynolds in the Leigh-Browne Collection; and William H. Marshall and the University of Pennsylvania *Library Chronicle* for permission to reprint his excellent annotation to Reynolds' "Pulpit Oratory" series from *The Yellow Dwarf*.

I also thank my colleagues at Vermont, John H. Kent for assisting me with Greek quotations and Maurice E. Kohler for verifying translation from French. Miss Mary B. Fell, formerly Reference Librarian in the Bailey Library at Vermont, was unusually helpful in clarifying some obscure allusions.

I am also indebted to the University of Vermont for a Summer Research Grant to provide time and for an Institutional Research Grant to cover some of the clerical expenses.

L.M.J.

Burlington, Vermont
January 1966

CONTENTS

SELECTED PROSE OF
JOHN HAMILTON REYNOLDS

INTRODUCTION

During his later years John Hamilton Reynolds described himself as one who had "walked through life with a skeleton of reputation without a particle of name."[1] For a man who had once cherished the idea of fame as much as his intimate friend Keats, that loss was a bitter disappointment. He would have been pleased if he could have anticipated that after the lapse of a century scholars would be moderately successful in tracking his life and works.[2]

Born at Shrewsbury on September 9, 1794, the son of George (1764?–1853) and Charlotte Cox Reynolds (1761–1848), he had one older sister, his favorite Jane (1791–1846), and three younger sisters, Mariane (1797–1894), Eliza Beckford (1799–1870), and Charlotte (1802–1884). In 1803 he entered Shrewsbury School, remaining until 1806 when his father, who was a writing master and school master, moved the family to London. From March 4, 1806, until 1810 he was educated at St. Paul's School, where he relieved the academic routine by attending the theater[3] and by reading and dreaming over the ballads in Percy's *Reliques*.[4] During the years that he worked as a junior clerk in the Amicable Insurance office from about July 18, 1810, until April 24, 1816, he began his first attempts at literature, submitting verses to *The Gentleman's Magazine* from October 1812 and publishing *Safie* (1814), an imitation of Byron's metrical tales; *The Eden of Imagination* (1814), a long reflective poem showing Wordsworth's influence; and an *Ode* (1815) on the overthrow of Napoleon. In 1814 he began his long career of writing regularly for periodicals by contributing several poems, a prose "Character of Hamlet," and probably the unsigned theatrical reviews to John Martin's *Inquirer, or Literary Miscellany*, a quarterly magazine running for only three numbers. It is a minor misfortune that these early prose pieces,

[1] Hyder E. Rollins, *The Keats Circle, Letters and Papers, 1816–1878*, 2 vols. (Cambridge, Mass., 1948), II, 468.
[2] The following summary of Reynolds' career draws heavily on earlier scholarship, which is itemized below, in the Selected Bibliography.
[3] Dramatic Review, *The Champion*, May 25, 1817.
[4] *The London Magazine*, 4 (July 1821): 8–9.

I

first identified by George L. Marsh and never seen by this writer, seem lost irrecoverably, since bombing in World War II destroyed the volume in the British Museum, and the prospect of finding another copy is slight.

Several of Reynolds' poems reveal that about 1814 the death of a girl whom he loved clouded his life for a time, but we can hardly suppose that the tragedy scarred him permanently since he fell in love again within two years. More happily, in 1814 he met Benjamin Bailey through James Rice; the three quickly became close friends. In the next year Rice introduced Reynolds and Bailey to the Leigh sisters of Sidmouth, Mary, Sarah, and Thomasine. During March 1815 the three young men wrote over a hundred poems in a commonplace book of the Leigh girls, and on December 25, 1816, Reynolds and Bailey presented to Thomasine Leigh a manuscript, "Poems by Two Friends," containing twenty-five poems by Reynolds and thirty-two by Bailey. The Leighs introduced Reynolds to their friend Eliza Powell Drewe of Exeter, with whom he fell in love by the summer of 1816, though their marriage was delayed for six years probably because of Reynolds' need to establish himself financially.

Meanwhile, having left the Amicable Insurance office, Reynolds decided to try his fortune at journalism and literature, contributing regularly to John Scott's *The Champion* literary essays, theatrical reviews, and original verses, as well as assisting generally in the conduct of the periodical. Having been encouraged earlier by Byron's praise of *Safie*, in the summer of 1816 he pinned his young hopes to *The Naiad*, a long poem dedicated to a new and equally ambitious friend, Benjamin Robert Haydon, and published by Taylor and Hessey in August. The anxiously awaited letter from Wordsworth, to whom he had sent a copy through Haydon, momentarily disappointed him with a large measure of censure relieved by only slight praise. But that temporary disappointment soon gave way to revived ambition as he entered the finest five years of his life with his introduction to Keats in October 1816.

The familiar story of their close friendship as revealed in Keats's letters need not be repeated in detail here. It is sufficient to recall that, quickly recognizing Keats's genius and unusual virtues, he associated intimately with him; that he introduced Keats to a circle of valuable friends including Rice, Bailey, Charles Wentworth Dilke, Charles Brown,

John Martin, John Taylor, James Augustus Hessey, and Richard Wood-house; that he stimulated Keats to write *Isabella*, *Robin Hood*, the epistle *To J. H. Reynolds, Esq.*, and numerous short pieces; that his discussions and correspondence elicited from Keats some of his finest letters on poetry; and that he championed Keats's reputation vigorously, reviewing *Poems* of 1817 and *Endymion* favorably, encouraging sympathetic reviews from others, preventing him from publishing the first brash preface to *Endymion*, and generally counteracting some of the unfortunate aspects of Leigh Hunt's influence. In evaluating Reynolds' unselfishness and clear-sightedness, we should remember that Hunt praised Reynolds equally with Keats and Shelley in "Young Poets," and that Hazlitt read an entire poem by Reynolds in a public lecture, while merely echoing faintly a line from Keats. Yet Reynolds never confused his talent with his friend's genius. The association with Keats, however, stimulated his own work, as he continued to produce substantial material for the periodicals, and at the same time wrote most of the poems which later went into his finest collection of poetry, *The Garden of Florence* (1821).

On November 4, 1817, Reynolds became an articled pupil in the law office of Francis Fladgate (1773–1821), a relative of his friend Rice, and thereafter divided his attention between literature and law in such a manner that eventually both his interests suffered. He began early to vacillate between interest in the law and objection to the dreariness of the profession, as we can see from the sharp difference between Keats's extended reassurance to him five months after his entry that all knowledge, including even dull civil law, has value[5] and Keats's remark about a year later that "Reynolds is completely limed in the law: he is not only reconcil'd to it but hobbyhorses upon it."[6]

Reynolds retained his post on *The Champion* at least until December 28, 1817, though he induced Keats to substitute as theatrical critic for one week before that date. Early in 1818 his resolution to concentrate on the law was partially thwarted by extended illness and partially broken by his writing three articles and three sonnets for John Hunt's *Yellow Dwarf*. While on vacation from his legal work in the autumn, he submitted a defense of *Endymion* to the *Alfred*, *West of England Journal* at Exeter, which Hunt reprinted in *The Examiner*. During the next three years he

---

[5] *The Letters of John Keats*, ed. Hyder E. Rollins, 2 vols. (Cambridge, Mass., 1958), I, 276–277.
[6] *Ibid.*, II, 78.

may have neglected his legal business to some extent, for he contributed to *The Scots Magazine* from December 1818 through August 1820; wrote for *The Edinburgh Review* in 1818 or 1819; and produced a parody of Wordsworth's *Peter Bell* on April 15, 1819, a farce entitled *One, Two, Three, Four, Five: By Advertisement* on July 17, 1819, the pseudo-autobiographical memoirs of Peter Corcoran called *The Fancy* in 1820, and *The Garden of Florence* in 1821.

After serving as Peter G. Patmore's attorney in the legal action following the death of John Scott in the duel in 1821, he joined the staff of *The London Magazine* in July, having contributed occasionally before that date. For the next three and a half years, in addition to assisting Taylor and Hessey with the editing, he wrote most of the theatrical reviews, a series of epistolary articles under the pseudonym Edward Herbert, other literary articles, reviews of current books, and a few poems.

After Reynolds' death Charles Dilke called these years "the only true period of his literary life,"[7] an overstatement which we may correct without intending to deny the value of his *London* achievement. The fault in the judgment is that it deprecates Reynolds' accomplishment from 1816 through 1820 when he produced all the poetry, essays, and criticism outlined in the preceding paragraphs, when he associated freely with Keats and with Hazlitt, Lamb, Hunt, and a host of minor authors, and when he received recognition for his work ranging all the way from Hunt's ranking him as a poet along with Keats and Shelley to John Gibson Lockhart's decision that his prose was better than Hazlitt's. But in making the remark, Dilke was undoubtedly thinking of the long decline after 1825, not of the period preceding 1821, and we can certainly agree that the *London* years were glorious ones. Not only did he have the satisfaction of publishing prose worthy of its close association with the greatest prose geniuses of the age, Hazlitt and Lamb; he also met convivially in the hospitable quarters of Taylor and Hessey with Hazlitt, Lamb, De Quincey, Bryan Waller Procter, John Clare, and the numerous other *London* contributors. Though he had lost Keats, he had gained his future brother-in-law Thomas Hood, and that second literary friendship flourished in a way only relatively less memorable than the first with the greater poet.

But the association with *The London* was not without its disadvantage;

7 *Notes and Queries*, October 4, 1856, p. 275.

4

the old problem of conflict between law and literature recurred, and the difficulty encountered in producing a large volume of literary work while conducting a legal practice is painfully apparent in the series of letters which he exchanged with the publisher John Taylor in 1823 and 1824.

On leaving *The London*, he first paid his disrespects to John Wilson in a sparkling satire in *The Westminster Review* and then scored his greatest popular success in 1825 by collaborating with Hood on *Odes and Addresses to Great People*, a work which has sometimes been judged second to the Smiths' *Rejected Addresses* among the burlesque verses of the period. From 1828 until June 8, 1831, he owned a share of *The Athenaeum*, which he unluckily sold in protest at Dilke's cutting the price in half, a step which he must have lamented sorely as the magazine prospered, since his financial situation grew ever more desperate. But, though he received no share of *The Athenaeum's* profits, he augmented his legal income by contributing steadily to the magazine through 1837. As journalistic and ephemeral as most of that work was, Reynolds nevertheless deserves much credit for the articles which he wrote as Dilke's chief gun in *The Athenaeum's* campaign against corrupt "puffing" of new books. His dramatic writing, *A New Entertainment* in 1833 and *Confounded Foreigners* in 1838, can be mentioned only to be dismissed; his theatrical pieces from the farce of 1819 through the productions for Charles Mathews in the twenties to the two farces of the thirties were never more than hackwork, calculated attempts to make money by offering shallow amusement.

He had married Eliza Powell Drewe on August 31, 1822. Except for financial pressures, the twenties and early thirties were rather happy years for the young couple; all the evidence we have indicates that the enduring love of John and Eliza confirmed John Taylor's glowing prediction of a perfect match. Hereafter the story grows darker and darker. For ten years he had shared in the happiness which followed the marriage of his favorite sister Jane and his closest friend Hood. Then in 1835 his brother-in-law quarreled bitterly with the Reynolds family at the bedside of the desperately ill Jane. Although Reynolds personally escaped Hood's animosity, he must have grieved deeply at such strife among those he loved.[8] And, if that were not enough to crush him, in the same

---

[8] Peter F. Morgan, "John Hamilton Reynolds and Thomas Hood," *Keats–Shelley Journal*, 11 (Winter 1962): 90–91.

year his beloved daughter Lucy, the only child remaining after the earlier loss of an infant, died at the age of ten. From the recent research of Peter F. Morgan, we now know that about August 1838 Reynolds descended from steady contributing to the respected *Athenaeum* to editing *The New Sporting Magazine*, a task which he continued through December 1840. Although one can sense his own ever lively pen brightening the magazine a little from time to time, for the most part he allowed even that journal to deteriorate by embroiling it in a bitter quarrel with Charles James Apperley and other sporting writers. One suspects that the rueful accounts in his own "Turfiana" series of the danger of losing money to defaulting bookmakers had some foundation in personal experience. Whatever the immediate cause, the long-dreaded financial crash finally came with a certificate of bankruptcy on October 26, 1838.

Reynolds' subsequent management of Hood's legal dispute with his publisher evidently left much to be desired, and it seems very probable that Morgan is correct in suggesting that the dismissal of Reynolds as Hood's solicitor in June 1841 marked a break in the old friendship. Until the last five years of his life Reynolds clung precariously to the small prestige of a free-lance author by contributing occasionally to *Ainsworth's Magazine*, *The New Monthly*, and *Bentley's Miscellany*. Then in 1847, abandoning the private legal practice which he had always managed poorly, he secured an appointment as assistant clerk of the County Court at Newport in the Isle of Wight, where he spent the last five years before his death on November 15, 1852.

After having procrastinated his own biography of Keats for twenty-five years, he was cheered somewhat during this period of exile by the opportunity to render Richard M. Milnes invaluable assistance in preparing the first extensive life. Otherwise, according to Rowland E. Prothero, Lord Ernle, in *The Letters and Journals of Lord Byron*, these years brought a drastic deterioration: he was "a broken-down, discontented man ... who professed himself an Unitarian and a bitter Radical, and whose drunken habits placed him beyond the pale of society."[9] Probably unconscious prejudices caused some overstatement in Lord Ernle's report: surely not everyone will agree with the implication that it is disreputable to be either a Unitarian or a radical, and the fact that Lord Ernle's Tory parents and their friends thought these convictions partial

[9] Six vols. (London, 1898–1901), III, 46n.

6

grounds for ostracizing Reynolds reveals more about them than about Reynolds. As Willard B. Pope has shown, evidence from the Hampshire *Independent* and from local tradition in the Isle of Wight reveals that Reynolds lived a responsible life there and that he earned respect from many.[10] After discounting the exaggeration, however, we may still accept Lord Ernle's account of the heavy drinking and unhappiness.

But what was the man like in his prime? We may begin to answer the question by admitting that he had minor faults even then. He lacked Keats's high degree of sympathetic tolerance for the failings of his friends. After two years of intimacy with Haydon almost as close as Keats's, he became embroiled in an acrimonious dispute with the painter over so trifling a matter as failure to reply to a dinner invitation, a bitter quarrel which ended in "one of the most cutting letters" Keats ever read in its exposure of Haydon's weaknesses.[11] At the other extreme he exaggerated good manners to the point of some deceit even more than Keats in his relations with Hunt, maintaining the pose of respect and cordial friendship in social contacts and public statements, while slashing away savagely at Hunt's shortcomings in private conversation and correspondence with others. In a letter to John Taylor, for the most emphatic example, he speaks of "the vain and heartless eternity of Mr Leigh Hunt's indecent discoursings" and of "the irksome, wearing consciousness of a disgusting presence, than which I know of nothing more dispiriting."[12] It is no wonder that Hunt was so confused as to write Hazlitt, "Reynolds is a machine I don't see the meaning of."[13]

Reynolds was not always sufficiently penetrating in appraising character: he denounced Fanny Brawne as "the poor idle Thing of womankind, to whom he [Keats] has so unaccountably attached himself,"[14] failing to see that underneath the facade of stylishness and youthful frivolity lay a staunchly devoted and loyal woman. In extenuation of that faulty judgment, however, the reader should consult Reynolds' "The Ravens; or, The Force of Conscience" from *The Champion*, which

[10] "John Hamilton Reynolds, the Friend of Keats," *Wessex*, 3 (1935): 3–15.

[11] *Letters of Keats*, I, 205. The letter itself is conspicuously absent from Haydon's diary, where much other significant correspondence was preserved.

[12] *The Keats Circle*, I, 156.

[13] Peter P. Howe, *The Life of William Hazlitt*, third edition (London, 1947), p. 291.

[14] *The Keats Circle*, I, 156.

reveals that his hostility toward stylishness in women was a fervent conviction held for years.

On the other hand, there is the intelligent, witty, and lively boon companion who lives unforgettably in Keats's letters. What Reynolds meant to Keats can be recalled succinctly by noting a casual remark about a party of the sort that Keats did not ordinarily relish: "it was made pleasant by Reynolds being there."[15] After a year of close friendship, Keats grew very critical of the narrowness, dullness, and jealousy of the Reynolds women, especially the sisters, but he specifically exempted Reynolds from his later attacks. Though "John Reynolds is very dull at home," he remains "the playfullest" of Keats's inner circle of companions when away from home.[16] Even as he deplored the quarrel with Haydon, Keats judged Reynolds to be "on the right side of the question."[17] In an age when surname without courtesy title was the common mode of address for friends, Keats went further and broke out repeatedly in his letters with Christian name or nickname—John or Jack.

Hood reported that Reynolds' "wit bubbles up of itself" and that "generally, his jests, set off by a happy manner, are only ticklesome, but now and then they are sharp-flavoured,—like the sharpness of the pineapple."[18] Dilke praised his "wit and brilliancy," adding that Reynolds was "one of the most brilliant men" he had ever known.[19] These are merely samples of the many testimonials to the flashing but ingratiating wit which was his chief characteristic. Wit can be cutting; all too often the price of a jest is the injured feelings of the target. How then could Reynolds have employed it so constantly and at the same time have bound to himself so firmly some of the most sensitive men of the age? Hood's "set off by a happy manner" provides a partial answer, which fortunately John Clare explains at length:

Reynolds was always the soul of these dinner parties [given by Taylor and Hessey for the contributors to *The London*] he was the most good-natured fellow I ever met with his face was the three-in-one of fun wit & punning personified he woud punch you with his puns very keenly without ever hurting your feelings for if you lookd in his face you coud not be offended & you might retort as you

[15] *Letters of Keats*, II, 82.
[16] *Ibid.*, II, 15, 245.
[17] *Ibid.*, I, 205.
[18] *The Works of Thomas Hood*, ed. Thomas Hood, Jr., 7 vols. (London, 1862–1863), II, 381.
[19] *Notes and Queries*, p. 275.

pleasd—nothing coud put him out of humour either with himself or others . . . he sits as a careless listener at table looking on with quick knapping sort of eye that turns towards you as quick as lightning when he has a pun joke or story to give you they are never made up or studied they are flashes of the moment & mostly happy . . . his teeth are always looking through a laugh that sits as easy on his unpuckerd lips as if he were born laughing he is a man of genius & if his talents were properly applied he would do something I verily believe that he might win the favours of fame with a pun—but be as it will wether she is inclind to smile or frown upon he is quite at home wi content the present is all with him he carries none of the Author about him a hearty laugh which there is no resisting at his jokes & puns seems to be more recompense than he expected & he seems startld into wonder at it & muses a moment as if he turnd the joke over agen in his mind to find the merry thought that made the laughter.[20]

Clare wrote much more in the same highly laudatory vein, but these extracts suffice to show how Reynolds' spontaneity, warmth, and geniality converted his extraordinary wit into a richly humane humor.

Since the engaging personality and keen mind so apparent in his conversation also pervade much of his writing, it seems strange that he should now be so little read. One of the reasons for the relative neglect was his own extreme modesty. To Keats he wrote, "Do *you* get Fame,—and I shall have it in being your affectionate and steady friend."[21] Time and again he repeated that renunciation of any attempt to secure fame for his own work: in "The Pilgrimage of Living Poets," in "Farewell to the Muses," with faint indirection in the two fine sonnets in *The Fancy*, and in the Preface to *The Garden of Florence*. Perhaps posterity is not much to be blamed for taking him at his own word when that word was so often repeated.

Another reason is that he wrote so often anonymously or under pseudonyms. Twice during his life, in 1824 and again in 1837, he planned to collect his prose and publish it in book form, but the plans were never executed. Unlike Hood, he had no surviving children to collect his works after his death and assure them a fair chance at continuing attention. Twentieth century scholars have done valuable service in identifying a large bulk of his work, but rare indeed is the reader who will expend

[20] *The Prose of John Clare*, edd. J. W. and Anne Tibble (London, 1951), pp. 86–87.
[21] *Letters of Keats*, I, 377.

the time and energy necessary to track that work through the fine print of old periodicals.

Although one shares Ian Jack's regret in *The Oxford History of English Literature, 1815–1832* that a complete edition of Reynolds' poems has not been published, it should be noted that the poetry has at least been given some chance. John Masefield reprinted *The Fancy* in 1905; George L. Marsh published many of the best poems (but only two truncated essays) in *John Hamilton Reynolds: Poetry and Prose* in 1928; and the latest *Oxford Book of Nineteenth Century Verse* (1964) reprints *Peter Bell*. But the prose has not heretofore been reprinted in any substantial way, though it offers a range of critiques, satires, and essays worthy of the attention of all who are seriously interested in Romantic literature.

In assessing Reynolds' achievement as a critic, we may begin by saying what he was not. Never the meticulous scholar that his friend Charles Dilke was, he was not much interested in bibliographical and textual matters. He delighted in finding and sharing with his readers rare old books like *The Court and City Gamester* and Sir Thomas Parkyns' *Progymnasmata*, and he liked to dip into John Stowe, Joseph Strutt, Richard Carew, and John Nichols for choice morsels of earlier times, but his occasional antiquarianism was a hobby rather than a sustained pursuit. Expressing a distaste for the pedantry of professional scholarship, he sought to develop a liberal and humane view in his criticism, searching for basic characteristics in authors and works and pervasive distinctions among them. Like Hazlitt he was always eager to pose a comparison and to discriminate significant differences: Fletcher and Shakespeare, Shakespeare and Milton, Spenser and Milton, Goldsmith and Rogers, Richard III and Sir Giles Overreach, Othello and Ludovico Sforza, Hamlet and Romeo.

As a well-read and largely self-educated man who was ever lively himself, Reynolds attempted to locate qualities in literature which assure it continued life. At bottom he is a subjective critic: he reacts and then tries to account for his reaction. He is highly enthusiastic; he once feared that he would exhaust the printer's supply of exclamation marks, and the apprehension was a reasonable one. At times his enthusiasm seems excessive; some of his panegyrics on Nature as opposed to Art, on female innocence, and on love make one wonder whose opium he borrowed. But usually he succeeds in communicating his own enthusiasm to his reader, and as a result his criticism remains alive.

Without attempting to catalogue all authors, we may note some features of his treatment of major subjects from earlier literature. Our interest in the essay on Chaucer is diminished somewhat by mistaken attributions of *The Flower and the Leaf* and *The Plowman's Tale*, but we can scarcely blame him for errors shared with virtually all his contemporaries. Though his eloquence in praising Chaucer's delight in Nature perhaps captures the spirit of the subject, that characteristically Romantic section is more emotional than intellectual. He is perceptive enough, however, to give at least some attention to Chaucer's irony, as in his remarks on the Friar's arranging many a marriage "at his owene cost" and on the mock naïveté of Chaucer's repeated protestations of inability to do justice to a subject.

The eulogy of Milton's delight in romance once more shows the Romantic critic as he glories in the marvelous incidents and colorful descriptions of medieval tales. But again Reynolds' mind is at work as well as his heart. He strikes a neat balance in his contrast between Spenser's fanciful and Milton's restrained sensuousness; he sees the effect of Milton's repeating words and phrases so that "the sound steals back upon the ear like an echo," apparently without knowing of Dryden's discussion of "the turn"; and he provides apt illustrations for Milton's versatility in cadences from "the rushing sound of the trumpet" to "the mellow breathings of the flute." Moreover, he proves his ability as a sprightly phrase maker with such lines as "Poetry was to him the power of setting virtue to music" and "Adam himself is but Milton undressed."

Because of his post as theatrical critic, Reynolds criticized the drama most frequently, and the touchstone for nearly all his dramatic criticism was Shakespeare. He worshiped Shakespeare, and "worshiped" is only faintly metaphorical, for no one has ever surpassed Reynolds in Shakespeare idolatry. He often used religious terms to express the extent of his devotion, on one occasion, for instance, describing Shakespeare as the "divinity of the world of imagination." Not content to call Shakespeare "the god of our idolatry," he speaks only half-jokingly of "Shakespearian Orthodoxy," alludes to the Spanish Inquisition, and charges any who fall from the faith with heresy. He denies criticism any right "to purse its little brow in the presence of Shakespeare," and declares that Shakespeare has "very few imperfections,—and perhaps even these might vanish from our minds, if *we* had the *perfection* properly to scan them." All this idolatry sometimes led to mere eulogy, but, like those other idolaters Hazlitt and Coleridge, Reynolds was most interested in psychological analysis of the characters, and his studies of many of the characters are perceptive and thought-provoking. His worship of Shakespeare also lies behind his interesting refutation in *The Scots Magazine* of Hazlitt's argument that Shakespeare's comedies are markedly inferior to his tragedies, as well as behind his frequent Lamb-like arguments, which he nowhere credits to Lamb, that the plays can be appreciated fully only in the closet and not in the theater.

Reynolds' treatment of Ben Jonson displays sound caution; while suspicious of the old cliché that Jonson's learning subdued his wit, he avoids the temptation to discard an old truth for the sake of some eccentric approach to catch attention. His generally discriminating praise of several of the other Elizabethan and Jacobean dramatists re-enforces and extends the work of Lamb's *Specimens* of 1809 in arousing interest in those relatively neglected poets. The reviews of contemporary productions of Restoration and eighteenth century drama from Thomas Otway through Richard Brinsley Sheridan provide an appreciable body of literary criticism, since his usual inclination in *The Champion* was to evaluate and analyze the plays, while relegating appraisal of the acting to a subordinate position. His strictures on the poverty of the drama in his own day are just and sometimes entertaining, though this edition includes only a few examples of those articles, as the wit of the attack seldom compensates adequately for our lack of interest in the target.

Reynolds deserves study as a critic of his contemporaries even more than as a critic of earlier literature. He has always been best known for his unselfish championing of Keats, and appropriately so. Only comparatively less important are his appraisals of Hazlitt, continuing from the review of *Characters of Shakespear's Plays* in 1817 through the elaborate critique of *Lectures on the English Comic Writers* in 1818–1819 and the judgment of the man and his prose in "Living Authors, a Dream" in 1820 to the posthumous summing-up in the notice of *Conversations of James Northcote* in 1830. Though never so intimate with Hazlitt as with Keats, doubtless in part because of the difference in age and in part because of Hazlitt's temperament, Reynolds shared with Keats a recognition of his genius that bordered on reverence. As Keats judged Hazlitt's "depth of taste" one of the three finest achievements of the period, so Reynolds proclaimed him "the first prose writer of the age." Not only did he praise Hazlitt's books; he quoted from him repeatedly and imitated his style so closely and so successfully that it is sometimes difficult to determine whether an essay is by master or disciple. Reynolds was independent enough to disagree occasionally, as in the rejection of Hazlitt's contention that "Romeo is Hamlet in love" and in the refutation of Hazlitt's relative disparagement of Shakespeare's comedies, but, when he does disagree, he is deferential and acutely conscious of his own boldness.

As a critic of Wordsworth, Reynolds ought not to be remembered just by *Peter Bell*, splendidly hilarious as that parody is. Appreciation of *Peter Bell* can be heightened by the realization that Reynolds was for years one of the strongest advocates of what he judged to be the best of Wordsworth. His first initialed article for *The Champion* in 1815 defends Wordsworth with an ardor which was sustained and even surpassed the next year in "Pilgrimage of the Living Poets," "Popular Poetry, Periodical Criticism," and the review of the *Thanksgiving Ode*. His scattered comments on Wordsworth after *Peter Bell* always show respect for the poet's genius as well as awareness of his faults. Reynolds' judgment was not always perfect: like Keats, he at first rated *The Excursion* much higher than readers now think just, and either he or posterity is wrong about the *Thanskgiving Ode*, which he considered great poetry. But he recognized the merit of the sonnets and the greatness of *Tintern Abbey*, which he honored by imitating in his own *Devon*.

On Coleridge Reynolds was less successful. Without disapproving entirely of his rebuking Coleridge for allowing metaphysics to supplant poetry and his condemning Coleridge's mystification, we must object to the way in which he applied those charges to damn both *Kubla Khan* and *Christabel*. It may be some slight compensation, however, that Coleridge always fascinated him, that fascination appearing most clearly in the limited praise of *Zapolya*. Reynolds always dealt harshly with Southey, who became for him, as for Hazlitt, a kind of political symbol of all he detested in the Tories. He reacted to Byron in the manner of a great many periodical critics, qualifying high praise with some moral reservations.

In a second category of his prose achievement, satire, Reynolds was most successful when he designed some kind of frame, some controlling structure. Though the casual satire without any such firm structure which he scattered throughout his essays added spice to many of them, it seldom achieved much force or intricacy. The limitations of his casual satire can be seen in several early pieces. The account of the deficiencies of country actors in "The Exeter Theatre" enlivens that familiar essay, but it is rather relaxed and lacks the zest of his best satirical work. The attack on the Bluestockings in the theatrical review of Cibber's *The Refusal* is too directly didactic. It seems tame when compared with Hazlitt's more forceful direct attacks and dwindles into journalism when set against such a masterpiece as Byron's dramatic attack through Donna Inez in *Don Juan*. Significantly, Reynolds was somewhat more successful later in *The London Magazine* when he dramatized the attack through the character of the Blue, Prudence Morton. The attack on the affectation of stylish women in another theatrical review, *The Ravens*, resembles his treatment of the Blues in *The Refusal*: though it is not quite a homily because of Reynolds' dramatic sketching of the fashionable woman, it is still too close to moral preachment to be thoroughly effective.

The satirical articles on Evangelical preachers in *The Yellow Dwarf* also lack any controlling structure. Reynolds develops these attacks in the manner of lengthy editorials, moving rather loosely from one satirical thrust to the next as he describes his opponents ironically and quotes their arguments in order to refute them caustically. The essays do have merit: as the best of what might be called Reynolds' unstructured satire, they deserve Keats's praise of "very capital articles." The satirical portraits of "the snug Doctor in Divinity," the "sycophant Curate," and "the *high Evangelical*" are reminiscent of the best seventeenth century "characters" (Reynolds himself uses the term to label the sketches) in their skillful selection of concrete details to reveal dramatically the general characteristics of a class. Nevertheless, the limited success of this "Pulpit Oratory" series falls short of Reynolds' best prose satires, which all sprang from some one ingenious conception, varied though the different conceptions were.

Fortunately very early in his career Reynolds saw the advantages of a unifying structure for satire. In April 1816 the dream vision of "The Pilgrimage of Living Poets to the Stream of Castaly" furnished him with the classical waters of inspiration as a central device to rank contemporary poets and to discriminate the individual qualities of their poetry. The scheme encouraged him to exercise his wit by seeking variety within a rigid framework: melancholy Byron, bearing a Grecian urn, mingled his own tears with the Castalian water; martial Scott drew but a shallow draft with an old helmet, though his portion received a pleasant sparkle from the warlike metal shining through it; bewildered Southey scooped only a little in a gold vessel and rode off jerkily with it toward St. James's; superficial Rogers caught only a few drops, which he planned to dilute with common water; Crabbe plunged a rude wooden bowl into the stream and promised to brew strong ale for the country people with his share; and Coleridge "went to the depths, where he might have caught the purest water had he not unfortunately clouded it with sand which he himself disturbed" and later confused himself by analyzing "the sand's propensity to mount and curl itself in water." The true Castalian stream having served for these and other serious contenders for poetic fame, Reynolds then moved easily to the idea of a false brook, which permitted him to mock such poetasters as William Hayley, John Wilson, Amos Cottle, and especially William Lisle Bowles, who was "laboriously engaged in filling fourteen nut-shells." The result of this fanciful exploitation of the basic idea of the Castalian stream was a firmly organized minor satire which was both entertaining and critically revealing.

Eight months later Reynolds followed up that initial success with an even more original and elaborate framework which allowed both greater flexibility and sharper drama. In "Boswell's Visit" he contrived a clever anachronism in which he had Dr. Johnson and other members of "The Literary Club" pass judgment on the poets of the early nineteenth century. Some of the reader's pleasure derives from Reynolds' success as a literary mimic in imitating Dr. Johnson's ponderous abstractions, balanced sentence structures, and dogmatic assertions. But Reynolds did more than merely imitate prose style: his thorough understanding of Boswell's *Life* combined with his own imaginative flair enabled him to re-create Johnson's inner circle. We see again Boswell's deference and Johnson's prejudices, his Tory convictions, his abiding concern with moral issues in both literature and life, his emphasis on common sense, and his delight in spirited argument. The tactful, suave, and persuasive remarks of Sir Joshua Reynolds are set off against the more abrupt and weightier pronouncements of Burke. Without straining, except in the unrelieved eulogy of Wordsworth which does not quite agree with our expectation of what Dr. Johnson would decide, "Boswell's Visit" applies the principles and prejudices of Johnson and his friends to nineteenth century authors. Reynolds shows special ingenuity in using Dr. Johnson's concern for morality to satirize Byron's and Scott's bold, bad heroes and in using Dr. Johnson's insistence on common sense to satirize Coleridge's metaphysics and mystification, though the resulting disparagement of *Christabel* and *Kubla Khan* is less than just to Coleridge. On the whole, "Boswell's Visit" is one of Reynolds' most satisfying satires: though neither so laughable as the Preface to *Peter Bell* nor so clever as "Professor Wilson's Danciad," its drama and richness offer substantial compensations.

The parody of *Peter Bell* has always been, and doubtless will continue to be, Reynolds' best known satire. Here the controlling idea looms especially large because the piece was a very successful literary hoax. Everything centers upon the pretense that Wordsworth is the author, and the reader's appreciation is enhanced by his awareness of the swiftness and cleverness with which Reynolds produced the parody before Wordsworth could publish the genuine poem. Although the entire parody deserves its lasting recognition, most readers can probably agree with Coleridge that the prose of the preface is even better than the verse. Imitating the inflated and pompous tone of much of Wordsworth's prose, he exaggerates absurdly to ridicule Wordsworth's defects laughably, and at the same time incisively: his egotism, his complacent Toryism, his eccentric dwelling on the lowly, and his redundancy. Reynolds controls the irony admirably, not mentioning Shakespeare by name, but depending on the reader's knowledge of a quotation to reveal the conceit of the pseudo-Wordsworth's declaring him to be "a poet scarcely inferior to myself," and allowing the incongruous shift from Wordsworth's pose of serene objectivity to the heated denunciation of Francis Jeffrey to secure its effect dramatically without any unnecessary guidance. Reynolds' *Peter Bell* will always serve as an illuminating example of how parody can best achieve the ends of economy and forcefulness in literary criticism.

"The Literary Police Office," in which Reynolds tried to repeat with a different structure his successes seven years earlier in "The Pilgrimage of Living Poets" and "Boswell's Visit," falls somewhat short of its predecessors as satire. The framework is ingenious enough: the idea of haling contemporary authors before a magistrate and charging them with various literary offenses offered excellent possibilities. Reynolds strove diligently to provide wide scope: the several dozen figures satirized range from Wordsworth and Coleridge down to Lord Thurlow and Thomas Dibdin. But for the most part he is too good-natured; he walks on eggs in attempting to satirize without injuring the feelings of those attacked. As a result, though the piece is still lively and entertaining, it fails to exploit to the full the potentialities of the original conception.

Almost as successful as *Peter Bell*, on the other hand, was the later hoax on John Wilson, "Professor Wilson's *Danciad*," which has been virtually unknown and unappreciated. It can never have as wide an audience as *Peter Bell* because of the difference in the satirical targets; everyone knows Wordsworth, while John Wilson has maintained only a shred of reputation through literary history, and that largely infamous. Nevertheless the article affords some of Reynolds' finest satire to those equipped to savor it.

As coeditor of *Blackwood's* with Lockhart, Wilson shared the responsibility for all the vicious attacks on the Cockneys: Hunt, Keats, Hazlitt, Procter, and others. In 1820 he had been elected to the Chair of Moral Philosophy at the University of Edinburgh despite the scurrilous material which he had written and sanctioned, the absence of any real scholarly qualification for the post, and the genuine claim in philosophy of the rival candidate, Sir William Hamilton. Having already protested that appointment in an essay for *The London* entitled "Exmouth Wrestling," Reynolds was stirred in 1824 to renew the attack by *Blackwood's* itself. In "Noctes Ambrosianae" of April[22] the writer attempted to ridicule the flowery rhetoric of Reynolds' account of Thurtell's trial in *The London*[23] by quoting several highly enthusiastic passages and pretending to find them ludicrous. For some unknown reason the writer attributed the article not to Reynolds, though Edward Herbert was a transparent pseudonym, but to "Tims," the name which *Blackwood's* used elsewhere for Peter George Patmore. In the absurdly bad recent poem *The Danciad*

[22] 15: 375–377.
[23] 9: 165–185. Not included in this selection.

Reynolds found the perfect way of thrusting that confusion of authorship back at *Blackwood's* by pretending to mistake the dancing master "Professor" Thomas Wilson for the august Professor of Moral Philosophy John Wilson.

The hoax permitted Reynolds to damn John Wilson soundly, while claiming ironically to be his warm friend and ardent champion. The wretched doggerel on dancing (from which Reynolds quotes perhaps too abundantly) "is not exactly in the style" of Wilson's earlier works, "but in moral philosophy, pointed invective, and dramatic spirit, it perhaps far outstrips them all." Pretended praise of the dancing master's moralizing strikes sharply at the hypocritical incongruity between Wilson's lectures and his anonymous defamations in *Blackwood's*. Mock eulogy condemns Wilson much more effectively than direct counter-attack ever could have: "Those who have thought his buoyant spirits and pliant abilities a little unbecoming the chair, will now see that not without an object have those amiable gaieties been encouraged. The present work is a key to many of those extravagant sallies, which, until its appearance, were unaccountable even to his friends." The dancing master's cryptic reference to an obscure publishing firm named "Hogg and Co." enables Reynolds to broaden the attack to James Hogg, Wilson's cohort in "Noctes Ambrosianae," and at the same time to amuse the reader with the extraordinary coincidence of the parallels between the London and the Edinburgh Wilsons. Throughout the article varied and subtle ironies combine with pervading liveliness and joviality to form a satire which deserves resurrection from the dusty pages of *The Westminster Review*.

Although in prose Reynolds accomplished most in literary criticism and satire, he also succeeded substantially in the familiar essay. The Edward Herbert papers, comprising much of that subsidiary achievement, deserve analysis and evaluation. Curiously, Reynolds is both Edward Herbert and Tom Morton. When Herbert describes the journey on the stage coach and the trips to Greenwich Hospital, the green room of the theater, and the cockpit, he clearly draws from Reynolds' first-hand experience, and he is even made a lawyer in the first article on the coronation, though Reynolds later dropped that profession either because he forgot it or because it would have interfered with the contrast between unsophisticated Herbert and the rakish young law student,

Tom Morton. Tom is an exaggeration of certain tendencies in Reynolds five years earlier, with his exuberance, his love of sports, and his craving for all kinds of experiences ranging from Lancelot Andrewes' sermons to the shady side of London life.

The other Mortons are types who are developed somewhat didactically and sentimentally. We know that we are being preached at with the model of a perfect wife when Mrs. Morton subordinates herself excessively to her husband despite her superior intellect, and we are not warmed so much as Reynolds' contemporary female readers doubtless were by her pride in her husband's good looks on their wedding day or by her preserving a lock of his hair before it became gray. Agnes is made too much the perfection of modest maidenhood to contrast with the bold bluestocking, Prudence. But on the whole Reynolds manages specific detail well enough to make the characters credible, and he relieves the sentiment with enough mellow humor to make them appealing. The small detail and the humor often combine, as in the incident where the enthusiastic card player Mr. Morton insists excitedly the next day, when everyone else has forgotten it, that Herbert should not continue to worry about leading the wrong card, that it really was of no consequence at all.

There are also weaknesses in the accounts of the unusual scenes which occupy more than half of all the Herbert essays. Even in the better letters—and I have excluded from this volume the detailed reports of the coronation and Thurtell's trial—Reynolds describes so minutely that occasionally the reader's interest flags, as in parts of "Greenwich Hospital" and "The Cockpit Royal." Sometimes in the descriptions also he hammers away too insistently at a combination of sentiment and didacticism, as in the portrayal of the serene patience of the sailor paralyzed from the waist down.

But despite such weaknesses which were characteristic of the age, the framework is satisfying in itself, and it adds a human interest to generally animated descriptions of out-of-the-way places and events. We accompany Herbert and the Mortons to Greenwich Hospital, to the green room of the theater, and to the cockpit, and we are pleased both to learn of new places and incidents and to observe the reaction of Herbert's sensitive intellect to them.

In addition to the Herbert letters, Reynolds wrote a number of other essays for *The London*, from which three have been selected for this collection: "Exmouth Wrestling," "Bradgate Park," and "The Cook's Oracle." Written before Reynolds devised the Herbert framework, "Exmouth Wrestling" resembles quite closely in substance and tone the central Herbert papers ("The Literary Police Office" and the two others not reprinted here use the framework only superficially and would be just as effective without it). In the first part the author meditates wistfully on the pleasures of anticipating vacations and then describes rather whimsically some English scenes: the departure from the London coach house and the arrival at Exmouth. The second part resembles the Edward Herbert pattern even more strongly with its account of the rustic wrestling matches where Reynolds uses a rare old book on wrestling to lend a measure of dignity by placing the sport firmly in the English tradition and to give the reader a sense of the blending of past and present. He later repeats the same technique in two of the Herbert letters with an unusual passage from Sir Richard Steele in "Greenwich Hospital" and a rare seventeenth century volume in "The Cockpit Royal." On the whole, "Exmouth Wrestling" is an excellent essay, not inferior to the Herbert papers which it anticipates, and the initial section on vacations is perhaps the finest passage in all Reynolds' familiar essays.

"Bradgate Park" is not far removed from the Herbert pattern; it too offers a balance between past and present, as Reynolds uses the ancient estate as a starting point for elaborating reveries about Lady Jane Grey and sixteenth century chivalry. Ascham's *The Scholemaster* parallels the old volumes introduced into the other essays. The characterization of the virtuous old gamekeeper and his family and the description of the grounds and forest direct the reader's thoughts to the present at times, but here the stress differs from the norm in that instead of using the past to enrich appreciation of a present scene, Reynolds uses the present scene as an instrument for conjuring up the past. The primary concern is clearly the romantic dreaming of Lady Jane Grey, and the misty sentiment of that passage makes the essay a little less successful than the central Herbert pieces.

A third essay, "The Cook's Oracle," is not at all like the Edward Herbert pattern, nor like anything else in literature except some aspects of "A Dissertation upon Roast Pig," which it preceded by a year. Though it purports to be a review of Dr. Kitchiner's cookbook, it is really a humorous and imaginative personal essay on the naïveté of Dr. Kitchiner, the art of cooking, and the pleasures of the table. In general the mingling of irony with gourmandising suggests Lamb's greater essay, and in particular the Swiftian quality of the passage treating the roasting of a goose alive in order to enhance its flavor parallels Lamb's Jesuitical disputation on whether it is justifiable to whip a pig to death if the pain is counterbalanced by the intensification of the pleasure upon man's palate. "The Cook's Oracle" is not the masterpiece that Lamb's "Dissertation" is because it lacks Lamb's firm organization and it is too dependent on a multitude of quotations. But to admit that it is not the greatest is not to deny it great merit. One of Reynolds' finest comic productions, it can provide readers today as much pleasure as it did the author's contemporaries.

At the height of his success Reynolds wrote in *The London* of his prose, "What am I toiling for?—why do I covet experience, when half a century will set myself and any given dead idiot on a par?"[24] I believe that posterity will prove him wrong.

[24] 6: 163.

NOTE ON THE EDITING

I have attempted to stay as close as possible to Reynolds' intention by reproducing the texts from periodicals as printed there with the exceptions that I have corrected obvious typographical errors silently, that in the one case of "Boswell's Visit" I have supplied paragraphing for the special purpose explained in the first note to that article, and that I have not included quotation marks for quotations set apart from the text since reduced type serves that purpose. Although I realize that Reynolds' manuscripts may have been altered by editors or compositors in the mechanical details of punctuation, spelling, capitalization, and use of italics, I believe that the soundest procedure is to allow every reader to do his own speculating about that possibility by avoiding the introduction of yet another editor's changes which would separate the reader even further from Reynolds' original composition. The title of each passage indicates whether an article is a complete piece or a selection: *From* before the title indicates a selection. Dots of suspension are used only to indicate omissions within extracts. The dates after the titles are of course my additions.

As a general policy, I have sought to identify in my notes only those quotations which Reynolds considered long enough or important enough to set apart from his text. For all uninitialed essays, the first note to each cites the evidence of Reynolds' authorship. The starred notes that appear at the bottom of the page are of course Reynolds' own.

In selecting from the theatrical reviews in *The Champion*, I have concentrated on literary criticism of the earlier drama, often excising commentary on forgotten subordinate actors. I have included a number of the better articles on the four most famous performers of the period, whose careers are still of interest: Sarah Siddons, John Philip Kemble, Edmund Kean, and Eliza O'Neill. From the treatment of the feeble current drama, I have reprinted reviews of Maturin's two plays, a few representative attacks, and several extracts which have some value as miniature familiar essays.

ESSAYS AND REVIEWS

ESSAYS AND LITERARY REVIEWS

FROM *THE CHAMPION*

Mr. *Wordsworth's Poetry.* *December 9, 1815*

Mr. Champion,—Perhaps you may not be disinclined to permit me to continue a little further, the remarks on Mr. Wordsworth's Poetry, which have, from time to time, appeared in the *Champion*. It is an important subject, nearly concerning the character of the present age for taste, for feeling—in fact, for every moral and mental quality that can do it honor in future estimation, or conduce to its present enjoyment of the worthiest means of gratification.

Mr. Wordsworth has the power of calling forth the retired thoughts and fleeting recollections of the mind, more exquisitely than any poet of later times. He breathes the same air of philosophy that Milton and Jeremy Taylor breathed before him;—though, in the latter, there is indeed a singularly rich enthusiasm that defies similarity. Mr. Wordsworth's sublimities are of the same nature with the sublimities of these noble Poets—bold in their rise and steady and beautiful in their elevation.

We have generally remarked, that persons of deep intellect, beautiful fancies, and gentle affections, are readers of Mr. Wordsworth's Poetry.— It is true, there are not in him, that haughty melancholy and troubled spirit which so peculiarly distinguish Lord Byron,—nor the wild and melodious fancy, the wanton pleasantry, or lightsome mirthfullness of Moore;—neither are there the gentlemanly prettinesses, and snatches of antiquity of Scott;—(who, by the way, is nothing better than an artful libeller of chivalrous heroes.) The truth is, Mr. Wordsworth describes natural feelings and natural beauties,—his thoughts come from him, purified through the heart.—He indulges in calm reasonings and rich reflections, and invites us to feast, concluding that we have the same appetites with himself.—Of the Lyrical ballads,—we can imagine him to have composed many in the fields, with all his feelings fresh about him. —We can imagine him to have suffered his memory to wander at times so long in the fairy grounds of Childhood,—that the present seemed to fade, and the past seemed to brighten into life. We can believe that he may often have wept, over his own pure and fine reflections, such tears as were made sacred by the charm of his own mind. We never touch on the Lyrical Ballads without feeling that we are busied with the innocent and the beautiful. There have been no Pastoral Poems so truly sweet since the days of Sydney—none in which the simplicities of poetry and philosophy are so gracefully blended. The pieces by Shenstone, mis-named Pastoral, are totally destitute of feeling. We can get no other idea than that the shepherd walked about very discontented,—very amorous, and very affected. Shenstone deserves all the hard things that have been said of him by Gray and Dr. Johnson,—for it is very clear that he wrote merely from "vanity and vexation of spirit." All his descriptions of rural happiness are artificial. He would make us believe that the fields are for ever green, the sheep for ever feeding, and that the shepherds have nothing to do but to make love and play on a pipe.

To those who have been close observers of nature, the poetry of Mr. Wordsworth is indeed a treasure. We have never heard the sound of a closing gate* on a still summer's evening, or the "tremulous sob of the complaining owl" breaking the silence of night—without recollecting his descriptions with a thrilling delight. They have melody

> —like of a hidden brook
> In the leafy month of June—,
> That to the sleeping woods all night.
> Singeth a quiet tune.
>
> Coleridge's *Ancient Mariner*.[1]

The Lyrical Ballads had, on their first appearance, much to contend against. They introduced a new system to the world, and one that, if received, could not fail to overthrow the artificial one so long adopted. They came forward in the dress of nature, not tricked out in a fantastical habit, and sought to revive gentle tastes, quiet feelings, and innocent affections. But "the million" saw nothing beyond the surface,—they could not reach where the calm philosophy rested;—these Poems, there-

---

* "Sound of clos'd gate, across the water borne,—
Hurrying the feeding hare through rustling corn."

These lines are from Mr. Wordsworth's Poem, entitled, "*An Evening Walk*," &c., which was published in his youthful days, and is now become very scarce.

fore, were violently opposed, and, as it would seem, overpowered. But they remained alive in the hearts and minds of a few, and have been quietly gaining strength up to the present hour.

We are convinced that the name of Wordsworth will

> In Fame's eternal volume shine for aye.

It is associated in our minds with all that is great and beautiful in human intellect. In the following extract from the Supplementary Essay, printed in his two volumes of poems lately re-published—it will be seen that he feels within him that mental elevation which must command posterity.

The love, the admiration, the indifference, the slight, the aversion, and even the contempt, with which these poems have been received, knowing, as I do, the source within mine own mind, from which they proceeded, and the labour and pains, which, when labour and pains appeared needful, have been bestowed upon them,—must all, if I think consistently, be received as pledges and tokens, bearing the same general impression though widely different in value;—they are all proofs that for the present time I have not laboured in vain, and afford assurances, more or less authentic, that the products of my industry will endure.[2]

We cannot conclude without protesting against the expensive manner in which the two last of Mr. Wordsworth's Poems have been published. Mr. Wordsworth writes for persons of intellect and feeling, and not for brainless young men, and ladies of fashion.—In the quarto volume Mr. Wordsworth is altogether out of the reach of common readers;—he is as much above their pockets as their understandings.

R.

On the Early Dramatic Poets, I. *January 7, 1816*

> The great world, in a little world of fancy,
> Is here abstracted.
>
> Ford's *Fancies Chaste and Noble.*[3]

We look back upon the early Dramatic Literature of our country, with that sort of delight, with which we reflect upon the pure and beautiful and solitary light of the morning. It stirs up within us, fresh thoughts and delightful feelings; and makes us at once meditative on the realities of nature. The Drama, at the time of Elizabeth and James, was the day-dawn of our Poetry, and had an openness and grandeur which have never, in succeeding times, been surpassed. In the present age, it is certainly in its eventide,—and all the light that beams, is but the reflected brightness of a Power that is gone. Nor do we see a promise of any

> —reappearing star,
> Like a glory from afar.

The ancient play-writers are scarcely known by name in these days, much less by the beauty of their poetry. To a few, indeed, their unshrinking boldness and intense feeling are neither strange, nor unadmired:—but, in general, they are slightly mentioned, and more slightly read or thought of. The world do not like to look in a mirror that reflects too clearly; and it is very common for curiosity to shrink from what is great and good: these works are therefore shunned as things that "have in them something dangerous."

We have, however, long loved the naked simplicity and majestic strength of these old authors;—we have felt that they gazed at their fellow-creatures, and faithfully pourtrayed their vices and their virtues. They were familiar with the excellencies and errors of humanity, and drew them as strongly as if they were things of substance. At the same time, with these they mingled the richest fancies and the most eloquent thoughtfulness. Their characters are always boldly struck off,—and no touch is omitted that would heighten the general effect. Thus we are beguiled to the perusal by the diversity of language and character—and the fine freedom of the style is as a spell that wins us to its power. There is no escape from the hands of nature.

Our old dramatists were as various as great in their powers; they could work up a scene of sorrow the most tender, or the most terrifying;—and they could revel in all the luxuriances of wit, and the pleasantries of fancy. They never gave us a mere outline of a picture, but threw in the fine tints that lifted it to perfection. Grief is shewn by other signs than tears and sighs and groans;—its inward workings and fearful apathies are faithfully described: the agonies of silent suffering are most perfectly told in two or three quiet lines; and the breaking heart or the troubled mind is delicately and faithfully depicted. A clumsy hand may rough-hew a statue,—but it requires that of a master to give it roundness and expression. The wit of these poets is also something beyond mere words: it is full of contrast and spirit; and possesses in itself a lasting vitality. Even where incident is wanting, the dialogue hath an innate gaiety that keeps interest awake. There is, indeed, no rest for the mind that devotes itself to the works of these writers;—it must be either disturbed or delighted, for sorrow or merriment is sure to be acting a first part in them. When the plot is interesting, the characters appear to be actuated by such feelings as their situations would naturally give birth to; and where the incidents become in any wise tame, the language immediately becomes rich with poetical description.

The great objection that has been urged against these writers, by those who have carefully looked into their works, is the impurity of their language. That there is a considerable looseness in their dialogue at times, it would be folly to deny, and wickedness to defend;—but, assuredly, something may be said in its palliation. In the first place, it is their undeviating custom to utter their thoughts plainly and unshrink-ingly;—they do not dress up indelicacy in a lovely garment, nor hide the frightful visage of vice in a mask;—they seek for no blandishments of language to soften the vigour of their ideas;—as they are conceived, so are they uttered;—and it is surely better to meet the enemy face to face, than to be started upon unawares. Then, it must be remembered, that morality is the great and positive end of all they write;—the impurities, therefore, only float at the top of the stream;—the water runs pure beneath them. The manners of the time, also, not only admitted, but demanded an indelicate wit. It is true, the present time is fairer in its expressions, but are its manners better or its characters brighter? We say—no. Vice is clothed in a finer habit, but it is therefore the more insin-uating. We are become more polished, but our morals are perhaps weak-ened:—for refinement is seldom had, unless at the sacrifice of strength.

There is something amiable in the partnership productions of these authors: they freely joined their abilities, and contributed to one work, boldly and unsparingly.* No pretty cavils occurred to injure their

---

* It is worth observing, that one of these joint performances, was nearly proving very fatal to the authors. Ben Jonson, Chapman, and Marston were accused of reflecting on the Scots, in their play of *"Eastward Hoe!"* for which they were committed to prison, and were in danger of losing their ears and noses.

labours—their minds were deeply engaged in their works, and could not afford time to disagree. It does not appear that a selfish avarice for solitary praise was common with them. We have no example in later times of these friendly conjunctions of genius. A fondness for individuality has long been popular, and mankind, in literature as in life, seem to have ceased to be social.

We shall now proceed to substantiate our opinions by severally examining the powers of the best dramatic writers that lived in the age of Elizabeth and James. We shall occasionally give short extracts from their works, by way of more directly illustrating our assertions; but as the room that we can spare is very limited, we shall be most choice in our selections.

Shakspeare, as the sun of the system, must be first noticed. He *is* (it would be foolish to say that he *was*) the finished anatomist of the heart. He has the power of reconciling the improbable with the probable,—the gay with the wretched,—the airy with the earthly. He can finely mingle rapture with melancholy, and passion with humour. The elements seem subservient to him;—and the human character, with its feelings, and failings, and energies, appears to be at the disposal of his will. Knowledge with him is innate,—and conception and execution seem to be the blended work of a moment. He is a sort of supernatural mirror, that not only shews us what *is*, but displays to us also what will *be*. All this may, very probably, have been often thought of before,—for Shakspeare is on the lips, and in the hearts and souls of all;—but, as he is the noblest, every one should pay him reverence; and it is not because he is known and loved that he should be passed by unmentioned or unhonoured.

It is not our intention to notice every writer in the order, which his merit might place him in. We shall give our ideas of the finest writers of "the olden time" without attention to pre-eminence of talent,—thus, we may leave some of the best to the last.

The plays of Beaumont and Fletcher display more of the Shakspearian luxuriance of poetry, than the works of any other writers of their time. These fine Dramatists have the art of ennobling whatever they touch;—the wildest fictions, and the most improbable personages, partake of the splendour of their intellects; and the scenes and characters of nature

30

lose none of their truth and freshness in description. The *actual* is faithfully represented, and the *ideal* is rendered more light and lovely. Reflection becomes embodied in language, and the romantic beauties of the pastoral world are deliciously described in their poetry. Fletcher had the finer fancy of the two; he has given greater proofs of his love of nature, and seems to have been more at home in the visionary, the picturesque, and the passionate. The wit of Fletcher is also excellent,— though it has not the rapidity of Shakspeare's, nor the soundness of Ben Jonson's.—Though the incidents of these two old Dramatists are at times languid and improbable, there is always a richness of poetry that makes up for the defects; their language is never without a romantic sweetness. We shall extract largely, for a newspaper, from their works, and we feel assured that our readers will be delighted with the passages which we shall produce.

"*The Two Noble Kinsmen*" breathes the freshest poetry. The following passage is exquisite for delicate melancholy:—

> No, Palamon:—
> Those hopes are prisoners with us: here we are,
> And here the graces of our youth must wither,
> Like a too timely spring; here age must find us,
> And, which is heaviest, Palamon, unmarried;
> The sweet embraces of a loving wife
> Loaden with kisses, arm'd with thousand cupids,
> Shall never clasp our necks! no issue know us,
> No figures of ourselves shall we e'er see,
> To glad our age, and like young eagles teach 'em
> Boldly to gaze against bright arms, and say
> Remember what your fathers were, and conquer!
> The fair-eyed maids shall weep our blandishments,
> And in their songs curse ever blinded fortune,
> Till she for shame see what a wrong she has done
> To youth and nature: this is all our world;
> We shall know nothing here but one another;
> Hear nothing, but the clock that tells our woes;
> The vine shall grow, but we shall never see it;
> Summer shall come, and with her all delights,
> But dead cold winter must inhabit here still.[4]

31

The characters which Emilia draws of Arcite and Palamon are also well worth extracting:—

> Arcite is gently visaged, yet his eye
> Is like an engine bent, or a sharp weapon
> In a soft sheath; mercy, and manly courage,
> Are bedfellows in his visage. Palamon
> Has a most menacing aspect; his brow
> Is graved, and seems to bury what it frowns on;
> Yet sometimes 'tis not so, but alters to
> The quality of his thoughts; long time his eye
> Will dwell upon his object; melancholy
> Becomes him nobly; so does Arcite's mirth;
> But Palamon's sadness is a kind of mirth,
> So mingled, as if mirth did make him sad,
> And sadness, merry;* those darker humours that
> Stick misbecomingly on others, on him
> Live in fair dwelling.[5]

In the same play we have the following lovely image:

> *Emil.* Of all flowers
> Methinks the rose is best.
> *Serv.* Why, gentle Madam?
> *Emil.* It is the very emblem of a maid:
> For when the west wind courts her gently,
> How modestly she blows, and paints the sun
> With her chaste blushes! When the north comes near her,
> Rude and impatient, then, like chastity,
> She locks her beauties in her bud again,
> And leaves him to base briars.[6]

The tragedy of " *The Two Noble Kinsmen* " is, we think, richer in poetical passages than any other work of these poets. In *"The Lovers' Progress"* † there is a sweet description of love.

---

* This has much of the character of *Hamlet* about it.

† This tragedy (*The Lovers' Progress*) was left unfinished by Fletcher, and was perfected either by Massinger or Shirley;—most probably the former. There is, however, a peculiar sweetness and truth in the passage we have extracted, that persuades us, it was from the hand of Fletcher.

—can Heaven be pleased with these things?
To see two hearts that have been twined together,
Married in friendship, to the world two wonders,
Of one growth, of one nourishment, one health,
Thus mortally divorced for one weak woman?
Can Love be pleased? Love is a gentle spirit;
The wind that blows the April flowers not softer;
She's drawn with doves to shew her peacefulness;
Lions and bloody pards are Mars's servants.
Would you serve Love? do it with humbleness,
Without a noise, with still prayers, and soft murmurs:
Upon her altars offer your obedience,
And not your broils; she's won with tears, not terrors;
That fire you kindle to her deity,
Is only grateful when it's blown with sighs,
And holy incense flung with white hand innocence;
You wound her now; you are too superstitious;
No sacrifice of blood or death she longs for.[7]

We must steal room for one short passage from the tragi-comedy of
"*The Queen of Corinth*," but it must be our last. We could have wished
to have given some of the fanciful and pastoral parts of "*The Faithful
Shepard*," and a few extracts from "*The Island Princess*,"—"*The Humourous
Lieutenant*",—"*Valentinian*," and "*Nice Valour*;"—particularly a song
from the latter, which Milton closely imitated in *Il Penserso*.—A scene in
"*The Wife for a Month*," in which Alphonso is poisoned, is certainly
equal to the death-scene in "*King John*," or that in "*Valentinian*:" but
we cannot spare room for it:—

Wherefore sits
My Phoebe shadow'd in a sable cloud?
Those pearly drops which thou let'st fall like beads,
Numb'ring on them thy vestal orisons,
Alas, are spent in vain! I love thee still;
In midst of all these showers, thou sweetlier scent'st,
Like a green meadow on an April day,
In which the sun and west-wind play together,
Striving to catch and drink the balmy drops.[8]

Ben Jonson is a name well known to every lover of the drama: it
revives within us every idea of wit, and taste, and learning. His fancy is

of a rich kind,—though his extensive knowledge of the classical authors of the earliest times, had perhaps somewhat confined it. Still, however, it continually sports forth in the wildest and loveliest manner,—and spurns the chains which art would entwine around it. We know that it has been customary to accuse this poet of *always* injuring his imagination by his pedantry; but there are numerous passages in his works that would overthrow this unjust accusation. His wit is full of that immortal fire which time cannot subdue. In *The Alchemist*, and *Volpone*, there is a richness of character, added to a conversational humour, that cannot be surpassed; it absolutely feasts the mind. Though he succeeded well in the serious, and the imaginative, his talent evidently lay in the ludicrous and the learned. Yet the following passage from Ben Jonson's *Sad Shepard*, will prove to what a height his imagination could elevate itself, in spite of the weight of learning which his enemies have complained of. An old shepherd is instructing the followers of Robin Hood how to find a witch:—

> Within a gloomy dimble she doth dwell,
> Down in a pit o'ergrown with brakes and briars,
> Close by the ruins of a shaken abbey,
> Torn with an earthquake down unto the ground,
> 'Mongst graves, and grots, near an old charnel house,
> Where you shall find her sitting in her fourm,
> As fearful, and melancholic, as that
> She is about; with catterpillar's kells,
> And knotty cobwebs, rounded in with spells.
> Thence she steals forth to relief, in the fogs,
> And rotten mists, upon the fens and bogs,
> Down to the drowned lands of Lincolnshire;
> To make ewes cast their lambs, swine eat their farrow!
> The housewife's pan not work, nor the milk churn!
> Writhe children's wrists, and suck their breath in sleep!
> Get vials of their blood! and where the sea
> Casts up his shiny ooze, search for a weed
> To open locks with, and to rivet charms,
> Planted about her, in the wicked seat
> Of all her mischiefs, which are manifold.[9]

This passage may match with the noble descriptions of Shakspeare and Fletcher. We will give one other short extract: it is the opening passage of a scene in the comedy of "*The New Inn,*" and is delightfully written: we wish that it was in our power to produce the whole scene, which is full of graceful learning and elegant wit.

> There is no life on earth, but being in love!
> There are no studies, no delights, no business,
> No intercourse, or trade of sense, or soul,
> But what is love! I was the laziest creature,
> The most unprofitable sign of nothing,
> The veriest drone, and slept away my life
> Beyond the dormouse, till I was in love!
> And now I can out-wake the nightingale,
> Out-watch an usurer, and outwalk him too,
> Stalk like a ghost that haunted 'bout a treasure;
> And all that fancied treasure, it is love![10]

One more extract, and we have done. It is the luxurious speech of Epicure Mammon, in the *Alchemist*, who is led to believe that he will obtain the philosopher's stone:—

> My meat shall all come in, in Indian shells,
> Dishes of agate set in gold, and studded
> With emeralds, sapphires, hyacinths, and rubies;
> The tongues of carps, dormice, and camels' heels,
> Boil'd i' the spirit of Sol, and dissolv'd in pearl,
> (Apicius' diet 'gainst the epilepsy)
> And I will eat these broths with spoons of amber,
> Headed with diamant and carbuncle.
> My footboy shall eat pheasants, calver'd salmons,
> Knots, godwits, lampreys; I myself will have
> The beards of barbels serv'd:—instead of salads,
> Oil'd mushrooms; and the swelling unctious paps
> Of a fat pregnant sow, newly cut off,
> Drest with an exquisite and poignant sauce;
> For which I'll say unto my cook, "There's gold,
> Go forth, and be a Knight."[11]

The character of Epicure Mammon is a masterpiece; his inordinate love of wordiness, furnishes a splendid vehicle for conveying his greediness for sumptuous food, and store of money. Image after image comes trooping forth, and the language is withal finely harmonized. It is to be lamented that such a poet as Ben Jonson should have been vilely abused by the writers of his own days, and ours;—we can only recommend the able pamphlet of Mr. Gilchrist, as an antidote to such infamous calumnies. We feel convinced that "the learned Ben" will pass triumphantly down the stream of time,—and that he will leave his accusers, mere wrecks on his passage.

Massinger is a poet of very great ability.* His plots are admirably managed;—and characters and manners are strongly drawn by him. He gives the most delicate portraitures of female gentleness and fidelity, —and depicts an elevated mind in the most commanding and dignified manner. His versification is exquisitely beautiful, and is generally one continual flow of harmony;—it resembles the calm and majestic gliding of a river. In these days, it would not be possible to refine the language of his best passages; they have in them an imperishable sweetness—the changes of time and manners touch them not. But the wit of Massinger is by no means so brilliant, as that of many of his contemporaries,—nor is his humour so chaste: and it is perhaps owing to these deficiencies that his impurities are more glaring:—he is also destitute of passion. His descriptions of nature,—and his finished and faithful delineations of noble minds,—and his general eloquence of sorrow, place him, however, amongst the finest poets of his age: though inferior to some of them in wit, he is seldom beneath them in stateliness and grace. The length to which this article has already extended (though as yet we have noticed but three of the old writers)—will preclude us from extracting as largely as we ourselves could wish, or Massinger's merits would justify.

The following description from "*The Great Duke of Florence*,"—which, by the way, is the finest specimen of elegant comedy, that our language can boast,—is highly beautiful:

---

* In Mr. Gifford's "Introduction" to his excellent edition of the plays of Massinger, there is a very pathetic and interesting passage on the misfortunes of the poet. We think it well worth extracting: "Other writers for the stage, not superior to him in abilities, had their periods of good fortune, their bright as well as their stormy hours; but Massinger seems to have enjoyed no gleam of sunshine; his life was all one wintry day, and 'shadows, clouds, and Darkness,' rested upon it." p. lxxvi.

Massinger seems to have been a man of "singular gentleness and modesty," and it does not appear that he ever made an enemy:—adversity of course frowned on him. He led a life of dependence and penury —and it is therefore a wonder that he preserved his elegance of mind, and suavity of temper.

—We might walk
In solitary groves, or in choice gardens;
From the variety of curious flowers
Contemplate nature's workmanship, and wonders;
And then, for change, near to the murmurs of
Some bubbling fountain, I might hear you sing,
And, from the well tun'd accents of your tongue,
In my imagination conceive
With what melodious harmony a quire
Of angels sing above their Maker's praises.
And then with chaste discourse, as we return'd,
Imp feathers to the broken wings of Time.[12]

The funeral procession in "*The Fatal Dowry*" (on which tragedy Rowe founded his "Fair Penitent") is thus poetically described:—

How like a silent stream, shaded by night,
And gliding softly with our windy sighs,
Moves the whole frame of this solemnity![13]

The complaint against slavery in the following passage is very fine:—

—The noble horse,
That, in his fiery youth, from his wide nostrils
Neigh'd courage to his rider, and brake through
Groves of opposed pikes, bearing his lord
Safe to triumphant victory; old or wounded
Was set at liberty, and freed from service;—
The Athenian mules, that from the quarry drew
Marble, hew'd for the temples of the gods,
The great work ended, were dismiss'd and fed
At the public cost; nay, faithful dogs have found
Their sepulchres; but man, to man more cruel,
Appoints no end to the suffrings of his slave.[14]

The speech of Sforza, over the body of Marcelia, from "*The Duke of Milan*," is very beautiful.

How pale and wan she looks! O pardon me,
That I presume (dyed o'er with bloody guilt,
Which makes me, I confess, far, far unworthy)
To touch this snow white hand. How cold it is,

> This once was cupid's fire-brand, and still
> 'Tis so to me. How slow her pulses beat too!
> Yet in this temper, she is all perfection,
> And mistress of a heart so full of sweetness,
> The blood of virgins, in their pride of youth,
> Are balls of snow or ice compared unto her.[15]

We shall close our extracts with the following most sweet image. It is as delicate and tender, as if Shakspeare had breathed it in his happiest moments:—

> What's that? oh, nothing but the whispering wind
> Breathes through your churlish hawthorn that grew rude,
> As if it chid the gentle breath that kiss'd it.

We must now conclude this article for the present. At an early opportunity, we shall return to the subject; and amongst the writers yet to be noticed are Ford, Webster, Middleton, Marston, Heywood, Dekker, &c.

It will be seen, therefore, that some of the brightest ornaments of our Dramatic Literature remain still to be mentioned. Ford, indeed, appears to us not to be surpassed in feeling and melancholy, by *any* of the poets of whom we have just spoken.

R.

On the Early English Dramatists. No. II. March 3, 1816

In our first Essay on the Early Dramatic Poets of our country, we noticed those whose names all readers of the present day are familiar with. It is now our intention to proceed in the review,—and some of the poets we shall have to remark upon, (although their names are less generally known), will be found to have just claims on the admiration of all who find anything romantic or feeling in Beaumont and Fletcher, —witty or learned in Ben Jonson—and majestic or pathetic in Massinger. The present essay will include Marston, Marlowe, Dekker, and Ford;— the next (which will be the last) will take in Webster, Chapman, Middleton, Heywood, and one or two others.[16]

Marston was a dramatic satirist. In most of his plays we find some character that is the moving scourge of the vice and follies of his time. He was an inferior sort of dramatic Chaucer,—for he was chiefly distinguished as a close observer of men and manners. At times his ideas are of the most elevated kind, but then his language is often so uncouth, as greatly to disfigure them. Marston has, however, given us, in his *Antonio and Mellida*, some fine thoughts, and real feeling, finely expressed;—but we generally find that he strays at last into satirical humour. We shall select one or two of the best parts which can be found in his works. *Pietro Jacomo*, when disguised as a hermit in the play of *The Malcontent*, speaks the following beautiful passage—

> *P. Jac.* Now had the mounting sun's all ripening wings
> Swept the cold sweat of night from earth's dark breast,
> When I, whom men call hermit of the rock,
> Forsook my cell, and mounted up a cliff,
> Against whose base the heady Neptune dash'd
> His high-curled brows; there 'twas I eased my limbs;
> When lo! my entrails melted with the moan
> Someone, who far 'bove me was climb'd, did make.[17]

How sweet is the description of day-break in the history of *Antonio and Mellida*!—

> Is not yon gleam the shudd'ring morn, that flakes,
> With silver tincture, the east verge of heaven?[18]

The passage in *Antonio's Revenge* is even finer.

> —See, the dapple grey coursers of the morn
> Beat up the light with their bright silver hoofs,
> And chase it through the sky.[19]

Such perfect passages as these are not commonly to be met with in Marston—one more, which is from the *Insatiate Countess*, and we shall quit him.

> *Executioner.* Madam, tie up your hair.
> *Isabella.* O these golden nets,
> That have ensnared so many wanton youths!
> Not one, but has been held a thread of life.
> And superstitiously depended on.
> What else?

Executioner. Madam, I must intreat you blind your eyes.
Isabella. I have lived too long in darkness, my friend:
And yet mine eyes, with their majestic light,
Have got new muses in a poet's spright.
They've been more gaz'd at than the god of day;
Their brightness never could be flattered:
Yet thou command'st a fixed cloud of lawn
To eclipse eternally these minutes of light.
I am prepared.[20]

Marlowe was a writer of great power: with a mind formed for minute description and general observation, he had at the same time, a language always appropriately expressive. There is seldom anything of inaction in his serious plays.—He can either be great or graceful,—terrific in his flights into the imaginative world, or sweet and natural in his wanderings amidst familiar objects and noiseless scenes: he is as successful in his management of high thoughts and mystical acts, as he is in his workings up of human feelings and passions. The death-scene of *Faustus* is grandly awful. His description has a gloom about it which clouds the heart of the reader:—in the death-language of *Faustus*, there is a desperate and hopeless horror,—a madness of fear and memory. The imagination can almost discern the mists and terrors of hell in the background. This scene proves how well Marlowe could deal with the wild and the unearthly; his conceptions are not unworthy of his subject, and his language does justice to his conceptions. But in other plays, his genius shews itself in a fairer and milder way; we have many of the most exquisite descriptions of all that is beautiful in nature.—There, is, however, much that must be objected to in the works of Marlowe;—his attempts at humour are contemptible—his language is at times too turgid—and some of his traits of character are too disgusting to be borne. *Eleazer* and the *Mother* in *Lust's Dominion* are absolutely detestable,[21] we can afford room but for one extract, which shall be from *Doctor Faustus*.

After a long exclamation of horror—the watch gives notice that the hour of twelve is near approaching—Faustus goes on thus in his hopelessness—

All beasts are happy, for when they die,
Their souls are soon dissolved in elements.

> But mine must live still, to be plagued in hell.
> Cursed be the parents that engendered me:
> No, Faustus, curse thyself, curse Lucifer,
> That hath deprived thee of the joys in Heaven.
> > (*The Clock strikes Twelve.*)
> It strikes, it strikes; now, body, turn to air,
> Or Lucifer will bear thee quick to Hell.
> O soul, be changed into small water drops,
> And fall into the ocean; ne'er be found.
> > (*Thunder, and enter the Devils.*)
> O mercy, Heaven, look not so fierce on me.
> Adders and serpents, let me breathe awhile;
> Ugly hell gape not; come not Lucifer;
> I'll burn my books: Oh Mephistophilis.[22]

We now come to a Poet of great ability—to one who, in spite of sorrow, and want and imprisonment, left behind him works of the most spirited and fanciful order:—Dekker had all the greatness and all the misery of genius. He wrote for bread, and yet with a freedom and fire which would infer unbroken ease of heart and mind. Many of his years were worn away in a jail,—and still he could not descend to any common employment, that might have been more profitable and less precarious. He had much of Fletcher's richness of fancy, and is liberal in his scatterings of the flowers of poetry. Had fortune favoured him, we have no hesitation in asserting, that Dekker would have successfully contended with the most powerful of his contemporaries: poverty and confinement must have injured his mind, though his works would induce us to think otherwise. *Old Fortunatus* is a wonderful performance. We must content ourselves with making some extracts from this alone: it is rich in beauties.

There is great beauty in the speech of *Fortunatus* to his sons, on his return from travel.

> In some courts shall you see Ambition,
> Sit, piecing Dedalus' old waxen wings;
> But being clapt on, and they about to fly,
> Even when their hopes are busied in the clouds,
> They melt against the sun of majesty,
> And down they tumble to destruction.

> By travel, boys, I have seen all these things,
> Fantastic compliment stalks up and down
> Trickt in outlandish feathers; all his words,
> His looks, his oaths, are all ridiculous,
> All apish, childish, and Italianate.[23]

The following "exstacy of love," spoken by the mad-hearted *Orleans*, is admirable:—

> Thou art a traitor to that white and red,
> Which, sitting on her cheeks (being Cupid's throne),
> In my heart's soveraine; O, when she is dead,
> This wonder (beauty) shall be found in none.
> Now Agripyne's not mine, I vow to be
> In love with nothing but Deformity.
> O fair Deformity, I muse all eyes
> Are not enamoured of thee: thou didst never
> Murder men's hearts, or let them pine like wax
> Melting in the sun of thy destiny;
> Thou art a faithful nurse to chastity;
> Thy beauty is not like to Agripyne's,
> For care, and age, and sickness her's deface,
> But thine's eternal: O, Deformity,
> Thy fairness is not like to Agripyne's,
> For (dead) her beauty will no beauty have,
> But thy face looks most lovely in the grave.[24]

This is one of the tortures of reason;—this is the very essence of spirit. Ford is the Poet of these most after our own hearts. The sweetness and melancholy of his thoughts can only be equalled by the mild and mournful music of his language. Ford excells not, perhaps generally, in what is fanciful and imaginative. (Though the contest between the Lover and the Nightingale in the *Lover's Melody* is delicious). His mind sojourns in the breast of man, and the passions, and feelings, and affections living there, are what he busies himself with. His thinking is fine and powerful without exertion, and his language is emphatic in its very simplicity. He is quite equal to Shakspeare (and this is giving the fulness of praise) in his delineation of the rapturous attachment of youthful souls, and the lonely and fatal sorrows which time heaps on it:—or in the portraiture of the high and noble heart that is lost in its own greatness. The fearful and ardent passion which *Giovanni* cherishes for his sister *Annabella*, is most beautifully and strongly told;[25]—the false reasoning with which he justifies it to his own mind,—the delicacy and yet enthusiasm with which he breaks it to her—the last fatal interview in which he destroys her—and *Annabella's* mildness, and loveliness and simplicity, and, we might also say purity in guilt, are described in poetry which is pathos itself. It is impossible to read of these poor lost enthusiasts without feeling a pity for them, unmingled with aught of disgust—and perhaps no other writer,—Shakspeare excepted,—could have drawn a brother and sister loving each other, as *Giovanni* and *Annabella* love, without making them wholly disgusting. Ford has contrived to throw an air of purity around all they say,—they seem to live but for each other, and to walk in the light of their own affections. We should shrink from the madness of their passion, if it were not that they beguile us to linger and forget, by the music of their discourse;—their fondness seems fate,—and our own hearts are charmed till we deem their fatal passion a spotless purity.

The *Broken Heart* is nearly equal to the Play we have been just admiring, in its poetry,—and is superior to it in plot. The characters in it are most faithfully and forcibly drawn;—the gentle and wasting *Penthea* is sweetly interesting—and the pure-spiritedness of *Ithocles* is well described: but *Calantha* is the perfection of female character;—she has the mind of a hero, with the heart of a woman,—and her intense feeling can only be equalled by her patient and silent suffering. There is not, we think, any scene in the English Drama superior to this one, in which her weight of sorrow breaks her heart:—what can be finer than the following four lines,—they are the strong traits of her own character, and from her own lips;—

> Be such mere women, who with shrieks and outcries,
> Can vow a present end to all their sorrows;
> Yet live to vow new pleasures, and outlive them;
> They are the silent griefs that cut the heart-strings.[26]

Our limits will not allow us to speak severally of the remaining Plays of Ford:—they are unequal in merit. We do not much admire the historical drama of *Perkin Warbeck*.—The author seems to have lost his spirit in his confinement,—for into close confinement did history put him. *Fancies Chaste and Noble* and *The Lady's Trial*, are of a light nature—the heart of Ford was fond of gloom. Darkness was his light.

The conversation which *Giovanni* holds with *Annabella*, just before he destroys her, is inimitably beautiful—we wish we could extract the whole scene:—

> *Gio.* Look up, look here; what see you in my face?
> *Anna.* Distraction, and a troubled conscience.
> *Gio.* Death and a swift repining wrath—yet look,
> What see you in mine eyes?
> *Anna.* Methinks you weep.
> *Gio.* I do, indeed; these are the funeral tears
> Shed on your grave: these furrow'd up my cheeks,
> When first I lov'd and knew not how to woo.
> Fair Annabella, should I here repeat
> The story of my life, we might lose time.
> Be record all the spirits of the air,
> And all things else that are, that day and night,
> Early and late, the tribute which my heart
> Hath paid to Annabella's sacred love,
> Hath been these tears which are her mourners now.
> Never till now did nature do her best,
> To shew a matchless beauty to the world,
> Which in an instant, ere it scarce was seen,
> The jealous destinies required again.
> Pray, Annabella, pray; since we must part,
> Go thou, white in thy soul, to fill a throne
> Of innocence and sanctity in Heaven.[27]

The preceding passage is not more beautiful than the rest of the scene. But to quote from Ford is to do him an injustice,—he is regular in his merit throughout each scene—the stream of his thoughts runs evenly, and sweetly, and mournfully.

For the present we must rest. Our next Essay (which will be the last) will notice the remaining fine poets of the age of Elizabeth. They have been long in the shade, but we shall yet see them placed in the sunshine. It has been well observed by Bacon, "Nature is often hidden, sometimes overcome, seldom extinguished."[28]

J.H.R.

The Pilgrimage of Living Poets to the Stream of Castaly.[29]
April 7, 1816

Who now shall give unto me words and sound
Equal unto this haughty enterprise?

Spenser B. 2 C. 10.[30]

I am one of those unfortunate youths to whom the Muse has glanced a sparkling of her light,—one of those who pant for distinction, but have not within them that immortal power which alone can command it. There are many,—some, Sir, may be known to you,—who feel keenly and earnestly the eloquence of heart and mind in others, but who cannot, from some inability or unobtrusiveness, clearly express their own thoughts and feelings:—whose lives are but long and silent dreams of romantic pleasure and poetic wonderment;—who almost adore the matchless fancies of genuine bards,—and love them as interpreters and guardians of those visionary delights which are the perpetual inmates of their bosoms. I know not whether I make myself clear to you;—if I do not, you will see that my confusion arises rather from a defective power than a defective will. I love the Poets: I live in the light of their fancies. It is my best delight to wander forth on summer evenings, when the air is fresh and clear,—and the leaves of the trees are making music with it,—and the birds are busy with their wings, fluttering themselves to rest,—and a brook is murmuring along almost inaudibly, and the sun is going quietly down:—it is at this time delicious to muse over the works of our best bards. Some time last year, I had roamed in an evening like to one of those I have spoken of; and, after dwelling on the fairy beauties of Spenser, and from thence passing to the poets of my own time, and to comparing the latter with some that had gone before, I cast myself on a romantic bank by a brook side. The silence around me, —save the home-returning bee with its "drowsy hum,"—and the moaning sound of distant cattle,—and the low, sullen gurgling of waters —lulled me into a sleep. The light of my thoughts gilded my dream;— my vision was a proof of mental existence when the bodily sense had passed away. I have a great desire to attempt giving publicity to my dream, but I have before told you how limited are my powers of expression;—so I must rely upon your goodness, in receiving the crude description, or not.

Methought—(this, I believe, is the established language of dreams)—methought I was walking idly along a romantic vale, which was surrounded with majestic and rugged mountains;—a small stream struggled through it, and its waves seemed the brightest chrystal I had ever witnessed. I sat me down on its margin, which was rocky and beautiful—(so far my vision was copied directly from life).—As I mused, a female figure rose like a silvery mist from the waters, and advanced, with a countenance full of life, and a form of living air:—her garments floated round her like waves, and her hair basked on her shoulders—

like sunny beams on alabaster rocks.

There was a touch of immortality in her eyes,—and, indeed, her visage altogether was animated with a more than earthly glory. She approached me with smiles, and told me she was the guardian of the stream that flowed near,—and that the stream itself was the true *Castalian*, which so many "rave of, though they know it not." I turned with fresh delight to gaze on the water; its music sounded heavenly to me,—I fancied that there was a pleasant *dactylic* motion in its waves. The Spirit said, that from the love I bore to her favourite, Spenser, she would permit me to see (myself unseen) the annual procession of living bards to fetch water from the stream on that day:—I looked her my thanks as well as I was able;—it was out of my power to express them;—so you see my old complaint did not forsake me even on the brink of immortality. She likewise informed me, that it was customary for each Poet, as he received his portion, to say in what manner he intended to use it. The voice of the Spirit was such as fancy has heard in some wild and lovely spot among the hills or lakes of this world at twilight time:—I felt my soul full of music while listening to it, and held my breath in very excess of delight. Suddenly I heard the sound of approaching feet, and a confused mingling of voices;—the Spirit touched me into invisibility, and then softly faded into sunny air herself.

In a little time I saw a motley crowd advancing confusedly to the stream:—I soon perceived that they were each provided with vessels to bear away some portion of the immortal waters. They all paused at

46

a little distance from the spot on which I was reclining; and then each walked singly and slowly from the throng and dipped his vessel in the blue wild wave of Castaly. As well as I can recollect, I will endeavour to describe the manner and words of the most interesting of our living poets on this most interesting occasion. The air about the spot seemed brighter with their presence, and the waves danced along with a livelier delight:—Pegasus might be seen coursing the winds in wild rapture on one of the neighbouring mountains,—and sounds of glad and viewless wings were heard at intervals in the air, as if "troops of spirits were revelling over head and rejoicing at the scene."

And first, methought, a lonely and melancholy figure slowly moved forth and silently filled a Grecian urn:—I knew by the look of nobility, and the hurried and turbulent plunge with which the vessel was dashed into the stream, that the owner was Lord Byron. He shed some tears while gazing on the water, and they seemed to make it purer and fairer:—he declared that he would keep the urn by him, untouched "for some years;"—but he had scarcely spoken, ere he had sprinkled forth some careless drops on the earth. He suddenly retreated.

There then advanced a polite personage very oddly clad;—he had a breast plate on,—and over that a Scotch plaid—and, strange to say, with these, silk-stockings and dress shoes:—this gentleman brought an old helmet for his vessel:—I guessed him to be Walter Scott. His helmet did not hold enough for a very deep draught, but the water it contained took a pleasant sparkle from the warlike metal which shone through its shallowness. He said he had disposed of his portion on advantageous terms.

Next came Thomas Moore. You might have known him by the wild lustre of his eye, and the fine freedom of his air; he gaily dipped a goblet in the tide, and vowed, in his high spirited manner, that he would turn his share to nectar:—he departed with smiles. I heard the wings play pleasantly in the air while *he* was bending over the stream.

I now perceived a person advance whom I knew to be Southey. His brow was bound by a wreath of faded laurel, which had every mark of town growth. He appeared quite bewildered, and scarcely could remember his way to the inspiring stream. His voice was chaunting the praises of kings and courts as he advanced—but he dropt some little poems behind him, as he passed me, which were very opposite in tone to what

47

he himself uttered.[31] He was compelled to stoop before he could reach the water,—and the gold vessel, which he used, procured but little at last. He declared that his intention was to make sack of what he obtained. On retiring, he mounted a cream-coloured horse, which was in waiting, —and set off in uneven paces for St. James's.

Then appeared Rogers with a glass in his hand, which, from the cypher engraved thereon, had evidently once belonged to Oliver Goldsmith. He caught but a few drops, and these he meant to make the most of, by mingling them with common water.

Crabbe, with a firm step and a steady countenance, walked sedately to the stream, and plunged a wooden bowl into it:—he observed that he should make strong ale for the country people, of all that he took away;—and that, after the first *brewing*, he should charitably allow Mr. Fitzgerald[32] to make small beer for his own use.

In a pensive attitude Montgomery sauntered to the water's brink;— he there mused awhile,—uttered a few somethings of half poetry and half prayer,[33]—dipped a little mug of Sheffield ware in the wave, and retired in tears.

With a wild yet nervous step Campbell came from the throng;— light visions started up in the fair distances as he moved, and the figure of *Hope*[34] could be faintly discerned amidst them,—she smiled on him as he advanced. He dipped his bowl in the stream with a fine bold air, and expressed his intention of analysing part of the water which he procured.[35]

Next came Hunt, with a rich fanciful goblet in his hand, finely enamelled with Italian landscapes;[36] he held the cup to his breast as he approached, and his eyes sparkled with frank delight. After catching a wave, in which a sun-beam seemed freshly melted, he intimated that he should water hearts-ease and many favourite flowers with it. The sky appeared of a deep blue as he was retiring.

Lord Strangford would now have advanced but the voice of the Spirit forebad him,—as he did not come for the water on his own account.[37]

Coleridge, Lamb, and Lloyd[38] walked forth arm-in-arm, and moved gently to the stream:—they conversed, as they passed, on the beauties of the country,—on its peaceful associations, and on the purity of domestic affections. Their conversation then turned to poetry,—and,

48

from the simplicity of the remarks of Lloyd and Lamb, I found that their very hearts were wedded to innocence and peace;—Coleridge talked in a higher strain,—but he at last confused himself with the abstruseness of his own observations:—he hinted at a metaphysical Poem he was about to write in 100 books,—Lamb remarked to him that he should prefer one of his affectionate and feeling sonnets to all his wanderings of mind. Each of these Poets held in his hand a simple porrenger—declaring, that it brought the finest recollections of frugal fare and country quiet:—Lamb and Lloyd dipped in a bright but rather shallow part of the stream;—Coleridge went to the depths, where he might have caught the purest water, had he not unfortunately clouded it with the sand which he himself disturbed at bottom. Lamb and Lloyd stated that they should take their porrengers home and share their contents with the amiable and simple hearts dwelling there;—Coleridge was not positive as to the use to which he should apply his portion of the stream, till he had ascertained what were the physical reasons for the sand's propensity to mount and curl itself in water: he thought, however, of clubbing it with the portions of his companions and making a lake of the whole.—These three Poets left the stream in the same manner they approached it.

Last came a calm and majestic figure moving serenely towards the stream:—the Celandines and small flowers sprang up to catch the pressure of his feet,—the sun-light fell with a finer glow around,—spirits rustled most mirthfully and musically in the air, and a wing every now and then twinkled into sight,—(like the autumn leaf that trembles and flashes up to the sun)—and its feathers of wavy gold were almost too sparkling to be looked upon;—the waters of Castaly ran brighter as he approached, and seemed to play and dimple with pleasure at his presence. It was Wordsworth! In his hand he held a vase of pure chrystal, —and, when he had reached the brink of the stream, the wave proudly swelled itself into his cup:—at this moment the sunny air above his brow, became embodied,—and the glowing and lightsome Spirit shone into being, and dropt a garland on his forehead;—sounds etherial swelled, and trembled, and revelled in the air,—and forms of light played in and out of sight,—and all around seemed like a living world of breathing poetry. Wordsworth bent with reverence over the vase, and declared that the waters he had obtained should be the refreshment of his soul;—he then raised his countenance,—which had become illumined from the wave over which he had bowed,—and retired with a calm dignity.

The sounds of stirring wings now ceased,—the air became less bright, —and the flowers died away upon the banks. No other Poet remained to obtain water from the Castalian stream,—but still it sparkled and played along, with a soul-like and melodious sound.—On a sudden I heard a confusion of tongues behind me;—on turning round, I found that it arose from a mistaken set of gentlemen who were chattering and bustling and dipping at a little brook, which they deemed was the true Castalian;—their splashing and vociferation and bustle, can only be imagined by those who have seen a flock of geese wash themselves in a pond with gabbling importance. There was Spencer, with a goblet, lent to him by a lady of quality,[39]—and Hayley,[40] simpering, and bowing, and reaching with a tea-cup at the water,—and Wilson[41] with a child's pap-spoon,—and Bowles laboriously engaged in filling fourteen nut-shells,[42]—and Lewis slowly and mysteriously plunging an old skull into the brook:—while poor Cottle[43] fumed and angered, but scarcely reached the stream at last. There were no encouraging signs in the elements,—no delightful sounds of attendant spirits,—no springing up of flowers to cheer these worthies in their pursuits:—they seemed perfectly satisfied with their own greatness, and were flattered into industry by their own vanity and loudness. After some time, the perpetual activity of tongues fatigued my ear, and I turned myself from the noisy crowd, towards the silent Heavens:—There, to my astonished and delighted eyes, appeared Shakspeare, surrounded with excessive light, with Spenser on one hand, and Milton on the other,—and with the best of our early Bards thronging about him. One glance of his eye scared the silly multitude from the brook;—then, amidst unearthly music, he calmly ascended, and was lost in the splendours of the sky.—At this moment I awoke. The evening was getting chill around me;—the breeze was coldly whispering through the foliage, and the deer were couching to rest on the spangled grass. I arose,—and musing on the wonders of my dream,—slowly bent my way homewards.

J.H.R.

The Reply of William Lisle Bowles to Reynolds' Satire. May 12, 1816[44]

To the Editor of *The Champion*.

Bremhill Parsonage, near Calne, Wilts.

Sir,—When the name of an individual is brought into a public paper, any observation, in reply from that individual, is generally admitted in the same paper, by the liberal and generous courtesy of its conductor. —A correspondent of the *Champion* has facetiously described the numerous Poetical Characters of the present day, as dipping for water in the "clear Castalian well," whilst to me is assigned (*Horresco referens*) a place among the *gabbling geese*, at a brook mistaken for the real stream! Of this I have no right to complain, and it is a matter of indifference to me, whether I am introduced among the geese or the swans. It is a satisfaction to me, that I could appeal to those who appear highest and most adorned, in this assembled society, for a very different character than that which, as a Poet, is here given me. I could appeal to your favorite Wordsworth himself,—and none estimates his poetical talents higher: I could appeal to those who speak with delight of the feeling and affectionate sonnets "of one of their number;"[45] I could appeal to the writer of these "feeling and affectionate sonnets," who has publicly said, they were written in "*imitation*" of some others, and of which no one has been so ready to speak warmly,[46] both in public and private;—I could appeal to him, who, as a Poet in the present day, stands next to Spenser in imagination, and who exceeds him in pathos, whether I am entitled to such a place and character as is assigned to me in the description.

I think, Sir, I could venture to appeal to your own judgment and candour, after you had given a quiet and dispassionate review of these small poems, (which are so contemptuously spoken of) because I am convinced that those writings cannot be quite so *contemptible*, of which there have been published eleven editions, of nearly one thousand to fifteen hundred copies each; and which have been indebted to no particle of their success, either from romantic narratives or detraction of the fair fame of others. The writer in your paper is one of the readers of those poems which he condemns,—one of upwards of ten thousand!

This, Sir, you may call self-applause. No,—it is not;—it is a plain fact.

Those who know me, know how very far I am from deserving the character of "gabbling importance," or that of ever seeking to depreciate others;—nor should I have troubled you on this occasion but on another account.

Living in the country, I should have never seen or heard of your examination of our Poets;—occupied solely, as a parochial clergyman, neither my morning studies, or my evening walks, would have been disturbed by the knowledge of your correspondent's satire; but, as Sheridan says, there is generally a "—good natured friend" on those occasions,—so I would wish that "good natured friend" to know, through the medium of the same paper which he has been at the pains to convey to me, that the unmanly and despicable littleness, which could prompt his anxieties on this occasion, (lest I should be ignorant of the important contents of your paper) in my mind, is far more offensive than the article he has been so studious to convey. I am, Sir,

Your Obedient Servant,

W. L. Bowles

P.S.   May I take the liberty of requesting your acceptance of my first small volume, which contains the "*nut-shells.*" I almost venture to think you have not read them: if, on an occasional perusal, at your leisure, you agree with your correspondent, "*a la bonne heure!*" If not, I trust I may rely on the equity of a manly judgment for your taking some opportunity of doing a piece of justice to one who may have received (in your unbiassed opinion) unmerited abuse.

On Chaucer.   May 26, 1816

—Call up him who left untold
The story of Cambuscan bold.

Milton.[47]

Chaucer is the clear and breathing Poet of the months of April and May—of morning—of meadows, and birds and their harbours,—of

52

internal feelings as connected with external nature—of strong individual character—and of the noble wonders of romance.

He is a stern but faithful painter of things about him:—we can always see that he sketches and works up his views from nature. He feels intensely through his eyes. A leaf is described by him so clearly, that its crispness and glossy greenness come directly before the sight. A little path winds through his poetry as naturally as it does through a field, and all the idleness of a romantic stroller creeps over the heart as the poet speaks of it. Chaucer delights to be up, and out, before the sun— while the stars are coldly white in the cold white sky—while the trees are still, and the waters are looking through the silent air to heaven, and the dew is twinkling, and all the world seems wrapt in cheerful and quiet thought. He loves to see the sun bound up into heaven, and to talk gloriously of Phoebus's splendour—of his steeds, and of his rolling chariot wheels. Chaucer is happy at all times, but more so in the listening morning, than in the busy day. The song of the Nightingale* swells and flows freely forth—and breaks into a trembling and sparkling sweetness,—and sinks to a mellow murmuring,—and again fills out and passes into wild and deep sobs,—as perfectly in *his* bosom as in the bird's. In the exquisite poem of the "Flower and the Leaf,"[48] Chaucer has described the manner of idling about the field, and of turning the head to try if the Nightingale could be "perceived any where;"—and he has also told us of his sudden and feeling astonishment when the bird sang forth—

—that alle the wood yrong.[49]

He says that the song thoroughly ravished him, and that he knew not where he was—that he thought from the fulness of the notes, that the Nightingale sang close by his ear. He then looks about, and finds her seated in a fresh green laurel tree. What can surpass the idea of the poetess of birds pouring forth the music of her soul from the thick of laurel leaves! The song flowing through the tree of song!

---

* The song of the Nightingale forms one of our best spring delights, and we always feel a kindness towards those who speak of it in their poetry. Chaucer makes it the luscious food of his heart. Crashaw and Ford, since his day, have breathed poetically of it. The former has indeed caught the very life and sweetness of the bird in his "Music's Duel." And Coleridge, in our own day, has sung not unworthily of all that is full and soul-formed in music. His poem of "The Nightingale" is a delicious piece of moonlight harmony.

3+

> Where she sat in a fresh green laury tree,
> On the further side, even right by me,
> That gave so passing a delicious smell,
> According to the Eglantere full well.[50]

Here is the perfect harmony of song, and scent, and color!—Here is a beautiful blending of living poetry, with its author and its honours!—Here is the most finished description of the breathing music of birds and trees!—Chaucer has added a pillar to the temple of universal harmony. We have little doubt but that this passage was a favourite with Milton,* who felt intensely the pulse of music—and who knew that it was living in the lightest leaf of nature.

The plain style in which Chaucer spoke, carries every idea home to the bosom. What can be more to the purpose than his description of the Yeman in the prologue to the Canterbury Tales—

> A nut head had he,—with a brown visage.[51]

This is Titian in verse. Or what can be more fanciful or true than the account of the young squire?

> So hot he loved, that by nightertale,†
> He slept no more than doth the Nightingale.[52]

"The Frere" is exquisitely described—"a wanton and a mery:"—

> He had ymade ful many a marriage,
> Of young women at his owen coste.[53]

We cannot but equally admire the Merchant with his "forked beard;"—and the Clerk, with his horse—"lean as is a rake," and with his books ever in his head,—with his love of silence and moral virtue;—the Frankelier, with his daisy-coloured beard;—the "peure Parson;"—the slender Reve;—the Sumpnour with his "fire-red face";—and the "gentil Pardonere":—All these characters are struck out with a truth which none but a painter of poets could achieve. They are also beautifully grouped. There is a pure bold strength about Chaucer's descriptions which cannot be found in any other writer.

---

* We purpose making a few observations on Milton, who appears to have ever been thinking to music. Our remarks will relate to his harmony of idea and expression.

† Night-time.

Chaucer always throws his own intense feelings into his favourite characters. He makes all his persons young of spirit;—there is a noble blitheness in the hearts of his favourites, which stamps them the legitimate offspring of Chaucer, and this blitheness is continually caught from nature;—it is ever as "fresh as the sun," or as "crisp as the leaf." Can any thing be more rural, or beautiful, or true, than the Plowman's prologue to his Tale?—

> The Plowman plucked up his plowe,
> When Midsomer moone was comen in,
> And saied his beastes should eat enowe,
> And lie in grasse up to the chin.[54]

The feeling in this passage is exquisitely pure, and proves how well the poetical nature of Chaucer could mingle with the nature of the character which he pourtrayed.

Chaucer delighted in the rich wonders of romance. He gloried in the trappings and fiery carriage of noble steeds,—in the splendour of castle banquetings,—in womanly dress and beauty,—in the wonderment of a believing crowd,—and in supernatural incidents. The Squire's Tale is perhaps the most beautiful fragment in English poetry. Milton loved to remember it, and to talk of it; Spenser blended it with his Faery Queen. The story is easily told:—"The King of Araby sendeth to Cambuscan, King of Sarra, a horse and a sword of rare quality, and to his daughter Canace, a glass and a ring, by the virtue whereof she understandeth the language of all fowles."[55] The description of Cambuscan sitting clothed in rich vestments, and with his diadem on, "full high in his palace," is glorious. Chaucer then gives us sumptuous notions of the feast, by repeatedly declaring his want of power to describe it:—

> Of which if I shall tellen all the array,
> Then would it occupy a summer's day.[56]

After the third course, while the minstrels are playing deliciously at the board, a Knight on a steed of brass enters the hall.—How richly beautiful is the following description!—

> And in his hand a broad mirrour of glass;
> Upon his thumb he had of gold a ring,
> And by his side a naked sword hanging;
> And up he rideth to the high board.

In all the hall ne was there spoke a word
For marvel of this Knight; him to behold
Full busily they waiten, young and old.[57]

This a perfect picture. The King sitting high in his grandeur—the minstrels pausing over their harps—the groups of ladies and youths—the Knight on his steed of brass riding majestically through all. The Knight then speaks of virtues of the gift:—next comes an account of the wonder of the people at the marvellous horse. In the second part Canace rises in the morning early, when—

The vapour which that fro the erthe glode,
Maketh the sun to seem rody and brode.[58]

Canace finds a falcon in a tree complaining piteously, and, by the help of her ring, converses with the bird and comprehends its answers. The falcon tells a dolorous tale, and Canace takes it home with her.

And by her beddes hed she made a mew,
And covered it with velouettes blew,
In sign of truth that is in woman seen,
And all without the mew is painted green.[59]

After this the tale suddenly breaks off. We have given a pretty minute account of this beautiful, romantic fragment, because we think it is calculated to make all lovers of poetry betake themselves to Chaucer. It has all the magnificent fiction of the finest Arabian tales;—it sets the heart a dreaming of the days of Launcelot, who, by the way, is feelingly remembered by Chaucer in this story, as the only man that could rightly tell of dances, and fresh countenances, and subtle looks, and pretty dissemblings,—

No man but Launcelot,—and he is dead![60]

The Squire's Tale is made for summer reading in noble halls;—it takes the fancy captive. Many have often lamented that this romance was left unfinished; but who might venture to touch this glorious fragment!

The Knight's Tale is also very beautiful; Chaucer was indebted for it to Boccaccio. Many passages in the poem are translated literally from the Italian. We shall give one or two short extracts.

The busy lark, the messenger of day,
Saluteth in her song the morwe gray,

56

> And fiery Phoebus riseth up so bright,
> That all the Orient laugheth of the sight,
> And with his streams drieth in the greves,
> The silver drops hanging in the leaves.[61]

This is the morning itself, and not a description of it. The temple of Mars is strongly and terrifically painted—

> The *Northerne Light* in at the doore shone,
> For window on the wall ne was there none.[62]

Chaucer thus illumines the temple,—which is formed with pillars of iron, and gates of "adamant eterne,"—with the most deadly light. What is seen in this place is the horror of horrors,

> *The smiler with knife under the cloak,*
> The shepen brenning with the black smoke;
> The treason of the murdering in the bed,
> The open werre, with wounds all bebledde;
> Conteke with bloody knife, and sharp menace:
> All full of chirking was that sorry place.
> The sleer of himself yet saw I there,
> His heart blood hath bathed all his hair,
> *The cold death, with mouth gaping upright.*[63]

The last line of the foregoing passage is very powerful and terrific. One would think that Burns had read this description, when he wrote his tale of "Tam O'Shanter;"—what Tam sees in Kirk Alloway very much resembles what we have just extracted.

A little further on, Chaucer tells us of—

> The sow fretting the child right in the cradle.[64]

After these horrors, we will give one pleasant passage to cheer the mind of the reader—

> A mantlet upon his shoulders hanging,
> Bretful of rubies red, as fire sparkling;
> His crisp hair, like ringes was yronne,
> And that was yelwe, and glittered as the sun.[65]

We have now, we believe, extracted largely enough to support the praise which we poured forth upon Chaucer, in the opening of this article. His versification is peculiarly harmonious:—the following lines, taken at random, will shew how sound follows sense with him:—

He was a very parfit, gentil, knight.

A morwe, when the day began to spring,
Up rose our host.

In darkness, and horrible, and strong prison.[66]

There is also a very delightful humour in the Poet's way of dismissing his reader, when he has told things in every particular,—with

—my wit is shorte, ye may well understand.

or—

But for to tellin you all their beauty,
It lith not in my tongue, ne in my cunning;
I dare not undertake so high a thing . . .
I am not such; I mote speak as I can.

or—

—ye get no more of me.[67]

The poetry of Chaucer is not read by a large portion of what are called the readers of Poetry. The truth is, that his style is forbidding at the first glance; but we would recommend all who love purity of thought, and the clear light of feeling, to devote half an hour to the apparent difficulties of his mode of expression. His verse must be lingered upon. We confess that many parts of Chaucer are disgusting from their unveiled grossness; and this, we have little doubt, has helped to render him unpopular. Forgotten he *can* never be. Many of the old Poets have passed into obscurity from their carelessness about selection;—Browne, whose pastorals, in many parts, are exquisite;—Crashaw, of whom we have spoken in a note,—Habington, Cartwright, Suckling, and many others, are neglected for this reason. Chaucer disdained selection—but the intensity of his genius has carried him safe through all time. The flame of glory is around his name, and nothing can darken it. With all his faults, he is able to defy oblivion.

J.H.R.

On Egotism in Literature.[68] *June 2, 1816*

Egotism is a quality which is very generally decried, and very universally relished. Conversation seldom takes a more interesting turn than when it follows the personal histories of the speakers. We knew a man who was not merely disagreeable, but absolutely disgusting, if he opened his mouth on any other subject than the mischievous pranks of his boyhood: on these, however, he could charm the ears of all listeners.— Egotism is sometimes a fine, and generally a useful property in a writer. An indifferent Poet may acquire a wonderful popularity, simply by versifying his own troubles, passions, and moods; but an author must have great genius who can delight his readers with works in which he himself makes little or no appearance. His imagination must have a rare and noble power to effect this;—it must be able to make that his own, in which he has no concern, and of which he has had no experience—for it is only in proportion as the original feeling is genuine, strong, and clear, that it can produce a vivid, distinct, and durable impression of itself on the minds of others.

Egotism is a very common result of the changes and disappointments of the world,—for these lead one to trust in nothing, and take pleasure in nothing but what is within one's own breast. Melancholy is its proper mood,—and therefore a wit is seldom an egotist. A hasty view of some of our Poets will shew how much they have been beholden to this quality.

Shakspeare certainly was no egotist. He never shines through his characters. All his persons speak like real men and women, and their conversation seems to spring up from the circumstances of the moment. In all other dramas, except his, we can perceive the author through the scene, and hear him prompting;—but Shakspeare, after the plays were written, would seem to have no claim to them. There is, however, every variety of egotism in the different characters of Shakspeare's plays;— and as they come upon us like actual beings, we take *their* egotism, instead of searching for the author's. Who does not love the egotism of Jaques?[69] Of him, who colours the air with the sombre light of his own thoughts,—who shades the forest of Arden with the gloom of his own mind. His philosophical egotism lifts him above every other character in the play. He thinks alone. He reads alone. In solitude, life is to him the world of reflection. Meditation elevates him, in his own feelings and ideas, above the creatures breathing around. He laughs in the very face of mankind. Jaques is seen seldom:—he seems but the shadow of a man: —but then we think of him for ever—and the whole Court talk of him. Hamlet is another Jaques;—but his life lies at Court, and not in the woods. The great charm of Hamlet, is his proneness to selfish thought-fulness. The finest parts of Othello are where he speaks of his fiery love of battle,—or of his own personal appearance;—his farewell to the pride, pomp, and circumstance of war is truly heart-breaking, because it is the genuine burst of selfish sorrow. Desdemona loves him for his egotism—that is, for his ardent recitals of his own feelings and dangers; —*he* loves *her* for the fondness she bears to such feelings. Brutus is sternly egotistical:—his feelings and thoughts lie within him like square hard rocks. We are more interested in his struggles of cold philosophy, than in the struggles of Rome itself. Macbeth becomes doubly interesting after the murder,—because crime drives him more into himself. He becomes distrustful of all,—and goes apart in his sorrow and fear, to talk to his own thoughts. The light is reproachful to him,—society is a spy upon him;—his palace is the hall of suspicion,—his couch is a couch of fire. He is a moody philosopher, in solitude,—a gloomy abstract, in the scenes of pomp and revelry,—a plaything in the hands of super-stition. We might pursue this search after egotism, through most of the characters of Shakspeare, if it were necessary; but we have said enough on some of the principal characters to answer our purpose.

Chaucer was a direct Egotist. His descriptions of the early morning, the song of young birds, the breathing of flowers, and the fresh rustling of trees, would not be half so delightful, if they were not blended with his own feelings.

Spenser is not so much so. We lose sight of him amidst the rich and sunny gardens of his faery scenes. He is hid by sparkling streams and shooting fountains. The knights—and the ladies on their steeds—and the romantic vallies—and the sea, and the sea-shore,—win us to forget Spenser himself. How much should we have loved these scenes the more, if he had come forth occasionally,—like Venus with her handmaids,— amid the smiling company of his own feelings. But his subject, we fear, would not allow of it. Spenser is, without exception, the purest and yet richest sensualist amongst all the poets. He says more of the persons of women than any other writer, and yet he never says too much. He is always gratifying the senses—but his gratifications serve to purify, by their very refinement. Spenser, if he had written *Paradise Lost*, (which, however, is a whimsical supposition) would scarcely ever have been able to call himself from Eve's personal beauty:—her hair and her eyes would have been his favourite themes. He would have shewn us Paradise itself;—but his Satan would have been deformed, and his Adam would have been voluptuous. Milton does not differ, however, so much from Spenser, as at first may appear. Milton, we think, had the same feelings with Spenser,—but then his mind corrected them;—Spenser's mind approved of sensual delight,—it sanctioned every kind of pleasure. Classical knowledge gave Milton a passionate love for the beautiful and the romantic,—but then it made his heart more pure and his mind more lofty. He became fond of tales of Arcady—and filled his memory with deeds of heroism and innocence. Diana was to him more estimable than Venus. He did not thus wholly give up his sensual feelings,—but he gratified them in the best manner:—he fed them upon music and Italian poetry. Spenser went into the love tales of the ancients,—and wandered amid the most voluptuous of the Heathen deities. He knelt at the shrine of Venus. Spenser is ever in the most lovely spots—but then his pleasures and his reflections are, though beautiful, mortal. Milton is on this world, and on the richest parts of it,—but his soul is up with heaven,—and there is nothing earthly in his thoughts. We have rather wandered from our subject in this comparison, but in passing from Spenser to Milton, we could not avoid luxuriating a little in reflections on their peculiarities. Milton was an egotist;—though the classical veil which hangs over his poetry, hides him from common sight. Lycidas is one of the most pathetic pieces we know of. It is the elegant sorrow of a scholar and a young enthusiast. It is a long, uninterrupted, piece of delightful egotism:—for it serves to shew the feeling, the learning, the refinement, and the pleasures of the Poet. Milton is seen in every part of his works. What can be nobler than the language of Satan!—But Satan never talked so till Milton taught him. Adam himself is but Milton undressed, in personal appearance, as well as mind.

Pope is more liked in his satires, than in any other parts of his poetry; because he struck them more from himself. His satires are the offspring of his irritated feelings;—they come directly from his heart, and tell tales of himself. They are Pope melted into verse. The egotism of Dr. Young is interesting from its severity. Otway dramatized his own sorrows; and therefore it is, that he was so successful in the pathetic. Dr. Johnson was a thorough egotist: his misgivings—his asperities—his downright, *adamant* assertions—his weighty reasonings—his charitable kindnesses—were all egotistical. He was, however, on the whole, a melon of human nature,—for under a rough outside he had the very kindliest feelings at heart. Cowley, Collins, and Falconer, (we take these names quite at random from many), were egotistical. In our own time, we can instance one or two poets who are also peculiarly so;—that is (for we are desirous of being well understood), who derive their poetry immediately from their own circumstances, and the feelings arising from these circumstances;—and who are never themselves out of the eye of the reader. Wordsworth lets us at once into the most powerful and most noble of his thoughts and habits, as well as the minuter feelings. The "moods" of a great poet's mind[70] are valuable at all times. He tells us what delight he experiences at finding a nest "with five blue eggs."[71] The lightest objects become beautiful and eloquent by the radiance of his mind;—his imagination sheds a lustre over the dreaming days of childhood. He entices us through a green shrubbery, and refreshes us on the way with the melodies of nature; and we are suddenly surprised at finding ourselves at the steps of the Temple of Philosophy, the pillars of which he has himself decked with wreaths of flowers. Lord Byron is another egotist. He has become popular by his egotism. The public would not have read *Childe Harold*, or the *Corsair*, or the *Giaour*, if it were forbidden them to speculate on the original of the characters. The little pieces to Thyrza are the favourites of all his Lordship's poems, because they appear to be records of his private feelings. Montgomery, Coleridge, and Bowles, are egotists.

We also know one writer of the present day,[72] who delights his readers with the most able and ingenious speculations, and who is never so eloquent as when he speaks of his own feelings. He then seems to rise above this earth, and to float in an air and in a light of his own:—his youth comes back upon him. His heart lives in a vision. He talks the purest poetry.

We wish (to speak of ourselves, and so to conclude in a way perfectly harmonious with our subject) that we could be as egotistical in our writings, as we are in our feelings and fancies. Our readers would like us the better.

J.H.R.

On The Spectator. *June 16, 1816*

In our boyish days we read the *Spectator* through with the greatest delight, and we remember that no volume of a periodical work ever took such an absolute possession of our hearts, or won so much of our time of leisure, as the second volume of this pleasant book. It was our companion in the fields,—it was the first and the best friend that nourished our amiabilities. The other evening we took it up by chance, after having neglected it for some years. It is impossible for us to describe the host of happy thoughts and gentle feelings that started into life as we returned to the old country residence of Sir Roger de Coverley, and once more mingled with the sociable and whimsical creatures which are to be met with there. Those who have loved some rural spot in their young days, and visited it after years of absence, can alone have an idea of our pleasure at retracing scenes and characters which we had long been kept apart from. There is nothing so pleasant as the association of ideas. No man leads so sweet a life, as he who keeps those feelings green round the heart which were first sown in the happy days of boyhood. The memory of things long gone is in itself an existence. It charms away actual burdens;—it calls up feelings in our bosoms as instantaneously as if they had been touched by a wand of enchantment,—like the spirits of romance, they rise to music of their own making, and circled by light of their own shedding;—it makes a fairy-land of early scenes,—and gives a beauty and a sweetness to sorrow. The second volume of the *Spectator* sent our hearts wandering over innocent days and brought to us the hours—

Of splendour in the grass, of glory in the flower.[73]

We found ourselves seated with the short-faced moralist, and with the good old white-haired Knight, enjoying once more their pleasant discourse. We have never seen, in the course of our reading, any mention made of this volume in particular. To us it appears to be not only by very far the most excellent portion of the work, but to be the most amiable description of a happy country retirement, and of kindly and peculiar characters that we ever met with. It is as good as gentle music played on the water on summer evenings. It is like a smooth green field in spring. Though it cannot be expected that we should be able to create a fondness for it in others equal to that which we ourselves enjoy; yet we will just hastily run over the principal incidents and characters, to prove that we have some cause for our enthusiasm.

First there is the Spectator's arrival at Sir Roger's country residence, and the joy of the servants at the old Knight's return. Then there is the venerable Chaplain, with his plain sense, sociable temper, and a turn for back-gammon. Sir Roger understands, too, that he is a good scholar, though he does not shew it. He always dreaded lest he should be insulted with Latin and Greek at his own table. Next we meet with Will Wimble, who meddles with every thing but thinking: nothing can be more amusing than his note to Sir Roger,—it is full of kindness, simplicity, and ignorance. He hunts and fishes away his life out of pure good nature; he does kindly acts all round the country, and makes a May-fly to a miracle. Will's way of telling the *Spectator* of his having sprung a cock pheasant in the woods is very characteristic,—and it is pleasant to listen to him when he talks of the Jack-fish, and of his late invention for improving the Quail Pipe. Will Wimble is one of the most agreeable pieces of nothing in the world. Who would wish him a bit wiser, or a bit better? The picture gallery is a delightful place.

Sir Roger gives an excellent account of his ancestry in his simple manner. There is the Gentleman who distinguished himself in the tilt-yard at Whitehall, which, as Sir Roger shrewdly observes, "might be exactly where the coffee-house is now." His predecessor had also a turn for music, as the base viol hanging at his basket-hilt-sword could testify. Next there is the Maid of Honour, who brought ten children into the family, and who had written out in her own hand, and left, the best receipt in England both for an hasty pudding and a white pot. How well Sir Roger then describes the soft gentleman of the family, who is drawn sitting with one hand on a desk, writing *and looking as it were* another way, like an easy writer or a sonneteer;—he ruined every body, but never said a rude thing;—nothing can be better than the good old knight's innocent satire on this kind of personage. "He left the estate 10,000 £ in debt, but, however, by all hands, I have been informed that he was every way the finest gentleman in the world."—Lastly, there is Sir Humphry de Coverley, the honour of the house,—a man of his word, and a knight of the shire. We do not like to quit the picture gallery.* We next come to the Spectator's account of Sir Roger's behaviour in Church,—of his standing up and looking about him after a nap, to observe whether any other person has been guilty of the same, —of his lengthening out a verse in the psalms, half a minute after the rest of the congregation,—of his earnest manner of pronouncing *Amen*, and of his plan of counting the congregation, to see if any of his tenants are missing. The walk at a distance from Sir Roger's house, which is sacred to the Widow, is beautifully described. It is the spot which shaded him in the hopeless hours of his affection,—and every bough and leaf is dear to him. It is the pleasure-ground of his associations. The bower of his heart. There is a fine touch of character in the following observation which Sir Roger makes to the Spectator,—"You are to know this was the place wherein I used to muse upon her; and by that custom I can never come into it, but the same tender sentiments revive in my mind, as if I had actually walked with that beautiful creature under these shades." The Knight's account of his life is very amiably told here. He is deluded into the passion by learning that the widow looked upon him as the tamest and most human of all the brutes in the country. This Widow, as far as we can gather from Sir Roger's descriptions, seems very affected. She is a reading lady, and very far gone in the pleasures of friendship;— she has certainly the finest hand of any woman in the world. The hall of the old Knight is well described, with its trophies of deer horns, and otter's skin stuffed with hay. How amusing is it to see Sir Roger's pride pointing out the fox's nose on the stable door with the brass nail driven through it: it cost him 15 hours hard riding, carried him through half a dozen counties, killed him a brace of geldings, and lost above half his dogs.—This was looked upon by the Knight as the greatest exploit in his life. The hare-hunt is admirably told. The jolly Knight rides on a white gelding, encompassed by his tenants and servants: the scene is enspiriting,—the weather is bright and cheerful,—and the dogs are

* It is very probable that this Number of the *Spectator* suggested the picture gallery scene in Sheridan's Comedy of *The School for Scandal*.

musical to perfection. Next we have a description of Moll White, the witch, and of her cat, who is reported to have spoken twice in her life. Then we have Sir Roger's phillipic against confidants,—with the illustration of Will the huntsman and his lover. We love the account of Sir Roger riding to the assizes with the Spectator,—and of Will Wimble riding before them in the company of Tom Touchy, a fellow famous for taking the law of every body, and the yeoman who just comes within the game act, and kills his own dinner twice or thrice a week. The Knight's boldness in court is excellently set forth, in his speech to the judge. Lastly,—there is the entertaining account of Sir Roger meeting with the Gipsey. The old Knight's good heart shines out in all he does or says: he is all humanity. His feelings are ever more powerful than his thoughts; he will therefore say a kind thing though it subjects him to a laugh. There is an air of chivalry about him; he seems the last of a noble knightly race. When he dies, it is evident that no one remains to keep alive the old English dignity of the family. We shall proceed no further in our mention of this volume; what we have already pointed out will, we think, justify our enthusiastic notice of it. We look upon it to be a piece of perfection of its kind.

I.H.R.[74]

On Milton. *July 7, 1816*[75]

In a note to an Essay, which was published in the Reader a few weeks back, we promised to offer a remark or two upon Milton: it is our intention in this number to fulfill that promise.

Milton, of all poets that ever existed, had the highest idea of his art: he brought every thing to enrich it. He never set his mind to poetry lightly, or looked upon it as a mere elegant amusement; he thought intensely, and applied himself to it, as to a noble labour, which would dignify and benefit all after ages. Poetry was to him the power of setting virtue to music;—it was to him the means of giving melody to high thought and heroic atchievements. All Milton's feelings and thoughts, and studies were blended together, and infused into his poetry. His religion gave him a glorious loftiness of thinking, and it went through his language in all its state and beauty. His classical learning also was always enriching his language. The ancient mythologies supplied him with names and images which are sublime even in sound alone. His expressions are always perfect. They are at times like the full rushing sound of a trumpet, and at times like the mellow breathings of a flute. In the following passage there is one specimen of his strength, and one of his softness; we cannot decide which is the best.

> . . . unfurl'd
> The imperial ensign; which full high advanc'd,
> Shone like a meteor streaming to the wind,
> With gems and golden lustre rich emblaz'd
> Seraphic arms and trophies; all the while
> *Sonorous metal blowing martial sounds:*
> At which the universal host up-sent
> *A shout that tore Hell's Conclave, and beyond*
> *Frighted the reign of Chaos, and old Night.*
> All in a moment through the gloom were seen
> Ten thousand banners rise into the air
> With orient colours waving: with them rose
> A forest huge of spears; and thronging helms
> Appeared, and serried shields in thick array,
> Of depth immeasurable: *Anon they move*
> *In perfect phalanx to the Dorian mood*
> *Of flutes and soft recorders.*[76]

Milton could write with a Grecian severity, or with an Italian softness, with equal ease and correctness. It is scarcely possible to read the last lines of this passage without beating time to the music of it. The glorious imagination of Milton gave life and reality to all his descriptions. His poetry is perfect Music and Painting. The Sister Arts hold their homes in his mind. There is one short passage in Paradise Regained which is given to the eye as powerfully as if it had been the work of an Italian painter.

Dusk faces, with white silken turbans wreath'd.[77]

This is rich in the contrast of colours. We will, at the same time, extract a passage which is the very sweetest music; it has all the gentle undulations of water, and murmurs as soft a sound.

> ... Thy words
> Attentive, and with more delighted ear,
> Divine instructor, I have heard, than when
> *Cherubick songs by night from neighboring hills,*
> *Aerial music send.*[78]

The early romances also gave a high and heroic air to the poetry of Milton. He had evidently read them with an enthusiastic delight; and they had ever after floated round his heart like visions. How beautiful are the following lines in Paradise Regained!

> Such forces met not, nor so wide a camp,
> When Agrican with all his Northern Powers,
> Besieged Albracca, as romances tell,
> The City of Gallaphrone, from thence to win
> The fairest of her sex, Angelica,
> His daughter, sought by many prowest Knights,
> Both Paynim, and the Peers of Charlemain.[79]

Milton speaks of the romance of Chaucer with the same delight. He is never satisfied with merely alluding to a tale of Chivalry; he must mention some of the names, and dwell on the incidents. In the poetry of Milton every line seems made of gold. Image rises upon image like the steps of a temple,—and the divinity is at the height.

> —Like Maia's son he stood,
> And shook his plumes, that heavenly fragrance fill'd,
> The circuit wide. Straight knew him all the bands,
> Of Angels under watch; *and to his state;*
> *And to his message high, in honour rise;*
> *For on some message high, they guess'd him bound.*
> Their glittering tents he pass'd, and now is come,
> Into the blissful field, *through groves of myrrh,*
> *And flowering odours, cassia, nard, and balm;*
> *A Wilderness of sweets;* for nature here,
> Wanton'd as in her prime, and play'd at will
> Her virgin fancies, pouring forth more sweet,
> *Wild above rule or art, enormous bliss.*[80]

Nothing could go beyond this. Milton ever describes Nature in the loveliest manner. He adorns her, without depriving her of her simplicity.

> . . . But rather to tell how, if art could tell,
> How from that sapphire fount the crisped brooks,
> Rolling on orient pearls and sands of gold,
> With mazy errour under pendant shades
> Ran Nectar.[81]

In these lines the author unconsciously describes his own poetry. Again:—

> Betwixt them lawns, or level downs, and flocks,
> Grazing the tender herb, were interposed,
> Or palmy hillock; or the flowery lap
> Of some irriguous valley spread her store,
> *Flowers of all hue, and without thorn the rose.*
> Another side, umbrageous grots and caves
> Of cool recess, *o'er which the mantling vine*
> *Lays forth her purple grape, and gently creeps*
> *Luxuriant.*[82]

This is Paradise. Harmony is every where. Perhaps, one of the finest touches in the descriptions of Paradise is in the fifth book, where Raphael is feasting with Adam in the bower.—

> —Rais'd of grassy turf,
> Their table was, and mossy seats had round,
> And on her ample square from side to side,
> All autumn piled, *though Spring and Autumn here,*
> *Danc'd hand in hand.*[83]

Nature was always the mistress of Milton's heart, and he loved to clothe and ornament her with classical garments. He sought her every where. His thoughts went, like pilgrims, over deserts to pay her adoration. His mind traversed the ancient world in search of honours for her. Lycidas is a beautiful specimen of youthful sorrow, flowing through classical feelings.—The "melodious tears" of the poet are shed into an ancient urn. How beautiful! How classical! How sweet and melancholy is the following passage! It is one that we can repeat to ourselves till our very hearts seem to beat to music,—till the fables of the older time seem to rise up embodied before us.

> Oh fountain Arethuse . . .[84]

69

Milton did not feel the less, because he expressed himself thus learnedly. His mind had dwelt so long with the ancients, that it learnt at last to think as they did. Who cannot see a true and pure affection in the two following lines, through their romantic style of expression.

> For we were nurst upon the self-same hill,
> Fed the same flock by fountain, shade, and rill.[85]

We shall conclude these cursory remarks upon Milton, with an extract or two from his works, which will prove how forcible and concise,—how elegantly descriptive,—or how nobly pathetic he could be when he chose. The first passage is stern and sad to the last degree. Every line tells in it, and tells mournfully. In the second extract, the harmony is most perfect. In the repetition of the images, the sound steals back softly upon the ear like an echo. The last passage can hardly be read without tears. When read aloud, its very sound has a deep despair in it.

> To whom the tempter, inly wrack'd replied.[86]

Popular Poetry—Periodical Criticism, & c.
October 13, 1816[87]

> Whose mind is but the mind of his own eyes,
> He is a slave,—the meanest we can meet!
>
> Wordsworth.[88]

Away, then, with the senseless iteration of the word, *popular*, applied to new works in Poetry, as if there were no test of excellence in this first of the Fine Arts, but that all men should run after its productions, as if urged by an appetite, or constrained by a spell! The qualities of writing best fitted for eager reception are either such as startle the world into attention by their audacity and extravagance, or they are chiefly of a superficial kind, lying upon the surfaces of manners; or arising out of a selection and arrangement of incidents, by which the mind is kept upon the stretch of curiosity, and the fancy amused without the trouble of thought.[89]

This is very justly said, and preparatory to noticing in our next number, a poem by a living author, which but for personal circumstances of interruption, we should have noticed much sooner, we shall here offer an opinion or two on the worth and meaning of this sort of popularity. By the device of a separate article we shall get rid of a long introduction, —to which, we fear, we are too prone,—and be able to enter at once on the actual business of the work to be reviewed,[90] without incurring the pain of sacrificing any of the ideas suggested by it.

We think it is clear that Genius has essentially nothing to do with what is called popularity:—no more than gold in its native bed has to do with a Bank note in a clerk's bill-book. When there were the most splendid and abundant displays of genius, the thing now named popularity could not have existed:—the state of society then would not allow of it. Paper and Gold, as we have found, in our time, cannot circulate together; that is to say, if the first fixes the standard of value in the public estimation. The same may be affirmed of Popularity and Genius: —the latter must be either withdrawn or debased, when it is not allowed to pass but according to the current *par* of the former. The resemblance might be pushed further than perhaps good taste will permit that a simile shall be carried. The Paper system has been productive of facilities and distributions: it has given importance to the mass: it has put means in the hands of the many:—it has spread country-houses and shooting-boxes over the face of the country, and filled roads with curricles and gigs. But in the mean time, moated castles and coaches and six have vanished. So Magazines and Reviews have pushed Epics from their stools and shelves. Modern improvements are excellent things,—as every one who has lately bought stoves or dining tables must know: but we have the convenient in lieu of the romantic and prodigious. Spenser would never have written this line,

A gentle knight was pricking on the plaine,[91]

if, in his official capacity, he had been accustomed to Acts of Parliament for enclosing waste lands, and establishing turnpikes. Still less would he have dared to make his "lovely ladie" ride "upon a lowly *asse*," if he had had before his eyes the fear of the Reviewers, who took offence at the habits of Mr. Wordsworth's *Wanderer*. To ridicule the latter as a "Scotch Peddlar," does not seem more obvious or demanded criticism, than it would be to sneer at the heavenly *Una's* "palfrey slow," as a donkey or Jerusalem poney. How admirably would Shakspeare's expression of "Lethe's wharf"[92] "minister occasion to these gentlemen

7 I

of such sensible and nimble lungs!"[93] To him, for instance, who favoured the public with the egregious criticism on *The Tale of Rimini* that appeared in the *Quarterly*![94] What would they say to the phrase in the second line that follows?

> The noble hart, that harbours vertuous thought,
> And is *with child* of glorious great intent.
>
> Spenser.[95]

The medium through which, in poetry, the heart is to be affected,—is language; a thing subject to endless fluctuations and arbitrary associations. The genius of the poet melts these down for his purpose; but they retain their shape and quality to him who is not capable of exerting, within his own mind, a corresponding energy.[96]

This cannot our Reviewers.

It seems then, true, that times of general extension are most unfavourable times for great elevations. Since battles have been decided by arms which every body can wield, very superior personal strength has not merely ceased to be applicable,—it has even ceased to be possessed by heroes. It is not that we mean to join in an outcry against the ignorance and malevolence of criticism: there may be much of both qualities in it at present,—or it may overflow with candour and wisdom. Upon the whole, we believe that its rules will be found correct for general practice in common cases; but how will the most correct general rules bear upon genius which must be an exception to what is general? In former times the rules were taken from the examples,—although there can be no doubt they existed in them:—the poet made the critic,—and this seems the natural order of creation,—for, though the *Edinburgh Review* has done great good in its way, we do not believe that it has ever had, or ever will have, the slightest share in forming a single poet. We make ourselves very sure that its Editor would personally put slight faith in the pretensions to genius, that might be preferred in favour of anyone who could be materially influenced in his practice by the admonitions of its poetical department. We have no doubt that, notwithstanding all he has said to the undervaluing of Mr. Wordsworth's productions, he feels that the author in question cannot be reduced even to a level with the other best poets of the day,[97] until some one of his works has been advertised with an annexed encomium extracted from a quarterly criticism.*

Criticism, as it is called, chiefly consists in giving rules by the observance of which Mr. Higgins may write well to his correspondents, and his wife may deliver her opinion like a sensible woman at a tea table. What, as we have said, have these to do with the "*tricks* of strong imagination;" what prerogative can they have over those

> —that apprehend
> More than cool reason ever comprehends?[99]

The power that "bodies forth the forms of things unknown;"—the glorious faculty that

> Turns them to shapes, and gives to airy nothing
> A local habitation and a name,—[100]

Is to be regarded as oracular in its manifestations:—the crowd of people must reverentially accept them as they are given, acknowledging the deficiency to be in themselves wherever there is a want of satisfaction or intelligibility. Their faults are for higher correction than the common race of minds can furnish;—their beauties and sublimities are for the elevation and glorification of common feelings and perceptions. Mankind must bring their opinions with implicit humility to be modelled by these;—for these cannot be modelled by the opinions of mankind. The present generation is much in need of this lesson:—and, above all, its small, smart men are to be decried as nuisances. They have a cant phrase or a pert remark for every thing that takes a deeper turn than their own shallow skimming;—they pun upon the last word of a sentence as an excellent reply to the matter of the whole; they oppose to excited sensibility a horse-laugh,—and triumphantly carry away the suffrages of an evening party by a dexterous wink of their left eye. These creatures may teize genius to death; as the jack-daw destroyed the bull, on whose back he perched, by his chattering and pecking. Periodical

---

* It is a remarkable, and pathetical-ludicrous caprice with which things are ordered in the world, to see Mr. Coleridge's poem advertised with the guarantee to the purchaser of half a line of approbation from Lord Byron:—"*This wild—and singularly beautiful poem!*"—Lord Byron. This is what the Old Bailey lawyers term calling testimony to character; an expedient that rather savours of a desperate case. Lord Byron in the witness box, in behalf of Mr. Coleridge![98]

criticism fastening upon words and lines; applying dictionary inter-
pretations to imagination's abstractions; questioning poetical phrases
by the regulations of daily parlance; and putting the comprehension
of dull heads in the place of judge without appeal over the vivacities of
"seething brains:"—this, and the cold, nauseous saws of *sensible* people;
and the impertinences of *clever* people; and the cautious scepticism of
stupidity; and the malevolence of mortified ignorance,—all unite to
form what is commonly called the public voice in matters of taste and
talent,—and this delectable union must be addressed to secure *popularity*! As good mingles with the evil,—what is popular may also happen
to be very commendable:—but still it comes to this,—that Mr. and Mrs.
Higgins must be pleased!—It is true, they adore Shakspeare, and admire
Milton:—but, in regard to the past, they adore and admire on better
authority than their own;—nay, here they are often contented to adore
and admire without understanding. "Every author, as far as he is great,
and at the same time *original*, has had the task of creating the taste by
which he is to be enjoyed."[101] The value of opinion as to the past is, that
the taste has been created for all, or is professed by all as a matter of
pride,—not on the frail and blind judgment of the multitude, but
according to the dogmas of superior spirits who survive after the multitude has perished, and thus collectively joining their different eras,
form a cloud of witnesses instructing us as to what has gone before us.
We speak of the times of Addison, Pope, and Swift,—that of Cowley,
Dryden, and Milton,—that of Spenser, Sidney, Raleigh, and Shakspeare.
Their respective times are now *theirs*;—they make them what they seem
to us;—they fashion out their epochs, giving them their form and
pressure,—and the periods exist in our imaginations modelled according
to the greatest minds they produced. In this consists the charm of the
past:—we see it, as Moscow used to be seen at a distance,—altogether a
city of golden spires and magnificent cupolas: the little narrow dirty
streets where dwell the diminutive dealers in small ware, are hidden
from the view. When we speak of Athens, we think of Pericles, and
Socrates, and Phidias: when we speak of Rome we think of Cicero, and
Horace, and the Gracchi: ancient Asia rises before the eyes of our fancy
in all the pomp of elephants, and royal tents, and millions of warriors
in golden armour. But as to the present it is very different: we move in
the midst of the buz and bustle of common people and affairs; we cannot

see what is above our own level,—and the rumbling of a cartwheel is sufficient to make us deaf to the music of the spheres. "If we consider what are the cares that occupy the passing day, and how remote is the practice and course of life from the sources of sublimity in the soul of man, can it be wondered that there is little existing preparation for a poet charged with a new mission to extend its kingdom, and to augment and spread its enjoyments?"[102]

The evil would be, comparatively speaking, small, if it only extended to the present undervaluing of "the profound and the exquisite in feeling,—the lofty and universal in thought and imagination." In an enlightened time, like ours, when reviews and magazines and new poems push the needle case and the ball of patent cotton from our ladies' work tables, there must be, and there is, a doating fondness, as well as a disdainful rejection. The dear creatures must have their dear men;— and where is the man of talent that would not be seduced from his abstractions and reserves by the prospect of being admitted into such fascinating and flattering intimacy. All the honours of the world, all its caresses, all its comforts, are put in his view; and he has only to fall down and worship the Golden Calf Popularity to become possessed of all. Even the high priest of the true God could not resist this sort of temptation;—and, on the other hand, "but a small quantity of brain is necessary to procure a considerable quantity of admiration, provided the aspirant will accomodate himself to the likings and fashions of his day."[103]

Genius is the introduction of a new element into the intellectual universe:— or, if that be not allowed, it is the application of powers to objects on which they had not been before exercised,—or the employment of them in such a manner as to produce effects hitherto unknown. What is all this but an advance, or rather conquest made of the soul by the Poet? Is it to be supposed that the reader can make progress of this kind, like an Indian prince or general—stretched on his palanquin, and borne by his slaves.[104]

But at present we resist what is strange to us, as something that is inferior to us:—we question it,—not ourselves. We like best what tries us least;—and he who comes prepared to address what we are, is sure to be received more favourably than he who would render us something we are not. As these are times of reasoning and general good sense, we have much to say in behalf of our tastes and decisions,—and thus partly appalled, partly convinced, partly purchased, men of talent bring themselves to exert their powers agreeably to the received and general set of associations, so as to chime in with the temporary standard of manners, to tickle the irritation of novelty, without piercing that surface of sentiment, which is skinned thinly but widely over an advanced state of society.

Wordsworth's Thanksgiving Ode.[105]   October 20, 1816

Considering the subject of Mr. Wordsworth's Poem, this tardy notice of it might be deemed out of time, were not its author one who writes more for "all time," than for any particular time present. There is no one so little dependent as he is on occasion,—and on what are commonly called means. Indeed, both his attributed faults, and superlative excellence, chiefly proceed from this circumstance, that, whatever his subject may be, the soul and imagination of the poet make the all in all of the performance. Every thing that proceeds from him is an emanation of himself:—he creates it in his own image,—and, without meaning to suggest any improper analogy, we would say, that *he* it is who sees that it is good. This is the proper exercise and sole province of genius,—which exists, in quality of its divinity, in itself and for itself. It makes no advances or concessions:—it is the privilege of all that may come to worship it; —those who will not, may enjoy the perversity for their pains,—those who cannot, may keep themselves in countenance by their numbers.

Mr. Wordsworth, we have heard, and on good authority, is not a popular poet:—we are very sure he is an admired one; and as to popularity, though it is a desirable thing for any weekly newspaper, yet we do not know that it is absolutely necessary for the Cartoons, or the Samson Agonistes. However, on this delicate subject we, perhaps, too frankly expressed ourselves last week:—at all events we need not now add to these remarks.

Asking, therefore, no further questions about popularity, let us simply inquire whether there is one of our readers who will confess himself dead to the charm of any of the following passages, and yet profess to be alive to the beauties of those works which the canons of criticism have established in the rank of master models and examples of poetical skill, grace, and power? The Ode in question, is a devout and patriotic hymn for the morning of the day appointed for a general thanksgiving, with reference chiefly to the splendid victory of Waterloo, —the successful termination of the war being the immediate and inevitable consequence of that great exploit. Mr. Wordsworth, in a prose dissertation, has said of poetry that it is "the spontaneous overflow of powerful feelings:—it takes its origin from emotion remembered in tranquillity."[106] Where can be found a more sublime illustration of this assertion, than in the opening of the poem now under notice;—and in reading it, we will do well to recollect another of his fine explanations of the poetic mind,—in which he terms it "the mirror of the fairest and most interesting qualities of nature."[107]

> Hail universal Source of pure delight!
> Thou who canst shed the bliss of gratitude
> On hearts howe'er insensible or rude,
> Whether thy orient visitations smite
> The haughty towers where monarchs dwell;
> Or thou, impartial Sun, with presence bright
> Cheer'st the low threshold of the peasant's cell!
> Not unrejoiced I see thee climb the sky,
> In naked splendour, clear from mist or haze,
> Or cloud approaching to divert the rays,
> Which even in deepest winter testify
>   Thy power and majesty,
> Dazzling the vision that presumes to gaze.
> Well does thine aspect usher in this day;
> As aptly suits therewith that timed pace,
> Framed in subjection to the chains
> That bind thee to the path which God ordains
>   That thou shalt trace,
> Till, with the heaven and earth, thou pass away!
> Nor less the stillness of these frosty plains,
> Their utter stillness,—and the silent grace
> Of yon etherial summits white with snow,
> Whose tranquil pomp, and spotless purity,

> Report of storms gone by
> To us who tread below,—
> Do with the service of this day accord.
> —Divinest object which the uplifted eye
> Of mortal man is suffered to behold;—
> Thou, who upon yon snow-clad heights hast poured
> Meek splendour, nor forget'st the humble vale;
> Thou, who dost warm earth's universal mould,—
> And for thy bounty wert not unadored
> By pious men of old;—
> Once more, heart-cheering Sun, I bid thee hail!
> Bright be thy course today,—let not this promise fail![108]

Whatever may be thought and felt of such poetry as this, we are quite sure that all will agree it is not likely to be ever deemed or called *popular* poetry. Mr. Wordsworth's warmest admirers will be the most earnest to affirm this. We shall give an example, from the works of another, and an earlier author—an author too of some note[109]—of poetry which we presume to think very admirable,—but which it would also be ridiculous to dignify with the epithet *popular*. Mr. Murray, who has disposed of so many editions of Lord Byron's works, would not have cause to envy the copy right of such verses as follow.

> Many are the sayings of the wise
> In antient and in modern books enroll'd,
> Extolling patience as the truest fortitude,
> And to the bearing well of all calamities
> All chances incident to man's frail life,
> Consolatories writ
> With studied argument, and much persuasion sought,
> Lenient of grief and anxious thought:
> But with th'afflicted in his pangs their sound
> Little prevails, or rather seems a tune
> Harsh and of dissonant mood from his complaint,
> Unless he feel within
> Some source of consolation from above,
> Secret refreshings that repair his strength,
> And fainting spirits uphold.
> God of our Fathers! what is man?
> That thou towards him with hand so various,

Or might I say contrarious,
Temperest thy providence, through his short course,
Not evenly, as thou rul'st
The angelic orders, and inferior creatures mute,
Irrational and brute.
Nor do I name of men the common rout,
That wandering loose about,
Grow up and perish as the summer fly,
Heads without name no more remembered;
But such as thou hast solemnly elected,
With gifts and graces eminently adorned,
To some great work, thy glory,
And people's safety,—which in part they effect.[110]

We apologize to our readers for being so tedious:—we know that we make the above long quotation at considerable risk,—particularly during the present dull time for newspapers: and we are sure our publisher[111] will see it with grief of soul. But when one is a good deal piqued in behalf of favourite opinions, hazard is not much thought of. We have been vexed and mortified, even nigh unto death, by sensible ladies and reading gentlemen on the subject of Mr. Wordsworth's poetry. One fair correspondent writes, from the neighbourhood of that seat of taste, Edinburgh, to know whether we really do, in our hearts, think, that Mr. Wordsworth has ever composed anything so pretty as the *Pleasures of Hope*?[112] A judicious friend is puzzled to know the meaning of one of Mr. Wordsworth's lines;—and a witty one asks if "*Harry Gill's*" teeth are yet done chattering.[113]—Now, to cut short all this, we have given them the last extract,—no matter whence taken, and from whom:—and we warrant it to them as excellent, standard poetry, of the first genius, and of immortal fame. Neither their sentiments or ours have any thing at all to do with this decision:—it *is* so—the thing is settled,—and we warn them that it can only now be denied to the shame of the dunce who denies it. If any one, lady or gentleman, will step forward and declare conscientiously, that they *doat* upon the lines beginning "Many are the sayings of the wise:"—that they could read them from morning to night; that they could do nothing but read them; that Lord Byron's *Farewell*[114] was not half so touching: that his verses to the *Star of the Legion of Honour*[115] were not so sublime:—if they will declare that they feel quite struck by these lines,—and add, after making this declaration *sincerely*, that they cannot see any high degree of power and beauty in the great body of Mr. Wordsworth's poetry,—we pledge ourselves never to write another line, or say another word in admiration of it.

If we have already said enough to excite some suspicions of the truth in a certain class of breasts—such as are full of quick sensibilities, but which have not been sufficiently scrupulous in questioning the nature of their excitement—we would recommend to these persons,—as nothing is more difficult of cure than a taste debauched from simplicity and truth,—to read the opening passage of Mr. Wordsworth's Ode *twice or three times over*. If they will read it aloud, and with an intonation characterized by feeling, the process will be assisted. They will then, if we are not much mistaken, speedily feel the growing charm spreading and warming within them; the charm which proceeds from "the unostentatious beauties of a pure style." But at this stage of the recovery, it is most essential for them to avoid all relapses of tea-table criticisms; to repress all inward movements of self-sufficiency; and, we think, it would be no more than prudent, to keep, at this time, any thick pamphlet-looking work, with blue covers, out of sight for a day or two. We only advise this latter precaution, however, till the patient has acquired a little strength. "In the higher poetry," says our author, "an enlightened critic chiefly looks for a reflection of the wisdom of the heart and the grandeur of the imagination."[116] But one can only recognize the fidelity of the images by sympathizing with the qualities:— and this leads us to state of Mr. Wordsworth's poetry, that it must actually bring the mind of the reader *up* to a full and thorough participation and communion with itself, in all its views, enjoyments, and discoveries,—or it has no effect upon him at all. In this it essentially differs from the greatest number of examples of modern poetry. These, —instead of encouraging, inviting, and strengthening the minds of those who engage in them, to make an advance of themselves,—seize their readers off their legs as it were, carry them away hastily for a temporary excursion, independently entirely of their own powers— whirl them about with violence amidst a hubbub of words, false sentiments, and misplaced ornaments,—and end by setting them down precisely where they found them,—not having made an inch of mental progression, or acquired one new insight into the properties or combinations of nature. It requires no explanation to point out the superior difficulties of Mr. Wordsworth's task;—he gives the intellectual part of those who apply to him, something serious and severe to do:—how should he be popular with the million? He turns the soul inward, to muse upon and enjoy its own realities:—if nature has made it in any case empty, what can the poet do? If the arbitrary and artificial fashions of society, and the common occupations, of sordid life, have made it the victim of low or false impressions,—have entangled it in false analogies, and given it, at the same time, an unshakeable self-confidence, —what can the poet do? This last consideration may serve to convince, how ill-adapted a very late period of society is, for the immediate appreciation of the original efforts of any great contemplative genius. People are all then proud of their own knowledge, and their own attainments: it follows that they are then most likely to withstand any attempt to extend that dominion over their spirits, "by which they are to be humbled and humanized, in order that they may be purified and exalted."[117] At an earlier period of human affairs, men's hearts are more full of generous confidence, and of that elevated disposition from which proceeds a frank submission;—then, too, the voices of the naturally incapable have no means of assuming a disgusting and fatal ascendency.

We do not feel that we have any thing to do as critics in this instance, but to explain the general principles of our favourable opinion, and to leave examples of the poetry to speak for themselves. We have quoted the opening of the Ode, which we consider distinguished by a majesty of thought and expression, not less elevated and imposing for being also benign and harmonious. "The *depth*, and not the tumult of the soul"[118] —(to quote one of our author's own fine lines)—is apparent in the next passage,—which follows the other, increasing the swell of the music.

> Mid the deep quiet of this morning hour,
> All nature seems to hear me while I speak,—
> By feelings urged, that do not vainly seek
> Apt language, ready as the tuneful notes
> That stream in blithe succession from the throats
>   Of birds in leafy bower,
> Warbling a farewell to a vernal shower.[119]

Milton, in his fragment of the History of England, says, "I have determined, in speaking of the antient and rejected British fables, to bestow the telling over even of these reputed tales, be it for nothing else but in favour of our English Poets and rhetoricians, who by their art well know how to use them judiciously."[120] Some of our present enlighteners of public opinion, will feel great contempt for this regard paid to the imaginative honours and decorations of our country; as they will sneer at the following burst of tender feeling towards her.

> Land of our fathers! previous unto me
> Since the first joys of thinking infancy;
> When of thy gallant chivalry I read,
> And hugged the volume on my sleepless bed!
> O England!—dearer far than life is dear,
> If I forget thy prowess, never more
> Be thy ungrateful son allowed to hear
> Thy green leaves rustle, or thy torrents war.[121]

If all this be childishness, as some will say it is, it only proves that "the child is father to the man."

The following passage, descriptive of the spreading of the good news, affords a remarkable example of what we mentioned in the beginning of this article;—*viz.* Mr. Wordsworth's power independently of subject, —his originality in the handling of all subjects,—and his habit of embellishing purely from the stores of his own imagination.

> Fly ministers of Fame,
> Whate'er your means, whatever help ye claim,
> Bear through the world these tidings of delight!
> —Hours, Days, and Months, have borne them in the sight
> Of mortals, travelling faster than the shower,
> That landward stretches from the sea,
> The morning's splendours to devour;
> But this appearance scattered extacy.
> . . .
> Such glad assurance suddenly went forth—
> It pierced the caverns of the sluggish North—
> It found no barrier on the ridge
> Of Andes—frozen gulphs became its bridge—
> The vast Pacific gladdens with the freight—

Upon the lakes of Asia 'tis bestowed—
The Arabian desert shapes a willing road,
    Across her burning breast,
For this refreshing incense from the West!
    —Where snakes and lions breed,
Where towns and cities thick as stars appear
Wherever fruits are gathered, and where'er
The up-turned soil receives the hopeful seed—
While the Sun rules, and cross the shades of night—
The unwearied Arrow hath pursued its flight!
The eyes of good men thankfully give heed,
    And in its sparkling progress read
How virtue triumphs, from her bondage freed![122]

The regular reader of the *Champion* knows how cordially we join in feeling with the admirers and celebrators of the victory to which this fine poem is devoted. Yet there is a beatific abandonment, and a spiritual fullness of faith about Mr. Wordsworth, which we can only contemplate with envying wonder, being ourselves far behind him in this respect, encompassed with fears, doubts, and misgivings.[123] We do not mean, however, to enter here on any political considerations:—suffice it for us to say, that the twenty first of his Sonnets devoted to Liberty, in the 2d volume of the last edition of His Lyrical Ballads, & c. speaks the language of our present poor frame exactly. He has now, however, outgrown all his weaknesses, and supplied all his barrenness. He has been caught up into the third heaven—whether in the body or out of the body we cannot tell—but unassisted earthly vision, when he takes this course, cannot follow him further than the clouds. It is in the excess of this saintly rapture that he describes the "blest angels," welcoming the hideous defeat of the French "with a choral shout!"[124] We wish we could be admitted with him into these regions of perfect confidence and perfect joy. But alas! we still remain where he was when he wrote the following beautiful and touching lines:—

England! the time is come when thou shouldst wean
Thy heart from its emasculating food;
The truth should now be better understood;
Old things have been unsettled; we have seen
Fair seed time,—BETTER HARVEST MIGHT HAVE BEEN

BUT FOR THY TRESPASSES:—and at this day
If for Greece, Egypt, India, Africa,
Aught good were destined, *Thou wouldst step between.*
England! all nations in this charge agree:
But worse,—MORE IGNORANT IN LOVE AND HATE,
FAR, FAR MORE ABJECT IS THINE ENEMY:
THEREFORE THE WISE PRAY FOR THEE, tho' the freight
Of thy offences be a heavy weight:
Oh grief! that earth's best hopes rest all with thee.[125]

Boswell's Visit. December 1, 1816[126]

There needs no ghost come from the grave, my lord
to tell us this.

Hamlet.[127]

The other evening, after having passed some cold and critical hours at the theatre, I returned home, and went full of asperity and fatigue to rest. My thoughts soon began to die away in sleep,—but not till I had taken a classical stretch of the limbs over the long-wished for bed;—Catullus deserves immortality, if only for that glorious line which records the luxurious enjoyment—

Desideratoque acquiescimus lecto.[128]

As oblivion began to steal its mist over my mind,—as the glittering dresses began to dance away from my eyes,—the double drum to cease rolling its thunder into my ears,—the audience in the pit and boxes to clatter their applause,—and the gods in the gallery, "to keep a dreadful pother o'er our heads;"—as the lamps of my recollections went down,—and Nature proceeded to drop her dark curtain over my senses: lo! I was disturbed with a knock at the door of my chamber. Duncan could not have started more, when Macbeth politely introduced the knife into his body, than I did at these frightful sounds. "Whence is that sound?"

The voice of my servant returned me to my serenity. "I forgot to tell you Sir, the *Devil* of the Office has been here this evening, and that he says *Copy* must be had in the morning."—

"Oh?" said I, turning round sulkily, "Copy in the morning! the Devil!"—Here was havoc made with my rest! Here was an infernal visit!—I closed my eyes, and attempted to squeeze them into sleep.—I repeated numbers!—I counted sheep:—it would not do. The Devil haunted my mind, and "bawled for copy." I questioned Oblivion in the words of Macbeth:—

> Canst thou not minister to a mind diseased;
> Pluck from the memory a rooted sorrow;
> *Raze out the written troubles of the brain.*[129]

But no! Recollection sat bolt upright in my head, and dwelt on "the very fiend's arch mock." At length worn out with long and useless cogitation, I dropped into a slumber:—or rather, to speak poetically, "slumber laid his leaden mace upon my head." I was in an instant provided with the needful copy for the morning: "A happiness that often dreaming hits on, which Reason and Sanity could not so prosperously be delivered of." I fancied that I was hopelessly sitting over my papers, beseeching my sulky mind to help me out of the difficulty; when up stepped the figure of Boswell, piping hot from the shades; with a ponderous look of importance on his brow, and a little roll of paper in his hand.

"Sir!" said he to me, "The little devil has told me of your difficulty; and I come, like a second Perseus, to your assistance. Here, Sir! here is matter that must satisfy the very devil himself. My name, Sir, is Boswell. I am now from the shades.—There, Sir, occasionally do the celebrated Members of the Old Literary Club assemble:—I have copied for you a conversation of Dr. Johnson, (that rock on which I once chained the Promethean Public, and on which I myself acted as vulture), yes, Sir, of Dr. Johnson, Sir Joshua Reynolds, Burke, and myself, on your living men of genius. You marvel; but I assure you many of the works even of your most celebrated characters, drop into the shades. Take this paper, and print the contents:—the public will then, Sir, be contented with your paper. I may—'see you again at Philippi!'" He vanished, in a Scotch mist. I instantly opened the scroll, and read it so attentively, that when I awoke, my memory enabled me to copy it word for word;—and the devil was not disappointed!

—Doctor Johnson and myself were first at the Club. He looked unusually morose; and I ventured to remark to him that something must have ruffled his immortal temper. He looked angry. I said—"Nay, Sir! I do not mean that you are dull, but that you are serious."

His features relaxed from their severity.—"Well, Bozzy, Bozzy! but I do not wish to be subjected to the charge of immoderate dissatisfaction. I am serious, but not dull. Do not give me reason to think you dull, and not serious."

"I only observed"—

"Sir! you only observed what humanity should have razed from your tongue. It is cruelty to touch upon those metamorphoses of the features, which expose pain of heart. Do not, Sir, accustom yourself to keep watch over the irritability of the mind: you will one day or other write mine down as a tempestuous temper."

I felt hurt that I had annoyed this great man with my petty observations: I therefore took his hand, and assured him that "I did not mean—"

"No, (interrupted he) I know you did not: you never do!"—

Thus ended our little difference. I asked him what he thought of his own fame. "Sir, I think it is universal, and I am satisfied. But you have held the trumpet to Fame's mouth. I have signalized my mind:—you have immortalized my body. I have shewn the vigours of the human intellect, and have pointed out the frailties of human passion:—you have told the world all about my love of my tea and my cat,—you have shewn me doating equally on the Indian beverage and the whiskered quadruped."

Here Sir Joshua Reynolds joined us. He entered with a copy of the "Catalogue Raisonee"[130] in his hand. He asked Dr. Johnson if he had read it.

"I have, Sir! It is the essence of weakness. It is the only tribute which Folly could pay to the immortality of Genius. But, Sir, it is a cloud which will steal over modern art, and darken it in the eyes of the world."—

"I see," said Sir Joshua, "that, much ribaldry is thrown over all the possessors of old pictures."—

"Sir!—if painters abuse their patrons,—particularly trade-painters,—the patrons will abandon the painters. Abuse will never scare away Fame!—Neither will insolence procure it. Sir, I take it that the author of the book is a fool and a licenced painter."—

I hinted to the great critic that it was not quite right to join the two names.—

86

"Sir!" said he to me hastily,—"The author has joined the two names: —not I. He wantons in all the cant of the art, and feels not one atom of its inspiration:—He may be an academician: and I think he is."—

"But," said I,—"is there not some wit in the pamphlet?"—

"No, Sir! The author is not one of Shakspeare's fools. He is not a fool and a wit at the same time. He says a great deal,—and nothing to the purpose. His weakness is a weapon in the hands of his rashness:—He enriches his folly with his indecency. Sir! The pamphlet is a witless pamphlet!"—

Sir Joshua agreed with the doctor in despising the thing:—and I agreed with both.—"What think you, Sir! of Campbell as a poet?"—I put this question to him with some alarm;—knowing that Campbell was a Scotchman,—and knowing the good man's antipathy to the Scotch.—

"I think Campbell a poet. He has written little,—but he has written well. He succeeds in the lofty,—and excels in the pathetic. I read his 'Gertrude of Wyoming'[131] lately,—and think it a pleasing poem:— He has made Pennsylvania a pretty place, Sir!"

"Do you think, Sir,"—said I,—"that he should write oftener?"—

"Yes, Sir!—unless he thinks he should write worse. He seems to me an idle man,—which is not national in him!—But Campbell is a poet— and I like him well!"—

Sir Joshua asked the great man if he had read any of Moore's works.—

"I have read them, Sir, and I like their fancies vastly. But they are too classical for the young, and too luxurious for the old:—They confuse youth with a mystic depravity; and elevate age with amorous recollections."—

"But," said Sir Joshua, "You speak now of his early poems:—There is surely great feeling and unblemished fancy in his later productions."—

"His Irish melodies are, indeed, the melodies of Ireland. They are national:—and not like Twiss's melodies of Scotland,[132] which ought to be called The Discords of Twiss. Sir! Moore is a patriot as well as a poet! He makes me love his country. But he should not continue to circulate the melodious immoralities of his boyhood.[133] When once the muse forfeits her chastity—she stains her beauty, and insults her comeliness. Moore, Sir, writes such songs, as will sing of themselves:—Twiss writes such, as no one can sing."—

I observed that Moore appeared to have read the old theological writers well.

"Sir! he has:—and in his boyish books, he tacked the notes of old divinity on the verses of young desire. Sir! he made Anacreon[134] and Martin Luther join hands, and dance a reel together. He made Beda hold a candle to the devil."—

Sir Joshua Reynolds thought that Moore was more powerful in the fanciful than in the pathetic. I ventured to support the same opinion.

"You are both wrong. Moore is as commanding in his pathos, as he is captivating in his fancy:—He would sooner make me weep than dance."—

I spoke of his sociality!—

"Sir," said the great moralist, "Moore is a sprightly man."

I observed that it was said he sang well.—

"Sir!" said the doctor, angrily, "That has nothing to do with the nature of his poetry. Singing is not genius. Moore's immortality will not depend on his own voice,—but on the voice of distant ages. You stray from the argument."—

I was silent, for a time, after this rebuke from the illustrious man, and felt hurt that I had hazarded an opinion which Dr. Johnson disapproved. But Sir Joshua Reynolds spoke of Crabbe as a powerful writer of the pathetic.—

"Aye!—Crabbe was known to me, when I was mortal. He is a stern and vigorous chronicler of the poor. His lines are very pleasant to me— and I remember his name with affection. Crabbe will never be universally liked;—for he writes too plainly for the fanciful, and too purely for the voluptuous. His muse walks about on the earth:—she has no wings. Some of his descriptions of simple rustic beauty would have suited your pencil, my friend!"

Sir Joshua said that he was fearful of painting from poetry,—after his failure in Dante.

"True, Sir!—I did not like your attack on Ugolino!"

Here I mentioned the name of Rogers—and spoke of my admiration of it.—

"Bozzy!—Bozzy! You are admiring Goldsmith, and don't know it. Rogers is an elegant poacher on the manor,—of which *Goldy* is the lord. The pleasures of memory are melancholy things to me:—He might as well call them the comforts of unhappiness. Rogers pleases without informing, and pains without improving. Sir! you may like Rogers,—but you must not love him."—

"But surely, Sir! he is very graceful and very classical."—

"Yes, Sir! but so is a dancing Apollo in an Italian ballet: you are amused, but never instructed. Rogers writes good polished notes, but his verses are gloomy and hollow: he puts brass headed nails on a coffin. He clouds the future with shadows of the past. He is eternally melodious, but never sublime. His poetry is dull with perpetual sweetness, and doleful, from its superabundance of pleasure. He has the fault of never being faulty.—Sir! Rogers is not a great poet."

"What think you, Doctor, of Southey? Is he not a great poet?" I felt that I had put a lucky question to him; for his features bespoke the workings of his mind.

"Southey, Sir! is a vast writer. He inundates one with a deluge of prose and verse. I would not be the muse of this bard for all the honours she may get. Her place is a place of all-work. Southey, Sir, is a court poet: and I *now* think that a man cannot speak freely and truly there, at the same time. He has genius, but he wants moderation. His mind thinks more than his hand can write;—and his hand writes much more than posterity will read."

Sir Joshua thought that his genius was "beautiful, and singularly wild and original."[135]

"Yes, Sir! It is beautiful from its originality,—and original, from its singular wildness. To write mad improbabilities is 'as easy as lying.'—But posterity will question their worth, and act accordingly. The Curse of Kehama is a pleasant fiction,—and the lies are well gilded:—the *Lay of the Laureate* is not so pleasant a one. Southey will never succeed, when he lavishes divinity on a review, and enthusiasm on a potentate."

"But surely, Sir!" (I was very careful how I crossed the great moralist with any unlucky opinion):—"but surely sir! The rapidity with which Mr. Southey writes, may be taken as a pretty good proof of the genuine feeling that actuates him?"—

"No Sir! The velocity of his pen is no evidence of its vigour:—A dove flies swiftly,—but it is not a powerful bird. Care never accompanies perpetual quickness, and perfection must depend upon care."—

"Yet surely Sir!" said I—"you will allow that a poet must be inspired who writes so freely?"—

"No Sir! I will not. Haste is not inspiration. Our friend here, Sir Joshua, might paint fifty pictures in a day;—but no one would care fifty pence about them. Sir! A man must not be a spendthrift of his intellect;— or he will very soon be brainless."—

"Why there may yet—"

"Come—come—no more of this useless contention. Southey will not write better,—though he write faster;—and though *you* argue in his favour."

I did not chuse now to push the conversation on this subject any further,—as I well knew the great critic's obstinacy of thinking:—I still feel, however, that I had the best of the argument,—though "I grant,— it does not appear so." I now asked Dr. Johnson if he admired Gifford.—

"Gifford is an arrogant man;—but he is well read and the Editor of a Tory review.[136] He has translated Juvenal;[137] but his third and tenth satires are not equal to mine. Sir! He is the whipper-in of a whole pack of writers."

Sir Joshua did not admire his petulance.

"Sir! you will never find a Flogger to be an amiable man:—the ferocity of his employment makes him flinty and rugged."

I hazarded an opinion that Gifford wrote little feeling poems well,— but the doctor turned sharply to me—

"Not he, sir!—He writes little poems to pretty women, and persuades himself that he is tender. Sir! he cares not one jot about Anna;—though he ventilates his poetry with her name. Gifford is a satirist, and would have us believe that he is also an amorist. Sir! he does not translate as well as I do!"

"Do you think"—said I—"he will live after death?"

"It is not for me to judge"—(and here an awful seriousness crept over the good man's countenance) "who will live, and who will not. Death, Sir! may come unawares to the name as well as the body. I do not like to talk of death now;—though I have done with it:—Rogers,—when he comes here,—will make it one of his 'pleasures of memory'."

Sir Joshua. "But you cannot fear, where there is no danger?—"

"Yes Sir! I can,—I fear from custom."

"But"—said I—

"Sir! I won't talk of death."

As the subject was evidently unpleasant to him, I changed by speaking of Walter Scott.

Sir Joshua. "I have always admired the richness of Scott's descriptions, and really look on him as the painter of poets. He colours richly, and from nature."

Johnson.—"Walter Scott is a pretty poet, Sir! but he puts too many trees into his scenery, for Scotch scenery. He makes a Tivoli of the Highlands."

I remarked that he ought to be a little ornamental.

"But, Sir! you may dress up a truth so finely, that it will look like a lie. Walter is, however, a nice writer:—he reminds one of chivalrous times—and I love him for it. I have read his Lay, and think it a good thing."

Sir Joshua.—"Have you read *Marmion*? The battle is full of fire."—

Johnson.—"So a battle ought to be:—Walter Scott makes a stupendous battle. Marmion, Sir, is a very magnificent rascal."

I observed that it was a very bold character—

Johnson.—"Sir! you might as well talk of the character of a highwayman. Marmion is a bold, black villain:—you must not say character. Macheath[138] is not a good character:—he is Marmion without his fine clothes and name."

Sir Joshua.—"Scott risks his fame I think by editing."—

Johnson—"He does Sir!—He writes too much to win an untarnished fame. He sacrifices worth to quantity, which will injure his immortality. Fame, Sir! is but the reflection of genius in the stream of time."

Sir Joshua.—"I think Walter Scott amongst poets, is what Westall is amongst painters,—an elegant mannerist."

Johnson. "Sir! I remember the features of Walter's heroes so well, that I should know one, if I saw him in a crowd of other robbers. Marmion, and Bertram,[139] and William of Deloraine are brothers. They are black-bearded ruffians, and do not know their letters."—

Here Burke joined us, and I looked forward to a lively conversation. I asked Dr. Johnson what he thought of Amos Cottle,—[140]

"Sir! I never heard of him."

J.H.R.

Boswell's Visit. (Continued). December 15, 1816

The ghost of Caesar hath appear'd to me,
Two several times.—

Julius Caesar.[141]

It was visible that Doctor Johnson was much gratified at seeing Burke enter, for his eyes sparkled with an uncommon vivacity, and his limbs became restless with pleasure.

Burke—"Well, Doctor, there seems to be something like a calm in the political world which we have left."

Johnson—"Yes, Sir, and after the tempests which have flourished, such a calm was to be coveted. Repose is the natural follower of immoderate agitation. Nations have their hours of sleep."

Burke—"But sleep betokens internal serenity;—and it cannot be expected that England should be wholly at rest yet."

Johnson—"Yes Sir, she may be. Violent exertion provokes a perfect inactivity. Expended strength must be replenished;—and repose is replenishment."

Burke—"But if a nation has over-exerted itself,—then repose is dangerous and wearisome. I should think that this might be seen in little, in the human body,—which may, by excessive labour, even subdue its capability of enjoying rest."

Johnson—"Sir, it may for a time. But quietness must ultimately be acquirable."

Burke—"What think you of the Insolvent Act, which has been passed in the house above?"

Johnson.—"Sir, I never was a friend to the incarceration of unfortunate men. Imprisonment is cruelty and folly. A body is locked up from the world, to which it was born;—and is deprived of the power of recovering itself from insolvency to affluence."

Burke—"I would rather at any time suffer death, than the loss of that liberty, which is the breath of the soul."

Johnson—"I would not Sir,—I loath confinement—but I ever feared death. Death is perpetual bondage."—

I here perceived by the serious aspect of the great moralist, that an unpleasant set of reflections were likely to ensue;—so I ventured to interfere, with a question on a different subject. It may be supposed that I spoke with all humility, when it is remembered how much I reverenced the high intellects of these two powerful characters:—and let no one accuse me of an improper boldness in thus breaking in on them. My motives must be considered, before I am accused of meddling rashly and unnecessarily. I stepped forward and asked the Doctor what he thought of Coleridge.

Johnson—"Why Sir, I think him a strange fellow."

Boswell—"But do you think him a better metaphysician than a poet?"

Johnson—"Sir, it is impossible to separate his fancy from his ponderous logic. He has made negus of his poetry and his metaphysical prose. I have read some of his early poems with pleasure, because they were written before he had bewildered himself with the intricacies of philosophy. He is very rich in the good gold of feeling,—but he hoards it up. Two or three of his Odes are lofty."

Boswell—"But have you read his *Christabel, Sir?*"

Johnson—"I have Sir—and it is a very dull enigma. He has put nonsense into fine words, and made her proud. I do not like to be puzzled to no purpose:—and it is a downright insolence in Mr. Coleridge to pester us with his two incomprehensible women. Sir, Geraldine is not to be made out:—she may be Joanna Southcote[142] for all I know. Then what can be said of the dreams.[143] They are arrant stuff. If Coleridge annoys us with more, the world will wish him a dreamless sleep. Sir, he might as well kick you."

Burke—"His politics appear to be very changeable."

Johnson—"Yes Sir, but he seems to be wise in his late opinion on that head."

Sir Joshua—"I think his description of the shadow of pleasure's dome floating midway on the waves of a river, gives you a grand idea of the size of the structure. It seems to me very picturesque."

Johnson—"But, Sir, I can make nothing of the dream. Any man may say an occasional good thing, but that will not embalm his eternal follies. He talks of a *sunny* dome, with caves of *ice*;—Sir, such a building could not exist. Fancy turns away with disgust from such an absurdity."

Boswell—"Lord Byron has spoken well of the poems, Doctor."

Johnson—"Sir, if he chuses to say a silly thing, I am not bound to abide by it. He may write an eulogy on Idiotcy, but I shall be bold to deem him mad. Sir, he may write ten yards of complimentary prose, on ten inches of insane poetry, if he likes; and I will neither read the first, nor admire the last. Let us hear no more of Coleridge."

Burke then observed that Lord Byron had enriched his coronet with a wreath of fresh laurel, a thing which Peers were seldom accustomed to do.

Johnson—"Lord Byron is a powerful writer;—but he seems an unfortunate man. He has certainly made his name endurable with time;—which is a clever deed in a lord. I like the Childe Harold best, because it has more thought. But the heroes of all his lordship's poems are but romantic ruffians. Lara is no better than O'Leary, except by birth:—and the Giaour is an impetuous varlet, whose pranks would in England have procured for him an exalted death on the top of Horse-monger Lane. I hear something of a Prisoner of Chillon; I hope it will turn out to be the despicable Childe, who after many disguises, is to be confined at last. The Corsair would enrich a dungeon."—

Burke. "But there, Doctor, you go contrary to your former opinion; you now advocate the cause of bodily imprisonment."—

Johnson. "Sir! I said that I did not like the confinement of *unfortunate* men: but I am not averse to the confinement of *wicked* men. Crime and disappointment are different things. If you were to borrow a hundred pounds of me, and found yourself unable to repay me by unlooked-for failures; I would not therefore deprive you of freedom, to glut my baffled avarice: but if I found out that you had picked my pocket of the money, I would trounce you, Sir! with a well-merited dungeon."

I ventured to admire Lord Byron's pictures of the sunny shores of Greece—

Johnson. "Lord Byron is a classical writer. I like his words on Athens and its suburbs."—

Boswell. "How do you like his descriptions of rural scenes in general?"—

Johnson. "I think them good: but you know that I hate the country. He has lavished pretty language on a dull subject. I wish, Sir! he had immortalized Fleet Street in his Spenserian verses. Why did he not lay the scene of his Corsair in the Strand, and make him a river pirate:—

We should then have seen Poetical Justice done to him at the Thames Police Office."—

Boswell. "Surely, Sir! that would have injured the splendour and interest of the poem."—

Johnson. "Not it, Sir! the Thames is as good as the Hellespont; only it is too near home."—

Burke remarked, that many English scenes were romantic and beautiful,—and that it was wonderful that they were not more often resorted to by the poets.

Johnson. "Sir! a genius might extract beauty from the Fleet Prison, if he chose to set about it."—

Boswell. "That he might, Sir! for loveliness is not exempt from confinement."—I could not refrain from this harmless jest, because I felt that it was a very fair one,—and because I longed to brighten the conversation, as much as lay in my power. No man I hold, can be blameable in uttering a good witticism. At any rate, I was guilty of no rudeness, for my jest escaped the observation of the party, in whose presence it sparkled. I now asked Dr. Johnson if he admired Montgomery.—

Johnson. "Yes Sir! he is an unaffectedly pious and pathetic writer;—and I love to read his works."

Sir Joshua thought that there was a fine air of humanity spread over his poetry.

Johnson—"Montgomery is a feeling man;—and his poetry comes simply from his heart. 'The World before the Flood' is a grand poem. The power of music over the wandering Cain is well described. Sir! Montgomery is very dear to me."

Burke observed, that of all modern poets, Wordsworth appeared to him the greatest.

Johnson—"Wordsworth, Sir, is a glorious poet.—I should like to write his life, whenever it is to be written. I would read Milton well, before I sat down to the task. I never read Wordsworth, but I think of Milton."—

As I was desirous of putting in a word in this interesting conversation, I remarked that I never read Milton but I thought of Wordsworth.

Johnson—"Sir! you talk foolishly. You merely turn my sentence wrong side outward. You might as well say that you never heard of Alfred without thinking of his fool."

I was unfortunate in my last observation, and refrained from answering the powerful Lexicographer, lest I should anger him further.—Burke asked the Doctor what he thought of Sir N. Wraxall.[144]

Johnson—"Sir! he is tedious. Besides he has a most prolific invention, which is greatly dangerous to historical fame. I should not be pleased, if I were compelled to believe all he tells. Sir! He has written a good romance of the eighteenth and nineteenth centuries."

Sir Joshua laughed at the irritable and *questionable* answers which Sir Nathaniel had given to the Edinburgh Review.[145]

Johnson—"Yes—yes—He had better have sat quietly in the pillory of that journal. All his writhings have only exposed him the more, to their unmerciful peltings."

I now thought that I had a good opportunity of urging the strength of my country's literature:—and therefore praised the Edinburgh Review as a most powerful work.

Johnson—"It is written well—but it is becoming less violent every day. I think I should have made a good Edinburgh Reviewer:—What think you, Bozzy?"

Boswell—"Sir! I should have been proud of your contributions to our national literature."

Johnson—"But, Sir, I should have steered clear of Scotticisms." The good man smiled while he spoke;—and I smiled to keep him in countenance. The conversation now turned on the respectability of authors writing for money:—Burke thought it a degradation in them.

Johnson—"Sir, it is no degradation. A man of genius has a right to benefit himself, as well as others, by his powers. It would be no honour to an author, to sit writing an epic poem without soles to his shoes, merely because he thought it a degradation to receive money. Sir! I would as soon clothe myself with the profits of my intellect,—as with the receipts of a shop. No man should starve himself to maintain his dignity. Sir! I would sell my abilities to the greatest advantage, provided I did not act dishonestly."—

This was certainly——

Here the paper abruptly concluded.—The rest was either torn off, or never written.

J.H.R.

The Arithmetic of Poetry. *February 16, 1817*[146]

I lisp'd in numbers, for the numbers came.

Pope.[147]

In shoals the hours their constant numbers bring,
Like insects looking to the advancing spring.

We have made some curious extracts from the works of our modern Poets, which we intend offering to our readers! Though we are aware that it would be more merciful to the fame of our living bards, to make burnt offerings of them; yet, as the selection may put the ridicule home to some of the authors' minds, we shall not insult the fire with such stuff. A poet now-a-days turns cocker[148] when he writes, and ingeniously hangs the fetters of rhymes over the addition table: It is in the hope of cutting a better figure that he is so constant to his numbers. The numeration table is a figurative fable to him, if he would but read it,—for there he will find that all the numbers lead to nothing in the end. Addison, when writing the Spectator, seems to have been annoyed with some bard, who, like Michael Cassio, was—"forsooth a great arithmetician:"[149] At least so we conclude from following observation:—

It is necessary to have read the multiplication table, fully to understand the author's works.

We have no doubt that we could, with very little trouble, point out the whole course of studies which a modern poet pursues. He reads the Tutor's Assistant all the week and *muses* over that book of the Bible called "Numbers," on Sundays:—thus,—and we can account for his being so deeply *versed* in arithmetic. We take it that Mr. Coleridge deserves to be made King of these poor bewildered bards,—as Bamfylde Moore Carew[150] was made King of the beggars. We shall now draw out our numbers,—taking care to put the Christabel at the head of the *feebles*. We have often heard of the *Lake Poets*,—in future we shall merely hear of the *School Poets*. More sublimity will be found in the Tutor's Assistant than in the lake of Grasmere; and "3 times 3 are 9," will strike deeper sensation into the heart than the Vale of Chamouny or Mount Blanc.

"And where are they?—I pray you tell,"
She answered, "Seven are we;
And two of us at Conway dwell,
And two are gone to sea,
Two of us in the churchyard dwell—"

Wordsworth.[151]

Not five yards from the mountain path,
      This thorn you on your left espy;
And to the left, three yards beyond
You see a little muddy pond,
      Of water never dry;
I've measur'd it from side to side,
'Tis three long and two wide.

Ditto.[152]

Since one, the tallest of the five,
Took me from the Palfrey's back.

Coleridge [153]

—She makes answer to the clock,
Four for the quarters, and twelve for the hour;
Ever and aye, moonshine and shower,
Sixteen short howls not over loud.—

Ditto.[154]

We were seven—who now are one,
Six in youth and one in age,
Finish'd as they had begun,
Proud of persecution's rage;
One in fire and two in field.

Lord Byron's *Prisoner of Chillon*.[155]

There are seven pillars of gothic mould.

Ditto.[156]

It was ten of April morn by the chime.

Campbell.[157]

The suns of twenty summers danced along.

Ditto.

A thousand wild waves on the shore.

Ditto.

98

Nine and twenty Knights of fame,
Hung their shields in Branksome hall;
Nine and twenty Squires of name,
Brought them their steeds from bower to stall;
Nine and twenty yeomen tall.—

Walter Scott.[158]

Ten squires, ten yeomen, mail clad men,
Waited the beck of the warders ten:—
Thirty steeds, both fleet and white.—

Ditto.[159]

And sometimes over thirty desarts drear—

Southey.

One, two,
Buckle my shoe;
Three, four,
Open the door, &c.

I'll take care of number one.

Both these supposed to have been written by the Laureate.

A second passes, and a third wanes on.

Southey.

He stept o'er benches one and two,
Oh' lovely maid I go with you;
He stept o'er benches two and three,
Oh' lovely maid I go with thee.

Lewis.

Keats's "Poems." *March 9, 1817*[160]

Here is a little volume filled throughout with very graceful and genuine poetry. The author is a very young man, and one, as we augur from the present work, that is likely to make a great addition to those who would overthrow that artificial taste which French criticism has long planted amongst us. At a time when nothing is talked of but the power and passion of Lord Byron, and the playful and elegant fancy of

99

Moore, and the correctness of Rogers, and the sublimity and pathos of Campbell (these terms we should conceive are kept ready composed in the Edinburgh Review-shop) a young man starts suddenly before us, with a genius that is likely to eclipse them all. He comes fresh from nature,—and the originals of his images are to be found in her keeping. Young writers are in general in their early productions imitators of their favourite poet; like young birds that in their first songs, mock the notes of those warblers, they hear the most, and love the best; but this youthful poet appears to have tuned his voice in solitudes,—to have sung from the pure inspiration of nature. In the simple meadows he has proved that he can

> —See shapes of light aerial lymning [sic]
> And catch soft floating from a faint heard hymning.[161]

We find in his poetry the glorious effect of summer days and leafy spots on rich feelings, which are in themselves a summer. He relies directly and wholly on nature. He marries poesy to genuine simplicity. He makes her artless,—yet abstains carefully from giving her an uncomely homeliness:—that is, he shows he can be familiar with nature, yet perfectly strange to the habits of common life. Mr. Keats is faced, or "we have no judgment in an honest face;" to look at natural objects with his mind, as Shakspeare and Chaucer did,—and not merely with his eye as nearly all modern poets do;—to clothe his poetry with a grand intellectual light,—and to lay his name in the lap of immortality. Our readers will think that we are speaking too highly of this young poet,— but luckily we have the power of making good the ground on which we prophesy so hardily. We shall extract largely from his volume:—it will be seen how familiar he is with all that is green, light, and beautiful in nature;—and with what an originality his mind dwells on all great or graceful objects. His imagination is very powerful,—and one thing we have observed with pleasure, that it never attempts to soar on undue occasions. The imagination, like the eagle on the rock, should keep its eye constantly on the sun,—and should never be started heavenward, unless something magnificent marred its solitude. Again, though Mr. Keats' poetry is remarkably abstracted, it is never out of reach of the mind; there are one or two established writers[162] of this day who think that mystery is the soul of poetry—that artlessness is a vice—and that nothing can be graceful that is not metaphysical;—and even young writers have sunk into this error, and endeavoured to puzzle the world with a confused sensibility. We must however hasten to the consideration of the little volume before us, and not fill up our columns with observations, which extracts will render unnecessary.

The first poem in the book seems to have originated in a ramble in some romantic spot, "with boughs pavillioned." The poet describes a delightful time, and a little world of trees,—and refreshing streams,— and hedges of filberts and wild briar, and clumps of woodbine

> —taking the wind
> Upon their summer thrones.[163]

and flowers opening in their early sunlight. He connects the love of poetry with these natural luxuries.

> For what has made the sage or poet write,
> But the fair paradise of Nature's light?[164]

This leads him to speak of some of our olden tales; and here we must extract the passages describing those of Psyche, and Narcissus. The first is exquisitely written,

> So felt he, who first told, how Psyche went
> On the smooth wind to realms of wonderment;
> What Psyche felt, and Love, when their full lips
> First touch'd; what amorous and fondling nips
> They gave each other's cheeks; with all their sighs,
> And how they kist each other's tremulous eyes;
> The silver lamp—the ravishment—the wonder—
> The darkness—loneliness—the fearful thunder;
> Their woes gone by, and both to heaven upflown,
> To bow for gratitude before Jove's throne.[165]

The following passage is not less beautiful,

> What first inspired a bard of old to sing
> Narcissus pining o'er the untainted spring?
> In some delicious ramble he had found
> A little space, with boughs all woven round;
> And in the midst of all, a clearer pool
> Than e'er reflected in its pleasant cool,

> The blue sky, here and there serenely peeping
> Through tendril wreaths fantastically creeping.
> And on the bank a lonely flower he spied,
> A meek and forlorn flower, with nought of pride,
> Drooping its beauty o'er the watery clearness,
> To woo its own sad image into nearness:
> Deaf to light Zephyrus it would not move;
> But still would seem to droop, to pine, to love.
> So while the poet stood in this sweet spot,
> Some fainter gleamings o'er his fancy shot;
> Nor was it long e'er he had told the tale
> Of young Narcissus, and sad Echo's Vale.[166]

This poem concludes with a brief but beautiful recital of the tale of Endymion,—to which indeed the whole poem seems to lean.[167] The address to the Moon is extremely fine.

> Or by the moon lifting her silver rim
> Above a cloud, and with a gradual swim
> Coming into the blue with all her light.
> O maker of sweet poets, dear delight
> Of this fair world, and all its gentle livers;
> Spangler of clouds, halo of chrystal rivers;
> Mingler with leaves, and dew and tumbling streams,
> Closer of lovely eyes to lovely dreams,
> Lover of loneliness, and wandering,
> Of upcast eye, and tender pondering!
> Thee must I praise above all other glories
> That smile us on to tell delightful stories.[168]

The 'Specimen of an induction to a poem,' is exceedingly spirited,—as is the fragment of a Tale of Romance immediately following it; but we cannot stay to notice them particularly. These four lines from the latter piece are very sweet.

> The side-long view of swelling leafiness,
> Which the glad setting sun in gold doth dress;
> Whence ever and anon the jay outsprings,
> And scales upon the beauty of its wings.[169]

The three poems following,[170] addressed to Ladies, and the one to Hope are very inferior to their companions;—but Mr. Keats informs us they were written at an earlier period than the rest. The imitation of Spenser is rich. The opening stanza is a fair specimen.

> Now Morning from her orient chamber came
> And her first footstep touch'd a verdant hill;
> Crowning its lawny crest with amber flame,
> Silv'ring the untainted gushes of its rill;
> Which, pure from mossy beds, did down distill,
> And after parting beds of simple flowers,
> By many streams a little lake did fill,
> Which round its marge reflected woven bowers,
> And, in its middle space a sky that never lours.

The two Epistles to his friends, and one to his brother are written with great ease and power. We shall extract two passages, both equally beautiful.

> But might I now each passing moment give
> To the coy muse, with me she would not live
> In this dark city, nor would condescend
> Mid contradictions her delights to lend.
> Should e'er the fine-eyed maid to me be kind,
> Ah! surely it must be where'er I find
> Some flowery spot, sequester'd, wild, romantic,
> That often must have seen a poet frantic;
> Where oaks, that erst the Druid knew, are growing,
> And flowers, the glory of one day, are blowing;
> Where the dark-leav'd laburnum's drooping clusters
> Reflect athwart the stream their yellow lustres,
> And intertwined the Cassia's arms unite,
> With its own drooping buds, but very white.
> Where on one side are covert branches hung,
> 'Mong which the nightingales have always sung
> In leafy quiet: where to pry aloof,
> Atween the pillars of the sylvan roof,
> Would be to find where violet beds were nestling,
> And where the bee with cowslip-bells was wrestling.
> There must be too a ruin dark and gloomy,
> To say "joy not too much in all that's bloomy."[171]

The next passage is from the opening of the poet's letter to a friend.

Oft have you seen a swan superbly frowning,
And with proud breast his own white shadow crowning;
He slants his neck beneath the waters bright
So silently, it seems a beam of light
Come from the galaxy: anon he sports,—
With outspread wings the Naiad Zephyr courts,
Or ruffles all the surface of the lake
In striving from the chrystal face to take
Some diamond water drops, and them to treasure
In milky nest, and sip them off at leisure.
But not a moment can he there insure them,
Nor to such downy rest can he allure them;
For down they rush as though they would be free,
And drop like hours into eternity.
Just like that bird am I in loss of time,
Whene'er I venture on the stream of rhyme;
With shatter'd boat, oar snapt, and canvass rent,
I slowly sail, scarce knowing my intent;
Still scooping up the water with my fingers,
In which a trembling diamond never lingers.[172]

Except in a little confusion of metaphor towards the end, the above passage is exquisitely imagined and executed.

A few Sonnets follow these epistles, and, with the exception of Milton's and Wordsworth's, we think them the most powerful ones in the whole range of English poetry. We extract the first in the collection, with the assurance that the rest are equally great.

To My Brother George
Many the wonders I this day have seen;
The sun, when first he kist away the tears
That filled the eyes of morn;—the laurell'd peers
Who from the feathery gold of evening lean;—
The ocean with its vastness, its blue green,
Its ships, its rocks, its caves, its hopes, its fears,—
Its voice mysterious, which whoso hears
Must think on what will be, and what has been.
E'en now, dear George, while this for you I write,

> Cynthia is from her silken curtains peeping
> So scantly, that it seems her bridal night,
> And she her half discover'd revels keeping.
> But what, without the social thought of thee,
> Would be the wonders of the sky and sea?

We have been highly pleased with the Sonnet which speaks—

> Of fair hair'd Milton's eloquent distress,
> And all his love for gentle Lycid drown'd;—
> Of lovely Laura in her light green dress,
> And faithful Petrarch gloriously crown'd.[173]

But the last poem in the volume, to which we are now come, is the most powerful and the most perfect. It is entitled "Sleep and Poetry." The poet passed a wakeful night at a brother poet's[174] house, and has in this piece embodied the thoughts which passed over his mind. He gives his opinion of the Elizabethan age,—of the [*sic*] Pope's school,—and of the poetry of the present day. We scarcely know what to select,—we are so confused with beauties. In speaking of poetry, we find the following splendid passage:—

> —Also imaginings will hover
> Round my fire-side, and haply there discover
> Vistas of solemn beauty, where I'd wander
> In happy silence, like the clear meander
> Through its lone vale; where I found a spot
> Of awfuller shade, or an enchanted grot,
> Or a green hill o'erspread with chequer'd dress
> Of flowers, and fearful from its loveliness,
> Write on my tablets all that was permitted,
> All that was for human senses fitted.
> Then the events of this wide world I'd seize
> Like a strong giant, and my spirit tease
> Till at its shoulders it should proudly see
> Wings to find out an immortality.[175]

The following passage relating to the same event, is even greater. It is the very magic of imagination.

> —For lo! I see afar,
> O'ersailing the blue cragginess a car

> And steeds with streamy manes—the charioteer
> Looks out upon the winds with glorious fear:
> And now the numerous tramplings quiver lightly
> Along a huge cloud's ridge; and now with sprightly
> Wheel downward come they into fresher skies,
> Tipt round with silver from the sun's bright eyes.
> Still downward with capacious whirl they glide;
> And now I see them on a green hill's side,
> In breezy rest among the nodding stalks,
> The charioteer with wondrous gesture talks
> To trees and mountains;—[176]

We have not room to extract the passages on Pope and his followers, who,

> —With a puling force,
> Sway'd them about upon a rocking horse,
> And thought it Pegasus.[177]

Nor can we give those on modern poets. We shall conclude our extracts with the following perfect and beautiful lines on the busts and pictures which hung around the room in which he was resting.

> Sappho's meek head was there half smiling down
> At nothing; just as though the earnest frown
> Of over thinking had that moment gone
> From off her brow, and left her all alone.
>
> Great Alfred's too, with anxious, pitying eyes,
> As if he always listen'd to the sighs
> Of the goaded world; and Kosciusko's worn
> By horrid suffrance—mightily forlorn.
>
> Petrarch, outstepping from the shady green,
> Starts at the sight of Laura; nor can wean
> His eyes from her sweet face. Most happy they!
> For over them was seen a free display
> Of outspread wings, and from between them shone
> The face of Poesy: from off her throne
> She overlook'd things that I scarce could tell.[178]

We conclude with earnestly recommending the work to all our readers. It is not without defects, which may be easily mentioned, and as easily rectified. The author, from his natural freedom of versification, at times passes to an absolute faultiness of measure:—This he should avoid. He should also abstain from the use of compound epithets as much as possible. He has a few of the faults which youth must have;[179]— he is apt occasionally to make his descriptions overwrought,—But on the whole we never saw a book which had so little reason to plead youth as its excuse. The best poets of the day might not blush to own it.

We have had two Sonnets presented to us, which were written by Mr. Keats, and which are not printed in the present volume. We have great pleasure in giving them to the public,—as well on account of their own power and beauty, as of the grandeur of the subjects; on which we have ourselves so often made observations.

To Haydon, with a Sonnet written on seeing the Elgin Marbles

Haydon! forgive me that I cannot speak
Definitively on these mighty things;
Forgive me that I have not Eagle's wings—
That what I want I know not where to seek:
And think that I would not be over meek
In rolling out upfollow'd thunderings,
Even to the steep of Heliconian springs,
Were I of ample strength for such a freak—
Think too, that all those numbers should be thine;
Whose else? In this who touch thy vesture's hem?
For when men star'd at what was most divine
With browless idiotism—o'erwise phlegm—
Thou hadst beheld the Hesperean shine
Of their star in the East, and gone to worship them.

On seeing the Elgin Marbles

My spirit is too weak—Mortality
Weighs heavily on me like unwilling sleep,
And each imagin'd pinnacle and steep
Of godlike hardship tells me I must die
Like a sick Eagle looking at the sky.
Yet 'tis a gentle luxury to weep
That I have not the cloudy winds to keep
Fresh for the opening of the morning's eye.

Such dim-conceived glories of the brain
Bring round the heart an undescribable feud;
So do these wonders a most dizzy pain,
That mingles Grecian grandeur with the rude
Wasting of old Time—with a billowy main—
A sun—a shadow of a magnitude.

Ben Jonson. May 4, 1817[180]

Still to be neat, still to be drest,
As you were going to a feast;
Still to be powder'd, still perfumed:
Lady, it is to be presumed,
Though art's hid causes are not found,
All is not sweet, all is not sound.

Give me a look, give me a face,
That makes simplicity a grace;
Robes loosely flowing, hair as free:
Such sweet neglect more taketh me,
Than all the adulteries of art;
They strike mine eyes, but not my heart.

Ben Jonson's *Silent Woman*

This is one of the very few productions of this once celebrated author, which by their singular elegance and neatness, form a striking contrast to the prevalent coarseness of his tedious effusions.

Dr. Aikin's Essay on Song Writing.[181]

In matters of literature and taste we were never inclined to pay a very humble deference to what is called *the judgment of the public*. The multiplication of nothings will not make a single unit, neither do the voices of weak men become oracular because the blockheads war in unison. It were indeed a "speculation intelligent" to define honestly what is public opinion! Agreeably to notions we sometime hence held, it was at best but one voice and many echoes; a sort of extensive fit of gaping, in which, as in real life, the emptiest head had not unfrequently the honor of precedency.—But the most established faiths may be sometimes shaken; and we candidly admit that Dr. Aikin has shewn us, in the passage above extracted, that a voice may be sometimes the response to an echo, and that the multiplication of nothings will amount to something in the end:—estimate the value of the Doctor's authority and we have it.[182]

As, however, it is not impossible, but that our previous errors may have misled some confiding reader, we hold it but honest to shew the grounds of our recantation; and we cannot do so more effectually than by proving that the "opinion" the Doctor has here hazarded, is nothing but the concentration of the very vulgarest prejudices of the last century. We wish it, to be distinctly understood that we are not intending in this article a general and indiscriminate defence of the poet. That he has defects, gross and palpable defects, none can be more sensible of, and if we do not instance them, it is because they are without the limits we have prescribed ourselves on the present occasion. A few illustrated observations on the charges generally preferred against him, can alone be brought within reasonable bounds; we shall, therefore, confine ourselves to those generally, if not altogether to the Doctor's assertion that the song in The Silent Woman is but "a strain of rareness,"—the jewel in the toad's head:—and indeed when he proceeds to talk of "the prevalent coarseness, & c." it is something of a gratuitous and *original* folly, and consequently does not fall immediately within the reach of our proposed inquiry.

There are few writers of whom men are more accustomed to talk by rote than Ben Jonson: but as the hardiest and most determined enemies of his fame, neither ventured to deny the extent or profundity of his learning, the richness of his imagination, the raciness of his humour, his truth and wonderful discrimination of character, the strength and masculine vigour of his language:—when these excellencies were beyond the cavilling of "the hounds that hunt," it only remained for those "that follow and make up the cry" to pull [*sic—for pule?*] about a want of judgement, taste, and elegance.

The judgment of any man is of all others the point on which there will be, most probably, the greatest difference of opinion. It is difficult of positive and full illustration, in a work much less voluminous than the subject of the controversy. But we incline to believe that Jonson's defects, such as they are, arose rather from a *severity* of judgment than a want of it. He would touch and retouch to work up to the niceties of his own discriminative taste, until, as Cartwright has observed, "the file would not make *smooth* but *wear*."[183] We have indeed sometimes to regret that what is bold and vigorous is also bare and naked: but this originated in the school in which he had studied, and the object he ever proposed to himself in his dramatic writings, to better and instruct, as well as to delight mankind. Still the subject is open to reasonable discussion: but when we look into the Minor Pieces of our poet we cannot but wonder at the blind infatuation of those men who have ventured their authority to abuse his taste and elegance.

To come at once to our subject, and passing over things as notorious as his song to Celia, "Drink to me only with thine eyes," with which the reader must be acquainted, and "The Sad Shepherd," with which it would be offensive to presume his ignorance,—The Penates (as Mr. Gifford has named it) is assuredly one of the most elegant dramatic trifles in the language, and "The Satyr," abounds in all that is playful. "The Gipsies Metamorphosed," the reader may remember, is interesting in a high degree from the sketches of character it contains of some of the most distinguished persons of the court of James: and it is scarcely possible to conceive a series of compliments more full of discrimination, more ingenious or more poetical. Perhaps the second and third songs might have suited Dr. Aikin's purpose:—

> The Faery beam upon you,
> The stars to glister on you;
> A moon of light,
> In the noon of night,
> 'Till the fire-drake hath o'ergone you!
>
> The wheel of fortune guide you,
> The boy with the bow beside you;
> Run aye in the way,
> Till the bird of day,
> And the luckier lot betide you!
>
> Third Song
> To the old, long life and treasure;
> To the young, all health and pleasure;
> To the fair, their face
> With eternal grace;
> And the soul to be loved at leisure.

To the witty, all clear mirrors;
To the foolish, their dark errors;
　　To the loving sprite,
　　A secure delight;
To the jealous, his own false terrors.

And we are not satisfied that there is any thing very *coarse*, or that Lady Purbeck, to whom it was addressed, thought it very *tedious* to be told, with a hundred other elegant things,

Though your either cheek discloses
Mingled baths of milk and roses;
Though your lips be banks of blisses,
Where he plants, and gathers kisses,
　　&c. &c. &c.

The Vision of Delight too is inimitably beautiful: and so are innumerable poems in The Forest and Underwoods. Here is a third, fourth, and fifth "singular evidence."

Come, my Celia, let us prove,
While we may, the sports of love;
Time will not be ours for ever:
He at length our good will sever.
Spend not then his gifts in vain,
Suns that set may rise again;
But if once we loose this light,
'Tis with us perpetual night.
Why should we defer our joys?
Fame and rumour are but toys.
Cannot we delude the eyes
Of a few poor household spies;
Or his easier ears beguile,
So removed by our wile?
'Tis no sin love's fruits to steal,
But the sweet theft to reveal:
To be taken, to be seen,
These have crimes accounted been.

III

Her Triumph

2

Do but look on her eyes, they do light
All that Love's world compriseth!
Do but look on her hair, it is bright
As Love's star when it riseth!
Do but mark, her forehead's smoother
Than words that sooth her:
And from her arched brows, such a grace
Sheds itself through the face:
As alone there triumphs to the life
All the gain, all the good of the element's strife.

3

Have you seen but a bright lily grow,
Before rude hands have touch'd it?
Have you mark'd but the fall o' the snow
Before the soil hath smutch'd it?
Have you felt the wool of the bever?
Or swan's down ever?
Or have smelt o' the bud of the briar?
Or the nard in the fire?
Or have tasted the bag of the bee?
O so white! O so soft! O so sweet is she!

A Song

Oh do not wanton with those eyes,
Lest I be sick with seeing;
Nor cast them down, but let them rise,
Lest shame destroy their being.

O be not angry with those fires,
For then their threats will kill me;
Nor look too kind on my desires,
For then my hopes will spill me.

O do not steep them in my tears,
For so will sorrow slay me;
Nor spread them as distract with fears;
Mine own enough betray me.

Innumerable other poems of equal beauty suggest themselves to us: but this article has already extended to an almost unreasonable length, for which we can only hope the poems we have extracted will sufficiently apologize:—unless indeed the reader decides with the Doctor that they are "coarse" or "tedious," and that the song in The Silent Woman is really "a singular evidence" shining amidst such rubbish "like a rich jewel in an Ethiop's ear." Whatever that decision may be, we shall not, however, forego our "resolved judgment," and to us these little poems seem literally steeped in the richest harmony. It has been suggested to us that our musical composer would do well to bring them forward: but where is the correspondent genius that would feel their excellence! And indeed such is their exquisite modulation that to us accompaniment seems altogether superfluous. We can liken [them] to nothing so well as those shells found on "the beached margent of the sea" whence flow perpetual music; as if Sycorax held, shell-bound within them, some delicate spirit of the waters: as if some gentle and immortal creature, after listening to Arion, had retired there to feed on memory and rapturous imitation.

"Characters of Shakespeare's Plays." By William Hazlitt.—Hunter.—1817. July 20, 1817[184]

This is the only work ever written on Shakespeare, that can be deemed worthy of Shakespeare;—some remarks in Schlegel's German lectures[185] only excepted. Now this is a sweeping assertion,—and yet it is true. All the commentators ("a plague upon them") preyed only on the expressions of Shakespeare, and wholly disregarded his spirit and feeling. But here we have a noble criticism on the very heart of our bard,—or rather on the hearts of those who took their greatness and perfection immediately from his. In the work before us, there are no little questionings of words and phrases—no petty cavillings about black-letter books, or worn-out and worthless customs,—but instead of such trifling, we meet with a masterly and beautiful essay on the imagination, the fancy, and the feeling of the poet,—and a fine display of the mental anatomy of all the principal characters which he created. With Shakespeare all was creation. He never drew the mere outline of persons or things,—never was satisfied with calling up shadows only;—all his characters are beings of downright flesh and blood,—and these of the very best kind. We do not become acquainted with high *Macbeth*,—*Othello*,—the romantic *Romeo*, that soul of all lovers,—our gentle *Hamlet*, "for we must call him ours,"—the old mad *Lear*, whose sorrows are sent forth into the open air, when thunder is abroad,—*Falstaff* the round man, the huge tun of man, fat Jack,—*Richard*,—*Brutus*,—*Prospero*;—we do not know these by the poet's description. No. He gives them life, spirit, utterance,—he sends them "into this breathing world," and leaves them to speak for themselves. There is little doubt but that *Hamlet*,—when once he held his existence, uttered many a saw and common saying, which Shakespeare would have expunged if he had possessed the power of so doing. But it seems that the poet had very little control of his creatures,—and certain it is that most of the characters are as head-strong, as other men, in their several opinions and pursuits, and have a decided consciousness of their own existence. *Hotspur*, for instance, holds not a described passion,—a shadowy madness of humour;—his passions and fancies are the things themselves. His captiousness when he cannot remember the name of a certain castle,—and his sudden calmness when the name is told him,— are realities of the temper. *Hotspur* would have cuffed Shakespeare's cheek, if he had ventured to curb him in his wild humours. It is a well known fact, that the poet was compelled to kill *Mercutio*,—because he "had in him something dangerous," which his wisdom feared.— Shakespeare is the divinity of the world of imagination,—and assuredly many of his creatures play most fantastic tricks before him:—but in this, they do but mock their fellows of the earth. Shakespeare holds the glass to nature,—and mankind dance the mirror before it:—he makes us see double. His characters, and nature's men, grow "like a double cherry on the stalk." We have heard it remarked by a friend, who *reads* Shakespeare,—and *really* to read Shakespeare, is "to be one man picked out of ten thousand,"[186]—that he was always correct in the costume of language. This is an excellent observation. *Othello's* discourse hath always something glowing and lofty in it, like his clime and race. It is either nobly declamatory, or short and fiercely conjectural. His language is always as open as the day,—as wide as the casing air,—when his mind is unhurt;—but he becomes confined, bound in, in his discourse, when his suspicion is awakened. It was ever the way of suspicion to be thus. *Romeo*,—how exquisitely his language becomes him!—his words are silver sweet. The conversation between him and *Juliet* in the garden is perfect music. It is uttered in the thick of fruit trees, with the moonlight flowing over them. It is impossible to hear a happy sigh,—or walk in a soft twilight, or look at the moon,—that pale thing of the skies,—and not think of *Romeo's* love. There is no doubt that *Romeo* was a poet, from the colour of his love:—we wish he had written "a book of songs and sonnets" for our summer reading. The language of *Shylock* seems a translation from the Hebrew,—or the Hebrew itself. It has a strange fierceness in it. It seems to have been caught in a wilderness,—and never to have been tamed. It is "warlike as the wolf for what it eats." *Lear* talks awingly. His madness inspires him,—and he seems to marry his nature to the elements. He calls upon the old heavens to assist him, "for he is old himself." He is the spirit of age in his troubles—and the thunder and lightning break about the skies as he speaks. Again,—*Hamlet* says what he pleases,—for he is a great reader,—and "knows all qualities with a learned spirit." He talks of Niobe, and Hecuba, and Hercules,—because he had become familiar with them in books;—we do not find any allusions of this kind in *Falstaff*, or *Hal*, or *Poins*, who were revellers and not readers. *Hamlet's* heart sits quietly o'er its melancholy, like a bird on its nest. His words always set us thinking,—and depress our spirits. Every thing seems hushed while he is speaking, so sweet and lonely is his discourse. It will be seen by these instances, how true the remark is, which we cited. Young poets, we think, should have a portrait of Nature, Shakespeare's mistress, hung up near their books,[187]—in the same way that painters have a picture of Fornarina, Raphael's mistress, suspended amidst their works of art.

The work before us is one, of all others, which we longed to see written, and now it is come we must make the most of it. It is a sort of mental biography of Shakespeare's characters. The author has written it, with that spirit and intensity which prove him to be worthy of the task. We shall not detain our readers longer from this delightful work, but proceed to feed them with some of the most eloquent passages of the work. The following remarks on *Cymbeline* are very true and beautiful.

The pathos in *Cymbeline* is not violent or tragical, but of the most pleasing and amiable kind ... The scene in which Pisanio gives Imogen his master's letter, accusing her of incontinency on the treacherous suggestions of Iachimo, is as touching as it is possible for any thing to be.[188]

Mr. Hazlitt has done justice to the characters of Shakespeare's women; of whom we were always fond. We are glad *Imogen* was of Britain, for she should be the leading star of her country women. How beautiful she must have been! See what *Iachimo*, the keen Italian, thinks of her.

> —Cytherea,
> How bravely thou becomst thy bed! Fresh lily,
> And whiter than the Sheets! That I might touch,—
> But kiss, one kiss—Tis her breathing that
> Perfumes the chamber thus: The flame o' th' taper
> Bows towards her, and would under-keep her lids
> To see the enclosed lights now canopied
> Under the windows, white and azure, laced
> With blue of Heav'ns own tint.[189]

There is no poetry beyond this:—This is the heaven's need [*sic;* for "meed"?] of poetry. Our Author's Essay on *Macbeth* is admirably written,—particularly the following parts of it.—

Macbeth, generally speaking, is done upon a stronger, and more systematic principle of contrast, than any other of Shakespeare's plays ... The whole play is an unruly chaos of strange and forbidden things, where the ground rocks under our feet ...

This tragedy is alike distinguished for the lofty imagination it displays ... The impression which her lofty determination of character makes on the mind of *Macbeth*, is well described where he exclaims—

> Bring forth men children only;
> For thy undaunted mettle should compose
> Nothing but males![190]

Mr. Hazlitt has written very finely on *Othello*, which we think a noble but difficult subject. It is full of all the varieties of character,— and is a little world of passion in itself. *Iago* is finely interpreted. The most affecting thing in this tragedy,—or rather the thing that stirs our nerves most,—is the scene in which *Desdemona* opens her heart to *Iago*, on the subject of *Othello's* change of mind;—his pretended sympathy is more than *Patience* can bear. We never read this, but we instantly compare it with *Cleopatra's* applying the asp to her bosom. Love in *Othello* is destroyed in the same way. The opening remarks on tragedy are extremely good.

It has been said, that tragedy purifies the affections by terror and pity ... It exercises the understanding upon things out of ourselves, while it leaves the affections unemployed, or engrossed with their own immediate, narrow interests![191]

We have run this article to a great length, and yet we have not said as much as we could wish. In our next number we shall continue it.

"*Characters of Shakespeare's Plays.*"—*By William Hazlitt.—* (*Continued*). *July 27, 1817*

The play *Troilus and Cressida*, which we think was unavoidably spoiled by having too much of the classical infused into it, is no very great favourite with us:—of course we speak thus of it, as compared with the rest of Shakespeare's plays,—for it has enough of poetry in it, after all the declamation of the Trojans and Greeks, to weigh down twenty plays of any other writer. *Cressida* in Shakespeare is a more volatile creature than the *Cressida* of Chaucer;—she is a little natural coquet, that follows her passions (if passions they may be called) where ever they lead,—so that it cannot be expected her heart should sojourn long at one place. The *Cressida* of Chaucer hath a wisdom in the management of her pleasures, and knows to take advantage of the time. Mr. Hazlitt has described the difference that exists between the genius of Shakespeare and that of Chaucer, with great ability.

There is no *double entendre* in the characters of Chaucer: they are either quite serious or quite comic ... His genius was dramatic, as Chaucer's was historical.[192]

How noble a play is *Anthony and Cleopatra*!—it swells with poetry, as with a passion. It is History caught in its voluptuous hour, over which Shakespeare has thrown a Vulcan-web, and exposed it to all eyes. The spirit of *Anthony*, like a pearl, is dissolved in the voluptuous cup of *Cleopatra*. She is all that is luxurious;—beautiful, indolent, and possessed of a most gorgeous imagination. She is of the East; and not to be satiated with pomp and pleasure. In the Remarks we meet with the following passage, which is as true, as Fame.

The character of *Cleopatra* is a master-piece . . . The luxurious pomp and gorgeous extravagance of the Egyptian Queen, are displayed in all their force and lustre, as well as the irregular grandeur of the soul of *Mark Anthony*."

Again,—

Cleopatra's whole character is the triumph of the voluptuous . . . Where most she satisfies.[193]

What a spirit and fire in her conversation with *Anthony's* messenger, who brings her the unwelcome news of his marriage with *Octavia*! How all the pride of beauty and of high rank breaks out in her promised reward to him!—

> —There's gold, and here
> My bluest veins to kiss.[194]

She had great and unpardonable faults, but the beauty of her death almost redeems them. She learns from the depth of her despair, the strength of her affections. She keeps her Queen-like state in the last disgrace, and her sense of the pleasurable in the last moments of her life. She tastes a luxury in death. After applying the asp, she says with fondness—

> Dost thou not see my baby at the breast,
> That sucks the nurse asleep?—
> As sweet as balm, as soft as air, as gentle.
> Oh Anthony!—[195]

All continuations of characters in the plays of Shakespeare have an harmonious connection. There is no contradiction in action or description,—let the character be introduced, or mentioned a thousand times. For instance, Anthony says, after being defeated by Augustus—

> —I struck
> The lean and wrinkled Cassius, and twas I,
> That the mad Brutus ended.[196]

Now, in *Julius Caesar*, almost the first thing we hear, is of "that lean *Cassius;*"—and nearly the last, that *Brutus* hath "rid like a madman through the gates of Rome." How fine a knowledge of human nature has Shakespeare here shewn,—in making the philosophic *Brutus*, wild, when once excited. The flint when struck produces the keenest fire. Shakespeare in the play, speaks not as of a Chariot, but of *"Caesar's wheeled seat;"*—How processional is this! How steadily grand! It has something like Grecian Sculpture in it.

Mr. Hazlitt's essay on *Hamlet* is not quite so great as we expected,—and yet it is very great:—But our disappointment may arise from the almost idolatrous enthusiasm which we feel for the play. Hamlet!—the graceful and melancholy Prince!—The disappointed, blighted Love!—The soul of youth!—How is it possible to write up to our conceptions of this matchless work?—"He is himself,—alone!"—The following passage is beautifully written, and with this we shall pass the play,—for it is pain to dwell on intense feelings, without having the power of breathing them with expression.

Hamlet is a name . . . This is the true *Hamlet*.[197]

But we must begin to make short work of these interesting essays. The remarks on the *Tempest* and the *Midsummer Night's Dream* are extremely graceful and poetical. They are all fairy like, and are fit to associate with Oberon, and his flower-haunting court. The essay on *Romeo and Juliet* is, to our feelings, the best in the volume. The soul of passion is infused into it; and every sentence weighs on the heart like a feeling. The youth of lovers is shed over it. It shakes one like a realized dream of Hope. We must find room for the following beautiful passage, —which is, however, equalled in many other parts of the essay:—

All that was to come of life was theirs . . . As are the desires and the hopes of youthful passion, such is the keenness of its disappointments, and their baleful effect.[198]

With the above exquisite passage,—which has a passion in it, almost beyond description,—we must close our extracts. We could have wished to have noticed the remaining plays, amongst which are *Lear*, *Twelfth Night*, and *As You Like It*,—but our limits will not allow of it. What we have said and extracted, however, will send most of our readers to the work itself, which we again pronounce to be the only true work ever written on Shakespeare.

Zapolya. A Christmas Tale. By S. T. Coleridge.
Fenner, 1817. November 16, 1817[199]

How glorious is our old Drama!—how eternal a monument has old English genius built up! enough in all conscience for one nation, when other nations are blank; except perhaps in the *Dramatis Personae*, a fit of compliments or curses, or of sentiment. What can this country expect more?—more it will not have. The ages of romance are fled, gone for ever, we are

> Sitting by the shores of old romance[200]

never again to spread a sail over its waters—strange fancies we may see, and carping imaginations: but never more will Poet look into these regions as a little child, and tell of them with a child's simplicity. No more will poet sing,

> Lithinith and lestinith, and
> Holdith still your tongue,
> And ye shall herin strange talking
> Of Gamelyn the yonge.[201]

No Juliet will any more yearn from her window, saying

> O for a Falconer's voice
> To lure this tassel gentle back again![202]

For

> Metaphor is dead—and hath not left his peer.[203]

Yet should there not be an echo of the old thunder in these days? We think over all things in the drama shape of late-birth—*Manfred* is full of fine things, but we do not feel the Poem—*Fazio* is well.[204] *John Woodvil* is excellent;[205] most particularly in the delicacy of its characters. It is a spice of the antique, and of course is full of poetry and wit. This very unassuming Tragedy we believe has few readers, and therefore we cannot resist treating ours with a few lines from it . . .[206]

After having looked through Zapolya, we were insensibly led into these few remarks and quotations—which have created a state of feeling, not at all favourable to the Poem. We could not look in vain for poetry—but the mystery is, how the Author of the following passage, could be content to write whole pages of dulness.

O she was innocent!
And to be innocent is nature's wisdom!
The fledge dove knows the prowlers of the air,
Fear'd soon as seen, and flutters back to shelter.
And the young steed recoils upon its haunches,
The never yet seen adder's hiss first heard.
O surer than suspicion's hundred eyes,
Is that fine sense, which to the pure in heart,
By mere oppugnancy of their own goodness,
Reveals the approach of evil.[207]

There is but one explanation—he *can* write thus: but he has been time immemorial an admirer of Bowles's sonnets: a sort of Della Cruscan spell has ever tied the tips of his wings together:—it has damn'd him with the most vile epithets:—such as "self-expected," "tyrant-quelling" and made him personify everlastingly, Memory, Destruction, Contemplation, Blasphemy, &c. without [our] hearing any thing like "Warder of the Brain" or a "fiery-wheel'd throne." A genuine admirer of Mr. Coleridge's Poetry could never take up his books without cursing the hour in which he took to Bowles's Sonnets. Such a misfortune should not have befallen Mr. Coleridge—as a writer who would wish to please: for where he ought to be admired there are few to wonder at, and fewer to feel with him;—very few to whom images present themselves in the genuine sibylline[208] attitude. We meet with but one here and there who is able to enter fully into his fantastic thought region; or be intense over his phantom-illustrations. He seems as enamoured of a serpent's coil, as of nightingale; and would think it no small delight to be eye-bound, for a short season, by a rattle-snake: unless he might prefer the idea of a mountain setting out from the Galaxy on New Year's Day, for the express purpose of crushing him at Whitsuntide.

His nicety in these particulars is unrivalled. It may be that the best way of ascertaining the particular powers of poets, is, if possible, to follow their different graspings at things, less in keeping and taste, than what are at length adopted. For instance, we can imagine in what a different manner the idea of death operated on the minds of Shakspeare and Milton. With the latter it was a positive deadly power; with the former a mere absence of life: Milton began with death, and from it thought into the varieties of life;—Shakspeare looked at the grass, the flowers, and feminine beauty, and sighed because he could not hide from himself that all would end in death. Look at the lamentation of the one over Lycidas, and of the other over Fidele. Milton, who like Wordsworth, set himself, in early youth, a great task, had acquired a restless habit of mind, a continual breathlessness after the savoriest essences: he read for them—he thought for them—he dreamt of them—and established himself among them in such a way, that (except, certainly, a high moment of religion), he seldom experienced an unmixed pathos of time, and place, and individuality. Therefore, in Lycidas, he strays after all sorts of beauty: his grief is

> Breaking the silence of the seas,
> Amongst the farthest Hebrides.[209]

But Shakespeare, a child of the moment, living only in the present, has no combinations from the distance. He finds the "prettiest daisied plot," and does not lift his eyes from it. His reflections are merely, that all things must die; and this presses so heavily on him, that the delicious burial is, as it is.[210] Now Mr. Coleridge is the greatest puzzle for this kind of unravelment that has ever lived: we are completely at a loss on enquiring how and why he writes thus and thus. It were to be wished that some acute critic would point out the probable differences in temper and taste, between the authors of *Laodamia* and *Kubla Khan*. It would bring us a step or two towards Mr. Coleridge, and make us more at home in *Zapolya*. This drama the author says is in humble imitation of the *Winter's Tale*. Here is a rebel usurping it over his king and brother, killing him and driving his sister-in-law, with her infant, out into the woods; where she remains till all is cleared up. *Kiuprili*, a household patriot, one of those virtuous souls we meet with in many a melodrame, after having braved the usurper,—been put under lock and key,—and escaped by means of his young friend *Ragozzi*, and a mute,

> One that can shoot a precipice like a bird,[211]

exiles himself with the queen into a dreary forest,—where they become the terror of all the country round.—But it is needless to sketch out the story;—for the reader may come at the main part directly, from these last lines of *Zapolya's* speech to her infant at the end of the prelude.

> —And thou snatched hence
> Poor friendless fugitive! with a mother's wailing,
> Offspring of royal Andreas, shalt return
> With trump and timbrel clang, and popular shout,
> In triumph to the palace of thy fathers![212]

Emerick, the usurper, is, like most other usurpers in plays,—a man who in real life would be laughed at and made a butt of. There is an innocent, pretty she-orphan, who says of her good mistress.

> As far back as I wot of,
> All her commands were gracious sweet requests,
> How could it be then, but that her requests
> Must needs have sounded to me as commands.[213]

Then there is young master *Laska*, who is in for a commodity of cowardice and *malvolioism*: we have seen such a fellow in the shape of Liston in many a gothic chamber. Then there is old *Bathory*, a mountaineer, and *Bethlem Bathory*, who turns out to be young *Prince Andreas*. Aye! but how did his mother lose him! What a question, good Sir! Are you to come at all this criss-cross romance in plain prose, and moreover for some tenpenny matter! There are besides *Pestalutz*, an assassin,— *Casimir*, son of *Kiuprili*; and the lady, his wife; and one *Lord Rudolph*. Now all these several and singular, should make us feel their views and dispositions; should let us know whether they hate or love, &c.—in real earnest:—but they do not. The queen's grief has not touch'd us; nor do we admire old *Kiuprili* for all his patriotism and exile: and furthermore, we hold that *Glycine* would fall in love with a prince in disguise, if he fell in her way. We will let the chief characters give specimens of their abilities.

> *Scene,—a wooded park and mountains.*
> *Enter Zapolya, with an infant in her arms.*
> *Zapo.* Hush! dear one! hush! My trembling arms disturb *thee*!
> Thou, the protector of the helpless! thou,
> The widow's husband and the orphan's father,
> Direct my steps! Ah whither? O send down
> Thy angel to a houseless babe and mother
> Driven forth into the cruel wilderness!

Hush, sweet one! Thou art no Hagar's offspring: thou art
The rightful heir of an anointed King!
What sounds are those? It is the vesper chaunt
Of labouring men returning to their home!
Their queen has no home! Hear me, heavenly father!
And let this darkness—
Be as the shadow of thy outspread wings,
To hide and shield us! Start'st thou in thy slumbers?
Thou canst not dream of savage Emerick. Hush!
Betray not thy poor mother! for if they seize thee
I shall grow mad indeed, and they'll believe
Thy wicked uncle's lie.[214]

Kiuprili does not utter many more sensible morcels than this—

O most of all, most miserable nation,
For whom the imperial power, enormous bubble!
Is blown and kept aloft, or burst and shatter'd
By the bribed breath of a lewd soldiery.[215]

Bethlem speaks to Lady Sarolta, about his mother and infancy as
follows—

—Eyes fair as thine
Have gazed on me with tears of love and anguish,
Which these eyes saw not, or beheld unconscious:
And tones of anxious fondness, passionate prayers
Have been talk'd to me! but this tongue ne'er soothed
A mother's ear, lisping a mother's name![216]

Lady Sarolta is very poetical: to one she says—

Thy fancied heaven, dear girl, like that above thee,
In its mere self a cold, drear, colorless void,
Seen from below, and in the large, becomes
The bright blue ether, and the seat of gods![217]

to another,—

I oft have passed your cottage, and still praised
Its beauty, and that trim orchard plot, whose blossoms
The gusts of April shower'd aslant its thatch.[218]

124

The following are two very characteristic parts,—

The Queen to her infant.

Thou did'st kiss thy father's lifeless lips,
And in thy helpless hand sweet slumberer!
Still clasp'st the signet of thy royalty.
As I removed the seal, the heavy arm
Dropt from the couch aslant, and the stiff finger
Seemed pointing at my feet. Provident Heaven!
So, I was standing on the secret door.[219]

Bethlem exclaims,—

O that I were diffused among the waters
That pierce into the secret depths of earth,
And find their way in darkness! Would that I
Could spread myself upon the homeless winds![220]

There occur two songs—neither of them very good.

However "when all is done," this *Christmas Tale* will not do from Mr. Coleridge. It is the old story of legitimacy worked up for the use of Schools. We care not though how many of the same kind he gives us, providing always they contain as much of his old sublimity as this does. The passage about innocence already quoted, would, we have no doubt, call an old manuscript play into print without much else to recommend it. It is his cant, and not his poetry, that we object to,—and we are sorry to see the former increases as fast as the latter dies away.

We have no doubt, however, that there are some who fondle his elfin luxuries; and for that reason he is a poet. His genius takes to the elements in a ghostly way, and engenders a shadowy result. The first faint thoughts of other men, are more distinct than his, when achieved in writing. His mode of coming at things is not to be understood: we cannot trace his fancy a voyaging; or if we could, we should never guess of what colour "the vaporous drop profound" would be, when condensed by his imagination. Can we thus follow other men's "spiriting?" —Yes. We know the temper of Shakespeare's soul when he sighed—

Ye Nymphs called Naiads of the wandering brooks,
With your sedge crowns and ever harmless looks.[221]

We can analize Wordsworth's mood when he says to the small celandine.

> —the thrifty cottager,
> Who stirs little out of doors,
> Joys to see thee near her home.[222]

This sort of poetry comes into our hearts by the same path, that the authors went seeking for it. It is quite another thing with Mr. Coleridge; we know how beautiful his sketches are, without having any real human sensibility in us convinced. It is a pleasant thing to discover any favorite haunt of a writer: one of Mr. Coleridge's may be seen, by these two pictures—the one from *Christabel*, the last from *Zapolya*. The ceiling of Christabel's chamber was

> —all made out of the carver's brain;
> The lamp by two fold silver chains,
> Hung dangling by an angel's feet.[223]

In the *Christmas Tale* we find—

> Ascend yon flight of stairs!
> Midway the corridor a silver lamp
> Hangs o'er the entrance of Sarolta's chamber,
> And facing it, the low arch'd oratory.[224]

DRAMATIC REVIEWS FROM

THE CHAMPION

December 9, 1815
Covent Garden Theatre.[1]
The Orphan.[2]

The poetry of Otway is certainly more pathetic than that of any writer since the days of Elizabeth,—more immediately expressive of passion and tenderness, and more unaffected in its description of nature. It represents love in so amiable a light, that we look upon any shadow of intruding grief, as something more than usually gloomy. It first enchants us with delectable images, and sweet and graceful fancies, conveyed in a language which is turned into music itself; and then at once overwhelms our animated feelings with sorrows the most natural, and the most touching. Otway was familiar with the heart;—he felt finely, and suffered deeply. His portraitures of domestic happiness and calamity are therefore perfect. His female characters are drawn with a truth and delicacy the most delightful. He gave them as beings in whom gentleness and gracefulness were inherent,—as beings whose thoughts and feelings harmonized with their persons;—warm, disinterested, and trustful in their affections,—lonely and lovely in their distresses.— Spenser hath finely said that—

> —As it falleth,—in the gentlest hearts
> Imperious Love hath highest set his throne.[3]

This is as true as it is poetical, and is what the lightest observer of human nature must have perceived.—Otway has made all his female characters illustrative of it, and we feel the beauty of the picture.

After the foregoing remarks, we need hardly say, that the tragedy of the *Orphan* is a favourite with us. We have long wished for its revival,— but with fears,—lest the squeamish taste of the public should affect disgust at its verbal impurities. It has, however, been brought forward,

127

and, much to our surprise, warmly welcomed. A novel, called *English Adventures*, is said (in the history of Brandon) to have furnished the plot of this tragedy. This may be the case, but we are more inclined to think, that Otway caught it from Tailor's old comedy of *The Hog hath lost his Pearl*.[4] The main incident is the same in both.

Miss O'Neill[5] was the *Monimia*, and never have we witnessed a performance of such exquisite delicacy and pathos. She was *Monimia* to the life! If Otway could have seen her, we are certain that he would have felt all his ideas of the character at once embodied. We saw before us a beautiful and benign creature, whose heart, with all its hopes, and feelings, and fears, was resigned to one object;—we saw an affectionate and unassuming woman, giving herself wholly up to an ardent and an innocent passion,—resting her very life and fame upon it. While Miss O'Neill was on the stage, we were lost in the illusion,—for it was next to impossible to believe her any other than the *Orphan*; her very nature seemed blended with the character. She sought not, by any artful manoeuvres or misplaced energies, to make the representation attractive;—her whole aim was to represent the fond and confiding *Monimia* —and she succeeded. Her step was marked with a sweet timidity,—her figure won respect by its simple grace,—and her look was the very language of modesty.—Indeed, nothing could more strongly prove the chastity of her demeanour, than the enthusiastic applause that followed any passage that referred to her innocence. In the delineation of this character, Miss O'Neill has given the finest specimen of her talents we have yet seen.

We sincerely hope that she will confine herself to characters resembling this. She seems made up of tenderness, and we cannot believe that she could call into action that fierceness and sublimity of thought, and wild energy of heart, which are necessary for the representation of *Lady Macbeth*;—nor would she well express *Constance's* majesty of sorrow. She is not a Mrs. Siddons. Miss O'Neill is actuated by human feelings and human passions,—Mrs. Siddons gave identity to the most sublime imaginations.—Mrs. Siddons was most successful in the *active*—Miss O'Neill excels in the *passive*:—the latter is the mistress of the heart— the former was the Empress over the mind. In short, we wish to see Miss O'Neill personifying only the sorrowful, and lovely, and loving of her sex. We cannot remember any actress that could match with her, in depicting the passion of love. While it is unthwarted, she seems to revel in the innocence of her happiness. At the occurrence of any little anxieties, or unexpected enjoyments, she gives each variety of feeling most delicately and faithfully,—we may discern the tear and the smile in her eye at the same moment;—but when her hope is annihilated, there is a silent horror on her features, that makes the heart feel itself desolate.

In the scenes where *Monimia* appears with her brother, Miss O'Neill was very successful; and her explanation with *Polydore* was altogether the most pathetic piece of acting we ever witnessed.

Mr. Young sustained the character of *Chamont* most ably. He struck off the fiery temper and generous nature of the young soldier with an energy, which we scarcely believed him possessed of. He seems at home in a turbulent and noble character. *Chamont* is a second *Cassius* in temper and courage, but without the latter's keenness of intellect.

Castalio was given by Mr. C. Kemble:—it was, on the whole, pretty good. But his style of acting wants variety; he should check his features in their eternal trick of frowning, and should endeavour to feel what he is representing. At present, when he would be impressive, he is boisterous,—and when he would appear sorrowful, he is cold. At the end of the third act he took great pains to prove his lungs stronger than his judgment. Mr. Conway, in *Polydore*, was very tall, very noisy, and very affected.

December 9, 1815
Drury Lane Theatre.
The Honey-moon.[6]

We shrink, in utter hopelessness, from the task of noticing all the novelties which the theatres now produce.* The wonder is, what comes of the many pieces with the fair sounding titles, two or three of which

* *What's a man of Fashion*, a farce; *Where to find a Friend*, a comedy; *My Spouse and I*, a farce; *Bobinet the Bandit*, a comic melo-drama, have all just shewn themselves in our mortal sphere lately, and have either disappeared for ever, or are on the point of doing so, or *ought to be* on the point of doing so, "—Like a flower crusht with a blast is dead,/ And e'er full time hangs down his smiling head." (*Sir John Beaumont*). *Who's Who*, a farce, seems to have a rather stronger principle of vitality.

are produced every week, and received, as those faithless rogues, the managers, declare, with "enthusiastic approbation by an overflowing audience." A new comedy on Monday, a new farce on Tuesday,—yet, by Saturday, it would seem that both are too old to bear further wear and tear. They succeed each other like the dishes of a French dinner,—excess of variety is to make up for a deficiency in substantial quality,—but we confess that our British tastes lead us to regret the absence of every thing that is worth a cut-and-come-again. We shall not put our fair readers in possession of our sentiments on the Turkish practice of substituting a passing acquaintance with many ladies, for a lasting intimacy with one,—but we are sure that the public reputation and taste are likely to be degraded by the dramatic libertinism, to which the managers are the panders. It seems, however, that they find it easier to bring forward many that are worthless, than one that is worthy,—and it would not be easy to refute the man's logic, who said, the other day, to the Judges, when they were about to sentence him for keeping a house of varieties, that he had made twenty thousand pounds by the trade, and did not see but what it was as reputable as many others that bore better names.

Our complaint is of course limited to the dramatic productions of living writers: we cannot draw one good play from the present time, and the curiosity of our people is therefore allayed with trash:—but, thanks to the talents of Miss O'Neill, and Mr. Kean,[7]—which cannot be so well displayed in melo-drama and sentimental comedy,—we have excellent revivals of old ones. One of these is the subject of the previous article,—and we are glad to see Drury Lane announcing Beaumont and Fletcher's play of the *Beggar's Bush* for next Thursday.

Mr. Kean has appeared as the *Duke Aranza*, in the comedy of the *Honey Moon*. It is certainly taking a great skip from *Bajazet*.[8] In the latter part, the storm of noise breaks out from defeated weakness,—in the former, dignity of spirit, and a calm firmness of manner, must deserve, gradually acquire, and fastly keep a victory. As we cannot say much from ourselves in favour of Mr. Kean's general representation of this character, we shall repeat the warm eulogium which we heard expressed in the pit,—as the people were crowding out when the play was over:

"Well, Tom, how do you like it?"

"Oh, it was *very* fine:—Kean's *dancing* is genius itself, by G——."

A man behind us was in the ecstasies of one prolonged "bravo!" all the time this exertion of strength and agility was going forward. It probably merited his acknowledgments, for we confess we never saw any thing similar to it in a drawing-room. Elliston, however, danced differently,—and, in our simple judgments, better. We are sure, that such dancing, as Mr. Kean's, would never have won *Juliana's* heart;— she, in her representative, Mrs. Davison, seemed to have quite a different notion of what constitutes the grace of this elegant accomplishment.

To say the whole truth, our admiration of Mr. Kean's powers, which we have so often and so strongly expressed, cannot blind us to the fact, that, in this part, he has failed. He is beaten in it completely by Mr. Elliston, and therefore he has failed:—yet, it is true, that many of the passages were given by him with great force and point,—but the appearance of peculiar force, and the display of marked point, are quite at variance with the spirit of the character. Both in its genuine nature, and its assumed disguise, it is one of simple intrinsic superiority, winning the affections by its unruffled propriety of demeanour, no less than subduing the refractory passions by its energetic determination of will. This is a character that is sure soon to gain an ascendency over woman for whom it may cherish love; for such a woman is at once addressed by it in her vanity, her respect, and her fear; and the result must be the sense of doating attachment and implicit submission in the female breast. Women are kept in the orbit of love and duty, by something of the power of repulsion,—(not too much)—mingling with that of attraction. This is far from charging them with any deficiency of high-mindedness,—but rather the contrary: they love only when they are made to feel a superiority of quality, as men admire heroes and geniuses; —but men will throw their hearts beneath them.

The *Duke*, in Mr. Kean's hands, did not seem well calculated to correct the faults of *Juliana*, though very much so to break her heart. There was, in Elliston's representation of the part, a shining out of fondness and admiration of her person,—and even a good-humoured enjoyment of her excesses, not abating a jot the determination to restrain them;— these were necessary to subdue the hostility of the Lady's pride and vanity,—without gaining which there could be no thorough conquest of her mind. The force of Mr. Kean's manner, also, though it has scope in high tragedy, of which we know little or nothing but what we see on the stage,—is at variance with what we regard as the stamp and assurance of the Gentleman in disposition and habit.

Mrs. Davison's *Juliana* seemed to be something faded in freshness from what we remember it; the fabric, too, looked coarser.

Mr. Perley, as *Jaquez*, the mock duke, made vulgar burlesque of that which Mr. Collins presented as a rich piece of nature. Knight, too, was upon the extravagant order in the peasant *Lopez*. It seemed to have been previously arranged between Mr. Kean and him, that the former should smack the hand of his visitor very hard, and the latter make wry faces at each blow. By what possible conception of the duke's character, can this dainty device be justified?

December 24, 1815
Drury Lane Theatre.
From My Spouse and I.

How is it that none of our living bards write for the Stage?—Coleridge, some time back, gave one fine proof that he had the ability,⁹—but his long after-silence has shewn that it has sunk into inactivity. Moore, we suppose, is busied with his forthcoming Poem,¹⁰—and it is more than probable that Southey is hard at work on a new-year's Ode. Lord Byron, however, is, we think, eminently fitted to produce a Tragedy, which "the world would not willingly let die." He is full of powerful feeling, and has a fondness for the mysterious and the terrible:—indeed, the characters and situations in his tales are all of the Dramatic cast. We earnestly call upon him, endowed as he is with every requisite for the task, to give the world a Drama that shall redeem the glory of this age.

January 14, 1816
Drury Lane Theatre.
From A New Way to Pay Old Debts.

Here is another revival from the excellent works of our early dramatists. It is a matter of no little delight to us, to find that the public have feeling and taste enough to welcome what is excellent. The managers could not perhaps have turned to a better writer than Massinger for dramatic effect;—he is very skilful in the management of his plots, and very powerful in the delineation of character. The comedy which has been selected is full of interesting and domestic incident, and has one or two characters in it, which are of a very powerful cast.*

Sir Giles Overreach is the *Richard* of common life: He has all the latter's enthusiasm, and industry, and personal courage,—with, perhaps, less of subtlety and reflection, he has more of vanity, and avarice, and naked ferocity. *Overreach* is, indeed, avowedly brutal to his closest relatives, and unguardedly talkative on the subject of his crimes; *Richard*, on the contrary, is seemingly kind to those about him, and wholly reserved in his villainies:—the first calculates only on present occurrences,—the last looks out after future mishaps and successes. We were about to say that Mr. Kean in this performance had surpassed his *Richard*,—but reflection checked the assertion:—we must not forget the deep and eloquent thoughtfulness,—the silent and piercing looks, and the matchless persuasion of tone and manner, which he contrived to throw into his performance of the tyrant King. We have however, no hesitation in saying, that the delineation of *Overreach* is second only to *Richard*. From the moment that Mr. Kean appeared on the stage, we felt that he was at home in this character,—his eye told us so. In the early scenes of this comedy, there is little room for energy; we do not become acquainted with the real baseness of the character until the second act. In the opening of that act, the conversation between *Marrall* and *Sir Giles* was admirably given.—The broad humour, coarse cunning, and fawning manners of the former, were exquisitely contrasted with the biting cruelty and excessive avarice of the latter. We saw at once villainy,— and the tool of villainy;—and could discern the mutual hatred that lurked under smiling looks and fair words. Mr. Kean was excellent in the scene in which *Sir Giles* urges his daughter to throw out lures to *Lord Lovell*:—he walked around her,—and fed his eyes upon her splendour and her beauty,—and inwardly gladdened, as if secure in his hopes:

* *Sir Giles Overreach* and *Marrall* are said to have been drawn from living characters. We think that Massinger was considerably indebted to Middleton, for some of the peculiarities of *Overreach*. There is a character in *A Trick to Catch the Old One*, to which it bears a strong resemblance. Mr. Gifford has not noticed it in his edition of Massinger.

nothing could be more dreadful than the loose and heartless manner with which he bade her to be free of her favours to the young Lord, or the fierceness with which he treated her modesty and sorrow. The moment that *Lovell* appears, *Sir Giles* casts aside his violence and meets him smilingly:—Mr. Kean's quick change of voice and manner was admirable,—he turned from frowning to fawning in an instant, and subdued the harsh loudness of his tone, to a sound of gentleness and courtesy the most winning. When the young Lord salutes *Margaret*, the savage delight with which he spoke the following words was inimitable;

> That kiss
> Came twanging off,—I like it.[11]

Mr. Kean was also good in his assumed kindness to *Wellborn*, when fortune again dawns on the latter. The scene in which *Overreach* lays bare the course of his crimes, and describes his own "character in little" to *Lord Lovell*, was finely given. We were electrified by this great actor's style of delivering the following lines, in answer to a question touching his conscience—

> *Lov.* Are you not frighted with the imprecations
> And curses of whole families, made wretched
> By your sinister practises?
> *Over.* Yes, as rocks are,
> When foamy billows split themselves against
> Their flinty ribs; or as the moon is moved,
> When wolves, with hunger pined, howl at her brightness.[12]

But in the last act, Mr. Kean rose above every thing that we have mentioned. He became all energy. His heart seemed to live on its hopes of grandeur and nobility; and as he failed in his plots against *Wellborn*, his fury maddened itself into a restless joy at the prospect of his daughter's marriage. We never heard any thing spoken more exultingly than the following.

> —They come! I hear the music,
> A lane there for my Lord![13]

His last look at *Margaret*, when he finds that she has married contrary to his wish and expectation, was full of hatred, fierceness, and hopeless-ness:—his clinging gaze left her not, till all his vital powers were withered up, and he sunk lifeless into the arms of his servants. Mr. Kean, in this performance, has certainly added some fresh leaves to the green wreath of his fame. We have no doubt but that this revived comedy will be found very attractive;—it has been the vehicle of some of the finest acting we ever witnessed. We see no reason, however, for the feeble gait which Mr. Kean assumes in this character—and he himself, at times, threw it aside. We think, also, that he delivered one part with a wrong emphasis:—he says, in answer to *Lovell*, who declares that he only waits for *Margaret's* leave to wed:—

> She *shall* seal it to my Lord, and make me happy![14]

Mr. Kean spoke it as we have marked it, but it appears to us, that the stress should be put on the word "seal." These, however, are but trifling objections, and we have nothing else to urge.

January 21, 1816
Covent Garden Theatre.
From A Midsummer Night's Dream.

This is the finest piece of poetical luxury to be found in any language. It is rich in delicate descriptions, and graceful fancies; and it is full of the happiest contrasts of broad humour with beautiful and finished mirth. Shakspeare has in this play, given up his imagination to the wildest and loveliest enchantments:—He wanders amid flowery scenes, and calls forth little frolicksome beings from every thing around him; his descriptions transport us to Elfin land, and we seem to dwell only in a world of imagination. The four fantastic spirits which *Titania* calls to attend on *Bottom*, are creatures directly of the fancy: *Cobweb* is a floating being, more light than air, whose wings can only play in the breath of the Poet; —*Mustard-seed* is a living and pleasant whimsicality,—*Moth* is an intelligent and tricksy insect,—and *Pease-blossom* rises at a thought, on its coloured pinions, before the sight,—we deem it, some flowery being that has just flown off its stalk. Then there are *Oberon* and *Titania*, the fairy King and Queen, with their pretty jealousies and lovely little revenges!—The first talks a language which would grace the lips of

Apollo himself,—and the last is a beautiful moonlight reveller, that lives among roses and lilies and cowslips, and is continually calling around her, "quaint spirits" and airy forms. Her romantic passion for *Bottom* is the most delectable exaggeration that can be imagined;—she talks of "fair large ears" and of "the sleek smooth head" so lovingly, that we begin to look upon the head of an ass as something not uncomely: but her directions to the fairies are the most exquisitely rich—

> *Titania.* Be kind and courteous to this gentleman:—
> Hop in his walks and gambol in his eyes;
> Feed him with apricocks and dewberries,
> With purple grapes, green figs, and mulberries;
> The honey-bags steal from the humble bees,
> And for night-tapers, crop their waxen thighs,
> And light them at the fiery glow-worm's eyes,
> To have my love to bed, and to arise;
> And pluck the wings from painted butterflies,
> To fan the moon-beams from his sleeping eyes;
> Nod to him elves, and do him courtesies.[15]

Who would not "confess himself an ass" all his life, to listen to such music as *Titania* breathes? It is most amusing to find that *Bottom*, after his sleep, remembers only the last-mentioned order of his enamoured Queen,—he calls to *Monsieur Cobweb*—

Kill me a red-hipp'd humble-bee on the top of a thistle; and, good Monsieur, bring me the honey-bag.[16]

He asks for what he himself knows to be luscious,—apricocks, and dewberries, and green figs are quite out of his knowledge. The character of *Bottom* is admirably finished. Shakspeare has made him pompous, busy, vain, and ignorant,—yet with a large portion of vulgar wit, and a marvellous relish for the luxuries. He is perfectly happy and unabashed in the company of the fairies, and orders the attendant spirits about him, most freely and conceitedly.—When he is restored, however, to himself, and imagines that he has been dreaming, he has not the power of putting his vision into expression. His ideas are much too rich for his language.

Bottom is looked upon as a finished wit, and an accomplished gentleman, by the "hard-handed men of Athens." He acts the first part in the play, and gives directions for the performance, and hints at Court patronage in the most knowing manner. Nothing can be more humorous than his delivery of five or six intelligible lines to *Quince*, and the rest, when the play is being cast, to convince them of his superiority.—*Bottom* was certainly a favourite with its author:—Shakspeare loved to draw a character in which pride was mingled with ignorance, and cunning with humour. But what can we say of *Puck*? He seems to be a gay, vivid, mischievous thought which the poet gave being to. He is a spirit of excessive velocity, of which property, by the bye, he continually reminds us; for instance—

> I go, I go; look, how I go;
> Swifter than arrow from the Tartar's bow.
>
> Act 3 Sc. 2.[17]

And again—

> I'll put a girdle round about the earth,
> In forty minutes.
>
> Act 2 Sc. 2.[18]

Puck is a Fairy King's messenger, and is ever ready to start on momentous business:—he loves to be at work, his mischievous nature is admirably shewn in his joy at scaring *Quince* and the whole company, and in the trick he plays off upon *Bottom*. There is a most delicious vivacity in his speech and action, rendering them wholly above those of earthly creatures. We can fancy him darting off upon his errand, and glancing back again ere the grass gets steady from which he had hurried. In short, he is a dew-drop of the fancy, which reflects the newest and loveliest lights, but which, if touched—

> Slips in a moment out of life.[19]

Into one of the speeches of *Titania*, Shakspeare has thrown the whole spirit of his imagination. The Fairy Queen, in mentioning the mother of her Indian boy, says that she would, while gossiping on the yellow sands, imitate the vessels,—

> —and sail upon the land,
> To fetch me trifles, and return again,
> As from a voyage, rich with merchandize,
> *But she, being mortal, of that boy did die.*[20]

The last line makes fine food for the fancy. What kind of creature can that boy be, which a thing that floats and revels on the light air is too mortal to survive the birth of?—But we might go on admiring thus for ever. Then we have the whimsical play, with its accommodating wall and polite lion;—and the magnificent *Theseus*, who would have been a matchless personage, if he had never spoken any thing more than his first speech in the fifth act.

The lovers, *Hermia*, and *Lysander*, and *Demetrius*, and *Helena*, would be very tiresome people, if it were not that they "discourse most eloquent music,"—and at the same time are a relief to the splendid and romantic wonders of the Faery Court. Their affections, which set and change sides so easily, provoke but little interest; Cupid's shaft must have been—

> Quench'd in the chaste beams of the wat'ry moon,[21]

ere it pierced their hearts, and thus made them as cold and as changeable as Dian herself.

But we forget that we have yet to notice Mr. Harris's[22] *Midsummer Night's Dream*:—we must step out of this ideal world.—At the recollection of the Covent-garden fairies, away fly all these sparkling fancies;—farewell to the beings that can "creep into acorn cups and hide them there"—farewell to the delicate and fanciful queen,—to the dazzling little haunters of the moonlight,—to the matchless *Oberon*,—and to the quaint spirit *Puck*:—fancy's occupation's gone!

It will be seen that we do not think the *Midsummer Night's Dream* can be acted;—it is a property of the imagination, and ought not to be trespassed on by machinists and scene painters. A Poet might see it acted on some fresh green spot on a moonlight night,—but it cannot be touched in reality. We have no doubt that Wordsworth could *get it up* better and quicker than all the labourers of the theatre put together. Since, however, this piece has been tortured into form, we must give some account of it;—but, as *Cassio* says, "it likes us not." In the first place, the Play has been cut down to three Acts, and many of the incidents are entirely altered.—Then much of the fine poetry is struck out, and the wandering lovers are turned into arrant singers:—*Hermia* and *Demetrius* seemed to have strayed out of *Narensky*,[23] or the *Devil's Bridge*, or,—any other modern Opera. Some of the scenes are picturesque, but we remember to have seen most of them before; and the procession before *Theseus* has stolen much of its splendour from the one in *Coriolanus*. Its glories are those of Carlton House²⁴ rather than those of Athens.

January 28, 1816
Drury-Lane Theatre.
From Love for Love.

This comedy is full of the most spirited wit from beginning to end, and has in it one or [two] extremely masterly characters; but there is a want of interest in the plot; and the indelicacy of the dialogue is for ever disgusting us. It has been said, and we think justly, that all the female characters in Congreve's comedies are destitute of moral principle: certain it is, that in the play before us, we do not find one woman of purity. *Mrs. Frail* and *Mrs. Foresight* explain away their characters to each other, the moment they appear,—and their after-discourse, throughout the piece, by no means raises our ideas of their virtue;— *Miss Prue* is a rude, loose-hearted country girl,—very free in her speech and manner, and with a fine natural taste for intriguing;—and even *Angelica*,—though evidently meant for a lovely woman,—is not exempt from this charge of indelicacy.—Her general gaiety often wantons into immodesty, and she is always ready with an answer to any of *Sir Sampson Legend's* indecent witticisms. The comedy of *Love for Love* is undoubtedly better fitted for the closet than the stage; we relish its wit more in the reading than in the representation, and the pruriences are less offensive when they are not aided by the shrewd look and tone of the actor. Congreve is one of the finest wits that England ever produced; his language sparkles and breaks from him like the waters of a fountain, and gives a delicious freshness to the spirits: he wrote his comedies with great rapidity,—and, indeed, the dialogues bear evident marks of the gaiety and quickness with which they were put together;—his pen seems to have been a feather plucked from the wing of Mercury's heel.

The comedy of *Love for Love* has been revived with the whole strength

139

of the house; and the warm reception it has met with, proves that genuine comedy still retains its charm with the public . . .

Munden's *Foresight* was, perhaps, the richest piece of humorous acting that he ever gave. This character is one that feeds upon the "signs and wonders of the elements," and is happy or miserable as the day's omens are good or bad. *Foresight* is joy itself, if he finds that his stocking has been put on wrong side outward, but his heart is fit to break, the moment that he discovers a pin with its point towards him:—if he gets out of bed backwards, he is happy; but then he stumbles on his way down stairs, and that is frightful:—Sun, moon, and stars are the gods of his idolatry,—and Astrology is indeed to him, a science of "the first magnitude." Munden's quiet stare of wonder,—and sudden commotion of features, were astonishingly useful; and his usual twist of the mouth, which sent each word out like a cork from the turn of its screw, had a powerful effect.

March 17, 1816
Drury-Lane Theatre.
The Duke of Milan.

The tragedy of the *Duke of Milan* is written with great vigour, and is highly interesting to the reader. As Massinger has drawn it, however, the incidents in the last act are not altogether fit for representation.— An audience would shrink with horror from the scene in which Francisco paints the lips, cheeks, and hands of the dead Marcelia.—This act is too dreadful and disgusting a tyranny over the dead, for humanity to witness. In the revival, this incident is of course changed—but the alteration is not very cleverly made.

Ludovico Sforza is, indeed, a noble character. His ardent love for his wife, *Marcelia*, which feeds upon all his thoughts, and looks even beyond present existence:—his resolute notions of honour and courage:—his wildness at *Marcelia's* altered manner on his return from Pavia:—his abject cravings for her forgiveness:—his sudden murder of her on suspicion of her dishonour:—and his mad caresses of the lifeless form in the delusions of his ruined mind—are all most ably drawn. It will be seen that many of these traits of character are apparently similar to some of *Othello's*.—On examination, however, a difference will be found: the affection of *Sforza* is ardent and confiding,—it can only be turned by the coldness of the object which it rests upon—it then becomes a quick, executing hate. The love of *Othello* is the love of an eastern heart— doating impatient, and terrific;—open to the hints of others,—taking, and calculating upon, the merest shadows as substances,—and laying a long train of revenge, which he has resolution enough to fire with his own hand. *Othello's* love is the love of a lustful savage—*Sforza's* of a passionate and fine-feeling man.—*Sforza* laments over the defiled mind of *Marcelia*, and deems her lost, because he supposes her guilty in intent, —*Othello* madly weeps over the knowledge of *Desdemona's* actual impurity—*Othello's* is chiefly the love of the body,—*Sforza's* is chiefly the love of the mind.

Mr. Kean was the representative of *Sforza*. We were in fear lest he should express the agitations and suspicions of this character, in the manner which he is accustomed to adopt in *Othello*;—we strongly suspected that he would not draw the nice line of difference—that, in short, he would be too violent in his affection and sorrow, and their suspicions.—But we found that our fears were groundless: Mr. Kean played the character admirably. He was all affection in the first scene with *Marcelia*—and his sinkings into despondency on the arrival of the couriers that bring him bad news, were beautifully relieved by the sparklings and flashes of fondness that broke over his features and eyes when he turned towards *Marcelia*:—we saw a fine struggle between sadness and love. In the midst of his dejection—he exclaims,

—Silence that harsh music.[25]

The pleasing air which they were playing while he spoke this, gave,— in the contrast with the despairing tone of his voice,—a fine effect to the passage. He played the scene with *Francisco*, where he commissions him to destroy his wife, should he fail in his suit to the emperor, with very great power. In ennumerating her excellences, his manner of delivering the following lines was full of feeling—

> Add too, her goodness,
> Her tenderness of me, her care to please me,

> Her unsuspected chastity, ne'er equall'd;
> Her innocence, her honour:—Oh! I am lost,
> In the ocean of her virtues and her graces,
> When I think of them.[26]

His interview with *Charles* was the least effective;—this, however, might be owing to the emperor, who was most assuredly the dullest piece of stage royalty we ever witnessed,—and we cannot speak more unfavourably than by saying so. Mr. Kean occasionally delighted us till the last act, and then, as usual, he was all excellence. His affectionate watching over the body of his murdered wife, who, he thinks, is but sleeping,—was earnestness itself.—And his sorrowful address to the doctor—

> —How sound she sleeps!
> Heaven keep her from a lethargy!—How long
> (But answer me with comfort I beseech you)
> Does your judgment tell you that her sleep will last.[27]

The melancholy and almost hopeless tone of his voice was well assisted by the eagerness of his eyes and the earnestness of his features. After a long speech, in which he becomes furious in his exclamations against *Francisco,*—his manner of falling from the height of turbulence to a sad calmness, lest he should disturb *Marcelia,* was wonderfully fine: he electrified the house with these three words—

> —I am hush'd![28]

The audience seemed to look for something new at his death—but he disdained to give any exertions then, which the part would not justify. He died serenely.

Mr. Kean, in this character, has added to his own. We think it a very perfect performance.

Mr. Rae played *Francisco* most indifferently. An intelligent friend remarked to us the other day, that he thought we had of late, spoken too well of this gentleman:—we certainly owe Mr. Rae a grudge for so speedily justifying our friend's observation. Mrs. Bartley was very bad in *Marcelia*: we never before saw affectation so finished, nor heard whining carried to such a pitch.

The dresses were good in general: and one new scene was introduced.

March 24, 1816
Covent Garden Theatre.
From The School for Scandal.

There is little doubt but that we owe it to the love of novelty in the public, that Miss O'Neill has been instigated to perform the part of *Lady Teazle*. The last time we saw her, she acted *Calista*,—and truly the house was very poorly attended;—the old characters had been played till all the town had seen them, and the *Fair Penitent*[29] was a tedious, heartless creature which no one cared for. The managers therefore resolved to put her forth in comedy, and the excellent play of the *School for Scandal* was fixed upon. With all our admiration of this play, we cannot but see faults in the character in which Miss O'Neill has appeared. *Lady Teazle* is too fashionable, witty, and lady-like a creature, for a young girl who was educated by an old fox hunter, and whose sole engagements were to thrum the sportsman to sleep after a chace, or to "comb Aunt Deborah's lap-dog."—The change from the hoydenish girl of the squire's house, to the thorough intriguing woman of fashion is too quick to be natural: though we admit [the] sex possesses an admirable facility of transformation. There are, however, in the part, most exquisite scenes with the lady and her husband, *Sir Peter*;—his pettishness and uxoriousness are excellently contrasted with her general good-humour, and archness, and affectation of fashionable simplicity—(which is nothing but art after all.)—Notwithstanding the rumours which were circulated, as to the success of Miss O'Neill, in the part of *Lady Teazle*, in Dublin; we went to the theatre with anxiety,—for we feared that she would lose sight of nature in a character of gaiety; her tears, and shrieks, and sobs, we knew to be good,—we knew nothing of her smiles and laughter. She, however, performed very cleverly, and never stepped, we think, beyond the bounds of nature: probably she was a good way short of it. Her action was that of a lady accustomed to high life and a carriage; it was free and graceful;—and her voice was always musical, though now and then monotonous. Her manner of coaxing *Sir Peter* was very elegantly humourous. Yet some characters in more *sentimental comedy* (if we may use the term) might be found better suited to this lady's talents;—for, after all, we like her better in serious parts. She is always commanding in her delineation of a lovely and helpless woman sunk, in unmerited sorrow,—and in such sorrow, patient, and tender, and trustful. It is necessary to remark to her, that she owes all her popularity to her truth and her unaffectedness;—the best style of her acting is what all persons, whether well educated or not, can judge correctly of; it is a style so closely imitative of nature, that, while beholding it, we can easily forget that there is any thing of imitation in it. The lowest artizan can tell whether the afflictions of an unfortunate woman are faithfully pourtrayed or not;—every tailor and tailor's journeyman can sympathise with the anxieties and distresses of *Mrs. Beverley*,[30]—because each, it is most probable, knows what female attachment is;—and genuine female attachment will be found almost equally pure, in all classes, though not so refined. The lofty and terrific imaginations,—the artful thoughtfulness, and high anxiety for glory, in *Lady Macbeth*, are qualities which none but the great-minded can comprehend or delight in. One or two of the plays of Shakspeare have, we think, but one or two true readers in the world,—or rather but one or two persons fit to read them.

Miss O'Neill seemed to have a just idea of *Lady Teazle*. But her powers seemed exercised out of their most proper element. Yet she played gaily, and imitated carelessness;—she chattered her little scraps of scandal with an infinite deal of vivacity; she appeared to pay greater attention to her fan than her husband,—put on a very pretty air of vanity,—and looked eager to glide into vice itself for the sake of fashion. We have little doubt but that Sheridan copied the characters in this comedy from life:—the same love of petty malice,—the same anxiety to murder characters and libel beauty or innocence—the same selfish and varied roguery,—may be found in all circles. A *Lady Sneerwell*, or a *Joseph Surface*, or a *Mrs. Candour* might be picked out at any dowager's rout in town. In truth, the whole comedy is delightfully spirited, and bears a sufficient resemblance to life to be natural and keen, without being disgustingly severe—It has nearly all the rapid wit of Congreve and Farquhar without any of their indelicacy:—We agree with the remarks of an ingenious modern writer, that "the perpetual flow of wit in the *School for Scandal*, may familiarize it so much with some auditors, that they cannot be made sensible of its perfect enjoyment." It is our hope, that Miss O'Neill will avoid anything approaching to imitation;—we have fancied that her voice now and then seeks to resemble that of Mrs. Siddons. Miss O'Neill should be more careful to avoid this fault, because she is indebted for much of her popularity to her general freedom from it. The moment she becomes a mannerist, her fame and her excellence are gone.

May 12, 1816
Drury-Lane Theatre.
From *The New Tragedy of Bertram; or, The Castle of St. Aldobrand.*[31]

The author of this tragedy has certainly read the works of Lord Byron, with earnestness and effect: he has mused over the Poet's fierce and gloomy thinking, till he has sunk into the same moodiness himself.— The hero of the work, which we are to review, is the *Corsair*, in his most turbulent moments;—*Bertram* breaks on the sight with the same black hair and black bosom, and with his heart clothed in a terrific obscurity. He is the same bitter despiser of human nature—the same scoffer at religion and its ministers—the captain of pirates:—in short, *Conrad*, with another name, and with even a darker nature.

This tragedy is the best production we have witnessed for some years. The plot of it is powerfully interesting;—the characters are ably dashed out;—and the language is generally good, and, in many parts, exceedingly beautiful. The piece opens with the wreck of *Bertram's* vessel: he is cast on the shore, and is received by the monks of the convent of St. Anselm. His gloomy and savage brow—his utter dreariness of heart, which spreads itself even over his love of life—his sullen silence, broken only by stormy gusts of passion—his scathed figure—his arms—his wild black locks—his fierce glaring eye—all combine to raise their wonder and their pity. It turns out that *Imogene*, the lady of his love, thinking him lost, had wedded the Lord of St. Aldobrand, his greatest enemy. *Bertram* is conducted to the castle, where he meets, and makes himself known to *Imogene*. He ultimately destroys her husband;—she goes mad, and dies of a broken heart,—and he kills himself with a sword, wrested from the hand of a soldier, who had advanced to secure him. These are the main incidents of the piece:—we do not think it worth the while to give a minute account of the refined confidante of *Imogene*—or the

145

good Lord of St. Aldobrand—or of the singing pirates—or the active monks, with their energetic and pious leader. The three first acts are uncommonly interesting: the two last are, comparatively, flat. The truth is, that the mysteries are unfolded too quickly,—and that the excess of passion and poetry, in the early scenes, leaves the mind incapable of enjoying any thing that is quietly good at the end. The beauty of the language in many parts drew from the audience shouts of approbation and delight;—we were much struck with one or two of the images. For instance,—*Bertram*, when he is about to destroy the Lord of St. Aldobrand, compares *Imogene* to a flower which decks his rugged path, and which he, in his tiger leap, must crush. When Imogene faints on his cold bosom, he likens her to

A withered lily on its icy bed.[32]

This is also very taking,—but we think it questionable. All the characters talk poetically, which is a fault; *Bertram* may be permitted to utter bright fancies—and the lady *Imogene* may be gently graceful in her discourse:—nay, even a snatch of the ornamental may be allowed to the harmless Lord of St. Aldobrand—but confidantes have no right to splendid language: it is set down that if their mistresses are mad in white satin, they must be content with white muslin:—nor do we approve of romantic priors—men who walk about with bald heads, bare feet, and flowery words,—mingling fiction with piety, and prettinesses with austerity. The prior of St. Anselm is a terrible hand at fine speaking; and outdoes Dr. Slop himself in his liberality of malediction. Some alterations might be easily made, we think, in the language of the secondary characters, and in some of the characters themselves. The tragedy is worth every attention. The style is, on the whole, rather of the artful than the natural kind:—and the images of the author are too apt to be imitative of each other. The serpent ever affords him a simile for any thing wicked or wily;—and a flower is the certain expression of innocence or delicacy.

Of the performers, we can with great justice and pleasure speak in high terms. Mr. Kean was *Bertram*. We recommend our readers to see him as soon as possible—to see his performance of this bold bad man while yet it is fresh and powerful in his mind. We think better of him than ever. His rude fierce sorrow is beautifully relieved by the fine tenderness of his lingering affection:—his love rests on his heart, though all other feelings madden or blacken around it. It is a drop of dew on a withered flower—the sound of a lute in a rugged cave,—a swan upon a dark and troubled water. It is beautiful to observe how one virtue will gild a thousand crimes. There was something exquisitely touching in his voice when he said—

> Imogene's tear may rest upon my cheek,
> But may not dew my grave.[33]

These, we believe, were the words—but we quote from memory. At the end of the second act he very beautifully illustrated the following lines of Lord Byron:—

> Where late I saw thy favourite child,
> I thought my jealous heart would break;—
> But when the unconscious infant smiled,—
> I kiss'd it, for its mother's sake:—
> I kiss'd it, and repress'd my sighs
> It's father in its face to see;—
> But then it had its mother's eyes;—
> And they were all to love and me.[34]

Mr. Kean embodied these lines in the most pathetic acting. He electrified the audience with his genius throughout the piece;—twice he gave touches, which were finer than even he had led expectation to look for.—The first was in the first act. He is speaking of his deadly enemy, and his speaking changes to noisy raving;—he savagely imagines his enemy fixed in his grasp—never was any thing finer than his wild way of expressing the dying gaspings of his opponent. There was destruction in his eye, and death in his clutchings. The second was a quieter though not less beautiful piece of acting:—after the murder, and while in chains, he fell into a long, abstracting, thoughtfulness;—he paused with fixed eye for some minutes;—the Prior moved gently and slowly towards him,—and put his hand kindly and softly on his shoulder.—That light touch seemed to convulse his very heart. He started—gazed fearfully and wildly—and then sank into a sorrowful inactivity. The audience seemed shot;—the start was answered throughout the house . . .

We have nothing to say of the Prologue or Epilogue—except, that in the latter a fling was made at the Covent-garden rope dancer. We intend taking an early opportunity of saying a few words on the degradations of the modern stage. Madame Sacchi is an expensive piece of buffoonery —a terrifying indelicacy—an insult to the English people. We see by the bills that a new tragedy is in preparation at Covent Garden Theatre. What?—insult the Boards, over which Madame Sacchi has revelled, with any thing classic?

August 25, 1816
The New English Opera House.
The Beggar's Opera.

That Opera of all Operas, the *Beggar's Opera,* was played to a very full house on Thursday evening last. We should never be absent from the representation of this matchless piece, if we could wholly follow our own inclinations: and we know of no dramatic work, upon which so many new things may be said. It is quite a luxury to a critic. There is every quality in it, which an Opera ought to possess;—it is full of character, incident, humour, music, and poetry. The character is admirably purloined from that class, which is supposed to be tolerably destitute of it;— the incidents are of the most various kinds, such as brandy-drinking— love-making—filching—quarrelling, &c. and are all worked up with infinite skill;—the humour is every where,—and broad and bold enough for every understanding;—nothing can surpass the simplicity of the music, which is a selection from the best national airs. The poetry is delightfully expressive:—it has a fine mixture of feeling and impudence, —of passion and vulgarity;—it would seem to have been composed by one of *the Fancy,*[35] who had left off robbing, and taken to reading. It must have come from the St. Giles's side of Parnassus, and, during the composition of it, the real juniper juice must have been the waters of inspiration. Throughout the Opera, there is a peculiar blending of the purest pathos with the most hardened villainy,—of the most enchanting tenderness and the wildest gaiety, with all that is low and *knowing* in cunning and guilt. Timid beauty and impudent roguery go together like friends. It is Miss O'Neill arm in arm with *Dutch Sam.* How inimitably well drawn are the various characters in this Opera! *Macheath,* that strange compound of the gentleman, the Debauchee and the Highway-man;—*Peachum* and *Lockit*, the two creatures with human forms, harpy hands, and iron hearts;—*Mrs. Peachum*,—the loose, old, brazen *Mrs. Peachum*,—that friend to strong waters and nimble pickpockets. The two separate gangs of Highwaymen and harlots;—*Filch*, the prince of slang fellows,—the heir-apparent to the rope,—the perfect specimen of a meditative, cunning, successful, confident blackguard:—all these char-acters are made by the skill of the Poet, to live, move, drink, and swindle to the very life. But what shall we say of *Polly*,—"the pretty, pretty Poll;"—the sweet and simple creature that walks amidst ruffians, cheats, and women of the town, circled with the light of her own innocence;—she looks like a dove surrounded by hawks and ravens. How charmingly she talks!—How delicately and expressively she sings! How beautifully and faithfully she loves! Her conversation goes to the heart, and her voice comes from it. She is a perfect picture. She seems the bright young figure of a Corregio, surrounded with the dreariness and blackness of a Rembrandt. She is the Una of common life amidst the Satyrs:—a flower growing lonely and lovely in a wilderness,—with only weeds and ser-pents around it. She is too fair and good every way, for her company; and yet we would not willingly see her out of it;—for she becomes doubly interesting by the contrast. But it is high time that we should turn to the representation of this Opera; we could go on chattering for ever on its beauties.

Mr. Incledon played *Macheath*;—but he did not play it well. He was too serious,—yet his looks convinced us that he had not ever been too sober. He is a great deal too corpulent and sedate for *Macheath*, who even in prison, ought to be "as careless and genteel as ever." A performer in this part should always betray a want of principle in his acting,—but never shew a want of gaiety. *Macheath* is a man who would be hung with silk stockings on his feet, and a belcher handkerchief over his face:—he would die game and genteel. Incledon will of course play this part in America, where its merits and peculiarities will be so thoroughly understood. That lively girl, Fanny Kelly, acted *Lucy* with infinite spirit, and put on the vixen to the life. We never saw a more insolent, pettish, charming little wench in the world; she seemed to have passed all her days in Newgate, in the society of convicts and turnkeys,—and never to have passed outside the doors, except when a man was to be hung or pilloried. Her way of singing "Why how now—Madam Flirt?"—was glorious:—Billingsgate could not go beyond it. And her manner of offering a glass of prepared *strong waters* to *Miss Polly* in the prison, was a fine specimen of St. Giles's politeness. We did not think that any thing could have taken from the sweetness and interestingness of *Polly*;—but we were mistaken:—Miss L. Kelly completely ruined the character. She did more in one night towards spoiling *Polly* than all the villains and vagabonds and wretches of London could do in an age. She worships affectation with an idolatrous enthusiasm,—and she sings worse than a Peacock. We have seen the late Miss Bolton (now Lady Thurlow) and Miss Stephens in the part;—they both looked, loved, and sang like angels. They gave the airs with the true pathos and simplicity: we never shall forget their exquisitely pathetic way of putting *Polly's* pretty and gentle appeal to *Macheath*, when she is abused by *Lucy*:—

> How can you see me made
> The sport of such a gypsey?[36]

No one but *Macheath*, who never was touched by any thing less than a Bow-street officer, could have resisted this delicate and feeling reproach. Miss L. Kelly surely thought she was playing the old Duenna[37] instead of *Polly*. She is no singer,—and she ought to be no player. We wish the part of *Polly* had been left out for this night, as Hamlet once was at an Irish Theatre. Any thing is better than murder. The actor who played *Filch* (a Mr. Herring, we believe) had nothing of *Filch* about him but the strings of his small-clothes.

September 8, 1816
The Exeter Theatre.[38]

Critics must occasionally breathe the fresh air like other men,—for they are liable to the same feelings, ailings, and pleasures with others. They are fallible in their health,—though it is next to impossible that they should be so in their judgements. From the late hours which it is their *duty* to keep, they are perhaps more open than others to weariness and discomfort; and what can be a finer remedy for these, than fresh air and beautiful scenes.—The truth is, we have been taking a jaunt into the country;—so our readers may expect that we shall be more spirited and free in our remarks to come, than we have been hitherto. We shall be quickened: we shall avoid what Hamlet fell into by having "foregone all custom of exercise." Our future observations will be true and powerful,—not rash and splenetic. It should be remembered that one of our predecessors passed a month in the country very much to the edification of his readers;—the Spectator never produced any thing half so pleasant, witty, or natural, as his papers from the country-house of our old friend Sir Roger De Coverley. They tasted of the fields and farm-yards. There was a rural homeliness,—a liveliness,—a humanity breathing through them, which the cold city would have chilled. They were as fresh as grass; and were put together as tidily as trusses of new hay. Some of our best poets dwell in the country. Wordsworth writes amid majestic mountains and lovely lakes; and his poetry catches the inspiration of the place. Moore lives in a romantic spot,—and the flowers of his song are culled fresh from his own bowers. Scott resides in a wild and beautiful part of Scotland,—and who will say that the wildness and beauty of the scenery have not rushed into his verses. The country is, in truth, the nursery of good writing:—why then should not critics get vigour and spirits in a rural retirement?—What we are about to disclose now, will, we rather think, remind our readers of the worthy old tallow-chandler in the Idler, who could not rest quiet in his country retreat, but must come to town on a *melting-day*, and assist his successor in his business.— We could not remain comfortable in our chairs the other evening, when we learnt that the Exeter Theatre would be open;—for we were within the reach of it. Nothing could keep our troubled spirits from walking. We hungered after our old occupation. It need hardly be said we went to the house;—and we shall now pretty well prove that we had not resolution enough to abstain from making a few remarks upon the performance. This Theatre has indeed more than ordinary claims on our notice;—for it gave us Mr. Kean. It is small, comfortable, and pretty; —it might perhaps be made a little more ornamental. Mr. Kean had been performing in it but very lately,—so that after the storm that had lived within its walls, there was now a tolerable calm;—that is, to drop all metaphor, so immediately after the late full houses, there were not above thirty people present.—"A beggarly account of empty boxes."

The performers—but let us have Shakspeare's description of a strolling company.—"The best actors in the world, either for tragedy, comedy, history, pastoral, pastoral-comical, historical-pastoral, tragical-historical, tragical-comical, historical-pastoral, scene individable, or poem un-limited: Seneca cannot be too heavy, nor Plautus too light. For the law of writ and the liberty, these are the only men." Here indeed we have them set down "in little." Your country actors will do any thing or say any thing. They will act you a hero,—aye and in "King Cambyses' vein;" —they will dance a hornpipe, and sing a comic song between acts;— they will bustle about in a farce; and yet you shall never lose sight of the man who first set out before you. The men very often look as if they had fallen from the profession of waiters and ostlers,—and the women seem, for the most part, to have descended from the posts of bar-maids and barrow-women:—but they will dash at any thing, when they are well tinselled and frilled. The life of a thorough-bred country actor, is, we think, harder than that of a post-horse or a watchman. He is *hacked* on all roads,—and up and wearied on all nights. His days hang heavy on him; his nights wear him out; and yet how merry the rogue is! He thinks less, if possible, than he eats; and he sleeps less than he thinks;— but he undoubtedly drinks more than all. Care dodges his footsteps— but he laughs in the very face of care. He acts to empty benches, with as much careless vivacity, as he would to a house tumbling about his ears with auditors. He is a living jest. But we would not have our readers believe that the Exeter Company are altogether of this cast.—No: there is a Mr. Palmer Fisher, who played *Sheva* in *The Jew* with great truth and effect. He has a good deal of feeling, and no bad turn for quiet humour. A Mr. Clifford in *Jubal* was also very amusing. He reminded us repeatedly of poor Lovegrove,—and yet he did not imitate him. He is certainly a very easy, merry, rough, honest fellow;—at least he seems to be so. We should have no objection to see both these gentlemen on a London theatre. They would bear transplanting well.—But after these,—"all is dark." The remainder of the company act miserably;—"and the stony-hearted villains know it well enough." They are stiff, dull and awkward, —"If I be not ashamed of them, I am a souced [sic] gurnet." A Mr. Forrester in the *Lover*, is a deadly enemy to grace and gentility;—he tears the passion to tatters. He turns good grammar into bad,—and in a voice which jars on the ear like the loose string of a viol. Then there is a

Mr. Richards very remarkable for the fulness of his body, and the emptiness of his mind. He talks very drowsily,—

> His whole function suiting
> With forms to his conceit.[39]

The gentleman who pretended to perform the part of *young Radcliffe* had most violent starts of passion. He was not a little terrifying at times. The Ladies (God wot) were very much in earnest. Mrs. Clifford stretched out her arms, and declaimed,—as we have seen some actresses do before her. But her voice is a most original one; it has a twang peculiar to itself. Miss Rennels and Mrs. Comesford are both very plaintive, and very odd.—So much for country actors.

> Sad happy race! soon rais'd and soon depress'd,
> Your days all pass'd in jeopardy and jest;
> Poor without prudence, with afflictions vain,
> Not warn'd by misery, not enrich'd by gain;
> Whom Justice pitying, chides from place to place,
> A wandering, careless, wretched, merry race.[40]

October 13, 1816
Drury-Lane Theatre.
The First Part of Henry IV.—Mr. Stephen Kemble in Falstaff.

We wished the other evening, at the theatre, for the presence of three friends,[41] to whom we had been lately reading the first part of *Henry the 4th*,—and to whom we had been also asserting that Shakspeare's plays suffered in the representation. They would, we feel assured, have been convinced of the truth of our assertion,—for the performance of this admirable play made wondrous havoc with the wit, and spirit, and poetry, which are so excellent and evident on a perusal. We do not much like to see Shakspeare tortured on the stage:—what has he done to deserve it?

Henry the 4th is a feast for the Reader, which nothing can come up to;—it is a banquet, to which his wit,—his independence, his enthusiasm,—his memory, his fancy,—may sit down, like a set of friends, and make a

153

glorious repast at. The Fancy absolutely turns Alderman, when such a sumptuous turtle as *Falstaff* is served up to it. He comes on garnished with jokes. We cut at him,—and come again. *Hotspur* is a cayenned dish for the spirit. *Hal, Poins, Bardolph,*—that ignis fatuus *Bardolph,*—the carriers,—are all delicacies in their way. We say that these pleasantries are peculiarly grateful to the reader,—but they become comparatively unpalatable on the stage. The truth is,—nothing on the stage is left to the imagination:—every thing is forced into a reality. The wit is uttered, —the poetry is declaimed,—the characters are "bodied forth,"—and we have nought left to dream over. How is it possible that *Hal* and *Poins* (we read over these short merry names, as we do the syllables that describe a laugh) can be dressed up, and shaped forth, as they ought to be. They are spirits of the night. They live on their own mad-cap tricks,—and can even join in a robbery on the King's highway to our great delight and perfect satisfaction. We have apartments fitted up in our imagination for them, and they should have no other home. They are the will-o'-th'-whisps of the fancy,—and go shining, and dazzling, and gliding about, and go out, if touched. Then there is *Falstaff.*—"The substantials, Sir Giles, the substantials." Oh! thou inimitable creature—how dost thou lard the spirits!—how inestimable is thy lying! how delicious is thy cowardice!* Thy figure is a pun on the human form,—thy mirth is of a downright *suetty* quality, thy very vices are the foundation stones of a jest,—thou art a knight,—and yet a pleasant fellow!—We cannot sit to see *Falstaff* stuffed out for the stage. Flesh and blood cannot bear it. We scarcely know what parts of this matchless play will be hurt the least in the acting;—perhaps some of *Hotspur's* fiery speeches,—because they luckily open the way to a little ranting:—and an actor is never so happy as when he can "tear a passion" with some propriety.

We could go on in our praisings of the characters, language, and incidents of this play, "for ever and a day," if our paper would allow of it, and our readers would bear with us:—but we begin to find that we

---

* A curious essay fell into our hands the other day, in which the Author attempted to prove that Falstaff was no coward![42] It might as well be said that he was no fat man,—that he was Romeo's Apothecary in figure,—and that all the allusions to his corpulence were to be taken by their opposites,—so that the humour of the piece depended on the contrast. And he were not as arrant a coward as ever breathed,—we are "no true men." As Peachum says, "he could neither stand himself, nor make others stand." Oh! your Falstaff is huge enough to make "Ossa like a wart,"—and certainly "the most fearful wild fowl living."

must turn to a consideration of the comedy as acted, or the limits of the first will be passed, and the patience of the last worn out. The actors, for the most part, seemed to be in a conspiracy against the spirit of Shakspeare:—they all attacked it at once, as Cassius and his comrades struck Caesar in the Senate House. Mr. S. Kemble gave the Brutus-blow. Rae in *Hotspur* was, throughout, in the most deliberate rage we ever witnessed. He had read *Hamlet* to some purpose, for in the very tempest and whirlwind of his passion, he begot a calmness which was truly enviable. We missed all the snatches of fury and turbulent courage, which Shakspeare has dashed into the part. Mr. Rae should not distort such characters. *King Henry* in the hands of Bengough was made a tolerable part. Mr. Penley acted the *Prince of Wales* very badly;—we never saw but One[43] who did the part worse. *Bardolph* and *Poins* were not so despicable. We purposely mention Mr. Stephen Kemble last, because we wish to speak at some length on his performance, and because we would not have any thing remain to draw our attention from him. Our readers, we believe, are pretty generally aware that Mr. S. Kemble plays the part in his own proper person, and without the aid of stuffed garments. He certainly looks *Falstaff* well. His round, well-fed face is of a piece with his enormous shoulders:—with those who generally act *Falstaff*, the head is too diminutive for the rest of the form. It looks like a pea on a pumpkin. It is too thin, and resembles Pitt's head on Fox's shoulders:—or one might suppose that the head and body had become rivals in a love affair, —and that the head had suffered a disappointment. Mr. S. Kemble, however, is only *Falstaff* in figure. He has no turn for humour,—no cunning—no briskness in his abuse. The wit of Shakspeare freezes on his lips. In the very boxing match (as it may be termed) of repartee between *Hal* and *Falstaff*, Mr. S. Kemble is beat hollow. He is never *up* in time. He repeatedly reminds us of Mrs. Siddons,—and we think, he would play *Queen Catharine* admirably. Though his voice is in itself powerful and deep, he continually drawls, in all the styles of all the Kembles. The great fault of Mr. S. Kemble is the earnestness with which he acts the part;—*Falstaff* ought to be always on the look out for a pun or a lie:— he is never what he seems. Mr. S. Kemble's manner resembled that of the young Prince repenting before his father;—and it must be allowed that it is as improper that *Falstaff* should imitate a Prince, as that a Prince should resemble *Falstaff*. Indeed the whole play was miserably acted, with the exception of that episodical joke of *Hal* with *Francis*,—which we always take to be one of the finest touches in the play,—and the copper looks of *Bardolph* which quite warmed us. In the last article we wrote, we wished for one or two of the Exeter Performers at London;—we can now balance the account,—for we wish one or two of the London Performers at Exeter, with all our hearts. One thing we were glad to see, and that was, that the Committee of Drury-Lane had, citizens-like, re-elected Mr. Carr as the representative of their chief Magistrate:—he sustained it with all his accustomed dignity.—We certainly think Mr. S. Kemble's performance of *Falstaff* a failure altogether.

But (to conclude as we set out) *Falstaff* cannot be acted, except in the imagination. John Kemble once thought of the part, but he forgot himself when he did so. He is no more fit for *Falstaff* than Miss O'Neill is for *Coriolanus*. His humour, (for he has humour) is too sedentary,—too indolent,—too scholastic:—it has a touch of melancholy in it, and would be as heavy and unwieldy as the body of *Falstaff* itself. It is a *Hamlet*-kind of humour:—a compound of satire, merriment, and sadness. John Kemble could never throw aside his stateliness and his air of philosophy for a whole evening:—he would give life to some strange amphibious creature;—something that was half a Brutus, and half a Daniel Lambert. His discourse would be a lay-sermon on corpulence and cunning—and his voice, a melancholy reproach to the wit he was preaching.—We never met but with one subject on which we felt so great an inclination to speculate. John Kemble in *Falstaff*!

> —They can no more atone,
> Than violentest contrariety.[44]

How sanctified would he look! How stupendously would he move!—Who would care for seeing Stonehenge after him?—Of all the magnificent objects, he would be the most magnificent. And yet we should assent to what he says, in one part, to *Bardolph*:—"Note it!—Am I not vilely fallen away of late?"—Why "Bottom's translation" was nothing to it. We should not see "*Old, Old Sir John*,"—the fat, dissolute, merry, lying crafty *Sir John*,—the huge hill of flesh,—the wag of Eastcheap,—the soul in lard,—the reservoir of sack!—but in his stead, the creature, *Falstaff* himself promised to be,—one who had left off sack,—and lived cleanly as a gentleman ought. It would be *Falstaff* turned methodist. We do not think Mr. Kean could play the part,—though we have no objection to his trying it. The Laureate might do it, as far as the sack was concerned,—and his "devotion to the true Prince,"—but then he is a poet,—and poets are not robust.—These however are mere speculations. *Falstaff* appears to us to be out of the reach of human powers;— or at any rate, no one has yet been born with sufficient fat and intellect to give him to the life.

October 13, 1816
Covent Garden Theatre.
From The Broken Sword.[45]

As long as the public in general will be content to gratify their eyes to the exclusion of all their other senses and faculties, so long must the few who have no relish for mere "ocular demonstrations" rest satisfied with half the entertainment the theatre used formerly to afford them. We are among the number of those who most lament the substitution of sound and shew for common sense; to us it is doubly irksome, being not only a deprivation of pleasure, but as we are frequently compelled by duty, to keep our unwilling seats, and force our reluctant attentions to that incongruous heap of absurdities 'ycleped a "Melodramatic Spectacle."

We do not greatly blame the managers for the production of such things—their taste naturally lies in their pockets,—but we sorely rue the taste of the town that suffers them.

For our own parts, liberal and tolerant as we are in our sentiments on ordinary occasions, we must confess ourselves bigots of the right Spanish breed in matters of this kind.—Were we exalted to the Papal Chair of criticism (and critics possess the same attribute of infallibility with his holiness) we should certainly pronounce against these heresies in taste, the same sentence that our holy brother used in religious differences of opinion, only reversing the *order* of the punishment—we would have them *damned here* and trust to their being *burnt hereafter.*—

Since however we live in so tolerant an age, that it would be in vain for us to preach up persecution against the whole sect of these dissenters from the Shakspearian Orthodoxy, it would be unjust to attack one for the offences of the whole. The only consideration therefore as to the piece before us must be, how far it is better or worse than others of the same breed, for there are degrees of differences even in these things.— The *Broken Sword* must be tried by its Peers. In the first place, in the article of shew and scenery, the principal requisites of a melodrame, it is particularly deficient:—no fortress stormed,—no castle fired,—no bridge blown up,—no march of Heroes, or procession of Vestals,—bating one meagre troop of dancing nymphs;—none of the "pomp, pride, and circumstance of glorious war;" no "drums, trumpets, blunderbusses, guns, and thunder." Our nostrils are not once refreshed with the smell of powder through the whole piece.—There is but one bit of common murder, and an attempt at another, or as Walton's Angler would call it,—"a bite, and a nibble."—No "helm nor hauberk's twisted mail." No sultans,—no caliphs,—no Turks,—no Tartars. Nothing in the shape of—"Knights, Paynim,—or the peers of Charlemain." The whole dramatis personae consist of two colonels,—two young women,—a dumb child and a half-pay officer,—a galley slave and a duke . . .

The style of language is an indifferent English, and the sentiment and pathos genuine French. There is an anniversary of mourning and a festival of mirth celebrating by the same folks at the same time:—as if Shrove Tuesday and Ash Wednesday had agreed to make but one day of it.— You catch the distant notes of high mass, which is being solemnized behind the scenes, and are at the same moment regaled with a waltzing party in front. This is John Buncle dramatized.[46]

October 20, 1816
Covent Garden Theatre.
From Othello.—Mr. Macready.

Othello is decidedly one of "the children of the sun, with whom revenge is virtue."[47] His heart is rapid and excessive in its feelings, and passes with the swiftness of lightning from the most perfect serenity of reason, to the wildest and most ferocious madness of passion. His gentleness is only

> The torrent's smoothness ere it dash below.

Othello is a soldier, with all the spirit of war in his soul, and with all the splendours of war in his person. His wreathed turban—his dark face glowing under it,—his light, rich, graceful habit, studded with beads,—his good sabre curving on his thigh—his dark bare arms—his fiery and lofty speech,—all render him a being who carries our eyes along with him, when he moves before us,—and who clings to our memories when he is absent. How beautiful does the gentleness of *Desdemona* appear in the midst of *Othello's* turbulent passions:—it is a goddess surrounded by the Eumenides. We pass our eyes from the fierce grandeur of the Moor, and feel a relief by resting them on the calm and angelic purity of *Desdemona*;—we lower our gaze from the sunflower, and repose it on the lily which grows beside it. Nothing can be finer than the difference which exists in the qualities of *Othello's* and *Desdemona's* loves. *Othello's* love is ardent, heroic, and restless:—*Desdemona's* is devoted, timid, and reposing. *Othello's* passion has something of warlike pomp in it: it reminds us of sieges, battles, and victories:—*Desdemona's* affection seems to float on the wings of peace,—and to know no restlessness. *Othello* loves like an Eastern Monarch:—he reigns over our heart. *Desdemona* is a sweet and unaffected woman in her tenderness: she lives silent and happy in the glory of *Othello*, and is a perfect stranger to suspicion. Her heart slumbers in its own constancy, and never dreams of a revolt in the trustfulness of her lord. In this contrast we see the admirable skill of Shakspeare. He has written such a picture as Titian would have painted; that is, he has combined the light and the lovely, with the gloomy and the grand. He has made the dark glow, and the light shine. The loves of *Othello* and *Desdemona* are well illustrated by that rich line in Milton—

> Dusk faces, with white silken turbans wreath'd.[48]

At least they seem to us to be so. It is always a very unpleasant task to turn from the characters of Shakspeare, as we find them in his books and our own imaginations, to the representatives of the characters as we see them on the stage; and it is for this reason, that we so continually dwell on the originals, and hasten over the copies . . .

But to return to *Iago*,—the part ought to be played with a mixed air of familiarity, shrewdness and dissatisfaction. *Iago* is deeply versed in the tricks and manners of the world; yet he is not a scholar;—his knowledge arises from experience, and not from study. He has a penetrating eye, and looks quite through the deeds of men.—Thwarted ambition appears to us to be the groundwork of all his vices. He had a heart fit for a French Emperor,—but it could not succeed at first.

October 27, 1816
Drury-Lane Theatre.
From Hamlet—Mr. Kean.

Mr. Kean's performance of *Hamlet* is a very noble work. We all know that this character is one of intense thought; that it is for ever meditating on the crimes, frailties, and sorrows of this world: and therefore it is, that so few actors arrive at excellence in the part. The great beauty of Mr. Kean's acting is its mental energy. He plays directly and intensely from his mind, and does not put his whole reliance, as many actors do, on his dress or his person. In *Hamlet*—"'Tis not alone his inky cloak,"— but we see the gentle sadness which is sitting on his heart—the deep agitation which springs partly from suspicion, and partly from super- natural appearances—the philosophy, which dallies with the dearest purposes of his soul—the tardiness in acting, arising from his meditative disposition—the false madness, which hides itself in raving—the affec- tion—the nobility—the enthusiasm of *Hamlet*. We look upon it, that *Hamlet* has more of the poet in him, than any character in the whole range of the drama. He has a taste for the grand, the beautiful, and the reflective. Witness his scenes with the *Ghost*,—his rich exclamation, beginning—"What a piece of work is man;"—his report and treatment of the players,—his melancholy feelings at the grave of *Ophelia*. *Hamlet* is a perfect character, let the critics rail at him as they will. What in him appears indifference, is in truth, internal perturbation which seeks to hide itself under an apparent ease;—what seems unfeelingness, is the deepest feeling in him. His situations at Court, with none but courtier's eyes on him, compel him to "put an antic disposition on." *Hamlet*, if he had turned his mind to writing, might have produced something like Dante's *Divine Comedy*:—the character of *Hamlet* is in the same key with this wild and terrific satire. We scarcely ever felt any thing more seriously and reflectively, than the mournful thoughts which *Hamlet* utters over the skull of Yorick. There is more feeling in the simple ejaculation of "Alas! Poor Yorick!" which goes into the heart like the music of past days, than whole volumes of such sentiment as Mackenzie could write. *Hamlet* is the man of feeling[49] in soul, and not in words. Mr. Kean was very effective with the skull, and at one part he gave a complete Hamlet-touch of his own:—he held up the skull, and turned it round before the eyes of those in the boxes, and then with a malicious satisfaction, he exclaimed, "Go, get you to my lady's chamber: tell her, let her paint an inch thick, to this complexion must she come at last." The dreadful satire of this seemed not to touch a single person; though it ought to have gone like a shot into the hearts of hundreds. Would it not have a great moral effect, if the skull of one of the great comedians, who used to set the house "in a roar," were procured and used on this occasion, the audience and the actors being perfectly informed of it? Then would the player see to what he must come, let him rave and strut as he would; —then would the spectators truly feel what the finest creatures of mirth must moulder to. This would be reading the world "a great moral lesson," with a vengeance.

But we must say something more of Mr. Kean. The scenes in which we admired him most, were, the meeting with *Ophelia*, and the interview with his mother. In the first, he betrayed a heart-broken sorrow under the shade of his forced madness, which was most powerfully affecting:—in the last, his voice and manner assumed an enthusiastic earnestness which bore away all before it. In the first act, Mr. Kean was rather tame; but we have no objection to a little coldness at the commencement, when we find that an actor can catch the spirit as he proceeds. He may begin with as small a spark as he chooses, so that he kindles in his course, and flames ere he dies away.—A fire, caught thus from the witchery of the scene, is a pretty good security for the genuineness of the actor's feelings, and the greatness of his intellect. Mr. Kean is indeed worthy to act Shakspeare:—And this is paying him the highest compliment we can imagine. His feelings seem always to be as powerful as his thoughts;—and his actions and looks are the perfect and eager interpreters of his mind. He throws an air of reality over his acting, by his strong and rapid manner. His mind appears to be a muscular part of him. Mr. Kean managed the fencing match with great grace and skill; —and his death was as usual very effective.—He seemed to struggle with the poison as he would wrestle in his "custom of exercise;"—but his groans became weaker and weaker, till death "quite o'ercrowed the spirits." Many of the new readings, which Mr. Kean introduces, are certainly wrong,—but they are for the most part, extremely ingenious. We do not, however, altogether approve of a player making Shaks- peare a mark for his ingenuity to shoot at.—Reasonable alterations are all very well,—but experimental readings are as dangerous to the actor, as they are insulting to the poet. We often feel vexed with Mr. Kean, when he hazards some new pronunciation, which deserves to be success- ful only for its novelty. It is difficult to excuse even a great genius, when he takes such liberties;—a man of ordinary capacity cannot be pardoned . . .

Miss Kelly played *Ophelia*;—and we have learned something by this performance, which we were ignorant of before,—that Miss Kelly can play a character badly. "Oh I warrant you,—how she mammock'd it!" When *Hamlet* raved at her about the nunnery, we fully expected that she would take him a box on the ear,—or abuse him again in like manner. Miss Kelly must surely have been acting Lucy Lockit[50] at some private theatre the same evening, and had not been able to get the termagant out of her mind;—for *Ophelia* was at times as like *Lucy*, as star is to star. The acting was too bold,—and the singing was too bad.

November 3, 1816
Drury-Lane Theatre.
Timon of Athens.

Timon of Athens,—though it abounds with passages of beautiful poetry, and admits of much splendour in costume and richness of scenery,— will not be popular. The tragedy in itself is of too noble a quality to square with the taste and understanding of a modern audience. And the learned Committee of Managers have taken all the pains in their power, to render it inattractive, by surrounding Mr. Kean (who is the representative of *Timon*) with all the inferior actors of the company. If we see Mr. Kean for five minutes, we are sure to suffer for it, by having to undergo the tortures of Mr. Bernard, Mr. Penley, and Mr. Holland for a quarter of an hour. The play is indeed got up with all the *weakness* of the house,—and cannot fail to prove unamusing and unprofitable; a thing much to be coveted, we believe, in the present prosperous time. Most of our readers are familiar with the character of *Timon*, though they may not be aware of their knowledge;—*Childe Harold* is but a modern image of *Timon*,—with less of liberality and humanity in his days of nobility,—and with more of vice and infidelity in his fall. *Timon* hath a bold and lavishing spirit,—when he is carousing in his halls, or hunting in his forests;—he would give the world away, if it were his to give, and a breath could give it. *Timon* as carelessly wastes away his own wealth, as a minister wastes the wealth of others. When finds himself—

> Deserted at his utmost need,
> By those his former bounty fed;—[51]

his heart hardens against mankind. His spirit lives on its own pride,—when he finds that the friends who propped it, have fallen away. Then do the woods, the caves, and the deserts become *Timon's* home,—and wolves form his society. Man is the beast of prey that he shuns. We see *Timon* in the early part of the play sitting at the banquet, with robes of purple and gold flowing from his shoulders,—while his halls are spangled with lamps,—and the goblets glow on the board,—and music floats on its melodious wings through the air,—and guests sit around in gallant habits,—and fair young girls come playing around in bright white groups, like the bloom from trees,—or like a company of butterflies revelling through flowers,—or like showers of dew, when the air plays with the rose-tree,—or April drops sparkling through a sunbeam. We see *Timon* in the latter part of the tragedy, stripped of all his splendour, and clothed in a wolf-skin;—he roams about,—beneath the "moss'd trees, that have outlived the eagles." The stars, that visit the heavens in the night, are his lamps,—the brook ministers to his thirst,—the winds are his choristers,—the leaves are his dancers. *Timon*—who lived in all the pomp of Athens,—is become a naked wanderer, and his own attendant. *Timon* is a man of extremes. He is profuse in his generosity, and extravagant in his misanthropy. In his prosperity, he is never happy, unless he is surrounded by crowds of friends;—in his retirement, the appearance of one man sets him raving. His life is fretted away. It has been well observed "that in the speeches of *Timon*, after he is undeceived, all the hostile figures of language are exhausted,—it is a dictionary of eloquent imprecations." It must be confessed that such a character, placed in such scenes, cannot but afford an actor many opportunities of shining out, and "taking all eyes captive." Mr. Kean is very great in his own peculiar talent, in the part,—but he is not altogether what *Timon* is. We ought to have the recollection of *Timon's* splendour and greatness, preserved even in his fall, by the dignity of his person, which no altered fortune ought to overcome. Mr. Kean seems quite another person, when he lays aside his robes, and takes to his skins. At first he appears to us, as a gallant young nobleman, who has a fine taste for every thing that is elegant and spirited;—but, after his change of garments, we see only a savage little gentleman in buff, who abuses gold and man, with a most industrious severity,—and who is totally without dignity, which is the saving grace of the character. *Timon* is a satirist in the woods, and even in his most severe and abusive moments, something of his former nobility ought to exist. One of the best things in Mr. Kean, was his way of delivering the following lines,—which are exquisitely beautiful:— indeed we do not know but that we praise the delivery of them, as much for the feeling and strength of the passage, as for the skill of the actor. We do verily believe, that one great reason of our liking Mr. Kean as we do, is, that we have seen him so often in Shakspeare's plays, that he has become associated with Shakspeare in our recollections. But to the passage.—

> —But myself,
> Who had the world as my confectionary;
> The mouths, the tongues, the eyes, and hearts of men
> At duty, more than I could frame employment;
> That numberless upon me stuck, as leaves
> Do on the oak, have with one winter's brush
> Fell from their boughs, and left me open, bare,
> For every storm that blows.[52]

Here, Mr. Kean's voice swelled with disgust and fury till the last half line,—and then it seemed spent with its own exertions,—and it caught a hollow, deserted, sorrowful tone with it, which was greatly affecting. It had all the dreariness of winter in it. We were most pleased with Mr. Kean in the scenes previous to his flight from Athens:—and we were much struck with the effect of his rushing on the stage, and looking back upon Athens, which is in the distance, with all the hatred of his heart, gathered into his countenance. It is here that he throws off his "vile lendings,"—and begins "to sophisticate." The scene is beautiful,—and appears to us to be taken from a view, which our readers will find in Hobhouse's travels. The Acropolis rises grandly in the distance, under a soft golden sky, which ever seems to bend over Greece, as though it loved it. The foreground is dark and rich, and unencumbered,—which makes Athens smile the brighter upon us. The scene is truly picturesque and classical. The worst of it is, we are not allowed to gaze at the scene for a sufficient time;—it ought to be shewn us again after the play. *Timon* is a fine romantic character;—and we love him, if only for his feeling in the following passage:—

> Then Timon, presently prepare thy grave,—
> Lie where the light foam of the sea may beat
> Thy grave stone daily.[53]

Mr. Kean did not seem to speak these lines, as if he felt them: a fault, which we cannot easily forgive. He made amends however in the following passage, which is the last speech of *Timon*, and which is poetry of the right Shakspearian quality. It is the last romantic exclamation of a fine and disappointed heart!—

> Come not to me again: but say to Athens,
> Timon hath made his everlasting mansion
> Upon the beached verge of the salt flood;
> Which once a day, with his embossed froth,
> The turbulent surge shall cover.[54]

Such extracts as these make the thorny path of criticism, a flowery one;—Duty puts on a smiling aspect, as she leads us up it,—

> —Fragrance in our footing treads.—[55]

165

Mr. Kean ought to be praised for ushering us thus into the paradise of Shakspeare, where flowers wreath themselves amongst the fruits,—and blend the ornamental with the useful. If we have not spoken so well of Mr. Kean, as might be expected, from our known opinion of his genius;—it is not because we think he has mistaken the part, but because we think that nature has not enriched him with power to embody his conceptions:—here, we speak of his general execution of the character, and not of his manner in particular passages. Mr. Kean, in one part, descended to imitation,—which is a crime in genius. He threw his spear, —on his return from hunting,—into the hands of an attendant, who was prepared to receive it,—in the way that Kemble in *Coriolanus* tosses his shield to a soldier that is expecting it. The trick is ridiculous at best;— it is worse than ridiculous when it is given at second-hand.

Upon glancing our eyes over a bill of the play, which lies before us, we perceive another reason why the tragedy of *Timon* can not be a popular one. It has not a single female to bless itself with. There are trumpets, and trees, and thieves, and poets, and spears, and soldiers to be had by dozens,—but not a woman is to be met with for any consideration. To our tastes, this is a very serious objection to the play. We love to see a female glide in before the lamps,—with her hair richly clustering around her forehead, and her dress starred with spangles: she gives a grace to tragedy:— and helps to break our hearts with a becoming elegance. *Timon* and *Alcibiades* and *Apemantus*, are all "very pretty fellows in their way,"—but we should think better of them if they had been lovers after an honest fashion. To be sure, the females which Shakspeare has introduced in *Timon* are better away,—nor could we expect that the Committee would provide others of fairer character to fill their places:—the play is a downright *male-play*, and nothing can be done to amend it. If such pieces only are to be revived, let our managers "bring forth men children only."—But we will not endure this banishment of women,—and this selfish and unjust encouragement of men:— one glance at the light figure and lovely face of Mrs. Horn,—is worth "a wilderness of Penleys." Beauty and grace are too estimable to be given up without a word. They are the divinities of human nature; and earth would lose half its radiance without them. The characters in *Timon of Athens* are just such as we should find in the world, were women excluded from the haunts of men;—they are vain, vulgar, and cynical:—men would jar with each other, if women did not breathe harmony amidst them. And here it is, that we see Shakspeare's power of depicting human nature in all its qualities. The stage looks as unseemly without its "chief ornament," as the boxes would appear, if on some evening during a general mourning, none but men were to fill them. We have heard the Grecian armour in this revival, very much extolled; —but we confess ourselves to have been so dull as not to have particularly admired it:—however we do not doubt that it was "complete steel." The *Cynic Apemantus* was growled out in a most set and sour fashion by Mr. Bengough, of whose talents, if this be a specimen, we augur but badly. Mr. Bengough always reminds us of the honest country gentle-man,—which is not very desirable, when we wish to see a Grecian Misanthrope. His voice sounds like the twanging of a damp bow-string; —and his actions resemble those of a fish out of water. Wallack looked *Alcibiades* very prettily,—and indeed acted the part "with good emphasis, and excellent discretion." We really like Wallack in general,— though he would not be looked upon as a less wise person, if he were to shake his head more sparingly. Mr. Harley's voice was very entertaining: —It caused many a laugh, by its singular, rich, smallness. Prior foretold it admirably in his poetry,—

> Fine by degrees, and beautifully less.

Wordsworth perhaps alluded to it when he spoke of "the wandering voice." The tone of the young man in The Arabian Nights' Entertain-ments, who is heard reading, all solitary, amidst a marble people at midnight,—had not half the effect. Mr. Harley's voice is something between merriment and suffocation. It is ever happy and active. Lord Byron did not exactly hit it when he wrote

> The voiceless thought, that will not speak but weep.[56]

He should have written

> The thoughtless voice that will not weep but speak.

Had Mr. Harley been an Ancient Roman, how anxiously would *Coriolanus* have petitioned him,—"your voice, Sir?"—Mr. Harley is indeed the *vox populi*,—and he cannot fail to be a favourite. Mr. Holland, as the *Old Steward*, hummed like a weary bee, well might Timon say to him "sermon me no further." The character is naturally a heavy one,—and Mr. Holland certainly gave additional weight to it. Mr. Penley and Mr. Barnard "kept on in even current." Their course lay through the waters of dullness,—and they floated over them most comfortably. The dancing girls in helmets, cut very pretty figures;—they looked as if they had just skipped out of a Fairy Tale. One of them reminded us of Brito-marte.

The scenery is pleasing,—though little of it is new. Timon's cave is beautifully picturesque; the boughs hanging loosely over its mouth, were very natural; and it was delightful to see Timon breaking forth from between the clustering leaves. It reminded us of the richness of summer. The cave looked like a cave, which on the stage is seldom the case; it more often resembles an arch of Westminster Bridge, or the Highgate Tunnel.

November 3, 1816
Covent Garden Theatre.
Coriolanus.—Miss O'Neill, and Mr. Kemble.

The play bills very shrewdly assure us, that Miss O'Neill, in her performance of Volumnia, has surpassed the expectations of her warmest admirers:—now, if her admirers are to be considered as persons of taste and judgment, we must reasonably conclude that their expectations were very moderate as to her success in the delineation of the Roman Matron. The puff in the bills is a very ingenious one,—but it is a puff. Miss O'Neill is too young and too lightly graceful, for *Volumnia*:—she looks the daughter of *Coriolanus*, instead of the mother. She is fortified with dress,—but it will not give her a matronly appearance;—her loveliness and her elegance will shine out in spite of her endeavours to be dignified, serious, and powerful. Her dress is a curious specimen of gothic architecture. We do sincerely hope that Miss O'Neill will not trifle with her talents thus. She should play the youthful and the feeling, and the beautiful,—and not the sedate, the commanding, and the aged: —her forte lies in the tender and the graceful,—and not in the majestic and the severe. Miss O'Neill is better calculated to personate a beautiful

Italian lady than a stern Roman Matron. We saw nothing in her whole performance, that was worth particularizing. Mr. Kemble played with finer spirit, and greater bodily energy, than we ever before remember. He is *Coriolanus* to the life. All his soul seems to rush into the character, and to animate the actor with powers which he would not otherwise be possessed of. If the present season is to be the last of his acting, we feel assured that he will retire worthy of himself. His corporeal strength still seems constant to him,—and his intellectual power is in no way diminished. We could sit for ever, to see him personate *Coriolanus*,— for he carries us to Rome itself. He stands before our eyes, like the figure of Brutus re-animated. His scarlet robe hangs over him, as if it gloried in the form which it decked. We do not see Kemble,—but *Coriolanus*. He is worthy to have trophies carried before his steps,—and choral songs chaunted in his presence,—and captives led in chains behind him,— and crowds of citizens shouting round his majestic person. He wears the oaken garland,—and he becomes it. He passes under a triumphal arch,— and his figure adorns it. Let but Mr. Kemble retire from the stage in this character, and he will leave a name in the memories of the public, which glory will love, and which time cannot wear away.

We intend devoting a long article to Mr. Kemble in the course of a few weeks.

February 2, 1817
Covent Garden Theatre.
The Ravens; or, The Force of Conscience.

A very few years ago,—that is,—in the facetious day of Mr. Dibdin[57] and Mr. Reynolds,[58]—our stage was honoured monthly with some finished folly on the follies of the day. Nonsense was poured in at the ears of the audience as they sat in a dozing state,—much in the same liberal manner that the deadly liquid was infused into old Hamlet's,— and the senses of the former were poisoned as completely as those of the latter. Repetition was then the soul of wit. One play would stand its ground solely through the means of a character, who was eternally requesting others to "*keep moving.*" Another piece entirely depended on "*what Mrs. Grundy would say.*" A third (the phrase was an excellent joke in the theatre at that time, though it is none at this) amused the people with a perpetual demand of "what's to pay:"—while a fourth relied confidently and successfully on a tall thin gentleman in black (we should imagine it to be the author, if it were not for the phrase) who sleepily and continually reminded all parties "that he had an idea." Comedies, with solitary witticisms of the above mentioned nature, were sure of success. Crowds followed them. The standing jest was chalked on the walls,—and bellowed in the streets,—and echoed in the galleries, and tortured into songs;—and the actors were hailed with shouts,—and the authors were mistaken for wits. And Mr. Reynolds may flatter himself, if he can and chooses to sophisticate with the notion that his fame grows with his growth and strengthens with his,—weakness; for he is at this day laughed at, in more ways than one. Dibdin, we take it has punned his humour into a consumption. He never wrote a good thing in his life, —except one or two jokes from Joe Miller,—in which he clearly proved that his memory was more quick and serviceable than his invention. We hear nothing of him now. Where is he?—Our remarks on these *Phraseologists* would not perhaps very greatly gratify them,—if we were abruptly to close here,—but, as something may turn out to their advantage by a comparison of them and their works, with the writers and writings of our own day, we shall not withhold from them the negative praise which such a comparison yields. By the side of Mr. Pocock,[59] Mr. Dibdin is a Godhead:—and Mr. Reynolds is surely a Congreve when opposed to Mr. Lamb,[60]—honourable as the latter is.—But we still find "in the lowest deep, a lower deep,"—that is,—we see worse writers than Mr. Pocock and Mr. Lamb (it would seem impossible):—men with intellects in their bodies "no bigger than pins-heads," we allude to the senseless translators of French melo-dramas. The stage is now oppressed with the imbecility of French sentiment to a lamentable degree. Wit is never aimed at, humour is:—but never hit. All the iteration of a Cherry,[61] a Dibdin, or a Morton,[62]—were downright sense to the sickly sentimentality of the melo dramatists of France. Even the imitated iteration of a Pocock was sufferable;—"We could have borne that too:" —but we sit down heart-sick at the playhouse now-a-days to a dramatic robbery, where the thieves are taken with *bird-lime*;[63]—or to a feeling murder, which allows of a needless mystery and a moral saying. Thanks to our intercourse with France,—all our present afterpieces are of the true *Parisian cut*. The dramas of the French are full of exquisite opposites. Peasant girls preach morality and scorn to practise it. Tradesmen weep behind their counters, with pens behind their ears,—and keep account of their feelings by double entry. They are always sinning in act, and reforming in word,—and never turn over a new leaf,—except of the ledger. Spoons are stolen and merchants are murdered,—but then the birds of the air take cognizance of it.—If a man were drowned,—interesting information would be had, from "the fishes in the sea." Birds and beasts "and such like deer" were not sent us for nothing. The nonsense of French melodrames appears to be stealing on us rapidly;—according to all appearances, we may expect a pretty hard winter. We confess ourselves heartily weary of plays purloined from the police offices;—and why indeed do our managers go abroad for such things:—have we not very genteel robberies of our own?—Is there not a marvellous pretty choice of rogueries in England?—"Stands Bow-street where it did?"—Lavender or Vickery would dramatize a little incident of Bill Soames or Nimming Ned.[64]—in a way that would startle all the magpies and ravens in the world. We suppose that the managers imagine England does not grow enough of villainy for home-consumption,—and therefore import from the grand mart, Paris. If such dull pieces of inquiry into petty thefts and unaccountable murders are to be persevered in,—the managers will find that their rogues will have private examinations. For mercy's sake, let us go back, good masters, to the times, when characters had an idea, though but one,—and when the absence of burlesqued feeling did not blush to make us hear "what Mrs. Grundy would say." We go about, amongst these hard-hearted and empty-headed set of writers, much in the same perplexed way that Old Lear went backwards and forwards betwixt "those Pelican daughters" that gradually curtailed him of his rights. At first we would fly from that Goneril,—Cherry,—but then that Regan, Pocock, treats us worse, and we return to the Goneril, Cherry: "not to be worst, stands in some rank of praise." Kenney[65] did promise to be a Kent to us,—but he is disguised and we find him not near us: "let us not go mad,—sweet heavens, let us not go mad." We declare to the managers that, rather than bear with the dull stuff of the French stage,—(dull, as handed to us)—we would readily endure play-struck children, and perpetual pantomimes,

—and the horses,—and the elephant,—and Mr. Macready in *Othello*;[66]—in fact, any absurdity and monstrosity, silently and gratefully. But it is high time we should say something of the new piece of,—*The Ravens, or The Force of Conscience*,—which we were compelled to see the other night. It is well for the managers that we have a sense of duty,—otherwise this same drama would not be noticed. Wordsworth is wrong when he says of duty—

> Flowers laugh before thee on their beds,
> And fragrance in thy footing treads.[67]

We had not the luck of sitting near an old woman the other evening, or we should have asked what the sight of two ravens flying over the stage might portend. We think there is some sign, and not a very fortunate one, tacked to such a thing. "A foolish figure,—but farewell it."

The Ravens is a long dull imitation of *The Maid and the Magpie*;—the first act of it is chiefly passed in a counting-house, and the second in a wood. The whole plot depends on a murder, which the birds bring to light, and on a bankruptcy:—the latter incident is by no means new at the present day,—nor is the former, as far as dramas go. There is a very correct representation of a manufacturer paying his men their wages, on a Saturday evening;—we do not recollect ever having met with this incident in a dramatized state before. It is not over-poweringly interesting on the stage. The most ridiculous part of the business, is the tender feeling of the *Merchant* himself, Mr. Fawcett, who chequers the moments as they pass with merchandise and melancholy. He weeps, as he dabbles in the day-book,—and gives a loose to his feelings, over the ledger. In the same breath he calculates the profit and loss of a love-match and a building contract. Nothing can be more ludicrous than his extravagance of sorrow:—he calls for candles, in a voice that would touch the tenderness of the most particular sentimentalist. Mr. Fawcett was extremely puzzled in the way of his profession,—but luckily for him, it was a part of his business to undergo murder at the beginning of the second act. Mr. Terry acted the character of a ruined merchant with all the air of insulted excellence:—he ought not to be pent in the unhealthy dungeon of a French melodrame. The two murderers were represented by Farley and Emery; the first is a rugged ruffian, with black hair and every other characteristic of a villain,—the last is fair-haired, and a coward, who seems to be in possession of his brother's share of conscience, as well as his own. After the murder is committed, on rushes Emery, with a justifiable confusion, mistaking himself for *Macbeth*, and exclaiming, "Thou canst not say I did it." The crime has sublimed into a state of eloquent remorse. He talks of the thunder and lightning, and the ravens with a most laudable loftiness. Mr. Blanchard played a love-sick *Ostler* rather humorously,—but the character hardly justified his acting. Miss S. Booth represented a tender young lady after a French fashion,—and not much to our taste. We hate French girls,—or English girls with French manners and dresses:—particularly the latter.[68] They are always giving themselves airs,—and shewing their ancles and their teeth. They wear a profusion of flowers in their hair and hearts,—and nothing else. Their talent is for dancing,—in religion and morality, as well as in a ball-room. They love themselves best, and then like those best, who flatter them most. Truth is rudeness with them,—and lying and silliness gallantry. They libel the human dress in all possible ways,—either by "cutting their petticoats all round about," or by building up their hair like a rook's nest,[69] or a round house. Their words are without thought, —their habits without modesty,—their affection is an affectation. We wish our English girls would return to their own fair ways, and not suffer their hearts and heads to remain British prisoners in France. We rejoice that it is in our power in this article to instance one or two with whom dress is a modest ornament,—and dancing the most comely grace. The three Miss Dennetts*—though introduced in a French piece,—are attired in the most sweet and simple style, and never in the least violate grace and decorum. Their dance in the present melo-drame is with castanets, and the very perfection, as usual, of all that is elegant and harmonious. The Miss Dennetts always remind you that they are dancing to music, and the air might almost be guessed by their movements, though it

---

* *The Courier*, we understand, has paid us the compliment of objecting to the remarks of ourselves and some brother critics on the three Miss Dennetts. We take this first opportunity of noticing it, because such objections from such a quarter are striking proofs of the justice of our opinions. We are glad that our writings do not come within the comprehension of the *Courier*, because we may be then sure that they may be understood by every one else. The *Courier* observes, that "Prose ought not to be poetry, and poetry ought to be sense." Now it really surprises us to hear of sense and poetry spoken of together, in a paper in which Mr. Croker writes. It only proves that to preach and to practise are two different things. We would recommend the Editor to suggest in a future paper that "Poetry ought not to be Prose," and then we shall see how far Mr. Croker may be benefited by good advice. We still think highly of the Miss Dennetts, and we shall be rash enough to say so, in spite of the anger of so intellectual a thing as the *Courier*.[70]

were not heard. They are truly fanciful, and wreathe their dance like three wood-nymphs, sporting on the margin of some romantic wood:—we might look for Sylvanus in the back ground, sleeping amongst the leaves.—They would be sweet figures for an Italian landscape, and would look at home in a picture of Claude's:—there should they be, revelling near marble columns, with the grass under their light feet, and the water mocking them at a little distance,—and trees with golden foliage springing around them,—and fair hills afar off—and a blue and cloudless sky above them.—We really like them better and better.

By the way, we had forgotten Mrs. Davenport and the rest of the machinery. There is, however, something very magnificent and powerful in all.

February 9, 1817
Drury-Lane Theatre.
From Mrs. Alsop.

This same town is amazingly fond of whims,—in plays, politics, and poetry,—and is ever giving and taking away, at a moment's notice, "that bubble reputation." Extravagance of manner, and a seeming beauty of phraseology are, in modern patriots and poets, the high roads to popularity. Perfection depends on appearances. Our consistent Laureate,[71] who has indeed "seen old Proteus rising"—lifted his poetry higher in the hearts of men by his uneven measures and sanctified phrases, than by the most patient of his thoughts. The town lauded him because they could not understand him:—They will now leave him, because they can. The Prince rewarded him with pensions, and what is called honour, —for his ability in veering:—"Sir! He can turn and turn." The Laureate's fame is a whim. Is the Laureate a player, a politician, or a poet? In politics, this extravagance does greater wonders,—it obtains a wilder popularity. Counsellor Phillips,[72]—for instance,—who made one good speech, and who has hashed it up as an oratorical dish ever since,—cajoled the town in a very pretty manner. His eloquence is a whim,—and so is his fame. We have mentioned these three players,— Mrs. Mardyn, the Laureate, and Counsellor Phillips,—to show that however loudly the public greet the tinsel imitation of intellect,—the admiration can only last till "The gilding frets away." It is certainly a very difficult thing, to discover at first sight, the true genius from the counterfeit.—We cannot clip it, as we would a shilling, and expose the valueless brass;—we must wait till we perceive it will not bear "hard use" . . .

[Mrs. Alsop's] walk is most uneasy;—if she were doing penance with peas in her shoes, she could not be more awkward:—this is not the only thing in which she hobbles.—Her laugh is of the most limping nature; and she will laugh for five minutes with a cold earnestness. She cuts you off half a yard of laugh with the same indifferent ease that a haberdasher's girl serves you with a like quantity of threepenny ribbon. Her voice drawls over her words,—like a wounded snake over weeds:—this monotony could not be perceived at first,—but time teaches it to us with a vengeance. We now find her words, night after night, "drag their slow length along" very much to the annoyance of our ears and patience. These defects are of the same kind with those which we noticed in Mrs. Mardyn:—and Mrs. Alsop has not the same face and figure to plead in her favour. In the *Country Girl*[73] (we cannot for the wit, pardon the ribaldry of this comedy) Mrs. Alsop played *Peggy*. The part is a very dull one to us. The *unnatural* nature of the shrewd simpleton is quite ridiculous and disgusting. There is one admirable scene in this comedy,— and that is where Sparkish, Harcourt, and Belville, talk of the theatre. The wit is of the right taste, and is a true specimen of what was had at the time, when there were "men of parts about town." We like to see one or two smart fellows in cocked hats and silk stockings, *playing at repartee* on the stage: such a sight always brings before our minds, we scarcely know why, Congreve and Wycherly, and the wits of their day. There is nothing equal to being reminded of the past, particularly of persons and things, that we come at a knowledge of, through our minds only.

March 2, 1817
Covent Garden Theatre.
The Stranger.[74] *Miss O'Neill.*

We were present during the past week, at Miss O'Neill's return to the theatre after her long illness and absence. She chose to reappear as

Mrs. Haller. We are truly sorry to see that this interesting actress, lavishes her abilities so often on the mawkish sentimentality of German plays:—her taste is in the high road to ruin. All recommendation from us will doubtless be of no avail with Miss O'Neill,—for the audience applaud her in the wanderings of her talent, and the theatre is enriched by the abuse of her powers. We do not therefore notice this performance for the sake of admonishing a rash actress,—but merely for the purpose of giving a few of our opinions of German plays. The characters in the *Stranger* are "most foul, strange and unnatural,"—from Mrs. Haller, a countess *translated*, as Peter Quince says, into a housekeeper,—"dressing the dinner instead of herself,"—a creature that goes moping about with tears in her eyes, and her hands in her pockets,—preaching virtue and giving the lie with her actions to her own sermon;—down to the affected, sentimental fool of a servant, that mocks the misanthropy of the stranger, his master.

As to the play itself, it is in truth one of the worst of a species of drama, the best of which is far from excellent. It is *essentially* German—that is, not merely German in its original language, but of a certain style, which, whether exported from abroad, or imitated at home, is directly in opposition to truth and nature. Our own country can furnish several specimens of German artists. Our Lewises, Dimonds, and Skeffingtons,[75] what are they but so many Spital-fields playwrights, who think it the perfection of their art to imitate the clumsy, grotesque, and unnatural figures of foreign manufactures!—Bertram, and the Robbers are among the better specimens of German plays—The Stranger, Lovers' Vows,[76] and the late production of Adelaide[77] among the worst. There are certain characteristics of their class of drama common to all, they are all nearly of the same stuff, and nearly of the same pattern, the plan of them is simple. Let there be some heart-breaking scene of domestic misery presented to our view—be it a fond husband deserted by a faithless wife, a generous son disinherited by his father, or a sick mother turned out of doors to perish by hunger, and thus discovered by her own son. What can be more interesting?—Then let the hero as the *natural* consequence of such a situation be driven to some act of desperation, for which the laws of his country would award him a halter—but let him "so offend to make offence a skill," that is, let his crime be varnished over with so much pretty morality, and appear to be so naturally resulting from the circumstances in which he is placed, that the audience, dear souls! are won over to sympathy, and "quite forget his vices in his woe;"—instead of the merited rope, he comes off with their applause, leaving them with a pitying tear for his misfortunes, and an approving smile for the spirit which makes him break through the petty prejudices of society. A thread of this kind will be found to run through the whole web of them. The words and actions of their person-ages are ever at variance, and trying to break from one another, like ill-coupled hounds. They are as discordant as a man who should play one tune and sing another. The mouths of these gentry should be sent to the pulpit for our edification, and their ears to the pillory for our example. A friend once suggested to the manager, the idea of getting up these pieces with a double set of performers,—one set to *act* the parts, and the other to *speak* them, whereby the whole would be rendered much less inconsistent than by giving such words and such actions to the same individual; and it is probable this idea might have been carried into effect, but that performers could not be procured to take upon themselves the unrelieved odium of the dumb shew.

In the play of *Lovers' Vows* all the principal characters represent the unluckiest specimens of virtue and morality that can well be imagined. There is a most virtuous female, who becomes a mother, without having been a wife. The Baron, her seducer, the most conscientious of men, makes her a promise of marriage, and keeps it with another. There is his daughter, intended as a pattern of female delicacy and artless inno-cence, who makes an unsolicited tender of her hand—and *Frederick*, our hero, a most honourable youth ("so are they all, all honourable men,") is induced by the inevitable force of circumstance to turn his genius to the road. They are all "as virtuously given as gentlefolks need to be;" this their fine speaking sufficiently attests, but somehow or other they "fall into misfortune," as *Macheath* phrases it, and "no sight," as the old Roman tells us (and the Gallery assures us of it), "is more grateful to the gods[78] than a brave man struggling with the storms of fate."

The present play of the *Stranger* is no less vicious.—A wife forsakes a husband for no reason on earth, and the husband receives her back, because her well-painted crimes are varnished over with sentimentality. But to sum up the whole characteristics of this and most of the plays of the same school—the primary situations are improbable, the circumstances arising from them unnatural, the sentiment corresponds not with the situation, and the action still less with the sentiment—the whole is a tissue of extravagant inconsistencies and absurdities, and the language, like a broken down football, notwithstanding its present mean and squalid appearance, shews evident signs of having originally been gaudily coloured, and highly inflated;—it is like a coat of one of his Majesty's beef-eaters, after a third translation.

March 16, 1817
Drury Lane Theatre.
From Manuel.[79]

It is much better to read the new tragedy, than to see it, and no very good thing to do either. A perfect tragedy, or one approaching near to perfection, is a very difficult work to write; it cannot be struck off at a heat. Walter Scott may sit frivolously down to his verses, and make them as fast as his pen can move,—or Lord Byron may write complete satires on mankind in a morning:—but it requires great powers of mind, and a strenuous application of those powers to produce a good tragedy. The writer has to study effect and *keeping*, at the same time, in his characters, his incidents, and his language. He has to deal with all the lofty passions of the human mind, and to create an ardour in his audience, sufficient to make them go along with the wonders of the scenes. We know of no writer, except Shakspeare, who had made his scenes *casts* from life, or rather life itself. Macbeth, and Lear, and Othello are real beings:—they do not describe remorse, madness, and jealousy in superb speeches, but they labour under them severally, and we are made witnesses of excessive mental suffering. The deepest parts of Shakspeare are made up of the most common expressions. He is often most powerful when most colloquial. All other writers make too great a parade of language to give real passion. They fill their characters with swelling ejaculations and endless descriptions, and where the feeling of the scene should be highest, they produce nothing but "the perilous stuff" of big words. They draw (as Goldsmith should have said) "men as they ought *not* to be, not as they are." We are now approaching near to the kind of writers in which Mr. Maturin is to be found:—he is a fine extravagant manufacturer of murderous gentlemen with poetical souls, and romantic ladies with no souls at all. The tragedy of *Manuel* is not so good as *Bertram*, inasmuch as it is more improbable, more inflated, and much less interesting. It has all the defects of the former piece, with very few of the beauties. The language of Mr. Maturin seems to have been flattered into madness:—it often reminds us of Bottom's speech to his Athenian fellows. If it goes on improving as rapidly, as it has commenced, it may turn out a dangerous rival to the oratory of Counsellor Phillips, and find favour in the eyes of nonsense. The following four lines taken from *Manuel* will give some idea of what we allude to:—

> Thy tears, for which my heart sheds drop by drop,
> (And soon may weep in blood) against a father's,
> Wrung from the agony of his pallid brow,
> Are weigh'd in the soul's balance, and found wanting.[80]

The last line of this monstrous passage leads us to the consideration of another and more serious fault in our author. He is continually weaving, the very language of scripture, in with his violent fiction. This we do not like. He has no right, particularly as a clergyman, to surround the simple and beautiful passages of the sacred writings, with the proud and distorted poetry of his own heated imagination. The theatre cannot as yet boast of the church as "its immortal bride;" and we think it rather a rash thing for any curate to make preparations for the wedding. The tragedy is indeed wrought up after a very German fashion, that is, every thing is *excessive*. The old father loves his son passionately for five acts without intermission, and repeatedly forgets his dutiful daughter, and abuses his kind enduring friends;—the daughter is a very personification of duty, and goes about saying most gorgeous things of and for her parent,—*ecce signum,*—

> Go then; but know what enemy awaits thee:
> The shield of Manuel is his daughter's breast;
> Her streaming hair his banner; and his pledge
> The hand her agony rais'd to thee in vain.
> Bear on thy shield emblazed a virgin's heart,
> Broken for thee.[81]

"This is the very exstacy of love!"—All the characters are said to be Spanish, but this is an unkind disguise; we meet only with German hearts under Spanish cloaks. The whole piece may be a tragical swindle for all we know. Manuel may turn out to be old Moor;[82]—and the kinsman prove to be Francis;—and the daughter, Amelia;—and the son, Frederick;—this however is but a hint of ours. We would, "an if we could," give the plot of this tragedy, but it is too exquisitely mysterious for our simple understandings to unravel. There is a murder, and a festival, and a trial, and a tournament, and a good number of deaths of various sorts. There are, however, a few good passages in this tragedy, in spite of all the faults we have mentioned; they are for the most part overwrought, but they betoken a strong imagination, and great power of expression.

March 23, 1817
Covent Garden Theatre.
From Cymbeline.

This is the most elegant play of Shakspeare's,—the most poetical,—the most naturally romantic. It has great variety in language and character, and gives us all the splendour of a court, and all the simplicity of the country. In some scenes it is pastoral to the highest degree. There is that exquisite description of *Imogene's* beauty as she is lying asleep in her chamber;—this one passage is sufficiently great to justify, as Beaumont would say, the rest of the piece being dull throughout.

> Cytherea,
> How bravely thou becomest thy bed—sweet lily, &c.[83]

The scenes in the wood in which the two young princes appear as hunters of deer, with the old soldier "preaching natural sermons" to them,—are uncommonly delightful. These two youths in their simplicity resemble *Miranda* in the *Tempest*.

April 6, 1817
Drury Lane Theatre.
From The Double Gallant.[84]

A good comedy is nearly a stranger to the London theatres:—ballets, German tragedies and melodrames have possessed themselves of the stage. Now we think that we have discovered the cause of this lamentable usurpation, and we shall not make a secret of our knowledge. The English have been so long engaged in a fierce and tumultuous warfare, that they feel "sound and fury" to be necessary to their comfort, and become weary and languid with any thing quiet.[85] As they can no longer enjoy the excitement of genuine battle and bloodshed, they must be content to put up with the best imitations of it. A loud chorus, a blown up castle, a trampling of horses, a crash of music, a murder, a combat, a clash of swords, a gun's report,—will throw an English audience into raptures. The noisier the play is, the better it is thought, and the more profitable it turns out. The managers must "cry havock, and let slip the dogs of war,"—or they might shut their doors and put their lamps out. The poorest people love a good warlike play, and will in the very teeth of poverty, "pack up their tatters, and follow the drum." They roar "like nightingales" at a gunpowder pantomime, and at the appearance of a sword with a man to it, or a cocked hat with a man under it, applaud to the very echo, that does applaud again. Comedy is an amusement only to a happy people. The heart must be at rest, to banquet freely on good wit. Good wit in short sends the English people to sleep, or takes away their senses. It is like hot weather to them, and makes them faint, and languid. It oppresses them. There are two reasons for the want of a good modern comedy: the first is, that the audience could not understand it, or would not relish it,—and the second is, that none of our present playwrights could make one, if they would. We have at this day some of the best comic actors ever known, and yet we seldom are gratified with a display of their abilities.

To Mrs. Mardyn, Mrs. Alsop, and Mrs. Davison we are indebted, we believe, for the revival of Cibber's comedy of *The Double Gallant*. It is a lively comedy, but it is by no means equal to others of the age in which it was written. We dislike the name of Cibber exceedingly, either from Pope's notice of him, or from his own vanity, or (more likely than either) from his being Poet Laureate:—If our reason be not one of these, we know not what it is. The wit of this comedy is never keen and vivid,—but it is never weak or unnatural. It does not depend, as that of modern works does, on a single human folly or extravagance, or on the repetition of a senseless and cant phrase.—There is a description of foolish oddities, which being either local, personal, or temporary, are unfit subjects for comic representation. Wit and humour disgrace themselves by stooping to pick them up, or in attempting to preserve them. Should they chance, by their ridiculous notoriety, to obtain the applause of their own brief day, they have nothing to preserve their memories beyond it. The humour of them is transient: it must die in the age that gives birth to it. It has nothing in common with the past or the succeeding.—Precisely of this description is the "stap my vitals" of the *Trip to Scarborough*, and the "what's to pay," and "push along," &c. of the plays of our living dramatists. But there are certain follies and eccentricities, the seeds of which are inherent in our very nature and kind. These, as they gradually unfold themselves, and shoot up, assume, like the vegetable kingdom, a vast variety of form and colour, according to the soil in which they are sown, and the circumstances of their growth. To furnish specimens of these is the legitimate employment of the comic muse. The complaint of the present day is, that there no longer exists any new genius, nor even a single undiscovered species that may be drawn forth for the entertainment of the fastidious critic. This is a complaint, however, that dullness, which cannot find new stores, and indolence, which will not combine old, must ever put forth.

There are excellent materials for an excellent comedy, if one of our authors could select and combine them, and the English would properly appreciate the work when finished. The *Double Gallant* (for it is high time we should return to it) is a sprightly collection of intrigues, carried on after the fashion of the time. Married ladies walking, masked in the park, and talking and coquetting with "pretty fellows,"—and reasonably jealous husbands, on speaking terms with high-bred chambermaids, —and fashionable rascals with silk stockings and no principles,—and unmarried ladies plotting with gallants, with all the air of women of intrigue. These,—these are the characters of which the *Double Gallant* is composed. There are not many acute observations, or flashes of wit to be seen in this comedy; but a good thing is occasionally to be met with.

One truth is very well brought in:—the two ladies are, with a polite antipathy to each other, speaking of their lovers, and gently reviling each other;—one turns apart and observes, "How civilly we women hate each other."

April 13, 1817
Drury Lane Theatre.

At this house an afterpiece has been produced, from the pen of Mr. Knight the performer. It is founded on Southey's ballad of *Mary the Maid of the Inn*, and is wrought with great ingenuity. Every one likes it that sees it, which is good evidence of its merit. Mr. Southey is extremely fortunate in his dramatic pursuits;—this is the second piece, in which his brains have been concerned, which has been well received by the public. Wat Tyler[86] is somewhat more heroic than this little afterpiece— but both are pregnant with the Laureate's homely pathos. He will be applying to the Chancellor perhaps in a few years to get the present work checked, from motives of an unforeseen delicacy.

April 27, 1817
Covent Garden, and Drury Lane.
Mr. Kemble and Mr. Kean.

On Monday last we were present at Mr. Kean's representation of *Richard the Third*,—and on Tuesday we saw Mr. Kemble perform the part of *King John*;—so that we are now pretty well qualified to speak of the comparative merits of the two great tragedians. Mr. Kean, as the crook-backed tyrant, was by no means so great as we have at other times seen him,—at least, in the early, and silently guilty scenes;—but in the last act, in which Richard's mind is torn with the desertions of high friends and the workings of powerful thought, he was as great as ever. We do not think Mr. Kean can repress his feelings when once they are grandly called upon;—indeed we have heard from good authority that he never performs a noble and ambitious part, without being stirred into a belief, by his own mental impetuosity, that he is the very character he assumes:—and indeed all his actions prove it to us. There never was anything on the stage equal to his whole figure and attitude in *Richard the Third* on the eve of battle. He stands more like a grand picture from the pencil of one of the old masters, than any thing living in this common place age:—That is, his features are more keen,—more intense in their complexion,—more quietly impressive,—than those of any modern English face. There is very little expression, generally speaking, in the countenances of the present race of men,—certainly none in comparison with those calm, eloquent breathing faces of the early Italians, which are brought down to us by the hand of Titian. Mr. Kean stands, in the scene we have alluded to, surrounded by his generals, but communing only with his own gigantic thought. His eye,—dark wild and piercing,—is fixed, but on no visible object;—it looks upon the air, and seems to live upon things past, or to come. It seems to hold the concentrated rays of the mind, and to have a deep and desolate feeling of its own. His eyebrows come down edgy and contracted:—his face is pale and full of loneliness;—and his lips are compressed with an immense feeling.—The effect of all this is perfected by a fine flow of hair, falling round his face upon his shoulders, and lying there in rich black curls. This scene ought to be longer, the beauty of it is too fleeting. We are convinced, now that we have seen Mr. Kean and Mr. Kemble so closely together,—that the style of the former is the warm, the moving, the intellectual, the true one;—and that the style of the latter is the fixed, the cold, and the false one. Kean impresses us with all the enthusiasm of life,—Kemble yields to us only a picture of dignified decay. Kean fills the stage with a mental gaiety, and spurs the souls of his hearers into a delightful madness:—while Kemble only becomes elaborate in giving all the *methodism* of acting, and raises in his audience nought but a stately indifference or a stoical delight. Kean is all spirit and life, and could "wallow naked in December's snow, by the bare remembrance of the summer's heat;"—he never chills,—but holds on, in his matchless race, untried. Kemble must give his limbs a quarter of an hour's notice ere they will consent to stir,—and prepare for the turn of his head five minutes before it is required. His mind appears to have been kept cold all the day, for the use of the summer night, in that ice-house his body,— and is served up as a chilling luxury to the helpless senses of people of fashion. Kemble could "hold a fire in his hand, by thinking on the frosty Caucasus." He never forgets himself,—and so becomes lively by mistake, —nor suffers his voice by accident to give up its conventicle sing-song, and take to natural speaking. He is of marble,—and therefore never disgraces the stuff he is made of, by any undue warmth, lightness or motion. Of all characters however which Mr. Kemble acts, there is none so heavy, stiff, hard and unwieldy as his King John;—and we very much wonder that he should not have had more respect for his fame than to have chosen this part to play in the night after Kean's *Richard the Third*. This change from violent heat to excessive cold, may be very national, but it is extremely trying and dangerous. Mr. Kemble will do himself more mischief by sticking up these pillars of ice in the very face of Kean's fire, than by any other unwise thing he could do:—they will thaw, and run to waste. In these remarks on Mr. Kemble we have noticed the defective side of his style only,—and in comparing his style with Mr. Kean's, we can only do so;—but in a future paper,[87] we shall take an opportunity of remarking upon his performance of one of his Roman characters, and consequently pointing out what we consider the merits of his acting. In parts, such as *Penruddock*, or *Brutus*, or *Coriolanus*, which are in themselves settled, cold, or lofty, there is no one to equal Kemble. His *Penruddock* is the only specimen of baffled affection surviving the strife of time, on the stage. His heart there, though broken, seems to "brokenly live on." He strikes sorrow into us by the dint of his very frozenness. He looks like some magnificent creature hurled out by the hand of Despair into a fearful solitude, to which his spirit, by its own greatness, becomes reconciled. His *Brutus* and *Coriolanus* are great and majestic, and remind us of "the most high and palmy state of Rome." These kinds of characters, however, are in themselves artificial, and of course quite secondary to those of natural feeling and passion. If a Temple were erected in honour of the drama, the difference between Kean and Kemble would be immediately seen;—Kemble would take his stand by the side of some great column, at the head of the steps, and look down upon the crowds beneath him with an eye of confident grandeur:—Kean would come down from the pillars, and bustle amongst the people.

May 25, 1817
Covent Garden Theatre.
Mr. Kemble.

We find that some remarks, which appeared in our paper lately on Mr. Kemble's acting, as contrasted with Mr. Kean's, have given great offence to many persons,—among whom are a few for whose judgments we hold a high regard. Now as we do not wish to hang loosely on the good opinions of men of true taste, nor of "women neither,"—and as we are little inclined to have our observations misconstrued, and our feelings unfairly reviled,—and above all, as we are really anxious to pay respect to one who has gone gracefully and greatly through life, and who is about to retire from a scene of which he has long been the "chief guest,"—we take this early opportunity of noticing the beauties of Mr. Kemble's acting (which we promised to do), and of cheerfully perform-ing a duty to a man who was the best delight of our boyish days. If we had suffered Mr. Kemble to pass away from our eyes, without trying to pay the debt we owe him,—our hearts would be mean,—our thoughts would be blackened,—our criticisms would be vile,—"and all things unbecoming." We look back through a crowd of actors that throng together in the avenues of our memory,—and there Kemble stands like "the life o' the building." We remember well the time, when at half past five, we were jostling at the pit door with fat and happy tradesmen, sentimental milliners, lads, clerks, and country cousins,—to get a sight of Kemble in *Macbeth* or *Coriolanus*. We were then quite boyish, with hearts tip-top full of enthusiasm,—ignorant of this iron world,—unstruck by disappointment, filled with a young delight, that must have had something to rest upon:—we had read of the Romans in our school-books,—we had felt their grandeur by listening to Shakespeare's *Brutus* and *Cassius*. How eagerly did we press forward as the bars of the doors clanked!—How ardently did we wrestle with our enthusiastic neigh-bours! How hurryingly did our hands rush into the hot pocket in search of the well-known price! Our seat in the pit was doubly dear to us, since it was earned by the sweat of our brow. The theatre did then look to us like a happy place; it *was* one. The misty obscurity,—the callings of parted friends,—the solitary and cold servants, like *Penruddock's* bailiff, "keeping possession,"—the humming joy of the newly filled gallery,—

the fruit women,—the dark green curtain,—all these were glorious! Then the gradual lighting, and rising of the lamps,—the warmth which sat in all eyes,—the rustling of the play-bills,—the first bell,—the music, —the second bell, and the slowly ascending curtain![88] But the entrance of *Coriolanus*, when the dingy rabble dashed back, like something immortal descending in amongst black, brawling, revelling mortals,— was the perfection of excited feeling. We really, in going into these remembrances, seem to be enjoying the delight again:—"Ah! happy days,—once more, who would not be a boy!" In recollecting all these, we are affecting nothing in saying, that we are recalling sensations, which we thought, from our nightly duty now at the theatre, were gone for ever. We never were happier, nor gayer. The red Roman garment is floating before our eyes still, nearly as palpably as that which now is worn. We could rise this moment, late as it is, and go to the theatre, if we could be sure of a good, wild squeeze, and of seeing *Coriolanus* start before us full of pride, and high beauty,—and all in his pomp of costume. To Kemble we are indebted for this romantic delight,—for a delight which can never exist again. Criticism is a pelican thing, that feeds upon the bosom that hath bred it. It chills the warm currents that visit the heart. It nourishes dissatisfaction, and directs the eye to *causes*, instead of *effects*, thus "o'er-informing the soul." Criticism leads to a cold, calculating knowledge of the world,—and "knowledge of the world makes man perfidious;"—it bears away that beautiful and blessed consciousness of joy, arising from an unconsciousness of the innocent means that make it. For all these we detest it. Critics are but useless Ministers to philosophy, therefore we could wish to be none. "But we are tied to a stake, and, bear-like, we must fight our course, or die."

In the part of *Coriolanus*, Kemble stands unrivalled. In *Brutus*, the same. In the *Stranger*, *Penruddock*, *Zanga*,[89] and *Cato*, the same. His figure, in the Roman characters, is all strength and dignity, and looks like embodied eloquence.[90] His head is finely formed, and his features are fixed in one great expression. The dresses which Mr. Kemble wears, fall about his form with peculiar richness and beauty,—in broad wavy folds, like the draperies of Raphael, which have more expression and meaning than the best portraits Lawrence ever painted. The cloak in *Coriolanus*, for instance, hangs in exquisite curves, never losing the true line of beauty. Kemble's acting, in the young and impetuous Roman, can never be forgotten by those who have once seen it:—The haughtiness of the man, the valour and wildness of the soldier, the proud affection of the Roman Son,—are given with a truth and a strength which cannot be surpassed. His uncontrollable bursts of passion in the very teeth of the tribunes, when they brand him with the name of Traitor, as contrasted with the coolness of *Cominius*, and the generosity, humour, and friendliness of old *Menenius*,—are most admirable. Kemble *looks* the character to perfection. He is the only man on the stage that could boast before the people, that "on fair ground he could beat forty of them,"—and not be laughed at. In this character he is a tower of strength to Covent-garden Theatre, "which they, upon the adverse faction,[91] want." We had nearly omitted to notice his fine acting in the scene with *Aufidius*, where *Claremont*[92] murders him;—his manner of rushing up to the Volscian, with an eye piercing as steel, and a heart "made too great for what contains it," and the tone of voice, half gladness and half passion, in which he recounts his own victory over a whole town of the enemy, are indeed perfectly overpowering. By the way, *Claremont* seems to relish the part of *Volusius* marvellously, and to kill Kemble with a great deal of gusto:—He has, perhaps, in his casual readings of Shakespeare, stumbled upon that passage,—"An eagle towering in his pride of place, was by a mousing owl hawked at, and killed." The *Brutus* and the *Cato* of Mr. Kemble are very fine, but they are more tame, and necessarily so. They have more philosophy in their natures,—and "are not easily moved," and "being moved, perplexed in the extreme." The great beauty of Mr. Kemble's acting is its classicality,—its association with the highest characters of the highest nations,—its stern grandeur and sustained loftiness. We never lose our respect for Mr. Kemble while he remains before us,—and his figure "almost dares you to forget." He might stand on the stage for an hour together, and not weary us,—but there we should be gazing at him, as at a fine piece of Grecian sculpture, —and dreaming of great ages and magnificent characters all the time. He seems to be some forgotten Roman, left undebased and unhurt, in the vast and lonely ruin of his country. He has all the look of a solitary one of a great people, that flourished "in the most high and palmy state of Rome," out-living all, and bearing about with him a majestic and mournful patriotism, which no loneliness can extinguish. His eye proudly converses with Liberty. "If it were not as good a deed as to drink" to remember this man, when he shall quit the theatre, and "to give him a statue with his ancestors," we are no true men. His acting is remarkable for its stateliness, and for its declamation;—but the former is always commanding, and the latter is ever beautiful. His familiar touches of character are never vulgar, and they are the more felt because they are so decidedly relieved. His style is that of Rembrandt,—full of strong light and shade,—rich in its vast contrast. He is slow,—but sure; —and if he never startles his audience with an unexpected beauty,— he never forgets himself, "when some necessary part of the play is to be remembered." He is a great man,—and we are sorry that his theatrical life is drawing to a close. There is something so affecting in the word *last*, that we never like to see it, even on trivial occasions;—but when coupled with the parting of a great and glorious old favourite, it becomes unusually melancholy. We forget all his faults now that we come to say farewell to him,—and we own our feeling, that "no man shall have a nobler memory." In dissolving our partnership of delight with him, we would wish to express our obligations to him for the active part he has taken in the concern,—and to wish him a possessor of that happiness in retirement, which he has so long given to us in public.—We cannot do better, in concluding this article, than extract a passage from the Tatler, which is peculiarly applicable on the present occasion.

All admirers of true *Tragedy*, it is hoped, will have the gratitude to be present on the last day of his acting, who, if he does not happen to please them, will have it even then to say, that it is his first offence.

June 8, 1817
Covent Garden Theatre.
Macbeth.—Mrs. Siddons.

We had the good fortune to sit very near Mrs. Siddons on Thursday evening last, when she played the part of *Lady Macbeth* for Mr. C. Kemble's benefit. The ochestra[93] was opened for the public,—and the music transferred to the stage;—here we were accommodated, without the sacrifice of time, strength, and clothing. To have obtained a seat in the pit, the only good place next to the ochestra, we must have jostled in the lobbies at 3 o'clock in the afternoon, and have manfully fought our way to the pay office;—now the fact is, we are no great friends to waiting and suffocation,—and we honestly confess that we have lost all relish for a respectable squeeze. In the ochestra, therefore, we took our seats, quietly and comfortably,—but we felt some compunctious visitings of nature when *Lady Macbeth* exclaimed.

> —Would'st thou have that,
> Which thou esteem'st the ornament of life,
> And live a coward in thine own esteem.[94]

It struck upon the chords of our conscience. We were indeed moved with the sublimity of Mrs. Siddons's performance,—for there was not a syllable which we did not catch,—not a look which we did not perceive and fully feel. She is not feeble,—at least not on the stage;—but her spirit in its own element seems to defy decay. Her soul is regal,—and makes joyful the palace in which it dwells:—It wears "without corrival all its dignities."—We never perfectly caught the wondrous eloquence of her eye before her last performance;—we never were near enough to *see* it speak,—and the truth is that all great actors can only be truly observed and felt within the three or four front seats of the pit;—all who gaze from a greater distance, are out of their sphere. The low, sudden exclamations of intense passion or subdued feeling,—the quick, keen glances of anger, suspicion, or hate,—are "not for the million." The eye of Mrs. Siddons, like the guiding star on the sea, lights us over the troubled waters of life to that magic island of which Shakespeare is the Prospero. It has a full and noble light, and its lustre remains un-mellowed on the memory. We shall never forget one or two glances which we saw the other evening;—they seemed to be shot, like arrows from her soul: particularly the look at *Macbeth*, when she smilingly passes the fear-surprised guests, and exclaims "Are you a man?"—To us it appeared, as though a supernatural creature, with a most magical "speculation in the eyes,"—uttered this question. Again, in that grandest scene in the whole range of English Tragedy, when she is waiting for the murder of the king:—"Had he not resembled my father as he slept, —I had done it!"—We never expect to see the shadow of such playing as this. As to Miss O'Neill,—she is a handsome woman,—and plays very prettily to our fancies and our affections;—but she is no more like Mrs.

Siddons,—than we to Hercules. Mrs. Siddons is above us,—almost too high for our imaginations. Miss O'Neill is of the earth,—and we are never startled at learning that she has visited my Lady this,—or Miss that. Mrs. Siddons sits enthroned in our recollections,—like a Queen. Miss O'Neill is a simple woman, except when she reminds us of "German *distraction*." We have heard it observed that the voice of Mrs. Siddons is weakened and changed. But we thank our good chance that we were too near to be aware of it. It seems to us as great as ever. The sleeping scene was extremely well acted. All was slumbrous. We never saw a finer audience, nor ever saw an audience more delighted. Mrs. Siddons has the good fortune always to be attended by the ladies,—more numerously than any other actress,—which is a pretty strong proof that "she towers above her sex." Kemble played *Macbeth* with greater spirit than we have ever seen him;—his mind seemed to be stirred by some fine recollection of the days when he and his sister, and brother, stood as three "that Rome might well be proud of." Another reason might be, the sight of so full a house. Another, and perhaps the greatest, might be the knowledge of Talma[95] being in the house. We sat close by this great French Tragedian,—and had some occasional conversation with him. He appeared to us extremely sensible and unassuming,—and was much pleased with the performance of the evening. His face is fine, and expressive,—with a broad and eloquent forehead, and a dark and speaking eye. Kemble played as though he had heard "the trumpet's sound." He gained spirit as he proceeded,—and acted the last scenes with all the life of youth,—and as though his soul was fanned by the wing of Shakespeare's spirit. His way of delivering the passage on the Queen's death,—which we cannot refrain from giving,—seemed to us quite new and beautiful.

> To-morrow, and to-morrow, and to-morrow,
> Creeps in this pretty pace, from day to day,
> To the last syllable of recorded Time,—
> And all our yesterdays have lighted fools
> The way to dusty death. Out, out brief candle.
> Life is a walking shadow, a poor player,
> That frets and struts his hours upon the stage,
> And then is heard no more of. It is a tale
> Told by an idiot,—full of sound and fury,
> Signifying,—nothing![96]

Mr. Kemble spoke this at first with slow sorrow, till he reached the last word of the first line, when he burst into hurried disgust, and went finely and rapidly on to the last. The conclusion of this speech is fraught with dreariness. It sounds like the echo of a shattered world. The nearer and nearer the time approaches, at which we are to part wholly with Mr. Kemble,—the more reluctant do we feel at parting with him. There is no melancholy to equal the one we feel at parting with an old favourite. "Take him for all in all, we shall not look upon his like again:"—we wish this quotation had never been used before. It must be sterling, for it has been in circulation a long while, and has not yet lost aught of its value. Mr. C. Kemble played *Macduff* with very great feeling,—and proved himself worthy of his family;—but how should it be otherwise, —"The sons of Cornelia did not disgrace their mother." His manner of receiving the account of the death of his wife and children, was unaffectedly pathetic. We must be very chary of him, when his brother leaves us,—for he will be the last of a noble house. The best proof that could be given of his public talents and his private worth was before us the other evening. The house was full.

Here our praises must stop,—for after these the tragedy was badly filled. *Claremont* seems always awed into apathy by some presence or misfortune,—and Barrymore barks *Banquo* into our ears, "as it were any dog." The chorusses were not well managed, which we cannot forgive, loving the music as we really do.

July 6, 1817
Covent Garden Theatre.
From *The Exile—Miss Booth's Benefit.*

The play chosen for the evening was the *Exile*, a rude, romantic, and wretched Russian piece. We believe it was written by Reynolds, and a worse name could not be uttered[97] . . . We mean to say nothing against Mr. Reynolds, more than we would utter against the whole of the present living English dramatists, than whom it is impossible to find a race more miserable. There is no idea of fame existing in the souls of our dramatic authors: popularity alone is courted,—and fame and popularity are as different as night and day, or Reynolds and Shakspeare, which are the same at the distances.[98] Fame is life eternal on earth.—Indeed, we have very set notions on this great subject.—It has nothing to do with mortal existence. It is something on earth, not earthy. It is an immortal echo of the voice of excellence sounding through the halls of time. Poets that enjoy great applause during their sojourn with us, ere they go away, like flowers that have gladdened our eyes and perfumed the air we breathed,—are seldom the great possessors of true fame. The favour of the world is a dangerous compliment to human intellect, when lavished on living exertion, for it generally leads its object from the great pursuit. The poet that hears the voice of the world ringing in his ears, is too apt to turn to that voice, and to become a truant to poesy, his immortal mistress! He tunes his song to temporary tastes, and is intoxicated with a fair, momentary, and fleeting reputation. He listens to the breath of the Syren, and is seduced from his course. It is in solitude—in trouble—in a patient poverty—that we generally find those works are produced which "are for all time." Great intellects are naturally above those of their surrounding kind, and are led on to exertion by their own intensity;—they delight in high works, and finding their own age unfit to enjoy them, are content to trust them to posterity. Of course none but sterling minds can persevere in this solitary path to immortality. Nothing but industrious and noble ambition could toil a life away to be a guardian spirit for ever to the world it dwelt on. Fame is the reflection of genius in the stream of time.[99] Fame is every thing to majestic and inspired minds:—

> —The spur, that the clear spirit doth raise,
> To spurn delights, and live laborious days.[100]

But they had a fine consciousness of their own powers, that sustained them in all the severities of life,—and the world has since done them justice. In our own country, the wits of Queen Anne's time enjoyed an unbounded popularity, which seemed to endanger the sovereignty of pure fame;—but they are now fast "falling from their high estate," and their age is no longer allowed to be "the most high and palmy." They were in their own day, possessors of power unquestioned, and sat smiling under acknowledged laurels;—but they enjoyed all "the future in the instant."

July 13, 1817
Covent Garden Theatre.
Miss O'Neill—Desdemona.

There was every reason to believe that Miss O'Neill would never appear in the character of *Desdemona*,—for almost all people of taste and feeling desired and advised it, and the part was most peculiarly suited to her powers. Actors and actresses are perhaps the most head-strong beings under the sun, as far as the pomps and vanities of their profession go,— and would as soon *think* of dying, or *thinking*, as taking advice,—particu- larly if it were good. They have always an idea that they know more than others,—and look upon the stage as their own little world, over which they hold a sort of blended sovereignty. They are bigotted to their own old plans of government,—and take great care to oppose all invasions of improvement. Perhaps one of the causes of John Kemble's receiving such homage from his brothers, was, his preserving the hard and ancient laws of his ancestors:—the theatre would have rejoiced to have been able to "hail him the father of a line of kings." It was very clear at the dinner[101] the other day, how strongly all the royal players set their faces against that turbulent little Buonaparte, Kean, who leaped up to the throne, out of the very lap of obscurity,—tore the crown and sceptre from all the more orderly kings,—("for them, the gracious Duncan hath he murdered") rushed wildly into the society of fame, fortune and power,—and to all his nights and days to come, "gave solely sovereign sway and masterdom." We think Kean is likely to maintain his seat;—he cannot fail to hold it, so long as he continues to make the spirit of Shakspeare his Prime Minister. Kean has thrown off the garment of our dramatic Caesar, over which others have been eloquent,—and has stirred the hearts of the people with a sight of the royal form itself. We should very much like to know whether this "king in little" can take advice;—we would not ourselves be rash enough to offer it, but we should be glad to see the experiment made by others on him. Let somebody recommend him to play *King Lear*. The fatal passion, the strange credulity,—the madness,—and the death of that old king would suit him as well, as the sweet tenderness,—the womanly submission,— the faith, the gentleness, and the suffering of *Desdemona* are wrought for Miss O'Neill. She has been advised to play this character ever since she appeared, and of course without effect; we can only attribute her performing it now to the cessation of that advice. She has been endeavouring to wean our admiration from herself of late, by all the means in her power. We very much feared that her taste in itself was bad,—nor do we altogether withdraw that opinion now,—but as she has thought proper to play something feeling and sensible, we will give her all the benefit of the act and not urge the question as to her defects for the present. What we know of *Desdemona*, as Shakspeare has introduced us to her, is, that she is a young and ardent and lovely creature, who fell in love with a noble Moor "for the dangers he had passed,"—whose affections were intimately blended with her enthusiasm,—and whose imagination could throw the light of the mind over the countenance she loved. Her whole soul is gathered into one passion,—from which all her thoughts and actions stray like rays. Her own timidity and tenderness threw a lustre of their own over the heroism and the fire of *Othello*. She sees in him a being superior to all troubles and tempests,—one who had outlived battles and sieges and long wanderings. She feels the helplessness of her own nature, and gives it over, without reserve, to the care of the noble *Othello*. She is all simplicity and devotedness. Her heart gives all its feelings to her lip,—and can afford to do it. She confesses her love before the whole senate,—and when her father casts her from him, she seems to find her peace in the bosom of *Othello*. She waits for the arrival of *Othello* at Cyprus, with all that abstractedness of mind, which dwells in lovers who are parted:—it is then that she tells the sweet truth—

> I am not merry,
> But I do beguile the thing I am
> By seeming so.—[102]

She pleads for *Cassio*, when he is disgraced, with all her heart,—and this very openness is the best symbol of her innocence. Guilt walks about cloaked and masked,—but innocence wears the light of day on its face,—and knows no care. She never can believe that *Othello* is jealous, till he directly accuses her of crime,—and even then she keeps her "constant, loving nature," and gives herself up to sorrow only. At her death, we feel as if some pure and etherial creature had left the earth, on which she had [been] dwelling to better our natures. We feel,—as a lover would feel at seeing the evening star vanish from his eyes, while gazing on it. *Desdemona* is ever before us, "shining sweetly nigh." The light of purity is about her,—serene, lovely, and soft. *Desdemona* is the lilly which the lion crushes in its walk. We never hear much of her personal beauty,— and yet we are sure that she is beautiful. Miss O'Neill is very like her we understand,—only her hair and eyes should be darker. Wordsworth seems to have seen *Desdemona*, by the last verse of his poem, beginning "she was a phantom of delight:"[103]—if that description be not like her, we confess that we have no idea of "the gentle lady married to the Moor."

Miss O'Neill plays *Desdemona* in her very best manner,—and this is very high praise. We see in her a perfect woman,—and there is not a more beautiful sight in the world. Miss O'Neill's person, which appears to have been touched by illness to a more delicate beauty, is a very lovely comment on the text of the play:—It justifies all that is thought of her. Her voice,—which has always a melancholy about it,—a kind of sweet sullenness,—is *Desdemona's* to the life:—It uttered every thing to perfection, except the exclamation,—"But,—here's my husband!"— and in this, it had not enough of the rapture of affection in it. *Desdemona's* enthusiasm always starts into life, when she is speaking of *Othello*,— particularly when she is holding him up as her pride. The voice of Miss O'Neill could do this passage justice, if it chose. Her death-scene was not particularly fine. She will not perhaps please the galleries so much in this character, as in the *Apostate*,[104] but she will delight and win the hearts of all feeling people. We wonder whether she has a love of Fame within her;—but this may as well not be considered now.

Mr. Young is perhaps the very worst *Othello* we ever witnessed. His voice and his action gave a quiet lie to his fiery language;—and his face seemed to be merely that of a looker on. He does not seem to have got the taste of Campbell's ode[105] out of his mouth,—nor the promise to Kemble,—that he would march over feelings, like daisies, for the rest of his life,—out of his memory. The only thing he said, that seemed to be real, was his answer to *Iago* who observed that he was moved,—"no, not much moved, not much moved." Mr. Young did not look like *Othello*:—One might almost think that one of the dingy gentlemen of his Majesty's band, had strayed unawares into Covent Garden Theatre, and had not overcome his surprize at finding himself a Moor of consequence. We expected every minute to see him flourish a tambourine over his head,—and thump the parchment in the face of the audience. His face had no more expression than India-rubber,—and, like Alexander Selkirk's birds, "his tameness was shocking to us." Mr. Young could certainly play the part better,—but unfortunately Mr. Kean has taken up the enthusiastic and true way of acting it,—and it would be highly unbecoming in Mr. Young to follow his steps; he, therefore, acts "as if a man were author of himself,—and knew no other kin."

Charles Kemble's *Cassio* is a finished piece of acting. Mr. Booth's *Iago* is not. We wish it were.

October 12, 1817
Drury Lane Theatre.
From The Refusal [Character of a Blue-stocking][106]

Mrs. Alsop, as Sophronia, was the exact personification of all *blue-stocking* ladies. If there is a despicable character in women, it is the professed petticoat philosopher. She assumes every thing on the credit of her little shadowy knowledge, and her sex;—and says rude things, and fancies them intellectual severities. She neglects her domestic duties, which she ought to pursue,—for books and sciences, which she cannot understand. She gives her opinion on matters of taste, with a dangerous freedom,—and is more violent, in proportion to her ignorance of the subject on which she decides. She thinks the society of women beneath her, and thinks lightly of all men, unless they are literary, particularly her husband. She collects authors about her, like lap-dogs,—and fondles a sick versifyer, or an ailing metaphysician, with all the care [with which] a dowager nurses her favorite Pompey.—Her mornings are passed over Reviews, Quarto Poems, and books of ill-used philosophy. Her afternoons are worn away with a substantial dinner and pretended thinking. —Her nights are burnt to death with wax candles and flaming opinions. She lives the nuisance of her family and friends, the learned tormentor of herself, and the laugh of those who know her at second hand.

October 19, 1817
Covent Garden Theatre.
From She Stoops to Conquer.

The comedy of *She Stoops to Conquer* is a much better one to read than to see;—this is the case with the best of our dramatic works, and we have had occasion to remark it over and over again. There is a peculiarity in the humour of this delightful comedy, which we shall attempt to explain. Comedy partakes necessarily of the habits and fortunes of the author, as well as of the customs of the time in which he lives; and it would be an easy and a pleasant task, if we had room, to account for every change which has taken place in comedy, from the keenness and careless vivacity of the age of Shakespeare, to the tediousness and emptiness of the present day. In the time of Elizabeth, authors were favourites of the Court, and at the same time breathed their wit in a sort of easy intellectual wrestle over their pipes and ale. This happy mixture of high and humble life gave a freedom to their wit, a blended pride and homeliness, an ease and vigour, which have never since been equalled. In this day, authors are ashamed of their profession, and the Court does not countenance it; they are therefore for the most part men of other occupations, and having little time to think for themselves, pick up the puns of their acquaintance, and build on the plots of novels and romances. They are content to pilfer, rather than invent, and study quantity rather than quality. Sheridan was the last* of our genuine comic writers: and his life seems imaged in his plays. There is all the wildness, the spirit, the romance of his youth, playing in his scenes. His dialogues run on with all the grace and carelessness of young vines, and bear as joyous and intoxicating a fruit. You may trace in his comedies, all the author's uncertainty, and passion for wine and pleasure. His language at times reels round in a happy intoxication, and his wit starts and stops by fits. If an author would but write from what he sees, feels, or experiences, he would be sure of being successful. Goldsmith was a genuine writer; he had no deceit about him. The comedy of *She Stoops to Conquer* is filled

---

* We ought perhaps to include Colman, but he has himself so shamefully abused powers, which might have "thrown a light across his age," that we feel little inclined to remember him.—It must be a poor spirit that would rather be "a wit among lords, than a lord among wits."

with natural characters thrown into improbable situations; but the language wears throughout that easy humour, which came in with Steele and died with Goldsmith. The cause of our relishing this natural humour so heartily, is the apparent unconsciousness of it in the characters which create it, and our supposed superiority in being able to perceive and enjoy it. Our self-importance is appealed to, and the appeal is therefore not to be withstood. We admire old Isaac Bickerstaff in the Tatler on account of his simplicity, and delight in Sir Roger de Coverley because his virtue is unassuming, and our understandings are apparently superior to his. Goldsmith travelled over Switzerland, and won his way by the music of his flute. This solitary and wandering life gave him an insight into character, a deeper relish for home, and at the same time that haunting idea of travelling, which fashioned his style, and constituted the charm of all his works. In spite of his love of domestic comfort and domestic humour, he could not, from his habits, let the characters of his imagination rest; they are sent forth.

The Citizen of the World is one who has journeyed from China;—the Vicar of Wakefield, in the second or third chapter, sets out with all his family from one village to another;—And this is told in a more charming manner than any other part of the book:—Even little Beau Tibbs has his jaunts to Vauxhall, and places of a like distance, in all the pomp of travel. In the Comedy of *She Stoops to Conquer* the author has not omitted his little failing, he has accordingly made his heroes come in from a journey;—And all the faults of the play are attributed to the love of romance and difficulty which the author has imbibed from experience. The language of this Comedy is full of simple humour, and has that air of comfort and home, which can only be relished at a quiet fireside. The Comedy itself is more like an essay pilfered from a number of *The Citizen of the World*, than a piece formed expressly for the stage. The dialogue is too homely and familiar for the Theatre,—and does not at all square with the situations, into which the speakers are thrown: All these little "rubs and botches in the work" are smoothed away in the reading, because we then think of the author,—and that explains all. He seems to have infused all the benevolence of his nature into his characters,—all the spirit and confusion of his wanderings into their situations,—and to have breathed the gentle music of his flute into their language. He must always be admitted to our thoughts, when we read his works. We know not whether we have made ourselves clear to our readers, in this attempt at explaining the peculiar character of this Comedy;—what we would come to, is that the humour is too domestic, and the characters too natural for the stage;—the little improbabilities of the plots are also unsuitable:—but, that they are the best things in life, by the fireside, or in the company of a few friends.

The play has however been got up in the best style possible at Covent Garden,—and takes, as the theatrical phrase is, much better than we expected;—though we have heard many persons express their wonder at the vapid manner of its acting. Charles Kemble is an excellent *Marlow*. We know not which to applaud most, his modesty or his effrontery. When he is stammering before Miss Hardcastle, his downcast look, his trembling knees, his imbecile hand, all betray a timidity which appears unconquerable;—but the way in which all these glide away, at the sight of his mistress, whom he mistakes for the bar-maid, is as easy as it is delightful. The clouds vanish from his face, the tremulousness flies from his limbs, confidence laughs in his eye. He, in an instant, becomes all impudence, life, love, and whim. At the end of the character, he became a little too sentimental, which we were not so well pleased with, because the character did not quite call for it . . .

Mrs. Davenport was very industrious in *Mrs. Hardcastle*, "grinding her bones to make her bread." After her journey amidst the horseponds, or to speak more classically, her tour to the Lakes,—she came before us in all the dirt and experience of travel. After all her difficulties, she was, as the author intended her to be, quite at home. If she had been dragged through Lethe water, with all other lake travellers tied to her heels, she could not have looked more forlorn and sensitive. But who shall describe *Tony Lumpkin?*—Liston in *Tony Lumpkin*! What can we say, worthy of his flaxen wig and rosy, round phiz; where is the language to do justice to the awkward lounge of his country legs, or the lack-a-daisical dancing of his hands.—His head moves up and down, like that of a mourning coach horse, with all the conscious pride of its hanging curls:—and his eyes leer about in the most irresistible manner. He is the bumpkin squire to a nicety. His ease at the inn, with those who detest anything low-lived (amongst which is the refined beggar who never suffers his bear to dance to any but the genteelest tunes, "water parted," or "the minuet in *Ariadne*,") is all that it should be. He speaks of *Bet*

Bouncer with a voice steeped in bumpkin pride and delight. But it is impossible to give an idea of his endeavouring to read the letter:—this is ignorance in all its "pomp, pride, and circumstance." He rubs the paper on his arms and on his coat, and holds it closer and closer to his eyes, as though his power of deciphering the contents might come with a little trouble. The humour of Liston, like the humour of Goldsmith, goes on quietly and heartily without any molestation. Its riches are fineless. It is a sure "balm to hurt minds;"—a first course at the banquet of nature;—"chief nourisher in life's feast." Let all those who are wearied with the harassing labours of the day,—who are fretted with the perpetual cunning of their fellow-creatures,—bend their course to Covent Garden, where Liston and the new chandelier are "smoothing the raven down of darkness till it smiles."—The humour of Liston is a kind of anti-attrition to the wheels of life. He pours an unfailing oil of gladness over the wounded heart, and helps to clear away the thorns and brambles from "this working day world." He is a public good!

November 2, 1817
Drury Lane Theatre.
From The Beggar's Opera. Miss Byrne.

The Beggar's Opera was one of the first plays we ever saw, and we still think it the best. Gay has laid bare all the vice, cunning, folly, and dissipation of rogues, pickpockets, and women of the town,—and, one would think, the subject would condemn it without hope of reprieve,— but he has thrown in such heaps of wit and sweet music,—has made his characters tell their own tale of villainy and craft so keenly, and with such a stinging sarcasm on the more polished of their kind, that our admiration will not let it decay or die. Gay was a poor fabulist,—but he was an admirable historian. He appeared to labour with difficulty in wringing an effect out of the political assemblies of brutes, or the intrigues of birds,—and to feel a trouble in screwing the stories of natural history up into a moral;—but he took the hawks, the bears, and the wolves of the human kind,—exposed them at their own desperate meetings, and fearful passions and pleasures,—and wrenched a moral out of all they thought, said, or did,—out of the very heart of crime. *The Beggar's Opera* shews us the world of low life in its full market-day. Business is going on swimmingly. It is high change with vice,—and pickpockets and highwaymen are conversing on the chances of their trade, and the value and failures of their merchandize, like other established dealers. Brandy, watches, snuff-boxes, handkerchiefs and women are the chief topics of their conversation, and the principal treasures and traffic of their meetings. But in all this, there is a fearful air of danger and distrust,—a kind of absence of daylight in all that is acted or plotted, which will not let our thoughts of ruin rest. The characters suspect each other,—and are bitter and sarcastic from the vigour of their suspicion. Their days seem days of uneasy sleep, or dangerous obscurity; their nights are nights of bitterness, plunder, or loud and desperate debauchery. There is a perfect *keeping* in the whole opera. The characters, the incidents, the dialogue, have all a *slang* about them,—a hurry, as if springing out of continual danger and dread,—a keenness of the lowest yet finest order. The very songs have a strange restlessness in them,— and break off shortly,—as though they were to be sung by those, who were hunted from place to place, and had not time to sing them out. They are a curious kind of poetry. They bear with them a lingering sweetness even in their most dissipated garb, like unfortunate girls that cannot lose, in spite of vice and tawdry, some marks of their early beauty. They seem to be a poetry that has seen better days: a poetry seduced! There is no opera in which music is so necessary, or in which it steals in with such sweetness and pathos:—and no opera can be perfect in which the music does not come to us as a relief or a support. We question however whether we could endure all the dark revelry, low intrigue, and fierce pursuits of the personages that fill this extraordinary opera—if there were not some creature of innocence and tender delight to soothe our imaginations, and soften off the severity and boldness of the characters and the dialogue, into the extreme tenderness of the poetry and the music:—but luckily there is one. In the very nest of infamy, amidst the abandoned of both sexes,—associating with curl-pated Hugh[107] (a fellow whom we see before us, by the help of his name, in all the impudence of cork-screw ringlets, frock coat, and quarterns of gin)—with Nimming Ned, Jemmy from town (what an idea does this name give us of Moulsey Hurst,[108] and cautious sparring!) and sundry other gentlemen of a like name and nature,—lives Polly:—"Oh pretty, pretty, Poll!"—She hath as sweet a nature as the tenderest lover in romance, and her delicacy is reflected in the dark glass of her associates, like a star in the still and midnight sea. She is indeed a rich jewel in an Ethiop's ear. Her love for Macheath is ardent, constant, disinterested;— it cannot be weakened even by his impudent sleights, or his *slang* attentions to a brazen vixen before her face. In her parents' upbraidings, she knows no change, in her husband's danger she cherishes no distrust, in his neglect, she feels no fear. She loves him,—and that love excuses all his faults and follies,—lifts her out of all the little hypocrisy and selfishness of the interested part of her sex,—concentrates all her feelings, thoughts, and anxieties in one object,—and preserves her, "*come agnelina*," even as a lamb amidst a herd of wolves,—"a young lamb's heart amid the full grown flock." *The Beggar's Opera* is like one of Rembrandt's pictures,—and Polly tips the universal darkness with a heavenly light.

December 14, 1817
Drury Lane Theatre.
Hamlet. Mr. D. Fisher.

What has *Hamlet* done, that he should be held up to mockery on an unfeeling stage, and all his inmost and most passionate sensations turned into pageants and the shews of grief?—What thoughts hath he ever embodied against human nature, that it should put all its bravery on to oppress him?—Where did he wander but in gentle labyrinths of the brain, weighed down with dreary meditation and a wasting sorrow,— that he should now be tortured into substance, and embittered with "superior toil and heavier weight of cares?"—Is not his person the most shadowy and graceful in our recollections?—Does not his voice tremble in our ears with the most exquisite and softened tenderness, like the breath of days gone by?—Are not his sayings become proverbs of the heart, and his thoughts the star-light of our minds?—Is not his nature the most gentle, the most generous, the most amiable—And can we ever forget him? He is for certain the most beautiful and melodious work of human nature, that ever was doomed to be jarred by the rude hands of Time and Fate. He is a prince, but then one that bears his faculties so meek, that Love follows his person, and Pity waits upon his discourse. He should inhabit only the noiseless palace of the mind, and have no attendants but the humblest and most revering thoughts. In him we see all that makes us attached to human nature,—all that melts our hearts to the purest and most disinterested sorrow. In him, ambition is baffled; life disrelished; joy subdued; love obscured; parental affection severed; hope for ever clouded,—and youth struck down. The morning of existence is in him dark as the night. The star of his life hath disappeared. He is alone in a desert world. *Hamlet* is indeed the balm of hurt minds. With him we find the melancholy society that harmonizes with a bruised spirit:—His pure and eloquent sorrow drops on our wounds like the honey dew of slumber. To a person who has been blighted in some splendid dream of youth, or cast back, by the disdainful and regardless hand of fate, from some precious purpose of his manhood,— the discourse of *Hamlet* is sweet and musical as the divine breath of Apollo. *Hamlet* stands at bay with his desperate circumstances. He acts or relapses from action, as meditative and desponding men would do in common life,—and not as though he were the mere idle coinage of the Poet's brain.[109] He becomes sceptical when he should be resolute, and distracted where he should be wary. When he ought to strike, he dallies with philosophy;—where he should rush forward, he lingers and becomes lost in the mazes of intellectual speculation. His feelings are refined through his mind, till they are robbed of all their strength. *Hamlet's* dilatoriness is fed by the questionings of a great spirit,—and thence also arise his inconsistencies. Thence is he ethical when he should be revengeful—thence is he lonely and indolent when he should be terrific. Passion with him is smothered by surmise,—"nothing is, but what is not." It has been said by a great authority in these matters, that "Romeo is Hamlet in love."[110] This, we think is not the case. Romeo is a voluptuous dreamer, that bares his heart to the summer airs of love, and pants for nothing else. He luxuriates in an indolent earthly heaven. *Hamlet* is a great and intellectual spirit that hath "fallen on evil days;"— and whose powers are chained in with stern thoughts. The soul of Romeo is dissolved in Juliet's eyes, like the pearl of Egypt in the luscious [wine?]:—and his heart is made drunk with ever flowing pleasure. He is driven to desperation, because he is torn from the fountain of his joy. Hamlet is borne down with excess of passion,—oppressed into inaction by the vastness of his mind. He is ever the same caviller and lonely one. Romeo is uncertain, and hath had his joyous hours. He is wholly a creature of the heart; Hamlet is one of the mind.—To explain the distinction, by naming objects in actual existence, and in our own time: —We might say there is the same difference between Mrs. Siddons and Miss O'Neill, as between Hamlet and Romeo.[111] The feelings of Romeo float him beyond the reach of his thoughts;—the thoughts of Hamlet annul his feelings.

There are a thousand passages in this divine tragedy, which mingle with the most familiar and deepest of our thoughts. The poetry is prophetic of feelings to come. We confess that we can cling to it, as to life, mingling it with our being, and with our dearest and finest pleasures. Why are we compelled to see it on the stage,—to hear it forced from lips which cannot relish it, and to behold it tricked up, in all the pride, pomp and circumstance of courtly grief? A black satin cloak, and a hat and feather, are not sufficient to make a man a Hamlet. In such garments, there must be a feeling heart,—a fine and graceful person,—a noble and original mind to remind us of the youthful, gentle, broken-hearted, Danish prince:—and even then, Hamlet would be wanting. The actors will think us very unreasonable creatures to expect so much, and approve so little: and on looking into our own thoughts, we really fear we must sit down quietly under their displeasure:—at least so far as Shakespeare is concerned.—As for Morton,[112] and the rest of those theatrical may-flies, that buz for an hour in the sunny light of the new chandelier,—we expect little and can afford to applaud more.

The critic of the Times[113] ("Oh cursed sprite, that ever we were born to set it right!") says that Mr. D. Fisher plays *Hamlet* in a better style than he acts *Richard* or *Macbeth*. We do not think so. Parts of his *Richard* were very fair and spirited:—but his *Hamlet* throughout is stiff, dreary and monotonous. His language never thaws:—it suits well with the coldness of the weather, and the fogginess of the house. His tongue now and then stiffens so deplorably, as to be quite lame of speech and halting in its emphasis. It gives a sort of old nobility of tone, very lofty and very empty. He makes too much of his person,—and sets his heart more upon his own leg, than his mind upon his father's murder. His black hose appear to be of greater consequence, than his uncle's black acts. And his feathers oppress him more than his thoughts. He wears a flaxen wig, or else he indulges in the luxuries of his own light hair, which is not of the true Hamlet colour. We ought not to be in doubt whether the person before us is *Hamlet* or the grave-digger. To tell the truth, we are disappointed in Mr. D. Fisher in the leading parts of tragedy:—He would play second parts to perfection, but then he wishes of course to be what is called first hand. Kean is coming back on Monday, and will set all these matters right. He is the man of might!

December 28, 1817
Drury Lane Theatre.
Richard Duke of York.[114]

The Committee of Drury Lane have thought proper to give the name of Richard to the last-born of their ancient house, without considering that they have a child still living that bears the same title: a confusion has very naturally arisen in the minds of those, who have been introduced to both, as to *which is which*—and we will venture to say that more than half of the spectators believe, in the innocence of their hearts, that there are not two Duke Richards, but one Duke Richard. "'Tis yet to know" with many, that this same Duke of York is the father of their old savage, crafty and courageous favourite, Richard the Third. The present ingenious compilation, or rather the essence of three of Shakspeare's historical dramas,[115]—only throws us back into the breaking of the stormy day of the Lancastrian strife. We have on the stage been used to the noon-tide of the struggle, and to its tempestuous night. It is the morning of the Plantagenets. The white rose is but just budding on the tree,—and we have known it only when it was wide dispersed, and flaunting in the busy air, or when it was struck and the leaves beat from the stem. Perhaps there is not a more interesting time in history, than this pelican strife,—for it has a locality which none of us can mistake, at the same time that it relishes of romance in its wildness and chivalrous encounters. We read, of royal deeds of valour and endurance, and of the personal conflicts between armed and youthful princes under waving and crested banners,—till we might almost think the most knightly days were come again;—but then we read of Tewkesbury and Gloucester,—and of cities and towns which lie all about us; and we find the most romantic occurrences realized in our minds. What might almost have been deemed an airy nothing,—acquires at once a local habitation and a name. The meeting with such places as the Temple Hall and Crosby House, flatly contradicts the half formed notion that "'Tis but our fantasies,"—and we readily "let belief take hold of us." We have no doubt but that Shakespeare intended to have written a complete dramatic history of England,—for from Richard the Second to Richard the Third the links are unbroken. The three parts of Henry the 6th fall in between the two Richards. They are written with infinite vigour, but their regularity tied the hand of Shakespeare. Particular facts kept him in the high road, and would not suffer him to turn down leafy and winding lanes, or to break wildly and at once into the breathing fields. The poetry is for the most part ironed and manacled with a chain of facts, and cannot get free:—it cannot escape from the prison house of history, nor often move without our being disturbed with the clanking of its fetters. The poetry of Shakespeare is generally free as is the wind;—a perfect thing of the elements:—winged and sweetly coloured. Poetry must be free! It is of the air, not of the earth,—and the higher it soars, the nearer it gets to its home. The Poetry of Romeo and Juliet, of Hamlet, of Macbeth, is the poetry of Shakespeare's soul,—full of love and divine romance;—It knows no stop in its delight, but "goeth where it listeth:"—remaining however in all men's hearts a perpetual and golden dream. The poetry of *Lear, Othello, Cymbeline,* &c. is the poetry of human passions and affections,—made almost etherial by the power of the Poet. Again, the poetry of *Richard, John,* and the *Henries,* is the blending of the imaginative with the historical:—it is poetry!—but oftentimes poetry wandering on the London road. We hate to say a word against a word of Shakespeare's,—and we can only do so by comparing himself with himself:—on going into the three parts of *Henry the Sixth,* for themselves;—we extract[116] all dispraise and accusation,—and declare them to be perfect works—Indeed they are such. We live again in the olden time. The Duke of York plucks the pale rose before our eyes. *Talbot* stands before us,—majestic,—huge,—appalling,—"in his habit as he lived." *Henry,* the weak, careless and good *Henry,* totters palpably under his

crown. The temple hall is in our sight. By way of making some repara-
tion for having put these plays last in our estimate,—and for the real
pleasure of contradicting the critical remarks which we in our petty
wisdom have urged,—and for the simple and intense delight we take
in copying, and feeding upon, noble passages in Shakespeare,—we will
here give one of the speeches of *Richard, Duke of York,* which is in itself rich enough to buy an immortality for any man.

> Oft have I seen a corse from whence the ghost
> Hath timely parted, meagre, pale, the blood
> Being all descended to the labouring heart;
> Who, in the conflict that it holds with death,
> Attracts the same for aidance 'gainst the enemy,
> Which with the heart there cools, and ne'er returneth
> To blush, and beautify the cheek again.
> But see—His face is black and full of blood:
> His eye-balls further out than when he lived;
> Staring full ghastly, like a strangled man:
> His hair uprear'd, his nostrils stretch'd with struggling,
> His hands abroad display'd, like one that grasp'd
> And tugg'd for life, and was by strength subdued.
> Look on the sheet—his hair, you see, is sticking,
> His well proportion'd beard made rough and rugged.
> Like to the summer corn by tempest lodged.
> —Oh thou soft natural death, that art joint twin
> To sweetest slumber! No rough bearded comet
> Glares on thy mild departure—the dull owl
> Beats not against thy casement—the hoarse wolf
> Scents not thy carrion. Pity winds thy corse,
> While horror waits on princes.[117]

We haste now to look at the manner in which this compilation has
been made,—for we feel that criticism has no right to purse its little
brow in the presence of Shakespeare. He has to our belief very few
imperfections,—and perhaps even these might vanish from our minds,
if *we* had the *perfection* properly to scan them. The play, as it is compressed, is most interesting, clear, and vigorous. It bears us from the
beginning to the middle of that tremendous struggle,—and very
properly stops at the death of the first of the *Richards. Richard, Duke of
York,* has all the quickness, resolution, and ability,—which would

naturally exist in a man, that was inwardly stirred to wrestle for the crown. He has not that rushing stream of thoughts and purposes, which characterized *Richard the Third*, his son, who was born in the cause;— of an aspiring father; and with all the excitement of a parent's and a brother's death, urging him on. The individuality of Shakespeare's characters is most strongly exemplified in the two *Richards*:—but in what is it not?—Perhaps the faults of the compilation are these; first, the characters are too hastily introduced and dispatched and their language clipped too closely. They are "curtailed of their fair pro- portions." *Jack Cade* and his rabble are put into straight-waistcoats, as a body might say,—and the armourer and his man are cut short in their dispute most abruptly and unsatisfactorily. We see nothing of *Talbot*,— and missing him, is like walking among the Elgin Marbles, and seeing an empty place where the Theseus had reclined. In the next place, the poetry is too much *modernized*. We speak of it, as we heard it. Again, the events are not harmonized well,—and Shakespeare felt that they could not be put together in less than fifteen acts,—"and we would take the ghost's word for a thousand pounds."[118] The present play appears to go on by fits and starts,—and to be made up too much of unmatch- able events. It is inlaid with facts of a different colour,—and we can see the cracks which the joiner's hand could not help leaving. After these little objections, all our observations on the compilation are full of praise. Great ingenuity is displayed,—and we should think Kean had a hand in it.[119] The author has extracted veins of gold from a huge mine,— and he is liberal enough to share it with other people. The workings of *Richard's* mind are brought out, as it were by the hand of the anatomist, —and all the useless parts are cut away and laid aside.—But with all, we fear that the public will not take the obligation as it is meant, and as it ought to be received. The English people do not care one fig about Shakespeare,—only as he flatters their pride and their prejudices:—we are not sure that this has not been remarked before, though we do not remember where, nevertheless, it is our firm opinion. But let us say a few words of the actors.—

Kean stands like a tower. He is "all power, passion, self-will." His insinuations flow from his lip "as musical, as is Apollo's lute." It is impossible to point out any peculiar and little felicities,—where the whole piece of acting is of no mingled web. If we were to single a favourite part, we should chuse that in which he parts with his son, *Young Rutland*, just before the battle. It was pathetic to oppression. Our hearts swelled with the feeling of tears, which is a deeper feeling, than the starting of them in the eye. His tongue lingered on the following passage, as fondly as his eyes clung to the object which occasioned them; and as tenderly as the heart dwells and doats on some long loved object.

> Bring in my dear boy Rutland.
> *(Enter Rutland with attendants.)*
> My darling! let me kiss thee ere I go—
> I know not if I ere shall see thee more,
> If I should fall, I leave thee to my brothers,
> All valiant men; and I will charge them all,
> On my last blessing, to take care of thee,
> As of their souls.[120]

His death was very great:—but Kean always "dies as erring man do die." The bodily functions wither up,—and the mental faculties hold out, till they crack. It is an extinguishment, not a decay. The hand is agonized with death; the lip trembles, with the last breath,—as we see the autumn leaf thrill in the cold wind of evening. The very eye-lid dies. The acting of Kean is Shakesperian;—he will fully understand what we mean. There is little to be said of the rest. Pope as a *Cardinal* (how aptly chosen) balances a red hat. Holland wears insipid white hair, and is even more insipid than the hair which he carries. Rae plays the adulterous *Suffolk*, and proves how likely he is to act amiss. Wallack, as *Young Clifford*, "towers above his sex." Mr. Maywood is more miserable in *Henry the Sixth*, than winter, or wet nights, or Death on a pale horse,[121] or want of money, or deceitful friends, or any other crying evil. The comic parts are sadly mangled, owing to illness of Munden and Oxberry. *Jack Cade* dies of a locked jaw;—and *Dick* the butcher is become a grave man. Mrs. Glover chews the blank verse past all endurance:—her Comedy is round and comfortable; her Tragedy is worse than death.

One thing we are convinced of, on looking over the three parts of *Henry*, from which this play is gleaned;—which is,—that Shakespeare was the only lonely and perfectly happy creature God ever formed. He never could have a mate,—being most unmatchable.

ESSAYS FROM *THE YELLOW DWARF*

Pulpit Oratory, No. I.[1] *February 7, 1818*

—Palmer, steer aright,
And keep an even course; for yonder way
We needs must pass (God do us well acquight!)
That is the gulf of greediness, they say,
That deep engorgeth all this worldë's prey.

Spenser.[2]

In the Speech which was delivered the other day to both Houses of Parliament, as coming immediately from the Throne, an increase of Churches was particularly recommended; and the reason for this proposed addition was alledged to be the increase of population.[3] This has a good colour, and looks well in the eyes of the devoted; but there is an under-feeling which the framers of this pious exhortation dared not trust the light with, which, however, it would have been more useful, as well as more honest, openly to have confessed. The fact is, we believe, that the Chapels of the Sectarists have so thickened in and around the metropolis, and the seceders from the established religion have consequently become so numerous, that the Dignitaries of the Church begin to tremble for the security of their followers, and start, as from a troubled sleep, to redeem the losses occasioned by a long and luxurious inactivity. The political religionists have joined hands with their fellow reapers, the religious politicians, and have raised a loud cry, like that of the Brobdingnag peasantry, before they enter the fields of the earth, to do a great work. The alledged reason for building the houses of worship is not the true one; nay, it is the very opposite to the true one. Instead of the increase of population being the thing that calls for a larger throng of Churches, it is wished that there should be an increase of Churches, in order to recall the departed, and restore the number of orthodox Christians. It is proposed to build high towers, from which the orthodox-keepers may shout and halloo the scared herd back within the national

211

pale of established Christianity. Are the Churches already erected filled to an overflow? Do the Chapels of Ease, names derived perhaps from the nature of their ministry, shake with the heavy press of episcopal worshippers? Is the call for more Churches loud among the laity?—No. The aisles, for the most part, of our Cathedrals, and of our Churches and Chapels, are but barely sprinkled with the remnants of a congregation, and do but echo with the indolent tread of a murmuring pew-opener, who has become insolent from inactivity, and proud from example. The galleries of most of the parochial Chapels are nearly as deserted as the gallery of the House of Commons in the Christmas holidays, or Westminster Hall in the long vacation. The people are silent, and satisfied with the number of their Churches: if they complain, it is against the carelessness, luxury, pride, and indolence of the Priests, and not of the want of proper places to kneel and breathe their hearts in. We are far from being among those who do not love the Established Church; we only hold ourselves against those who abuse it, under the cloak of petitioning for its safety. Do our State guardians remember that Caesar was destroyed by those very hands which were stretched in humility towards him, and at the very time they were so stretched. Let not religion be bound up with politics, like the fasces of the Romans, to be a rod for the subduing of the people. All the secessions from the established religion are attributable and traceable to the errors—to the despicable as well as deplorable inactivity and forlorn haughtiness of its appointed promoters and guardians. Their principles are gorged by their interests, and their religious humility lies fawning at the feet of their worldly pride. They bow their heads only toward the high places, and take in the good things of this world with the same enthusiastic earnestness that they talk of and laud the good things of the world to come. From the day of their ordination, in all their works and wanderings—in their thoughts, their hopes, and their aims—they keep the old huge holy home at Lambeth as the great and perfect end. They know that there, by the side of the river, for all sacrifices of conscience, for all dutiful concessions to the high and noble of their time, there is "a harbour and an ultimate repose."[4] There are, however, long before the reaching of this dignified bay,—which holds, in rich and eternal rest, the proud craft of the wearied Church,—sundry snug berth-places, creeks, and corners, which afford very cozey comforts and pleasant luxuries to those who do not go through with the grand voyage. All Bishops, Priests, and Deacons, are well off. Their temporal wealth, food, and delights, are taken as much care of as their eternal. They live in a pretty division between heaven and earth, and devote all the spare hours from the comforts of their bodies, to the good of their souls. They repose in indolent quiet under the dignified shade of branching pillars, as though they were divine shepherds; and they idly watch the Thirty-nine Articles, as though such were a flock of innocent sheep. Danger does not rouse them into action, but it makes them disturbed and vociferous. Pampered pride and indolence carry the day, all the world to nothing. There are the Priests who live richly in the great Episcopal Sees, stall-fed on the oiled cakes of the Cathedral, revelling in gorgeous food, and proudly sleeping and feeding a life away.[5] They look to themselves, and pray for their palates; and, as Gray well says, "leave us leisure to be good."[6] You might as well try to teach a tiger his Catechism, or make the wolf and the panther subscribe to the Thirty-nine Articles, as try to rouse them from their lethargy. There is the snug Doctor in Divinity, who raises his tythes and lowers his voice in proportion, Sunday after Sunday,—who puts his name and his guinea down on the books of the Religious Tract Society, and gives away the Bible which he has not time to explain,—who feeds at great tables, and talks sweet things over his tea,—who pays a tythe of his income to his Curate for preaching two sermons in a week, gabbling prayers oftener, christening children, churching women, catching colds at buryings, and speaking well of the Rector in all companies. Of what great religious good is such a Divine? Does he ameliorate our sorrows, soften our worldly difficulties, touch us with humility, or strengthen us with solid advice?—Are his feelings the dear blessings of our hearts, or his advice the day-dream of our existence?—Do we listen to him as to some serene and good shepherd, that plays divine music into our natures as we roam around him?—No, no; he calls us his flock, but he cares not if the wolf take us day by day, and by twos and threes, so that he be not disturbed after his dinner. He calls us his brethren; but meet him, ponderously pondering and pacing through the street, taking, with his well-fed wig and broad black skirts, "ample room and verge enough,"[7] and then call him brother, or expect him to call you or treat you as a brother, and see how he will act.[8] He lives, and has a living; and you must get on as you can, and pray when you please. Again, there is the sycophantic Curate, who has his way to make in the Church and in the world. He is comely, and of pleasant visage—excellent in his apparel and in his hair,—has eyes of youth,—bears himself like a worthy gentleman, "and smells all April and May."[9] He walks the street with a smile playing ever gently over his face, and with a rose in his well-shaped three-cornered hat, the flower of the Trinity. His words are smooth and sweet as the honey of Hybla to his superiors and patron, but they become edgy, sharp, and contracted, to inferiors destitute of expectancy. He laughs at the jests of monied men, and is profoundly humble before all elderly maiden ladies. On a limited stipend he contrives to be pompous among the weak, pleasant with the rich, gay with the gay. In the morning he is engaged in petty controversies at charity-school committees,—snarling and biting over his morsels of power,—playing the dog in a little obscure tragedy,—and doing his mischief in a quiet way. In the evening, he is tricked up in silken hose and looks, for the tea-table of some parish-patroness,—or sitting in his little study, and losing himself in a rapid dream of degrees, incumbents, livings, divine honours, church per-quisites, Bampton-lectures,[10] professorships, deaconries, deaneries, lawn sleeves, mitres, palaces. His imagination goes the round, till it reels in its own speculations, and becomes infuriated,—maddened,—lost,—in its strange, dizzy, and sacred intoxication. He goes to bed with an inebriated imagination, and rises in the morning to inspirit a jaded mind with little provocatives of petty power. There is yet one other character, "to end this strange eventful history,"[11] which we like less than all,—it is that of what is termed the *high Evangelical*. We know more than one of this kind. They are true Church-born Ministers, dipped in a bath of Metho-distic enthusiasm. They rave at all discontent, but that of their own creating. National troubles and oppressions are beat down and destroyed on the very cushions before them; but they furnish a very sufficient misery in the stead,—the misery of self-debasement and self-horror. They keep up an extempore cant, with a forced fervour, for hours together, and ring the changes upon belief, humility, and moral worth.[12] They make two of the cardinal virtues reel round without their associate, —pushing Faith and Hope to all lengths, and banishing Charity from her old society. They are devout adorers of the existing state of things, and of the powers that sway. With their arms do they labour in their calling and "sweet religion, make a rhapsody of words!"[13] Their endeavour is to be popular,—their glory, to be pointed out as the eloquent Mr. *This*, or the great Mr. *That*, who is so followed. Young men are bowed down with the weight of their language and the beauty of their reasoning,—and young girls are lost in the flowery mazes of their figures, and the dazzling and lustrous paths of their piety. Old women think them very sweet in private prayer. They make religion truckle to politics, and they study national politics for their own private good.

We confess that our catalogue of the Clergy is not very favourable, but, generally speaking, it is deplorably true. There be those that we have known preach, who having neither worldly mischief in their hearts, nor worldly dignity in their eyes, have gone on, from the cradle to the grave, in one sweet course of charity, wisdom, and unadulterated good. Advice flowed from their lips, like a stream of heavenly music, and floated into the heart, never thence to pass away. Their souls performed a daily pilgrimage to the God of the just, and returned rich with measureless content and joy. Their thoughts were born of the heart,—in the heart,—and ever preserved a "mildness virginall." Their days were clothed with a beautiful, calm, and just Christianity, which shed a deathless light over their own souls, and "took all hearts captive."[14] Free from envy, hatred, and malice,—full of love for the good, and pity and charity for the erring,—filled from the crown to the toe with the very gentleness of childhood, and an almost pastoral simplicity, they "kept the noiseless tenor of their way,"[15]—doing good, like the dews of the earth, by their own light, and with a perfect and gracious silence. We know at this moment of one[16] who is about to enter holy orders, with a heart pure for the truth, and a mind ardent and strong and just. If he has any failings, they are such as bind us closer to him. He is destitute of selfishness, loves his God, and feels for all mankind. His youth has been tried with heaped up sorrows,—afflictions have been rained upon his nature: yet he is still strong, for his mind was sinewy enough to endure the weight of misery, depression, and falsehood, which fate, in its spite of superior mortality, piled upon it. He is still young; but ere his days are told, we look to see his name placed with the best, and of a kin with the noblest.

We wish from our heart of hearts that the Clergy had no stains upon their cloth,—that they were as worthy of the cause as it merits, or we could wish them to be. The desire of letting the world a little into the secret of this class of beings, has led us to resolve upon giving some account of the most popular individuals of the Established Faith. As Government have thought proper to advise the growth of Churches, let us see whether the Ministers "grow with their growth, and strengthen with their strength."[17] The Prince Regent has taken the great stone edifices under his especial care,—we, as part of the people, will not be found wanting with those who are to fill them with religion. If Churches are to be erected, it will not be amiss to ascertain who are the worthiest, and the wisest, to be promoted to them: and we pledge ourselves to be impartial, strict, honest in our opinions. We are not likely to be led aside by an overweening love towards Mr. Wilberforce,[18] or a politic passion for the gracious Mr. Vansittart,[19] or a lawful tenderness towards Mr. Butterworth,[20] or a respectful love for my Lord Sidmouth,[21] to turn aside from saying what we really think of the talents of our popular Preachers. We have no party ends to answer, and may therefore be trusted. What we think, we shall speak right out, and rest our claims to attention on the truth of our motives and opinions.

The length to which this article has extended, prevents us making any observations on the talents of the popular Preacher in the Bedford-row Chapel; but we intend to select him for the subject of our next week's Paper.

Caius.

Pulpit Oratory, No. II. February 14, 1818

He is the happy man, whose life e'en now
Shows somewhat of that happier life to come;
Who, doom'd to an obscure but tranquil state,
Is pleas'd with it, and, were he free to choose,
Would make his fate his choice; whom peace, the fruit
Of virtue, and whom virtue, fruit of faith,
Prepare for happiness; bespeaks him one
Content indeed to sojourn while he must
Below the skies, but having there his home.

Cowper.[22]

FROM *THE YELLOW DWARF*

The Rev. Daniel Wilson, A. M.[23]

The Chapel, according to St. John, in Bedford-row, is crowded on mornings and evenings by all descriptions of persons, from the lady who sits up to her eyes in rouge and religion, and on a softened seat,— to the poor half-starved devout mechanic, whose cheek has become lank from an excess of faith and a want of food, and who is compelled to stand during the service at a pew door,—looking yearningly to the Preacher, and, "with a greedy ear, devouring up his discourse."[24] Those who are becoming more ardent in their religious feelings than the Church warrants, and who still want the resolution, perhaps from worldly and political motives, to absolve themselves from its orderly services and limited earnestness, find in this goodly building a Priest to their heart's content. Mr. Wilson is a popular man. The devouter adherents to the Established Church approve him, because he has passed through a Bishop's hands fairly, preaches in a Chapel of Ease, and rallies his language and the Scriptures in favour of Kings and Ministerial Powers, and the beauty and serene perfection of our national peace. The Methodists think well of him, because he draws ghastly pictures over the pages of Scripture,—riots in the jargon of true repentance,—appeals to the passions, the weaknesses, the miseries of mankind,—and trusts to the moment for words to clothe his mechanical enthusiasm in.[25] Mr. Wilson ascends his pulpit, sure of his congregation: he knows that whatever he shall say, will be received by his audience as fine eloquent truths from a dear and virtuous man. He reads his prayers before his sermon in a soft yet confident voice, as though he knew he were speaking before a listening and loving congregation, and had wholly forgot that he were standing before his God. He has evidently an eye to the silent applause of his auditors, for he starts in the most gathered up and guarded manner possible,—never elevating his voice or his hand till time has gained a certain ground. His enthusiasm is hard and appalling, with more of rudeness in it than fervour. He lodges an assertion in the mind, like a bullet, and pauses to observe its overpowering effect. When he becomes vehement, he calls his hands into action, and labours as though he would convince the cushion as well as the congregation; and his features have all the expression of mental superiority, and the confidence of unbounded victory. It has been said by a great moralist, that there is no art to find the mind's construction in the look,—but had he seen the face of this earnest Minister, he would perhaps have blotted out the line. The features of Mr. Wilson are sharp, prominent, and particular: they seem formed to cut their way through all impediments up into a Bishopric. His voice is weak in its upper tones, but full and effective in its lower ones,—which perhaps answers his purpose better than if it were perfect throughout. In his appeals of tenderness,—in his allusions to youth and childhood,—in his reminiscences of beauty and sweetness, a maudlin whine creeps over his tones, as though his voice were nigh fainting with its own gentleness and pity. It dies away divinely, in a sort of holy aromatic pain. Mr. Wilson has a great command of words, and therefore preaches extempore; that is, he gives the grain and chaff together, and so avoids the trouble of previous preparation. Extempore preaching is a bad thing, in the pulpit as well as in Parliament. It should be remembered, that a Congregation is listening for advice, explanation, and truth; and how can a Minister say that he will talk to the purpose for an hour together? To be sure, he has a few notes before him, to keep him to the bare subject,—he speaks by the card, or equivocation would undo him. But if he must make notes, why cannot he write a pithy, earnest, and sensible sermon, at once, and not trust to the first things that come uppermost at the hour of trial? Thus, he would be commanding, and not diffuse,—he would be eloquent, and not incoherent. Mr. Wilson keeps his hearers about him for an hour and more, by dint of starts, assertion, pause, and repetition,—and he might give the essence of his discourse in a few minutes. Goldsmith's description of Burke in his *Retaliation*,[26] might be transferred with great truth to this popular Divine.—We have spoken thus far of Mr. Wilson's manner and physical peculiarities; we shall proceed to say a few words on things of a more serious consequence,—"we mean the matter that he reads, my Lord."[27] If he told grand and awful truths, and appealed independently to the hearts of men, without bowing to worldly motives and political views, we should not care if his voice were harsh as that of the bittern in the marsh, and his features sharp as those of a shark. Personal imperfections fade like the mists of the morning before intellectual honesty and moral hardihood. Mr. Wilson, in one of his sermons on *True Repentance*, paints the following picture:—

Go, penitent, to the garden of Gethsemane and the hill of Calvary, and see if any sorrow was like that of the dying Saviour. View the surrounding multitude. Mark how they mock the Holy Sufferer. Observe the blessed Jesus, as he is suspended on the accursed tree. Place yourself under the cross with the weeping Mary. The sun is darkened. The rocks are rent,—the graves are opened,—the bodies of the saints arise,—the veil of the Temple is rent in twain. The Son of God expires. At this moment the soldier draws near. The Saviour is dead already. Still he transpierces him, with wanton indignity, with his spear. *Look, and look again, at the dreadful scene.*

This is nothing less than an appeal to the terrors of mankind, in order to subdue it to a sacred servility. This is a cold sententious display of horrors, to startle the heart into a strange and miserable repentance. Religion should be dressed in smiles, not frowns;—it should raise and bless the soul, not depress and confound it. We meet with a passage, sequent to the one we have quoted, which carries this terrifying principle to a greater extent:—

But this is not all. You and I, my brethren, have a share in this death. *It was not so much the soldier that pierced Christ, as our sins.* This is the true cause of our Saviour's death.

Mr. Wilson well knows, that if his hearers can be brought to listen to language like this, they will infallibly bow down to the truth and weight of it. They will thenceforth abandon themselves to comfortless lamentation, and crowd about the author of their religious trouble, as though they felt safe only in his presence. He will halloo them together, and drive them on through the darkness, like a bewildered flock. A poet, a painter, and a priest, show their ingenuity when they severally aim at giving the wretchedness of humanity in their works,—for the English people will go any lengths to be made gloriously miserable. They adore trouble, whether of a poetic or a religious kind,—though they prefer the latter, because it is more genuine. It is this same malicious enjoyment of the uncomfortable, that keeps a bad Minister in his place, whether in the Church or in the Government. Again,—they like to have their passions appealed to, and detest and shrink from all attacks upon their reason. It is this innate love of ignorance that has made faith so powerful in the world,—so great an ingredient in all religious things. We witnessed a curious instance of this enjoyment, at hearing of the ignorance of their fellow creatures, in a set of people assembled at a lecture the other evening. The Lecturer read the following lines, among others of Cowper's:—

> Just knows, and knows no more, her Bible true,
> A truth the brilliant Frenchman never knew.[28]

And his audience instantaneously burst into a joyous applause at the Frenchman's ignorance.[29]

Mr. Wilson has thoroughly caught the knack of introducing the perfections of our Government into his holy discourses;—"Fear God, and honour the King,"[30] is his motto. If he speaks of religion, he musters up an army of terrors,—but when he comes upon the subject of State governance, "he roars you as gently as a sucking dove,"[31]—talks of national blessings, freedom, and the rewards of merit,—sinks all troubles and embarrassments in a well of honours and emoluments,— and raves vehemently for popular contentment. The following passage from a discourse delivered by Mr. Wilson, and headed with a text from Timothy,—"Godliness with contentment, is *great gain*,"[32] will let our readers into his style of thinking and speaking, more speedily than we could by any description of ours:—

And in these respects, what country can be compared to our own? Where are the laborious classes, which are always the most numerous in every community, placed on so good a footing and so much protected as here? Where are the highest honours and emoluments so easily open to real talent and modest merit as here? Where is the poor man's property guarded with so much care, and his legal rights and freedom defended with such jealousy, as here? Where are all the legitimate ends of government so largely and prominently attained as here? Now, to forget all these and a thousand other blessings,—and, in a season of public calamity, when a wet harvest has increased the embarrassments arising from a bad trade, to come forward and calumniate the Government under which we live, and to hold [sic] a language that would go to overturn all law and authority, is just the same as for a man to destroy his plough and fire his barns, because he thinks he has discovered some trivial defects in them, or because an unfavourable season has shortened his gains.

This attempt at taking the *onus* from the right shoulders and putting it upon those of nature, is in the true cant of religious policy. Here we find the voice of the Court echoing in the pulpit, and sounding up the aisle of a place for the worship of God.—We have taken the lines from

Cowper, at the head of this article, because they do not apply;—Mr. Wilson will not be hurt by the reading of them. In a worldly way, he is going the King's high-road,—and, we have no doubt, will come in for the blessings of earth in his future days,—which he may call, if he pleases, the rewards of the life to come.

Caius.

Pulpit Oratory, No. III. February 28, 1818

Who clothes you with, piety, meekness, humility, charity, patience, and all the Christian virtues? Who feeds your souls with the milk of brotherly love, and diets them with all the dainty food of holiness, which at once cleanses them of all impure carnal affections, and fattens them with the truly rich Spirit of Grace. Who does this?—"Aye, who indeed?" cries the Host.—

Fielding.[33]

The Rev. Henry G. White, M. A.[34]
One of the Preachers at the Asylum.

Mr. Abraham Adams was surely the most amiable Parson that ever existed. His simplicity clothes him even as with a garment. At fifty years of age, the Bishop had rewarded all his virtue and excellent qualities with a handsome income of twenty-three pounds a year;[35] "which, however, he could not make any great figure with, because he lived in a dear country, and was a little encumbered with a wife and six children."[36] He had no idea of anything beyond religion, content, and his pocket Aeschylus. We wish it had been our good fortune to have lived in the same parish with him, to have enjoyed the unaffected piety and worth of his conversation, and to have met him walking about the fields in that valuable cassock, which it was his misfortune to tear in getting over a style ten years before. We have no such Clergymen among us now-a-days, and none to remind us in the least of that amiable creature, to whom Fielding has given us so perfect an introduction. He was content to be a Curate, which no one now is. He never dropped a murmur from his lips, though he had four sermons to preach on a Sunday,—for he was doing his duty. Mr. White, the Gentleman of whom we are about to say a few words, is, as far as we can trace anything of him, the very reverse of Parson Adams. In the pulpit, he has an intolerable share of vanity,—and his voice, like the peacock, seems to swell in the contemplation of its own grace and beauty. He preaches at one or two churches and chapels in the course of the day,—but then he meets a new congregation at each,—receiving good store of money from each, and most probably makes the same sermon serve over and over again. Parson Adams looked upon all the Clergy as his brothers, but Mr. White seems to know the difference and degrees of men. Mr. White has just succeeded in pushing himself, or in getting others to push him, into a good deal of notice. He wrote little pompous prefaces to Phillips's two-penny Speeches, and printed a long answer to a review of one of his Sermons in the *Gentleman's Magazine*.[37] A copy of his face has been stuck in Brother Asperne's Magazine,[38] and the original has been used as a Sunday ornament at the Chapel of the Asylum. Parson Adams once offered, in the simplicity of that heart, to read a couple of sermons to a bookseller as a sample, the consequence of which was, that the trader declined the offer of the sermons and the delivery together. Mr. White goes to the market better: he cultivates a good name in the hearts of the ladies, and opens a subscription at a reduced price. He goes to Mr. Asperne at the entreaties of his weeping congregation, and silently gives up the MS. to the best advantage. If he were to endeavour to read it to the worthy trader, it would put Freemasonry to the pinch. Mr. White is nearly as popular a man as Mr. Wilson,—only he is by no means so tedious, and nothing near so incoherent: the reason of this is, that Mr. White writes his sermon, and Mr. Wilson manufactures his discourses as he goes on. If the latter Minister sufficiently melts the hearts of his followers, and makes damp pews in the chapel at Bedford-row, the former Divine is altogether as touching in Great Tower-street, and once a week sows St. George's-fields with orient pearl. Mr. White is a subtle weaver of sermons. He spins, like the spider, an endless web of sophistries from the tender inwards of his head,—from the intestines of his higher house,—and hangs them, all glittering with dazzling phrases, over the walls of the Asylum Chapel, to delight enraptured eyes on Sunday evenings. His style of speaking is nearly theatrical, and quite the reverse of the unaffected. We are sick to death of the display of a white handkerchief, and a white hand, and a white forehead, so repeatedly and ridiculously made by the popular Preachers. We know not whether very many of our readers have seen the copy of Mr. White's countenance, which the *European Magazine* of the last year contains,—we will dare say that many have not. The features are broad, hard, and not intellectual; —the eyes are heavy,—and the form of the head such as to portend great thickness of thought.[39] His smile in the pulpit is extremely sickening. Mr. White seems to us a man who guides himself by circumstances (as most ingenious clergymen* do), and we therefore find him at present a sweet and dutiful Divine, delivering most profiting discourses. We have no reason to suppose that he would not veer round, if he saw good cause for so doing. This oily state of mind is not quite so good as the settled solid principle which keeps its station. Parson Adams, if he had been thrust upon a mass of ice, and floated about the Polar Sea in a cold solitude, would have pulled out a sermon, "which he always carried about with him for fear of accidents," and have read page after page on the good of a temperate life. Mr. White would have taken out his hand-kerchief, or set about affecting a congregation of white bears. The mind of the late excellent Bishop of Llandaff[41] was a singular example of that intrepid firmness, which carried him steadily through all temptation. If he could have relaxed, he would have slept in Lambeth pride;[42] but though he had ambition, he had not poverty of mind to feed it. In men's despite, he was a Bishop. Freedom kept perpetual and golden holiday in his heart. He had an *extempore* mind in the Sciences, which is next to miraculous. Mr. White is, apparently, by no means so rigid; and if he wishes to ascend the steps of temples made by hands, he is likely to succeed by making himself easy. In a sermon, called "The Day of Tears," preached on the death of the late unfortunate Princess,[43] Mr. White called forth all his sweetest words, and fine-pointed his sentences, till they almost fainted away. He was, as the occasion required, very loyal, very flowery, and very admonishing. We have heard, that the congregation followed him into the vestry, and begged him to publish. "He was no orator, as Wilson was,—but as they saw him, a plain, blunt man."[44] What could he do? He printed.[45] From this sermon we extract the

* There was a curious specimen of this ministerial devotion in a creeping Curate, in the *Times* of Wednesday last. Mr. Mitchell, of Twickenham, we believe, advertized that he was not the person mentioned in the list of those who had given alms as enemies of Arbitrary Imprisonment. There was no such stuff in his thoughts. He disclaimed all such dangerous charity and opinions.[40]

following passage, which shews, as Mr. White says, that national sin produces national suffering:—

Ah! the alarming question! Truly, my brethren, it is a painful search for the preacher to make, when he feels it his duty to probe the wound under which his country writhes in wailing and grief; but it were the most faithless compromise of my duty, were I to attempt to bind up the wound without first examining its depth; and to pour in the oil of consolation, without previously pointing out to you the only means by which it can be radically healed, and recovery completed. The wound is sin, the remedy must be repentance and amendment. We are struck down to the ground; our glory is laid low; and the chastisements of an offended God lie heavily upon us. O it is a heartrending thought, that a Princess so eminently gifted to grace and govern our country, may have been taken from us, as a punishment of our unyielding ingratitude to Heaven, and of our perverse violations of the righteous laws of Heaven's Almighty King! And what punishment could have been inflicted that could pierce more deeply the very vitals of that country's peace and hope?—She has taken possession of the eternal inheritance which her Saviour's righteousness has secured to her. To us remain weeping, *and mourning, and shame, and confusion of face.*

Government, like the bookseller in *Joseph Andrews*, objects to all divinity that will not sell. It is not orthodox, unless it is supple. We should think the passage we have just quoted, must be balm to the hearts of ruling political men. Mr. White will have one of the new Churches, or it will go hard. If he does not feel an airy mitre already gall his brow, in divine dreams, we are bad guessers. We have said a good deal about Parson Adams in this article, of whom we will venture to say all our readers have heard, and whom more than half absolutely love. Objections may be urged against us, for thus introducing an ideal character (and the Clergy are making him more and more ideal every day), but we do it with the best motives: and Mr. White would secure to himself a more eternal wealth, if he were to make it his study to give an identity to a character so pure, so innocent, so amiable, so good. It is one that vaunteth not itself,—is not puffed up. In it, righteousness and truth have met together; gentleness and peace have kissed each other.

Caius.

REVIEW FROM *THE ALFRED*

The Quarterly Review—Mr. Keats.[1] *October 6, 1818*

We have met with a singular instance, in the last number of the Quarterly Review, of that unfeeling arrogance, and cold ignorance, which so strangely marked the minds and hearts of Government sychophants and Government writers. The Poem of a young man of genius, which evinces more natural power than any other work of this day, is abused and cried down, in terms which would disgrace any other pens than those used in the defence of an Oliver or a Castles.[2] We have read the Poetic Romance of Endymion (the book in question) with no little delight; and could hardly believe that it was written by so young a man as the preface infers.[3] Mr. Keats, the author of it, is a genius of the highest order; and no one but a Lottery Commissioner and Government Pensioner (both of which Mr. William Gifford, the Editor of the Quarterly Review, is) could, with a false and remorseless pen, have striven to frustrate hopes and aims, so youthful and so high as this young Poet nurses. The Monthly Reviewers, it will be remembered, endeavoured, some few years back, to crush the rising heart of young Kirk White;[4] and indeed they in part generated that melancholy which ultimately destroyed him; but the world saw the cruelty, and, with one voice, hailed the genius which malignity would have repressed, and lifted it to fame. Reviewers are creatures "that stab men in the dark:"—young and enthusiastic spirits are their dearest prey. Our readers will not easily forget the brutality with which the Quarterly Reviewers, in a late number of their ministerial book, commented on the work of an intelligent and patriotic woman, whose ardour and independence happened to be high enough to make them her enemies.[5] The language used by these Government critics, was lower than man would dare to utter to female ears;[6] but Party knows no distinctions,—no proprieties, —and a woman is the best prey for its malignity, because it is the gentlest and the most undefended. We certainly think that Criticism might vent its petty passions on other subjects; that it might chuse its objects from the vain, the dangerous, and the powerful, and not from the young and the unprotected.

> It should strike hearts of age and care,
> And spare the youthful and the fair.

The cause of the unmerciful condemnation which has been passed on Mr. Keats, is pretty apparent to all who have watched the intrigues of literature, and the wily and unsparing contrivances of political parties. This young and powerful writer was noticed, some little time back, in the Examiner;[7] and pointed out, by its Editor, as one who was likely to revive the early vigour of English poetry. Such a prediction was a fine, but dangerous compliment, to Mr. Keats: it exposed him instantly to the malice of the Quarterly Review. Certain it is, that hundreds of fashionable and flippant readers, will henceforth set down this young Poet as a pitiable and nonsensical writer, merely on the assertions of some single heartless critic, who has just energy enough to despise what is good, because it would militate against his pleasantry, if he were to praise it.

The genius of Mr. Keats is peculiarly classical; and, with the exception of a few faults, which are the natural followers of youth, his imaginations and his language have a spirit and an intensity which we should in vain look for in half the popular poets of the day. Lord Byron is a splendid and noble egotist.—He visits Classical shores; roams over romantic lands, and wanders through magnificent forests; courses the dark and restless waves of the sea, and rocks his spirit on the midnight lakes; but no spot is conveyed to our minds, that is not peopled by the gloomy and ghastly feelings of one proud and solitary man. It is as if he and the world were the only two things which the air clothed.—His lines are majestic vanities;—his poetry always is marked with a haughty selfishness;—he writes loftily, because he is the spirit of an ancient family;—he is liked by most of his readers, because he is a Lord. If a common man were to dare to be as moody, as contemptuous, and as misanthropical, the world would laugh at him. There must be a coronet marked on all his little pieces of poetical insolence, or the world would not countenance them. Mr. Keats has none of this egotism[8]—this daring selfishness, which is a stain on the robe of poesy—His feelings are full, earnest, and original, as those of the olden writers were and are; they are made for all time, not for the drawing-room and the moment. Mr. Keats always speaks of, and describes nature, with an awe and a humility, but with a deep and almost breathless affection.—He knows that Nature is better and older than he is, and he does not put himself on an equality with her. You do not see him, when you see her. The moon, and the mountainous foliage of the woods, and the azure sky, and the ruined and magic temple; the rock, the desert, and the sea; the leaf of the forest, and the embossed foam of the most living ocean, are the spirits of his poetry; but he does not bring them in his own hand, or obtrude his person before you, when you are looking at them. Poetry is a thing of generalities—a wanderer amid persons and things—not a pauser over one thing, or with one person. The mind of Mr. Keats, like the minds of our older poets, goes round the universe in its speculations and its dreams. It does not set itself a task. The manners of the world, the fictions and the wonders of other worlds, are its subjects; not the pleasures of hope,[9] or the pleasures of memory.[10] The true poet confines his imagination to no one thing—his soul is an invisible ode to the passions—He does not make a home for his mind in one land—its productions are an universal story, not an eastern tale. The fancies of Moore are exquisitely beautiful, as fancies, but they are always of one colour;—his feelings are pathetic, but they are "still harping on my daughter." The true pathetic is to be found in the reflections on things, not in the moods and miseries of one person. There is not one poet of the present day, that enjoys any popularity that will live; each writes for his booksellers and the ladies of fashion, and not for the voice of centuries. Time is a lover of old books, and he suffers few new ones to become old. Posterity is a difficult mark to hit, and few minds can send the arrow full home. Wordsworth might have safely cleared the rapids in the stream of time, but he lost himself by looking at his own image in the waters. Coleridge stands bewildered in the cross-road of fame;—his genius will commit suicide, and be buried in it. Southey is Poet Laureate, "so there is no heed to be taken of him." Campbell has relied on two stools, "The Pleasures of Hope," and "Gertrude of Wyoming," but he will come to the ground, after the fashion of the old proverb. The journey of fame is an endless one; and does Mr. Rogers think that pumps and silk stockings (which his genius wears) will last him the whole way? Poetry is the coyest creature that ever was wooed by man: she has something of the coquette in her; for she flirts with many, and seldom loves one.

Mr. Keats has certainly not perfected anything yet; but he has the power, we think, within him, and it is in consequence of such an opinion that we have written these few hasty observations. If he should ever see this, he will not regret to find that all the country is not made up of Quarterly Reviewers. All that we wish is, that our Readers could read the Poem, as we have done, before they assent to its condemnation— they will find passages of singular feeling, force, and pathos. We have the highest hopes of this young Poet. We are obscure men, it is true, and not gifted with that perilous power of mind, and truth of judgment which are possessed by Mr. Croker,[11] Mr. Canning, Mr. Barrow, or Mr. Gifford, (all "honourable men," and writers in the Quarterly Review). We live far from the world of letters,—out of the pale of fashionable criticism,—aloof from the atmosphere of a Court; but we are sur- rounded by a beautiful country, and love Poetry, which we read out of doors, as well as in. We think we see glimpses of a high mind in this young man, and surely the feeling is better that urges us to nourish its strength, than that which prompts the Quarterly Reviewer to crush it in its youth, and for ever. If however, the mind of Mr. Keats be of the quality we think it to be of, it will not be cast down by this wanton and empty attack. Malice is a thing of the scorpion kind—It drives the sting into its own heart. The very passages which the Quarterly Review quotes as ridiculous, have in them the beauty that sent us to the Poem itself.[12] We shall close these observations with a few extracts from the romance itself:—If our Readers do not see the spirit and beauty in them to justify our remarks, we confess ourselves bad judges, and never more worthy to be trusted.

The following address to Sleep, is full of repose and feeling:—

> O magic sleep! Oh comfortable bird,
> That broodest o'er the troubled sea of the mind,
> Till it is hush'd and smooth! O unconfined
> Restraint! Imprisoned Liberty! Great key
> To golden palaces, strange minstrelsy,
> Fountains grotesque, new trees, bespangled caves,
> Echoing grottoes, full of tumbling waves,
> And moonlight![13]

This is beautiful—but there is something finer,

—That men, who might have tower'd in the van
Of all the congregated world to fan
And winnow from the coming step of time,
All chaff of custom, wipe away all slime
Left by men slugs and human serpentry;
Have been content to let occasion die,
Whilst they did sleep in Love's Elysium.
And truly I would rather be struck dumb,
Than speak again this ardent listlessness:
For I have ever thought that it might bless
The world with benefits unknowingly;
As does the nightingale up-perched high,
And cloister'd among cool and bunched leaves,
She sings but to her love, nor e'er conceives
How tiptoe night holds back her dark grey hood.[14]

The turn of this is truly Shakesperian, which Mr. Keats will feel to be the highest compliment we can pay him, if we know any thing of his mind. We cannot refrain from giving the following short passage, which appears to us scarcely to be surpassed in the whole range of English Poetry. It has all the naked and solitary vigour of old sculpture, with all the energy and life of Old Poetry:—

—At this, with madden'd stare,
And lifted hands, and trembling lips he stood,
Like old Deucalion mounted o'er the flood,
Or blind Orion hungry for the morn.[15]

Again, we give some exquisitely classical lines, clear and reposing as a Grecian sky—soft and lovely as the waves of Ilyssus.

—Here is wine,
Alive with sparkles—Never I aver,
Since Ariadne was a vintager,
So cool a purple; taste these juicy pears,
Sent me by sad Vertumnus, when his fears
Were high about Pomona: here is cream,
Deepening to richness from a snowy gleam;
Sweeter than that nurse Amalthea skimm'd
For the boy Jupiter.[16]

This is the very fruit of poetry.—A melting repast for the imagination. We can only give one more extract—our limits are reached. Mr. Keats is speaking of the story of Endymion itself. Nothing can be more imaginative than what follows:—

> —Ye who have yearn'd
> With too much passion, will here stay and pity,
> For the mere sake of truth; as 'tis a ditty
> Not of these days, but long ago 'twas told
> By a cavern'd wind unto a forest old;
> And then the forest told it in a dream
> To a sleeping lake, whose cool and level gleam
> A Poet caught as he was journeying
> To Phoebus' shrine and in it he did fling
> His weary limbs, bathing an hour's space,
> And after, straight in that inspired place
> He sang the story up into the air,
> Giving it universal freedom.[17]

We have no more room for extracts. Does the author of such poetry as this deserve to be made the sport of so servile a dolt as a Quarterly Reviewer?—No. Two things have struck us on the perusal of this singular poem. The first is, that Mr. Keats excels, in what Milton excelled—the power of putting a spirit of life and novelty into the Heathen Mythology. The second is, that in the structure of his verse, and the sinewy quality of his thoughts, Mr. Keats greatly resembles old Chapman, the nervous translator of Homer. His mind has "thews and limbs like to its ancestors." Mr. Gifford, who knows something of the old dramatists, ought to have paused before he sanctioned the abuse of a spirit kindred with them. If he could not feel, he ought to know better.

ESSAYS AND REVIEWS FROM

THE SCOTS MAGAZINE

Mr Hazlitt's Lectures on the Comic Genius of England,[1]
December 1818
Lecture First.—On Wit and Humour.
*Lecture Second.—On the Comic Characters of Shakespeare
and Ben Jonson.*

Mr Hazlitt is, we believe, pretty generally allowed to be one of the
most vigorous and spirited writers of the present age. His style is, for
the most part, stern and decisive,—which may, perhaps, have arisen
from the critical turn which all, or nearly all, his works have taken;
but it has, at times, breaks of lightness and gaiety, and occasional
passages of tenderness and delicate feeling, which are made doubly
beautiful from their contrast with what is abrupt and determined around
them. His language now and then starts away from its rigid and laborious
solidity, and passes at once with the utmost ease and pleasantry into a
free, airy, and beautiful enthusiasm, which has immediate control over
all hearts, even as with a spell, and which leaves a feeling of music on
the mind, of the most exquisite and internal kind. If any thing, perhaps
Mr Hazlitt's prose occasionally approaches too closely to the limits of
poetry. There is too much of passion,—too much of deep, internal
sentiment,—too much of the ethereal spirit of romance, to admit of
Mr Hazlitt's prose holding on in an even and regular course. We state
this objection, however, merely as critics:—if we could assert our own
private feelings on the subject, we should abandon ourselves to the
lawless beauty which we have just opposed. None of our readers, we
take it for granted, can be unacquainted with Mr Hazlitt's work on the
characters of Shakespeare's Plays; which, for a keen, intense feeling of
beauty,—and a felicity and spirit of expression, has seldom been
equalled. It has been the lot of Shakespeare, more than any other
author, to have suffered from the "damn'd good nature of friends."

Commentators on commentators have piled their cumbrous loads of dull remark and heavy conjecture on his immortal plays to a most colossal height; and nothing but the buoyancy and excessive life of the poetry could bear it up against such leaden and pitiful oppressions. It is really a matter of some marvel, that the name even of Shakespeare has not become obscured from the pains with which feeble and foolish hands have scribbled their nothings over it. His productions have suffered, as the painter's picture did when exposed publicly for amendment; every idle observer has swelled into a critic, and suggested an improvement. The original is hardly discernible for the annotations. Mr Hazlitt is not a commentator: he is too much a man of genius to be such. He writes enthusiastically and forcibly,—the only way in which a critic on Shakespeare ought to write; and he trusts to his feelings for a just language, and does not turn to his ingenuity for sagacious and original conceits, or conjectural improvements. He shews us what he loves in those deathless plays,—and all that is worthy of our love; and we are spared the petty suggestions of verbal corrections, and the precious betrayals of anachronisms and errors in natural history. Mr Hazlitt, very wisely we think, has sunk the critic in the eulogist,—and has been delighted to expatiate on what is beautiful, instead of seeking to expose trifles in which Shakespeare hath erred. Of the Lectures on the English Poets, which were delivered last winter at the Surrey Institution, we think very highly: they are written with admirable spirit and ability, and abound in passages of singular feeling and sweetness of expression. Mr Hazlitt is more at home with the old poets than with those of a later date; and with them his enthusiasm is of a higher spirit, and his style is of a more free and undaunted nature. He speaks of Chaucer, and Shakespeare, and Milton, and Spenser, and Dante, as though they were of old fellowship. Even his remarks on Collins, and Gray, and Burns, are more unconstrained than those which follow upon the modern living poets. The dead have become blended with, and spiritualized in, their poetry;—and they are no longer mortal men. They have passed into fame, and we can only hear their names echoing about the air-clad world, day after day, and for ever. The living poets are *men*, and we see them sitting well-dressed at the theatre, or encounter them in the Park, or at a panorama, or we jostle with them in Fleet Street, and the Strand. We meet them at dinners, and see them eat good things, and hear them utter bad ones with an equal alacrity. Their appearance, and converse, and occupation, are continually at variance with their fanciful or misanthropical poetry; and we cannot judge them as the spirits of the mind, because we see them eternally as *men* of a good bodily substance. If Mr Hazlitt had written as cleverly of the modern writers as of the olden ones,—who are become, and must ever remain to us, "a faith and a religion," we should have thought his Lectures heartless, poor, and mechanical, and should have put no faith in his opinions. He has, however, fallen off where he ought to fall off; and we have therefore a right to trust to his voice when it is loud in praise, or when it "cries havoc, and lets slip the dogs of war." We have repeatedly read these Lectures on the poets of our country, and have found a fresh delight in every reperusal. We now come to the subject immediately before us.—

Mr Hazlitt is at this very time delivering a course of lectures on the comic genius of England,[2] and, for the sake of our readers, and we may say of ourselves, we have made a point of attending them, and we propose in this number and in our succeeding ones, to give as full a review of them as the time and our limited means will admit. The lectures, which have as yet been delivered, are three in number;—and of two of these we shall speak in the present article. The first is an introductory one on Wit and Humour; it is full of very sound observation, and is more successful in its definitions, than works of a similar nature are generally found to be. Explanation is commonly a painful and serious business; and on the subjects of which this lecture treats, nothing could be worse than anything like severe and laborious disquisition; wit suffers in description, and what can a lecture on wit be, but a description of it? The great difficulty, therefore, attendant on the task, appears to be that of keeping up the interest of the subject in the history and anatomy of it. Mr Hazlitt seems to us to have succeeded very admirably in this, and to have told us what wit and humour are in a language very nearly allied to them; he has caught the spirit of his subject, in the course of talking upon it,—and begets an inspiration as he goes on. This is the true trick of wit; wit creates fresh objects out of its own creations; it can start upon nothing,—and work that nothing up into a thing, "huge as the leviathan;" it can make a mountain of a mole hill,—and call spirits from the vasty deep, and make them come when it calls. Wit can govern the ventages of ever so small a pipe,—give it breath,—and make it discourse most eloquent music. It is indeed "apprehensive, quick, foretive,[3] full of nimble, fiery, and delectable shapes." It is the dance and banquet of the mind; the tipsy joy and jollity of the imagination;—the mad wag of the heart. Wit and humour are like Don Quixote and Sancho,—and the world could as soon do without the one as the other. The very attempt at describing what is so instantaneous and imaginative,—of settling what so luxuriously revels and finely exists in evasion,—is of itself enough to sober the mind, and make its efforts feeble, laboured, and inanimate. We should laugh at that man as a fool, even though he were a critic, who should think of chaining down and dissecting Ariel, and yet the task of securing and anatomizing wit is hardly a less idle endeavour. Mr. Hazlitt seems to have felt the difficulties of his labour,—but he has set about mastering them in a way, which none but a man of real genius could discover; he works his passage through this strait of Scylla and Charybdis with infinite skill and facility. Dangers were about, and on the watch for him, but he seems pretty easily to have evaded them; he treats his subject admirably; he attributes much to the effect of contrast, and this is true. He says,

The principle of contrast is, however, the same in all the stages, in the simply laughable, the ludicrous, the ridiculous; and the effect is only the more complete, the more durably and pointedly this principle operates.[4]

He then proceeds to enumerate some of the objects, which, by their violence and contrariety, furnish examples in these different kinds. This passage we think is very pleasant and ingenious.

We laugh at absurdity,—we laugh at deformity ... What is sport in one, is death to another.[5]

There is a sort of inveterate attachment to what is odd and opposite in high wrought wit or humour, that maintains perverse propriety, and is the very perfection of all its kind. It is only a determined passion for and attention to absurdity. Of this Mr Hazlitt thus speaks.—

There is nothing more powerfully humorous than what is called *keeping* in comic character ... It is one of the striking weaknesses and greatest happinesses of our nature.[6]

234

Mr Hazlitt gives the following instances of comic character. We bring them forward because of the pleasant associations which they cannot fail to awaken in the reader's mind.

Malvolio's punishment and apprehensions are as comic from our knowing that they are not real, as Christopher Sly's drunken transformation and short-lived dream of happiness is for the like reason. Parson Adams' fall into the tub at the Squire's, or his being discovered in bed with Mrs. Slip-slop, though pitiable, are laughable accidents: or do we read with much gravity of the loss of his Aeschylus, serious as it was to him at the time?[7]

Who does not know Malvolio?—That smiling, pampered, cross-gartered, vain man! Are not his soliloquies the finest egotisms in the world? Who could have faith in letters after his beguiling and alluring sheet of deceit! He knows her O's and her A's,—but he was a dreamer! His love was ideal, and his punishment was such. He was only a little more glaring in his conceits than other lovers,—but he does not forsake the tribe, or throw aside a single absurdity or point by which that tribe is recognized. Women have led men into richer follies than those of Malvolio; only it has been their luck to escape his violent exposure. Parson Adams is the man of men: the first of men, and of parsons. He has all the perversity and folly of humanity, but he has ten times more than its common share of innocence and honesty. How simple he is, but then how affectionate! We knew a little boy who once protested, that he had met this worthy curate in a street of Shrewsbury,[8]—and nothing could do away this childish idea. We can readily imagine this to have occurred. He would not, perhaps, be met with at Cambridge or Oxford; but he is as real as life can be.

We give another defining passage on wit, which appears to get nearer the *bull's eye* than what we have already extracted.

Wit is, in fact, the eloquence of indifference; or an ingenious and striking exposition of those evanescent and glancing impressions of things which affect us more from surprise or contrast to the train of our ordinary and literal pre-conceptions, than from any thing in the things themselves, exciting our necessary sympathy or lasting hatred. The favourite employment of wit is to add littleness to littleness, and heap contempt on insignificance, by all the arts of petty and incessant warfare. Or if it ever affects to aggrandize and use the language of hyperbole, it is only to betray its derision by a fatal comparison, as in the mock heroic; or if it treats of serious passion, it must do it so as to lower the tone of intense and high wrought sentiment by the introduction of burlesque and familiar circumstance.[9]

There are some admirable illustrations of this definition given from Butler's Hudibras,—a poem which is so much an essence of wit, that to be properly relished, it can only be taken in quotations. It is not possible to read Hudibras through,—or a book of it at a time,—and not be perplexed with the excess of wit and sense. The line is sure to stagger us,—its fellow is as sure to repeat the blow before we have in any way recovered, and the rhyme comes in at the end, and never fails in settling the business. Hudibras is, perhaps, the happiest book of reference, for those who are fashioning an essay on wit, that can be found in the English language.

We cannot dwell longer on this lecture, though we have by no means said so much as we had at first intended, or exactly pointed out the passages which we had set down as worthy of notice: But our observations on the remaining lectures would be unjustly curtailed, if we were to linger over the first so long as we could wish. Some ingenious stories are told, which greatly enliven the descriptions. We ought, however, not to think of turning to the second lecture, without first giving the following spirited passage on the difference between wit and humour.

I ought, I believe, to have noticed before, in speaking of the difference between wit and humour, that wit is often pretended absurdity, where the person overacts or exaggerates a certain character, with a conscious design to expose it, as if it were another person; as when Mandrake, in the Twin Rivals, says, "This glass is too big, carry it away; I'll drink out of the bottle." On the contrary, when Sir Hugh Evans says, very innocently, "Od's plessed, I will not be absence at the grace," though there is here a great deal of humour, there is no wit. Wit is, in fact, a voluntary effort of the mind or exercise of the invention, shewing the absurd and ludicrous consciously, whether in ourselves or another. Cross-readings, where the blunders are designed, are wit, but if any one were to light upon them through ignorance or accident, it would be merely ludicrous. This kind of wit of the humourist, where the person makes a butt of himself purposely, and with his eyes open, and exhibits his own absurdities or foibles purposely in the most pointed and glaring lights, runs through the whole of the flagrant character of Falstaff, and is, in truth, the principle on which it is founded. It is an irony directed against himself.[10]

The second lecture is on the Comic Characters of Shakespeare and Ben Jonson. Here Mr Hazlitt gets into his own element. The plays of Shakespeare seem, indeed, to be his natural home,—and his genius returns to it with that affectionate and unconstrained delight, which a man feels on stepping over his own threshold, after the irksomeness and fatigue of travel through dull roads or a dreary country. Mr Hazlitt starts, however, on this part of his subject with opinions, which we cannot by any means assent to; and we will state, as well as we can, the reasons which lead us to differ with one of whose judgment we in general think so highly. He deems the comedies of Shakespeare very inferior to his tragedies. There is little doubt, we think, but that Mr Hazlitt has been led into this belief from his almost idolatrous passion for the tragic of Shakespeare:—a perfect love of which, like the perfect love for one woman, would exclude a passionate affection for every other object. He has wandered through the enthusiastic raptures and fancies of Romeo,—the philosophical dallying and bitter melancholy of Hamlet,— the gloomy ambition, lonely fears, and brave death of Macbeth,—the eastern pomp, pride, and circumstance of Othello,—the staggering passion of Lear,—till he can see nothing intense, nothing real, nothing exuberant, in any other works, as compared with these. Shakespeare and Nature went hand in hand through all things,—and we should, therefore, infer, that he stood no chance of falling off in his comic creations. He has even in his tragic works introduced passages of the most exquisite lightness and pleasantry, for he well knew that "the web of our lives is of a mingled yarn,"—that in the world of reality joy and sorrow take turns in being uppermost. He has joined passion with mirth, and revelry with austerity;—and the world bears him out in the propriety. Sorrow with him every now and then relapses into a heedless and luxurious gaiety, and the bitterest severity suddenly dances off into the most light whimsicality and joyous folly; and "thus runs the world away." It would be idle to say, that the height of the comic at all equals the height of the tragic,—but we do say, that Shakespeare has reached the heights of both. After speaking in most eloquent terms of the tragic plays, Mr Hazlitt thus proceeds:

Whereas I think, on the other hand . . . unless he could do it better than any body else.[11]

This is all cleverly done; but in the support of what we hold to be an erring opinion. It is carried a great deal too far. It would be folly to dissent for an instant from one word that is said in praise of the tragedies, for they are a race of passionate Titans against whom it were madness to rebel.[12] They tyrannize over the heart, and hold all the feelings in a severe bondage. The sublimities of Shakespeare reach to heaven,—and awe the imagination into a dreaming imbecility. The pathos of his tragic characters is of the sweetest and the deepest kind,—and it is made doubly sweet by the melodious poetry which clings like air around it. It is music,—and music in a dream. Into the heart it floats,— melting every feeling in its course, and leaving a bewitching melody through all its progress, never after to pass away! There are the same degrees of greatness, however, though of a different nature, in the comedies of Shakespeare; and it is not because we adore the tragic powers of this great heart-master that we should utterly forsake or cry down the comic ones. To our notion, Shakespeare, in his comedies, is worth a world of Cervantes' and Congreves. The whole set of plays is a harmony of humanity; and to reject any portion of them, is but to betray a disposition to make things out of tune and harsh. It would be a difficult task to point out where the line is drawn between the tragedies and comedies; they run into each other with matchless sweetness; are involved,—blended,—married, each to the other. The romantic wanders into the comic, and scatters its favours far and near. The ludicrous ventures in amongst the stern and the awful, and "holds its own." Some of the comic characters in the tragedies almost share honours with the serious heroes of the piece, and are quite "as much followed." Mercutio is a most pleasant fellow; and if he did not die so soon, we are not sure that he might not have "cut into little stars," better than Romeo himself. Certain it is, that Romeo makes no great figure till after the death of Mercutio. The grave-diggers' scene in Hamlet might be pointed out as an illustration of all the plays; in it, mirth and sorrow, —carelessness and pain,—philosophy and rugged cunning, unite, blend, and make indeed a goodly piece of work of it. It is a short tragi-comedy, —as life is! After the protracted meditation on human fate, and the bitter invectives against the events of the world, uttered, and lingered over by young Prince Hamlet, this work of grave-digging comes in as a good comment; and the pleasantries of the two labourers take off the intensity of the thought. The grave-digger turns up the fresh earth, and throws down a skull and a joke at the same moment. He seems to be occupied in a sort of human gardening; and takes delight in his occupation. He sings at grave-making. The fool in Lear eases the passion into our hearts. He makes merry with anguish; but he now and then jogs the hand that holds the knife. All his jests are bitter things well wrapt up. If the fool were not by, Lear would destroy himself under the first bewildering blows of fate. He would resort to death to do him justice, and relieve his naked helplessness. He would plunge out of his troubles,—away from his pelican daughters, into death;—a regal suicide! But the fool is by, to distort events, and make a mock of anguish; and he humanely eases the passionate fury and agony of the old man into madness! Richard the Third is a wit; which is not the common character of kings. Twelfth Night, The Midsummer Night's Dream, As You Like It, The Taming of the Shrew, Much Ado about Nothing, which are all professed comedies, are equal in their way to any thing in nature. They are full of a romantic pleasure which fairly intoxicates the spirits. They make the heart drunk with full and fast cups of wit and fancies. Shakespeare administers to us as quickly, and overcomes our senses as hastily, as Iago passes the replenished cups to Cassio, plunging him into inebriety. The two parts of Henry the Fourth, Henry the Fifth, Cymbeline, The Tempest, which are called *plays*, are the links which unite the tragedy and comedy of Shakespeare. They are perfect in their kind: the comic genius, perhaps, predominates. What we would shew from this slight review of some of the characters, and some of the plays of Shakespeare, is, that the comic is in the same degree of excellence as the tragic;—that the latter cannot well be severed from the former;— that they are so completely two for a pair, that it would be as ridiculous for a man to have a favourite leg, or a lady to pet and spoil one of her eyes, as for the reader to adopt the tragic and reject the comic, or take the comic and forsake the tragic. They must be loved together, by any one who can love either of them. They are united, and no man may put them asunder.

But, "we have staid too long" from the lecture. To return,—Mr Hazlitt is very happy in his remarks on Shallow and Silence.

In point of understanding and attainments Shallow sinks low enough; and yet his cousin Silence is a foil to him; he is the shadow of a shade, glimmers on the very verge of downright imbecility, and totters on the brink of nothing. "He has been merry twice and once ere now," and is hardly persuaded to break his silence in a song. Shallow "has heard the chimes at midnight," and roared out glees and catches at taverns and inns of court when he was young. So at least he tells his cousin Silence, and Falstaff encourages the loftiness of his pretensions. Shallow would be thought a great man among his dependents and followers: Silence is nobody—not even in his own opinion: yet he sits in the orchard, and eats his carraways and pippins among the rest.[13]

This is delightful,—written in the very spirit of the Elizabethan age,— and quite true. Shallow and Silence seem, indeed, to be at the very lag end of human nature. Beyond them all is nothing; Shallow is but the echo of a man: Silence is not even that. The only person in all the plays of Shakespeare that nearly approaches to the nonentity of Silence is Goodman Dull in Love's Labour Lost. Dull is however conversational, which Silence is not,—but the Dulls were ever so. How pleasant is that address to him at the end of a long conversation of various parties! "Via, Goodman Dull, thou hast spoken no word all this while."—"No, Sir, nor understood none neither." What a fine and utter emptiness! What a rich indifference to everything. Mr Hazlitt thinks that the comedies of Shakespeare are not rich enough in the follies and fashions, and intrigues of artificial life. "I think," he says, "that comedy does not find its richest harvest till individual infirmities have passed into general manners; and it is the example of courts chiefly that stamps folly with credit and currency, or glosses over vice with meretricious lustre."[14] This, perhaps, may be true,—but the poet makes it up from the ample stores of nature. The following passage in further support of this is exceedingly happy and ingenious.

We find that the scenes of Shakespeare's comedies are mostly laid in the country, or are transferable there at pleasure: the genteel comedy exists only in towns and crowds of borrowed characters, who copy others as the satirist copies them, and who are only seen to be despised. "All beyond Hyde Park is a desart to it." While there the pastoral and poetic comedy begins to vegetate and flourish, unpruned, idle, and fantastic with impunity. It is hard to "lay waste a country gentleman" in a state of nature, whose humility may have run a little wild or to seed, or to lay violent hands on a young booby squire, my lady's eldest son and heir, whose absurdities have not yet arrived at years of discretion: but my Lord Foppington, who is "the prince of coxcombs," and "proud of being at the head of so prevailing a party," deserves his fate.[15]

Mr Hazlitt always speaks of Falstaff with delight,—as he deserves to be spoken of. He is truly the perfection of all comic invention; he carries with him a body, capacious enough for his humour, and his sack; he hungers after a capon and a quibble,—and devours every absurdity and delicacy that comes in his way. Old, unwieldy, and profane,—he is sprightly of temper, and alert of mind; he rolls after all sorts of jesting, —even if it can only be found in a robbery or a brothel. There is a kind of gluttony in his humour,—but at the same time, the utmost joyousness in his gluttony. His own body is the pillow for his own wit and humour, and for the wit and humour of every one else; all mention of him is the provocation of humour, and his memory is mirth itself; his tavern-bill is an excellent joke, from the mere recollection of the huge sleeper from whom it is purloined. There is a voraciousness in all he says or does; a full-fed, huge humour, in every word and action. "There is a fury in that gut." Schlegel, the German Lecturer, has well observed, that Falstaff has a whole court of amusing caricatures about him, who make their appearance by turns, without ever throwing him into the shade. Mr Hazlitt has an excellent essay on this glorious personage in his "Characters of Shakespeare's Plays," and he has done him justice in these lectures.

After some clever and acute observations on others of the comic characters of Shakespeare, Mr Hazlitt passes to a review of the powers of Ben Jonson. We agree with our lecturer in not thinking of old Ben so highly as certain verbal and editorial critics would have us. The world knows very little about him, though they cherish his name. He is so extremely scholastic,—so hard and crude,—so laboured and set,—that we are almost content to take his merits upon hearsay, and grant his fame by right of custom. There is great power in him; but it is power produced "at the sweat and labour of his brain." All is "forced up-hill work." He reins his humour in,—and rides it with noble mastery; but he surprises more with its formal pride and restrained courage,—and with its glittering housing and embossed trappings,—than with its free and unhidden, and simple beauty. It is a dangerous thing to say a word against the acknowledged heirs of fame,—but it is most cowardly to overlaud them, or to eulogize them for virtues which they do not possess. Great poets and men of a rapturous imagination do not read, or do not doat upon Ben Jonson. Collegians, and learned men, and critics, are his readers and supporters. There is a controversy about him, and on this his fame greatly exists. He feeds commentators,—and they in return "nod to him and do him courtesy." Many passages in his plays are exceedingly splendid,—but their beauties are built up at great cost and difficulty. They are piled on each other with the utmost caution and exactness. His ideas are enriched by repetition,—and his fancies come in clusters, or not at all. Mr Hazlitt well contrasts him with Shakespeare.

Ben Jonson is a great borrower from the works of others, and a plagiarist even from nature; so little freedom is there in his imitations of her, and he appears to receive her bounty like an alms. His works read like translations, from a certain cramp manner and want of adaptation. Shakespeare, even when he takes whole passages from books, does it with that spirit, felicity, and mastery over his subject, that instantly makes them his own, and shews more independence of mind and original thinking in what he plunders without scruple, than Ben Jonson often did in his most studied passages, forced from the sweat and labour of his brain. His style is as dry, as literal, and meagre, as Shakespeare's is exuberant, liberal, and unrestrained. The one labours hard, lashes himself up, and produces little pleasure with all his fidelity and tenaciousness of purpose: the other, without putting himself to any trouble or thinking about his success, performs wonders,—

> "Does mad and fantastic execution,
> Engaging and redeeming of himself,
> With such a careless force, and forceless cunning,
> As if that luck in very spite of cunning,
> Bade him win all."[16]

Mr Hazlitt well remarks that "each of his characters has a particular cue, a professional badge which he wears and is known by, and by nothing else."[17] There is, indeed, a mark set upon them, and the author dreads its being effaced, lest they should not afterwards be recognized. He starts one character with one peculiarity,—and they travel through the play as "one flesh," to the conclusion. Some of the smaller poems of Ben Jonson are very beautiful, and of exquisite workmanship. They are little classical gems, and magnificently set. It is but justice to give one...[18]

Mr Hazlitt concludes his second lecture with some very intelligent and just criticism on the Silent Woman, The Fox or Volpone, Every Man in his Humour, and the Alchymist. The character of Sir Epicure Mammon is in truth one of the best that Ben Jonson has drawn. His inordinate appetite for wordiness well suits his voracious love of sumptuous food and store of money. Image after image comes trooping forth in long and splendid array; and the language is withal of a very costly quality. We cannot refrain from quoting one of his speeches, which, for pomp and gorgeous effect, has never been surpassed . . .[19]

It is hard to descend to simple prose after all this exquisite ornament. Words tell for jewels:—and the whole passage glitters, like a Dowager's stomacher on a birth-day.

Mr Hazlitt's Lectures on the Comic Genius of England [II].
January 1819
Lecture III.—Cowley, Butler, Suckling, &c. &c.

We now come to the third Lecture, which is upon Cowley, Butler, Suckling, Etherege, &c. It is not less clever than its predecessors, but the subjects are not so vast, commanding, and attractive. There is a good deal of very just criticism on the metaphysical poets of the time of Charles the First,—who marred fair thoughts with the most extravagant conceits, and arrayed pathos and feeling in the most ridiculous masquerade dresses. They served poor poetry as fashion served the women; dressed it up in silks, and furbelows, and hoops, and obscured the simple beauty of the figure by the most cumbrous and perplexing loads of dress and ornament. Unfortunately the muses in that age went to Court,—and it was thought necessary to trick them out for the occasion. They were then ladies about town,—arrant coquettes,—masqued beauties. Any thing that was simply natural was insufficient; every quiet grace and beauty was banished society; poetry played fantastic tricks in the Mall and in the Park; all was dazzling, confused, and extravagant; and poetry paid compliments to philosophy and fashion; and philosophy and fashion paid them back tenfold; and feeling studied the mathematics; and pathos learned dancing; and imagination and fancy were reduced to the state of elegant trifles. Cowley was, however, a most delightful writer; but he lost himself everlastingly in his own conceits and speculations. Donne, who preceded him, wrote some beautiful little pieces, and would have been a lasting favourite if he had given his powers fair play. He became, however, a passionate logician. The finest and most impassioned openings in his poetry die of excessive reasoning, or are stifled with heavy and lumbering conceits. Mr Hazlitt quotes the following lines, and then gives their continuation. We shall be kinder to Donne, and only gather the blossom.

> Little think'st thou poor flower,
> Whom I have watch'd six or seven days,
> And seen thy birth, and seen what every hour,
> Gave to thy growth, thee to this height to raise,
> And now dost laugh and triumph on this bough,
> Little think'st thou
> That it will freeze anon, and that I shall
> To-morrow find thee fall'n,—or not at all![20]

There is a quiet pathos in these simple lines, which nothing can surpass, and which it was a crime in the author to sully with a cold and calculating after-thought. Again, there are three or four exquisite lines on the poet's wearing his late wife's hair about his arm, in a little poem called the Funeral.

> Whoever comes to shroud me, do not harm
> Nor question much
> That subtle wreath of hair about mine arm,
> The mystery, the sign you must not touch.[21]

Donne should have closed the poem here, and not have marred the mystery himself, by the meddling and abstruse reasons which he has thereafter given. Lovers should not trust their fancies to the world, or endeavour to account to themselves for every little romantic indulgence of their attachment. Mr Hazlitt beautifully observes, "The scholastic reason Donne brings, quick dissolves the charm of tender and touching grace in the sentiment itself."[22] He who wears a locket of his lady's hair next his heart, needs no confidante to heighten the charm; it is a spell over his thoughts and dreams, of which any exposure would hurt the mystery. Crashaw was an indifferent writer; but he has told the story of the Nightingale and the Musician with great precisian and skill. The story, as he tells it, is quite an essay on music.[23] Marvel and Shadwell are next noticed. Of the latter, we know little, and are contented to dwell

in ignorance. The former is worthy to live, on every account. Of Suckling, Mr Hazlitt thus speaks:

Suckling is also ranked, without sufficient warrant, among the metaphysical
poets. Sir John was "of the court, courtly," and his style almost entirely free from
the charge of pedantry and affectation. There are a few blemishes of this kind in
his works, but they are but few. His compositions are almost all of them short and
lively effusions of wit and gallantry, written in a familiar but spirited style,
without much design or effort. His shrewd and taunting address beginning "Why
so pale and wan, fond lover?" will sufficiently vouch for the truth of this account
of his extemporaneous pieces.[24]

Suckling deserves all this. He is one of the best writers of love and wit
poems in the language. His Muse was the lady of a knight, and "our
hostess kept her state;" but she bears marks of having been his mistress,
and occasionally lets slip an expression, or betrays an action, that bespeaks her origin. She is a laughing joyous lady of the ton, and all her
effusions are strictly in the mode, but infinitely gay and spirited. Millamant, the charming Millamant, hits off the character of Suckling in a
few words. After quoting two lines from one of his gayest little effusions,
she sighs out, "Natural, easy Suckling!" thus reducing criticism to a very
essence. His ballad on a wedding Mr Hazlitt describes "as his masterpiece. It is indeed unrivalled in its class of composition, for the voluptuous
purity of its sentiments, and the luxuriant freshness of the images."[25]
It is, indeed, wit and poetry in their nightgown and slippers. The only
fault in Suckling is, that he did not write more—he wrote so well. His
songs, when mentioned, awaken a smile and a sigh at once. Mr Hazlitt
next goes pretty fully into the merits and failings of Cowley. He quotes
one or two of his translations of Anacreon, and, for simplicity, feeling
and nerve, they are most inimitable. We never heard poetry spoken
with such effect as when Mr Hazlitt gave these odes to his auditors at
the Surrey Institution. Every line told.[26] The prose works of Cowley are
highly spoken of, and, indeed, we are always sorry, when we read them,
that he did not abandon verse, and take kindly to a species of composition in which he so eminently succeeded.
Butler's Hudibras is thus described:

The greatest single production of wit of this period, I might say of this country,
is Butler's Hudibras. It exhibits specimens of every variety of drollery and satire,

and those specimens (almost every one) master-strokes, and those master-strokes crowded together into almost every page. The proof of this is, that nearly one-half of his lines are got by heart, and quoted for mottos. In giving instances of different sorts of wit, or trying to recollect good things of this kind, they are the first which stand ready in the memory, and they are those which furnish the best tests and most striking illustrations of what we want. Dr. Campbell, in his Philosophy of Rhetoric, when treating of the subject of art, which he has done very neatly and sensibly, has constant recourse to two authors, Pope and Butler, the one for ornament, the other more for use. Butler is equally in the hands of the learned and the vulgar, for the sense is generally as solid as the images are amusing and grotesque.[27]

We have spoken already of Hudibras, so we shall not stay to eulogize it here; neither shall we indulge in extracts from the poem, though Mr Hazlitt has sadly tempted us to revel in the pleasure, by his happy inter-mixture of quotation and comment. He notices the power of the rhymes, and instances that whimsical couplet,

> And straight another with his flambeau,
> Gave Ralpho o'er the eye a damn'd blow.[28]

Mr Hazlitt thinks Butler's *Remains* as good, or nearly so, as his Hudibras. We cannot agree with him. They are more loose, feeble, and sketchy. One of the chief virtues in Hudibras, is its conciseness and instantaneous effect. It is a string of decided conclusions. Facts are strung together like onions. Mr Hazlitt concludes his Lecture with some short remarks on the dramatic writers of this time. He notices "the Man of Mode" of Sir George Etherege, which, for airy grace and pleasantry, has certainly no equal. We remember a description of the heroine of the piece, which is perfect in its way, and is equal, or nearly so, to Fielding's description of Fanny, in Joseph Andrews. Mr Hazlitt speaks highly of it. It runs thus:

Medley. First she's an heiress, vastly rich.
Dorimant. And handsome?
Medley. What alteration a twelvemonth may have bred in her I know not, but a year ago she was the beautifullest creature I ever saw; a fine, easy, clean shape, light brown hair in abundance; her features regular, her complexion clear and lively, large wanton eyes; but, above all, a mouth that has made me kiss it a thousand times in imagination; teeth white and even, and pretty pouting lips,

with a little moisture ever hanging on them, that look like the provence rose fresh on the bush, ere the morning sun has quite drawn up the dew.[29]

This is beautiful, and quite done off in the style of a court pastoral. But the character of Sir Fopling Flutter is the acmè of all coxcombry. He seems made up of feathers, and his breath is a mere French essence,—his wit is a vapour,—his affection is a mode,—his senses are of the air. Fashion is his god, and he worships it with a most mincing idolatry. We think with Mr Hazlitt, that this play would answer the pains of a revival. The comedies of Dryden, and the Rehearsal of Buckingham are finally noticed: we think little of either. The first are as wretched as indecency could make them. The last is tedious, but not brief.

Mr Hazlitt's Lectures on the Comic Genius of England. [III]
February 1819
*Lecture Fourth.—On Wycherley, Congreve, Vanbrugh,
and Farquhar.*
Lecture Fifth.—On the Periodical Essayists.

We resume our remarks on Mr Hazlitt's Lectures, which assuredly do not decrease in interest on a further acquaintance with them. Congreve's comedies are, perhaps, the finest specimens of classical English wit that can be produced; and we are well pleased to see them worthily spoken of by a critic so able and so eloquent as the lecturer, of whose works we are now writing. The spirit of Congreve's dialogues never goes down, but, on the contrary, it acquires fresh strength and elasticity the more it is exercised. The characters in these inimitable comedies play a game of repartee and elegant raillery, which is kept alive with all the ardour, vigour, and gaiety of children at *forfeits*. They speak in epigrams, and the last speaker is sure to have said the liveliest thing. The great charm of Congreve lies not so much in his characters as in their conversation, for he could not abstain from enriching the meanest servant, the valet, or the waiting-maid, with those jewels of wit which belonged more properly to their masters and mistresses. The polished gems of the mind are not usually lavished upon the poor and the dependant, any more than the ornaments of the person are given by a lady to her maid. The latter comes in for the forsaken petticoats and disinherited tuckers; but she is not troubled with pearls and diamonds, or overburthened with rubies and amethysts. All the characters in Congreve would tell for more, if they were not so opulent in wit and fine fancies. The splendour of their language dazzles the eyes and dazes the senses, and they become "dark with excessive light." Of Congreve our lecturer thus writes:

Congreve is the most distinct from the others, (Wycherly, Farquhar, and Vanbrugh,) and the most easily defined, both from what he possessed, and from what he wanted. He had by far the most wit and elegance, with less of other things, of humour, character, incident, &c. His style is inimitable, nay perfect. It is the highest reach of comic dialogue. Every sentence is replete with sense and satire, conveyed in the most polished and pointed terms. Every page presents a shower of brilliant conceits, is a tissue of epigrams in prose, is a new triumph of wit, a new conquest over dulness. The fire of artful raillery is nowhere else so well kept up. This style, which he was almost the first to introduce, and which he carried to the utmost pitch of classical refinement, reminds one exactly of Collins's description of wit as opposed to humour,

> Whose jewels in his crisped hair,
> Are placed each other's light to share.[30]

The play of Love for Love is one of the best of the whole set. It is happier in its plot, more varied in its characters, richer in its language. The scenes follow each other with a never-ending sprightliness and variety, and nothing is wanting in thought or word. In the very first scene the conversation between Valentine and his servant Jeremy would supply fifty modern comedies with wit. It is a skilful display of mental fencing; and, if Valentine makes many a classical hit, it is "like master, like man," for Jeremy is never unsuccessful in the return. Old Foresight is, indeed, "a marvel and a secret,"—a sort of hieroglyphic, which it pozes the eyes to read. His mind is evidently influenced by the changes of the moon, and his eyes are star-struck. You see in him the astrologer bewildered in the mysteries and sublimities of his science, and borne to the brink of madness by hosts of perplexing and vexatious planets. We know of nothing richer than his exclamation, when he is contemplating the insanity of Valentine, and writing down the wild rhapsodies of the supposed lunatic. He says that "what most men call mad, I call inspired." Munden represents this forlorn Man of Fate to perfection,—and, in the confusion of his dress, the awfulness of his gait, and the intensity of his face, he calls up Old Foresight "in his habit as he lived." Mrs Frail and Mrs Foresight are two entertaining wicked women; and their mutual exposures and reproaches are truly edifying. There are more Frails and Foresights in the world than the world is aware of. The Double Dealer and the Old Bachelor are very slightly spoken of by Mr Hazlitt,—with much less care, we think, than they deserve. We have not room, or we should be tempted to make up for the neglect, by a minute detail of their beauties. The Way of the World,—but Mr Hazlitt should be heard on this delightful play.

The Way of the World was the author's last and most carefully finished performance ... her treatment of Witwould and Petulant, and of her country admirer, Sir Wilful.[31]

After this follows a most admirable contrast of the heroine of artificial comedy with that of nature. The lecturer says, that we think as much of Millamant's dress as of her person; but that of Perdita and Rosalind our ideas take a better turn. The poet has painted them differently, in colours which "nature's own sweet and cunning hand laid on;—with health, with innocence, 'wild wit, invention ever new,' with pure red and white like the wilding's blossoms, with warbled wood notes like the feathered choirs, with thoughts fluttering on the wings of imagination, and hearts panting and breathless with eager delight. The interest we feel is in themselves,—the admiration they excite is for themselves."[32] Millamant is, indeed, by far the finest piece of fashionable workmanship that mortal hand ever wrought. She is as gay and light as a life of youthful triumphs can make her. All the court beauties were nothing to her; but she had the good luck to be painted by Congreve, and not by Sir Peter Lely. It is not fair to speak of Congreve's tragedy, or of his poems; the first is heavy, dull, and monotonous, the last are meagre and insipid.

Wycherly is next mentioned by Mr Hazlitt, and meets with "honour due." The character of Peggy, originally drawn by him,[33] is full of spirit and nature. The name of this joyous Hoyden recalls to our memories the image of one, who never made one heart unhappy but her own,—whose voice was the soul of humour and kindness, and whose arch humour and happy looks can never, never be forgotten. We need hardly mention the name of Mrs Jordan. Perhaps of all the actresses that ever made comedy comic, she was the sprightliest, the most natural, the best! We speak of her with mingled emotions of mirth and sorrow;— of mirth, because her name was the watchword of it,—of sorrow, because she is lost to us for ever. Mrs Jordan seemed as if she could never help her merriment. It was a part of her. It danced in her black eyes, and was continually meddling with her features, and at times burst from her in a rich gush of laughter. Like the courage of Acres, it oozed from the palms of her hands. From her heart it sprung at once to her lip, and played with every word as it was uttered. We shall never again see an actress of so unconscious a vivacity.

Of Vanbrugh, the following character is given in the lectures. It is far better than any thing we could give:

Vanbrugh comes next, and holds his own fully with the best . . . and executes the most difficult and rapid theatrical movements at a moment's warning.[34]

Mr Hazlitt contrasts Farquhar with Vanbrugh. The passage is extremely good.

But we have every sort of good will . . . of his society, and the sake of good-fellowship.[35]

The fifth lecture is on the periodical essayists,—and when it is recollected that, under this title, the names of Steele, Addison, Johnson, Goldsmith, &c. are included, it will be seen how rich in subject the present lecture is. After some excellent remarks on this style of writing, Mr Hazlitt gives a very able character of Montaigne, who was the father of the essayists. He then comes to the Tatler, of which he thus speaks:

The first of these papers that was attempted . . . The whole appearance of our dress and manners undergoes a delightful metamorphosis.[36]

The passage is long, but its goodness will atone for its length. We agree with our critic that there is a finer freshness, a more delightful originality and simplicity in the Tatler, than in the Spectator, as a whole work: But the second volume of the latter book seems to us as complete as any thing can be of the kind. It is a perfect pastoral . . .[37]

From Living Authors, A Dream. August 1820

> What things have we seen,
> Done at the Mermaid.

Beaumont.[38]

London, July 21.

Mr Editor,

There is a certain country gentleman spoken of in the Spectator, if my recollection serve me justly, who raises money by inveterate slumbers, and who gives out in a steady advertisement that he "intends to *sleep* next at the Cock and Bottle;" inviting all curious people, at so much per head, to come and see him in his trance. I am so far like this worthy *somnulent*, that I now advise your readers I purpose sleeping this month in the columns of your Magazine, and request a generous public at 2s. per head to read my dreams. I confess that since I encountered Boswell in a vision,[39] I have taken but profitless naps, and have rarely manufactured an interesting sentence, or wandered into a page of speculation. In vain have I tried to *drug* myself into a literary slumber, or to go to sleep with music in my ears for the sake of poetical visions. Laudanum would not turn a period—opiates could not catch a single metaphor,—the dying falls of music fell dead on my benumbed and senseless senses, and there seemed no sleep in me. I have, however, Mr Editor, at length had a sleep, with a valuable kernel of a dream in it; and as I know how much you prize the marvels of my pillow, I have carefully written down the "full, true, and particular account,"[40] and sent it you on the instant, so that, like its Newgate namesake, it may be printed, purchased, and read, almost before it has been conceived or uttered. It is curious on a Black Monday to find about the obscure streets of the west end of the town, that a moody moral has been wrenched out of a malefactor's mouth, and his untimely end and mournful confessions recorded long before he has had his irons knocked off. The freedom of the press is proverbial,—and wood-cuts of suspended mortality are ready, to any number, at the shortest notice. There dangles a set of indistinct bodies on broken ropes, in all the rude grandeur of bad engraving, bad ink, and bad paper. But I am straying from my subject; or, to speak in fitting language, walking in my sleep.

Perhaps it may not be amiss to tell you, Mr Editor, the cause of the poetical turn my dreaming mind has taken, as it certainly involves in it a few interesting particulars of certain public men, which may amuse many of your readers.

I am in the habit of seeking the society of literary people, and of noting their peculiarities of thought, manner, and person, with all the strength of observation I can command. I love to see one of the modern poets, celebrated in the Reviews and Ladies' schools for tender verses, fairly imprisoned in a circle of learned female critics, and beset by the sounds of many tongues, and exposed to the ogles of poetical old eyes, which roll before him as disrelishingly as peas grey with age, and dimmed with the "lateness of the season." While Mrs —— asks him with a whisper whether he has read Don Juan, and whether, with all its wickedness, it is not "a lovely poem;"—he, in a worse condition than the ladye Eve, has a second gentle toad pouring its flattery and its slimy criticism in at his other ear:—being the while in a mental sleep between each, and lost in indistinct dreams of poetry, old gentlewomen, and tea.

I have been tolerably fortunate in encountering most of our popular authors, at seasons like to this; not that I have ever seen them together in a body, like a complete set of Mrs. Barbauld's novelists, or Chalmers's English poets; but I have at one time met the worthy banker, who versified the pleasures of memory,[41] at one house, and sat down with Childe Harold to a vegetable dinner at another. I have heard, and thrilled while I hear[d] the round and rolling periods come from the mouth of the celebrated metaphysician and poet of the age, as from an ocean cavern,—grand—deep—eternal; or as from the sea itself. "He, of the pet lamb,"[42] has been before my eyes more than once with his solemn visage and more solemn discourse; not only in a room, but in Mr Haydon's "great picture,"[43]—though in the latter he differs from that which he is in the former,—being there bowed down with humility. He finds sermons in every thing. Nevertheless, he is "a great personage," and would be greater, if he did not think himself the greatest. The writer of John Woodvil[44] I have known well, and commend me to him for the vigour of his judgment, the nicety of his taste, and the fine severity of his wit. He cuts with his tongue the tumours of men's minds. His discourse amongst that of other men "sticks fiery off indeed." He is a bright little man,—the stilleto of conversation.

I remember sitting in the same box with Mr Moore at Covent Garden Theatre, on an evening when John Kemble played Zanga in Dr Young's Tragic Sermon upon Revenge.[45] It was just before the publication of Lallah Rookh, when all London was on tiptoe to catch the first flutter of those Arabian leaves, and when the west end of the town stood peeping with an anxious eye (as Justice Metaphor would say) in at the dusty windows and dim warehouse of Messrs Longman, Hurst, Rees, Orme, and Brown, to watch the progress towards publication of the Tales of the East. I remember the evening well, for I had rude curiosity enough to listen to the remarks he made to his lady-friends, and to note his "ways of pleasantness." *He* will remember Zanga: I saw one who reminded me more of the East; and I remember little of Zanga. His eyes sparkle in his head like two good things, and his heart seems dancing to the music of its own feelings.

I have seen Mr Campbell at the Royal Society's House, lecturing in mid-day, on poetry, to powdered heads, clouded canes, extensive bonnets, and flowered pelisses.[46] His intelligent countenance, and slight Scottish accent, gave an interest to his readings from the poets, which I cannot describe; but the time of day was as unfit for poetry in a room, as King John has declared it to be for the deeper accomplishment of murder. Enthusiasm cannot stand a glaring sun through a skylight,— nor are its nerves assured by the "gentle creations" of applause, rising lightly from French gloves and green benches. Poetical enthusiasm must hide itself in woods and solitudes by day. It abhors Albemarle Street. The only passage of Mr Campbell's Lecture that seemed to stir the hearts of his audience, in good truth, was his description of his first sight of the Apollo Belvidere in the Louvre at Paris. It *told* upon the fashionables before him, because they had all seen, in the common course of their life, the statue as he described it, and they now flattered themselves with believing that they had contemplated it with the same poetical idolatry and dreaming wonder of which he spake. The allusion was to a figure in France,—where they themselves had often cut one,— and that was enough. It was of Apollo, and they believed him to be a god and a gentleman. There was a flutter amongst the ribbons and silks, as though an unexpected gust of poetry had passed through them; and the old gentlemen tapped the floor with livelier canes, and nodded approval with heads of thrice brightened powder.

I fear, Mr Editor, I am rather straying from my subject, but it is almost impossible to speak of the "great men of the age," without becoming garrulous and fond over the recollections that attend them. They rise on the memory with attendant lights—I revel in the recollections of many authors. In short, there are few of the modern writers whom I have not seen, at some time or other. And it is my constant custom, as much so as the senior Mr Hamlet's habit of taking an afternoon's nap under the golden pippin and black cherry trees in his orchard at Denmark, to write in a ruled commonplace-book (of a reasonable size, neatly bound, ordered after the method of the great Mr Locke, to be had of two worthy booksellers, yclept Taylor and Hessey, 93, Fleet Street, price only 12s.) my observations of the day, particularly of the literary gentlemen whom it is in my good fortune to encounter,—not omitting the cut of their clothes, or the colours of their conversation.[47] I am thus enabled to refresh myself on a wet afternoon, or a chilly Sunday morning, with paying a visit to Mr Rogers,—indulging in the amiable and benevolent remarks of his memorable mind,—watching the shifting expressions of his speaking face,—and listening to the prodigious accounts of the flying editions of his first book, given by Messrs Cadell and Davies,—and preserved by the inspired author with laudable care and matchless poetical awe. Copyright is with him a real estate: It is not, as with others, a mere personal property, liable to the changes and the chances of the times;—it is "All that piece or parcel of arable land" that never passes away,—that is mowed season after season, and is always green,—that yields after-crop on after-crop! He may leave it to his children (if he has any) or to his friends, and they will be sure of an estate on which they can live. The writer of this would jump at such a devise, and he would preserve the publishers' returns with scrupulous industry and sacred zeal, in justice to the wishes of the inspired deviser. But you will think, Mr Editor, I am bestriding a dream already, and in sooth I fear I *have* taken a light canter upon a waking vision. "My uncle Toby dismounted immediately."

You will see and acknowledge that the virtues of my common-place-book are great; like the wonderful volume told of in that golden tale of the fairies, "The Golden Bough."[48] I can open its leaves, and see living figures moving therein; turn to one part of the book and see feasting, and splendour, and merriment; turn to another and *hear* intelligent conversation, and see the brightest persons in the world. In truth, Prince Tortocoli's volume could hardly have surprised him, so much as mine delights me. I look into it on high days with earnestness and rapture,—I open it on holidays with superstitious zeal, as a young girl prys into a legend book to know her love-fate.[49] I look in the index, if I happen to be *Lock*ish and Methodical, at the letter B, and against it I find "Byron, Lord, page ——." I turn to that page, and, lo! there he is!—"In his habit as he lives!" There is his low soft voice, like a stormy wind controlled; there is the fine breadth and paleness of his forehead,—the black *intense* curls of his lordly hair,—the haught-lip,—the dark and dreaming blue light of his eye. There is the humility of his manner, the extreme politeness of his carriage; there he abides! He may be chafing his wayward melancholy into anger in a back-room in Albemarle Street, or inditing faithless farewells in his chambers in Piccadilly with his fatal and black pen; or he may be distilling the poison plants of satire to drug the life-draught of a domestic;[50]—but he must arise at my bidding, and walk by me, or sit to me! He must flee from the gondolas and the guitars of Venice,—from the flowery masks of Paris,—if I but say to my book, "Call him, let me see him!" The spell on Manfred was not stronger: the spirit of Lara was not more charmed.

To resume, I can turn to the letter O, and under it I find (the letter being a fit forerunner of the person) the name of "Opie, Mrs."[51] I behold her at once, the pride of the *Blues*,—the gentle sharer of the *blue* throne with my Lady Morgan,—[52] the Fatima of Mr Murray's *Blue Chamber*![53] That *Abomelique* of books! Her decision upon those luckless authors who do not tread the party-coloured carpets of "the higher circles," is fatal, and unchangeable. It is not, What is the book? it is, "Who is the author?" If the latter be Mr Hazlitt, there is but one line of vituperation to be taken; if Mr Luttrell, (the silken writer of "Advice to Julia,")[54] be the person, he is a charming poet, and his book is pleasant and fanciful indeed. I like this lady's happy, sentimental, one-sided, little criticism prodigiously, and I turn to her leaf-home in my book, occasionally to hear her fashionable chimes playing the old established tune. Lady Morgan I have seen, and I have therefore taken a lodging for her in a room at the top of an obscure page. She has her harp there, which she pretends to play, and her books, which she professes to understand; and I leave her alone in her light summer *dishabille*, of which she is peculiarly fond, to write volumes on countries through which she has ravaged a tour, and to quote ingeniously from languages which she cannot comprehend, but which an ancestor of hers is said to have understood. And, marvellous it is, that in this family learning, she does not hear "ancestral voices prophesying war."

But let me not here omit the society of one, whose mind is the storehouse of all deep thoughts and proud imaginations.[55] If his early hopes, from their very ardour, have been broken and frustrated, still the memory of those hopes sheds a melancholy thoughtfulness over his mind, and over his countenance, which awakens in others a fellow pensiveness. He is the first prose writer of the age, and yet of manners simple and modest as a child. The world, by repeated blows, has stricken him into patience. He has learned to *endure*, in a hard school. His keen, yet serious face, encircled by its raven hair, has all the intellect and quiet power of one of Titian's portraits. His prose is lion-hearted, and lion-sinewed. His style of writing, however, it must be confessed, is very superior to his style of shaking hands. The first is all eagerness, intensity, and vigour; the last is cold, tame, and indecisive. He appears to abandon a bunch of melancholy fingers to your threatened squeeze, with some hope of their not coming to a *shake*. His hand strikes you as doubly chill, from its taking no interest in the ardour and nerve of your own. It swoons away. It appears to have something on its *mind*, or to be of an absent disposition. If Isaac Walton had received such a hand in the way of salutation at twilight after a day's hard fishing, he would have thought some wag had greeted him with four gudgeons and a *Miller's Thumb*. I wish he would "palpably confirm his grasp" in future, that my own paw may not be disconcerted or lured into the same lifeless habits. But what has this to do with his strong and impressive writings? Nothing. Only I find it recorded in my observant book, and therefore I cannot choose but remember it. He is a good hearted man, as well as a fine minded one,—good hearted still, in spite of rude usage, and the despoiled poetry of his youthful hopes. May he yet see a happy sunset after all the boisterous gustiness of his morning.*

* It is a curious fact, that the Indicator (a very clever little periodical work) has written a paper on the "shakings of the hand," and even remarked upon the very individual of whom I have spoken.[56] This is a curious coincidence. I did not see it till long after my own observations were written; and I only notice it now, for the sake of declaring, at the same time, that I am innocent of all literary theft.

Having thus stated to you the wonders of my matchless common-place-book, I come to the dream of which I spoke to you at the opening of this paper. I stated that I would account for the poetical colours which illuminated it, which I shall proceed at once to do, previous to giving a detail of the dream itself . . .[57]

Coleridge, Lamb, and Lloyd, walked forth arm in arm, and moved placidly to the water. They conversed as they passed on the beauty of the country,—on its peaceful associations,—and on the purity of the domestic affections. Coleridge talked in the grandest strain, and his voice was as deep and melodious as mournful music. His own conversation involved him in a web of magic thoughts. He passed from poetry to metaphysics, and lost himself in the labyrinths of abstruse systems. Lamb remarked, that he should prefer one of his affectionate and feeling sonnets to all his learned wanderings of mind. He thought that the rose that peeped at his cottage window suited Coleridge better than the volume of Jacob Behmen that encumbered his book-shelf. Each of these poets held in his hand a simple porrenger, such as is used in the Lyrical Ballads,—declaring that it was a homely and natural vessel borrowed from the utensils of daily life, and, therefore, fitted for poetical use. Lamb and Lloyd dipped in a bright but in a shallower part of the stream. Coleridge went to the depths, where he might have taken the purest water, had he not unfortunately clouded it with the sand, which he himself disturbed at bottom, by dipping too deeply. Lamb and Lloyd stated, that they should take their porrengers home, and share the contents with the simple and amiable hearts that were dear to them there. Coleridge was not certain as to what use he should apply his portion of the waters, till he had ascertained what were the physical reasons for the sand's propensity to mount and curl itself in the stream. The Spirit declared he might and could do what he pleased with it,—and then uttered to him with a smile—"Remember poetry!" Coleridge, Lamb, and Lloyd, separated by mutual consent, when they quitted the margin of the water.

Wordsworth, with a confident step, next advanced. The Spirit said, as she saw him, that no one had a greater right to approach her than himself,—that no one had so great a natural right to the water,—but that he applied it to such inferior purposes, and calumniated her favours by such fits of childishness and vanity, that she loved and yet regretted to see him. He began a long and very prosaic defence of his system; but in the course of it he became so egotistical, mystical, and abusive, that she reproved and silenced him. He made a bowl of the crown of his hat,* (it was so natural!) and scooped up the water with it. The Spirit smiled at his folly, but the poet preserved a serious countenance, and pronouncing certain lines from his own Excursion, he quitted the place.

* See the Excursion.[58]

PREFACES

Peter Bell, A Lyrical Ballad.   April 15, 1819[1]

I do affirm that I am the real Simon Pure

Bold Stroke for a Wife.[2]

It is now a period of one-and-twenty years since I first wrote some of the most perfect compositions (except certain pieces I have written in my later days) that ever dropped from poetical pen. My heart hath been right and powerful all its years. I never thought an evil or a weak thought in my life. It has been my aim and my achievement to deduce moral thunder from butter-cups, daisies,* celandines, and (as a poet, scarcely inferior to myself, hath it) "such small deer."[4] Out of sparrows' eggs I have hatched great truths,[5] and with sextons' barrows have I wheeled into human hearts, piles of the weightiest philosophy. I have persevered with a perseverance truly astonishing, in persons of not the most pursy purses;—but to a man of my inveterate morality and independent stamp, (of which Stamps I am proud to be a Distributor[6]) the sneers and scoffings of impious Scotchmen, and the neglect of my poor uninspired countrymen, fall as the dew upon the thorn, (on which plant I have written an immortal stanza or two[7]) and are as fleeting as the spray of the waterfall, (concerning which waterfall I have composed some great lines which the world will not let die.)—Accustomed to mountain solitudes, I can look with a calm and dispassionate eye upon that fiend-like, vulture-souled, adder-fanged critic,[8] whom I have not patience to name, and of whose Review[9] I loathe the title, and detest the contents.—Philosophy has taught me to forgive the misguided miscreant, and to speak of him only in terms of patience and pity. I love

---

* A favourite flower of mine. It was a favourite with Chaucer, but he did not understand its moral mystery as I do.

"Little Cyclops with one eye."
Poems by ME.[3]

my venerable Monarch and the Prince Regent.* My Ballads are the noblest pieces of verse in the whole range of English poetry: and I take this opportunity of telling the world I am a great man. Milton was also a great man. Ossian was a blind old fool.[10] Copies of my previous works may be had in any numbers, by application at my publisher.

Of *Peter Bell* I have only thus much to say: it completes the simple system of natural narrative, which I began so early as 1798. It is written in that pure unlaboured style, which can only be met with among labourers;—and I can safely say, that while its imaginations spring beyond the reach of the most imaginative, its occasional meaning occasionally falls far below the meanest capacity. As these are the days of counterfeits, I am compelled to caution my readers against them, "for such are abroad." However, I here declare this to be the true Peter; this to be the old original Bell. I commit my Ballad confidently to posterity. I love to read my own poetry: it does my heart good.

W.W.

N.B. The novel of Rob Roy is not so good as my Poem on the same subject ...[11]

Supplementary Essay[12]

I beg leave, once for all, to refer the Reader to my previous Poems, for illustrations of the names of the characters, and the severe simplicity contained in this affecting Ballad. I purpose, in the course of a few years, to write laborious lives of all the old people who enjoy sinecures in the text, or are pensioned off in the notes, of my Poetry. The Cumberland Beggar is dead. He could not crawl out of the way of a fierce and fatal post chaise, and so fell a sacrifice to the Philosophy of Nature. I shall commence the work in heavy quarto, like the Excursion, with that "old, old Man," (as the too joyous Spenser saith).—If ever I should be surprised into a second edition, I shall write an extra-supplementary Essay on the principles of simple Poetry. I now conclude, with merely extracting (from my own works) the following eloquent and just passage (my Prose is extremely good) contained in the two volumes lately published, and not yet wholly disposed of:—

---

* Mr. Vansittart, the Great Chancellor of the Exchequer, is a noble character:—and I consecrate this note to that illustrious financier.

A sketch of my own notion of the Constitution of Fame has been given; and as far as concerns myself, I have cause to be satisfied.—The love, the admiration, the indifference, the slight, the aversion, and even the contempt, with which these Poems have been received, knowing, as I do, the source within my own mind, from which they have proceeded; and the labour and pains which, when labour and pains appeared needful, have been bestowed upon them,—must all, if I think consistently, be received as pledges and tokens, bearing the same general impression though widely different in value;—they are all proofs that for the present time I have not laboured in vain; and afford assurances, more or less authentic, that the products of my industry will endure.

Lyrical Ballads, Vol. I, p. 368.[13]

The Fancy. June 1820[14]

It has been justly remarked by a great critic and biographer, that "the heroes of literary as well as civil history have been no less remarkable for what they have suffered, than for what they have atchieved." The Author of the present little volume is a strong instance of the truth of this remark; for few have squandered away the talents alloted to them so lavishly, and few have suffered more from their own melancholy imprudences. A short account of his life will, perhaps, not prove uninteresting to those who may be amused with the sallies of a sad mind, seeking relief from trouble in grotesque gaiety and elaborate extravagance.

Peter Corcoran* was born in the month of September, in the year 1794, at Shrewsbury, a town not very celebrated for men either of talent or genius, but proverbial for the pride and arrogance of its inhabitants, and for the excellence of its cakes. The parents of Peter were reputable, but by no means opulent; his father however had, by patient care and rigid frugality, saved a sufficiency to support himself and his wife comfortably and respectably: and he was enabled to place his son at the free-school in the town, and ultimately to give him that education at

---

* The father and mother of Peter were Irish, but they left Carlow on their marriage. Peter partook more of the spirit of his father's country than of his own; for the serenity of Shropshire did not appear to have chilled the blood in his veins. He used often to remark that Randall was the most *thorough bred* man alive,—being of *Irish parents* but born in *St. Giles's*.

College and the Inns of Court which is required to fit a young man for the bar. How far the propriety of this liberal exertion on the part of the father may be questioned, will be seen in the course of this short but decisive narrative. Peter was sent to school at seven years of age.

Mrs. Corcoran was often perplexed in her maternal feelings at suffering her son, in the tenderness and insecurity of his youth, to dare the dangers and vices of a public school; but her anxiety for his welfare and his renown overcame this natural apprehension, and she hushed to silence those fears which, had they been abandoned to their strength, would, perhaps, have prevented the loose life and early death which are now to be recorded. She would have taken him home, but she dreaded lest derision should fall upon her innocent son,—and lest her feelings as a mother should be laughed at as idle and weakly womanish. Peter was therefore permitted, at a very early age, to mingle with the world in little,—to tear grammars, break bounds, and pilfer orchards:—to fight nearly as soon as he could walk,—and to swear almost as soon as he could speak. He has often given a lively history of his labours and adventures, as the boy-servant of an elder boy;—how he used to get the tea-things set, clean the shoes, and dress any little nicety for supper;—how he was lowered, at the risk of his slim young neck, from the bed-room window, to *thin* Mr. Danna's garden for the next day's tart;—how he carried fighting cocks for his master in a bag to a bye field, for what he called "an afternoon's play;"—how he escaped on a fine moonlight night to steal trout, or bathe in the chill and rapid stream of the Severn. These are but a slender portion of his recitals, but they will serve to shew the probation he endured, and will be some excuse for the frailties, gaieties, and abandonment of his after existence.

Young Corcoran was never very much addicted to what he slangly termed "the hard-meat of the classics;" but he learned, as other boys learned,—the lesson of the day; and forgot, as other boys forgot,—the lesson of yesterday. It was not the fault of his masters that he thus became a night-prowler instead of a pedant; for he never ceased to speak of the unceasing application of the head master's rod, and of the gentlemanly kindness and care of his tutor,* (the third master) who, as Lord Byron

* This gentleman, the Rev. Mr. S——, behaved most kindly to Peter at all times;—a gentle master is the boy's first blessing under heaven:—and in this case Corcoran was blessed to the uttermost.

says, "was the best and worthiest friend he ever possessed; whose warnings he remembered but too well, though too late—when he had erred; and whose counsels he had only followed when he had done well or wisely."[15] This is, perhaps, not the place to enter into the question of the propriety of committing young spirits to the dangers of a public school. But it is much to be feared that the natural wildness of Peter's mind was nourished in one, rather than restrained; and that the fatalities of his after life might be traced to such a receptacle of violent liberty. A better boy at heart than Corcoran could not exist, but he had wild blood in his veins that would flood his nature,—and then self-controul was vain, and the controul of others disregarded or repelled with anger, as being impertinent. Peter was never idle. He was soon descried and allowed to be a most bitter lampooner of his school-fellows, if his spleen was provoked,—and to be an able celebrater of youthful and heroic atchievements whenever they called for song. His love of verse-making was thus early nourished; he reaped the rich harvest of boyish applause, and to a young spirit the caresses and welcomings of kindred spirits are the golden grain of the field of fame. His early poems were all either bitter, melancholy, or heroic,—much more so than could be expected in one so volatile, so daring, and so young. His father and mother hardly knew of his habits or his talents: they would, perhaps, have grieved over his rambling and predatory tricks; but would not have remarked his rhyming propensity, as it is more than probable they never saw a couplet in their lives. His mother was a kind but rather illiterate woman; his father always set down poetry as a synonyme for poverty. Perhaps he was right!

The school days of young Corcoran were soon over, for those light and careless times have swift wings, and abide not long with any of us. There was little variety in the events of each week:—the school—the playground—the fields;—the night—the window—the tree;—the dark wall —and the deep river;—these made up his existence. One hour he would be lost over his Phaedrus; the next might see him stripped and glowing with fierce young eyes, fighting a disorderly playmate "for love and glory." He was, perhaps, an impatient wooer of Latin prose; but who, so well as he, could beat "one of his size," or say a smart thing, beyond his years, to his master's daughter,—or to the maid, while he was washing on a Saturday night.

On quitting Shrewsbury (never again to return to it so happy!) he entered himself of Oxford, and there formed new acquaintances with the opulent and the extravagant. The innocent vices of his boyhood, for such they might comparatively be termed, were exchanged for the deeper failings of advanced years: and he plunged into the gaming and drinking habits of his associates with an enthusiasm strange and dangerous. From this fatal life he partly recovered himself, by the energy and natural goodness of his own heart; and just as illness had left him in possession of noble resolves and shuddering repentance, he became acquainted with a young lady, who strengthened his better thoughts, and freed him, when apparently irreclaimable, from the enthralling vices of his college life.

It appears that he had been visiting at the house of a friend near Hanover Square during the vacation, and it was here that he became attached to the virtues, the accomplishments, and the beauty of his friend's sister. Young Corcoran was just emerging from a severe illness, and the languor, generally attendant upon it, gave to his person and his features the softness and sadness which are so peculiarly touching to the tenderness of women. His very mind had become refined by suffering, and he was anxious to appear in her eyes intelligent, subdued, just, and unvulgar, and to hide from her knowledge the dissipation and emptiness of his school and college life. He now breathed a new and a cheerful existence. He read poetry to her; he wrote it. Her name crowned innumerable sonnets, and her image was mingled in many verses with pastoral fictions of retirement and happiness, and with classical wishes for unambitious ease—for the days of chivalry and romance, or the return of the golden age. The young lady of course became enamoured of these attentions, and she listened with a pleasing willingness to Peter's pledges of love, and to all those little ebullitions of tenderness of which young persons are in general innocently guilty, when they sit together, and look into each other's eyes.

The father of young Corcoran now permitted him to leave college, and to enter himself of Gray's Inn, though he had taken no degree, and was therefore subjecting himself to a harder town probation. Peter took lodgings in Vine Street Piccadilly, to be near the fair object of his attachment; and it may be supposed that he looked more into her face than into the Lord Chancellor's; and that he turned the curls on her forehead oftener than the leaves of Coke:—certain it is he made little way in his legal studies. He might be said hardly to know Blackstone from the Law-List.

Corcoran now wrote poetry vehemently, and flamed in the gorgeous pages of *La Belle Assemblée*, or pined in the sober and pensive columns of the *Gentleman's*. The magazines felt the ardour or the melancholy of his hand, month after month; and he has often said that nothing could equal the rapture,—the pride,—with which he perused his own productions,—reading over and over, with solitary glory,—"Lines to a Lady weeping," or "Verses on hearing Miss —— sing!" The following is a specimen of the effusions of his muse at this period;—it is a favourable one, being a piece written at the desire of his lady to an Italian air:—

Stanzas
Hark! Italy's music
  Melts over the sea;
Falling light from some lattice,
  Where cavaliers be:
And sweet lady voices
  Steal over the deep,
To hush all around us
  The billows to sleep.

Our gondola gently
  Goes over the wave;
As though it were dreaming
  To sounds that enslave:—
We listen—we listen!
  How blessed are we,
Who hear this dim music
  O'er Italy's sea!

About this time the young lady went on a visit to some friends in Kent; and there never was known, it has been said, so devoted and anguished a parting. Peter vowed, till he had not a vow left to bless himself with; and the lady wept, and promised to write unceasingly. There are some lines extant on this event; but they are not good. From the day of the lovers' separation may be dated the ruin and death of young Corcoran. He wrote warm letters, but the lady was not near to feed the flame of his constancy and ardour, and he therefore was driven by the eagerness and natural enthusiasm of his mind, to seek, in other pursuits, new and exciting pleasures: not that his love decreased,—but from inaction it slept.

It was in August, 1817, that young Corcoran strayed by chance into the Fives'-Court, to witness a sparring exhibition by the pugilists of the day. The sight so delighted him, that he thereafter could talk on no other subjects to his friends in the hours of conviviality; and he has often been known to rise from the table in the earnestness of his descriptions, to shew a favourite hit, or a scientific parry. He sought an acquaintance with all the eminent pugilists, and in their society he snatched, what he considered, "the life of life," planning combats, eulogizing heroic merit, and encouraging "the noble art of self-defence," with an ardour and a delight which knew of no repose.

The letters of young Corcoran now became less devoted to the cause of love, though still he snatched from the midnight an hour to write of the ability of Turner, and the genius of Randall, to his astonished mistress. He passed evening after evening at Belcher's house, (the Castle Tavern) the life of the company,—the favourite of his gallant associates! The songs which he wrote on his beloved topic were sung with rapture; and he himself often delighted a select party of *the Fancy* with an Irish melody* or a musical piece by the celebrated Mr. Dibdin.

Corcoran, at this period, never missed visiting a fight; and the eagerness with which he rushed about among the livery stables to possess himself of a rapid horse and gig, would have been noble in a better cause. He laid money on the favourite men, and lost it; and these failures generally compelled him to draw upon his father for supplies, which his indulgent parent granted, to the manifest detriment of his worldly comfort and private repose. Peter now and then made up a *match*, and

---

* Peter used to relate, with great glee, his singing Moore's favourite melody, "Though the last glimpse of Erin with sorrow I see," at Belcher's house one night, when Captain B——, the only critic in the room (except the fighting Oilman), protested against the bad English, as he called it, of the first line:—"Though the last *glimpse* of *hearing* with sorrow I *see!*" This was the same gentleman that would not pardon Ned Turner, who, having taken a glass of ale too much, struck him. The captain in the morning, although Ned protested that the ale had overpowered him, and that he was not himself, quoted, against all apologies for inebriation, the Latin words, "qui facit per *alium*, facit per se!"

266

put his *man* into training;—hiring a person to attend him, and allowing him all the expensive and nutritious *niceties*, which the insatiable appetite of the combatant might require. Fowls and port wine were thus handsomely demolished; and Peter occasionally found even these of no avail on the day of contest; but, on the contrary, he more than once saw the effects of two months sumptuous training ruined in twenty minutes.

With the *gloves*, Peter was allowed to be no despicable hand, for there is reason to believe that he had taken repeated lessons of a sparrer of peculiar skill and agility. Peter was *long*, light, and active,—possessed of good strength, and of no mean courage. He has made a good *set-to* with Eales, Tom Belcher, (the monarch of the *gloves!*) and Turner; and it is known that he has parried the difficult and ravaging hand even of Randall himself. His days were passed at this time in bed, or over *Boxiana*;[16] his nights were exhausted at the tavern, and afterwards in bitter and solitary repinings at a life which he had not the energy to remodel. In recording this fatal waywardness, it is deeply to be regretted that Corcoran had no friendly hand to assist him to the better path; no kind voice to tell him of the life he *should* adopt: he needed none to admonish him of the life he led,—for his midnight hour of solitude brought him the bitterest reproach he could experience.

The study of the law appeared a marked object for every light and unfortunate pursuit to aim a successful dart at. Peter now wholly neglected it. His days became useless to him from the weariness which the preceding nights of gaiety and dissipation had provoked,—and his jaded mind was compelled, in the same exciting sources, to seek a forced relief from enervation and despondency. He drank,—he betted,—he sang:—but the patient hour of self-reproach would come; and then he wretchedly felt what he had lost, and what he was losing, and made desperate resolutions,—to break them in the morning! His muse abandoned all hope of atchieving any thing great or good, and it was with this feeling that he wrote the following Sonnets. When it is recollected that they were composed by a despairing, self-ruined man, they may, to feeling breasts, assume a pathos, though in themselves they may have it not.

Sonnet

Were this a feather from an eagle's wing,
And thou, my tablet white! a marble tile

Taken from ancient Jove's majestic pile,—
And might I dip my feather in some spring,
Adown Mount Ida, thread-like, wandering:—
And were my thoughts brought from some starry isle
In heaven's blue sea,—I then might with a smile
Write down a hymn to Fame, and proudly sing!
But I am mortal; and I cannot write
Aught that may foil the fatal wing of Time.
Silent, I look at Fame: I cannot climb
To where her temple is—Not mine the might:—
I have some glimmering of what is sublime—
But, ah! it is a most inconstant light.

P.C.

Sonnet

I once had thought to have embalm'd my name
With Poesy:—to have serv'd the gentle Muses
With high sincerity:—but Fate refuses,
And I am now become most strangely tame,
And careless what becomes of Glory's game—
Who strives—who wins the wondrous prize—who loses!
Not that the heavy world my spirit bruises;
But I have not the heart to rush at Fame.
Magnificent and mental images
Have visited me oftentimes, and given
My mind to proud delights—but now it sees
Those visions going like the lights of even:
All intellectual grandeur dimly flees,—
And I am quiet at the stars of heaven!

P.C.

About this time he wrote a slang description of a fight which he had witnessed, to the lady while she was on a short visit at Esher, accompanied with his Sonnet to Randall. He received in return, as might be expected, a grave remonstrance. The lady says, with affectionate simplicity and frankness,—

Could you have seen the anxiety with which I glanced my eye over line after line, and page after page, in hopes of meeting with something that was intelligible, and (shall I add?) interesting; and had you witnessed my disappointment in beholding two whole sheets, and half a third, devoted to the subject of a "mill between Belasco and the Brummagem youth," you must, in spite of yourself, have pitied me.———Can it be possible, my dear Peter, that you *did* derive so much pleasure as you describe, and that you "lament that it is not given to poor human nature to forget such a sight at will, so as to have the gratification, arising from seeing such an exhibition for the first time, sixty times over"? Good heavens! you are quite enthusiastic! and on such a subject too!———I cannot thank you for the Sonnet. It is no doubt clever, but I was too sick of the subject to enjoy it.———[17]

Perhaps Peter was nettled at this return for his pains and his puns,* or (to use a term he has often used himself,) he was too much imbued with the pugilistic spirit to *receive without returning*. He replied in terms to deepen his offence—

My dear Kate,

I assure you I am not *fibbing*, when I say, I regret that my last letter proved so severe a *punisher* to you. You have, however, *returned upon* me pretty smartly. You have quite *hit me off* my pugilistic *legs*,—*doubled* me and my letter up at a *blow*,—and actually *floored* me. And though (as this may serve to show) you have not altogether "taken the *fight* out of me," yet you see I come very languidly *up to the scratch*; and this will be in all probability the last *round* in which I shall present myself before you in a *milling* attitude. You are *too much* for me. I am but a *light weight*, and you carry too much *gravity*. My *rallyings* are of no use. If I make a *good hit*, it does not *tell* upon you. You are too well *guarded*. I waste my wits and my wind to no purpose: if I try to *plant* a *tickler* upon your *ribs* that shall *shake your sides*, you laugh *at* me, instead of *with* me; and finally put in a *write*-hander upon me *by the post*, that disables my *jaw* and *drops* me. There is no *standing up* against such a *rum customer* as you are. So I shall in future keep myself out of the way of such *punishment*.

Alas, for poor *Fancy*!—If her flowers meet with so nipping a reception in the neighbourhood of *her own Moulsey*,[18] she may as well, (like Lord Castlereagh's crocodile,) put her hands into her breeches pockets; or turn them to any thing else, rather than double them into fists. She had better at once cut down her *gloves* into mittens, and put her fingers into *rings*, instead of going into them herself.

On the return of his young mistress to town, Corcoran for a while

* Application was made for Corcoran's first letter, which must have been a curious one, but without success. It seems to have happened to him, as it has to others, to have his works properly appreciated only when their poor author is in his grave.

absented himself from the haunts of pugilists and of *the Fancy*,—being in some sort influenced by her presence: but he was always unsettled and heedless, and he sat late, and forgot himself before her in the histories of his favourite subjects. Differences naturally arose between the lovers on his altered habits; but he had become hasty and intemperate, and she, from being disgusted at his follies and his faults, gradually alienated her heart from its first affection. The lady did not consider herself faithless, for Peter was not the same that she had loved previous to her Kentish visit. On one occasion he appeared before her in the day with two black eyes, and with other marks of the preceding night's skirmish on his way home. The lady from this moment forbade him her presence, nor could she ever afterwards be persuaded to relent, though he sued to her in that fond and penitent style, which bespoke in him an undecayed affection. Some lines appear in this selection which he wrote to her soon after this unfortunate event, thinking that she would listen to his humour, and forget his misconduct: but she returned the stanzas upon his hands, and from this identical copy the lines have been printed.*

His letters of expostulation to her were dictated by a steadier pen and a more sombre mind; but these met with the same fate. In one of his letters he says:—"You cannot imagine, my dearest Kate, what I suffer by the recollection of that idle quarrel, and the still more idle verses which it occasioned. If you continue unforgiving, I have no one left to make life cheerful. My own good opinion is lost. My nights are torture to me:—but I seem now to have no inducement to wish them better or quieter. I might, perhaps, escape from folly, if any one would rejoice at it, or 'welcome me back to the world.'" In another letter he writes, as if in the provocation of sorrow and despair:—"To-morrow I go to Randall's fight;—but I think if I were recalled by you, I could break my promise to my companions, and pass a day of happiness and forgiveness with you. Try me, my dear Kate!" It is most probable that she never attempted to reclaim him; but it is much to be lamented that an endeavour was not made by her:—for from her influence alone, could such a measure have been effected.

* Peter was a great admirer of Mr. Coleridge's poem of "Love," and he appears to have lost his mistress on the following fallacious principle:
"She loves me best whene'er I sing
The songs that make her grieve."

The health of Peter, which had been some time declining, now became rapidly altered for the worse; and he fell into the most dangerous state, apparently without a struggle on his part to avoid it. He was gay, active, and spirited to the last, with the exception of his nightly visits of melancholy, and occasional fits of despondency by day. In reality, life had lost its importance to him.

In the last weeks of his existence, he employed himself in writing light pieces of poetry for his own amusement;—thus living over again the pleasures of which in health he had so eagerly partaken. A few of these, and but a few, are now printed. The spirit of poor Corcoran was thus triumphant over pain, and thus did it remain till his departure. His father was with him at his death, and witnessed that heart-rending sight, the termination of a consumption, that complaint which flatters even its conclusion. Peter wished to see his mistress, but she declined the interview. *He* was, as Dr. Johnson says, "inextinguishably amorous, and she inexorably cruel."* He died very recently without a struggle, just after writing a Sonnet to *West-Country Dick*.

It is impossible to contemplate the youth, the talents, the fate of this young man, and not lament that he should not have applied himself to some pursuit steadily, so as to have filled a worthy station in life. At one time he seems to have partly recovered himself from the trammels of sad society; but the fascination of pugilism and its professors was too strong in his eyes, and he sealed his ruin and his death by a devotion to its pleasures. A fight was to him a resistless attraction, and he has often declared that he was never so thrilled with enthusiasm, as when that moment arrived at which the men stripped against a fine sun, and advanced like trained blood-horses, to start for the prize. Peter caught cold upon cold at these diversions; and certainly to an infatuated and unrestrained attention to such pursuits his death is attributable. Pugilism in itself is a manly and noble science,—but it is apt to seduce its admirers into evil ways and corrupting society.

The person of Peter Corcoran was tall and slim. His features were of a pleasing expression, particularly when they were excited by any sudden feeling of enthusiasm. If any belief could be placed in the system of Gall and Spurzheim,[19] the head of Corcoran would have explained

* Life of Hammond.

to any person skilled in the study of such system, that Peter's passion for fighting was greater than men in common possess. His organ of combativeness was unusually large, so much so as to be repeatedly remarked by indifferent observers. The very name of Corcoran is expressive of pugnacity, or an *intense inclination towards butting and battering*. Vide Calasio, in voce כרכרנם.*

His style of writing is not good; it is too broken, irresolute, and rugged,—and is too anxious in its search after smart expressions to be continuous or elevated in its substance. Corcoran was remarkably fond of puns, as his works will exemplify. He wrote with great rapidity, when he could bring himself to write at all; but he more often commenced than concluded works; and it was a common case for him, to plan and open a new piece at night which was neglected or forgotten in the morning.

He had few friends:—and it cannot be denied, in spite of his faults, that his mistress was harsh and relentless, beyond the run of women in general. Few ladies would have frowned so long, who appeared at one time to love so well. The woman that can retain her stern disregard through a long siege of letters and verses, is either singularly high-principled, or superlatively unfeeling. Peter, with all his heedlessness,

---

* There is a sort of *craniology* in names, by attending to which, a Biographer, who knows but little of his subject, may derive as much certain information as his betters.[20] Spenser, who read *Sackville's* νοῦς in his *nomen* (to express a meaning by the marriage of Greek and Latin,) says,
"Whose Muse, full of high thoughts invention,
Doth *like himself* heroically sound!"[21]
The name of our immortal Shakspeare is composed of two Hebrew words, signifying "beautiful plays." There was also a mysterious meaning in the Christian name of *Will*, often played upon and *riddle-me-riddle-me-ree'd* in the Author's sonnets, which ought to have set antiquarians upon the scent, long before Malone found the *Will* itself in a hayloft at Stratford! —Mr. Gifford might have learned that *Mass-singer* was a Catholic, without drawing heavy inferences like an editorial carthorse.—*Pope*, of course, could not help being a Papist,—if there be any help in it!—*Suckling* had too much of the milk of human kindness in him to fight, let Octavius Gilchrist say what he will.[22]—*Sprat* was, as Mr. Southey observes, the smallest of the poetical fry: How could he be otherwise?—*Gay* wrote the Beggar's Opera; his monosyllabic title promised to do it, and kept its word!—*Savage* foretells his fate, in his name.—The rich metal with which *Goldsmith* wrought his works is plainly foretold.—*Cowper* and *Cowley* were intended for pastoral poets, and *Somer-ville* was by nature cut out as the laureate of the *hunt*-ing box. *Bacon* could never have meddled with the spring of poetry. It was only by a dry-salted philosophy that he saved his name. *Broome* did all the dirty work of the muses, and *Mallet* was but a *tool* in the hands of Bolingbroke. The list might be continued for several pages, but the reader is referred to the Biographical Dictionary, *passim*. It may be stated in conclusion, that there was actually a celebrated Bruiser of the name of *Corcoran*, an Irishman, who lived in the time of Figg and Broughton. His name warranted his profession.

was the only constant lover of the two, for he remembered her on his death-bed. The lady still lives, and is married. When she reads this imperfect memoir of Corcoran, she will surely feel some contrition at having repulsed him to the last, instead of having lured him from the fatal and fascinating errors that generated his death.

The works selected for publication are but a small portion of those left in MS. by Peter; if this little volume should be well received by the Public, the Editor may be induced to offer what Addison has happily called, "more last words of Mr. Baxter."

The Garden of Florence and Other Poems.[23] 1821

(Advertisement.)

Many of the poems in this little volume, indeed the greater part of them, have been written for some years, and I very much fear that age has not improved them. Modern poetry is not, perhaps, bettered by being hoarded according to the directions of Horace;—for to be seen in its freshest colours, it should be "worn in its newest gloss."

The stories from Boccaccio (The Garden of Florence, and The Ladye of Provence) were to have been associated with tales from the same source, intended to have been written by a friend;—[24] but illness on his part, and distracting engagements on mine, prevented us from accomplishing our plan at the time; and Death now, to my deep sorrow, has frustrated it for ever!

He, who is gone, was one of the very kindest friends I possessed, and yet he was not kinder perhaps to me, than to others. His intense mind and powerful feeling would, I truly believe, have done the world some service, had his life been spared—but he was of too sensitive a nature—and thus he was destroyed! One story he completed, and that is to me now the most pathetic poem in existence![25]

The Ladye of Provence is taken from one of Boccaccio's stories, and the original incidents are pretty faithfully followed. The names have been changed, for the reason given in the old epitaph;—*Rossiglione* would not accomodate itself to the metre.

ESSAYS AND REVIEWS FROM

THE LONDON MAGAZINE

Exmouth Wrestling.[1] December 1820

Rosalind. —Shall we see this wrestling, coz?
Le Beau. You must, if you stay here, for here is the place appointed for the
wrestling, and they are ready to perform it.

As You Like It.[2]

A Londoner's life,—with all its wealth of theatres, picture-exhibitions,
parties (both tea and political) sports, beauty, and places under government,—would really be scarcely worth the possessing, if it were not for
that month of recreative wandering which is permitted, at one season
of the year, to master and clerk,—to knight, gentleman, and appren-
tice,—to all descriptions of city labourers in short, except the Editors of
newspapers and the hackney coachmen. The former must perservere,—
while others are permitted their breathing times,—to feed voracious
columns with fresh malice, night by night; while the latter are doomed
to bask in the middle of an autumnal street, owing to the absence of
those persons who, if in town, might take them to Mile End, or to the
gate of the Regent's Park, or to the bottom of Highgate-hill;—and thus
transport them at least to the brink of the country. For my own part,
I would rather dwell in Brentford for the remainder of my days, than
consent to abandon my claim to that month of country idleness and
enjoyment, which I look back upon with melancholy delight during the
months of October, November, December, January and February;—
and towards which I turn a longing and expectant eye through the whole
of March and its five sequent sisters of the Calendar.[3] Part of my pleasure,
as the time more nearly approaches, arises from the declaration I make
to my friends, that "*I shall be off in about a fortnight,*"—though, in my own
mind, I am pretty well assured that I shall not break from the trammels
of business, for four or five weeks. A traveller in the *pleasure line* is

always thus full of his subject. He requests his taylor to be careful that his clothes are at home by the Wednesday,—because, "he is going out of town." If he receives an invitation to dine with a friend, he excuses himself, with an air of carelessness and vivacity, by "fearing that he shall be out of town at the time." Law clerks, and other dependants, who derive their holiday from the graceless permission of their masters —who wring a fortnight or three weeks out of the long vacation, "by wearisome petition and slow leave"—indulge in the same pleasantry towards their acquaintance. They cannot take a part in a private play, *because they are going to pass some time at Stamford Hill,*—or are likely to be at *Calais*—which they call being on the *Continent*—at that precise time. Half of their relish of the holiday, is procured from the expectation of it, and from the importance which accrues from its mysterious announcement. To go, is something; but how much more is it, to enlarge,—to dwell,—to feed upon the promise! The core of the enjoyment is, in short, to "*stand* upon the *order* of your going."

It is impossible to describe the careless importance with which I pay the hackney coachman, who carries my person and my portmanteau to Piccadilly, or Charing Cross, on the evening of my departure! He asks me a sixpence too much, because he sees by my face that I am in good humour, and guesses moreover that I am going out of town, and shall forget the extortion long before my return:—I pay him the excess, and threaten, with a look half grave and half gay—like the face of that compound of skeleton and gentleman in Bowles's shop-window—to *have him up,*—well knowing that I shall have no opportunity. I underwent this very pleasure the beginning of last September,—and I recollect thinking the better of the coachman for discerning an extra sixpence in my eye. He saw me flushed with anxiety and happy expectation, and very properly made me pay for it. I know not whether others feel as I felt,—but I *remembered* the porter,—who pretended an anxiety for the safety of my luggage, and who, to evince his zeal, thrust the cape of my box coat from the lamp,—with a cheerful groat;—and I paid the balance of my fare to the book-keeper, at the office, with a prodigal hand,— as one who was paying the purchase money for a perpetual advowson in Paradise, or buying a cut out of that classical cake, the golden age! The ride through the streets, which you are quitting for their betters;— the sullen transitions (as Dr. Johnson would call them) of the hackney coaches;—the light and flimsily dressed passengers on the pavement, whose appearance you contrast, to their disadvantage, with the travel-girt bearings of your own body;—the names of the shopkeepers and their several callings, from whose eternal gilding you are glad to escape; —the bustle and impatience at the last coach-office in Piccadilly, where you deride, with a scoffer's eye, the retail travellers on the *Chelsea* and *the Chiswick*;—the stupid quiet of the water in the Green Park, which you contemptuously denominate *town-water*—and the scanty dusty appearance of the adjoining grass, which you also sneeringly call *town-grass*;—the determined imperfections of the pavement near Hamilton-place, which jolt your body about in all directions, as if purposing to have the last and the most of you,—and the quiet fall, after one conclusive shake, into the easy, loose, and pleasant gravel at Hyde-park corner:— these, all of these,—are delightful in their way, and serve as the prologue to the happy yet brief comedy you are about to enjoy.

I shall not continue thus minutely to trace a journey of 176 miles, which mine, according to a credible book of roads, is stated to be; though I believe a description of its casualties and ordinary events might not prove unamusing:⁴—but I shall say to my reader, as a Melo-drame murderer says to his glittering employer, *"conclude it done!"* The descent from the coach at the end of the journey is "another thing." You are conscious that enjoyment is in sight, but then your eyes have been twinkling in a mid-night wind, and know not what they do. The day is all before you,—but then you have been up all night. You jump down from the fore wheel on ten benumbed toes, and stagger forward as awkwardly as if you had jumped on ten of your neighbour's. Your hands are swelled and foolish, and you pretend to laugh at them while they are impotently fumbling after a shilling for the coachman, who "*leaves* you," as he calls it,—and who therefore stands, with a look of sly and inanimate patience, as if he would wait till your fingers came to themselves. Your coat is as wrinkled as though it had travelled till it was old, and it has become worked up in folds on your back, so that the buttons are nearly on your shoulders. You dare not look at your hat; the condition of which, however, you surmise by the *serpentining* of the rim,— which, if you are in the law,⁵ reminds you of "*This indenture of three parts.*" You declare to some of the passengers, that "you would have brought a travelling cap, if you had *known*."—For a about minute you stand helpless and stupid in the street, looking at the country people, with one eye to them, and one to your own consequence:—you are a traveller to all intents and purposes! The guard, with a body like a maggot, is standing on the wheel, pulling out the luggage and parcels from the foreboot, and you therefore request he will get you a blue bag, tied round with red tape, and with your direction on parchment, which is in the boot behind—while an old lady, at the same time, is urging him to search in one of the seats, inside the coach, for a small basket "as big as that little box he has now in his hand." He answers you, and others, like the waiter at an inn, with promising to attend to you directly,—and continues reading,—"So-and-so—Fore-street,—to be kept dry. Here, take this into the office. Um-um-aye—South-street. Let Jack run down with this:—carriage *is* paid. Bill, *jist* take this basket to Muster Newton's in the yard, and get 3s. 9d. for it."—And thus does he go on, in spite of the impatience of his poor wearied passengers, who are too tired to be angry, and who wait about in dust and dejection, till he condescends to approach one of them with.—"Well, Sir! what's yours?"—A black leathern portmanteau—a blue bag,—a parcel in brown paper—and an umbrella!—"Oh!" and then, in tedious and due course of time, you "get your own."

To quit the coach, and to come to the country—and my readers will have travelled at least a *stage* of prose to get to it—I must suppose the meetings of friends over, with the usual allowance of exclamations, such as—"you are really grown, or you appear to be so!"—and, "you are certainly thinner!"—and "dear! what a very odd hat you have!"— and "how natural your voice sounds!"—and,—the like. I must suppose, that all minor arrangements are over, and that, by the kindness of a few accompanying friends, I am at the seaside:—But why should I *suppose* what I have really enjoyed:—why should I not at once "unlock the cells of memory"—as sentimental correspondents express themselves,—and trust to faithful recollections. I am about to describe a scene, at which it was my good fortune to be present, and to describe which, in fact, was the cause of my writing the present paper. As I intend "to be faithful," I shall throw aside those little arts and prettinesses, in which essayists and prose writers indulge, and put together a few plain sentences, recording a few plain facts.

I was induced, during my stay in the West of England, in September last, to pass a fortnight at Exmouth,—a very pretty sea-side village, on which a very pleasant farce has been written.—That I did not make a difficulty of being *induced*, may be conjectured, when I confess to having pretty broadly hinted at such an excursion to my friends, and acknowledge that they threw aside all anxiety and thought, and made up a party for the purpose. The village is seated, as its name intimates, at the mouth of the river Ex;—some of its best houses are built on a high cliff, which commands the sea and the river, and from which some of the most splendid *sunsets* are to be seen that eye of man can desire. I would however, being one of humble desires, more particularly speak in commendation of a neat little brick built tenement, which stood near to the water, (I leave the reader to settle whether I mean the sea or the river,) and which had, I believe, the benefit of every wind that blew during the month of September.—Oh! we were a merry crew in our smart brick vessel, and laughed away many an hour, at which the clouds wept, and the wind howled! While the strings and tassels of our window-blinds shook and rattled,—and the blinds themselves flapped, like the rigging and sails of the barks which we saw before us;—and while the carpet actually rose and heaved, even as waves, around us;— we fleeted away the hours, as though the world were laughing without, and went merrily on our voyage, as vessels will go, "with youth at the prow, and pleasure at the helm." The wind did not howl in our hearts;— the rain did not fall upon, or damp our spirits!

I can never forget the perfect idleness and delight with which we discussed the morning's walk at breakfast,—or with which we accomplished what we had so discussed. I remember to have expended twelve pennyworth of coin in the purchase of a basket to hold shells, which we were to cull "I know not how oft:"—being thus prepared,—we never picked shell more! Our employments seemed to laugh at our promises. Our engagements played at cross purposes with our intentions. We only gathered shells when we had no convenience for carrying them home;— but, in truth, there is a pleasure in this waywardness of pleasure which only holiday hearts know. I can say that I have been delighted to stand within reach of the waves, and *feel* them weave "an untumultuous fringe of silver foam" around my feet;—to see the gulls busy in the distance;—to hear the tumult of the sea when it became angry;—to enjoy the vexed elements.—I am perhaps only telling what hundreds of readers have experienced and will acknowledge;—but, if I may judge of others by myself, there is some pleasure in being reminded at times of things which we know.

One morning,—(I seem to have indulged in generalities long enough,) —one morning, on sauntering to the window after breakfast, I perceived in a piece of flat meadow ground, an unusual assemblage of spars, posts, rails, remnants of tattered rigging, and cordage. The servant, with a voice of peculiar satisfaction, informed me, in answer to an inquiry which escaped me without *a direction*,—that there was going to be *"a wrastling,"* as she, in her county dialect, expressed herself. What! A match? said I,—evidently as much delighted as if I had been "native there,—and to the manner born." "Yes, Sir!" she replied—"And the Canns will be there—and young Brockenden,—and Thorne from Dawlish, and the Men from the Moors!"—Oh, if it be a fault to admire the sports and pastime of the poor—to delight in their manly games, and feats of courage and enterprize,—I must at once confess myself guilty of it to the fullest extent:—it is not for me to plead to the minor offence. I see all I can see, at all times, of skilful struggle between man and man;—and I glory in seeing it!—The communication of this enthusiastic serving-woman sounded to me pleasantly indeed;—I could not help thinking it somewhat poetical,—for there is a beauty even in common names, when clustered together thus, and connected with the idea of personal enterprize and superiority, which, I own, makes a strong impression on my feelings, and I believe is not without its effect upon those of others. "Young Brockenden," appeared a gallant name;— and, to my ears, there seemed something decisive in the name of "Thorne from Dawlish:"—But the "men from the Moors" came upon my imagination like a clan from the Highlands, or the sudden incursion of a band of freebooters upon a quiet hamlet. The muster hour was twelve o'clock;—and I panted for that hour!

In the mean time, I went continually to the window, and could plainly distinguish the labourers preparing the ring, and fitting up booths for the accommodations of those persons who might wish to guard against a wet day outwardly, and who would not object to it inwardly. I could almost fancy that I heard the hammers of the workmen "accomplishing the field;"—but I do not wish to *romance* on this interesting subject. The morning was certainly very unpropitious, for the clouds not only threatened, before breakfast, to try the security of the awnings,—but they made good their threats, after that meal, with one or two pretty effectual showers,—which however afflicted the heart more on account of the mischief which would ensue to the turf, than on the score of any other inconvenience. Persons began to assemble during the morning,—but the sports did not commence till one o'clock;—and, as some time elapsed between the hour at which the ring was ready, and that at which the wrestlers entered themselves for contest,—I shall fill up the pause for my readers, by giving them a few particulars of the sport, as practised in our earlier English days;—and I trust my learning will last me till the first *hat* may be supposed by my readers to "rise in air," and no longer.

The men of Devon and Cornwall have been celebrated, from time immemorial, for their skill and prowess in the art of wrestling. The boys may at the present day be seen struggling and practising at a very early age: and Carew says, in his quaint old style—"you shall hardly find an assembly of boys in Devon and Cornwall, where the most untowardly amongst them, will not so readily give you a muster of this exercise, as you are prone to require it."[6]

It is told by Strutt, that, in the reign of Henry III., the citizens of London, who delighted in the science, held their anniversary meeting near the Hospital of St. Matilda, at St. Giles's in the Fields, where the inhabitants of Westminster met, and wrestled with them for a ram. The Londoners were successful, which produced a challenge for Lammas-day. The challenge was accepted—and the parties encountered each other;—but the bailiff happening to quarrel, a strife ensued, in which some mischief was done.[7]

According to the accounts of that accurate historian Stowe, Clerkenwell was a celebrated spot for wrestling.[8] The Mayor, Sheriffs, and officers of the city, took an active part in this sport. It must have been a curious excuse that the Mayor could not attend the Mansion-house, as he was trying a fall with one of the magistrates of Westminster!

In a plate from an old picture, supposed to be considerably anterior to the time of Chaucer, and which is given in Strutt, two men are represented wrestling for a cock:[9]—it is curious that even at the present day the combatants wear a loose linen jacket, on the back of which is affixed the figure of a *cock* in cloth of a green or red colour. The prizes were, in early days, a ram, a small sum of money, or even something of greater value. Strutt quotes an extract from one of Robin Hood's songs, which touches on the rewards of the conquerors.

—Unto Bernisdale,
As he went by a bridge was a *wrasteling*,
And there taryed was he,
And there was all the best yemen,
Of all the west countrey.
A full fayre game there was set up;
A white bull up ypight;
A great courser with saddle and brydle,
With golde burnished full bryght:
A payre of gloves, a red golde ringe,
A pipe of wyne, good faye;
What man beareth him best, ywis,
The prize shall bear awaye.[10]

Carew, the old writer before referred to, thus quaintly describes the art of wrestling in the western parts of England;—it will be seen that some change has taken place in the science itself, in the present age, but the practice has certainly not declined.

The beholders then cast, or form themselves into a ring, in the empty space where-of the two champions step forth, stripped into their dublets and hosen, and untrussed, that they may so the better command the use of their lymmes; and first shaking hands, in token of friendship, they fall presently to the effect of anger; for each striveth how to take hold of the other with his best advantage, and to bear his adverse party downe; wherein, whosoever overthroweth his mate, in such sorte, as that either his backe, or the one shoulder, and contrary heele do touche the ground, is accounted to give the fall. If he be only endangered, and make a narrow escape, it is called a foyle. This pastime also hath its laws; for instance of taking hold above the girdle,—wearing a girdle to take hold by,— playing three pulls for tryal of the mastery, the fall giver to be exempted from playing again with the taker, but bound to answer his successor. Silver prizes, for this and other activities, were wont to be carried about, by certain *circumfer-anci*, or set up at bride ales; but time, or their abuse, hath worn them out of use.[11]

Strutt, whose name I have so repeatedly mentioned, and to whom I am so much indebted for information on the subject, gives a representation of two persons riding on the shoulders of two others, and so wrestling for the fall. He states this to have been a sport of the fourteenth century:[12]—I think I have been concerned in such a pastime at school within even a very few years,—and the great object was to secure, what was termed, "a good *horse*." This amusement seems trifling enough, and is certainly no trial of bodily strength, agility or skill.

—But I fancy that I see the *hat* thrown up, and therefore I proceed to give as correct an account as my memory will furnish, of the match at Exmouth, which was *played out*, to use the county phrase, with the utmost zeal and courage, in spite of falling rains and slippery grass. The ring was formed in a field called *The Marshes*,—a term sufficiently explanatory of the nature of the spot, without any further description of mine. The showers, however, lent a cruel aid to the natural wetness of the land, as if purposing to "try a fall" with these holiday folk. When I approached the ring, the rain was descending rapidly, but the people stood undauntedly around; and the sports were coming on steadily and profoundly. There was a large circle of wooden railing erected, forming the back to a single bench, and within this ring you were admitted on paying the sum of three pence. The crowd was compelled to stand as near to the rails as possible, and thus an open space was kept for the competitors. After the rules had been read, which I could not very well hear,—a hat was hurled into the air, and immediately followed by one from an acceptor of the challenge;—the wrestlers began to prepare immediately for the struggle. The first that stood in the middle of the ring, having been stripped to the shirt, and enclothed in the linen jacket with a green cock on the back,—which I have noticed to be the customary garment—was a young man of extremely prepossessing appearance. His figure, which, in its county garb, had not particularly impressed me with its size or strength, now struck me as highly powerful, compact, and beautiful. His limbs were well grown, and strongly set—yet rather slight than otherwise—and his body was easy, slim, yet peculiarly expressive of power. The fronts of his legs, from the knee to the ancle, were armed with thick carpeting, to protect him from the kicks of his antagonist; and even this strange armour did not give to his person the appearance of clumsiness. His neck was bare, and certainly very fine;—but the shape of his head struck me as being the most impressive and *poetical* (I use the term under correction), I had for a long time beheld—

being set off, I conceive, by the way in which his hair was arranged;—and this was dark,—hanging in thick *snakish* curls on each side his forehead, and down the back part of his head. Add to all this, a handsome melancholy thin countenance, and you will have at once some idea of the young man who now stood before me.

I turned to a countryman near me, and inquired who this youth might be, whose undaunted mien and comely port had so taken my favour captive. "Who is *that!*" said the man with a tone of surprise, accompanied with a look of profound pity at my ignorance,—"why, one of the *Canns* to be sure!"—In an instant I remembered the name, and his presence so well seconded the feeling which the enthusiasm of the servant had awakened, that I really had the sensation of a blush on my mind, at not recognizing in such a figure one of the names which were in the mouths of women and domestics as synonyms for prowess and valour, and which at the onset had sounded to me like fame!

Young Cann stood awhile in a calm and indifferent attitude,—and his opponent ploughed his heavy way towards him. This was a little bull-necked, thick-set man,—of prodigiously broad and weighty carriage. His carpeted limbs resembled the bolsters of a sofa,—and his throat was scarcely inferior in size. Cann pledged him in a cup of beer or cyder, (I will not call it a *wine cup*, as Mr. Campbell would, to exalt it from the vulgar truth into poetical respectability), and then giving the mug to one of the umpires, he clutched the little coast Hercules firmly with one hand, by the collar of his jacket, and received in return the tiger clutch of his eager antagonist. The struggle immediately commenced;—the umpires keeping a wary eye on the sport. Cann stood up nobly, watchfully—gallantly—meeting every movement of his opponent with a harder gripe of the jacket, and receiving the kicks of the little human *Cob* with an indifference quite astounding to all possessors of knees and shin-bones. The short man stood low, and far from Cann, and seemed rather to watch and labour for his safety than to dare for his enemy's downfall. He leaned forward, as if he were on *all fours*, and slipped and sprawled about, and abroad,—like a cat in walnut shells,—and with the same extraordinary pertinacity for keeping on his feet. This ungainly attitude was beautifully contrasted by Cann's upright muscular form, towering over it, and following, lion-like, the crouching and shifting manoeuvres of the tiger-like creature opposed to him. This struggle, in which a fine display of skill and strength was exhibited, lasted five minutes, when the parties were instantly separated by the umpires;— such being the time limited for the *single play* as it is termed. When a man has stood out two men, and thrown one, he is set down as a *double player*, and is entitled to strive among the select, on the second day, for the prizes. Of course all the Canns, and the best men from the Moors, and young Brockenden, and Thorne from Dawlish, made themselves *double players*. I shall not longer dwell on the various wrestling of the first day.

The second morning was any thing but "rosy fingered"—but still we were not to be terrified by threatening clouds from following the manly sport which the day was to decide. There were some slow and tedious contests for *double players* till very late in the afternoon,—when, as the evening closed, and the moon arose, the grand contest was commenced. One of the umpires approached the booth in which I stood, and requested of Mr. Roe (as I understood the name), not to postpone the sports till the morrow, "as the Canns were anxious to get back to their farms, and Thorne must return to Dawlish the same night, and the men wanted to go to the Moors!"—This appeal was commanding, and the kind Mr. Roe yielded to the wishes of the combatants. "To night be it then," said this amiable patron of the pleasures of the poor,—"and let not a moment be lost in matching the men, and calling them forth!"

The first shout of the master of the revels was—"the younger Cann, and Widdicomb of the Moors!"—and this was received with a low murmur, and a deep interest which almost smothered sound. The younger Cann was the stoutest of the brotherhood, finely formed, and fair-haired. He stripped and accoutred himself immediately; his brothers assisting in buckling his *leg-armour*, and fastening his jacket. There was evidently a great anxiety in this group, but still the utmost confidence in ultimate success;—and I could not help taking part in the interest of the brothers, and at the same time entertaining a full share of their faith in their champion's triumph. "And who," said I to a neighbour, "are these Canns!"—"They are farmers, and there are five brothers, all excellent wrestlers;—but you only see three here to night."—But the fine young wrestler stepped into the ring, and our conversation ceased.

The moon was now very clear, full and bright; and its light fell upon the noble person of Cann, and showed every curl of his hair. The Moor-man soon joined him—prepared for the conflict. He was a giant in size, and from what I gathered around me, a man of most savage nature. The popular feeling was painfully on Cann's side. After the cup had been pledged, the opponents seized each other with an iron grasp. Cann stood boldly, but cautiously up, as conscious that he had much to do;—and the Moor-man opposed him resolutely and grandly. The struggle was immediate, and Cann, with one terrific wrench, threw his antagonist to the earth;—but he fell so doubtfully on his shoulder, that it seemed uncertain whether he would fall on his back (which is necessary to victory), or recover himself by rolling on his face. Cann looked proudly down upon him, and saw him by a miraculous strain, which resembled that of a Titan in pain, save the fall, by wrenching himself down on his face. His shoulder and side were soiled;—but he was not deemed vanquished.

By the order of the umpires the struggle was renewed, when, owing, as I conceived, to the slippery state of the grass, Cann fell on his knees, and the Moorsman instantly hurled him on his back. All was uproar and confusion—but Cann was declared to have received a fall—and gloom spread itself over all! He could not be convinced of the justice of his judges (a common case when the verdict is adverse,) and it was in real pain of spirit that he pulled off the jacket.

Young Brockenden followed next with another man from the Moors; —and he received a doubtful fall, which was much cavilled at, but which the judges nevertheless gave against him.

It now grew late, and the clouds thickened around, so that the wrestling could scarcely be perceived. I left the sports somewhat unwillingly; but I could not distinguish the parties, and, in truth, I was dispirited at my favourite's being foiled. I heard that the brother Canns retrieved the fame of the family,—but the darkness of the night, and the state of the grass, gave no chance either to the spectators or to the wrestlers. In the morning, the ring,—the awning,—the scaffolding—had vanished; and the young fellows had separated—the Canns to their farms,—the Men to the Moors!

I have described this meeting as well and as faithfully as I could, in the hope that the account may interest many persons who are content to be excited by description only. At the same time, if this manly sport, among others, should be cried down and oppressed by the feeble and the fastidious, it may not be amiss to have some record of it preserved to feed the curious of after ages. I cannot conclude this paper better, than by noticing a very learned, quaint, and ingenious little work on the *Art of Wrestling*, which I met with by chance in a pamphlet-shop, and which I have read with much admiration.[13] I believe it is the genuine reprint of an old book—though certainly now published in a very graceless and forbidding shape.

The title page sets forth that the work is written by *Sir Thomas Parkyns*, of Bunny-Park, Nottinghamshire,—and certainly a more intense production, on the use of the sinews and muscles, cannot easily be pointed out. Sir Thomas lived in the early part of the last century,[14] and was remarkable for his skill in, and fondness for, the art of wrestling. He was strong in the loins, and a justice of peace for Nottinghamshire and Leicestershire. All his servants were trained to the sport, and he gave public exhibitions of it, taking an active part himself in tripping up his coachman, and giving his footman a heavy fall. He was fond of indulging in scraps of *Latin*, in which, however, he was not so powerful as in wrestling. Over a seat which stood by the road-side, he inscribed,—

Hic sedeas viator, si tu defessus es ambulando.[15]

And a judge happening to ascend his pad, during his circuit, by means of Sir Thomas's block, the event is thus classically recorded:

Hinc justiciarius Dormer equum ascendere solebat![16]

Sir Thomas studied physic for the good of his neighbours,—married two wives, one being the daughter of a London alderman,—indulged in a selection of stone-coffins during his life, for his choice to lie in after death,—left a guinea to be wrestled for on Midsummer-day, and a *something* to the ringers of Bunny church, among whom he had often formed one,—wrote a book,—and died in the year 1741, aged 78.

His little work, however, must not thus be dismissed.—Sir Thomas wrestles manfully with grammar, and is good at the *in-play* with metaphors and figures. The dedication—which, by the bye, gives the book to no one, and is, therefore, strikingly original—is "a fair specimen of the author's style," as the Reviews express themselves.—Take the following:—

For the most part, the first question I ask a scholar, (if I like his size and com-plexion, for I am an indifferent physiognomist, a judicious physician, and can prognosticate more from a *phyz*, than most physicians from waters) is, if his parents are alive? if not, what age they died at? For I admit no *Hereditary Gouts*, or *Scrofulous Tumours*; yet I'll readily accept of *Scorbutick Rheumatisms*, because the persons labouring under those maladies are generally strong and able to undergo the exercise of *wrestling*. I am so curious in my admission, I'll not hear of one hipp'd and out of joint, a *Valetudinarian* is my aversion, for I affirm, *Martial* [*Lib*. vi. *Ep*. 54.] is in the right on't: *Non est vivere sed valere vita*.[17] I receive no limber-hams, no darling sucking-bottles, who must not rise, at *Midsummer*, till eleven of the clock, and that the fire has aired his room and cloaths of his colliquative sweats, raised by high sauces, and spicy forced meats, where the cook does the office of stomach, with the emetick tea table, set out with bread and butter for his breakfast: I'll scarce admit a sheep-biter, none but beef-eaters will go down with me, who have robust, healthy, and sound bodies. This may serve as a sketch of that person fit to make a *wrestler*, by him who only desires a place in your friendship.

On the page immediately following the dedication there stand some notable lines, with an embellishment, which are thus described by the writer, in a style worthy of the mighty Baronet whose memory they celebrate. The following is a *fac-simile*:

"A Poem in defence of the Marble Effigies of *Sir Thomas Parkyns*, of Bunny Park, in the County of Nottingham, Bart. erected by him in his life time, in a Moralizing Posture, in his Chancel of the Church of Bunny: being the first Posture of Wrestling; an Emblem of the Divine and Human Struggle for the Glorious Mastery.

By Francis Hoffman."[18]

The poem itself is energetic, moral, and amiable,—fit elegy for a man of thews, and a Baronet:—But I must not thus dally so long with the opening beauties of the book. Sir Thomas Parkyns commences his instructive treatise with stating, that, after reading in Martial,—under Dr. Busby, at Westminster,—that the ancients always performed their exercise (like school-boys) before their full meal,—he advised all his scholars to take "light liquids easy of digestion," to meet this classical example. He then proceeds,—

Whilst at *Westminster*, I could not learn any thing from their irregular and rude *certamina* or *struggles*: and when I went to *Cambridge*, I then, as a spectator, only observed the vast difference betwixt the *Norfolk out-players*, and the *Cornish-huggers*, and that the latter could throw the other when they pleased. I do confess, the small knowledge I shew to have in my several pieces of architecture, &c. with my useful hydraulicks, and the use and application of the mathematicks here in *wrestling*, I owe to *Dr. Bathurst*, my tutor, and *Sir Isaac Newton*, mathematick professor, both of *Trinity College, Cambridge*: the latter, seeing my inclination that way, invited me to his public lectures, for which I thank him, though I was Fellow Commoner, and seldom, if ever, any such were called to them; but when I went to *Gray's Inn of Court*, and applied myself to the several masters of the *Academy*, to learn fencing and vaulting, I met with *Mr. Cornish*, (by name) my *inn-play* wrestling master; and when I found so much variety in the several holds, that it was impossible to remember half of them, without committing them to paper; and telling him my design, he said, he had taught five hundred scholars, but never any one could set them down; and that it would be in vain to attempt any such thing: however, once in two months, I shewed him what I had done, and then digested it in this method, which I here present you with.[19]

Sir Thomas continues, and is very urgent against "weakening by drink." Personifying the various strong liquors which wrestle with man, he thus pleasantly concludes his caution.

Ceres keeps school at all checquers, with her assistants, *Nottingham, Derby, Burton, Easingwould,* &c. At most public houses, *Stout* has the fullest school amongst the porters, carmen, chairmen, &c. *Paracelsus* admits for the most part, at the *Golden Stills*, his method he extracted from, and is an abridgment of, the two former, his journeymen assistants are, brandy, a *Frenchman*; usquebagh, an *Irishman*; rum, a Mollosonian, &c.[20]

In the middle of these, his prefatory remarks, Sir Thomas thus eloquently breaks out on the origin of the science, which he seems suddenly to think has rather been a sufferer in his opening observations. Certes he goes back sufficiently, and "can quote scripture to his purpose."

Though at the beginning of the preface I take notice, that wrestling was in vogue, great credit, estimation, and reputation, in *Martial* the poet's days, wrestling without all doubt is of greater antiquity, as appears, *Gen. chap.* xxxii. *ver.* 24, *Jacob* wrestled with an angel, whether it was real and corporal, or mystical, and spiritual in its signification, I leave *Pool* and the rest of the divines to determine.

But I advise all my scholars, *to avoid wrestling with angels*, for though they may maintain the struggle until break of day, and seem to lay their adversaries supine, and on their backs, they will have the foil, and be out of joint with *Jacob's* thigh.[21]

The concluding advice cannot be too strictly attended to.

The second division of the book, is a regular set of rules and directions for "Every Man his own Wrestler," and commences with several pages on strained ancles, (which allows for Sir Thomas's passion for physic to have its way,) and the best methods of avoiding or curing the Evil. High-heeled shoes meet with the kind Baronet's most serious and vehement displeasure, as being the causes of all sprains. He reasons so much to his own satisfaction in favour of low-heeled shoes, and brings such apposite illustrations of his arguments, that he suddenly breaks off into the following exclamation:—

For shame, let us leave off aiming at the out-doing our Maker in our true symmetry and proportion: let us *likewise*, for our own ease, to secure treading, and upright walking, (as he designed we should) shorten our heels. Since the women have lowered their top sails and head dresses, and find it a vain attempt of theirs in offering to *add one cubit to their stature*.[22]

Next follows much masterly advice on the mysteries of wrestling, with full instructions on those various holds and falls, which are most destructive and conclusive. The ignorant are clearly taught how to accomplish "the *Flying Horse*," which simply means pitching your friend over your head. "The *Flying Mare*," is a throw of nearly the same airy description. I really cannot follow Sir Thomas through all his dissertations on "*the hanging Trippet*," the "*in Clamp*," the "*back Clamp*," "*the Pinnion*," "*the Gripe*," "*the In-lock*," and "*the loose leg*:"—all points of profound, and serious, and erudite discussion:—The direction for the back clamp is, however, curious, though I think it scarcely solves the mystery for young students.

Back-Clamp.

When your adversary back-clamps you, which is when he clasps his heel in your ham, with a design to throw you backwards, fall in close to him with your arms about him, as for the gripes; bear upon him with your breast and chin, and kick your own breech with your own heel, with his feeble heel in your fort ham; and his head and shoulder will come to the ground first, that throwing him out of the line of direction.[23]

The passage explanatory of "the gripes," (a phrase likely to be misunderstood, and mentioned in the foregoing passage,) is also so erudite, that I cannot resist giving it:—

The Gripes.

1. Are *nothing but laying your right arm amongst his small ribs*, and putting your left hand to your right arm to augment your strength in griping; and when you gripe, get your head on the outside of his arm, then may you lift the better.

2. Never delay the gripe, but get that as soon as you can, and hold him strait, and your head close to his breast, that he doth not give his elbow, and stand low with your knees bent and toes out, and it will prevent buttock, back-lock, in-lock, and trip.[24]

Sir Thomas thus proceeds, ardently, through many pages, on *outplay* and *inplay*, but I shall have already exhausted all my reader's patience, and my Editor's room: though, if I consulted my own taste only, I should minutely discuss every page, and now and then endeavour to give Sir Thomas *the Flying Horse*, in some of his arguments and conclusions. I flatter myself I could certainly *back-clamp* him on many of his *out-play*, or *loose-leg* instructions. His last page contains some directions for a *Boxer*, but here (to our knowledge) he is off his feet, for he decidedly betrays too much of the wrestler throughout them. The two first articles of this chapter, though amiably intended, sufficiently expose his ignorance of the art, unless, as we must believe, the art has undergone material changes since he wrote.

Boxing.

1. By all means have the first blow with your head or fist at his breast rather than at his face; which is half the battle, by reason it strikes the wind out of his body.

2. If you have long hair soap it. The best holds are the pinnion with your arms at his shoulders, and your head in his face, or get your right arm under his chin,

and your left behind his neck, and let your arms close his neck straight, by holding each elbow with the contrary hand, and crush his neck, your fingers in his eyes, and your fingers of your right hand under his chin, and your left hand under the hinder part of his head; or twist his head round by putting your hand to the side of his face, and the other behind his head.[25]

Really, as to the second direction, if a man could patiently endure this *fingering* of the eyes and gullet, he must possess a courage of no common order. So much for *Sir Thomas Parkyns*, the writing, wrestling, boxing Nottingham Baronet.

In conclusion, I do pray and trust, that these manly sports, which keep alive the courage and character of the lower orders, will not be neglected or oppressed by those who have the power to excite and promote them. The existence of such pastimes is influential on the moral rectitude of the country. Men who possess such names as the *Canns*,* and *Thorne*, and *Brockenden*, dare not by private baseness or indecorum sully them. They live in the eye of a County, and have a fame to maintain, which can only exist on the purest food. Other men have these names like beacons before them; and hope leads them on!—The days, on which a wrestling match is held, are acknowledged holidays for miles round the spot,— and the youths come forth in fascinating new hats and overpowering *velveteens*,—and the damsels in their best and most destructive attire. I saw girls from all quarters of the county in the gayest of their dresses,— and certainly there was a fashion about their bonnets (if I do not err) in spite of what the Spectator has said, (vol. iii, No. 175.) or suffered to be said, to the disparagement of the Exeter ladies, that "they are always behind-hand in the fashion, and, worse than that, have things palmed upon them which are not fashionable."

Having mentioned the Spectator, I cannot do better than give his recommendatory words for encouraging wakes and country assemblies of this kind. He knew that the lasses got suitors, and the lads admirers at these pleasant and sportive meetings, and he thus concludes his paper, as I shall mine, with pointing out a reason all sufficient for their being nourished among us:—

* Mr. Wilson, the Plague-Poet, and *Moral Professor*, is very fond of running about the Highlands, wrestling and leaping with the distillers of his favourite beverage whiskey. We wish he would try a fall with the younger Cann, for we cannot help thinking it would "take the conceit out of him," and the better fit him for those serener pursuits, to which Blackwood's Magazine and the lecture-chair of Edinburgh particularly invite him.[26]

Love and marriage are the natural effects of these anniversary assemblies. I must, therefore, very much approve the method by which my correspondent tells me each sex endeavours to recommend itself to the other, since nothing seems more likely to promise a healthy offspring, or a happy cohabitation. And I believe I may assure my country friend, that there has been many a court lady, who would be contented to change her crazy young husband for Tom Short; and several men of quality, who would have parted with a tender yoke-fellow for Black Kate.

I am the more pleased with having love made the principal end and design of these meetings, as it seems to be most agreeable to the intent for which they were at first instituted, as we are informed by the learned Dr. Kennet, with whose words I shall conclude my present paper. "These wakes," says he, "were in imitation of the ancient ἀγαπά, or love-feasts, and were first established in England by Pope Gregory the Great, who, in an epistle to Melitus the Abbot, gave order that they should be kept in sheds or arbories made up with branches and boughs of trees round the church."[27]

He adds, that this laudable custom of wakes prevailed for many ages, till the wise Puritans began to exclaim against it as a remnant of popery; and by degrees the precise humour grew so popular, that at an Exeter assizes the Lord Chief Baron Walter made an order for the suppression of all wakes: but on Bishop Laud's complaining of this innovating humour, the King commanded the order to be reversed.

The Cook's Oracle.* October 1821

Dr. Kitchener has greatly recognised the genius of his name by taking boldly the path to which it points; disregarding all the usual seductions of life, he has kept his eye steadily on the larder, the *Mecca* of his appetite; and has unravelled all the mysteries and intricacies of *celery soup*, and *beef haricot*, to the eyes of a reading public. He has taken an extensive *kitchen range* over the whole world of stews, and broils, and roasts, and comes home to the fireside (from which, indeed, his body has never departed) boiling over with knowledge—stored with curiosities of bone

* The Cook's Oracle: containing Receipts for plain Cookery, &c. the whole being the Result of actual Experiments, instituted in the Kitchen of a Physician. London. Constable and Co. 1821.[28]

and sinew—a made-up human dish of cloves, mace, curry, catsup, cayenne, and the like. He has sailed over all the soups; has touched at all the quarters of the lamb; has been, in short, round the stomach world, and returns a second *Captain Cook*! Dr. Kitchener has written a book; and if he, good easy man, should think to surprise any friend or acquaintance by slily asking, "What book have I written?" he would be sure to be astounded with a successful reply, "a book on Cookery." His name is above all disguises. In the same way, a worthy old gentleman of our acquaintance, who was wont to lead his visitors around his kitchen garden (the Doctor will prick up his ears at this), which he had carefully and cunningly obscured with a laurel hedge, and who always said, with an exulting tone, "Now, you would be puzzled to say where the kitchen garden was situated;" once met with a stony-hearted man, who remorselessly answered, "Not I! over that hedge, to be sure." The Doctor might expect you, in answer to his query, to say; "A book, Sir! Why, perhaps you have plunged your whole soul into the ocean of an epic; or rolled your mind, with the success of a Sisyphus, up the hill of metaphysics; or played the sedate game of the mathematics, that Chinese puzzle to English minds! or gone a tour, with Dugald Stuart, in search of the picturesque;[29] or leaped double sentences, and waded through metaphors, in a grammatical steeple-chace with Colonel Thornton;[30] or turned literary cuckoo, and gone sucking the eggs of other people's books, and making the woods of the world echo with one solitary, complaining, *reviewing* note." Such might be the Doctor's notion of a reply, to which we fancy we see him *simmering* with delight, and saying, "No, Sir! I have not meddled either with the curry of poetry, or the cold meat of prose. I have not wasted over the slow fire of the metaphysics, or cut up the mathematics into thin slices—I have not lost myself amongst the *kick-shaws* of fine scenery, or pampered myself on the mock-turtle of metaphors. Neither have I dined at the table and the expense of other men's minds! No, Sir. I have written on cookery, on the kitchen, on the solids, 'the substantials, Sir Giles, the substantials!'"[31]

If it were not that critics are proverbial for having no bowels, we should hesitate at entering the paradise of pies and puddings which Dr. Kitchener has opened to us; for the steam of his rich sentences rises about our senses like the odours of flowers around the imagination of a poet; and larded beef goes nigh to lord it over our bewildered appetites.

But being steady men, of sober and temperate habits, and used to privations in the way of food, we shall not scruple at looking a leg of mutton in the face, or shaking hands with a shoulder of veal. "Minced collops" nothing daunt us; we brace our nerves, and are not over-whelmed with "cockle catsup!" When Bays asks his friend, "How do you do when you write?"[32] it would seem that he had the Cook's Oracle in his eye—for to men of any mastication, never was there a book that required more training for a quiet and useful perusal. Cod's-head rises before you in all its glory! while the oysters revolve around it, in their firmament of melted butter, like its well-ordered satellites! Moorgame, mackarel, muscles, fowls, eggs, and force-meat-balls, start up in all directions, and dance the hays in the imagination. We should recommend those readers with whom dinner is a habit, not to venture on the Doctor's pages, without seeing that their hunger, like a ferocious house-dog, is carefully tied up. To read four pages with an unchained appetite, would bring on dreadful dreams of being destroyed with spits, or drowned in mullagatawny soup, or of having your tongue neatly smothered in your own brains, and, as Matthews says, a lemon stuck in your mouth.[33] We cannot but conceive that such reading, in such unprepared minds, would have strange influences; and that the dreams of persons would be dished up to suit the various palates. The school-girl would, like the French goose, "be persuaded to roast itself." The indolent man would "steep a fortnight," and even then not be fit for use. The lover would dream that his heart was overdone. The author would be roasted alive in his own quills, and basted with cold ink. It were an endless task to follow this speculation; and, indeed, we are keeping our readers too long without the meal to which we have taken the liberty of inviting them. The dinner "bell invites" us—we go, and it is *done*.

The book, the Cook's Oracle, opens with a preface, as other books occasionally do; but "there the likeness ends;" for it continues with a whole bunch of introductions, treating of cooks, and invitations to dinner, and refusals, and "friendly advice," and weights and measures, and then we get fairly launched on the sea of boiling, broiling, roasting, stewing, and again return and cast anchor among the vegetables. It is impossible to say where the book begins; it is a heap of initiatory chapters—a parcel of graces before meat—a bunch of heads,—the asparagus of literature. You are not troubled with "more last words of Mr. Baxter," but are delighted, and *re*-delighted, with more first words of Dr. Kitchener. He makes several starts, like a restless race-horse, before he fairly gets upon the second course; or rather, like Lady Macbeth's dinner party, he stands much upon the order of his going. But now, to avoid sinking into the same trick, we will proceed without further preface to conduct our readers through the maze of pots, gridirons, and frying pans, which Dr. Kitchener has rendered a very poetical, or we should say, a very palatable amusement.

The *first* preface tells us, *inter alia*, that he has worked all the culinary problems which his book contains, in his own kitchen; and that, after this warm experience, he did not venture to print a sauce, or a stew, until he had read "two hundred cookery books," which, as he says, "he patiently pioneered through, before he set about recording the results of his own experiments!"[34] We scarcely thought there had been so many volumes written on the Dutch oven.

The *first* introduction begins thus:

The following receipts are not a mere marrowless collection of shreds, and patches, and cuttings, and pastings;—but a *bona fide* register of practical facts,—accumulated by a perseverance not to be subdued, or evaporated, by the igniferous terrors of a roasting fire in the dog-days,—in defiance of the odoriferous and calefacient repellents, of roasting,—boiling,—frying,—and broiling:—moreover, the author has submitted to a labour no preceding Cookery Book-maker, perhaps, ever attempted to encounter—having *eaten* each receipt, before he set it down in his book.[35]

We should like to see the Doctor, we confess, after this extraordinary statement. To have superintended the agitations of the pot,—to have hung affectionately over a revolving calf's heart,—to have patiently witnessed the noisy marriage of bubble and squeak,—to have coolly investigated the mystery of a haricot,—appears within the compass of any given old lady or gentleman, whose frame could stand the fire, and whose soul could rule the roast. But to have eaten the substantials of 440 closely printed pages, is "a thing to read of, not to tell." It calls for a man of iron interior, a man "alieni appetens, sui profusus."[36] It demands the rival of time; an *edax rerum!*[37] The Doctor does not tell us how he travelled from gridiron to frying-pan—from frying-pan to

Duch oven—from Dutch oven to spit—from spit to pot—from pot to fork: he leaves us to guess at his progress. We presume he ate his way, page by page, through fish, flesh, fowl, and vegetable; he would have left *us* dead among the soups and gravies. Had a whole army of martyrs accompanied him on this Russian retreat of the appetite, we should have found *them* strewing the way; and *him* alone, the Napoleon of the task, living and fattening at the end of the journey. The introduction goes on very learnedly, descanting upon Shakspeare, Descartes, Dr. Johnson, Mrs. Glasse,[38] Professor Bradley,[39] Pythagoras, Miss Seward,[40] and other persons equally illustrious. The Doctor's chief aim is to prove, we believe, that cookery is the most laudable pursuit, and the most pleasurable amusement of life. Much depends on the age of your domestics; for we are told, that "it is a good maxim to select servants not younger than THIRTY."[41] Is it so? Youth "thou art shamed!" This first introduction concludes with a long eulogy upon the Doctor's "laborious stove work;" and upon the spirit, temper, and ability, with which he has *dressed* his book. The Doctor appends to this introduction, a chapter called "Culinary Curiosities," in which he gives the following recipe for "persuading a goose to roast itself." We must say it out-horrors all the horrors we ever read of.

How to roast and eat a goose alive.—"Take a goose, or a duck, or some such lively creature, (but a goose is best of all for this purpose), pull off all her feathers, only the head and neck must be spared: then make a fire round about her, not too close to her, that the smoke do not choke her, and that the fire may not burn her too soon; nor too far off, that she may not escape free; within the circle of the fire let there be set small cups and pots full of water, wherein salt and honey are mingled; and let there be set also chargers full of sodden apples, cut into small pieces in the dish. The goose must be all larded, and basted over with butter, to make her the more fit to be eaten, and may roast the better: put then fire about her, but do not make too much haste, when as you see her begin to roast; for by walking about, and flying here and there, being cooped in by the fire that stops her way out, the unwearied goose is kept in;* she will fall to drink the water to quench her thirst, and cool her heart, and all her body, and the apple sauce will make her dung, and cleanse and empty her. And when she roasteth, and con-

---

* This cook of a goose, or goose of a cook, which ever it may be, strangely reminds us of the Doctor's own intense and enthusiastic bustle among the butter boats. We fancy we see him, and not the goose, "walking about, and flying here and there, being cooped in by the fire." By this time, we should suppose, he must be about "roasted enough."

sumes inwardly, always wet her head and heart with a wet sponge; and when you see her giddy with running, and begin to stumble, her heart wants moisture, and she is roasted enough. Take her up, set her before your guests, and she will cry as you cut off any part from her, and will be almost eaten up before she be dead: it is mighty pleasant to behold!!!" See *Wecker's Secrets of Nature*, in folio, London, 1660, pp. 148, 309.[42]

The next chapter, or introduction, (for we are not within forty spits' length of the cookery directions yet!) is entitled "Invitations to Dinner;" and commences thus:

In "the affairs of the mouth," the strictest punctuality is indispensable;—the gastronomer ought to be as accurate an observer of time, as the astronomer. The least delay produces fatal and irreparable misfortunes.[43]

It appearing, therefore, that delay is dangerous, as mammas say to their daughters on certain occasions, the Doctor directs that "the dining-room should be furnished with a good-going clock."[44] He then speaks of food "well done, when it is done," which leads to certain learned sentences upon indigestion. The sad disregard of dinner-hours generally observed meets with his most serious displeasure and rebuke; but to refuse an invitation to dinner is the capital crime, for which there is apparently no capital punishment.

Nothing can be more disobliging than a refusal which is not grounded on some very strong and unavoidable cause, except not coming at the appointed hour; according to the laws of conviviality, a certificate from a sheriff's officer, a doctor, or an undertaker, are the only pleas which are admissible. The duties which invitation imposes, do not fall only on the persons invited, but like all other social duties, are reciprocal.[45]

If you should, therefore, fortunately happen to be arrested, or have had the good luck to fracture a limb; or if, better than all, you should have taken a box in that awful theatre at which all must be present once and for ever; you may be pardoned refusing the invitation of some tiresome friend to take a chop: but there is no other excuse, no other available excuse, for absenting yourself; no mental inaptitude will save you. Late comers are thus rebuked:

There are some, who seldom keep an appointment;—we can assure them they as seldom "'scape without whipping"—and exciting those murmurs which inevitably proceed from the best regulated stomachs,—when they are empty and impatient to be filled.[46]

Carving is the next subject of the Doctor's care; but he resolutely, and somewhat vehemently, protests against your wielding the king of knives at any other table than your own; thus for ever excluding an author from the luxuries of table anatomy. After giving an erudite passage from the "Almanach des Gourmands," the Doctor wanders into anecdote, and becomes facetious after the following recipe.

I once heard a gentle hint on this subject given to a blue-mould fancier, who, by looking too long at a Stilton cheese, was at last completely overcome by his eye exciting his appetite, till it became quite ungovernable and unconscious of every thing but the *mity* object of his contemplation; he began to pick out in no small portions, the primest parts his eye could select from the centre of the cheese.

The good-natured founder of the feast, highly amused at the ecstacies each morsel created in its passage over the palate of the enraptured *Gourmand*, thus encouraged the perseverance of his guest—"Cut away, my dear sir, cut away, use no ceremony. I pray:—I hope you will pick out all the best of my cheese—the rind and the rotten will do very well for my wife and family!!"[47]

There is something so serene and simple in the above little story, that we recommend it to persons after dinner, in preference to those highly seasoned and spicy jests, which Mr. Joseph Miller has potted for the use of posterity.

The next introduction contains "Friendly Advice to Cooks and other Servants;" but we cannot help thinking that Dr. Swift has in some degree forestalled our own good Doctor in this department of literature; although, perhaps, Dr. Kitchener is the most sober of counsellors. The following, to be sure, is a little suspicious. "Enter into all their plans of economy, and endeavour to make the most of every thing, as well for your own honour as your master's profit."[48] This, without the note, would be unexceptionable; but the Doctor quotes from Dr. Trusler (all the Doctors are *redolent* of servants!) as follows:—"I am persuaded, that no servant ever *saved* her master sixpence, but she *found* it in the end in her own *pocket*."—"Have the *dust* removed," says Dr. Kitchener, "regularly every fortnight!"[49]—What *dust*?—Not that, we trust, which people are often entreated to "come down with."—The accumulation of soot has its dire evils; for "many good dinners have been spoiled, and many houses burned down, by the soot falling:"⁵⁰—thus the Doctor, very properly, puts the greater evil first. "Give notice to your employers when the contents of your coal cellar are *diminished* to a chaldron."⁵¹— *Diminished!* We should be glad to hear when our cellars had increased to this stock. There is no hope then for those chamber-gentlemen who fritter away their lives by sack or bushel! Dr. Kitchener is rather abstruse and particular in another of his directions:—"The *best rule for marketing*, is to pay *ready money* for every thing."⁵² This is a good rule with the elect:—but, is there no luxury in a baker's bill? Are butchers' reckonings nothing? Is there no virtue in a milk-tally? We cannot help thinking that *tick* was a great invention, and gives many a man a dinner that would otherwise go unfed.

The chapter on weights and measures is short, but deeply interesting and intense. There is an episode upon *trough nutmeg-graters* that would do the water-gruel generation good to hear.

And now the book begins *to boil*. The reader is told that meat takes twenty minutes to the pound; and that block-tin saucepans are the best. We can fish out little else, except a long and rather skilful calculation of the manner in which meat jockeys itself, and reduces its weight in the cooking. Buckle and Sam Chiffney⁵³ are nothing to "a leg of mutton with the shank bone taken out;" and it perhaps might not be amiss if the Newmarket profession were to consider how far it would be practicable to sustitute the *cauldron* for the *blanket*, and thus reduce by *steam*. We should suppose a young gentleman, with half an hour's boiling, would ride somewhere about feather-weight.

Baking is dismissed in a page and a half. We are sorry to find that some joints, when fallen into poverty and decay, are quite unworthy of credit: "When baking a joint of *poor* meat, before it has been half baked, I have seen *it* (what?) start from the bone, and shrivel up *scarcely to be believed*.⁵⁴

Roasting is the next object of Dr. Kitchener's anxious care; and if this chapter be generally read, we shall not be surprised to see people in future roasting their meat before their doors, and in their areas; for the Doctor says—

Roasting should be done in the open air, to ventilate the meat from its own fumes, and by the radiant heat, of a clear glowing fire,—otherwise it is in fact baked—

the machines the economical grate-makers call roasters, are in plain English, ovens.[55]

The Doctor then proceeds, not being content with telling you how to cook your victuals, to advise carefully as to the best method of cooking the *fire*. "The fire that is but just sufficient to receive the noble sirloin, will parch up a lighter joint;"[56] which is plainly a translation into the cook's own particular language of "temper the wind to the shorn lamb." The chapter does not conclude without observing that "every body knows the advantage of *slow boiling—slow roasting* is equally important"[57] This is an axiom.

Frying is a very graceful and lively species of cooking, though yielding perhaps, in its vivacity and music, to *broiling*—but of this more anon. We are sorry to find the Doctor endeavouring to take away from the originality of *frying*, classing it unkindly with the inferior sorts of boiling—calling it, in fact, the mere corpulence of boiling.

A fryingpan should be about four inches deep, with a perfectly flat and thick bottom, twelve inches long, and nine broad—with perpendicular sides, and must be half filled with fat: good frying is in fact—boiling in fat. To make sure that the pan is quite clean, rub a little fat over it—and then make it warm and wipe it out with a clean cloth.[58]

Broiling follows. We really begin to be enacting this sort of cookery ourselves, from the vigour and spirit with which we have rushed along in the company of Dr. Kitchener. *Broiling* is the poetry of cooking. The lyre-like shape of the instrument on which it is performed, and the brisk and pleasant sounds that arise momentarily, are rather musical than culinary. We are transported at the thought to that golden gridiron in the beef-steak club, which seems to confine the white cook in his burning cage, which generates wit, whim, and song, for hours together, and pleasantly blends the fanciful and the substantial in one laughing and robust harmony.

The Doctor is profound on the subject of vegetables. And when we consider the importance of it, we are not surprised to hear him earnestly exclaim, "I should as soon think of *roasting an animal alive*, as of boiling a *vegetable after it is dead*."[59] No one will question that the one is quite as pardonable as the other. Our readers cannot be too particular in looking to their brocoli and potatoes.

This branch of cookery, requires the most vigilant attention.

If vegetables are a minute or two too long over the fire,—they lose all their beauty and flavour.

If not thoroughly boiled tender, they are tremendously indigestible, and much more troublesome during their residence in the stomach, than under-done meats.[60]

We pass over the rudiments of dressing fish, and of compounding broths and soups, except with remarking, that a turbot is said to be better for *not* being fresh, and that "lean juicy beef, mutton, or veal, form the *basis of broth*."[61]

Gravies and sauces are not neglected. The Doctor writes—

However "les pompeuses Bagatelles de la Cuisine Masquée" may tickle the fancy of *demi-connoisseurs*, who leaving the substance, to pursue the shadow,— prefer wonderful and whimsical metamorphoses, and things extravagantly expensive to those which are intrinsically excellent,—in whose mouth—mutton can hardly hope for a welcome, unless accompanied by Venison sauce—or a rabbit any chance for a race down the red lane, without assuming the form of a frog or a spider;—or pork, without being either "goosified," or "lambified," and game and poultry in the shape of crawfish or hedgehogs;

These travesties rather show the patience than the science of the cook,—and the bad taste of those who prefer such baby tricks to old English nourishing and substantial plain cookery.

We could have made this the biggest book with half the trouble it has taken *me* to make it the best;—concentration and perspicuity have been my aim.[62]

We do not know what the Doctor understands as "a big book;" but to our notions (and we are experienced in the weights and measures of printed works), the Cook's Oracle is a tolerably huge and Gog-like production. We should have been glad to have had a calculation of what the MS. lost in the printing. In truth, a comparative scale of the wasting of meat and prose during the cooking, would be no uninteresting performance. For our parts, we can only remark, from experience, that these our articles in the London Magazine boil up like spinage. We fancy, when written, that we have a heap of leaves fit to feed thirty columns; and they absolutely and alarmingly shrink up to a page or two when dressed by the compositor.

The romantic fancy of cooks is thus restrained:

The imagination of most cooks, is so incessantly on the hunt for a relish,—

that they seem to think, they can not make sauce sufficiently savoury, without putting into it, every thing that ever was eaten;—and supposing every addition must be an improvement, they frequently overpower the natural flavour of their plain sauces by overloading them with salt and spices, &c.:—but, remember, these will be deteriorated by any addition, save only just salt enough to awaken the palate—the lover of "piquance," and compound flavours, may have recourse to "the Magazine of Taste."[63]

Again—

Why have clove and allspice,—or mace and nutmeg in the same sauce,—or marjoram,—thyme,—and savory;—or onions,—leeks,—eshallots—and garlick: one will very well supply the place of the other,—and the frugal cook may save something considerable by attending to this, to the advantage of her employers, and her own time and trouble.—You might as well, to make soup, order one quart of water from the Thames, another from the New River, a third from Hampstead, and a fourth from Chelsea, with a certain portion of spring and rain water.[64]

The Doctor himself, however, in spite of his correction of the cooks, is not entirely free from the fanciful. When you have opened a bottle of catsup, he says, "use only the best superfine *velvet taper* corks."[65] This is *drawing* a cork with the hand of a poet.

And now, will the reader believe it? the work commences afresh! After all our labour,—after all our travelling through boiling, broiling, roasting, &c. we find that we have the whole to go over again. To our utter dismay, page 142 begins anew with—*boiling*! It is little comfort to us that the joints and cuttings come in for their distinct treatment: we seem to have made no way; and sit down with as much despair as a young school-girl who, after three quarters of a year's dancing, is put back to the *Scotch step*. Beef has been spoken of before; but we have not at all made up our minds on the following subject:

Obs.—In Mrs. Mason's Ladies' Assistant this joint is called haunch-bone; in Henderson's Cookery, edge-bone; in Domestic Management, aitch-bone; in Reynolds' Cookery, ische-bone; in Mrs. Lydia Fisher's Prudent Housewife, ach-bone; in Mrs. M'Iver's Cookery, hook-bone. We have also seen it spelt each-bone, and ridge-bone, and we have also heard it called natch-bone.[66]

Of "half a calf's-head," Dr. Kitchener says, slily enough, "if you like it *full-dressed*, score it *superficially*; beat up the yolk of an egg, and rub it over the head with a *feather; powder it*," &c.[67] Such a calf's-head as this, so full-dressed, might be company for the best nobleman's ditto in the land.

It is quite impossible for us to accompany Dr. Kitchener regularly through "roasting, frying, vegetables," &c. as we are by no means sure that our readers would sanction the *encore*. We shall pick a bit here and a bit there, from the Doctor's dainty larder; and take care to choose, as the English do with a French bill of fare, from those niceties which are novelties.

"A pig," observes the Doctor, as though he were speaking of any other dull obstinate personage, "is a very troublesome subject to *roast*. Most persons have them *baked*; send a quarter of a pound of butter, and beg the baker to *baste* it well."[68] The following occurs to us to be as difficult a direction to fulfil as any of Sir Thomas Parkins's wrestling instructions: "Lay your *pig back to back* in the dish, with one half of the head on each side, and the ears one at each end, which you must take care to make nice and *crisp*, or you will get scolded, as the good man was who bought his wife a pig with one ear."[69] The point at the end is like the point of a spit. Again: "A sucking pig, like a young child, must not be left for an instant!"[70] Never was such affection manifested before for this little interesting and persecuted tribe.

If Isaac Walton be the greatest of writers on the *catching* of fish, Dr. Kitchener is, beyond doubt, triumphant over all who have written upon the *dressing* of them. The Doctor dwells upon "the fine pale red rose colour" of pickled salmon, till you doubt whether he is not admiring a carnation. "Cod's skull" becomes flowery and attractive; and fine "silver eels," when "stewed Wiggy's way," swim in beauty as well as butter. The Doctor points out the best method of killing this perversely living fish, observing, very justly, "that the humane executioner does certain criminals the favour to *hang* them, before he breaks them on the wheel."[71]

Of salmon, the Doctor rather quaintly and *pozingly* observes,—"the *thinnest* part of the fish is the *fattest*." "*If you have any left*, put it into a pye-dish, and cover it," &c.: the direction is conditional we perceive. Remember to choose your lobsters "*heavy and lively*." "Motion," says the Doctor, "is the *index* of their freshness."[72]

Upon oysters, Dr. Kitchener is eloquent indeed. He is, as it were, "*native* here, and to the manner born."

The true lover of an oyster, will have some regard for the feelings of his little favourite, and will never abandon it to the mercy of a bungling operator,—but will open it himself, and contrive to detach the fish from the shell so dexterously, that the oyster is hardly conscious he has been ejected from his lodging, till he feels the teeth of the piscivorous gourmand tickling him to death.[73]

Who would not be an oyster, to be thus surprised, to be thus pleasingly ejected from its tenement of mother of pearl,—to be thus tickled to death? When we are placed in our *shell*, we should have no objection to be astonished with a similar delicate and titillating opening!

Giblet soup requires to be eaten with the fingers. We were not aware that these handy instruments could be used successfully in the devouring of gravies and soups.

N. B. This is rather a family dish than a company one,—the bones cannot be well picked, without the help of alive pincers.

Since Tom Coryat introduced forks, A. D. 1642, it has not been the fashion to put "pickers and stealers" into soup.[74]

After giving a most elaborate recipe for mock turtle soup, he proceeds—

This soup was eaten by the committee of taste with unanimous applause, and they pronounced it a very satisfactory substitute for "the far fetcht and dear bought" turtle; which itself is indebted for its title of "sovereign of savouriness," to the rich soup with which it is surrounded; without its paraphernalia of double relishes, a "starved turtle," has not more intrinsic sapidity than a "FATTED CALF."[75]

And a little further on he observes—

Obs.—This is a delicious soup, within the reach of those who "eat to live;" but if it had been composed expressly for those who only "live to eat," I do not know how it could have been made more agreeable: as it is, the lover of good eating will "wish his throat a mile long, and every inch of it palate."[76]

Our readers will pant to have "Mr. Michael Kelly's sauce for boiled tripe, calf-head, or cow-heel." It is this:

Garlick vinegar, a tablespoonful,—of mustard, brown sugar, and black pepper, a teaspoonful each; stirred into half a pint of oiled melted butter.[77]

Gad'a mercy, what a gullet must be in the possession of Mr. Michael Kelly!

We think the following almost a superfluous direction to cooks:—
"Take your chops out of the fryingpan," p. 324; but then he tells you,
in another place, "to put your tongue into plenty of cold water;" p. 156,
which makes all even again.

After giving ample directions for the making of essence of anchovy,
the Doctor rather damps our ardour for entering upon it by the following observation: "*Mem. You cannot make essence of anchovy half so cheap
as you can buy it.*"[78]

The following passage is rather too close an imitation of one of the
puff-directions in the Critic:[79]

To a pint of the cleanest and strongest rectified spirit, (sold by Rickards,
Piccadilly,) add two drachms and a half of the sweet oil of orange peel, (sold by
Stewart, No. 11, Old Broad Street, near the Bank,) shake it up, &c.

Obs.—We do not offer this receipt as a rival to Mr. Johnson's curacoa—it is
only proposed as an humble substitute for that incomparable liqueur.[80]

The Doctor proceeds to luxuriate upon made dishes, &c.; in the
course of which he says,—"The sirloin of beef I divide into three parts;
I first have it nicely *boned!*"[81] This is rather a suspicious way of having
it at all. Mrs. Phillip's Irish stew has all the fascination of her country-
women. In treating of shin of beef, the Doctor gives us a proverb which
we never remember to have heard before:

Of all the fowls of the air, commend me to the shin of beef,—for there's
marrow for the master, meat for the mistress, gristles for the servants, and bones
for the dogs.[82]

On pounded cheese, the Doctor writes—"The *piquance* of this *buttery-
caseous* relish," &c.[83] Is not this a little *over-done*. The passage, however, on the frying of eggs, makes up for all.

Be sure the fryingpan is quite clean; when the fat is hot, break two or three
eggs into it; do not turn them, but, while they are frying, keep pouring some of
the fat over them with a spoon:—when the yolk just begins to look white, which
it will in about a couple of minutes, they are enough;—the white must not lose
its transparency, but the yolk be seen *blushing* through it:—if they are done nicely,
they will look as white and delicate as if they had been poached, take them up
with a tin slice, drain the fat from them, trim them neatly, and send them up
with the bacon round them.

The beauty of a poached egg, is for the yolk to be seen *blushing* through the white,—which should only be just sufficiently hardened, to form a transparent veil for the egg.[84]

So much for the Cook's Oracle. The style is a *piquant* sauce to the solid food of the instructions; and we never recollect reading sentences that relished so savourily. The Doctor appears to have written his work upon the back of a dripping pan, with the point of his spit,—so very cook-like does he dish up his remarks. If we were to be cast away upon a desert island, and could only carry one book ashore, we should take care to secure the Cook's Oracle; for, let victuals be ever so scarce, there are pages in that erudite book that are, as Congreve's Jeremy says, "a feast for an emperor."[85] Who could starve with such a larder of reading?

Edward Herbert's Letters to the Family of the Powells.
No. II.
Greenwich Hospital. November 1821
To Russell Powell, Esq.

My Dear Russell—The kind interest which all your family took in the letter which I addressed to your sister, descriptive of the Coronation,[86] has rendered the task of writing to any one of you the most delightful amusement of my evening hours; and I have now a double pleasure in witnessing the various scenes which make up the great drama of life in this metropolis, from a knowledge of the gratification I shall have in describing them, and the interest you will feel in hearing them described. You well know my restless and unappeasable hunger of mind, after all that is either curious or instructive in this world,—not regarding personal comfort, or even personal safety, in the attainment of any interesting object, and ever disciplining my temper and my mind to meet and mingle with all descriptions of persons, in order to the observing of their habits, their pleasures, or their peculiarities. I love to visit the great national buildings, which commemorate either the country's taste, or the country's charities and wealth;—I love to behold the revelries, the glories, the pastimes, of the rich and the great;—I take a deep interest in the amusements, the rude sports, the noisy vivacity of the poor. You know that my knowledge of London had previously arisen principally from the books which I had read, and that my actual experience of life had been gained chiefly from the small life of market towns and country revels. How often, Russell, have we ejaculated wishes to each other, when standing at a wrestling match, or looking upon the lads of single stick, or, when walking over the most celebrated houses "for miles round,"—that we could see and admire those higher and more exciting struggles and combats of the great city,—those theatres, temples, and palaces, of which we had so often read, even to dreaming— that we could watch and wonder at the workings of that tremendous hive, into which,—rash drone as I am!—I have at length ventured to creep. I am now, my dear Russell, seeing all that can be seen,—insinuating myself into scenes and amongst characters which half of London even know only by hearsay,—wandering amongst the noblest buildings around me,—harvesting, in truth, within the granary of my mind, food enough to last your hungry spirits through the winter. Russell! strange and opposite have been my researches of late.—I have been to the green-room of a principal theatre, and witnessed all the craft, hate, and envy, "found only on the stage," as my Lord Byron well expresses it in his sweet nuisance, Don Juan;—and I have penetrated into all the heartless eagerness, guileful ferocity, and desperate spirit of the cock-pit. Greenwich Hospital has opened to my eyes its majestic, enormous, and beautiful charities;—and the bear-garden has made me familiar with its strange, antique, and brutal mysteries. I have beheld the costly state and fineries of a court,—the strife, the terrors, the appalling fierceness of a bull-fight,—the pictorial wealth and stately formalities of Hampton palace,—the beautiful and exciting conflict of two great pugilists. Have not my pursuits been various, and my curiosity unwearied and determined?—My letters will now, if my health and leisure permit, give to you, my dear Russell, or to your sisters, if the subject should beseem them, faithful accounts of my *travels,*—accounts which will be novel at least; for I do not remember to have read any description of several of the scenes which I have enumerated.—The buildings, the theatres, the court, will have gaiety and beauty enough to interest the ladies' minds; for what female heart is proof against pointed lace, or can contemplate ruffles without emotion?—while the rougher diamonds of the cock-pit, the bear-garden, and such rude mines, will be rich jewels in the cap of your curiosity. I have, indeed, a scene in store which will be brighter and costlier than all the rest; but I dare not hint at it yet, lest I ruin my chance of being taken to it at all, or rashly endanger my safety while there:—rest, rest, perturbed Russell! until I shall in my wisdom see fit to exhibit this brilliant and matchless gem to your wondering, your delighted eyes.

I should not omit to inform you, that Mrs. Mallinson's letter of introduction to the Mortons has been to me most serviceable and successful, for they have taken me by the hand with the utmost friendship and liberality, and have obtained for me the sight of many London lions:— indeed, they appear to me to have access to all the chief *cages* of the city, and the *Hectors* and *Fannys* of this marvellous metropolis are familiar to them as household words. To render my letters the more intelligible to you, as the Mortons will make the principal dramatis personae of my epistolary drama, I will attempt as clear a description of them as I can accomplish; relying upon your ingenuity for colouring my sketch with the lively and gallant tints of your own imagination. I shall merely offer you the family in outline, after the style of Retsch's Faust,[87] being convinced that none but a masterly hand can safely venture upon a minute finishing. Mr. Morton, the father, is one of those gentle and silent characters, which are rather spirits of the household, than active and common mortal portions of it:—never mingling in the petty strifes and light joys of the moment,—but softening and quieting the former with a bland and pleasant placidity, and heightening the latter by a cheerful and generous regard. His age I should guess to be about fifty-six; you may perceive that Time is beginning to write a few faint lines upon his forehead, and that his eye begins to show that patient wisdom which only comes of the light of many years. His hair (which Mrs. Morton tells me was a raven black "when they were married," and of which she has one precious lock, neatly folded in fragrant paper, and kept in the innermost recess of her pocket book) is just dashed with a glossy white, which seems to light upon him more like the glory than the waste of age, and brightens, if possible, the serene sweetness of his forehead. He speaks very little, but he looks as if his thoughts ran on with the radiant solemnity of a river. His observations, indeed, when they do come forth, are remarkable only for their simplicity and humane gentleness;—and you feel convinced that they are, as the old play hath it, killed with kindness. His thoughts remain with him, but his feelings come forth and speak, and you may ever perceive that his mind discourses silently and with itself, while his heart is the active and eloquent minister to his tongue. I wish, Russell, you could see him sitting at his table, or at his fireside, and lighting the conversation with his pleasant looks. All customs, all pleasures, all regulations, take their exactness from his presence, and I never saw order wear so attractive a garb as that in which Mr. Morton clothes her. He has the most precise and quiet mode of taking his seat, or reading the newspaper (and quiet as he naturally is, he is yet deeply interested in the political agitations which ever disturb the heart of his country), or stirring the fire, or putting on his spectacles. He goes to an office somewhere in the city daily, but I do not see that his merchant-life distracts his home comforts, or molests his morning thoughts; whether it be that his peculiar temperament places all commercial fluctuation in a mild and softening atmosphere, or that he meets not with those temporary difficulties and perplexities which call daily at the most obscure and dusty dens of business, and afflict the nerves of the oldest and most staid merchant, I know not; but the rise and fall of stocks—the intricacies of the markets—the uncertainties and dangers of the shipping—the more polished difficulties, and changes, and higher mysteries of the court, abide not with Mr. Morton. He hears the din of the nation, and it stuns him not:—he sees the great game of the world played, and heeds not its rogueries, its ruin, or its fascinations. His heart is in his home, and in his family, and he does not ever look to the winners and the losers elsewhere. Such is Mr. Morton. To me he is unusually loquacious, which is a sure mark of his regarding me kindly;—and the other evening he took particular joy, during our rubber, in always having a king for my queen, and laughed outright in detecting a revoke which I committed; which was the most gratifying sign.—He, in general, pities the objects of his triumphs, and silently pines over his own success, which he ever thinks "runs too much on one side."

Mrs. Morton is a woman of the most superior mind and admirable manners; and I never hear her mentioned, even by *friends*, without expressions of the most untainted endearment. The silence and worldly inaptitude of her life-partner have called forth the powers of her mind, and given a constant exercise to her fine judgment. She has the most pleasing way of insinuating plain advice that I ever beheld; and I believe it is impossible to disregard the sweet persuasion and delicate earnestness of her voice and expression. She is younger than Mr. Morton by some years, and has a face still eloquent with beauty. The dark eye,—the happy forehead,—the pale cheek,—the mouth, made ever pleasant by a thousand amiable smiles, seem still to retain the sweeter virtues of youth, and enforce the wisdom of experience by giving it a charm which experience seldom possesses. Mrs. Morton is admirably well read in all the sound authors of our language, and can converse on subjects which seldom come under the consideration of women. She is mistress of the learned enthusiasm, holy poesy, and breathing piety of Bishop Taylor, and can lead you through the quaint periods of Sir Thomas Browne's rich and antique philosophy. Shakspeare and Spenser are familiar to her, in their deepest fancies, and most curious excellencies; and she is skilful in her knowledge of the works of the most eminent painters. She enlightens common walks, the idlest evening rambles, with talk, all breathing information, and pleasure, and truth. The distant gloomy landscape reminds her of this or that picture; and she points out the disposition of the lights and shades which frames the resemblance. She never delivers her opinions authoritatively, or with a consciousness of power, but suggests wisdom for the adoption of others;—and often so expresses an ingenious thought, that her husband, by a word or two, seems to originate rather than confirm it. It is her chief desire to make Mr. Morton appear superior to herself, and to that end, her voice and her manner are gentle and subdued in his presence, as though she took all her feelings, thoughts, and wishes, from his heart and mind:—though to those whose observation is acute, it is evident that her knowledge is far more profound than she chuses to lay open. By an ease of manner peculiar to herself she accommodates her mind to that of every person with whom she converses, and never offends an inferior capacity with the least sign of superiority. With all these higher qualifications of mind, she is at heart a very woman, and has all the delicate tenderness, and unfailing love, of her sex. The lock of hair which she preserves with the youthful mystery of a girl, awakens early pride and young joy within her, and sets her dreaming over Mr. Morton's marriage dress and manly person, and calls up the mode of his hair, and the astounding colour of his coat. "Your uncle was dressed in bright blue, and had ruffles of this breadth (measuring a width upon her sleeve, that never fails to exalt all the female eyebrows in the room), I think he was certainly the handsomest man of his time!—I wore that dress which you now and then contemplate in my drawer, and I cannot say I think the brides of the present age dress so becomingly as those of my own day." Such womanly reminiscences as these are always said with a mellowed tone of voice, and with a glisten of the eye, which show how much the devoted nature of the sex triumphs over the acquired formalities and tastes of life. Mrs. Morton sits at her table like a queen, in the true dignity of grace, and I am happy to say, Russell, that I stand well at her drawing-rooms and domestic court.

This excellent couple are without children of their own, but they have taken to their bosoms two nieces and a nephew, the daughters and son of Mr. Morton's brother, whom they cherish as their own, and upon whom they lavish all those paternal endearments which, in the want of an object to rest upon, so often irritate and embitter the married life. The eldest of these young ladies is naturally of a good heart, I believe; but she has so many acquired faults, so many lady-artifices and studied prettinesses, that I never know when she is thoroughly interested or earnestly moved. She is a polite adorer of literature and the drama,— and follows the stage more like a religion than a light and occasional amusement. From certain connexions she has become intimate with some of the performers, and the consequence is, that a morning visit from any tragedian is a sure forerunner of seriousness for the day, a support and a stay to her pensive looks, which she leans upon with a most dignified reserve. Miss Prudence Morton (she was the first of an intended series of the cardinal virtues, which, to her mother's deep disappointment, was broken in upon by the perverse arrival of two brothers into this breathing world) Miss Prudence Morton, I repeat her name, is a decided Blue, at least as far as youth and its established foibles will permit her to be. She is tall, and has dark earnest eyes, which at evening parties go through and through you in search of literary information. She loves to secure to her own reading the person and the attention of some young gentleman in the sonnet line, and to extract all the sweets from his brain as store for the cells of her own pericranium. She sits *at* him. She so disposes her attitude, that his bodily retreat is rendered impracticable. Her eyes are levelled against him, and she steadily fires down upon his helpless ears the twenty-pounders of her heavy interrogatories. "Have you seen Campbell's song in the last New Monthly, and is it not charming?[88]—Not seen it! I own I wonder at that. Mr. —— (naming some literary name) copied it out for me before it was in; and I like it amazingly.—O! and are those your lines in the LONDON? I know they are—but why do you use that signature? Not but that I could always detect you! Not yours! dear me! Well I thought them not quite pensive enough.—But I don't believe you.—O! What is Lord Byron about? Mr. —— (naming another literary name) tells me that he is writing a tragedy. I think Marino Faliero, horrid![89] Mr. —— (naming an actor) assures me it would never *get up*! Have you read Don Juan? I have not: but I think it abounds with beautiful passages, though it is a sad wicked book. O! what do you think of ——'s prose? Is it not flowery and beautiful? You never know whether it is poetry or prose, which is so vastly delightful."—This is a slight and meagre sketch of the style of Prudence's conversation, which I must, as usual, leave to the powers which you possess of making a miserable description opulent. She has great good-nature, the eternal palliative of all disagreeable qualities, and can at a quiet fireside make herself amusing and intelligent, but a stranger at tea, or an extra wax candle in the sconce, is the never-failing destroyer of all her natural freedom. And she straightway exalts herself into the wary, the wise, the literary Prudence. Some of her sayings are remembered, but considering the plentiful crop of her conversation, it is wonderful that a few scanty ears only are preserved. When her form is at its height she, like the lovely Marcia "towers above her sex,"[90] and that considerably, and I shall not easily forget the prodigious step and grasp with which she wheeled me down the stone-staircase of Mr. Morton's house the other day at dinner.

Agnes Morton, younger than either her brother or sister, is one of those sweet little fairy creatures which we seem to recognize as the realization of some dim poetic dream, or favourite beauty of the fancy. Her light blue eyes, softening beneath the shadowy yet even tracery of her eye-brows, gleam upon you with a modesty and tenderness almost unearthly:—and the airy figure, ever simply attired, seems framed only to be lighted about by such gently radiant eyes. Her very motion has feeling in it: and her voice is quite Shakspearian, being low and sweet, an excellent thing in woman. Indeed her elf-like shape, melodious tones, and retired looks, seem contrived by nature as contrasts to the gigantic figure, vehement voice, and vampire gaze of Miss Prudence. Agnes, worthy owner of that innocent appellation, hath the sweetest and simplest wisdom in the world: Agnes with her lamb-like heart, and "those dove's eyes," by gentleness carries all before her. She rules all hearts, as by some fairy spell. Her soft exclamations of attachment, disregard, or wonderment, are potent as acts of parliament, or wills of princes. You must not imagine, Russell, that I am heart-stricken more than becomes a respectful friend, though I fear my description rather borders on the style of the last new novel:—my affections are, as you know, wedded to books and life, and I see no very great probability of my ever deviating into the lover. Besides, the times are ill, my prospects are bounded, and Mr. Vansittart has set his face decidedly against Cupid.[91]

Thomas Morton, the nephew, or Tom as he is more familiarly and affectionately called by his near acquaintance and friends, (and I always think that pleasant monosyllabic appellation is a species of short-hand for kind-heartedness), is the life, delight, and perplexity of the household;—spirited, volatile, effervescing in health, and twenty years of age; he is at once the source of mirth, affection, and disorder. When you enter the house he, like Latimer's peculiar bishop, "is never idle;"[92] either the foil is in his hand, and he is pinking away at an old portrait of a great great uncle, whose canvas countenance he has already converted into a frightful rival of the nutmeg-grater; or with *muffles* on his knuckles, he is dipping away scientifically at the *day-lights* of a pier glass, or getting considerably the best of a corner-cupboard. One while you shall leave him reading one of Plutarch's lives, or burying his brain in the dark soil of Bishop Andrewes' Divinity;[93] but leave the room for ten minutes, and you will find him on your return trying the latest quadrille with six chairs and a plate warmer; or exercising his legal powers of oratory, and convincing a green baize table of the strength of his talents and his hand, and the inveterate justice of his cause. He has a fine manly person, which, however, he a little distorts by the decisive cut of his coat, and the Corinthian roundness of his collar,—but it is not at all unpleasant to behold his light lithe person disdaining the restraint and imprisonment of dress, and dancing about under the Merino and the buckram with all the loose liberty of a boy at school. His spirits, when excited, run riot, and trample upon fashion in their freedom. Buttons, stay-tape, and button-holes are set at defiance; and the natural man bursts through all his envious clouds, and asserts his untameable glory. Tom is intended for the law, if it shall please his volatile spirits to suffer such intention to run its unshackled course; but there is no vouching for so heedless and unreliable a mind, which at a moment's warning, or even none at all, might waste its sweets behind a grocer's counter, or inspire crossed-legs and a thimble on a raised board under a dim sky-light. He reads poetry to please Prudence; but he occasionally tries her patience by the vehemence and sameness of his quotations. He has an ill knack of wrenching a profound or romantic passage from its original beauty and meaning, and of applying it to some unlucky and ludicrous circumstance, to the utter dismay of his elder and more inspired sister. She looks upon him with her tragic eyes, a look of learned remonstrance; and he receives her rebuke with a burst of triumphant laughter, which sinks him only deeper in Miss Prudence's displeasure. To Agnes, Tom is all that is respectful, gentle, and sincere, recognizing her unobtrusive manner and exquisite softness of heart with all the generous and sensitive regard of his nature. The affectations and enormities of Prudence sit uneasily upon him; but the pretty manners and engaging looks of Agnes disarm his ridicule and tame his heedlessness. Mrs. Morton is continually annoyed at the follies and bursts of rash gaiety in Tom, but her inimitable discernment into character makes her perceive a virtue under all, which will yet surmount its present impediments. Prudence, with all her temporary afflictions, sets a proper value upon his services at theatres and parties,—Agnes loves him for his marked and unceasing gentleness and affection,—and old Mr. Morton silently delights to see how fine spirited a lad Tom is, and though often worn with his noisy mirth, and suffering in his furniture from Tom's turbulent exercises, still he never fails to take a pride in the boy, and to say "Aye, aye, let him be young—we were all young ourselves, and have all had our troublesome days. I myself, (he will sometimes continue, to the regular astonishment of Agnes) I myself was once dangerous to the glasses, and had my boisterous propensities. Tom is a kind nephew." And Tom *is* kind. He is kind even to me, Russell, who sometimes venture to sift advice over his fleeting failings: and his readiness to fly any where in my service, or accompany me on any of my extravagant wanderings, is so lively and pleasurable, that I should hate myself if I thought I had written one word which would in reality prejudice his frank character in your eyes.—There, I have given you a picture of the Mortons, and it is not "done in little," I think, but manufactured after the style of poor Dr. Primrose's family group,—huge, awkward, and unsatisfactory.[94] Tell me, when you write to me, whether you detect in my poor language Mr. Morton from Mrs. Morton, or Tom from Agnes. I own I pique myself on Prudence.

Many of my days, my dear Russell, are passed, as you will readily conjecture, in the society of this excellent family; and one or other of them generally accompanies me on my excursions in search of the picturesque, as it may be called, of this mighty city. At evening, we discuss the wonders we have seen, and many and various are the observations we make—each admiring, or severely commenting upon, the events of the day, after his or her own peculiar turn of mind. I remember the Coronation was food for many candle-light hours, for though I then was not so familiar with the Mortons, I saw them, and spoke to them, at that august ceremony. Mrs. Morton described the felicitous effect of the grouping and the colour of the scene, and thus opened to me the mystery of the beauty that delighted me; and I will say, that if I have been at all successful in describing any part of that magnificent procession, it is to Mrs. Morton that I am indebted for the learning, eloquence, and discernment she displayed in her account of it. Mr. Morton was not present, as he did not think that the pleasure compensated for the danger of attempting to be there; but he cheerfully used his interest and his purse in procuring tickets "for the girls," and listened, and still listens, with one of his own quiet smiles, to the unravelling of the brilliant and tangled threads of the subject, so perseveringly taken in hand by the rest of his family.

We were all sitting one afternoon over our fruit,—sipping it might be a temperate glass of Mr. Morton's *particular*, which leapt into the glass "with all its sun-set glow," ever at the same interval, and ever in the same moderate quantities; our discourse was at its meridian, and we sat basking in the warmth of bright talk, and could have been satisfied to have ever so sunned ourselves. Mrs. Morton was in the full plumage of wisdom,—Miss Prudence had laid aside those two dilating eyes, so wont to expand over a whole company,—Agnes sat with her little white hand in Mr. Morton's, and smoothing with the other the scanty silken hair which scarcely shadowed his forehead. Tom was cutting out an orange into a sick alderman, and finding in his labours their own exceeding great reward; for he could procure no one to eulogize his sculpture in fruitage—all present having often been treated with a sight of the same specimen of the ideal in art. I had my forefinger of my right hand pertinaciously hooked round the stem of my glass, in which bloomed that purple flower which I have gathered ever since I was no higher than a wine glass. We were all peculiarly happy, alternately talking, alternately listening,—when the perfect blue of the sky, and the intense lustre of the sun, carried our thoughts to the country, and I know not how it was that they travelled to Greenwich. One ignorant question of mine led on to one sweet remembrance of the ladies, and another, another—and my mind became excited in the narration I heard—and curiosity led to uttered desires—and desires grew to projected realizations, till in due course of scheming, we arrived at a determination to visit Greenwich Hospital on the following day. Mrs. Morton would fain have gone that very afternoon, that her *best* half (in her estimation) might partake of the pleasure; but Mr. Morton protested against it, declaring that he had seen the building many years ago, and that the evening damps were much against the journey home. The visit accordingly was postponed until the morrow; and the evening subsided into a quiet tea, and a patient rubber, in the course of which I led a small diamond that forced Mr. Morton's king of trumps, and crowned my misfortune by omitting to lead through the *honour*, which lost us the game, and which abducted from Mr. Morton a kindly and monitory moaning, till I left the house for the night. But on shaking my hand at parting, he told me that he believed we could not have won the game; and he begged I would not think more about it, although indeed any card would have been better than the diamond.

I wish I could begin this paragraph with the explosion of some such eloquent gun as commences the *deep* tragedy in the Critic; and thus convey to you a perfect and an instantaneous idea of the rich "saffron morning," without the usual flourish of sun and clouds, and all the established finery of blue firmament, and "gilding the eastern hemisphere," and singing birds and fresh zephyrs; but I have no way of breaking all this splendour to you, Russell, without having recourse to these popular terms: you will therefore have the kindness to imagine one of the brightest days that ever shone in the first chapter of a novel, and you will approach within thirty degrees of that admirable morning on which it was our fate to visit Greenwich Hospital. Our company fell off rather in the morning. Mr. Morton, as usual, came down to breakfast (I was invited to that meal, and was punctual) in his easy slippers, but otherwise neatly armed in cleanliness for his City duties. He shook my hand, and slightly recurred to our misfortunes the night before by hoping that I had thought no more of the diamond, as it was really not worth caring about. He rejoiced in the fineness of our day, and begged me to admire particularly Sir James Thornhill's paintings at Greenwich Hospital, which he remembered were very blue and very beautiful;[95] and he then wondered whether this Sir James Thornhill was any relation of the Baronet in the Vicar of Wakefield, for he never lost the impression, made in youth, that this tale was a true one, and that all its characters had lived precisely as Goldsmith has so exquisitely described them. When we were all assembled at the breakfast table, Prudence broke the ice of an apology, by hinting that she doubted whether the day "would last;" and, indeed, that she took no peculiar delight in seeing a great old building, full of lame uncultivated old men; and that, indeed, she expected Miss —— would call with the lines; and, indeed, that she could not altogether think herself well, for she had heard the clock strike *two*, and could not see very clearly with her eyes in the morning, giving them at the same moment a profound roll, as though they were revolving like satellites around her head, to convince us that her sight *was* affected. Mrs. Morton, foreseeing no great advantage from Miss Prudence's society under her then state of mind, very wisely begged her not to think of venturing in so dire a state of health; and Miss Prudence, with a sigh that seemed "to shatter all her bulk, and end her being," consented to give up the pleasure of Mr. Herbert's company, with the same species of reluctance that Richard displayed to receive the crown at the hands of the pertinacious Lord Mayor. Agnes looked pale, and was evidently affected with a head ache, though she made no complaints, and was anxious to assure us that it would be removed by the ride and the fresh air. Tom would have accompanied us, but he had some other engagement, which I guessed, by his shrewd winks and nods, was not of that order that, in the opinion of ladies, ought to supersede a visit to so noble a building as Greenwich Hospital. He wished he could make one with Herbert, but (squaring with his clenched hands, and scientifically touching at the tea-urn) he had business in hand that must be taken by the forelock. He took an opportunity, while the ladies were gone up to attire, to let me into the secret of "a bull bait down the Edgeware Road, near the four mile slab," which would be worth whole pailfuls of pensioners, and he was desirous of fleshing a young ring-tailed and tulip-eared puppy, of which he had the most extravagant expectations; not but that I should be entertained where I was going. In less than a quarter of an hour from the period of this assurance our breakfast party had separated; Mrs. Morton, Agnes, and myself, were seated in the carriage, rattling through the stony-hearted streets. Mr. Morton was steadily walking towards his counting-house, with a placid heart, and an umbrella under his arm, (for he never was betrayed by a fine morning into an abatement of this salutary provision against the malice of the clouds). Miss Prudence had arranged herself over a volume of Wordsworth, and a lace-frill, and sat like Lydia Languish over the tears of sensibility, ready for any one that should come: while Tom, with a blue neckerchief, and a white hat, was shaking his way down the Edgeware Road, in the taxed cart of one of the cognoscenti, discussing the breed of *pied* and *brindled*, and sitting with his two hands round the lugs of his little tulip-eared puppy, which sat up in restless state between his legs.

I shall not detain you, Russell, over the common adventures of the road; you will know that the principal incidents were the paying of turnpikes, a tax which those who prize smooth roads and easy riding seldom think an evil. We passed Charing Cross, a part of the world that echoes the word "Greenwich" unceasingly, and is kindly sending coaches there every quarter of an hour of the day. We passed over Westminster Bridge—we passed Astley's Theatre—we passed the Asylum—we passed the Elephant and Castle—we passed the Bricklayer's Arms—we passed the Robin Hood—we passed the Canal—the Three Compasses—the Seven Stars—all buildings and places very uninteresting to you, excepting so far as they show, being the leading objects of a given road out of London, that public houses, in proportion to other houses, are as about four to one—extravagant odds! as Tom would say.

How shall I give you an idea of the beauty of the far-famed Hospital of Greenwich, rising with its fair domes and stately walls, by the side of one of the noblest rivers in Europe?—In no way, I fear, save by sending you the "perspective view," sold by the boatswain in the painted Hall, done in a very masterly manner by some one, if I recollect rightly, connected with the Hospital. The beautiful park rises grandly on the *larboard* side of the building, to speak professionally, and seems to protect it from all rude storms, and tempests; as it, in turn, shields its old glorious inmates from the blasts and billows of the world. There are four divisions, all stately and majestic; and the court yards and kingly statue speak, like an English history, of the reign of George the Second. The very dress of the pensioner appears a sober record of the fashion of that day, and removes the wearer from the modern manners and look of the foolish mankind of this round-hatted generation. Every old sailor appears coeval with the foundation of the charity, and walks the deck of the building under his three cornered beaver, more like a formal gentleman out of one of Sir James Thornhill's pictures, than the living hulk of a man of war, laid up in the blessed harbour of his country. All the arrangements of this admirable charity are so well ordered that the sailor has his life embalmed in comfort, and preserved as much in its original shape and appearance as possible. The watches are set—the food is portioned out—the cooks are of the crew—the lieutenants pre-side—the bed-rooms are like cabins—the wainscotting is of oak—the very cloth of the dress is blue. It is life in a stone ship,—on an untroubled sea,—with no end to fresh meat and water,—a naval romance! There is no more to do than to take care of their munificent vessel; and I will do them the justice to say, that they are ever washing the decks. You can hardly go over the rooms without finding one man at his Bible—another at a sea voyage—another looking through a telescope at the vessels in the river: they are a silent, contemplative race, made so, it may be, by the eternal and higher noise of the sea, which has unfitted them for the lighter voices of their kind. But from this general character for reserve and retirement let me exempt honest Master Ball, as comely a man as ever wore checked shirt,—as conversational a man as ever piped all hands,—as cheerful a man as ever brake biscuit, or damped a tobacco-tinted tooth with a tumbler of cold grog. He is, if I mistake not, the boatswain of one of the long rooms, and sits there as jolly as though he should never be old; smiling on all comers, and looking over two shining bronzed cheeks with the most easy and winning assurance in the world. Mrs. Morton well remarked, that he looked as if he would give sickness no more quarter than the enemy. His forehead shone insufferably bright, and quite dazzled the eyes of the beholder; and his hands were crossed over the lower button of his waistcoat, which fastened as convex a little garment as ever bent round a comfortable body. Agnes thought the forehead was like that of Mr. Morton; but we all negatived her opinion, and left her to the solitary possession of it; which, however, woman-like, she tenaciously held. But I know not how it is, I am getting out of order, and am describing a character with which, at present, I have clearly no business.

The terrace that runs along the whole range of the building, between it and the water, is pleasantly situated, but, as it does not much abound with pensioners, it is by no means a striking attraction in my eyes. But in the walk below it, at the edge of the water, narrow, inconvenient, and thronging with water-men, sailors, and other bronzed men,—we all delighted to walk. There do the maimed and weather-tried tenants of the place saunter out their indolent and late holiday existence. There do they sit for hours, like Crabbe's Peter Ghrimes, but without his crimes, looking upon the flood.[96] There do they lean,—there stand,—there recline,—there sidle about. The passing of a packet,—the slow drifting of a merchantman,—the heavy slumber of a Dutch vessel,—the arrowy course of a wherry,—are all beheld and thought over with an unchangeable profundity and a deathless silence. It appears to me that words are of no use by the water side. The only object that calls up an extraordinary expression of surprise or distaste on the mahogany line of visages along the railing, is the aquatic innovation of a steam-boat;—*that* elevates the bristles of twenty or thirty pair of rugged old eyebrows, and crumples up so many dark brown cheeks till they look like a row of biffens.— But not a word passes. The long—rapid—smoking machine goes rattling by, convulsing the river, and agitating the lesser craft:—but much as it offends the eyes of the oldest sailors, it is passed and passes in a dignified silence. I was much amused, and nudged my good friends on each side to share in my amusement, by watching one hale old man, with a peculiar and shrewd cock of his tri-cornered beaver, probing, with his gimlet eye, the rusty hole in the bottom of a worn-out skiff. He stood sideways, peering into it with all the sagacity of the magpie's marrow-bone survey—now ogling it on this side—now contemplating it on that,

—and appearing to see in it something far deeper than our poor optics could discern. He looked closer and closer, and twined his glossy anti-quated fingers upon the small of his back,—and pursed his under lip,—and gave his head a more intense twist—till I really thought the hole might not be a mere hole, and that I ought not, as Mr. Puff says, to be "too sure that he was a beef-eater."[97] Five minutes elapsed, but the inquisition was not over;—indeed, it deepened and deepened, and just as I was satisfied the scrutiny was ripening to a purpose, and that the old man was arriving at his conclusion, he suddenly dispersed all our expectations by loosening his hands, giving the silver buckle of his right leg an easy elevation into the sun, and, whistling off the last notes of some ricketty tune, he left us with an empty stare at ourselves, the building, and the river. And this is, with these charming old men, an incident—a sample of life. Thus do they dwell, thus exist in doing nothing with more industrious exactness than any other kind of idlers in the world.

By the kindness of one of Mr. Morton's friends, who holds some place of trust in the Hospital, we were conducted to the chapel, one of the most beautiful places of worship I ever beheld, but possessing, perhaps, too much of architectural splendour for the sincerity and serenity of devotion. It had not the unobtrusive quiet of the little Oratory of War-wick Castle:[98] but the gothic style is to my feelings always more associ-ated with the sacred earnestness of prayer. A steady, sober pensioner, with a white willow wand in his hand, marshalled us up to the extreme end of the interior, and pointing to a huge painting by West, over the communion table, began his daily labour of description. The Preserva-tion of St. Paul from Shipwreck must be a brave subject for an old sailor to enlarge upon; and accordingly, our guide lifted up his voice and spake. He pointed out the mariners,—the sea,—the vessel; and nothing that I can say will afford you an idea of the deep rugged vigour of his voice. When he came to a word with an R in it,—it rattled in his mouth like a loose sail in a stiff wind; and his laborious expulsion of sound resembled the exertions attendant upon working a boat against a heavy sea. He resolutely adhered to his own mode of pronunciation, which made good havoc with many stout words, that had stood the storms of other tongues;—but so like the monotonous tones of the sea was this his delivery of sound, that I could have closed my eyes and fancied myself sitting near the mainmast, with all the world of ropes and booms creaking and rattling around me. The picture is a clever picture, but it has all the hardness and stiffness peculiar to West. The pulpit is not at all suited to the purity of the chapel. The ceiling is extremely rich. At the entrance there is an inner portico supported on beautiful columns of white marble, which caught the heart of Agnes, and was not displeasing to the severer eyes of her aunt and myself.

The Painted Hall faces the chapel, and is, to be sure, sufficiently splendid:—the ceiling is, as a very clever little account of Greenwich Hospital remarks, well described by Sir Rich. Steele. And as his language cannot fail to be more satisfactory than "any thing that I can say upon it," I have borrowed an old copy of that dull essayist, and transcribe for you part of the passage, as follows:—

In the middle of the ceiling is a very large oval frame, painted and carved in imitation of gold, with a great thickness rising in the inside to throw up the figures to the greater height; the oval is fastened to a great soffite adorned with roses, in imitation of copper. The whole is supported by eight gigantic figures of slaves, four on each side, as though they were carved in stone.

* * * * * * *

Each end of the ceiling is raised in perspective, with a balustrade and elliptic arches, supported by groups of stone figures, which form a gallery of the whole breadth of the hall; in the middle of which gallery (as though on the stocks,) going into the upper hall, is seen, in perspective, the tafferill of the Blenheim man-of war, with all her galleries, port-holes open, &c., to one side of which is a figure of Victory flying, with spoils taken from the enemy, and putting them on board the English man-of-war. Before the ships is a figure representing the city of London, with the arms, sword, and cap of maintenance, supported by Thame and Isis, with the other small rivers offering up their treasures to her; the river Tyne pouring forth sacks of coals. In the gallery, on each side of the ship, are the Arts and Sciences that relate to Navigation, with the great Archimedes, many old philosophers consulting the compass, &c.

At the other end, as you return out of the Hall, is a gallery in the same manner, in the middle of which is a stern of a beautiful galley filled with Spanish trophies; under which is the Humber with his pigs of lead; the Severn with the Avon falling into her, with other lesser rivers. In the north end of the gallery is the famous Tycho Brahe, that noble Danish knight, and great ornament of his profession and human nature. Near him is Copernicus, with his Pythagorean system in his hand: next to him is an old mathematician, holding a large table, and on it are described two principal figures of the incomparable Sir Isaac Newton, on which many extraordinary things in that art are built. On the other end of the gallery, to the south, is the learned Mr. Flamstead, Reg. Astron. Profess., with his ingenious disciple, Mr. T. Weston. In Mr. Flamstead's hand is a large scroll of paper, on which is drawn the great eclipse of the Sun that happened in April, 1715; near him is an old man with a pendulum, counting the seconds of time, as Mr. Flamstead makes his observations, with his great mural arch and tube, on the descent of the Moon on the Severn; which at certain times forms such a roll of tides, as the sailors corruptly call the Hygre, instead of the Eagre, and is very dangerous to all ships in its way. This is also expressed by rivers tumbling down, by the moon's influence, into the Severn. In this gallery are more arts and sciences relating to Navigation.[99]

Mr. Flamstead looks down, with his ingenious disciple, in a way to awe all sublunary objects. The mixture of gods, rivers, virtues, fame, king, queen, and Tycho Brahe, is sufficiently various to hit the taste of the most dainty admirer of variety. I do not, however, see in this description any account of the portrait of the first pensioner, the original man of blue, the Adam of Greenwich Hospital, whom death turned out of his waterside Paradise:—I see no mention of him, although the little stunted boatswain pointed him out in the ceiling, and dared us to get to any part of the hall without encountering the eyes of this seaman in the shrouds. I think, however, in spite of this, that he was blind. At the end of the hall are the portraits of George I. and his family, all little well-wigged princes, and formidable princesses, doubtless very staring likenesses. Sir James Thornhill figures away also himself, in a splendid suit, and enclouded in a wig of inestimable curl. "The whole of this celebrated work was not completed till 1727; and cost 6,635*l.* being after the rate of 8*l.* per yard for the ceiling, and 1*l.* per yard for the sides." This appears to me, Russell, to be very cheap workmanship, and might well be adopted by private families. The sides of the hall have representations of fluted columns, which, as the boatswain says, "you would believe were carved;—they are all as smooth as this wall." Mrs. Morton engraved a smile upon his copper visage, by examining closely, and very generously still professing a disbelief;—he drew his willow wand across it, winked at me, and re-assured her that it was "nothing but painted." Lord Nelson's car stands in one corner, and when it is remembered how great were the remains which it bore, through a grateful weeping people, to its last and eternal cabin, and how glorious was the wood of which it was constructed, it is affecting little to say that it inspires gentle, and proud, and melancholy thoughts.

The kitchen, and the dinner room, with their homely furniture and peasesoup atmosphere, are refreshing to behold, provided you have not allayed the cravings of your appetite; and the cleanliness observable around is the pleasantest provocative of hunger in the world. When we passed through these rooms, the scouring was going on, and there was a thorough sloppiness apparent over everything. The bread-room had a delightful wheaten odour, which took my senses mightily. Agnes, as she peeped with her pretty face through the grating at the imprisoned loaves, heaved a sigh as though she pitied the confinement of even a *half-quartern!*—so much like a prison did this huge pantry look, and so ready was her pity for any thing that reminded her of a prison.

We took a survey of the rooms, in which were the little cabins of this happy crew, all as smart and neat as the peaceful hearts and golden leisure of their tenants could make them. Each pensioner appeared to have brought with him the hammock from his favourite vessel; and the clean silence of the long apartments seemed one perpetual sabbath. On entering,—there sat our good friend Ball, reading near the window, with his comely blue legs crossed placidly over each other, and his bright old eyes twinkling with a roguish joy peculiar to himself. He did not rise up,—neither did he lay aside his volume—Robinson Crusoe, or Philip Quarll[100] it might be,—but he looked archly upon us, and answered our queries with an honest merriment that made me wish myself an old bald-headed sailor of some sixty years of age, sitting in a long room at Greenwich Hospital, and answering three inquisitive visitors without a care as to what queries were put to me. The little cabins, or bed-rooms, are small, and decked after the taste of the proprietors:—here you shall see a flaming ship,—there a picture of Nelson, done on glass, with desperate blue coats, and alarming yellow breeches, and sold by those foreign pedlars at a price which almost persuades one that they must have stolen the colours, or pilfered the pictures ready framed and glazed.

We were shown into some of the rooms of state, and were hurried from portrait to portrait in cruel haste. In one room we beheld Captain

Spearing, the marvellous gentleman that lived seven days in a coal-pit without food, and afterwards married and had nine children, as he by his own ingenious and entertaining narrative avoucheth.[101] The belief among the sailors, however, is, that a Robin Redbreast brought him food, but I do not altogether side with the pensioners in this creed. He looked so well and neat in his light flaxen wig, though upwards of ninety, as I was told, that I had serious thoughts of trying a coal-pit myself, and could well endure the Robin Redbreast's victuals to survive so well and flourish so merrily.

Age, indeed, in this matchless building, is as verdant and pleasant as youth elsewhere. You see white hairs in every direction—but no white faces. The venerable chaplain, whom I saw, had a cheerful vivacity, and a sprightly vein of conversation, quite captivating and instructive; and I am very sincere in wishing, Russell, that you and I could have a cozey dish of tea with him, and a long chat over the early governors and the golden days of Greenwich Hospital.

I have given you, my good friend, a very imperfect and hasty sketch of this great charity; but I would not tire you with the minute details, which you will read in the agreeable and intelligent little pamphlet, sold at the hospital (a copy of which I now send you).—We sauntered into the park, and buried ourselves for some hours in the green solitude of that solemn and peaceful retreat. The rich trees, spreading and mingling their ample foliage—the soft verdure of the grass—the deep and silent dells—the lofty and green eminences (commanding a view of the mighty city, and its spacious living river), all well and wondrously contrasted with the scene we had been witnessing, and disposed our hearts to feel brimmed with peace and grateful joy, and gently to marvel "why there was misery in a world so fair!" I shall never forget Mrs. Morton's voice, musical and eloquent in that blessed place, and Agnes letting her sweet nature breathe itself in unrestrained freedom. We returned to town, and recounted to Mr. Morton, late into the night, the wonders we had seen!

Forgive this letter of fearful length; not often will I so err; but the Mortons are described, and you will not have that description to undergo again. Miss Prudence had seen Mr. ——, the tragedian, and was profoundly pensive:—Tom was tired to death, and slept in his chair a sort of dog-sleep, learned, I believe, at the strife he had been witnessing.—

Farewell.—Love to all the Powells—not forgetting yourself, my dear Russell.

Your's faithfully,

Albany. Edward Herbert.

The Drama.[102] *January 1822*

Christmas, according to traditionary right, is made up of frost, perhaps snow; turkeys, mince-pies, and burnt brandy (oh for a game of snap-dragon! who'll play?); consequently cannot consist with thunder and rotten humidity, which sours your turkey, makes limp the puff-paste, and turns the oily cogniac from a privileged luxury, into an obvious necessary! This is what valetudinarians call fine open weather. I love to hear the roads ring like iron to the trotting hoofs; to listen to the heavy shoes of the rustic, who thumps his hollow shoulders with tingling hands. Then is the time for toasted cheese, for spiced ale, for the parting glass of hot elder wine, which gives the bed-ward shiverer a few minutes more reprieve ere he launches into the bleak atmosphere of unwarmed corridors;—then are sprats eaten, and scalloped oysters;—virtuous dames knit red worsted nets for their husbands' throats; chairs are drawn round the fire after dinner, and travelers twine hay-bands round their stirrup-irons. Mouths smoke, and chimney-pots,—another blanket is put on Mr. B.'s bed, "who could not sleep a wink for the cold all last night." The coats of horses stare, and the gardener mats carefully his forcing frames—

The bellman's drowsy charm
Blesses the doors from nightly harm.[103]

The village fidler scrapes with cheerful discord for his Christmas-box. —Through the gaping embrasures of Fort C——d the wind cuts shrilly; the turbid billows break with watery roar on the Goodwins, and the wild blast sweeps mightily, raging over Stanmore waste.—But now

The winds have suck'd up from the sea
Contagious fogs; which falling in the land

326

Have every pelting river made so proud,
That they have overborne their continents;
* * * * * * *
The fold stands empty in the drowned field,
The crows are fatted with the murrain'd flock;
The nine-men's morris is fill'd up with mud;
And the quaint mazes in the wanton green
For lack of tread, are undistinguishable;
The human mortals want their WINTER *here!*
No night is now with hymn or carol blest;
Therefore the moon, the governess of floods,
Pale in her anger washes all the air,
That rheumatic diseases do abound:
And thorough this distemperature we see
The seasons alter * * *
And on old Hyems' chin and icy crown
An odorous chaplet of sweet summer buds
Is, as in mockery, set.*

Drury Lane.

We are not aware of any novelties having appeared at this ill-directed place, except De Montfort, and the feminine debût to be noted below. "The splendid Coronation" has ceased to draw, and Mr. Kean has been forced into double harness with it, which at first we believe he declined. The treasury, however, was not much the better, and orders to well-dressed people for the dress circle are said to have been issued plentifully. Still we do not credit the vulgar notion, that Kean's day is over, that his trick is found out, &c.; but rather attribute the continued depression to a parsimony behind the scenes, which refuses to grant salaries in any way adequate to very moderate abilities.† A play cannot now be upheld by the talents of one man, let them be ever so brilliant—two or three good lamps enliven the darkness much better than the most eye-blinding flashes of lightning; and Kean is not to be kept on the stage

* At the time I write, I have an evening primrose to my nose; the strawberry plants are in bloom; violets were gathered a week ago of full perfume; gooseberry bushes and honeysuckles are covered with bursting leaflets; and the sparrows, poor fools! are building their nests.—*Dec.* 19.[104]

† It is rumoured that the munificence of the person appointed to treat with performers offered Mr. D——n, the justly celebrated Comedian, four pounds per week!![105]

constantly, throughout five acts, as you may a glass chandelier. Good-for-nothing people have a notion that the Drury Roscius has something to do with this beggarly array, and do not scruple to charge him with the "lowest players' vices—envy and jealousy, and miserable cravings after applause: one who in the exercise of his profession is jealous, even of the women performers that stand in his way, full of tricks, strategems, and finesse."—If these things were true, let him be whistled down the wind, a sport for chiding fortune; "for why should honour survive honesty?" But we have a better opinion of Mr. Kean's theatrical knowledge; he must be aware that his feeling and nature cut sadly against the coldness and impracticability of his colleagues, and that the audience soon get tired of his hectoring triumphs over their evident inferiority. There is no sport! he walks over the course; and tort-strung[106] must those powers be which are not enervated by this dangerous facility. To our mind some trifling symptoms of this degeneracy are, if we may use the figure, creaming over the style of Kean. Flattery before him, and weakness beside him, have swelled a proper self-appreciation into a dreaming security; he seems, generally speaking, to have composed a sort of off-hand compendious theory of setting giddy palms in motion, lively and imposing, flashy and shallow, which, though more affected than the graceful majesty of John Kemble, is termed nature by his parasites. All these pictorially-mean and petty gestures, (nearly as disgusting to a man of taste as a courtier's finical bow) come home to their trammeled comprehensions; and consequently the broadly expanded noble actions of John Philip are to them foolishness. We are running counter, we know, to the present doctrine in vogue; but we confess with Sir Joshua Reynolds, that it appears more honourable to fall in flying after M. Angelo than to succeed by creeping with Ostade and Brouwer.[107] C. Lamb himself has failed to change this studiously weighed opinion of ours; so has Hazlitt (though to differ from him is a good deal presumptuous, and not a little dangerous).* At present Mr. Kean too often resembles his double, Booth,[109] rather than himself;

* We have not forgotten Mr. Hazlitt's attack on our old friend Janus, in the Table Talk, and had thought to have taken up the cudgels, but W. assured us that he was quite satisfied:— 1. Because he had no mind to another drubbing.—2. Because most of the points answered themselves.—3. Because he had made the great Lion wag his tail.—And, 4. Because the satire of his Diogenes had immortalized the victim. "Better be damned, than mentioned not at all."[108]

the harmonizing glazings are scoured off in patches, and the dead colouring is left bare. It is the delicate, almost imperceptible finishing, that shows the master; the imitating pupils can *forward* the picture. K——'s lazy play is in singular unison with the developements of character in Müllner;[110] every word is anatomized and commented on; every expression must be marked and insisted on. The faculties of attention and comprehension are kept painfully tense—he is inflexible that his art shall be apprehended; there is an excess of consciousness; the audience admire and applaud, and few take the trouble to investigate whether they were moved by the keys of the heart or the head. I have as great a dislike to all this glitter and blaze as I have to a picture where every face and body is eruditely and indiscriminately foreshortened. Still Kean's worst is preferable to Young's best; and when the afflatus comes on him, as in Othello, he wrings the heart-strings even to breaking. To return to our starting place, (we have a sad knack of *bolting*, as Buckle would say,) if the popularity of this true genius is on the wane, he may lay it to his own sluggishness, and to the play-bill puffs which blush in red letters at their own grossness. "Mr. Kean's performance of Sir Giles Overreach exceeded even the effects of his first delineation of that character, and was honoured with repeated bursts of applause until the falling of the curtain! The whole of the play seeming also to contribute highly to the public satisfaction, it will be repeated to-morrow, being Mr. Kean's last appearance until the termination of the Christmas Holidays!!" This latter sentence is untrue—he has played Hastings and Macbeth twice each! after announcing Hastings ("*for this night only.*") People are sick of such quackery.

Dec. 16.—A fuller house was assembled than on any previous night in the season. The pit was crowded, and the front rows of the dress circle looked gay with silks, gold combs, flowers, variegated shawls, and rich-coloured jewels. The attraction was a Miss Edmiston in the part of Jane Shore,[111] supported by Kean in the wavering Hastings; and by the noisy partisans of that gentleman, who it seems had prognosticated success; therefore she was to succeed. The lady, who appears about seven and twenty, received the welcoming hubbub with all imaginable serenity. Her curtsey sank into a kneel, and drew, as was intended, a fresh tumult of applause. An affected drag in her step was construed, by those determined to think favourably, into a modest tremor; so was the inaudibility of her level speaking: we cold critics have the cruel faculty of detecting the truth, and to us there was too much of artifice in her gentleness. It is ill-advised to confess it perhaps; but the singular self-possession that marked "*this first appearance on any stage*" hardened our hearts considerably against her charms: the reader will, therefore, make allowance for a little *un*-gallantry towards an *unprotected* female, as folks say. We must pass the sentence of the law, though the tears run down our judge-like cheeks. Perhaps we were out of humour to see that our share of encouragement was needless, for she could do nothing to please us the whole night. We did not like her voice, we did not like her gesticulation, we did not like her pathetics, we did not like her heroics; and though her figure and features were good, we neither liked her in full dress nor in dishabille. Something of this lack-sympathy grew out of the character itself, and the whole indefinite diction of the play. A. Schlegel kindly says that "Rowe did not possess boldness and vigour, but sweetness and feeling; he could excite the softer emotions; and hence, in his Fair Penitent, Jane Shore, and Lady Jane Grey, he has successfully chosen female heroines and their weaknesses for his subject."[112] All we know of his Jane Grey is, that there is a very pretty print by Sherwin, of Mrs. ———, by way of frontispiece in Lowndes's New English Theatre, published *circa* 1780. We never read or saw The Fair Penitent, being amply contented with Massinger's original.[113] Of Jane Shore we can speak from several painful experiences which sit heavy on our memories. Rowe is reported to have meant it for a Drama in the spirit of Shakspeare—we cannot find any touch of the great artist either in the conduct, the cast of thought, or the language. Were you to take away the measure and the exterior ornaments from Hamlet, there would still be poetry and sweetness; but the elevation of Rowe resides in a sort of cautious mouthing far beneath the hot rants of Eleazar, Oedipus, and Alexander;[114] while his melody is little better than the monotonous recurrence of a Merlin's swing, or the easy trundle of a family coach. One of the personages is called Belmour, and this delicate appellation is a felicitous type of a Drama which "assumes to be poetry because it is not prose." If Miss Edmiston displayed little intuition into, or observation of, the secrets of nature in the guilty Jane, we must not argue thence her insufficiency; for of what use could the deepest insight into the genuine passions be in passages after this plan, with which, for the sake of better justifying our objections, we shall entreat the reader to contrast the death of Mrs. Frankford, the Woman killed with Kindness, of that prose Shakspeare, Old Heywood—straw versus flesh and blood. He will find the scene in Lamb and Campbell.[115]

> *Bel.*   How fare you, lady?
> *Jane.* My heart is thrill'd with horror,
> * * * *
> *Bel.*   Be of courage:
> Your husband lives: 'tis he, my worthiest friend—look up.
> *Jane.* I dare not!
> Oh! that my eyes could shut him out for ever.
> *Shore.* Am I so hateful, then, so deadly to thee,
> To blast thy eyes with horror? Since I'm grown
> A burden to the world, myself, and thee,
> Would I had ne'er survived to see thee more.
> *Jane.* Oh! thou most injured—dost thou live indeed?
> Fall then, ye mountains, on my guilty head!
> Hide me, ye rocks, within your secret caverns!
> Cast thy *black* veil upon my shame, oh night,
> And shield me with thy *sable* wing for ever![116]

Who will pretend that this has either originality or vraisemblance. Not to insist on such hollow talk as "black night and sable wing," it is throughout manifest that the writer has merely skimmed the surface; he puts down words instead of things; no distinction of character is to be found. "When we accurately examine the most of their (the dramatists of that day) tragical speeches, we shall find that they are seldom such as would be delivered by persons speaking or acting by themselves, without any restraint; we shall generally discover something in them which betrays a reference more or less to the spectator." Still Rowe must have his due; and it cannot be denied, that by incorporating his exposition or statement of the preliminary and actual situation of things with positive dramatic action, he has overcome that tedium which oppresses in the awkward prologues of Euripides, and the chief French writers both in Tragedy and the higher Comedy. We should not have been so wordy on this *leaden stock* piece, were it not that while many excellent plays of Thomas Heywood, Marston, Fletcher, Jonson, Ford, &c. lie dustily honoured in the collections of Dodsley and Reed,[117] or the

331

somewhat more popular editions of Gifford and Weber,[118] the stage libraries creak with a body of respectable doaters, who, like Tithonus, seem to preserve immortality in senile decrepitude.

The character of Alicia (to return,—we are always returning!) is in itself sufficiently ugly and coarse. Why should it be delivered over to Mrs. Merrilies, Mrs. (what is her name?) Egerton. Mr. Pope acted the noble-minded husband well. Mr. Cooper as the Lord Protector, ditto. Kean's Hastings saved the play.—Of De Montfort we would rather be silent. The great little man made the most desperate and oftimes brave attempts to career it on his part over the necks of the audience: but it is sorry work to ride a saddle without a horse.—Geraldi Duval, the laughable farce of Monsieur Tonson, and "*The splendid exhibition of the Coronation!*" have been alternated during the last month *as usual.*—

The Other Large House.
The stage proceedings here are best given from their own bills.—

The Play of The Two Gentlemen of Verona, again produced as great an effect on a brilliant and overflowing audience as any previous revival of Shakspeare. The introduction of his Sonnets and the Musick, were enthusiastically received, and the Carnival was not only deemed a most magnificent spectacle, but a classical embellishment of a Play of our Immortal Bard.—*The Two Gentlemen of Verona* will therefore be performed on Saturday, Monday, Wednesday, and Thursday, and four times a week till further notice.

The New Entertainment, called The Two Pages of Frederick the Great, continuing to be received throughout with the highest approbation and applause, will be repeated every evening.

In consequence of the increased demand for places, The Exile will be performed for the 29th and 30th times to-morrow and Tuesday.—

We shall not discharge our function thoroughly if we do not say one word on the first of the above load-stars. Let Mr. Reynolds[119] write original dramatic rhapsodies as long and as often as he pleases, and as the good-natured gallery will bear; but let him not attempt to darn Shakspeare's Plays that need no mending, and least of all such mending as Mr. Reynolds can give them.

The exterior ornaments are showered over the withered carcase of this Play with a brave prodigality; it is as if Sir Epicure Mammon sat in the treasury, "lord of the medicine."[120] Marble halls cooled with water jets, which catch, and fling back fresher, the languid richness of the orange blossoms; dark hoary woods; silent shrubbed lawns, trimmed, curled, and set in order,—lucid lakes, black-dashing torrents, and sunny casinos, form the back-ground to the well-formed figures of Miss M. Tree, Jones, and Abbott. Then shines forth the pantomimical triumph of that *Ami des Enfans* Mr. Farley,—"Go with him, and he will show" Apollonian temples, fiery mountains, allegorical palaces,—the circling seasons, conflicting elements, and "the serpent of Old Nile as when first she met Marc Antony, and pursed his heart up on the river Cydnus." When—

> The barge she sat in like a burnish'd throne
> Burn'd on the waters.[121]

When—

> On each side of her—
> Stood pretty dimpled boys, like smiling Cupids,
> With diverse-colour'd fans, whose wind did seem
> To glow the delicate cheeks which they did cool,
> And what they did, undid.[122]

In sober truth the Carnival, with its illuminations, processions, dances, and pageants, is surprisingly splendid, and would be admirable any where else but where it is; and the same may be said of the extraneous lyrical poetry, the sole effect of which is to distract the most determined attention, and retard the natural developement of the fable. The effect of the only song proper to the play, ("Who is Sylvia?") is marred beyond all conceivable indignation, by Bishop[123] and Reynolds together having, for the sake of a female voice in the glee, made the wretched Julia assist in praising her dreaded rival, while the ensuing dialogue is retained, as if to throw ridicule on their own folly. "*Host.* How now, you are sadder than you were before? How do you do, man? The music likes you not!—*Julia.* You mistake! The musician likes me not.—He plays false, father.—*Host.* How? out of tune on the strings?—*Julia.* Not so; but yet so false that he grieves my very heart-strings."[124] Is this the language of a person who has just sung her part at sight? This is not all: how can it be reconciled even to poetical possibility, that an utter stranger (which Julia absolutely is) both to the music and the words, should swim so toppingly off in her share of each. This comes of a Sir Thurio meddling, who does not know the distinction between a regular romantic Drama and an Opera. We should have thought any fool (Hamlet's grave digger to borrow) might have surmised, that if the great author of the detached poems in question had perceived the fitness of the introduction in any one of his artfully interwoven emanations, it would have been done. Sentences and descriptions may be good by themselves, yet impertinent as parts of a whole; because their mutual relations and dependencies are neglected or misunderstood. It was this rare comprehension of a whole which shed on the laurel crowns of Shakspeare and Raffaëlle that bloom, which shall remain fresh and dewy while a scene or group shall survive of their invention.

The actors come next, we believe? Miss Tree's Julia was in a higher taste, in a deeper gusto, than any of the other personations. She threw herself devotedly into the part, received passively the inspiration of her author, and, thus possessed wholly with his idea, poured forth into every gesture, look, and word, the genuine woman when she loves—yearningly timid, bashfully bold. Miss Tree has gradually gained to herself a superior and more permanent station than she originally made pretension to; and is now no longer a singer who can act, but an actress who can sing. Her figure round, yet slender—her limbs full, yet long—show to greater advantage her advantageously contrived androgynal vestments;—whose softly harmonised colours evidence much sentiment and feeling, either in herself or her adviser. Her light-bending attitudes when greedily yet fearfully drinking in the accents of her lover, may be contemplated as untiringly as the living lilies of Allegri and Parmegiana. Messrs. Abbott and Blanchard come next, for intelligence, spirit, and propriety in discharging their respective characters. Miss Beaumont was not half arch enough in Lucetta: she is a pretty girl, with an honest English expression spread over her face like a steady sunshine. Of Liston and Farren we cannot speak with commendation: yet they failed divergingly: Launce was not liked by the former, and Sir Thurio was at feud with the latter. Farren had not only missed his way, like Liston (who had the discretion to remain uncomfortably dubious), but dashed merrily along the lane of error. Does Mr. F. suppose that quizzing glasses were created in the opening of the sixteenth century? Or that if they were, a butterfly, like Sir Thurio, would have employed one on Valentine without brooking the buffet or the stab? Miss Hallande sings very loud; and well, we make no doubt, as great applause followed the heels, or the final cadential shakes of several vocal difficulties, which, with Johnson, we wished were impossibilities.* It would be very unfair, as well as ungrateful, to criticise the lively Jones's Valentine. He was altogether thrust into a misfit; and it showed no little talent that he never was offensive or liable to ridicule. This gentleman wears a long Spanish cloak better than any one on the stage; indeed, he graces every costume.

Of the "Two Pages," we can only say that it is an old story pleasantly retold. There was a very interesting piece on this subject, some years back (from the pen of Mr. Abbott, of this theatre) in which Terry as Frederic William, the father of Frederic the Great, was unapproachable.

Bradgate Park, the Residence of Lady Jane Grey.[125]
February 1822

The palsied hand of Ruin is on our House.

Real Old Play.

"If any one would choose to pay Antiquity a visit, and see her in her grand tiara of turrets, see her in all her gloomy glory,—not dragging on a graceless existence, in ruined cell, with disordered dress, and soiled visage; but clad in seemly habiliments, bearing a staid, proud, and glowing countenance, and dwelling in a home that seems charmed, and not distracted by time:—let such a one go to the wooded solitudes, the silent courts, the pictured walls, and rich embrowned floors of Warwick Castle."

This is the direction of a writer in the London Magazine.[126] Let me have permission also to speak my advice to the reader.

Reader!—Art thou a lover of those grand and melancholy places in which virtue hath thriven, or genius abided, or beauty reigned? Art

---

* The music was flashy and perishable. Mr. Bishop judges an English audience unworthy of his finer compositions. Rossini's lees are good enough for them! we believe he is right.

thou a melancholy worshipper of the memories of the great and good, and wouldst have thy worship solemnized by scenes which are covered with gentle recollections, and which seem by their decay to have sympathised with the fortunes of their mortal deities? Go thy ways to the lone and melancholy ruin in Bradgate Park—walk in the majestic solitude of its strange and romantic valley—and hear and *feel* the wild evening voice of its brook. Or shouldst thou desire to remain by thy home-fireside, and to read—aye—read *aloud* of a spot which innumerable circumstances may prevent thee from visiting and wandering in; listen to one who owes it no common remembrances,—who gathered in its quiet unassuming paradise no common peace,—who went to it sick in mind and body, and who came away from it refreshed, even as the pilgrim that hath reached the spring, and is returning.

It is now six or seven years, since, at the persuasion of some very kind friends, who, pitying the maladies, mental and bodily, to which I was a slave, craved of me to accompany them into Leicestershire, I first entered Bradgate Park. By some peculiar and early ties, my lady-friend was bound to this memorable place; and her family having sojourned on the borders of the park, she had in childhood become intimate with the deer-keeper (of whom I shall have hereafter to speak), and in his cottage she, her husband, and myself, were hospitably and quite happily accommodated. We remained there a month, and in that time I made a healthful acquaintance with the trees and with the air,—and indulged in a passion of the memory (if I may so stretch the phrase) for the birth-place, and the abode of the beautiful and the unfortunate Jane Grey— the daughter of the House of Suffolk—the lady of the noble Dudley— the friend and scholar of honest and kind-hearted Ascham—the sweet and girlish reader of the Greek and the Latin, the Chaldaic and the Arabic! I visited over and over again every nook of the building, crumbling, ruined, and confounded as it is; and I wandered into every sequestered and romantic angle and upland of the forest,—re-building, by aid of that goodly mason, the imagination, each broken tower and disordered wall, and honouring some conceived window with the image of the gracious young creature, leaning her head upon her slight hand, which her curls seemed to chain and imprison to her cheek, and reading the *Phaedon* in its mystic characters in the evening sun. Her pleasant tutor, for such I must call Master Ascham, hath writ that nothing could distract her from these her wondrous and *unsexlike* studies.[127] Not the chiding of parents, nor the noble pleasures of the forest chace,—nor the harmonies of youthful societies—nor the gallant example of her ladies, and the enchantment of the place. There she sat discoursing with the learned Greek, and fitting her young and patient heart for the philosophical regard of a bitter world which she had thereafter to encounter, and for the uncomplaining sufferance with which she met her fatal sorrows, and untimely death. How brief is beauty! This gentle lady had passed through the perils of infancy—the tediousness of strict scholastic labour—the chidings, the remonstrances, the anxieties of parental care—the fleeting joy of her girlish love—the welcome and tender devotions of Lord Guilford Dudley—her marriage—her wedded peace and happiness—the Mary-persecution—her fatal trial and condemnation—her husband's death on a scaffold—her own execution!—and all ere she was seventeen years of age. In this poor breath of life—this bitter instant—the most beautiful and sainted lady of England had suffered her birth and death. No mind that hath a thought—no heart that hath a feeling—but must in the lonely ruin of Bradgate Forest be made the better and wiser for its wholesome and searching associations. And I cannot conceive of that temperament so gay as not to quail on some jut of the rocks, or near some noising angle of the brook, and beget a seriousness and a sad vision of the hapless Jane; a seriousness better than all mirth—a vision such as doth "rise without a sleep," and sweeter than all that can be called realized joy.

I am becoming profuse too early in my remembrances of this lady, and am forgetting that all these thoughts upon fleeting mortality are as common to mankind as human calamity; and that even if they were not the tenants of every-day minds, they might be conjured up at the fireside, without dragging the reader to a far off forest, of which I have promised a description, and not a code of common morality framed within it. It is, however, next to impossible to write of this great ruin, and refrain from relapsing into recollections tender, visionary, and shaded. I will be as "faithful" as my *Polonius*-humour for diverging will permit; but let not the royal tempers of my readers run riot and distract, if I am somewhat tiresome and prolix in arriving at my conclusions. I will keep to the *pathway* of the forest as steadily as I may; but if a dell diverts me,—if a silent fragment of ruin, the tomb it may be of some early architectural beauty, lures me to step aside, and struggle for its mystic inscription—let me be endured and forgiven.

I remember it was a very beautiful autumnal evening (I am strictly faithful in my relation of facts, however I may wander in my meditations,) when we left Leicester, passed through the turbulent and *poaching* little village of Anstey—about three miles from Leicester, as I conjecture, though for greater certainty, as the law expresses it, I crave leave to refer to *Paterson*[128]—and descended the irregular and sloping field that leads down into the forest, and to the deer keeper's cottage. The sky was ruddy and rich, and looked as ripe as a harvest field, from the extreme heat and cloudlessness of the foregone day. The forest rose as it were from a depth beneath us, and displayed before our eyes clumps and extents of old noble trees,—openings of sallow and ripe grass,— the silver threading of a perplexed brooklet, which was as narrow and meandering as a fairy's silken clue, unwound to conduct some favoured princess to her palace: we beheld distant and sky-bound hills—caught glimpses of a shattered building, standing in warm brown fragments of colour, in the very brick work that seemed, and always seems to me, an *architectural history* of the age of Elizabeth; and below us, in the quiet depth of the entrance of the forest, stood the cottage of the keeper, all alone, and sending its white wood-smoke up as from some domestic altar, in token to Heaven of peasant devotion, and grateful content.

The keeper—worthy A—— (nay, why should I disguise a name which his manly, frank, and sensible mind may make him free to hear, and proud to have uttered?)—the keeper, Harry Adams,—I am now guilty of a familiarity which I never took in his presence,—had been on business to Leicester that day, it being market-day; and he rode just a-head of us on a switch-tailed old mare that might have carried old Roger Ascham for aught I could, by her apparent age, guess to the contrary. I drove a one-horse chaise, the first time I should think that ever so town-like a vehicle had *convulsed* its way through the pitfalls and fearful varieties of that amazing road. We talked little on our way, —and rode with extreme slowness; indeed the hump-backed lane set its deformities against a trot. Adams ploughed his way before us with a serene gravity; and so, thought I, have I often, quite in my boyhood, seen the English husbandman ride homeward through the outskirts of my native town,[129] slowly, pensively, and alone, when I have been straggling back from the river bank on a Saturday evening, where I had been cozening the silly perch all the live-long holiday afternoon: such was indeed my thought! And, oh! how easily and well are opposite scenes joined together by some gliding association—even as you see in a theatre the separate parts of a wood, or of a heath, shot on and blended, by unseen hands, and as by magic.

On arriving at the long old barred gate that *pretended* to protect the entrance to the farm-yard, our guide dismounted, and led his reverend mare through to an opposite wicket, disburthened her of her saddle and simple bridle, and showed her *serene* highness into the open park, where she just took one wholesome and orderly shake,—one look of luxurious indolence around her, and straight-way proceeded to the cropping of her evening meal. Adams returned to offer us assistance, though I am vain enough to account myself a decent hand at harnessing and un-harnessing a horse, from curb to crupper.

Our horse being accordingly housed in a comfortable spacious stable, but littered with dried fern, instead of straw, at which I know more than one scrupulous nag that would have turned up the nose, spurning such a bed, we entered our worthy friend's cottage. We entered it through a maze of children, "each under each," and quite as *tuneable* as the beagles of Theseus. The eldest was a fine healthy rosy girl, of about twelve years of age, with handsome and regular features, and possessing that natural and retired modesty which seldom fails to accompany true youthful grace and beauty. She stood somewhat apart, looking with her shy dark eyes askance at us, like one of her father's fawns, from which she perchance caught this her so pretty air the while it came fearfully at the dawn about the cottage, to get bread from her hand, and to fleet away at the sun-rise. This little girl held a baby-sister in her arms, as like to herself as blossom is to blossom. Around the doorway crowded breeches-brother, and petticoat-brother, and pinafore-sister, and frock-sister, and every species of this urchin genus, some with bread, and some without, but none wanting it! The bigger ones marveling at our coats and boxes,—the biggest "encumbering us with help,"—and the lesser ones clinging to the clean tucked-up gown of their pleasant and welcoming mother, who stood intreating and rejoicing at our entry, yet continually molested by unknown hands, which she removed from her garments only to have them return, as some peasant girl brushes away the giddy murmuring, still returning gnats that swarm round her comely head. In vain she pleaded, protested, rebuked. There they clung with their round, crumby, rosy cheeks, and plump buttery fingers; they were her children, and she was their mother, and tiresome as they might be to her I should like to see the person that could or would have put them asunder. Inside the cottage, an aged and respectable mother of the mother sat spinning at the wheel,—she was the only one in whom joy and curiosity slumbered. Years had destroyed the wonder which a stranger creates; and she heard the din of her grand children without, and lost not a turn of her wheel, or a thread of her flax. She seemed to me sacred to the age of the place—akin to the ruin,—silent as the old decaying oak that brooded over the cottage wicket, and almost as unconscious of our approach.

Our tea was delightful, our butter tasting as of country air, our cream rich as any that curded up to the silver brim of "a lordly dish" for Suffolk's Countess, in Bradgate's nobler days:—we sat in the tile-paved parlour, and had a talk of past times, to which I listened, and which gradually lighted up the manly countenance of Adams with gladness, and set his memory to work with great industry. I had leisure to note him curiously; and I thought I never saw the dignity of human nature so well asserted in humble life, as in the tall well-proportioned person of this keeper; in his strong, handsome, and evenly marked countenance; and in that frank unobtrusive manner with which nature had endowed him. His voice was extremely quiet, and his remarks were at once modest and sensible. I was much pleased to hear him eulogize the present Earl, then Lord Grey of Groby, and admire him for his condescension, and his higher powers of walking and shooting. Such a faithful and attached servant, so earnest in his wishes and intentions, so steady in the performance of his duties, I never beheld; and I sincerely hope that at the time I write this he is worthily remunerated, and relieved from many labours which often seemed to me to silently oppress him, though he never complained.

We arose each morning, not with the lark, perhaps, but long before the sun had dried up the dew from the glittering grass. My window looked out across the brook, and up towards the ruin, and I never so drank in the bright air as then, when I first unhasped my casement, and let in the noise of a thousand rooks, at the same time that I heartily admitted the cool spirit of the morning's breath. The throwing back of that jingling and diamond-paned window to its farthest limit, seemed to be the signal to the babbling geese, the lowing cattle in the park, the singing birds, the trees, wind-shaken,—all, to tell me that the day was up, and to rebuke me, with pastoral sounds, for staying so idly in my bed-chamber. I used to speak to the little Adamites under the window, and inquire how long they had been abroad: and certainly in comparison with these sleepless urchins, I showed off "poor indeed!"

And now, suppose that the morning meal is dispatched, let us, gentle reader, (thou art always by an author's courtesy so called; and, in my present mood, I am not minded to curtail thee of the title,) let us go into the park, and enjoy one of those happy walks, which that place affords better than any other place I ever visited. We will idle on our way and discourse pleasantly of all that may interest,—connecting the present with the past, and tenanting with creative thoughts the holy retreats of our melancholy ruin, so as almost to recall the times when they were indeed gay and perfect,—when the laugh went round by day, and the dance by night,—when at morn the hound was loosed, and the hawks unhooded,—and when at eve "the lamps shone o'er fair women and brave men." I will be to thee, gentle reader, a faithful guide, an honest narrator of the little I know.—Oh! that I could speak of the air, the water, and the light, in phrase as white and simple as that which characterises the discourse of goodly Master Walton, when he talketh of the angle rod, and the silver river Lea!

On stepping to the wicket of the farm-yard, you pass, or rather I passed (for I *must* speak by my memory), under an oak that is hollow with age;—perchance under that very tree hath Lady Jane passed;— under that tree read;—there thought and wept (for she had ever a soul sad with an over-wise consciousness);—I leaned against the wicket, and looked up into its forest of branches, *mazing* my mind in its knotty intricacies, as the philosopher would vainly master some tangled subject of the brain. The brook is within forty paces of this gate, and winds up, snakishly enough, to within the same distance from the ruin of the house. There is a nearer footway, well trodden, through the park; but that was not the way for me, and I chose rather to unthread the little slim palace of the water-spirit that haunts the solitude of the forest, than go as the crow flies, and the milkmaid walks. The tall and beautiful trees which line this delightful stream, hold out the most tempting spots for indolence and rest;—and I could not resist lying down at the foot of many a goodly trunk, and starting the wary trout from a similar though deeper enjoyment of solitude and shade.[130] At length I reached the famous ruin—ruin indeed!—The few relics of wall and tower that remain give you little idea of the original shape of the building, although it is described as having been square and with four towers. There appear to be some remains of a kitchen, and the side nearest the chapel (which is the most perfect) still partly triumphs over time. The walls on all sides, except this, have not only fallen, but crumbled into the very earth, and become covered with the soft and silent turf. You can walk on a kind of terrace of about eight feet in breadth, within which, as though sunk into the earth, is a place now called the Bowling-green; I could not myself help thinking that it must have been the tilt-yard, and more particularly, as the place pointed out to me as such did not in the least satisfy my feeling of that chivalrous spot. The pleasure-grounds are now distinguishable by their being a wilderness.—The uncultivated earth is rich and soft as ever; but the garden of man's care is eloquent of neglect, and seems to disdain any other but its first proud life.

Nichols writes exactly enough, in his Leicestershire History, thus:— "The careful observer may yet discover some traces of the tilt-yard; but the courts are now occupied by rabbits, and shaded with chestnut-trees and mulberries. The lover of the picturesque will be particularly struck with the approach from Thurcaston, especially at the keeper's lodge, where the view is truly enchanting. On the left appears a large grove of venerable trees. On the right are the ruins of the mansion, surmounted by rugged rocks and aged oaks; the forest hills, with the tower on the hill, called Old John, forming the back ground of the prospect: whilst the valley, through which the trout stream runs, extends in front, with clumps to shade the deer, and terminates in a narrow winding glen, thickly clothed with an umbrageous shade."[131] This passage, written in the good old *county* style, gives a very fair picture of the place;—and if it were only from the mention of the *rabbits*, I should be sure that the writer had visited the Ruin itself. That little grey race has fixed itself immoveably there, and defies extinction.

The chapel, which you reach through a mass of ruin, is the least touched by decay. You enter it, and are awed by the intense chill and silence of the place. All is white—solemn—exact. One tomb of the Suffolk family, with its two figures extended, in the usual monumental attitude, with pointing palms, is in a very fine state. It is impossible here to forget, that Lady Jane Grey must often have knelt in this sacred chapel, and have breathed her virgin prayers audibly within it:—no such voice hath ever broken its silence since;—nor will hymn be sung, or orison uttered, with so pure a zeal, in any of the coming years of its decay. The trees around this ruin seem older than any other trees in the forest. They appear musing over their age, and drowsing

> —With hoods, that fall low down
> Before their eyes, in fashion like to those
> Worn by the monks in Cologne.[132]

On the opposite side of the brook to that on which the ruin decays, stands a large barn-like building, which was originally used as the kitchen and offices of the mansion. Since that time, it has been converted to a kennel for stag hounds, and now it is utterly closed and neglected. The effect of this huge sombre building is in unison with the whole scene, making the heart grave and melancholy.

I turned again to the poor fragment of the ruin, and again stood by the side of that yard, which I still must think the tilt-yard. How often, methought, within a bowshot of that desolate place had bounded the armed horse, with glittering poictrel,[133] bearing his proud lord in rich apparel, and costly armour. The silence, now so profound, and vexed only by the lofty rook, had been torn by the daring trumpet,—and the turf, now touched but by the simple rabbit, had been spurned by the flashing hoof, or dinted by the dishonoured helm. I pictured in a dreaming mood a joust in Suffolk's days—and brought into the field the flower of that age's chivalry:—first, the Earl of Surrey, in his dancing plume—the Howard with his white charger—Seymour and Cromwell—and Dudley—all appareled like brave knights. They tilted like visions of the air, their imagined accomplishments gleaming and glancing in the sun—they shifted—triumphed—encountered—faded—all—all by turns, and with the inconstancy of dreams. I became delighted with the enchantment, and in the mad joy of fancy—the walls grew up before me—the lattices, flower-adorned, re-opened to my view—fair ladies, goodly nobles, filled terrace and gallery—and I saw the young, the gallant

Guilford, the impassioned, brave, and unfortunate Dudley, come fiery off in a joust—and ride with bared forehead to the lady of his love, bending as knights in romances are said to bend. And there *was* the lady—the lady Jane! Young as the veriest flower—beautiful as poet can imagine—her hair simply bound back, after the fashion of her time, so as to betray her expansive and pearl-white forehead—a costly close cap on the higher part of the head—and a long and *solemn* necklace wound in quaint fashion over her neck and bosom,—her gown, gold-embossed and fitted to her form, like some gentle armour. There she sat. I saw her smile upon Dudley, and straight, as though fancy were jealous of the splendours of that she had woven her web withal, the walls crumbled to air—the pageant faded—and in their room the rabbit nibbled beneath the shading fern—and the fawn bounded out of some weedy recess of the ruin.

It can never be forgotten, that here in Bradgate, the Lady Jane tasted all that was permitted to her of ease, and learning, and happiness. It was here that Ascham, who sojourned in the neighbourhood, was wont to come, and marvel at, and encourage the noble girl's accomplishments. She wrote a beautiful hand, and Ascham was skilful in penmanship. She read Greek, and Ascham, who once wished that friends could discourse in that brave tongue, gloried in her learned pastime. In one of his letters to a favourite German is the following pleasant description of our gentle girl.

Before I went into Germany, I came to Brodegate in Leicestershire, to take my leave of that noble Lady Jane Grey, to whom I was exceeding much beholding. Her parents, the Duke and Duchess, with all the household, gentlemen and gentlewomen, were hunting in the park. I found her in her chamber reading Phaedo Platonis in Greek, and that with as much delight, as some gentlemen would read a merry tale in Boccace. After salutation, and duty done, with some other talk, I asked her, why she would lose such pastime in the Park? Smiling, she answered me; "I wist, all their sport in the Park is but a shadow to that pleasure that I find in Plato. Alas! good folk, they never felt what true pleasure meant." "And how came you, Madam," quoth I, "to this deep knowledge of pleasure? And what did chiefly allure you unto it, seeing not many women, but very few men, have attained thereunto?" "I will tell you," quoth she, "and tell you a truth which perchance ye will marvel at. One of the greatest benefits that ever God gave me, is, that he sent me so sharp and severe parents, and so gentle a scholemaster. For when I am in presence either of father or mother, whether

I speak, keep silence, sit, stand, or go, eat, drink, be merry, or sad, be sewing, playing, dancing, or doing any thing else, I must do it, as it were, in such weight, measure, and number, even so perfectly, as God made the world; or else I am so sharply taunted, so cruelly threatened; yea, presently, sometimes with pinches, nips, and bobs, and other ways (which I will not name for the honour I bear them) so without measure misordered, that I think myself in hell, till time come that I must go to Mr. Elmer, who teacheth me so gently, so pleasantly, with such fair allurements to learning, that I think all the time nothing while I am with him. And when I am called from him, I fall on weeping, because whatsoever I do else, but learning, is full of grief, trouble, fear, and whole misliking unto me. And thus my book hath been so much my pleasure, and bringeth daily to me more pleasure and more, that in respect of it, all other pleasures in very deed be but trifles and trouble unto me."

I remember this talk gladly, both because it is so worthy of memory, and because also it was the last talk that ever I had, and the last time that ever I saw that noble and worthy Lady.

Ascham's Scholemaster, 8vo. 1743, p. 37.

This is wholesome prose, and worthy of its gracious subject: it seems idle to vex the sentiment which language, clothed in so fitting a costume, must awaken in the reader; and yet I cannot deny myself the introduction of a few stanzas, which were composed under the influence of the character to which they are dedicated.

Stanzas
To the Lady Jane Grey, at Bradgate.
This was thy home then, gentle Jane!
This thy green solitude;—and here
At evening, from thy gleaming pane,
Thine eye oft watch'd the dappled deer,
While the soft sun was in its wane,
Browsing beneath the brooklet clear:
The brook runs still, the sun sets now,
The deer yet browseth; where art thou?

Oh, gentle Dudley! Where art thou?
Have years so roll'd that not a track
Of even thy chamber lingereth now
To call thine image sweetlier back?

345

The careless chair at window bow,
The ruin'd lute, the crumbling wrack
Of broidery, the forgotten glove,
The learned book, thy virgin love;—

None, none of these abide to tell
Thy gentle tale,—yet it *is* told!
The silence of the breathless dell
Is musical of thee; the cold
And mournful water passeth well
Thy house's ruin, as of old,
And pineth with a watery sound
Its little hymn to thy lone ground!

The air is sainted;—never shone
More tender light on greener grass,
Than that which kisseth turf and stone
Of thy decayed house; alas!
The aged drowsing trees make moan
For thee, sweet girl! And many a lass
Pauseth at morn upon her way,
And grieveth for the Lady Grey.

Here was thy life! Here was thy bower,
By this light water! Thy hard death
Was far away in town and tower,
And cruel hands destroy'd thy breath:
Might they not let so young a flower
Bud all its beauty in life's wreath?
What must have been that guilty sense,
That had such fear of innocence!

But though thy young and bridal heart
Was tortured, thy brave spirit, still
Untroubled, left its mortal part,
And halloweth now each dell and hill:

It liveth by a gracious art
For ever here; and that wild thrill
The stranger feels of love and pain,
Is the present voice of the Lady Jane.

It may be supposed, that often and often during my stay at Bradgate, I wandered amid the ruins of this noble park; and many were the verses that I dedicated to the memory of my favourite Lady and Queen. I did not, however, entirely confine myself to this particular part of the forest, but sought out all the romantic beauties of valley and hill. The valley which leads from the ruin to the village of Newtown, is extremely beautiful, and seen, as I have seen it, in the misty and inconstant lustre of the morning, or warmed and enriched with the steady flood of the evening sunlight, it is quite a scene of enchantment. The sides of either hill are rocky, and fledged with the most luxuriant fern, from which the deer are continually starting; and trees of magnificent growth are in great profusion. The stream winds gracefully in the depth of the valley, through broken rocky ground,—

And to the sleepy woods all night singeth a quiet tune.[134]

Here I used oftimes to take my book, and read the hours away in such a golden idleness as I have never since enjoyed, and now never shall enjoy more! Here I read many a goodly poem, from which shortly thereafter I was ever utterly to be divorced. And here I sat discoursing with my friends on subjects to which now I dare never to recur. In turning to those times, I feel that I am changed; and my present sense of the idle romance of many of my then pleasures is perhaps one of those bitter apples of knowledge, the tasting of which has driven me out of Paradise! However, we cannot always be boys.

Let me return to Adams, and in conclusion give a slight account of his pursuits,—pastimes they seemed to me, shared as they were at the jolly autumn-tide, when the open air was all enjoyment: to him they were daily work—drear daily work! One morning I accompanied him to Groby Pool, a large piece of water within a few miles of the forest: thither he went to shoot wild ducks and to take pike. He took an assistant to row the boat, and with his active spaniels, we were soon coasting the reeds and dreary bulrushes of that immense sheet of water. The dogs dashed in and paddled, and struggled, and yelped their way, betraying their passage by their tongue, by the splash of water, and the severing of the reeds. A few ducks were soon scared from their ancient brooding-place, and the keeper fired. At that instant, as the echo of the gun shook its way across the waters, the air was *freckled* with water birds. One cloud of noisy frightened fowl arose tumultuously into the air, as though a great silence was broken for ever, and these creatures of the place were by one consent quitting their old and desolate habitation. The fishing did not prove successful, for though nets were cast, and the pool is well stocked, only fish of a moderate size were taken. Adams was quite disappointed with the day; but he was the *Nelson* of such sports, and always calculated on the *three-deckers* of pike and ducks—aye, and many of them.

Another day he took down his rifle piece, and quietly loaded it with ball. I enquired his pursuit, and he told me that he was about to shoot a buck. Of course, I determined on seeing the gallant beast die, if possible, and I therefore kept as near to him as he could permit. The task was tedious and difficult, and many hours were lost before the keeper could obtain his shot; for the herd, being extremely suspicious of his intentions, ever shun him with singular care. His assistant I found singing a melancholy low ditty of a few notes only, and pacing up and down with a measured *monotonous* pace (if I may use the expression); the deer began to herd, as though the music lulled and overcame them; and as the notes drew nearer, they huddled up more and more closely, till they appeared to be lost in the melancholy of the keeper's song, and heedless of the freedom of the park and the natural life and wild-ness of their natures. Suddenly, Adams, having selected with his eye the unfortunate creature whose speed was to be checked, gave a sort of war-whoop, at which sound the herd started from their melancholy trance, threw up their confused and mingled horns, and bounded away in one fleet single line. The keeper steadily leveled at a fine black gallant buck, and the aim was death. The fire flashed,—he plunged upward with a frantic motion of his body, and a mad toss and clash of his horns, and fell with his nostrils at the very brink of that brook to which in the pride of youth he had so often come for water. He was carefully carried home, and carved up by Adams, "as a dish fit for the gods!" I recollect grieving to see such goodly venison go from the cottage; but he was delighted in contemplating the haunch, and thinking what satisfaction it would give.

The inhabitants of the neighbouring villages are sad poachers, and much trouble and anxiety did they occasion to our good keeper, who could never rest morning, noon, or night, if he suspected them at the brook. Many a night late, have I seen him take down his gun from the rack, and sally out with his dog, because he had a notion of their haunts, and knew that the hour was likely: what but the sense and pride of doing and deserving well could recompense this man for the slavish and dangerous existence which he led? His rigid honesty was such that he wished me not to fish in the brook, that he might not sanction in any one under his own roof that practice which he sought to put down in others.

I have often walked out with him for the greater part of the day when he has been shooting; and he could not disguise his surprise that I should hold on with him untired, coming as he imagined I did from poor powerless London. He walked well and shot well; indeed, his aim was unerring, but I rather think he was not severe enough to his dogs for a game-keeper, not but that I honoured his character the more for this its *professional* weakness. When *Rattler*, a tall handsome galloping setter, with a liver and white skin, and curly head, raced over a field and pro-ceeded to bound a hedge or shoot a gate without leave, I have seen his master (almost delivered to wrath I confess) halloo and whistle him in,—take his long *napkin* of an ear in one hand, and *stretching* forth the other, like an orator, expostulate, as man would talk to man, on his undoglike conduct. His *"for shame"* awed even me. *Rattler* remembered the admonition for a time; but I fear a small whip would have been more impressive, much as I should have grieved to see so handsome a creature corrected. During our walk I spake to my guide of the Turks and of the Greeks, people of books, imaginary men, creatures for travelers to romance upon. Adams listened with visible delight, and put questions to me, credulous but sensible, to which I replied as faithfully and plainly as possible. He liked to hear of the habits of these nations, even though he was not quite convinced of their positive existence.

I have been in many scenes, and with those persons who are called lovers of the country, but never did I pass such a happy golden time as that which I whiled away in the humble hospitable cottage of Harry Adams.

Here I conclude my rambling history. But who can write of a wild and romantic forest, peopled with such associations as those which abide in Bradgate, and keep the straight and beaten path? Here and there I may in descriptive particulars be incorrect, but I am strictly faithful to my impressions, and write from recollections that were born between six and seven years ago. The memory of Lady Jane Grey made the place sacred to me, and therefore I thought that some record, however slight, might find readers who would take pleasure in the same. If I have thought correctly, I shall not have written wholly in vain.

E.H.

The Green-Room.
The Letters of Edward Herbert, No. III. March 1822
To Russell Powell, Esq.

My dear Russell,—It was my intention to have addressed this letter to your sister; but as I am apprehensive that the subject of it would prove but uninteresting to her, and as I know your passion for theatrical matters, I shall devote this sheet to you, and write to her anon upon some topic more pleasant and suitable to female curiosity. You will find that my letters contain a sort of narrative, broken into chapters as the post requires, so that I need not be wasting my time upon repeated prefaces. Having introduced you to my friends, the Mortons, I have only now to relate whatever occurs, that may prove entertaining. And so I proceed.

The stocking of Prudence Morton is, as I have hinted, subject "to all the skiey influences" in its colour—but setting this aside, she is naturally a kind-hearted and pleasant girl. I called one morning at the house of my friends, and was announced to Prudence only (her sister and her aunt being busied elsewhere)—she was sitting in state, over a little pink-lined and cotton-furnished box, and playing at needle and thread with a bit of muslin scarcely large enough to have made a tippet for a fly;—a volume of Southey's *Roderick*[135] was open on one side of her work-box. She received me with a little momentary disappointment, as though she had hoped for some one of a wider fame; but her natural kindness triumphed over her artificial manner, and in three minutes she laid aside her parody on work, pushed the little thread-closet towards the middle of the table, descended from her *blue* throne of state, and began to converse with me unaffectedly and amusingly, though still with something of her customary flightiness. She did not load the great guns of her visiting and company powers, and destroy me with her elegant vehemence,—but chatted like a girl in a parlour, with ease, playfulness, and spirit, and was content to discourse without aiming at effects. On my asking her whether she had seen Mr. Kean (with whom she was intimate, as I have before hinted, and of whose fame she was extremely chary), she turned her chair towards me, and said, "Seen him! Yes! the clever creature! He kindly called the other morning to ask how we were, and we had a delightful theatrical conversation. Not that I dislike Macready —but I never saw any picture so expressive as the fine countenance of Kean, when he is addressing you on dramatic subjects. Don't you think so? But oh! true—you never saw him in a room—you should go to the Green-Room with Tom, for he has the *entré* at all the houses—I wonder why they call it a Green-Room—for Tom says it is not green." This hint of the Green-Room was enough for me, and I picked it out of the tangled threads of Prudence's discourse, and made use of it. I found that Tom, in the leisure of his industrious idleness, passed many an hour at the theatres, and that his acquaintance with the performers secured him free ingress and egress at all seasonable times, as the leases specify, to and from the theatrical premises. I begged Prudence to arrange for my accompanying Tom some morning or evening, which she cheerfully undertook to do. And, indeed, so earnest was she on this subject, that she promised, if possible, to pack up her brother, and send him to me at the breakfast hour on the following morning. At this moment, Mrs. Morton and Agnes came in from a walk, and our conversation became general. I sat chatting upon pleasant little scandals, until within half an hour of dinner; and then Mr. Morton, who had returned from the City, true as the dial, would have me stay the day, as he had an inclination to try a rubber after tea. The hours passed cheerfully—we made up a table—but without Prudence and Tom, as usual. The first was finishing the *Bride of Lammermuir*,[136] with as many tears in her eyes as I had trumps in my hand; and Tom was plaiting a whip-thong, and whistling a York-shire tune out of time, and with many dreary pauses between. The thong was tied to the chair-rail, and he worked away like a saddler,—

pretending at the same time to read *Fearne on Contingent Remainders*,[137] which lay open (at the index) in his lap. Mrs. Morton revoked in the first deal, which made us all serious, until I trumped the best club, and by my bad play restored the cheerfulness of the table. Tom promised at the door, as he let me out, to be with me in the morning after breakfast; for Prudence had told him what I wished—but he begged me at the same time to give up "*that* union of the black handkerchief and buff waistcoat," which he protested was quite gothic.

Tom was with me at the stirring of my second cup of cocoa, and burst into my room as though he "would have told me half my Troy was burnt." I poured him out a cup of my patent beverage, which he would not taste, and pushed a chair towards him, which he as carelessly kicked away. All breakfast-time he was fretting me, and strutting his hour, about my best Brussels carpet, with his muddy buskin. Speeches from various plays were mouthed by him in a most tragic fury, and he turned to me at the conclusion of each separate passage, with a request that I would tell him "where *that* was;" I guessed awry, and so pestered him. He raved about as Octavian;[138] and I arose, intreating him to sit down; when he immediately saddened into Jaffier,[139] and threw himself on my Belvidera neck with all his weight. I had scarcely set him upright, and relieved myself from the oppressive pathos of this embrace, when he fenced at me with his fingers, and put in some mortal thrusts about the region of my waistcoat pocket. I half offended him by expressing doubts of his grace at this amusement—when he doubled up his affronted fingers, started into another attitude, and, with a quickness which I could not counteract, snatched a smart hit upon my chest bone, that staggered me up against my own breakfast table, convulsed the whole family of the tea-things, and made my milk-jug shed some natural tears. My awkwardness, and abrupt flight from the visitation of his knuckles, perfectly restored his good humour and his confidence—and he relapsed into a theatrical conversation. "I'll tell you what, Edward, you bury yourself here in this gothic spot, without having a notion of life—why an Abbey statue has ten times the *nous* about him, not barring Sir Cloudesley Shovel.[140] If, instead of sitting here in your poor's box, (I hate the Albany—it's so like a genteel King's Bench!) with as little to do as a money-taker after a charity sermon, you were to doff that morning gown, and accompany me to a rehearsal of ——'s play; I would engage you will say to me, Tom Morton, I thank you for breaking my monumental existence, and will hereafter follow wherever you shall choose to lead. Why you are like the man in the Arabian Nights, with a marble moiety."[141] And with this my young gentleman ran lightly through the figure of a quadrille—*dos-à-dos*-ing it with an arm chair, and concluding with a harlequin-roll of his head in its loose socket, and with a "Well, Edward, what say you?" "My dear fellow," said I, "if you will introduce me to the real interior of a London theatre, nothing will give me greater pleasure, and I will be out of my *shell* in two seconds; you know that I am anxious to see all the *lions*—and surely one of them must be kept behind the scenes of a metropolitan theatre." Tom, with no allowance for metaphor, only informed me that Kean once kept one, but that it was since dead! I rang my bell; my table was immediately cleared, and in a few minutes I was fitted with bright boots, like Dan in John Bull,[142] to accompany my heedless guide on his proposed walk. He dragged me into Piccadilly, at as rapid a rate as though we were going off by the Bath mail, and heard the carts *horning* their way up to the White Horse Cellar; but he did not so hastily pass the print-shop at the corner of Sackville-street; for there, as he assured me, was a portrait of old Fewterel worth looking at; and there, sure enough, was an awkward sprawling animal, painted as formidably as warlike man could desire. As we eagerly trod the pavement, Tom assuring me that the rehearsal must have begun some time back, I made inquiries of him as to his power, and the propriety, of introducing me, which he begged me to be perfectly easy about, muttering something about settling any door-keeper. We were soon at the stage door of Covent Garden theatre.

The porter permitted him to pass; and as he had firm hold of my arm, I was suffered to pass also, though I own I looked upon myself as an impertinent intruder, and could have been pleased to escape from the suspicious gaze of passing actors, actresses, musicians, servants, and the long living *et cetera* of a playhouse. One tall serious gentleman, in a well-shaped, but aged and napless hat, and in a coat that had evidently not been made without seams, passed me with a proud tragedy step and an inquiring stare, that made me quail within myself, and feel as if I was about to play Tom Thumb, to his Lord Grizzle.[143] Another, a young lady, gaily *pelissed*, nodded familiarly to Tom, and looked curiously at me, taking me, as I conceived, for some unwarrantable personage that had no business in that part of the house. Some viewed me with wonder, others with disregard, or so I read their looks, as they passed to and fro on the stone staircase that led from the entrance to the stage. But in spite of my feelings, Tom dragged me on to the *boards*, as they are termed, which I now trod for the first time in my life, and not much to my satisfaction, as I determined it. The first act of Tom's ascension to this Covent Garden throne, was to confer with Mr. ——, one of the great tragedians of that magnificent theatre, and arrange for my seeing the house, as it is termed. This gentleman, in a true Coriolanus key, ordered forth one of the *red coat men*, as he called them, and gave him directions to escort me on the view. We accordingly began our voyage of discovery —the servant preceding us with a lanthorn, and Tom and myself following with a silent and determined curiosity. We were first shown the two Green-Rooms, which certainly, by day, looked miserably enough; but as I shall have to speak of them anon in a better light, I shall not here pause to give an unfavourable account of them. I was then taken into several of the principal dressing-rooms; and one I could not but regard as a place of sweet interest, for the guide addressed me with, "This, Sir, was Miss O'Neill's room." There were two full-length mirrors in it, and I found it was impossible not to contemplate them with a foolish (perchance) and romantic delight, as having so often reflected the handsome form of that fair and far-famed woman. There— before those simple mirrors had stood Belvidera, and Monimia, and Isabella,[144] in all their gentle beauty and feminine bravery; there, methought, on the first tremulous night which was to mar or make her fame, had lingered this young and intelligent and charming creature, dreading all that she was about to dare,—and sighing in timid apprehension of her splendid trial! A thousand of these idle yet delightful daydreams of the moment flitted through my mind, as I looked upon the silent, yet not ineloquent furniture of this diminutive and simple room. I seemed to have a perfect vision of *Juliet*, reclining in strange and painful terror on her chair, just before she astounded the public with her gentle presence—and again, I as plainly beheld her, in my mind's eye, resting in all her heated agitation, and palpitating distress, after leaving the house in a tumult of sorrow, admiration, and intense feeling. I know not whether my friend Tom entered into any of these my sensations; I fear not; for he was intently considering his own symmetry in the mirrors, and his thoughts appeared to be of too domestic a kind to quit the all-satisfying home of his own person.

From these rooms we were conducted to the wardrobe, a truly curious scene; and here we found tailors and dress-makers as earnestly engaged, as if trade were only at its height in the loftiest part of the interior of the theatre, and that the motley artizans were engaged in some fashionable contract for supplying the army of Brutus with garments, or completing a large order for Virginius[145] for ready money only. The exactness with which the various dresses are kept is highly to be admired; and I could not fail to take a hint for the arrangement of my own habiliments, for which my little wardrobe has ever since been the better. Mr. Macready was at this time giving some directions about a Roman vest; and the *sincere* steel and the superfine stuff of which it was made really surprised me; for I, like a very country gentleman, had supposed that every ornament and property of a theatre was as unreal and slight as the keenest economy could make it. The trappings, however, of a Roman warrior of the true Covent Garden *breed*, are as solid, honest, and handsome, as old Cassius himself could desire; and I verily believe, that Mr. Charles Kemble, or Mr. Young, or Mr. Macready, as harnessed for the night and fairly accoutred, might safely have walked through Rome's Cheapside without being once suspected to be any other than Rome's true man. Macready's face perchance might have told an English story, —but I would vouch for it, that Charles Kemble, with his fine, earnest, and classic features, and his noble figure, might meet a Roman in the market-place, and be deemed a true dweller by the Tiber, and nothing native to the Thames. The dresses for all the plays are kept properly sorted and ticketed, and those needed for the night are duly laid forth in the previous morning.

From the wardrobe, we were conducted to the carpenters' room. The machinery by which the scenery is shifted, and by which the skies and ceilings of rooms are *laid on*, is almost fearful to look at; and I confess, that when I was walking about in the theatre's heaven, I had all the feeling of being half-mast high in a man of war, with all the sails, cordage, and pulleys, around me. Indeed, it is a question to me whether a ship is half so well rigged as a play-house. As you are nearly grown up, my dear Russell, I may inform you of the stuff that storms are made of, though I should pause at telling your little sisters such destructive facts.

With them, thank heaven, at present, thunder is thunder—lightning, lightning—and rain, rain. But if, to this moment, your faith has remained strong in the sincerity of theatrical elements, now lay aside your belief, for know that the wind is not wind, but brewed from an old barrel covered with silk, which by being turned quickly round *blows* fit to wreck a vessel. The thunder keeps its gloomy state in a large sheet of iron, and it only bellows to the ear when some rash intruder dares to shake its throne. A long hollow tube, lined on the inside with loose pegs, and filled with peas, will wet the *ears* through presently: it is held up-right, and the shower continues until all the peas have performed their journey through the pegs; and then it is but turning it down anew, and *"spunge,"* you are not *"dry again."* I saw no lightning, but the man assured me that it was not real; you may believe him or not, as you choose. Our guide was happy to find that the *wind* was a little discon-certed, for it allowed him to make one little but well-established joke, which Tom had heard four-and-twenty times, that "it took a deal of repairing, for in times like these it was very difficult to *raise the wind."* Having been conducted over and under the stage, and let into all the mystery of lamp, and trap, and fly, and wing, I was taken by Tom to the stage itself, where I beheld a rehearsal of ——'s play, going on as tamely as it possibly could on an Author's night. I could scarcely believe that that earnest gentleman in every-day attire was Mr. Macready; or that Charles Kemble was wearing a common hat and dress, and talking in a voice more familiar than Melpomene is said to sanction. Miss Foote looked as pretty, and as prettily dressed, as ever; and seemed to be ever thus armed, like Branksome's Knights.[146] I found the rehearsal tedious and unamusing; for each performer so studiously avoided emphasis or energy, and appeared to guard so cautiously against over-informing his companions, that the play was uttered with much less spirit than a spelling lesson at school, and I certainly never saw boys half so imperfect.

On quitting the theatre, Tom undertook to conduct me to a Green-Room at night, that my dramatic education might be advanced as much as possible; and in the mean time, we adjourned to my chambers to take our dinner and to pass the hours till the evening. Nothing could exceed the volatile spirit that characterized Tom's conversation. He was life itself. After dinner, when he had dipped his muzzle, as he himself called it, in a bottle of claret, he grew more and more communicative, and at length asked me if I knew ———. On my replying that I did, he said, "I have a Sonnet of his in my pocket-book which Prudence allowed me to copy from her album. It's very tender, but Prudence says not more tender than true. I don't particularly want it," continued he; "will you have it?" I gladly accepted the cast-off verses, and on reading them, I could not help fancying that you would like to put them into your book, and therefore here they are.

A Dream.

To ———.

The ring by unknown hands was brought to me,
As I lay prison'd in a dreary dream;
And while I cherish'd it, my thoughts of thee
Did tow'rds a grave most desolately stream.
Darkness had 'spoiled the adornment of thine eyes,
And from thy cheek the perfect spirit had gone,—
Thy lips had lost their lustre and their sighs,
And thou didst seem some beauty graved in stone.
Then I awoke, and wept that fate should so
Distemper my remembrances of thee,
Cruelly tainting even my dreams with woe,
And darkening my good thoughts with mystery:
And when I touch'd thy living hand, I seem'd
Still tangled in the terror I had dream'd!

If you had heard Tom read these lines, I think you would have forsworn pensive poetry for ever. He drawled his voice with such painful slowness, and afflicted the passages with such cruel emphasis, that literally the town crier would have been a man of pathos compared with him. We took coffee at eight, and soon afterwards started for the theatre.

In passing across the stage (not Covent Garden), I heard Miss Kelly's delightful voice making the very most of some waiting-maid prattle; and at each pause in the dialogue, the merriment of the audience broke upon my ear in a deep, subdued, yet pleasant murmur. Harley too was speaking; and his tones seemed to come from every part of the house at once, so quick and continual were his movements. I stood awhile at the side scene, and was pleased at seeing the earnestness with which these admirable performers entered into the cunning of the scene. The colouring is rather strong, or I should say, for ever let me see a Comedy from the *wing*. But I was now conducted into the Green-Room.

It is a square unfurnished-looking place, with benches on each side, fastened to the walls; and having at one end a huge mirror, capable of giving back the actor to himself, in all his glory; or, of showing the lady how fair, how wondrous fair, she is. A table stands near to this glass with a goblet and water (the only refreshment allowed), and these furnish a pretty excuse to the well-dressed to sun themselves in the lustre of the mirror. One hand is pouring out the water, while the other is trimming a curl, or adjusting a point of lace; and not till the eye is satisfied to the utmost, does the water ascend to the lip, and only then to be sipped and set down again. It is amusing to see the several characters sitting in easy and general conversation: Artaxerxes[147] giving an account to Dr. Cantwell[148] of his having caught cold at Lady Cork's party, while the Doctor is speaking of having been at the Somerset-house Exhibition. Mawworm[149] is giving a relation of a cold dinner to Mandane.[150] And Artabanes [151] and old Lady Lambert[152] are disputing about the sinking fund, though neither of them has a second idea on the subject. The performers sit around the room on benches, until they are in turn wanted on the stage, when a little boy, generally known as the call-boy, comes to the door and announces the name of the party required, a short time before it is necessary for the character to go on the stage. The boy receives the name from the prompter, or rather a number referring to the name; and it is his sole business to connect the Green-Room with the stage. In the very middle of an interesting conversation or anecdote, this imperative boy's voice utters at the entrance, "Miss Kelly!" or, "Mr. Harley!" or, "Mr. Dowton!" and the conversation is stopped—the anecdote ruined—and the party summoned rises, plumes her or his dress at the mirror, and goes to contribute amusement elsewhere. I confess discourse is not so sprightly as a stranger might expect in this ante-room of the drama;—but I was impressed with a high respect for the good sense, taste, and feeling, which marked the observations of all the principal performers with whom I conversed. In Miss Kelly there is a strength of mind, and a delicacy of taste, quite delightful; and the only drawback to the pleasure you take in her conversation is the detection, which you cannot avoid making, of a melancholy about her character and manner, forming a painful contrast with that arch pleasantry that attends her on the stage. Mr. Harley, too, is a shrewd and sensible man; and Wrench is the soul of gentlemanly whim and good fellowship. The stage manager is always in attendance until the performances are over.

At the conclusion of the play I took my departure;—for the whole mystery of this scene, when once tasted, is perfectly understood, and seen into. The sameness of sitting heroes and resting actresses becomes tiresome in an hour;—and, I confess, I was not sorry to take my leave. Before we retired, however, Tom received a paper from Harley, which gave him the utmost delight;—and when we reached the Albany he sang it to me (for it was a song) with admirable spirit and life.[153] At my earnest entreaty he favoured me with a copy, and with this I beg to conclude this letter.

The Exhibition.
A Song.
Come, come—I am willing
To down with my shilling,
The time to be killing
With varnish and paint;
So up the stone staircase
I corkscrew my carcase,—
As steep and as dark as
St. Paul's;—and as faint:
Tall women and towers,
And children with flowers,—
Twelve rosy old Hours,—
A study of cows;—
A view on the Humber,
And nags out of number,—
With other live lumber,
At Somerset House!
Tol de rol, &c.

One dandy Adonis,
And two noble cronies,

Beside rampant ponies
Reclining in curls;
And tumble-down torrents,
And pictures of Florence,
And portraits by Lawrence
Of lanky old Earls:
That a man! what a log!—
Turn to the catalogue!
How like a water-dog
After a souse!
That sky is too milky,—
That dress is too silky,—
How charming is Wilkie
At Somerset House!
      Tol de rol, &c.

I've seen the room fuller,
And yet felt it cooler;—
Lord! there's Mrs. Buller,
All pensive and red!
I wonder such fat ewes
Make paintings and statues,
I'll never to that use
Abandon my head!
Here, Wealth hath call'd her men,
Hairy Jews, balder men,
Grim gouty aldermen—
Wigs, beards, and brows!
I think 'tis a pity,
The hanging committee
Thus flatter the city,—
At Somerset House!
      Tol de rol, &c.

The sculpture invites me,
For marble delights me,—
Except when it spites me
In desolate busts;

A neat modell'd wax man,
Two babies by Flaxman,
The head of a tax-man
Whom nobody trusts!
Fighters who've fill'd a ring,
Two sleepy children,
Sweetly bewildering
Many a spouse:—
Oh! that Raphael or Titian
Could rise at my wishing
In this exhibition
At Somerset House!
      Tol de rol, &c.

There, my dear Russell, there is a song for you.—I have let you a little into the mystery of a London Theatre, such as the mystery is. If you find my description dull, you will be pleased to attribute the dulness to the subject;—if you are amused, I beg you to give *me* the credit for amusing you. With remembrances to all the Powells.
      Ever yours, &c.
Albany, ——18—.   Edward Herbert.

The Inside of a Stage Coach.
Letters of Edward Herbert. No. IV. August 1822
To P—— Powell.

My dear P—— It falls to my lot to assure you, à la Partridge, that I am not dead nor buried,—although a fever had nearly exposed me to being both the one and the other. In the thick of my visits and wonders, I started a pulse of 106, and took violently to my room and my despair. It is not necessary that I should tell you how I escaped that termination of complaints which ultimately I shall *not* escape. But here I am in a sea-port town,[154] posseting and nursing a recovery with all the arts of an experienced sufferer. Russell will lift up his two dandy-grey-russet eyes, and exclaim in his mild imprecatory manner, "Bless me!"—and your mother, with a light up-glance, will say, "P——, fetch me the receipt book,—Herbert ill! turn to *fever*—and copy Mrs. ——'s water-gruel out for him!"—But rest, rest, perturbed *spirits*! I am now certainly bettering, and shall not die to have another Barbara Allen written over me. At times, indeed, my spirits do not *trot* at the rate Tom Morton's pace it. The Mortons are in town, poor things—where I shall soon be, even though I am just set down here among the shingles, black boats, loitering pilots, and blue old bathing women. I hate sentimentality, but you must nevertheless expect a little of the romantic in this chattering apology for a letter. Let me be plaintive, *d's'ee*, as the Devon people say. I shall just talk as I please, not caring much whether you turn to the cover and sigh over the castaway elevenpence marked there;—for I am in a true Juliet mood, and pant "to speak and yet say nothing."[155]

I am now, P——, walking about in a yellow straw hat and India looking jacket, as pale as a moss-rose. What jessamine animals we sick gentlemen are!—When I think that I am now a poor solitary fish of a man, flung here on the beach to flap about by myself, I sigh to be any other thing—aye, even a dead pigeon in a pie, that is sure to have two or three friends by his side, with their mahogany coloured ankles in the same predicament. Here I walk, think, and grieve, to no purpose. What am I toiling for?—why do I covet experience, when half a century will set myself and any given dead idiot on a par?—and yet I am moralizing; —oh, what a dowlas web of wisdom is philosophy!

I am dull,—am I not?—dull as the Stranger![156] But being just arrived here, I am, as you will suppose, rather jaded in mind and body by the tediousness and fatigue of a long stage coach journey. I am, however, convinced that a few moderate and quiet walks in a wood, which stands on the side of a hill and just above the cottage in which I dwell, will restore the wonted elasticity of my mind, and set my stupidly sensitive and jarring nerves at rest. Like the strings of an Aeolian harp, my nerves are moved with a breath; nor can I find that anything short of a perfect quiet life procures me common ease. Even the very act of writing this letter,—attended as it is with the thoughts of you all, and home, and idle fears of fever, and the foolish dread of associating with strangers in a strange place,—shakes me, as the wind stirs a branch of the mountain ash in a troubled day. If my health should be of that stubborn quality, which, mule-like, will either stop short, or move in a retrograde fashion, —I shall faithfully remember my promise to your mother, and be careful against violent readings, revellings, or keen winds:—she always said I was delicate.—A book I shall then look upon as a dangerous companion, and shun it as I would the society of a badger or an authoress;—and as for an easterly wind, it may sing itself hoarse, before I will listen to its song,—and it may go whistle to its cloudy flocks for days together, and yet never prevail upon me to venture into a company so awfully pastoral. Be under no apprehensions on my account; for I have laid in good resolutions by the waggon-load, as an old lady heaps in her winter stock of coals;—I am quite determined to keep a strict eye on the weather, and to run from storms and showers as I would scamper from a herd of wild elephants. I am also pretty sure of passing a solitary and reflective life; for the family with whom I now lodge is the most regular and serene I ever beheld. It appears to move by Act of Parliament, and to think and speak by clock-work. It consists of an old gentleman, who was long master of a small trading vessel, and his wife and daughter. The father is far gone in good health and years; and having retired from the labours of life, is making up for his early troubles and tempests by an extraordinary stock of quiet and calms now. He appears, however, never to have been ruffled, but to have had his eye all the first part of his life on the compass, and all the last on his pipe or the weathercock. I have already watched him smoking, and he really seems charmed from all earthly vexation and care;—his thoughts appear to sleep within him; or to be so light, that he can collect them without an effort together, and whiff them away in the warm, silent, and momentary mists of his pipe. Whatever he says (but he speaks so seldom that I should think thirty words go to the day with him) is full of humanity and homely wisdom:—he appears to be able to grow all the observations necessary for his own use (so few are they) in his own heart. From the little I have seen of him I like him greatly. His person is spare, but well proportioned; and his hair begins to whiten around his brown visage, like the embers around the fire. The wife has been originally a pretty good talker, I guess,—but she seems to have learned moderation from her husband;— whenever she begins, she appears to prepare her tongue for a long and sedate voyage,—but a sigh from her daughter, or the perfect inattention and placid indifference of her gentle partner, arrests her progress and becalms her discourse. She is very cautious in her movements and her language, but her observations are a little too *historical*. The daughter,—whom they call Laura,—is sensible, unassuming, and pretty. She cultivates her mind with books,—at least, so her conversation leads me to believe;—and she seems to have read herself into a modest and delightful importance with her family. She is of a fair stature,—with light hair and blue eyes:—this almost sounds romantic!—Whatever she says has an instantaneous weight with mine host and hostess,—and she never, as far as I have been able to observe, abuses her power or their confidence. There is something extremely plaintive in her air,—and an apparently habitual and occasional absence of mind,—which I cannot account for: you know that I cannot bear to see the shadow of trouble on the mind of woman. The mother found an opportunity yesterday evening of assuring me that her family had existed in this part of the country for many generations,—and that her great aunt had very nearly married the lord of the manor. She also contrived to inform me that her husband's vessel was copper-bottomed and a surprizingly swift sailer,—and to insinuate that her daughter could read better than any girl of her age in the village, and was allowed to be the best getter-up of fine linen, far and near. She asked after my grandfather Paul with a significant sigh, and disclosed to me that he had been an admirer of hers in his youth. Heaven knows how!—The entrance of her husband cut short my attention and her speech at the same moment. You will be surprized at the stock of domestic knowledge and insight into character which I have already gained;—but you will remember that I was always given to observation of this nature.

My journey here was remarkable for nothing but its tedious length and finished dullness. As I left town at night, and did not choose to alight at supper-time, my fellow travellers were not revealed to me, till the cold moist morn peeped palely through the wet windows of the coach, and discovered to me a fat old gentleman in a dingy night-cap, sleeping to some regular nasal music of his own playing, and pillowing his heavy swaddled head on the well-stuffed bolster of his own body. His face was red and full, and seemed to have imbibed the colour of Port wine as industriously as his mouth had the beverage itself. His nose was the throne of good living, and there it sat in purple pride; and a wet

364

grey eye twinkled at intervals, like a stupid star in a foggy night. Next to this pampered sleeper sat a tall thin lady, holding a basket on her lap, and having a dark red handkerchief tied over a shabby travelling bonnet. Her eyes were wide awake, and fixed immoveably on the comfortless window. She now and then sighed or hemmed from dreariness, and moved a leg, or put back her straight hair with her hand, from utter lassitude. Occasionally she would take the tassel of the window, and smear away the moisture from the pane, though little was obtained by the act, beyond a momentary peep at one or two cold and solitary cottages, and a procession (as it would seem) of dingy pilgrim-trees. To be sure, the white morning could be seen wrapping all objects in a pale light, like a shroud, and the countenance of my tall and quiet traveller became more fixed, icy, and monumental. It gleamed up the avenue of her bonnet and handkerchief with a deathy, clammy paleness, which "looked not o' the earth," but told a silent tale of other worlds. The marble ghost in Don Juan could not have been more terrifically still, or more frightfully pallid. To me, this fair forlorn looked like some Aegyptian figure found in the pyramids, that held age to be a merit, and life to be "a thing to dream of, not to tell."[157] A bad temper appeared to have set its mark on her upper lip; and vexation had written a few legible lines on her forehead, which were plain and intelligible to the eyes of every person. By these two several whimsical specimens of slumbering fatness and wakeful leanness was one side of the coach occupied, in the proportion of two thirds to the Sleeping Beauty, and one third to the Enchanted Damosel. Next to myself, sat a little gentleman in black, with a hairy travelling-cap drawn down over his face, so as to hide all but the end of a keen nose, and a compressed lip. I fancy that I can generally find the character in the nose, and here I found enough of the hawk to warrant me in guessing at the possessor's profession. How well has Sterne described the want of purpose in a person, —"You have no nose, Sir!"[158] This duodecimo edition of a lawyer (for such I deemed him) was dozing, but his hand did not forsake a blue bag which rested between his knees, thus "holding fast," as the child-game saith, even in that predicament in which half the world would have "let go;" and his head continually dropped towards it, even in its sleepy helplessness. I amused myself with speculating on my companions till breakfast-time, when we all assembled round a well-stocked table; but each seemed suspicious of the other; and every cup of coffee was passed with a laudable caution, and every egg handed with a careful and silent mysteriousness. We returned to our coach, like culprits to a cell, not half so happy as convicts to a caravan; all, save the corpulent sleeper, who in vain attempted to provoke a conversation, and cultivate a better acquaintance. His observations, when generally made, were considered as the property of none, and were therefore left unanswered and disregarded by all. He at last retired into himself, and found in a renewed sleep that comfortable society which he had vainly sought in those about him. The jolting of the coach never mingled us; each stuck as perversely in his corner, as if banishment awaited the least infringement on a neighbour's rights, and death would be the consequence of sociality and freedom. I was rejoiced when I observed the guard and coachman for the last time, and felt the happy serenity of the home into which I passed, doubly sweet, as coming so immediately after the rattling, close, and unsocial vehicle in which I had travelled. I fear this account of my journey and my host may tire you; but, so soon after my arrival, I had little else to communicate, and I could not be silent longer, nor could I reconcile myself to helping you to the mere merrythought of a letter. I shall not, however, write again till I return to town, when I hope to be able to give a better account of the world and its progressings, and continue my old tales of real life, not *after* Mrs. Opie.[159]

For the present, my dear P——, adieu!—Assure Russell of my constant love for him—and to the kind hearts that beat about your fireside (we have fires here!) commend me in all sincerity and affection. I can hardly write, my materials are so miserable; my pen is surely a bit of an old anchor, and such bilge-water of ink never muddied the letter of an old sailor!—But through the roses of my window I see my host is beginning to tune his evening *pipe*, and I myself am inclined to get behind the silver veil of a fragrant cigar, and forget in its rolling vapours the hard world and all its ills. Yet, my dear P——, thee I can never forget; whole worlds of tobacco could never raise such a fume as to hide thee from thy faithful friend

Edward Herbert.

PS. I shall write to Russell from London, for I know he likes to have his letters *town made*.

The Cockpit Royal.
Edward Herbert's Letters to the Family of the Powells.
No. V. November 1822
To Russell Powell, Esq.

It has a strange quick jar upon the ear,
That *cocking*—.

Lord Byron.[160]

Dear Russell,—To write short and dispirited letters is one of the tokens of a distempered frame. I blush to find by the packet of anxious notes and tender enquiries, lately received from your family, that I have furnished them a messenger of alarm and disquiet, by my last brief but tedious epistle from the country. When women are ill, they bear their sufferings with silence and patience, but the moment we masters of the creation are nipped by ailments, we lose no time in hallooing to the world about our agony and magnanimity—and in writhing before visitors like giants in pain. I am sorry to say, my dear Russell, that experience daily proves to me, that in all great things we men are frightfully little—and that it is the weaker sex that rise with the difficulties of the time, and that display unaffected greatness and power, in the moments of anguish, disappointment, or despair. I gave to your sister the other day a melancholy report of myself—hinted at declining health and decaying hopes—spake of pain and its company of evil spirits—of sea-side solitude and melancholy readings:—I wish I had written no such foolery. Do you know, Russell, that a few morning rambles on the beach, and a few early excursions in the fishing boats, gave my feelings a new life on the instant, and made me better and blither than I ever in my life remember to have been. I arose with the sun (no common trick of mine); and while the sky was yet white, and the cold brisk waves came shuddering in with a green gloom upon the beach,—I scrambled into one of the old black fishing boats—and oh, how bravely did we spread the brown sail on the graceless pole of a mast, and dance off to our profitable sport! I assisted in putting out the nets—I assisted in managing the boat—I assisted in the pulling in. Such flapping and flashing in the light!—such tossing and breaking of waves! We would return before the day was warm—and I relished my breakfast with part of the spoils. Sometimes, however, I have done nothing but saunter among the shingles as the tide was swelling in, and take note of the grand labour of the sea—the labour which *has been*—and which *will be*!—What sights! what noble music! The white spread of the foam,—eternal, yet momentary;—the sound of the curled wave—sounding with time!—I became learned, Russell, in the mysteries of an ocean and its shores. I studied the patient strife, and forgot the world in all I saw and heard. If you would, indeed, steep your mind in quiet and in power, take a seat on a rock or on the loose dry stones of the shore—and *read* the waves!—If you would truly wed your senses to serenity—"feast them upon the wideness of the sea!"[161]—I only know this (to know something in these extremely wise times is not amiss). Yes,—I only know this,—that with all my love of merriment, bustle, and life—with all my passion for popular pleasures and exciting pastimes—I never was half so contented in any hour of my existence, as in that which found me overtaken by a ravenous wave that covered my feet with embossed foam, and set me tearing with might and main from a wave—that was dead and gone!—Well, Russell, the meaning of all this salt-water prose is, that I am now terribly well—and I must entreat you to break my sudden relapse into health to your distracted family with as much tenderness as possible,—to soften to your sister my unbecoming desertion of the romance of my letter;—to make them all, in short, think as favourably as they can of a gentleman, who gave promise of an approach towards the *interesting*, and who, at the very threshold of delicacy and youthful decay, has put the pale face in his pocket, turned round impudently on those who were sympathising with him, tripped up the heels of sensibility, and rushed back to life with the impudence and strength of an Irish giant. P—— will be good enough to let my last letter go for nothing:—It was,—as dear uncle Noll says, "too sentimental by half!"—

The sea air certainly has given the return-force to my frame, but I have much reason to believe that my mental elasticity has taken its spring from the reflections which a maimed old sailor lately awoke in me during some conversations I held with him. I cannot resist the temptation to which *we tourists* are constantly subjected, of giving you a sketch of this amiable and suffering creature, poor, pained, contented, gentle Tom Barnes! He was about thirty-five years of age—apparently healthy—certainly patient and cheerful:—but the position which he

invariably occupied too plainly told me that he was the victim of some
dreadful malady. On all sunny days, he was wheeled out in a sort of plain
wooden chaise, and placed opposite the cheering light and warmth—
and long before you reached him you saw him surrounded with children,
—a sure sign of worth! I was first attracted towards him by the mild
smile of his sunburnt and placid countenance, and by the extreme
urbanity of his manner as I passed him. He was nibbing a pen for a child.
He sat in a sailor's dress,—in his leathern hat, in his blue striped shirt,—
habited as when he trod the deck or walked the shore. The costume
of his once dear element was left to him, though he was divorced for
ever from boat and billow. His upper frame was nobly robust and
manly, and his face remarkably placid and handsome. I never saw softer
or bluer eyes in woman. I stopped one morning and discoursed with
him;—I stopped each succeeding day, and our discourse grew longer.
He informed me briefly of his malady. About eighteen years ago, in some
quay, on the Cornish coast (I forget its name, though he mentioned it)
he fell from a high part of a vessel, and was stupified, bruised, and wet
with his fall: his messmates took off his jacket and shirt, but left him in
his wet trowsers for two days totally neglected. He was brought home,
surgical aid was called in, but the lower part of his frame was thenceforth affected with paralysis beyond remedy. From that day, he has
been thus helpless and afflicted. From that, he has been downward-
dead—useless—except to sit in the sun—to lighten the fireside,—to show
the simple beauty of an ungrieving endurance,—to read through the
long and cheerless night! To hear him speak, was to hear true, pure,
unaffected wisdom—the philosophy, not of the schools, but of nature.
His face appeared to have received a softer expression from his long
inaction and serenity. His humanity seemed to have gone into his
features—to have taken steady and temperate watch in his calm blue
eyes. I learned from his townspeople (who invariably knew and loved
him) more of his history,—more of Tom Barnes;—and one or two anecdotes gave me a sensible delight—for they not only vouched for the
endearing qualities of the sea-sufferer himself, but extended my respect
for others of his species. He had been attached, in the heyday of his
youth and spirit, to one —— ——, a young woman, who lived by assisting ladies in their *plain-work,* as it is termed, and a miserable living it is!
—*She* must have been industrious, patient, and contented—for persons

not possessed of such qualities would quickly want employ—*He* must have been merry, volatile, handsome. I should like to have seen them in this spring-time of their love! Eighteen years are now gone by, and more! Tom Barnes has lost relatives, acquaintance, and friends—but this young woman (she can never grow old) is near, dear, and constant to him still, and her family are the only creatures that attend him. She talks to him of an evening, sits with her needlework by his side, and loves him at this very moment. He has also once been taken to a hospital, some fifty miles from his residence, at the expense of the Misses P——, and there he has had the first medical aid,—but to him, alas! aid, it has been none!—At this day he is continually hearing of the deaths of those sailors who so cruelly deserted him when he met with his accident—and he seems to lament, by his manner of recounting their dooms, that they should be so marked by Providence! His own fate he never repines at,— and he even recalls certain mischances, by which his progress was baffled in the royal navy, the West-India, and the East-India trades, with an air of wonder rather than sorrow;—invariably concluding with the remark, that his was "a number lot," and therefore not to be lamented or disputed. I am quite sure, Russell, that I gained strength of mind from my colloquies with this patient wreck of a man—and my resolution not to moan and mutter over trifling ailments and temporary pains gained vigour from the contemplation of this smiling sufferer of eighteen years' duration, who knew himself half perished,—the eternal prey to sloth and anguish,—yet could sit in the sun, gladden in the face of the sea, and look philosophy to the gay, the active, and the healthy of his kind.—Poor Tom Barnes! I would thou couldst read this honest description of thyself, and see how much good thou art able to do, even in thy lone and withering inactivity!

But to come to more serious matter. I turn from the sea and its wonders as abruptly as I bounded from sickness to health. Nor will you regret that I make so little ceremony in varying my subjects, for there is no one that surpasses Russell in an insatiable appetite for knowledge "with a difference." I remember, in one of my early letters, I made a kind of half promise to induct you into the mysteries of this metropolis; —and since my return to the placid comforts of the Albany once more, I am strongly reminded of my duty to you, my poor country solitary,— and more particularly since I have been carried by volatile Tom Morton to a fresh scene of London's singular drama. I shall, therefore, put on my habit of description—and retail to you, not only the particulars of what I witnessed, but my own impressions at the time. I can give you few of Tom's—who certainly sinks a good deal of his humanity and moral feeling in the enthusiasm of the moment. He has a way of settling these things with his conscience in a very summary mode; for when he has a mind to be profuse, or when he has, in his sporting speculations, "made his money," (to use his own expression) he sends off his initials and his guinea to some charitable subscription—and thus pays his toll for the liberty of passing through the turnpike of iniquity. He will hold five guineas in his hand, just received from some creature of folly like himself,—and calculate its application with the nicest mixture of propriety and profligacy:—"Let me see:—aye—four guineas to make good the stake on the fighting oil-man—and one guinea for the Irish sufferers:"—or, "If I win on Neat I shall back Randall through thick and thin, and do something for poor Mrs. Emery's family."—Thus you see, Russell, this young lawyer argues "in violentest contrarieties."[162] His charity walks hand in hand with the Fancy.

I was sitting, some evenings ago, in my room, at the first coming of the twilight, which in our Albany rooms is fond of paying early visits;—my head was indolently hung back upon the red morocco top of my easy chair, and my hands were hung like two dangling bell-ropes over each arm of my seat—and in this position I was ruminating on many things of little moment. I had thus leaned back in my chair, and resigned myself to the most luxurious idleness,—a kind of reading made easy,—when a knuckle, knocking at my door, intimated the arrival of some impatient visitor—and before I could muster voice enough to give Tate Wilkinson's[163] direction of "Come in!" the tooth of my door-lock was wrenched, and Tom Morton, with a newspaper in his hand, dashed in—and at once stood astounded, with his white hat elevated on his forehead, —admiring my amazing stupor.

"Why Edward! Edward Herbert! Asleep, by all that's sublime!—There he sits, deaf to time!—Edward, I say!—Come, bolt up from the morocco! I have news for your two *no-thoroughfare* ears, which ought to make you as lively as an eel with half his waistcoat off!—Here," said he, smacking a creased and dingy newspaper, with an air of vehement exultation—"here is that which will be life itself to *you*!"—I closed my book-mind quietly, or doubled it up, as Tom would say, and raising myself with difficulty into an erect posture—rubbed my eyes, uncrossed my tingling legs (which were just beginning to wake out of a nap), and begged, through the archway of a yawn, to know what this very sprightly piece of news consisted of. Tom pulled, or rather tossed off his hat, nodded to me a nod more eloquent than speech, and tipping an acute wink out of the left corner of his little impudent grey eye—proceeded at once to read aloud from the first column of the newspaper. He pronounced one word with an emphasis the most pointed—*cocking!*—and then paused to let loose wink the second, which, if possible, was more charged with mystery than the former,—"*cocking!*—there Edward!"—continued he—"there! cocking—at the Royal Cockpit, Tufton-street, Westminster!—there;"—and then he went strictly through a formal advertisement,—touching—"200 the main,"—and "byes," and "feeders"—and "gentlemen of Norwich," and "a deal of skimble-skamble stuff," which for the life of me I could not then retain, and therefore cannot now repeat.

When Tom had finished his formal information, he very readily and clearly, at my request, divested the announcement of its technicalities, and explained to me, that on such a day, being the morrow, a grand main of cocks was to be fought at the Royal Cockpit, at which, for 5s. the head (certainly not the heart), a man might be present. It required little of my volatile friend's rhetoric to induce me to promise my attendance, as I had never been present at any thing of the kind, higher than a full-feathered blustering skirmish of a couple of huge-combed, red-ruffled, long-tailed dunghills, amid a wilderness of poultry, in a farm-yard. I had seen no clean fighting—no beautiful sparring in silver—no blood-match! as Tom earnestly describes it. I was the more induced to accede to his request of accompanying him, from learning that he could introduce me to Mr. D——, one of the principal breeders of game cocks—a gentleman of the most winning manners—and one who could and would describe to me the characters present, and procure for me the sight of the coops and pens, where the birds were fed and kept previously to the day of battle.

I begged Tom Morton would by some means get me a sight of any book upon cocking, as I was extremely desirous of going to the scene of war with as much ready-made knowledge as I could, in the short time allowed me, acquire. He said, he himself had a tidy little work upon the subject, which would let me into the whole art of breeding, trimming, matching, and betting,—but that he would apply to his friend Mr. D——, who would inform him if there were any more erudite and desirable books on the sport. I gladly availed myself of Tom's pamphlet, and to my pleasure (certainly not to my surprise) he pulled it from his coat-pocket, and laid it down quietly on my table. We arranged all things for our meeting the next day—and it was settled that he should call upon me, and that I should be ready for him by half past one o'clock. The candles were brought in; and Tom, vowing that he had "to finish Preston on Abstracts,164 and to sharpen up a pair of Malay cock-spurs for his friend, before he went to *roost*,"—scrambled into his hat, touched my man-servant Robert, (an old trick of his,) so smartly on his parsley figured waistcoat as to startle him into a "hey, Mr. Thomas!"—and then, finally bowing formally and solemnly to me, departed.

I moralized in a lack-a-daisical manner, for about half an hour, upon the vices and backslidings of this life, and then betook myself to "The Directions for breeding Game Cocks, with Calculations for Betting," and passed the evening in cultivating an acquaintance with "moulting,"— "clutches of eggs,"—"stags,"—"long-law,"—"fighting in silver," and the like:—and long before the clock of St. James's church had timed eleven to the drowsy hackney-coachmen and watchmen of Piccadilly, I was fit to sit "at the mat," and risk my "guinea on Nash."

I think I cannot do better than treat you, Russell, in the same manner that I treated myself—and I shall, therefore, pick my way daintily through the book which Tom lent me (a neat little olive-coloured pamphlet, and writ in a friendly *Waltonish* tone), and thus prepare you, in some measure, for the cock-pit itself, to which, by your favour, I mean to introduce you.

And first, as to the choice of a bird.—Observe, Russell, how many points must be attended to:—

As to the exterior qualifications, his head should be thin and long, or if short, very taper; with a large full eye, his beak crooked and stout, his neck thick and long (for a cock with a long neck has a great advantage in his battle, particularly if his antagonist is one of those kind of cocks that will fight at no other place but the head): his body short and compact, with a round breast (as a sharp breasted cock carries a great deal of useless weight about him, and never has *a fine fore-*

hand); his thighs firm and thick, and placed well *up to the shoulder (for when a cock's thighs hang dangling behind him, be assured he never can maintain a long battle)*: his legs long and thick, and if they correspond with the colour of his beak, I think it a perfection; and his feet should be broad and thin, with very long claws.

With regard to his carriage, he should be upright, but not stiffly so; his walk should be stately, with his wings in some measure extended, and not plod along as I have seen some cocks do, *with their wings upon their backs like geese*.

As to the colour he is of, I think it immaterial, for there are good cocks of all colours; but he should be thin of feathers, short and very hard, which is another proof of his being healthy; as, on the contrary, if he has many, soft and long, it favours much of his having a bad constitution.

The parenthesis which I have underlined, appears to me to be as strongly put as it is possible to write it; and indeed there is a plain vigour in the style which takes one greatly. Remember, Russell, that a cock with all this stoutness of beak, length and thickness of leg, rotundity of breast, "fine forehand," firmness of neck, and extent of wing, ought to weigh no more than 4 lb. 8 or 10 oz. If he happens to have an ounce or two more in his composition, he is out of the pale of *un*civil society, and is excluded by all match-makers "from fighting within the articles." A bird, to be a bird "fit for the white-bag, the trimmed wing, the mat, and the silver spur,"—must be "high upon leg, light-fleshed, and large boned;" but still no more than 4 lb. 8 or 10 oz. Do not forget this.

There is a very expressive picture of two cocks in this little book, and, miserable draftsman as I am, I here subjoin a small sketch I have made from it. You will not forget that the battle is nearly at an end, so that the spirit of the birds is not outrageous. I wish your cousin Theodore were here; he would make the cocks crow again![165] The author of the pamphlet gives the following explanation of the plate:—

The winner represented in the Plate, was an elegant ginger cock, bred by Mr. B-d-l, but having had his wing broke in a battle, he gave him to a friend, and the cock afterwards became the property of a Mr. T-yl-r, for whom he won several battles, particularly this his last, (which he won when almost worn out) with the loss of one spur (early in the contest), against a cock he was not matched to fight: the party taking the advantage of showing one cock and fighting another, which they had the modesty to own after the battle was over.

There is much admirable and scientific writing about the education of the young and warlike game-fowl, in which I seem to detect some-

thing smacking of the Lancastrian method.[166] The art is to teach in classes, and to reconcile as many at a time, as is practicable, to their growing duties. It is surely pleasant to be safely instructed how to bring up a chicken in the way it should go. The Amateur writes—

I have heard many persons declare, who could have had no experience in breeding fowls, that they did not think it necessary that a hen should be confined while her chickens were young, and had just sense enough to say, that nature never designed it; but let me tell those naturalists (*naturals I may call them*), if a hen should lay a clutch of eggs secretly in January, as it is not uncommon for young hens to lay in that month and sit upon them, consequently, if there are any chickens hatched, it must be in February, when if she is not taken in doors, but left to range where she pleases, I am confident that the cold northerly winds and wet weather, which are usual at that season of the year, will destroy every one of them.

The little playfulness in the parenthesis, which is like the flirt of the cock's wing, gratifies me much. The shrewdness at the end of the next direction is, however, of a higher order—it is the cut of the spur. It is curious to observe how man's wit is fashioned and coloured by the subject of which it treats. The very style is cock-like! It is indeed well con*cock*ted!

Be sure also that they do not drink any soap suds, or get to any filthy place, for if they do, it engenders distempers in them which very often turns to that fatal one the roup, a disease for which *I have heard many remedies, but never found any so effectual as breaking their necks.*

I cannot in any way avoid giving you the very ingenious mode of quelling the intestine wars of this feathered and pugnacious race. It strikes me that a useful lesson might be learned from it applicable to states and kingdoms, as well as game-cocks. The "holding the weakest in your hand, and buffeting him," is, to be sure, an old trick, from school upwards: and perhaps there is not much of novelty in the imitative submission which is afterwards treated of; but the science is laid down in a masterly style.

Now to prevent their fighting from being attended with such disagreeable consequences after they have begun, divide them into as many parties as you can find separate apartments, leaving the strongest upon the ground, and when these have fully established their authority over each other (which you make them do in the course of two days, *by holding which you find the weakest in your hand, and buffetting him with your handkerchief while the other strikes him*, and if this wont do, *confine him without victuals for a few hours until he is cold, when being stiff and sore, and the other fresh, after a blow or two he will not attack him again*), you may put down the strongest from one of the parties that are shut up, who by being kept short of food, will submit directly to run under all those that are down; and when they are so far reconciled as to permit him to run amongst them, *put down the strongest from another party, which will submit in the same manner*, and by pursuing this method, in the course of a few days, *you will be able to get them all down*. When once settled, they will go very peaceably together, except by accident one of them should get disfigured, which if such a thing should happen, and they do not seem to be perfectly reconciled, send him to another walk for fear of a general quarrel.

The author is very particular in recommending you cautiously to try your *stags* (which are young cocks "and such small deer!"); and his language is so gentlemanly, that the most *hard-hearted* of humane people could not resist indulging in a few secret trial battles, after reading such persuasive advice. He begins one passage thus—

Now *permit me to recommend you to transact the business relative to trying your stags*, without mentioning it even to the person that feeds them.

One more quotation, and I lay aside the book. It is an anecdote, Russell,—or such the author calls it. He is reasoning, "beak and heel," against relying upon cocks in a second battle, however courageous and victorious they may have proved themselves in their first fight. He says, a bird is almost sure to receive some hurt, which neither time, training, nor feeding, can make him forget, when he comes "to be touched" a second time. A slight *hurry* (or hurt) is often remembered.

I recollect a circumstance (says this circumstantial artist) of this kind happening to a neighbouring gentleman, who having entered into an agreement to fight a week's play, at a very short notice, and not being able to get a sufficient number of cocks he could depend upon, had the temerity to weigh in some of his own stags, of about ten or eleven months old, and it so happened that one of them had to fight against the cock the other party depended most upon winning; but after a doubtful and bloody contest for near half an hour, contrary to the opinion of every one present, the stag came off victorious, which so elated his master, that he sent him to one of his best walks to run till the next season; *but what was very extraordinary, he moulted from a dark red to a very light ginger pile.* This strange metamorphose we were totally at a loss to account for, when we were informed by a person *who spoke pertinently upon the subject,* that it was owing to his having been so severely *handled in his battle,* that he had seen two or three instances of the same kind; and at the same time advised my friend never to fight him again, for it was almost reduced to a certainty that he would be beat if he happened to *fall in weight with a good cock.* But this piece of advice my friend did not attend to, having him weighed in the very next match he made, and in which he was killed, making hardly any defence, although as well to fight with regard to the feeding part, as it was possible for a cock to be.

In fighting a match, the author recommends a carefulness in the choice of a feeder (the person who is to give the bird his last training, food, and care), and of a setter-to (the *second,* in fact, of the cock in battle).—There are good and bad feeders—and good and bad setters-to.—"I have seen," says the writer, "many of the latter, who do not know when a cock wants rest, and when he should be made to fight."*

So much for the little learned tract which Tom put into my hands! The moment he left me, I turned to my book-shelves, and among several old and curious volumes, I fortunately dropped upon The Court and City Gamester,[168] a rare little storehouse of knowledge for those who would become masters in the arts of Whist, Racing, Tick-Tack, Ombre, Archery, Brag, Bankafalet, Put, and Cocking. The style "eats short," as old ladies say of Threadneedle-street biscuits; and to show you how differently the same subject may be treated by different

* There are betting tables and calculations of odds annexed to this little pamphlet, which put the Tutor's Assistant quite out of countenance. The subject, and the ability that marks the execution, lead me to think that *Cocker* had some hand in them.[167]

writers, I shall copy out this ancient artist's picture of a game-cock, "as he ought to be,—not as he is!" You will at once detect the hand of a gentleman, a cocker, and a scholar, in the work.

His head ought to be small, with a quick, large eye, and a strong back, and (as master Markham observes) must be crockt and big at the setting on, and in colour suitable to the plume of his feathers, whether black, yellow, or reddish, &c. The beam of his leg must be very strong, and, according to his plume, blue, grey, or yellow; his spurs rough, long, and sharp, a little bending and looking inward.

His colour ought to be either grey, yellow, or red, with a black breast; not but that there are many other coloured piles very excellent good, which you must find out by practice and observation, but the three former, by the experience of most, found ever the best; the pyed pile may serve indifferently, but the white and dun are rarely found good for any thing.

Note, that if your cock's neck be invested with a scarlet complexion, it is a sign he is strong, lusty, and couragious; but on the contrary, if pale and wan, it denotes the cock to be faint, and in health defective.

You may know his courage by his proud upright standing, and stately tread in walking; and if he croweth very frequently in the pen, it is a couragious demonstration.

His narrow heel, or sharpness of heel, is known no other-ways than by observation in fighting, and that is when upon every rising he so hits that he extracts blood from his opponent, gilding his spurs continually, and every blow threatening immediate death to his adversary.[169]

The whole essay is admirable, and certainly surpasses the Pamphleteer in its treatment of the Pip and Roup; but I cannot spare room for a critical comparison. I therefore shut the book of science, contenting myself and you with extracting only the following

Excellent and Elegant Copy of Verses upon Two Cocks Fighting,
By Dr. R. Wild.*

No sooner were the doubtful people set,
The match made up, and all that would had bet;

* Dr. Robert Wild, the author of the above poem, claims by our extract to be better known and remembered. He was a non-conformist *divine* and poet; and was born in 1609. In 1648 he was appointed rector of Aynho, in Northamptonshire, and was looked upon as a wit of his time. It is told of him that he and another preached probationary sermons for the living, and that on his being asked whether he had obtained it, he replied—"We have divided it; I have got the AY and he the NO." Wood speaks of him as a "Fat, jolly, and boon Presbyterian." Some of his poems were printed with the poems of Rochester, (no very creditable distinction,) and (apparently as an atonement) a few of his sermons survived him. He appears by his poem to have been a resolute cocker and a tolerable poet.

But strait the skilful judges of the play
Brought forth their sharp-heel'd warriors, and they
Were both in linnen bags, as if 'twere meet
Before they dy'd, to have their winding-sheet.
Into the pit they're brought, and being there
Upon the stage, the Norfolk Chanticleer
Looks stoutly at his ne'er before seen foe,
And like a challenger began to crow,
And clap his wings, as if he would display
His warlike colours, which were black and grey.
Mean time the wary Wisbich walks and breathes
His active body, and in fury wreathes
His comely crest, and often looking down,
He whets his angry beak upon the ground.
This done they meet, not like that coward breed
Of Aesop; these can better fight than feed;
They scorn the dunghill, 'tis their only prize,
To dig for pearls within each other's eyes.
They fought so nimbly, that 'twas hard to know,
To th' skilful, whether they did fight, or no;
If that the blood which dy'd the fatal floor,
Had not bore witness of't. Yet fought they more;
As if each wound were but a spur to prick
Their fury forward. Lightning's not more quick,
Or red, than were their eyes: 'Twas hard to know,
Whether 'twas blood or anger made them so.
I'm sure they had been out, had they not stood,
More safe, by being fenced in with blood.
Thus they vy'd blows; but yet (alas) at length,
Altho' their courage were full try'd, their strength,
And blood began to ebb. You that have seen
A watry combat on the sea, between
Two angry, roaring, boiling billows, how
They march, and meet, and dash their curled brow;
Swelling like graves, as tho' they did intend
T'intomb each other e'er the quarrel end;
But when the wind is down, and blust'ring weather,
They are made friends, and sweetly run together;
May think these champions such; their blood grows low,
And they, which leap'd before, now scarce can go:

Their wings, which lately, at each blow they clapp'd,
(As if they did applaud themselves) now flapp'd.
And having lost th' advantage of the heel,
Drunk with each other's blood, they only reel:
From either eyes such drops of blood did fall,
As if they wept them for their funeral.
And yet they fain would fight; they came so near,
Methought they meant into each other's ear
To whisper wounds; and when they could not rise,
They lay and look'd blows int' each other's eyes,
But now the tragick part! After this fit,
When Norfolk cock had got the best of it,
And Wisbich lay a dying, so that none,
Tho' sober, but might venture sev'n to one;
Contracting, like a dying taper, all
His strength, intending with the blow to fall,
He struggles up, and having taken wind,
Ventures a blow, and strikes the other blind.
And now poor Norfolk, having lost his eyes,
Fights only guided by antipathies:
With him (alas!) the proverb holds not true,
The blows his eyes ne'er saw, his heart must rue.
At length, by chance, he stumbled on his foe,
Not having any pow'r to strike a blow.
He falls upon him with his wounded head,
And makes his conqu'ror's wings his feather-bed.[170]

You now, Russell, know nearly as much as I knew before I visited the pit:—that is, you are a good theoretical cock-fancier. Yet I shall not let you rest here, but immediately proceed to the battle itself. Read on— or cast aside my letter, as your curiosity or disgust may prompt you. I must finish the work I have begun.

Tom Morton called punctually on the day, and at the appointed hour; dressed up dutifully for the sport, and well fitted to rival a horse-dealer or a groom—yet with a loose-hung gentility about him, that just left it a matter of doubt, whether you ought to ask him into your drawing-room or your stable. We took our way across the Park with hasty, eager feet, and were with very little difficulty soon conducted to the door of a dull old-fashioned building in Tufton-street, Westminster, around which were sauntering a sprinkle of old gentlemen, old hackney-masters, old sportsmen, old leathern-breeches, old top-boots, old canes, old nondescripts: all that was strange, and vitiated, and extravagant in age seemed collected about this spot; and I could not but remark how few I saw of the young, the rakish, and the depraved, present at a sport which was cruel enough for excitement, and uncertain enough for the purposes of gambling. One or two solitaries of a youthful appearance dangled about as half in shame and half in curiosity; but I detected none of the enthusiastic bustle, none of the wildness, spirit, and pleasure which light up "young bloods" at other of the ancient and rude sports of this country. One very respectable and aged gentleman on crutches struggled his way on the unmolested pavement to the door, as though the fires of his youth would not go out, and accident, or disease, could not warn him to subside into the proprieties of his years. The doors were at length opened, and we paid our entrance money, and received the check for admission. This check was cast in pewter, and had the figure of a fighting cock embossed upon it. But we entered the pit!

The cockpit is a large, lofty, and circular building, with seats rising as in an amphitheatre. In the middle of it is a round matted stage, of about eighteen or twenty feet diameter, as nearly as my eye can measure it, and rimmed with an edge eight or ten inches in height, to keep the cocks from falling over in their combats. There is a chalk ring in the centre of the matted stage, of, perhaps, a yard diameter, and another chalk mark within it much smaller, which is intended for the setting to, when the shattered birds are so enfeebled as to have no power of making hostile advances towards each other. This inner mark admits of their being placed beak to beak. A large and rude branched candlestick is suspended low down, immediately over the mat, which is used at the night battles.

When we entered there were very few persons in the pit; for as the gentlemen of the match were not seated, the principal followers of the sport were beguiling the time at a public-house opposite the cockpit. A tall, shambling, ill-dressed fellow was damping the mat with a mop, which he constantly dipped in a pail of water, and sparingly and most carefully sprinkled around him. This was to make it soft for the birds, and to prevent their slipping. We took out seats at the foot of a flight of stairs, that went up into one of the coops,—judging that that would be the best spot for seeing as much as was to be seen. There are two "tiring rooms"—of course, for the separate sides.—One room, or more properly, coop, is up the flight of stairs I have mentioned; the other is beneath it, and has an entrance without the pit.

At this time my friend Tom's friend, Mr. D——, arrived, and I was introduced to him at once. He was a young man (I was almost sorry for this, because it untied a theory of mine, respecting the sport being a propensity of age only, owing, as I had settled it, to its being easy of enjoyment, a sedentary amusement, not troublesome to the beholders, cruel enough to stir the blood, and open to money-stakes like a game at cards; played in fact at a table, and under shelter. However my theory is foolish). Mr. D——, as I said, was young, he was also lusty—fresh-coloured—cheerful;—open as day in his manners and in his conversation;—and free from that slang slyness which generally characterizes the sporting man. Tom told him that I was anxious to see and know all I could; and he immediately opened to me the curiosities of the place, with a lively liberty, and a power of description, which I wish in my heart I could have caught from him. Seeing that he was thus so pleasantly minded, I began boldly at the beginning, and begged to know something of the rules and regulations of cocking. He turned-to at them, in high feather, on the instant.

The birds, Russell (I am saying after him), are weighed and matched—and then marked and numbered. The descriptions are carefully set down, in order that the cock may not be changed; and the lightest cocks fight first in order. The key of the pens, in which the cocks are set and numbered, is left on the weighing-table on the day of weighing; or the opposite party may, if he pleases, put a lock on the door. The utmost possible care, in short, is taken, that the matched birds shall fight, and no substitutes be intruded.

Mr. D—— next gave me a very particular description of the modes of setting-to—of terminating difficult battles—of betting—and of parting the entangled birds; but as I really could not very clearly follow his rapid and spirited explanation, and as I am about to relate to you a battle as I myself saw it, I will not detain you here with my imperfect detail of his very perfect description.

But before the birds are pitted, Mr. D——'s account of a few of the characters must not be omitted. I cannot at all give you them in *colours*, as my new friend dashed them off; but I will follow him in a respectful *Indian-ink*, and at a distance; and you must make the most you can of what I am able to afford you.

There was a tall, sallow-faced, powdered man standing below us. He took snuff industriously, wore very yellow leathern breeches,—very brown aged top-boots,—and a black coat of the *same* colour. He was sixty years of age if he was a month—and I never saw a dull man so enlivened as he was with this his *betting hour*, and the approaching warfare. He had a word for every one near him, and a restlessness which would not allow him to wait for answers. I found that he was a hackney-coach proprietor, and that cockfighting was his only amusement. He thought playing at cards a waste of time,—a disgraceful kind of gambling,—and he could not endure the barbarities of a man-fight, which he called "seeing two human creatures knock each other to pieces for other people's sport." Cockfighting was the only game! He was steady in his business, when no cockfighting was on the carpet, and idle and tacit in a public-house parlour at nights.—But in the pit he was at home! Sovereigns were golden dust, which blew about in the breath of his opinion; and he rose into perfect life only in the presence of "a Shrop-shire Red," or "a Ginger Pile!"

Nearly opposite to this person was a very orderly, quiet, respectably dressed man, with a formal, low-crowned, broad-brimmed hat,—a black suit of clothes,—and a dark silk umbrella. He was trying to look demure and unmoved; but I was told that he was a clergyman, and that he would be "quite up in the stirrups" when the cocks were brought in. He forced himself to be at ease; but I saw his small, hungry, hazel eyes quite in a fever,—and his hot, thin, vein-embossed hand, rubbing the unconscious nob of his umbrella in a way to awaken it from the dead:—and yet all the time he was affecting the uninterested incurious man! The *cloth* was half in his mind!—He would fain still be a clergyman—but he had "no *spur* to prick the sides of his intent!"

Another person,—very small,—very dapper,—powdered like a gentle-man of the old school,—with glossy grey silk stockings, high ankled shoes, and buckles,—perked up against the pit,—affecting nothing,—caring for no one,—but living, revelling in the ancient sport. He bowed smartly around him, looked about with a couple of nimble bird-like eyes,—crowned one or two offered bets,—and sent the little white tip of his extremely thin pig-tail from shoulder to shoulder, with an alacrity which showed that he was "a hearty old cock" still; and had neither of his little silken legs in the grave!

The lame old gentleman was seated close to the mat, and sat pillowed in fatness on a truss of straw, which one of the feeders had procured for him, to make his position less painful. He closed a bet quietly, with the end of his crutch touching the ferule of the umbrella of a tall, gaunt, white-faced man in bright blue (a tailor, as I learned); and thus forcibly reminded me of the conjunction of the two horse-whip buts, in Hogarth's admirable picture of the Cockpit in *his* day:—except that this extended crutch gave to me a more poignant moral—a more sorrowful and acute truth!

In one part of the place I saw shabby old men, apparently wanting a meal, yet showing by their presence that they had mustered 5s. for an hour's sport here. In another spot I beheld blunt, sly, coarse Yorkshire-men, with brownish-red cheeks, short uneven features, thick bristly whiskers, and cold moist bleak-blue eyes—looking as though they were constantly out upon prey. I saw one gentlemanly, quiet, unaffected man of middle age, genteelly dressed, and begged to know who he could be in such a place—and I found that he was the celebrated Mr. ——, who killed —— —— in a duel. In short, there was no uninteresting personage present, and I was almost driven into myself to ascertain *my own* peculiarities,—to know what strange creature of whim, vice, and caprice inhabited Edward Herbert, since he was rooted in this garden of very singular human weeds!

I was continuing my enquiries into the characters around me, when a young man, of very slang, slight, but extremely prepossessing appearance, passed me, dressed in tight kerseymeres, with a handkerchief round his knee, neat white cotton stockings,—small shoes,—a blue check waiter-looking jacket, short about the waist,—and a gay 'kerchief knowingly tied on his neck. He was really a clean handsome-faced young fellow,—with thin but acute and regular features,—small light whiskers, —and with his hair closely cut, and neatly and 'cutely combed down upon his forehead. He had scarcely passed me before I felt something rustle and chuckle by my elbow; and turning round, saw a stout plump old ostler-looking man carry a white bag past me, which by the struggle and vehement motion inside, I guessed to be one of the brave birds for

384

the battle. The two men stepped upon the mat,—and the hubbub was huge and instantaneous.—"Two to one on Nash!"—"A guinea on Nash!" —"Nash a crown!"—only sounds like these were heard (for the bets are laid on the setters-to),—till the noise aroused a low *muscular*-brooding chuckle in the bag, which seemed to show that the inmate was rousing into anger even at the voice of man!

From the opposite door a similar procession entered. The setter-to (Fleming by name) was dressed much in the same manner, but he appeared less attractive than young Nash (the name of the young man I have just mentioned). He certainly was not so smart a fellow,—but there was an honesty and a neatness in his manner and look, which pleased me much. The chuckle of the cock in the one bag was answered deeply and savagely from the other—and the straw seemed spurned in the narrow cell, as though the spirit that struck it would not be contained.

Nash's bag was carefully untied, and Nash himself took out one of the handsomest birds I think I ever beheld. I must have leave to try *my* hand at a description of a game cock!

He was a red and black bird—slim,—masculine,—trimmed—yet with feathers glossy, as though the sun shone only upon his nervous wings. His neck arose out of the bag, snake-like,—terrible,—as if it would stretch upward to the ceiling;—his body followed compact—strong and beautiful—and his long dark-blue sinewy legs came forth,—clean,— handsome,—shapely,—determined,—iron-like! The silver spur was on each heel, of an inch and a half in length—tied on in the most delicate and neat manner. His large vigorous beak showed aquiline,—eagle-like; and his black dilating eyes took in all around him, and shone so intensely brilliant, that they looked like jewels. Their light was that of thoughtful, sedate, and savage courage! His comb was cut close—his neck trimmed —his wings clipped, pointed, and strong. The feathers on his back were of the very glossiest red, and appeared to be the only ones which were left untouched;—for the tail was docked triangular-wise like a hunter's. The gallant bird clucked defiance—and looked as if he "had in him something dangerous!" Nash gave him to Fleming, who held him up above his head,—examined his beak—his wings—his legs—while a person read to him the description of the bird from paper—and upon finding all correct, he delivered the rich feathered warrior back to Nash, and proceeded to produce his own bird for a similar examination.

But I must speak of the senior Nash,—the old man,—the feeder. When again may I have an opportunity of describing him? and what ought a paper upon "cocking" to be accounted worth,—if it fail to contain some sketch, however slight, of old Nash? He wore a smock-frock, and was clumsily though potently built;—his shoulders being ample, and of a rotundity resembling a wool-pack. His legs were not equal to his bulk. He was unconversational almost to a fault—and never made any the slightest remark that did not appertain to cocks and cocking. His narrow, damp, colourless eye, twinkled a cold satisfaction when a bird of promise made good work on the mat; and sometimes, though seldom, he was elevated into the proffer of a moderate bet—but generally he leaned over the rails of a small gallery, running parallel with his coop, and, stooping attentively toward the pit, watched the progress of the battle. I made a remark to Tom and Mr. D—— that I thought him extremely like a cock.—Tom was intent upon Fleming, and could not hear me; but Mr. D. was delighted at the observation, which seemed to him one of some aptitude. Old Nash's beaked nose drawn close down over his mouth,—his red forehead and gills,—his round body,—and blue thin legs;—and his silver-grey, scanty, feathery hair lying like a plumage over his head—all proved him cock-like! This man, thought I, has been cooped up in pens, or penned up in coops, until he has become shaped, coloured, mannered like the bird he has been feeding. I should scarcely have been surprised, if Mr. D—— had told me that old Nash crowed when the light first dawned over the ancient houses of Tufton-street, in a summer morning! I warrant me, he pecked bread and milk to some tune;—and perchance slept upon a perch!

But Fleming lifted his bird from the bag, and my whole mind was directed his way. This was a yellow bodied, black winged, handsome cock,—seemingly rather slight, but elastic and muscular. He was restless at the sight of his antagonist, but quite silent—and old Nash examined him most carefully by the paper, delivering him up to Fleming upon finding him answer to his description. The setters-to then smoothed their birds, handled them—wetted their fingers, and moistened their bandaged ankles where the spurs were fastened—held them up opposite to each other—and thus pampered their courage, and prepared them for the combat.

The mat was cleared of all persons except Fleming and young Nash. The betting went on vociferously. The setters-to taunted the birds with each other's presence—allowed them to strike at each other at a distance —put them on the mat facing each other—encouraged and fed their crowning and mantling until they were nearly dangerous to hold—and then loosed them against each other, for the fatal fight.

The first terrific dart into attitude was indeed strikingly grand and beautiful—and the wary sparring, watching, dodging, for the first cut, was extremely curious. They were beak-point to beak-point,—until they dashed up in one tremendous flirt—mingling their powerful rustling wings and nervous heels in one furious confused mass.—The leap,—the fire,—the passion of strength—the *certaminis gaudia*,[171]—were fierce and loud!—The parting was another kind of thing every way. I can compare the sound of the first flight to nothing less than that of a wet umbrella forced suddenly open. The separation was death-like. The yellow or rather the *ginger* bird staggered out of the close—drooping—dismantled —bleeding!—He was *struck*! Fleming and Nash severally took their birds, examined them for a moment, and then set them again opposite to each other. The handling of the cocks was as delicate as if they had been made of foam, froth, or any other most perishable matter. Fleming's bird staggered towards his opponent, but he was hit dreadfully— and ran like a drunken man, tottering on his breast,—sinking back on his tail!—while Nash's, full of fire and irritated courage, gave the finishing stroke that clove every particle of life in twain. The brave bird,— thus killed,—dropped at once from the "gallant bearing and proud mien,"[172] to the relaxed, draggled, motionless object that lay in bleeding ruin on the mat. My heart sickened within me! Can this be sport? thought I!—Is satisfaction to be reaped from this pampered and profligate butchery? I sighed and looked thoughtful—when the tumult of the betters startled me into a consciousness of the scene at which I was present, and made me feel how poorly timed was thought amid the characters around me.

The victor cock was carried by me in all his pride—slightly scarred,— but evidently made doubly fierce and muscular by the short encounter he had been engaged in. He seemed to have grown to double the size! His eyes were larger.

The paying backward and forward of money won and lost occupied the time until the two Nashes again descended with a new victim;—and then the usual noise—betting—clucking—and murder followed. I will not shock you with any further recital of battles, which varied in cruelty and duration, but invariably terminated in death to one side. Sometimes the first blow was fatal—at another time the contest was long and doubtful—and the cocks showed all the obstinate courage, weariness, distress, and breathlessness, which mark the struggles of experienced pugilists. I saw the beak open, the tongue palpitate—the wing drag on the mat. I noticed the legs tremble, and the body topple over upon the breast,—the eye grow dim,—and even a perspiration break out upon the feathers of the back. When a battle lasted long, and the cocks lay helpless near or upon each other, one of the feeders counted ten,—and then the birds were separated and set-to at the chalk. If the beaten bird does not fight while forty is counted, and the other pecks or shows sign of battle, the former is declared conquered.

Such is cockfighting. I began like the bird, in bravery and spirit, but I have drooped in the contest, and find myself struck down and helpless at the last. In vain would I try to sustain its character, to hold it up as an ancient and noble sport; my pen refuses the office,—its feather drags,—and my very gorge rises at the cold-blooded cruelty of its abettors and lovers. To see the rich and beautiful bird towering in his strength, mantling in his comeliness,—and in a moment to see him *bodkined*, and gnawed to death, in the presence of those who have pampered him up to an obstinate heroism and a stubborn savageness,—is more than heart can bear!—I saw the cocks go by me one minute, all life, and power, and beauty—I saw them pass the next—languid,—discoloured,—bleeding from the beak,—dead. The Gladiator scenes of Rome seemed to be wretchedly mocked here—and when all was over, what remained in the mind, but the dirty dregs of brutality and vice?

Tom vowed I looked pale:—it might be that I did. I grieved really to see *him* gratified. Mr. D—— discerned my feeling,—owned that "the sport was cruel,—perhaps too much!"—This was something—indeed, a great morality in a regular cock-fighter. To relieve me, he proposed showing me the coops; and I instantly accepted his proposal, and followed him up the stairs.

I entered the place with unpleasant feelings. A covering was hung before each pen; so that I *heard*, rather than saw, the cocks. But it was feeding time; and I beheld innumerable rocky beaks and sparkling eyes at work in the troughs—and the stroke of the beak in taking up the barley was like the knock of a manly knuckle on a table. Old Nash was mixing bread and milk for his fatal-feathered family. But I have done!

I have seen the *sport*! I have described it!—and I shall certainly never again do either the one or the other. You know I am not by any means a squeamish person;—but when I have come to reflect on the fighting and its consequences, all the glory of the contest has faded from me. I will not, however, add to the length of this letter, by indulging in a vain and common fit of moralizing.

Commend me to all my dear friends—and if you dare to say that you have heard from me, read to them my letter as far as the character of dear Tom Barnes, and then desist. I am glad to conclude with recurring to that kindly piece of humanity.

Yours, dear Russell, for ever,

Albany. Edward Herbert.

The Literary Police Office, Bow-street.
Edward Herbert's Letters to the Family of the Powells.
No. VIII.[173] *February 1823*
To Russell Powell, Esq.

Dogberry. One word, Sir: our Watch, Sir have, indeed, comprehended some auspicious persons, and we would have them this morning examined before your Worship.
Leonato. Take their examination yourself, and bring it me; I am now in great haste, as it may appear unto you.
Dogberry. It shall be suffigance.

*   *   *   *   *

Dogberry. Go, good partner, go; get you to Francis Seacoal: bid him bring his pen and inkhorn to the gaol. We are now to examination these men.
Verges. And we must do it wisely.
Dogberry. We will spare for no wit, I warrant you.

Much Ado about Nothing, Act III.[174]

Dear Russell!—I am much gratified that the Morning Herald, which I now intend to send you daily, gives you so much amusement; the

389

Police Reports are, as you correctly observe, written in a masterly style of humour and truth. Since you have urged me to ascertain the writer, I have left no stone unturned to fulfil your wishes, and I am happy to say, that I now rank that ingenious gentleman among my warmest friends. His name is not Vickery, as you surmise,—I would communicate it to you, but as yet he has not confided it to my keeping.

The other day this good gentleman consented to my proposal of accompanying him to one of the Police Offices. Bow-street was our chosen spot. I had told him of my anxious desire to be initiated into all the curious scenes of London; and he assured me that much whimsical work was to be inspected at a metropolitan Police Office. The day we chose for our visit was one of great interest and singularity—and my friend obtained for me a seat at the very foot of Sir Richard Birnie, and under the immediate nose, as I may say, of Mr. Minshull himself. I stayed the whole day, from the opening of the office, even unto the shutting up of the same. And at my particular request, my friend, the Reporter, adjourned in the evening to my chambers in the Albany, and there wrote his report for the Herald, permitting me at the same time to copy it, page by page, as he proceeded; I beg to inclose it to you for your immediate perusal, as the Herald, owing to the debates at the present *close* of parliament, will not be able to print it for some time. Oh! Russell, read it aloud to the friends of my heart!—You, with your acute remarks and pungent tones, will give the paper all its force and effect. I can vouch for the truth of the statement,—but indeed no one can doubt for a moment that the sketch is one from the very life.

My sheet of paper is large, but the report is extensive. I therefore copy it at once, that I may get all into one sheet, and save you that *double charge*, which is as serious in letters as in guns. Here is the Report.

Literary Police, Bow-street.

Yesterday the magistrates, Sir Richard Birnie, and Mr. Minshull, were employed the whole of the day in hearing charges preferred against literary offenders. Some of them were pregnant with great public interest; some were unworthy of notice.

William Wordsworth, a pedlar by trade, that hawks about shoe-laces and philosophy, was put to the bar, charged with stealing a poney, value 40s. from a Mrs. Foy, of Westmoreland; but as no one was near him at the time, and as he was *beside himself*, the charge could not be brought home. Another charge, however, was made against him, for converting to his own use a spade, with which Mr. Wilkinson had tilled his lands— but as Mr. Wilkinson was a gentleman of the Quaker persuasion, he would not appear to swear, and William also escaped on this charge.[175] There were several readers of William's books who were ready to swear, but their oaths could not be taken. The prisoner had several duplicates of little childish poems and toys about him, which he said he obtained from his grandmother. But it appearing that he had often imposed himself off as that old lady, he was remanded to allow of some inquiry. He conducted himself very extravagantly while before the magistrates, so as to give an idea that he was not quite right. He called himself the first man—king of the poets—and wanted to read passages from his own works to prove it. The officers had much difficulty in restraining him from getting out of the dock to beat the magistrates' brains out with a log of the Excursion. Jeffrey, the officer, was obliged to *pinion* him.

Samuel Taylor Coleridge was brought up for idling about the suburbs of town, without being able to give a satisfactory account of himself. He was taken up for sleeping at Highgate in the day-time. The magistrates committed him to the Muses' Treadmill for two months, to hard labour. It is supposed his *feet* will be all the better for this exercise. This is the same person, though much altered, who passed himself off as the Ancient Mariner, at a marriage in the metropolis some time back.

The Rev. Mr. Bowles was charged with stealing fourteen lines from an old gentleman's garden, of the name of Petrarch, at Putney. But he stating that he was not aware of his own dishonesty, and it appearing that the things were of little or no value—he was reproved and discharged. It was supposed that he had stolen these fourteen lines to hang himself with. This is the same person who was taken up on suspicion of being concerned in the attempted murder of Alexander Pope, at Twickenham, some time ago.[176] But it appearing that he had no idea of what he was doing, and was generally reckoned a harmless man—he was not detained. He said he could appear to his own character.[177]

O. Gilchrist gave information of having been shot at while playing a game at Bowles, in his garden at Stamford. It is supposed he would have fallen, but the *cloth* protected him. Several persons have been apprehended on suspicion—but nothing is to be *apprehended* from the gentleman who was most talked of as the ruffian in the neighbourhood.[178]

John Clare (a comely country-looking man, in a smock frock, and face to match) appeared to resist an order of filiation, made on the affidavit of one of the Muses with whom he had kept company, and who appeared to have been too liberal of her favours to him. The oath being persisted in, his innocence stood him in no stead; and he was ordered to set apart half-a-crown, out of sixpence a-day, to support the child. He pleaded poverty; but the magistrates explained to him that a poor soldier had been known to have managed such an allowance, and therefore they resisted his plea. Clare is said to have a wife, and ten little children all under the age of four years, which makes his case more reprehensible.[179]

Tom Moore underwent a long examination for picking the pocket of the public of nine shillings, in Paternoster Row, under the pretence of selling a book. But as it was proved that there were five partners concerned in this transaction, and that he was a mere instrument in their hands, he was on this charge discharged.[180] He was, however, put to the bar on several other complaints, one of which was from a pretty looking unfortunate girl, one of the family of the Muses, who stated that she had known him some years ago, when by the most plausible arts he completed her ruin.[181] She had since then been obliged to have recourse to the most distressing means for subsistence. She had been utterly deserted by him lately, and on her applying to him for relief, he had shut the door in her painted face, and informed her through the key-hole that he had married a religious woman out of the Magdalen, and was no longer a dealer in *Old Stores*.[182] The magistrates could afford this poor unfortunate no relief. Tom was also charged by one Dan Anacreon (a man himself of no very reputable character), for obtaining odes from him under false pretences:—on this charge he was *committed*. The odes were exhibited in the office, and appeared to be plated goods.[183]

Samuel Rogers, a youth of very prepossessing appearance, was placed at the bar on a charge of putting off several *forged notes* upon a banker in the City. The case involved much difficulty. The banker stated that he was of the same name with the prisoner, and was perpetually subjected to the annoyance of being mistaken for a poet; the notes, however, on being examined, were found to have nothing in them—and the charge of forgery therefore fell to the ground. The prisoner looked very pale throughout his examination, and was observed to conceal something under his coat towards the end of it—on being searched, it was found to be a brace of dedications; which, from a particular mark, were known to have been shot on the banker's grounds. The banker stated that he was compelled to put a *cheque* to these things, and having suffered much by such depredations, or decidations (we could not catch the precise word) he felt it imperative on him to prosecute. The prosecutor was therefore bound over (in sheepskin), and the prisoner was taken to the strong room.[184]

H. Smith, and James Smith, two brothers, were put to the bar on a very serious charge of forgery. The office was crowded by those who had suffered from the ingenious arts of these offenders. Some of the papers were produced at the time of examination, and were found to be executed in the most masterly manner. They seemed to be engraved on *steel*! The Rev. Mr. Crabbe could not swear to his hand-writing[185]— and one or two *forgees* were dead at the time of the forgeries;[186] upon which the magistrates observed, that post obits of this nature were dangerous cases to commit upon. However, Mr. Fitzgerald swore at the forgery upon him, and the prisoners were committed.[187] One of the brothers has, since his committal to Bridewell, escaped to the Continent.[188] The other is very penitent, and exhibits great cheerfulness in his confinement. He declares that his wife expects to be *confined* also in a few days, which will prove an increase to his comforts![189] Jem is a short thin melancholy man, with one eye, which is always bent on a joke.

Tom Dibdin was charged with robbing openly in the day-time, and was sent to the Bench.[190] He sat down with the magistrates.

Lord Byron, a young person, apparently of ferocious habits, was placed at the bar, under the care of Jeffrey and Gifford, two of the officers of the Literary Police, charged with a violent assault upon several literary gentlemen; when taken, he made a determined resistance, and beat the officers dreadfully. Jeffrey had his head bound up, in a blue and yellow handkerchief;[191] and Gifford carried his *arms* in a *sling*, like David the giant-killer.[192] The office was filled with bruised poets and broken prosers, all clamorous against the offender. It appeared, that going home on a certain day past, he was accosted by a Muse, and was prevailed upon to take a glass of something at the *Flying Horse and Pan-pipes*, which, getting into his head, made him unruly. On quitting the place, he was met by the party complaining, who remonstrated with him, and endeavoured to convince him of the badness of the company he was keeping; when, without a word, he began laying about him, mauling, and knocking down all that were far or near. Several men were brained for life, and poor Mr. Fitzgerald got an-ode on his head, which, it is supposed, will never be subdued; indeed, it increases every year.[193] The prisoner, for want of *Bayle*[194] (which he had lent to Mr. Leigh Hunt, to assist him in his philosophical pursuits), was committed to *Cold Bath Fields*, where it is feared he will soon put all the convicts into hot water. There was also an information lodged against him, by a lady of title, for keeping *unlawful game* in his house, without a licence—he was unable to pay the penalties immediately.[195] The prisoner looked scornfully at the Bench; and Southey declared he ought to be *hand cuffed*, but had not the courage to carry his declaration into effect. The prisoner, seeing one of Messrs. Longman's firm near him, protested, if they published his *pal* Tom Moore's Loves of the Angels to the world, he would make that deed and Heaven and Earth come together![196] The Bench shuddered at the thought, and Jeffrey was ordered to look to him. On retiring from the bar, the prisoner was very ferocious, and the officers were compelled to put his crooked spirit into a straight waistcoat. He was scarcely nineteen when he committed the offence for which *he* was committed.[197]

The Rev. Mr. Crabbe, an old man of very venerable appearance, was examined on a charge of having burglariously entered the parish poorhouse, and stolen therefrom a joint stool—a deal table—a wooden spoon—a smoke jack, and sundry kitchen and washhouse utensils. The case was clearly made out, and the parish was bound over to prosecute. It appeared on examination that this offender had been very hard upon the paupers in the house; and, indeed, while before the magistrates, he made several irreverent jokes upon the occasion.[198]

Sir Walter Scott, alias The Great Unknown, alias Bill Beacon, alias *Cunning Walter*, underwent a long private examination, on a sort of *novel* fraud, which was whispered to be one of a very extensive nature; nothing transpired after the examination, and the prisoner was ordered up for a further hearing.[199] Sir W. S. being a Baronet, and one of the

Bench being a Scotchman, the prisoner was allowed to be out on his own recognizance. He is a tall farmer-looking man—something of a Northern Cobbett. He is said to be the same person that was connected with the Longman gang in the great poetical robbery—[200] and that obtained the King's pardon, by turning King's evidence against his companions.

Sarah Siddons, a person well known about the theatres, was placed at the bar under suspicion of having disinterred the body of John Milton, a respectable scrivener, from the church-yard of Cripplegate. Some of the limbs were found in her possession.[201] She told a very plausible story, and much affected the Bench. But her powers this way were well known—and the magistrates wiped their eyes, and ordered her to find bail.

Robert Southey was informed against for sending out his poetical coals to Newcastle, without having the *metre's* ticket.[202] He offered to take an oath, that he had a right to do as he thought best—but the magistrates would not listen to him. His *sack*, however, was found to be *full measure*— which was much in his favour. The officers knew Rob well, and stated that he had often been at that bar before. He is the same person that knocked down Wesley in Paternoster-row, and that took away Lord Nelson's life in Albermarle-street.[203] On being called upon to account for his mode of living—he declared that he lived upon the lives of others—that he was the only man of unimpeachable morals in the world[204]—that he knew and revered the King, Mr. Croker, and the constitution; and that he would, if the magistrates pleased, write an Ode on the Police-office, which might be stuck up in some conspicuous place, to keep respectable people away. He was fined in the mitigated penalty of 1 *l.* and was ordered to be confined until the same was paid. He sold some waste paper, which his publishers held, and got out without a rag being left.

Charles Lamb was brought up, charged with the barbarous murder of the late Mr. Elia.[205] He was taken late in the evening, at a house of resort for characters of his description, in Fleet-street—and he had with him at the time of his caption a crape mask—a phosphorus (or hock) bottle—a dark lanthorn—a *skeleton* key—a centre bit (out of the haunch) —and a large clasp knife (and fork). The evidence was indisputable— and Mr. Lamb was committed. There appears to have been no apparent motive for this horrible murder, unless the prisoner had an eye to poor

Mr. Elia's situation in the London Magazine. The prisoner is a large gaunt-looking fellow, with a queer eye, and a broad overhanging brow. If no witnesses had come forward—his looks would *have appeared against him*!

Allan Cunningham, a dwarf, was brought up, under Tom Cribb's care (this is the second act of kindness of the champion), charged with a fraud upon a Mr. Cromek. Being young and little, he was handed over to the Philanthropic, as a fit place for such a heart as his.[206]

Barry Cornwall was brought up—charged by the officers with having created a crowd, and occasioned a disturbance, at Covent-Garden theatre. On expressing his contrition, and promising to offend again, he was reprimanded and discharged. He seemed to be a young man of very violent habits, and was near *flooring* the officer that stood by him.[207]

Thomas Campbell, a man well known about town, was charged with keeping a Little-go—for unlawful insurances in the lottery of Fame.[208] It was proved that he had taken in several poor authors to his concern—and he not being able to account for himself, was ordered to a year's hard labour, and to stand in the pillory in Conduit-street the first day of every month.

The Hon. Mr. Spencer—Lord John Russell—Lord and Lady Blessington—the Duke of Rutland—Lord Thurlow, and several others, all persons of no literary repute, were placed at the bar from the St. James's watch-house, charged with frequenting a masquerade at unlicensed rooms. They were brought up in their several motley dresses, and made the Literary Police Officers grin at the ridiculous figures they cut. Mr. Spencer was an Apollo—the wreath round his head was of artificial flowers, and he sang complimentary odes to ladies of fashion, which he accompanied on his *lyre*![209] Lord J. Russell was dressed up as Carlos in the Duenna: he supported the part pretty well, but he was obliged to do so, for the part would not support him.[210]—Lord Blessington appeared as Lord Colambre, out of Miss Edgeworth's novel of the Absentee, and did not look well[211]—his lady attempted the character of an authoress, and got some *credit* by writing on the ready *Rhine-o.*—[212] The Duke of Rutland made a very indifferent Mungo Park;[213] and Lord Thurlow was a middling Sir Philip Sidney dismounted!—[214] They all pleaded ignorance as an excuse for their bad works, and were fined a shilling each and discharged.

Just as the Bench had got through all these charges, and as the magistrates were rising, George Colman was brought in, charged with having attempted to destroy himself with poison. He talked a great deal of skimble skamble stuff—about the Law of Java—and the Upas-tree—but no one could understand him.[215] It appearing, however, that he had formerly been in his senses, and had lived in repute, he was given over to his friends, with strict injunctions, that pen, ink, and paper, and all such dangerous weapons should strictly be kept out of his reach. This was not the first attempt at suicide made by this unfortunate man.

There were some other cases of no public interest heard—and the magistrates rose and left the office. Nothing yet has transpired respecting the D'Israeli burglary:—[216] but Mrs. Opie is suspected of knowing something of poor Mrs. Donatty's death![217]

———

I have scarcely an inch of *lappel* left to say another word, and indeed my hand is already cramped with copying the report. I sincerely hope, my Dear Russell, that you will relish it, as it is intended;—nought is done in malice, but all in humour. Your kind mother will think it a pity to expose the names of the parties—but they are all too sensible to be affected by a trifle, which is merrily meant, and must pass away in a moment. Reason with her, Russell!—and as she knows Mr. Wordsworth, get her to intercede with him—for he is the only gentleman I fear. Farewell. With love to your sisters,

I am, ever and a day,

Your friend,

Edw. Herbert.

Albany, Jan. 1823.

PS.   A happy new year to you—and to those who see this letter.

ESSAY FROM *THE WESTMINSTER REVIEW*

Professor Wilson's Danciad.[1] *July 1824*

Art. XI. *The Danciad; or, Dancer's Monitor: being a descriptive Sketch in verse on the different Styles and Methods of dancing Quadrilles, Waltzes, Country Dances, &c. &c. as practised at various Public Balls and Assemblies; also on the Pretensions of certain Professors and Teachers of Dancing to that Title; on the Mode of Admission to, and of conducting various Places, termed Academies for Dancing; likewise on the Nature and Quality of what are frequently called Grand, Free, Select, Fancy-Dress, Friendly, Characteristic, Charity, and Dress Balls. Together with Observations on the Laws regarding Dancing, with Extracts from the Acts of Parliament relating thereto.* By Thomas Wilson, Author of various Works on Dancing, and several Dramatic Pieces. London, 1824.

The poetry of the head and the poetry of the heart, which until within a very few years, were so much be-praised and followed, have gone a little into decay; and those volatile wenches, the Muses, have flown, like the rheumatism or the gout, to other parts of the "human form divine."[2]

On the death of poor, pensive, and pugnacious Mr. Corcoran, poetry centred violently in the fists, and nothing would go down but imaginative punches in the head, and pictured black eyes: and every foolish bard threw his hat into the air and prepared for his *set-to*. We had odes to the Fives' Court, the Tennis Court, the Ring; sonnets to Moulsey Hurst, Brummagem Youths, and Champions of England, until the Art of Poetry and the Art of Self Defence seemed one and the same thing. Crib[3] and Tom Moore, Rogers and White-headed Bob, Dolly Smith and Wordsworth, became mingled in the imagination; and when the Fancy in any poem was alluded to, no soul could tell which was intended, that of Parnassus or Shepperton Bottom. Happily, this madness of the day was but the madness of a day—the Muses did not long go hand and glove with the Champions of England, and you might shortly ask a poet to see you without the risk of having your claret drawn. Poetry, thus turned abroad again, was glad to perch wherever she was able, and in her bewildered state, as a scared pigeon flies down a lawyer's chimney, or a lark drops into a Strand watch-box, she dashed into Warren's blacking manufactory, as a sanctuary, and dipping her wing in an eighteen-penny bottle, took up the cause of boots and shoes. Thus lowered in her own and other's estimation, she sat awhile in a solitude of brilliant jet, and has but lately gone from the shoe to the foot, and given promise of an amended life by abstaining from the bottle.

The poetry of the present moment is, therefore, the poetry of the feet; and so long as men can keep it out of the stomach, like the gout, it may give trouble, but can never prove fatal. We had apprehensions that in Doctor Kitchener's case it would fly there, but, happily, that evil is not yet consummated.[4] The feet, after all, are perhaps the proper home for the Muses: by the feet their language is regulated—by the feet do all poets invariably travel!—We remember being pozed for the moment by an eminent patron of the present age, who asked us if we saw any thing remarkable in his dinner table: we looked at it—it was a comely solid pillar and claw; we confessed, however, we saw nothing particular in the table. Ah! said he, with a sigh of melancholy rapture, and with his eye directed to the glorified mahogany—ah! under that table have been clustered some of the greatest and most intellectual legs of England! Porson's feet have been under that table![5]—The last sentence was pronounced with an unusual emphasis,—as though those immortal calves had left a lustre round the pillar and claw which time could not dull,— as though "the mind, the music breathing from" the ancles and insteps never could pass away. At the time, we thought this was a whimsical mode in our friend of looking at men of genius and intellect—we own it did appear to us to be an odd extremity to catch the mind in—but our friend saw further than we at the moment gave him credit for—he saw that in the great game of the mind the feet would one day turn up trumps!—That which he foresaw has at length come to pass. The legs and feet are the restless and happy palaces of Terpsichore and her eight sisters. Dancing has been often called the poetry of motion—there now can be no doubt of it.*

> *   Le Papillon danse
>   Mollement sur les bords d'un ruisseaux,
>   Puis il s'élance
>   Et ride sur les eaux.—
>   Les poissons sous les rives fleuries,
>   Les agneaux dans les prairies,
>   Les Bergers, et les troupeaux,
>   Jusqu'aux petits chiens dansent.   La Danse.[6]

An inspired work—a good book—as Mawworm[7] calls it, has very recently appeared, entitled "The Danciad, or Dancer's Monitor," and written by Mr. Professor Wilson, to whom we believe we are already indebted for several very pleasing poetical as well as dramatic perform-ances, the Isle of Palms,[8] the Children's Dance, the City of the Plague,[9] and other interesting publications. The present production is not exactly in the style of the works we have enumerated; but in moral philosophy, pointed invective, and dramatic spirit, it perhaps far outstrips any of them. It is deficient in that solitary horror and *city* agony of the plague poem, but atones for this deficiency by its severe wit and searching sarcasm. And while it bears away the palm from the Isle of Palms, by outdoing that simple poem in the easy gaiety of its measures; it possesses all the spirit and pathos of the Children's Dance. The syllables appear to catch the spirit of the subject, and to "come and foot it as they go."* Mr. Professor Wilson appears to be very familiar in this, as in some of his other works, which we have not here specified, with London persons, London vices, and London manners. He knows all qualities with a learned spirit. The only way at any time, we take it, to show mankind up, dregs and all, is to be able to mingle with the best as well as the worst company,—to be a saint with the saints, a philosopher with philosophers, a wrestler with wrestlers, a cockfighter with cockers, a poet with poets, a night-brawler with night-brawlers. It is the intimate knowledge of life displayed in this inestimable little pamphlet that recommends it so nimbly unto our gentle senses. We see that the professor, though really an absentee, knows every dancer in this metropolis, from a D'Egville down to a poney at Astley's.[11] Let us walk a minuet through these ornamental lines.

But first for the introductory part. Mr. Wilson sets out with a piece of novel information; he tells us that he is a teacher of dancing, at 18, Kirby-street, Hatton-garden. We thought he had been further north—and, indeed, we should be half disposed to doubt whether there were

---

* A mirthful tumult in which all partake?
  So dance the sunny atoms o'er a lake;
  So small clouds blend together in the sky;
  So when the evening gales the grove forsake
  The radiant lime leaves twinkle yet on high,
  So flutter new fledged birds to their own melody.

See Professor Wilson's *City of the Plague*.[10]

not two Simon Pures,[12] if we did not know how celebrated Mr. Professor Wilson has long been for feats of activity and spirit. This can be no other than he of the supple leg and agile arm!—aye,—and the poem itself will confirm our assertions. The dedication is in the professor's own style— modest and disinterested.

Dedication
To Teachers of Merit,

(Particularly those at whose request the Danciad was composed, and who are most capable of deciding how far the author has done justice to the subject) he respectfully dedicates this Work.

Academy for Dancing,
18, Kirby Street, Hatton Garden.
7th June, 1824.

We like a dedication with a date—and in all our experience of inscriptions (and as patrons of literature we know a little of things of the kind) we never saw one with so effective and picturesque a parenthesis. It is, in truth, more important with reference to its circumjacent prose than parentheses usually are. The preface follows (pardoned be the phrase) in that sort of sober pace which a dancer takes before he plunges, body and—heels, into a hornpipe. Our author shall here speak for himself.

The Danciad is founded on a dramatic prelude to the author's 89th Public Ball, [Lecture, we presume he means.] held the 30th October, 1822 (when the characters were represented by himself and three of his pupils), being intended as a descriptive sketch on the present state of ball-room dancing, teachers and professors of dancing, academies, public balls, &c. &c.

The sketch being approved, was afterwards shown, in manuscript, to several eminent philosophers, who strongly advised the author to continue the subject; as the various puffs and delusive advertisements of certain persons styling themselves "Professors of Dancing," tended to bring even the art itself into disrepute, and loudly called for exposure and reprehension; *however, what was every body's business was nobody's*; though all continued to complain of injuries sustained in consequence of such practices, yet none attempted to draw on them the attention of the public. The author was therefore urged to continue and extend his sketch; he in vain represented the difficulty of making it into a poem without new-modelling the subject, a task that he had neither time nor ability to execute. It was replied, that regularity of form was not regarded by them. *"Go on (they exclaimed) we care not about form,"* and to their suggestion he yielded.

401

So the author endeavoured to take up the cause,
By exposing mean tricks and explaining the laws;
To caution the public against some imposters,
Those self-named "Professors" 'yclept Dancing Masters.
How the task is performed, must be judged of by those
Who well know the art, and such quackery oppose.[13]

The eminent philosophers spoke out manfully and well. The tricks of these persons styling themselves "*professors*," crying aloud for reprehension, as Mr. Professor Wilson says they have done, ought to have been sooner attended to. And we only wonder that any man, with a foot to his soul, or a sole to his foot, should stand by, and endure the dance of existence without breaking out into the hornpipe of invective. Fortunately, the Juvenal of juveniles has been aroused in his lair in Kirby-street —and he has taken the necessary steps in an heroic measure for putting down the evil! He goes to the roots—to the feet of things—and leads you through all those palaces of the lamp, the Grand, the Select, the Characteristic, the Friendly, the Dress, the Free, the Subscription, and the Charity balls, with the persevering spirit of an Aladdin. The only fault we find with Mr. Professor Wilson in the Danciad—and it is a fault which has been seldom laid at his door—is his proneness to conceal the names of persons whom he wishes to hold up to shame, and the particulars of their private lives and connexions. We always admired the pleasant searching truth of the professor, when he chose to indulge in the private history of his offenders.

The first paragraph of the following passage is not exactly in the professor's usual vein—but the latter part is candid and agreeable, and goes strongly to make out the poet's identity.

He has entirely abstained from allusions to family circumstances, and personal misfortunes, which ought never to be the subject of ridicule, although they have been, too frequently, to the disgrace of some of our best authors; and perhaps he might in some measure have been justified in retaliating even personalities, after the illiberality of certain parties, and he can affirm without fear of contradiction, that

He's uninfluenced, aids no partial cause,
Nor strives to censure, to obtain applause.

The Author's motives for this publication will probably be attributed to various causes; some persons will accuse him of self-interest, but he is quite convinced, *if they had published as much, and as variously as he has, they would acquit him of that charge.* Books published by an humble individual (not a bookseller) seldom pay even for paper and printing, much less any remuneration for authorship; *he forms this opinion from his own experience,* believing it to be well known, &c.[14]

At page xi of the preface, the author very giddily and pleasantly flits round the inconstant flame of profit—that poor dancing light which is ever deceiving the poet's eye!

Not only has the author been without a rich patron and a dedication fee, but he has never received any pecuniary assistance from his subscribers in the publication of this work, *the conditions being, not to pay till delivery, and the price only 5s., whatever may be the size or extent of the book;* beyond which he has only this forlorn hope, as

> His subscribers belong to the family race
> Of the *Capers,* well known for their *figures* and *grace,*
> Who he hopes are too proud and too rich to abuse
> *A very good custom subscribers did use,*
> *When the copy's presented, the change to refuse.*

This expectation, he fears, is only one of the poet's golden dreams, which perhaps will never be realized.[15]

From the following extract it should seem that the professor has been induced to show the work in MS. to some of his friends, the contributors to Magazines or Reviews—and, indeed, to have received much encouragement in his task. We hope Sir Walter Scott has seen and approved it, and we are quite sure Wordsworth would give him wholesome advice on the old hills.

He fears the work will not please the critics, the subject being not only limited but technical: however, should it satisfy those for whom it was written, he shall consider himself fortunate; and should it not, after his best endeavours, meet their expectation, they will recollect it was their approval of a portion of the work that induced him to finish it.[16]

The preface ends at p. xxi, and bears the same date as the dedication. On the 7th of June, therefore, the professor was industrious to a degree. The poem, or rather the dramatic dialogue (for, like Pope's or Persius's

satires, the sarcasm is given in dialogues), opens with the *Dram. Pers.*,
as Sylvester Daggerwood calls it.[17]

> Belinda.
> Jemima.
> Aunt Frump.
> Lucy (*a Servant.*)
> Chassee (*a Dancing Master.*)

The last is clearly the Othello of the play.

The opening is familiar, yet certainly not very well on its feet; we all
know however that neither horse nor man can go till he is warm. Lucy,
the servant, it should be observed, speaks with a want of grammar
becoming her situation.

> *Lucy.* This way, Madam,—this way,—pray walk in,
> At nine, the Ball will certainly begin.
> *Bel.* It's now past eight—I think my watch is right,
> Do you expect much company here to-night?
> *Lucy.* We've plenty of fine ladies and smart beaux,
> Mostly pupils, and those that Master knows.
> *Bel.* I hope they'll not be late, for, I must own,
> I am melancholy when I am left alone.
> *Lucy.* There's several ladies dressing down below,
> Three of them came at least an hour ago:
> When I looked out just now I several more
> In coaches saw. (*Knocking heard.*) I hear them at the door.[18]

Belinda and Jemima now enter into a very eloquent discourse on
dancing; and go through it from the days

> When Bishop taught and Slingsby graced the stage![19]

down to the days of men styling themselves professors. And here
Jemima breaks out to some tune:

> Go round or thro' the town which way you will,
> You're sure to see some dancing-master's bill;
> On every wall or fence their bills are seen,
> From East to West, from Bow to Turnham Green;

They teach for prices any dance you chuse,
For less than shoe-blacks charge for blacking shoes;
They all "Professors" write, and on the wall.
They seem to vie with Vestris* and with Paul.†
Try them, see their pupils dance, then proclaim
Whether "Professor" does become their name.
One "gratis‡ gives a month," says "*come and try,*"
As they cry walnuts, "*taste before you buy,*"
Some advertise, that "if you do not learn
In certain time, *the money they'll return;*"
Quack doctors like, who advertise to say,
Their terms to patients are "*no cure no pay.*"
"*To give four months for three,*" there's one agrees,
By way of blessing, as they give with peas.
Others less modest still demand some pay,
And for one guinea, in six lessons they
Will teach completely any dance you will;
Minuet, gavotte, waltzing, or quadrille;
And some, who on their talents can't depend,
A picture§ of their room to shops they send,[20]

Surely this heavy truth!—again,

Others a letter from their names retrench,**
Or add, or else transpose, to make it *French*;
They shrug their shoulders, and cry "Sacre Dieu,"
But know no more of French than our Sue;

* Vestris the name of a celebrated family of French dancers, some of whom have been principals at the Italian Opera House for more than half a century; and Mr. Charles Vestris holds that situation at present, and is one of the best modern dancers. (Thomas Wilson).

† Paul a French dancer of uncommon agility, and who, when this work was begun, was one of the first dancers at the Italian Opera. (Thomas Wilson).

‡ The author begs he may not have the credit for invention of the captivating phrases above quoted, as they are really taken from bills and advertisements of certain professors of dancing, many of which are in his possession. (Thomas Wilson).

§ A practice resorted to by a certain professor, who prefixes several initials to his name. (Thomas Wilson).

** An eminent dancing-master, a subscriber to this work, complained to the author, that one of these quack teachers, whose name he mentioned, had obtained from him some of his schools; this was accomplished by retrenching two letters of his name, which rendered it the same as that of an established teacher in the neighbourhood, and engaging to teach the school at a reduced price. (Thomas Wilson).

> They gabble broken French, and try to pass
> For Frenchmen; but are often like the ass
> In fable told, who wore the lion's skin,
> And strove to take his fellow-creatures in;
> Was by his ears at last found out, and then
> Was scouted and disgraced by beasts and men.[21]

This is the true poetry. The simile of the Ass in the Lion's skin is striking and original.

The following hit at poor Mr. Walbourn, who recently danced the Dustman so vehemently at the Adelphi Theatre, is a palpable hit indeed.

> One prides himself on what you'd scarce suppose,*
> That he the manners of a dustman knows;
> To show his predilection for that trade,
> Has had his portrait as a dustman made,
> Which in his ball-room is conspicuous placed,
> To show his pupils his fine attic taste.
> He'd be offended, should he hear you say,
> He is not the greatest dustman of the day.[22]

The professor severely handles another artist of the toe for putting up the arms of Mrs. Olivia Serres on his shutters.

> Another thinks that Royalty† has charms,
> And on his shutters paints the Royal Arms;
> But e'er to see the royal guest dance there,
> Credulity itself would ev'n despair.

---

* It was formerly the pride of every dancing-master to be thought a gentleman, but that age, like the age of chivalry, is gone! for, several modern professors delight in being considered familiar with the lowest occupations; and one has had his full-length figure as a dustman placed conspicuously in his ball-room, and has distributed a metal portrait of himself as "the original dustman!" Others have stepped aside from the usual path, to imitate so enviable an example. What would the Noverres, the Gallinis, the Bishops, and the Slingsbys, have said to this? (Thomas Wilson).—Ah! what indeed! (R).

† The Prs. [Princess] of C.[umberland], in whose cause a patriotic M. P. eloquently but ineffectually spoke in the H.[ouse] of C.[ommons], and emphatically introduced the classical quotation—"Flectere si nequeo superos, Acheronta movebo."—Her highness resides in the professor's neighbourhood, but cannot be seriously presumed to have granted the licence. (Thomas Wilson)[23]

Bel. Perhaps he to the palace often goes,
To drill the monarch and to point his toes.
Jem. He, at the royal residence, 'tis said,
Was never seen—to knock would be afraid,
Lest the rude porter in an angry fit,
Should feel his ears, and tread upon his kit,
And make him soon be glad to stir his stumps
Thro' mud and water in his dancing pumps.[24]

There is an admirable picture of a pump-Pretender presenting himself unsuccessfully at Carlton Palace. His reception, or rather his dismissal is done with a pointed toe.

Mr. Wilson is angry, and with reason, at those pugnacious professors, who challenge all the world to try a foot with them: and yet he should recollect that it is hard to live by the toe, and that want will sometimes compel the most modest of feet to be extravagant. Distress will drive dancing masters as well as sailors to the pumps!

Jem. Another teacher* who for years I've known,
And who I am now almost ashamed to own,
Has imitated those I've just exposed,
And for five hundred pounds he has proposed
To dance a minuet with those who dare;
But tell it not to Vestris or Albert;
Nor at those schools where our professor's fame
Stands high, as such low tricks must sink his name,
And as a challenger bring loss and shame.[25]

At page 44, The Wilson begins to philosophize, and of course his "nature comes over him," in a very appalling manner. There is no

---

* The teacher alluded to, by resorting to the tricks of a juggler, has induced the author reluctantly to notice him. It appears that, in imitation of the professor who challenged any one to dance a hornpipe with him for one hundred guineas (see page 35 of the Danciad), the above teacher, as if resolving to go further, has challenged any one who dare to dance a minuet, in competition with him, for five hundred guineas. His conduct seems the more extraordinary, from his having always wished to be ranked with the first class of teachers, and reprobated the low devices of unfair practitioners. When asked his reasons for descending to this practice, he is said to have declared, "there was no living without it." What do Messrs. Byrne, Le Mercier, and Jenkins, and other members of the profession say to this? (Thomas Wilson).—Aye, marry! and what too would Slingsby say? (R).

Professor living who can combine wisdom with whim,* so effectively as our Author. He can moralize you like any Saint, and in the next breath can throw off an highland fling with the naked vigour of an Ettrick Shepherd.[27] He can lecture,—or he can leap:—but he would rather leap than lecture. His motto is from Moliere—"La philosophie est *quelque chose*—Mais—la danse!—Monsieur, la danse!''—[28]

Our Author is hard upon a poor Baker who tries to get his bread by teaching dancing. No mercy is shewn to the audacious Man of flour; but we are tempted to exclaim with Mr. Professor Wilson, and for the sake of the measure, in his own mode of pronunciation:

* All our readers have of course perused the Professor's previous poem on dancing called, "The Children's Dance," and published in the same Volume with the "City of the Plague." It is a little tender-hearted thing,—innocent as a wren,—yet wise as a Sir Isaac Newton. How prettily does the Poet describe his own little girl Miss Wilson, in her best shoes:—It seems the dance is by day and not by night, as in owlish England.

> All day the Earthern floors have felt their feet,
> Twinkling quick measures to the liquid sound
> Of their own small piped voices, shrilly sweet,—
> As hand in hand they wheel'd their giddy round.
> Ne'er fairy revels on the greensward mound
> To dreaming Bard, a lovelier shew displayed;—
> Titania's self did ne'er with lighter bound
> Dance o'er the diamonds of the dewy glade,
> Than danced at peep of morn, mine own dear Mountain Maid.

We must just call to our readers' recollection two other stanzas, written in all the poetry and philosophy of dancing.

> And lo! the crowded ball room is alive
> With restless motion and a humming noise,
> Like on a warm spring morn a sunny hive,
> When round their queen the waking bees rejoice,
> Sweet blends with graver tones the silvery voice
> Of children rushing eager to their seats,
> The Master proud of his fair flock employs
> His guiding beck that due attention meets,—
> List! through the silent room each anxious bosom beats!
> Most beautiful and touching is this scene!
> More blissful far to one than Fancy's bower!
> Arch'd are the walls with wreaths of Holly green,
> Whose dark red berries blush beside the flower
> That kindly comes to charm the wintry hour!
> The christmas rose, the glory white as snow!
> The dusky roof seems brighten'd by the power
> Of bloom and verdure mingling thus below,
> Whence many a taper's light sends forth a cheerful glow.[26]

This is indeed a splendid picture of a pump-room amidst the Hills. (R)

> Oh, Terps*ichore!* forgive our dusting friend,
> And grant him grace, perhaps he will amend![29]

We all know what a dancing master means when he prays for grace! At page 54, the professor evidently alludes to his friend the Ettrick shepherd; indeed, he is seldom either merry or severe without mentioning the worthy bard of the Scotch fleece.

> Some have become professors in the town,
> Because they'd names like teachers of renown;
> They're like those authors (*named by Hogg and Co.*)[30]
> Whose name is all the public of them know,
> Who learn a little dancing just to say
> They're dancing masters and their name display.

Mr. —— or we should rather say, M. Chassee, enters at p. 57. He is a little limping at first.

> [Belinda *and* Jemima *walk up the stage.*]
> *Chassee.* Two ladies here!—Hey!—Who is that I see
> Disguised;—'tis like Belinda. It cannot be.
> [Belinda *and* Jemima *discover themselves.*]
> *Bel.* Miss Jemima, Sir.—Mr. Chassee whose fame
> You have no doubt heard full half the town proclaim.
> *Chassee.* G. M. S. Chassee now I print my name.
> Didn't I near Temple Bar Belinda meet?
> *Bel.* I really, Sir, didn't know you in the street,
> Your parson's hat and dress to me were new,
> And strange at first I could not believe 'twas you.
> *Chassee.* That dress and hat are all my own design,
> There's not another in the town like mine;
> That is a proof of my ability,
> My taste and my originality.[31]

This is hard work—but anon we get upon a more *Macadamised* measure.

> *Chassee.* These quacks, I've challenged, aye, in every way,
> To dance with me, and their great skill display;
> They dare not answer me, but skulk away:
> Afraid to meet me, as you may suppose,
> These are the creatures, Miss, who me oppose.

Bel. Creatures, indeed! compared with those who know
What dancing really is, and who can show
They've execution, judgement, taste, and skill,
And can their public promise well fulfil.
A case in point their impudence will show,
How they pretend to what they do not know;
A friend told me (on whom I can rely),
That she proposed a minuet to try
With one who prints "professor" in his bill,
'Twas done to try the great professor's skill,
With this proposal he directly closed,
And took his place to dance, as was proposed;
But, strange! he knew the minuet no more,
Than one who had never seen the dance before,
As he knew neither figures, steps, nor grace,
For when he moved 'twas always out of place:
His feet seemed quite confused, and not to know
Which way to move, or where they ought to go:
He watched his partner, scraped about the dance,
And oft receded when he should advance:
At length the lady, quite disgusted, cried,
"I see this dance, Sir, you've not lately tried;"
Then took her seat, and to herself exclaimed,
"This to the public ought to be proclaimed."[32]

Chassee dances before Jemima at p. 69; and this leads to the following inimitable exposure.

[*Jemima dances; Chassee surprised and confused.*]
Jem. Now, Sir, excuse the liberty I take,
I've on your dancing some remarks to make,
I'll stand corrected, if I cannot show
That something of the art I really know;
I've been at dancing since six years of age,
And have for years had practice on the stage,
From false positions all your steps you take;
Third for fifth, and when the ballote you make,
Your feet are so confined with turned up toes,
That 'tis a ballote none could suppose;
Your arms ungraceful, then you bend your back
And head, when dancing, like a half filled sack,

410

You shake and wriggle, jerk about and swing,
Like children's puppets which they play with string;
If such your manner, taste, and execution,
Woe be to those who are under your tuition.
[*Chassee walks about agitated taking snuff.*]

This eloquent tirade drives poor Chassee to an exit. And then Jemima and Belinda keep up a rattling and incessant fire on all the naughty professors to the end of the work; closing, however, with a royal salute to those monarchs of the toe and heel—Le Blond, Le Gros, Noblet, Aumer, Ronzi, Vestris, D'Egville, and Oscar Byrne!—Stars in the forehead of Terps*ichore*! Spirits of the chalked firmament!

That this work is worthy of the pen of the great professor, no one we think will be rash enough to question; that it will work incalculable good in the due administration of the feet, it is impossible not to foresee. Pumps yet unborn shall partake the benefits of this invaluable poem. Embryo waltzers, and quadrille-queens in the bud, shall expand and flourish under the influence of the Wilson. Our eminent professor and poet will long deserve the blessings of the wise, the sprightly, and the good; he at once labours to make sound the head, to moralize the heart, and to elevate the feet. Those who have thought his buoyant spirits and pliant abilities a little unbecoming the chair, will now see that not without an object have those amiable gaieties been encouraged. The present work is a key to many of those extravagant sallies, which, until its appearance, were unaccountable even to his friends. We can only say, in bidding him farewell, that we wish the Author success from head to foot—whether in the professor's chair—or on the light fantastic toe!—In ball room or lecture room! May his tickets and philosophy go off with increasing spirit. And when that hour comes (and far distant may it be!) when the philosopher shall sleep as soundly as his auditory—and the dancer "take nothing by his motion!"—may all those fairy elves (who have duly paid their subscriptions) pay the last honour to their master—to him—

Who framed to grace their stature as it grew,
And train'd their fairy feet amid the morning dew![33]

ESSAYS AND REVIEWS FROM

THE ATHENAEUM

From Conversations of James Northcote, Esq., R. A. *By William Hazlitt. Post 8ᵛᵒ. London, 1830. Colburn & Bentley.*[1]
October 2, 1830

William Hazlitt, the editor of these "Conversations,"—at a period of life which scarcely exceeds what may be termed the middle age of man,—is suddenly gathered to his fathers; while the venerable North-cote, at the advanced age of eighty-two—firm in thought, and green in feeling—is at this very moment meditating and executing a life of his "fine old mouser," Titian![2] Such is the incomprehensible fate of those of the earth! The one was catching the soft and tremulous tones of wisdom and enthusiasm from aged lips, in all the confidence of life— and his own lips are on the instant hushed for ever! The inspired old man misses his hale companion, and stares at death. Alas! it is but too uncertain which of the flock the phantom butcher takes!

William Hazlitt was, throughout his troubled, many-coloured life, a thinking, feeling, dreaming, disappointed man! He studied as a painter —and the deep awe which the works of Titian and the other mighty masters of the art struck into his mind, paralyzed his hopes, and he abandoned his profession in despair. The faces of Titian's portraits haunted him, and never passed from him; and when he spoke of them, it was as though he had discoursed with high spirits, and had bent his eyes on some strange supernatural light. The same sense of perfection in poets and philosophers prevented him from travelling their paths with courageous vigour. The things were done!—the lists were made up! He copied only the pictures he adored, because they would be as records in absence; and he wrote not from inspiration or the hope of high achievement, but for "hard money" and a painful subsistence. To this cause is to be attributed certain acerbities, hasty asperities, abrupt assertions, angry and bitter lamentations, which cloud nearly all his writings, and which in the interested and the thoughtless have raised up so much of spleen and animosity. Hazlitt was the son of an Unitarian dissenter—he was therefore bred up in the fields of controversy. His politics, too, were those of the dissenter; and the more he suffered the buffets and contumely of the world, the more steadfastly he clung to his political opinions, strengthening them with storms. Had Hazlitt started in life with the sunshine of fortune upon his forehead, he would have been not only that which he was—a most original and powerful writer— but he would have been one of the most successful ones: the leaven of worldly prosperity was only wanting to make the bread perfect.

Various have been the productions of William Hazlitt. He has reported parliamentary prose, and lectured on English poetry. He has written masterly critiques on the drama, in which it was his invariable aim to be vigorously just. He has written reviews in the periodical works, essays, characteristics, satire. His criticism is always acute and clean—his satire poignant and bitter. The pamphlet which he wrote on Gifford, though deeply provoked, was, however, rugged and personal almost to a crime. His mind was soured—he had the eternal misery of seeing his anonymous writings cherished and admired, and of experiencing party rancour and detraction the moment he ventured to father his mental offspring. Many of his essays, scattered about among the pages of Magazines, are incomparably beautiful—beautiful from the tender melancholy which hangs about them—tuning the sentences to a sad cadence, which the heart feels, trembling and thrilling, to its inmost core. When he writes of Titian—of the learned Poussin's solemn land-scapes[3]—of his venerable father, with his unpretending virtues[4]—"of the drear melody of bedded reeds,"[5] in some old haunt—of the curlew wheeling and screaming around Winterslow Hut, where he so often abode,—that reader must be cold indeed that does not rise from the perusal "a sadder and a wiser man."[6]

Hazlitt was domestically unfortunate: he married hastily, and was unhappy at leisure. He parted from his wife—a warm-hearted, though eccentric woman—and entered into one of those convenient arrangements which are called Scotch marriages. Again he underwent a sort of Byronian separation.[7] He had, we believe, formed a deep and unhappy attachment, even at an unboyish age, which occasioned nothing but heavy disappointment in his friends, and led to despair in himself.[8] His passion was ever appalling, and under no control;—and he suffered for its unbridled vehemence and liberty.

But the grave has now closed upon William Hazlitt, and his errors, dangerous and troublous chiefly to himself, ought to, and will die with him. His mind, however, must have its tardy triumphs; for the works which it has produced, Posterity, in its slow but sure course of justice, will collect and value. Alas! late—late comes the decree for the suitors in Fame's fatal Chancery!

The work before us might now with great propriety be entitled "Conversations of James Northcote *and* William Hazlitt," for the latter has quite his share in the good quality as well as quantity of talk, and death levels all distinctions. The discourses are on painting and poetry—painters and poets—novelists and philosophers—romance and philosophy;—and we have gone through them with nearly unmingled pleasure and profit. Those who would *know* Sir Joshua Reynolds, Godwin, and Opie, *behind the scenes*—those who would nourish a *love* for pictures, a devoted passion for divine art—those who would hear of the great past in intellect and beauty, must feed on these high conversations.—"My God!" as old Northcote in his half-breathless enthusiasm would exclaim,—"who would have thought the old man had so much blood in his veins!"[9]

From Conversations of James Northcote (*continued*).
October 23, 1830

[After a long quotation in which both Hazlitt and Northcote attack Benjamin R. Haydon, Reynolds comments as follows.]

This is severe work upon a painter whose genius, however, is distinguishable through all his faults. He certainly abandons himself to the excessive in whatever he attempts or achieves;—he paints in the gigantic, and tortures nature; his writings on Art are arrogant and disputatious; his assertions and his complaints are "i' the Hercles vein";—but then his disappointments, his sufferings, aggravate his discontent and egotism; and in contemplating his character, it is impossible not to see and grieve

over great misdirected powers, and to feel and acknowledge that circumstances might have made him as pre-eminently superior in Art,
as they have unfortunately conspired to fret, baffle, and destroy him![10]

From Letters and Journals of Lord Byron. With Notices of his Life.
By Thomas Moore. Vol. II. London, 1831.
Murray.[11] *January 1, 1831*

Since the publication of our last number, in which we were enabled
to give our readers exclusively, a notice of this deeply interesting volume,
we have read the work with our utmost care and attention; and we
trust, we come to our critical task with minds fully qualified to form a
just estimate of the merits and demerits of the book. It is not our
intention, in the present article, to be very profuse of our own sentences;
—because we are quite sure, that the rare and racy observations, reflections, and biting severities, of Lord Byron, will be the most coveted by
all our readers. We will give the results of our attentive examination
of the volume, as concisely as we are able—and we shall then select
"full many a gem of purest ray," (*not* "serene,") to sparkle in our pages.

Mr. Moore has had a most difficult task to accomplish, in the editing
of a private correspondence so daring, reckless and personal, as that
which rushed from the pen of Lord Byron. The noble poet was a poet
in all things, and mighty in all things. He was a Juvenal on the foibles
of friends—a sort of savage Shakspeare on the common mishaps, deceits,
and occurrences of life. Where he saw or conjectured a doer of wrong,
he out-Swinged all men in the terrific potency of letter-writing.[12] His
words would burn a barn! To watch, to curtail, to omit, in a work like
the present, was no idle or easy matter; and we only wonder how it is,
that so much of the spirited and the beautiful has been retained, without
greater personal injury and offence. Mr. Moore, with one or two exceptions, appears to have applied himself to his labour without prejudices,
and with an earnest desire to show the real generous goodness which
lived in the heart of Lord Byron. His Lordship was a self-accuser in
every way—save in his actions; but often when his language is most
bitter and reproachful, he is doing some act of essential kindness, or

true magnanimity. The biographer has no great affection for Lady Byron, nor any particular respect for the memory of Lady Noel.[13] And when on the work of omission, Mr. Moore might well have cut out one or two distinguishing epithets, which take all the mystery out of the stars put in the place of a name. The spiteful pleasantries, too, on the wedding-day, and on the illness and recovery of his Lordship's mother-in-law, should scarcely have been preserved to gratify the sour palate of posterity. The blanks are sometimes ludicrously easy of solution— and we have, in our copy, filled in the names of Romilly, Lady Morgan, Schlegel, Southey, &c., to save other readers the trouble of guessing and searching for half a minute into the recesses of the volume.

The perusal of the work has impressed us with a higher idea of Lord Byron's genius, than even his poetry gave us. Indeed, the rude germs of many of his finest thoughts are traceable to his letters. Several of his noblest and loveliest statues, which now "enchant the world," may be seen in rough and unhewn masses in his epistles—nay, hewn in the rough, with all the form without the finish! The material—the marble is there—before it is carved into poetry. The extracts we shall give, will show the wit, the melancholy, the enthusiasm, the grandeur, the kindness of Lord Byron in many a bright variety. He can be gay, poignant, and poetical, almost in a breath; and his language is strong and impressive to the last degree. Few persons have possessed the power of praising so originally and well, or of censuring so concisely and forcibly. We know of nothing so delightful—and we speak from experience— as his good word uttered in his own good words;[14] and we certainly would endure any severity, in preference to suffering the eternal gibbet of his satire—in prose or verse.

The letters, which principally form this second volume, are addressed to Mr. Moore and Mr. Murray. How is it that, in a work of the character which this assumes, there appear none of the letters to Mr. Hobhouse, Mrs. Leigh, Lady Melbourne, and others who were intimate at heart with him, and to whom he wrote frequently and unreservedly? There should have been no interested or petty reserve, where the character and genius of Lord Byron were to be illustrated. Such letters do not belong to executors or legatees: they are the property of posterity; and posterity has a right to claim and keep it! There must have been some fine letters written to Mr. Shelley—where are they? The value of all that we attain is so great, that we cannot bear that children yet unborn should be destined to enjoy what is now in existence, and ought to be our own.

The present volume takes up his Lordship's life at the time when he had separated from Lady Byron, and was quitting this country. It shows him in his dissipation, in his solitude, and in his restlessness, at Venice. It details the particulars of his *two* attachments to two Venetians, and marks the growth of his poetry. It carries his Lordship to Greece, and to his death, in glory. We shall endeavour now to cull the jewels of the book . . .

With regard to what you say of retouching the Juans and the Hints, it is all very well; but I can't *furbish*. I am like the tiger (in poesy), if I miss the first spring, I go growling back to my jungle. There is no second; I can't correct; I can't, and I won't. Nobody ever succeeds in it, great or small. ** p. 381 . . .

Your first note was queer enough; but your two other letters, with Moore's and Gifford's opinions, set all right again. I told you before that I can never *recast* any thing. I am like the tiger: if I miss the first spring, I go grumbling back to my jungle again; but if I *do hit*, it is crushing. p. 556.

We have extracted the two passages, in which the one grand tiger character is given by Lord Byron to his poetry, because we think it is by far the truest and boldest picture that was ever dashed off, but also because it shows how much his Lordship himself valued it, and how able he was on repetition to improve it. Three or four such poetical lines of criticism as these are worth a complete set of the Edinburgh Review! . . .

Mr. Moore has been scrupulously careful of some of the living—and has protected them by the scissors against Lord Byron's lance of a pen. But the biographer has allowed all the ill-nature and sarcasm against Keats to be perpetuated,—without regard to the feelings of surviving relations and friends. The idle stuff of Keats dying of the Quarterly Review is preserved carefully—although it is well known that consumption, and not criticism, destroyed him. A Review is a very nauseous, but not a very poisonous drug—it has more of ipecacuanha than henbane in it.[15]

The passages in these letters, in which the modern poets are spoken of, are particularly interesting. To Rogers there is one very formal epistle—and it would seem that his Lordship's friendship for this poet had all the serene formality of a Pleasure of Memory. Rogers is called the Tithonus of Modern Poets. Campbell is corrected and coldly admired by Lord Byron. Southey is hated, reviled, and challenged. Wordsworth is sneered at—Coleridge is jeered at!—Moore is lauded to the Seventh Heaven. Scott is worthily beloved. Wilson and Hogg are flattered—being of the Blackwood party it would seem. Millman and Croly, and such "small deer," are treated after their kind.[16]

We have devoted an unusual portion of our paper to this article—but we were extremely anxious to give to our readers the essence of the book—and this we have, as far as our limits will allow, endeavoured to do. Much remaineth for "a second fytte," but we rather think we have given that sort of introduction which will induce the reader to form a friendship with the volume itself. How are places, men and things immortalized! Places and men too, that were already secured against the obliterating ravages of Time. Venice, where for ever dwell Shylock and Pierre, could have spared Lord Byron to some other sea-born city. And Chillon, wherein Bonivard breathed, and about which Rousseau wandered, all romance! needed no bi-formed immortality. Scott and Moore also can stand alone, and go alone, and require no poetical leading strings. Oh that we were of those lucky flies that have got *ambered* in these lustrous letters for the eyes of posterity!

The volume is massive. The printing and paper are the perfection of Davisonism[17] and Murrayism, and the portrait of Lord Byron, at the age of nineteen, although a little theatrical, and so far like the original, is very striking and effective. On closing the volume, we are impressed with two things;—that the Countess Guiccioli was, and is a most sensible and devoted woman,—and that Mr. Murray ought to have been a more punctual and communicative letter-writer. Between the two—the passion and the publisher—his Lordship was love-mad and letter-mad.

Letters of Edward Herbert. New Series, No. 1. January 7, 1832
To Russell Powell, Esq.

A change came o'er the spirit—!
Byron.

My dear Russell,—Our correspondence has held a truce for ten years:
—you have been a traveller in other climes, and have returned with a

wrinkled visage, an imperfect journal, and a loss of relations; and I, after nine years of *old*-newspaper reading, shooting, and fishing in the north of Devon, have returned to the changes, bitternesses, and frivolities of London. You ask me to revive our old gratification of an interchange of letters;—and as your communications cannot but *be* communications of interest to me—and as my observations on the past and the passing, after my decent banishment, cannot [but] be amusing to you;—why, Russell, let us at once barter epistles in the true spirit of merchants and letter-writers—that is, in the hope of being mutual gainers.[18]

But, first, let me gently protest against the strange use which was made of my letters in years bye-gone. Are you aware—yes, you must be —that they were printed, Russell? printed,—printed in the pages of the *London Magazine*. Never again, I entreat you, permit a lady-friend to copy or to peruse a letter of mine; I am not desirous of making a confidant of the public.

Oh! Russell, since I last wrote to you, what changes have taken place, in all that was dear and interesting to us!—and in these changes, how much is there at once to depress and to cheer. Great spirits have passed away, but others, that have been "standing on the forehead of the age to come,"[19] have advanced with the age; and life seems renewed,— with life,—out of death—proving that the Mind's Temple will ever be peopled, and its sublime service be ever going on. Do you still, after your sojourn in other climes, and "with other guess sort of people,"— do you still remember our old chat, in the old brown-panelled library, on Chaucer, Shakspeare, Spenser, Milton, and the after-trailing poetical lights; on Raphael and Titian, (the Spenser and Milton of painters); on Reynolds and Gainsborough, those early moderns; and on the Turner and the Stothard of our own day? And do you yet think of Handel, Mozart, and Haydn—those immortal masters of the learned and awful science of music? and can you forget Siddons and John Kemble? Never shall I, until this *greyish* head is put to rest for ever, forget the ardour, the partizanship, the affection, with which we agreed or differed on the mighty masters of poetry, painting, music, and the drama; and I cannot resist, in this letter, briefly touching on the losses and gains which the Arts, or rather the *Natures*, have suffered, since we last wrote to or conversed with each other. I, as you know, am now an active partner in the great bustling firm of the world; but, never to me will these divine topics, and the recollections of them, be other than the soul's comfort:—

> Not harsh and crabbed, as dull fools suppose,
> But musical as is Apollo's lute;
> And a perpetual feast of nectar'd sweets,
> Where no crude surfeit reigns![20]

Since I wrote to you, Byron—the daring, glaring, scaring Byron,— the pathetic, the unbelieving, the believing Byron,—the melodious, the moody, the pointed, the severe poet and Lord (for the nobility of the aristocrat struggled with the divinity of the poet, like Jacob with the Angel,) Byron, the splendid bard, the haught peer, the kindliest of men, has, since last we met, given Moore an opportunity of creating a Biography, and destroying an Autobiography.[21] Moore's Life is not *the* life. The true work is not yet achieved; and I fear, much as I like the Irish Melodist, that he will be rather remembered (as far as Byron-biography goes) for his destruction than for his creation. The destroyer of the Ephesian dome is remembered when the builder is forgotten.[22] Our poetical losses have been severe. Scott, "the Ariosto of the North," has sought the South—not to create poetry, but to seek health in a fame-crowned old age, and, perchance, to add one more long last novel to the rare catalogue of his romantic tales; wrung from him by "wearisome petition" of interested friends, or disinterested publishers.[23] There should—I say it in the sincerity of my heart—there should be no more! He has made Fame rich—he has left to her large and immortal possessions; in Literature, he "'gins to be a-weary of this life!" and he should not hazard his vast wealth by speculations, in times when his energies must, perforce, be not what they have been. As an author, he should use to the baby-writers about him, the last words of the old dying schoolmaster—"It grows dark! shut the book! boys, go and play!"

You will naturally ask me, in what way have our great vacancies been filled up; and I wish I could give you a satisfactory explanation. We have had accessions to our force of authorship; but then we have had no Wellingtons—no Marlboroughs—none above corporals or serjeants. L.E.L., a young lady of letters, has been for some years amorous and botanical;[24] but she clearly proves the truth of what one of her rose-predecessors has said, that "not even Love can live on flowers!"—

420

Passion smothered in lilies, is passion smothered to all intents and purposes: I wish we could have a leek and onion poet by way of a change. L.E.L. may be very amiable, but she looks upon all her readers as Children in the Wood, and hastens as quickly as possible, tenderly to "cover them with *leaves!*"[25]

There has been a sad waste of paper in new novels after the last fashion,—and, as Penruddock says, "Heaven send it may be the *last!*"[26] Since you left England, an enterprising publisher, of the name of Colburn, has issued sheets to the gluttonous world amply sufficient to paper the walls of the temple in which Martin has so splendidly depicted Belshazzar's feast,[27] or make a carpet for Salisbury plain. Fashion, or the apeing of fashion, has been the fashion in Literature; and no novel or poem would pass muster, unless completely furnished with titles, French phrases, silver forks, and bad English. I believe, Russell, that this *mode* of writing had its origin in the success of Lord Byron, who, setting the example of a Peer intertwining the laurel with the coronet, induced Debrett's great staring flock to consider that Literature was essential to the dignity of the Peerage.[28] Indeed, "the nobility and gentry" have of late patronized the publishers very extensively; and Mr. Colburn has now scarcely an author whose name is not to be found in the "Court Guide."

Mr. Bulwer, M.P., is perhaps the most popular novelist of the last ten years, and will, I verily believe, enjoy the immortality of another ten years. But, oh! Russell, how very much has fame fallen in the market, since the time of our early intercourse. This, I presume, is owing to the free-trade system; for since every person, even a Peer, may wag a pen for pay, a name is bought and sold in a week. Mr. Bulwer is considered the great polished Newgate novelist of the day:—his slang is so satin-ny in its texture, that it may be worn by the most delicate and fashionable of the softer sex; he can introduce Bob Booty,[29] in all the glory of oaths and side curls, to the Duchess of Bedford, without damaging the character of either great personage; and his Shock-Jem can visit the Jersey, and not be out of place. There is hardly a production from the pen of Mr. Bulwer, that is not redolent of the back slums; and his pictures, I assure you, are dark, glossy, coarse—everything but true. I quite long for his stories on Jerry Abershaw;[30] and on the murderer of the Marrs;—Patch, too, would make a pretty pattern.[31] Mr. Bulwer is now Editor of the *New Monthly Magazine*—avowedly so.[32] You will grieve to hear that both Charles the Tenth and Campbell have been dethroned since last I wrote to you.

I did intend to take a very learned review of all that has been done and undone in Literature during the last ten years; and then to have gone very laboriously and minutely through the history of the achievements and disgraces in the Fine Arts, in Music, and in the Drama;—but I must not teaze you with a long letter at the commencement of our *re*-correspondence. After a long fast, the appetite must be tenderly dealt with. In my next letter I will discourse with you on these great matters; and, I promise you, "much remaineth for a second fytte!"

The Ladies, I should tell you, have been dealing largely and profitably at the shop of the Muses. And the Hon. Mrs. Norton, a descendant from the great sire of Tom Sheridan and the "School for Scandal," has been proving that she has some of the true *ink* in her veins, and has *taken down* several big boys in Mr. Colburn's Great Burlington School.[33] Mrs. Hemans, too, has been kindly noticed by Mr. Murray, and has accomplished the difficult feat of a second edition.[34] Apollo is beginning to discharge his retinue of sprawling men-servants, and to have handmaids about his immortal person, to dust his rays and polish his bow and fire-irons. If the great He-Creatures intend to get into place again, they must take Mrs. Bramble's advice, and "have an eye to the maids."[35]

How are our old friends the Mortons? I intend calling upon them shortly—only I shall look about me as despondingly and reflectingly in that long-deserted mansion of theirs, as did Penruddock, when he stood in the splendid hall of his ancestor, and thought of his solitude, his cot, and his old familiar cobwebs.[36] Write to me soon, if I have not outwearied you, and I will undertake that my prose, like papers in a periodical, shall "be continued in my next."

Ever yours, my dear Russell,

Edward Herbert.

P.S. Newspapers, or rather Literary Papers, are falling in price. I hear there is a Journal published somewhere in London for Fourpence![37]

ESSAY FROM *THE NEW SPORTING MAGAZINE*

From Lamb and Pitman's Racquet Match.—Van Amburgh the Lion-tamer; the Mind, the Eye, and the Muscle.[1] *October 1838*

Masters! you ought to consider with yourselves;—to bring in, God shield us! a lion among ladies, is a most dreadful thing: for there is not a more fearful wild-fowl than your lion, living; and we ought to look to it.

Shakspeare.[2]

I would not miss the match for a thousand pounds.

The Road to Ruin.[3]

For a sportsman (and we speak this in the enlarged sense of the term) to see any thing supremely well done is the perfection of human pleasure —and we have, within the last few months, been present at two exhibitions of extreme power and lithe beauty, not, we will venture to say, to be outdone by any breathing beings in this our *little village*. There is always something of poetry in trained and active corporeal power;— Lord Byron described dancing, as "the poetry of motion;" but other exercises may well come under this description. Some of the attitudes of the pugilist and the wrestler are the *Homeric* or the *Miltonic* poetry of motion—as dancing is the Spenserian;—fencing is the *Martial*—or epigrammatic;—quoits are the *Rural* (after Clare and Bloomfield);— cricket is, perhaps, the Dramatic;—and the Barclay match[4] the Epic;— and oh! no one that had a soul for this peculiar poesy could have been dull to its influences at the times of their several displays on the occasions to which we have referred.

Our readers will now perchance be in the dark as to the subjects of our eulogy, and it is high time that we should possess such readers with the knowledge of them. A smile will perchance rise upon the reader's face at our coupling objects so opposite in name and nature as those we are about to introduce to him, but in these pages we reconcile "violentest contrarieties,"—and we feel it even natural to make "The *Lion* lie down with the *Lamb*."

We have seen,—for we must "leave our damnable faces and begin:" We have seen recently the great match at Racquetts (this word sounds like bathos after the "Hercules vein" of our opening, but the bathos is in the word and not in the subject) between Lamb and John Pitman. And we have also seen the power of Van Amburgh over lions—"*living lions*" (as Ducrow[5] impressively urges it), Bengal tigers, leopards, and panthers; and the two displays of inflexible resolution, muscular strength, and flexibility, calm self-possession, and above all, Eye-fascination,* are not to be surpassed in any possible human art, exercise, or mental accomplishment through the agency of the body.

* We intimately know a gentleman, who, with two others—one of them being Keats the deceased poet, and the other a gentleman now distinguished in the wise advancement of cheap and valuable literature—was once put in imminent peril in a field where a dangerous bull was pastured.[6] The cows were feeding leisurely around, but the bull met the party with his nose to the earth and with growls of fearful threatening. The trio only escaped by settled nerve, and *the power of the eye*; for they walked round the beast's lowered and menacing head within two yards of it's terror—composedly, slowly, and with fixed gaze on his eyes. Here the power of the well-nerved and *basilisk* organ perfected safety; for on reaching the farm-house, or a man from it, it was ascertained that a person had been previously (and but a short time previously) frightfully gored and savaged.—And he suffered this from attempted flight.

THE WRITINGS OF REYNOLDS

SELECTED BIBLIOGRAPHY

EDITOR'S NOTES

INDEX

THE WRITINGS OF REYNOLDS

PUBLISHED LETTERS

The Bookman, 64 (September 1923): 277–278. To Hood, dated March 13, 1840.

Champneys, Basil. *Memoirs and Correspondence of Coventry Patmore*. 2 vols. London, 1900. Two letters to P. G. Patmore, dated March 6 and 23, 1821, are included in the Appendix in vol. II.

Dilke, Charles W. *The Papers of a Critic, Selected by His Grandson, Sir Charles Wentworth Dilke, bart*. 2 vols. London, 1875. Two letters to Dilke, both dated February 15, 1831, I, 25–26.

Jones, Leonidas M. "New Letters, Articles, and Poems by John Hamilton Reynolds," *Keats-Shelley Journal*, 6 (Winter 1957): 98–101. Two letters to Haydon, dated August 26 and September 28, 1816, and a note to R. S. Mackenzie, dated September 21, 1844.

London *Times*, October 30, 1928, p. 19. To Francis Jeffrey, dated July 13, 1820.

Morgan, Peter F. "John Hamilton Reynolds and Thomas Hood," *Keats-Shelley Journal*, 11 (Winter 1962): 92–94. One letter to the printer of *The New Sporting Magazine*, dated February 1839. Two legal letters as Hood's solicitor to the attorney for A. H. Bailey, dated May 19, 1840, and March 26, 1841.

Rollins, Hyder E. *The Keats Circle, Letters and Papers, 1816–1878*. 2 vols. Cambridge, Mass., 1948. Contains the bulk of Reynolds' letters. A revised edition, which includes *More Letters and Papers of the Keats Circle* (1955), was published in 1965, too late for use in the preparation of this book.

MANUSCRIPT LETTERS

Leigh Browne Collection in the Keats Memorial House at Hampstead. To Mary Leigh, dated April 28, 1817. To Mary Leigh, undated. A joint letter by Reynolds, Bailey, and Rice to Sarah Leigh, dated November 24, 1815.

Houghton Library at Harvard: HCL. ENG. 936. II, 69. A note to Richard H. Barham, dated April 3, 1839.

Widener Library at Harvard. In a doctoral dissertation by Robert S. Newdick, "Studies in the Literary Works of Sir Thomas Noon Talfourd" (1930), a letter to Talfourd, dated May 1848. In 1930 the original was in the private collection of Major S. Butterworth, who then resided at Wood End, Queen's Crescent, Southsea, England.

MANUSCRIPT POEMS

By the kind permission of Mr. William R. Maidment, the Curator of the Keats Memorial House, and of Professor Willard B. Pope who catalogued the manuscript poems by Reynolds, I list all the poems in the Leigh Browne Collection which to the best of my knowledge were not published. Since 20 of the total of 64 poems by Reynolds in the collection have been located in various contemporary periodicals, it may well be that some of those listed here as unpublished have merely evaded the search of Reynolds scholars.

"Here around the Tower Decayed"
"Hoc Erat in Votis"
"I Had a Dream of Tears"
"Inscription for Rocks" (in collaboration with Bailey)
"J. H. Reynolds to His Friend J[ames] R[ice]"
"Lines on the Dunscombe Cliffs"
"Lines Written to One of Haydn's Airs"
"Lines Written under a Picture of Mrs. Tighe"
"A Matin Song"
"Oh Take the Lute"
"On Life"
"Over the Stream the Wild Flowers Bend"
"The Pr[ince's] Address on His Return to Pall Mall"
"Soft was the Night"
"Song" ("Fair one take this rose")
"Song" ("Her lips' softest murmur")
"Song" ("Larks have their little wings unfurled")
"Song To Be Introduced in a Poem"
"The Sonnet of Memory"
"Sonnet to Sleep"
"Stanzas" ("I hate the crowd")
"Stanzas" ("Oh take away those weeping eyes")
"Stanzas" ("That star! how fair it stands above the tree")
"Stanzas" ("The air is still, the day is done")
"Stanzas" ("The morn is breaking")
"Stanzas" ("This is indeed a world of tears")
"Stanzas" ("Though sorrow tinged my early hours")
"Stanzas" ("Where is now the heart that beat")
"The Maiden I Remember Now"
"The Moon Hath Shed"
"The Sun is Gone Down to the Western Sea"
"The Wolf That in Its Gloomy Solitude"
"Thy Feelings, the Flowers of Thy Bosom Faded"
"To ——" ("Lady! o'er thee I place this wreath")
"To ——" ("One tear to thee, my love!")
"To ——" ("Well—let us part—while part we may")
"To Ella" ("Well—if indeed that sigh be thine")
"To Friends"
"To Hope"
"To James Rice on His Birthday"
"To Maria"
"Touch Not That Harp"
"A War Song"
"Written in a Sister's Album"

Published Works

Except for the theatrical reviews and several unsigned literary reviews in *The Champion*, all the items listed below have been drawn from the following sources unless otherwise specified after an individual entry: George L. Marsh, "A Bibliography of the Writings of Keats's Friend Reynolds," *Studies in Philology*, 25 (October 1928): 491–510; Marsh, "Newly Identified Writings by John Hamilton Reynolds," *Keats–Shelley Journal*, 1 (January 1952): 47–55; and Leonidas M. Jones, "New Letters, Articles, and Poems by John Hamilton Reynolds," *Keats–Shelley Journal*, 6 (Winter 1957): 97–108.

The attribution of the theatrical reviews in *The Champion* requires some explanation. That Reynolds was a member of the staff of *The Champion* has long been known to Keatsian scholars. In *Life, Letters, and Literary Remains, of John Keats* (1848), Richard M. Milnes, who had consulted with Reynolds at length in preparing the book, explained a reference to the newspaper in one of Keats's letters as follows: "The 'Champion' herein mentioned was a periodical of considerable merit, in which Mr. Reynolds was engaged" (I, 91). Horace Smith listed Reynolds as a principal contributor in "A Graybeard's Gossip about His Literary Acquaintance," *New Monthly Magazine*, vol. 81 (1847), pt. 3, p. 415. Reynolds himself wrote Francis Jeffrey in 1820, "I wrote in the Champion newspaper during the years 1815 and 1816" (London *Times*, October 30, 1928, p. 19).

In 1928 George L. Marsh examined *The Champion* and found many articles and poems signed "J.H.R.," "I.H.R.," or "R.," all of which he assigned to Reynolds in "A Bibliography of the Writings of Keats's Friend Reynolds." In a subsequent article Marsh added to the list several unsigned poems in *The Champion* which also appear with Reynolds' signature or initials in the Leigh Browne Collection in the Keats Memorial House at Hampstead. Although the theatrical reviews during the period of Reynolds' connection with *The Champion* are not signed, Marsh concluded that Reynolds was "the paper's chief theatrical critic" for "possibly part of 1815 and certainly for 1816 and 1817" ("Newly Identified Writings," p. 49).

Keats's letters show that Reynolds was the dramatic critic for *The Champion* in December 1817 (I, 191, 195–196, 199, 201), but there is no external evidence to indicate when he began to serve in that capacity other than his own statement to Jeffrey that he wrote generally for the paper in 1815. Fortunately, evidence within the newspaper makes it possible to set the date with reasonable certainty. During 1815 Thomas Barnes wrote most of the theatrical reviews over the signature "S*," as we know from Derek Hudson's identification of that signature in *Thomas Barnes of the Times* (Cambridge, England, 1943), p. 21. The last theatrical column signed "S*" appeared on November 19, 1815. No theatrical reviews are included in the issues of November 26 and December 3. Since there are no articles signed "S*" after December 3, it seems probable that Barnes severed his connection with the journal at that time.

In the issue of December 10, 1815 (misdated as December 9), the first article initialed by Reynolds appeared in the Literature section. The theatrical review of the same week is unsigned, and the style suggests Reynolds' hand. In the review of the next week, there is demonstrable evidence of Reynolds' authorship in the following passage: "Many plays of Webster, Decker, Heywood, Marston, and Ford, can easily be fitted for the stage,—particularly those of the latter. The character of Calantha in *The Broken Heart*, for instance, is full of that pensive sorrow and silent dignity which Miss O'Neill so well pourtrays. Ford is a delightful poet;—he leads the heart about at will. Shakspeare does not surpass him in descriptions of quiet heart-breaking grief. His fancy too, is exquisitely rich. The contention between the nightingale and the musician in *The Lover's Melancholy* is beautifully told" (December 17, 1815, p. 405).

In two articles "On the Early Dramatic Poets," which he initialed in *The Champion* of January 7, 1816, pp. 6–7, and March 3, 1816, p. 70, Reynolds criticized all the dramatists mentioned in the quotation above except Webster and Heywood. In the second article he also promised to include remarks on Webster and Heywood in a later essay, though no later essay on the subject appeared. Reynolds' discussion of Ford in the second initialed article makes it clear that he also wrote the review of December 17, 1815. Compare the following passage with the quotation given above: "Ford is the Poet of these Elizabethan dramatists other than Shakspeare and Jonson most after our own hearts ... the contest between the Lover and the Nightingale ... is delicious ... He is quite equal to Shakspeare (and this is giving the fulness of praise) in his delineation of the rapturous attachment of youthful souls, and the lonely and fatal sorrows which time heaps on it ... *Calantha* is the perfection of female character; —she has the mind of a hero, with the heart of a woman,—and her intense feeling can only be equalled by her patient and silent suffering" (March 3, 1816, p. 70). Reynolds also praised Ford's description of the nightingale in his initialed essay on Chaucer, "The Reader, No. IV," *The Champion*, May 26, 1816, p. 166.

It seems reasonably certain, therefore, that Reynolds had been engaged by December 10, 1815, as a regular member of the staff to replace Barnes and that as the regular theatrical critic he wrote nearly all the notices through December 28, 1817. Occasionally he was relieved by substitutes. For April 14, 1816, Coleridge wrote "Critical Portraits of Actors: Mr. Terry, No. I," signed "Satyrane," a pseudonym he had used earlier in "A Tombless Epitaph" (l. 1) and for the series of letters in *The Friend*, which he republished in *Biographia Literaria*. This hitherto unidentified article by Coleridge undoubtedly resulted from Wordsworth's suggestion to the editor John Scott on February 25, 1816, that he "procure assistance" to allow himself more time to write poetry (*The Letters of William and Dorothy Wordsworth, the Middle Years*, ed. Ernest de Selincourt, 2 vols., Oxford, 1937, II, 712). Coleridge's assistance was short-lived, however, since no further articles from his pen appeared in the theatrical columns. That Reynolds resumed his position as regular theatrical critic the next week is revealed by the peculiar praise of Chaucer's ability to describe a leaf which appears both in that article of April 21, 1816, and in an initialed essay ("The Reader, No. IV," *The Champion*, May 26, 1816, p. 166).

When Reynolds took a vacation in Devonshire from August 26 through early October 1816, he was again relieved by one or more substitutes. The theatrical department was conducted somewhat irregularly. There was no review for September 1, but for the issue of September 8 Reynolds sent a long review of the Exeter theater. The notice of September 15 is by an unknown hand, while from September 22 through October 6 W. Carey substituted as the theatrical critic under the pseudonym "Algarotti"—identified in *The Annals of the Fine Arts*, 3 (1818): 512. Reynolds announced his return in the review of October 13.

In the next year, on August 24, 1817, Hazlitt substituted for one week with an unsigned article entitled "The Opera" (p. 269). No one has previously noticed that this article, which Hazlitt later reprinted over his signature in *The Yellow Dwarf*, was first published in *The Champion*. Since the standard practice in *The Champion* was for one author to write all the theatrical material for one week, it is very probable that

Hazlitt also wrote the other portion of the theatrical section, The English Opera House, an essay, entitled "Fire and Water," which has not heretofore been assigned to him.

Finally, just before he left the staff, Reynolds climaxed his singular good fortune in securing substitutes by persuading Keats to write the articles for December 21, 1817, and January 4, 1818. For a full discussion of Keats's contributions, see my "Keats's Theatrical Reviews in the Champion," Keats–Shelley Journal, 3 (Winter 1954): 55–65.

Except for the work of these substitutes, all the theatrical articles in The Champion from December 10, 1815, through December 28, 1817, have been attributed to Reynolds in this bibliography, since it seems reasonable to conclude, in the absence of any evidence to the contrary, that while he was the theatrical critic, he wrote the theatrical criticism. The omission of theatrical entries for some dates should not be ascribed to arbitrary exclusion; sometimes The Champion simply omitted the theatrical section.

"Ode to Friendship," The Gentleman's Magazine, vol. 82, pt. 2 (October 1812), p. 366. Signed "J.H.R."

Letter to the editor pointing out the similarity between a stanza by Anna Seward and an earlier one by Anne Finch, Countess of Winchelsea, The Gentleman's Magazine, vol. 82, pt. 2 (Supplement for 1812), p. 607. Signed "J.H.R."

"Lines to a Sister on Her Birthday," The Gentleman's Magazine, vol. 83, pt. 1 (February 1813), p. 160. Signed "J.H.R."

Safie. An Eastern Tale. London, 1814.

"A Paraphrase of Catullus's Address to His Vessel" (verse), The Inquirer, or Literary Miscellany, May 1814, p. 17. Signed "J.H.R."

"On the Character of Hamlet," The Inquirer, May 1814, p. 94. Signed "J.H.R."

"Stanzas to ✱✱✱," The Inquirer, May 1814, p. 104. Signed "J.H.R."
The same poem later appeared under the title "The Memory of the Beloved" in The London Chronicle, January 23/24, 1817, where it was again signed "J.H.R."

The Eden of the Imagination. A Poem. London, 1814.

"The Song of a Spanish Lover to His Mistress," The Inquirer, January 1815, p. 332. Signed "J.H.R."

"The Hand" (verse), The Gentleman's Magazine, vol. 85, pt. 1 (January 1815), p. 63. Signed "J.H.R."

"Sonnets to Greece" (two), The Champion, July 13, 1815. Unsigned, but they appear with Reynolds' initials in the Leigh Browne Collection.

An Ode. London, 1815.

Covent Garden Theatre, "The Orphan." Drury Lane Theatre, "The Honey-Moon." The Champion, December 10, 1815 (misdated as December 9), p. 397.

"Mr. Wordsworth's Poetry," The Champion, December 10, 1815, p. 398. Signed "R."

Covent Garden Theatre, "The New Comedy of Smiles and Tears." Drury Lane Theatre, "The Beggar's Bush: or, The Merchant of Bruges." The Champion, December 17, 1815, p. 405.

Drury Lane Theatre, "My Spouse and I," The Champion, December 24, 1815, p. 413.

"The New Pantomimes," The Champion, December 31, 1815, p. 421.

"Sonnet to Greece," The Champion, December 31, 1815. Signed "R.H.S.," but it appears in the Leigh Browne Collection with Reynolds' initials.

Drury Lane Theatre, "The Busy Body." "Othello;—Mrs. Barnes in Desdemona." The Champion, January 7, 1816, p. 5.

"On the Early Dramatic Poets," *The Champion*, January 7, 1816, pp. 6–7. Signed "R."

Drury Lane Theatre, "A New Way to Pay Old Debts," *The Champion*, January 14, 1816, p. 13.

Covent Garden Theatre, "A Midsummer Night's Dream," *The Champion*, January 21, 1816, p. 21.

Drury Lane Theatre, "Love for Love," *The Champion*, January 28, 1816, p. 29.

"Sonnet" ("Yes!—I have had my troubles,—For this heart"). Dated February 3, 1816, and signed "John Hamilton Reynolds" in the Reynolds Commonplace Book in the Bristol Central Library. Printed in Paul Kaufman, "The Reynolds–Hood Commonplace Book: a Fresh Appraisal," *Keats–Shelley Journal*, 10 (Winter 1961): 50.

Drury Lane Theatre, "Accusation; or the Family of Anglade." Covent Garden Theatre. *The Champion*, February 4, 1816, p. 37.

Covent Garden Theatre, "Measure for Measure," *The Champion*, February 11, 1816, p. 45.

Drury Lane Theatre, "Rosina—The Misses Halford." "A New Way To Pay Old Debts." "Macbeth." *The Champion*, February 18, 1816, p. 54.

"Stanzas Composed under an Oak That Grows over a Brook in Bradgate Forest," *The Champion*, February 18, 1816, p. 54. Signed "J.H.R."

"Sonnet to Wordsworth," *The Champion*, February 18, 1816, p. 54. Signed "J.H.R."

Drury Lane Theatre, "The Recruiting Officer." "What Next?" *The Champion*, March 3, 1816, p. 69 (mispaged as 59).

"On the Early English Dramatists, No. II," *The Champion*, March 3, 1816, p. 70. Signed "J.H.R."

Covent Garden Theatre, "The Fair Penitent—Miss O'Neill," *The Champion*, March 10, 1816, p. 78.

"To Spenser" (sonnet), *The Champion*, March 10, 1816, p. 78. Signed "I.H.R."

Drury Lane Theatre, "The Duke of Milan." Covent Garden Theatre, "Guy Mannering." *The Champion*, March 17, 1816, p. 85.

Covent Garden Theatre, "The School for Scandal," *The Champion*, March 24, 1816, p. 94.

"The Pilgrimage of Living Poets to the Stream of Castaly," *The Champion*, April 7, 1816, p. 110. Signed "J.H.R." Copied in *The British Lady's Magazine*, 3 (June 1816): 418–420, where it was again signed "J.H.R." Also reprinted as a preface to *British Melodies*, Norwich, ca. 1820.

Drury Lane Theatre, "Love in a Village.—Miss Nash in Rosetta," *The Champion*, April 21, 1816, p. 125.

Covent Garden Theatre, "Mr. Kemble's Re-appearance," *The Champion*, May 5, 1816, p. 141.

Drury Lane Theatre, "The New Tragedy of Bertram;—or, The Castle of St. Aldobrand," *The Champion*, May 12, 1816, p. 149.

Covent Garden Theatre, "The Jealous Wife;—Miss O'Neill as Mrs. Oakley," *The Champion*, May 19, 1816, p. 157.

Covent Garden Theatre, "The New Tragedy," *The Champion*, May 26, 1816, p. 165.

"The Reader, No. IV" (on Chaucer), *The Champion*, May 26, 1816, p. 166. Signed "J.H.R."

"The Reader, No. V" (on egotism in literature), *The Champion*, June 2, 1816, pp. 173–174. Signed "J.H.R."

"The Reader, No. VII" (on *The Spectator*), *The Champion*, June 16, 1816, p. 190. Signed "I.H.R."

Covent Garden Theatre, "Pizarro.—Miss O'Neill in Elvira," *The Champion*, June 23, 1816, p. 197.

"To Ella" (verse), *The Champion*, June 30, 1816, p. 206. Signed "R."

The New English Opera House, "The Duenna," *The Champion*, June 30, 1816, p. 206.

"The Reader, No. IX" (on Milton), *The Champion*, July 7, 1816, p. 214. For evidence of Reynolds' authorship of this unsigned article, see the first note to the reprint of it in this book.

The Haymarket Theatre, "The Man of the World." The New English Opera House, "The Siege of Belgrade." Italian Opera. *The Champion*, July 7, 1816, pp. 213–214.

The Haymarket Theatre, "The Jealous Wife, &c.," *The Champion*, July 14, 1816, p. 221.

The Haymarket Theatre, "The Heir at Law." The New English Opera House, "Artaxerxes." *The Champion*, July 21, 1816, pp. 229–230.

"From the Italian" (verse), *The Champion*, July 21, 1816, p. 230. Signed "J.H.R." Reprinted without signature in *The London Chronicle*, July 25/26, 1816.

The Haymarket Theatre, "Exit by Mistake." The New English Opera House, "A Man in Mourning for Himself." *The Champion*, July 28, 1816, p. 237.

"The Fairies" (verse), *The Champion*, August 4, 1816, p. 245. Signed "J.H.R."

The New English Opera House, "Artaxerxes—Mr. Incledon," *The Champion*, August 18, 1816, p. 261.

The Naiad: A Tale. With Other Poems. London, 1816.

The New English Opera House, "The Beggar's Opera," *The Champion*, August 25, 1816, p. 270.

The Exeter Theatre, *The Champion*, September 8, 1816, p. 285 (mispaged as 277).

"The Purple Beech" (verse), *The Champion*, September 15, 1816, p. 294. Signed "E.L.A.," but it appears with Reynolds' initials in the Leigh Browne Collection.

Drury Lane Theatre, "The First Part of Henry the Fourth.—Mr. Stephen Kemble in Falstaff." Covent Garden Theatre, "The Broken Sword." *The Champion*, October 13, 1816, pp. 325–326.

"Popular Poetry—Periodical Criticism, &c.," *The Champion*, October 13, 1816, pp. 326–327. For evidence of Reynolds' authorship, see the first note to the reprint of the article in this book.

Covent Garden Theatre, "Othello—Mr. Macready," *The Champion*, October 20, 1816, p. 333.

"Wordsworth's Thanksgiving Ode," *The Champion*, October 20, 1816, pp. 334–335. The sequel to "Popular Poetry" of the preceding week.

Drury Lane Theatre, "Hamlet—Mr. Kean." "Each for Himself." *The Champion*, October 27, 1816, p. 341.

Drury Lane Theatre, "Timon of Athens." Covent Garden Theatre, "Coriolanus.—Miss O'Neill and Mr. Kemble." *The Champion*, November 3, 1816, p. 350.

Drury Lane Theatre, "The Guardians," *The Champion*, November 10, 1816, pp. 357–358.

Covent Garden Theatre, "The Slave," *The Champion*, November 17, 1816, pp. 365–366.

Drury Lane Theatre, "Mr. Horn and Miss Merry," *The Champion*, November 24, 1816, p. 373.

"The Reader, No. XVI" (prose description of scenes along the Exe river), *The Champion*, November 24, 1816, pp. 373–374. Signed "J.H.R."

"Sonnet to Haydon," *The Champion*, November 24, 1816, p. 374. Signed "J.H.R."

Drury Lane Theatre, "The Iron Chest.—Mr. Kean in Sir Edward Mortimer," *The Champion*, December 1, 1816, p. 381.

"Boswell's Visit," *The Champion*, December 1, 15, 1816, pp. 381–382 and 397–398. Signed "J.H.R." at the end of both installments.

Covent Garden Theatre, "King John—Miss O'Neill and Mr. Kemble," *The Champion*, December 8, 1816, p. 390.

"Sonnet" (on Hunt's *The Story of Rimini*), *The Champion*, December 8, 1816, p. 390. Signed "R."

Drury Lane Theatre, "Lionel and Clarissa—Miss Mangeon." "Nota Bene—A New Farce." *The Champion*, December 15, 1816, p. 397.

Drury Lane Theatre, "Ramah Droog." Covent Garden Theatre. *The Champion*, December 22, 1816, p. 405.

"To ——" ("My eye in silent rapture prais'd"), *The Champion*, December 22, 1816, p. 406. The poem appears with Reynolds' initials in the Leigh Browne Collection.

Covent Garden Theatre, "The Pantomimes." Drury Lane Theatre. *The Champion*, December 29, 1816, p. 414.

"Song. To Albion," *The Champion*, December 29, 1816, p. 414. Signed "J.H.R."

Drury Lane Theatre, "The Pantomime, Harlequin Horner." "The Mountaineers." *The Champion*, January 5, 1817, pp. 5–6.

Drury Lane Theatre, "The Wonder.—Mrs. Alsop," *The Champion*, January 12, 1817, p. 14.

Covent Garden Theatre, "The Humourous Lieutenant; or Alexander's Successes," *The Champion*, January 19, 1817, p. 21.

Drury Lane Theatre, "Oroonoko," *The Champion*, January 26, 1817, p. 29.

Covent Garden Theatre, "The Ravens; or, the Force of Conscience," *The Champion*, February 2, 1817, p. 38.

Drury Lane Theatre, "Mrs. Alsop," *The Champion*, February 9, 1817, p. 46.

"Lines" ("Through these still woods"), *The Champion*, February 9, 1817, p. 46. Signed "J.H.R."

"Stanzas. Suggested by One of the Idylls of Bion," *The Champion*, February 9, 1817, p. 46. Signed "J.H.R."

Covent Garden Theatre, "Mr. Booth in Richard III," *The Champion*, February 16, 1817, p. 53.

"The Arithmetic of Poetry," *The Champion*, February 16, 1817, p. 54. For evidence of Reynolds' authorship, see the first note to the reprint of the article in this book.

Drury Lane Theatre, "Othello. Mr. Kean and Mr. Booth," *The Champion*, February 23, 1817, p. 61.

"Sonnet to Keats, on Reading His Sonnet Written in Chaucer," dated February 27, 1817, in the Woodhouse Commonplace Book. Published by Willard B. Pope in "John Hamilton Reynolds, The Friend of Keats," *Wessex*, 3 (1935): 5. More readily available in the reprint in *Keats–Shelley Journal*, 6 (Winter 1957): 96.

Covent Garden Theatre, "The Stranger. Miss O'Neill," *The Champion*, March 2, 1817, p. 70.

Drury Lane Theatre, "A Cure for the Heart Ache. Mr. P. Fisher," *The Champion*, March 9, 1817, p. 77.

"Poems by John Keats," *The Champion*, March 9, 1817, p. 78.

Drury Lane Theatre, "Manuel." Covent Garden Theatre, "Mr. Booth in Sir Giles Overreach." *The Champion*, March 16, 1817, p. 85.

"Sonnet" ("O Poetry, thou fairer maid"), *The Champion*, March 23, 1817, p. 93. Signed "J.H.R."

Covent Garden Theatre, "Cymbeline," *The Champion*, March 23, 1817, pp. 93–94.

"Sonnet. Composed on Seeing an Unexpected Snowy Morning," *The Champion*, March 30, 1817, p. 102. Signed "J.H.R."

Covent Garden Theatre, "The Curfew," *The Champion*, March 30, 1817, p. 102.

Drury Lane Theatre, "The Double Gallant," *The Champion*, April 6, 1817, p. 110.

Covent Garden Theatre, "Robinson Crusoe." Drury Lane Theatre. *The Champion*, April 13, 1817, p. 117.

Covent Garden Theatre, "The Conquest of Taranto, or St. Clara's Eve," *The Champion*, April 20, 1817, p. 125.

Covent Garden and Drury Lane, "Mr. Kemble and Mr. Kean," *The Champion*, April 27, 1817, p. 133.

Drury Lane Theatre, "Mrs. Hill in Lady Macbeth," *The Champion*, May 4, 1817, p. 141.

"Ben Jonson," *The Champion*, May 4, 1817, p. 142. For evidence of Reynolds' authorship, see the first note to the reprint of the article in this book.

Covent Garden Theatre, "The Apostate," *The Champion*, May 11, 1817, p. 150.

Drury Lane Theatre, "Surrender of Calais," *The Champion*, May 18, 1817, p. 157.

Covent Garden Theatre, "Mr. Kemble," *The Champion*, May 25, 1817, p. 166.

Covent Garden Theatre, "Macbeth.—Mrs. Siddons," *The Champion*, June 8, 1817, p. 182.

The English Opera House, "The Election," *The Champion*, June 15, 1817, p. 189.

"Stanzas" ("When the days of the summer"), *The Champion*, June 15, 1817, p. 190. Signed "J.H.R."

Drury Lane Theatre, "No Song No Supper.—Miss Cubitt." The Italian Opera. *The Champion*, June 22, 1817, p. 197.

"Mr. Kemble," *The Champion*, June 29, 1817, p. 206.

Covent Garden Theatre, "The Exile—Miss Booth's Benefit," *The Champion*, July 6, 1817, p. 214.

Covent Garden Theatre, "Miss O'Neill—Desdemona." The Haymarket Theatre. *The Champion*, July 13, 1817, p. 222.

"Characters of Shakespeare's Plays.—By William Hazlitt," *The Champion*, July 20, 27, 1817, pp. 230–231 and 237. Although the review is unsigned in some volumes of *The Champion*, the first installment is signed "R." in the set in the British Museum.

The Haymarket Theatre, *The Champion*, July 27, 1817, p. 237.

"Devon" (verse), *The Champion*, July 27, 1817, p. 238. Signed "J.H.R."

The Haymarket Theatre, "Teazing Made Easy." The English Opera House. *The Champion*, August 3, 1817, p. 245.

The English Opera House, "The Persian Hunters; or, The Rose of Gurgistan." The Haymarket Theatre, "The Actor of All Work." *The Champion*, August 17, 1817, p. 261.

The Summer Theatres, *The Champion*, August 31, 1817, p. 277.

"Whence is the secret charm" (verse), *The Champion*, August 31, 1817, p. 278. Signed "J.H.R."

Drury Lane Theatre, "Wild Oats. Mr. Stanley." Covent Garden Theatre, "The Belle's Strategem.—Miss Brunton." *The Champion*, September 14, 1817, p. 293.

Covent Garden Theatre, "Miss Brunton," *The Champion*, September 21, 1817, p. 301.

Drury Lane Theatre, "The Suspicious Husband," *The Champion*, September 28, 1817, pp. 308–309.

Covent Garden Theatre, "The Youthful Days of Frederick the Great." "Miss Brunton." *The Champion*, October 5, 1817, p. 317.

Drury Lane Theatre, "The Refusal." Covent Garden Theatre, "The Wonder." *The Champion*, October 12, 1817, p. 325.

Covent Garden Theatre, "She Stoops to Conquer." Drury Lane Theatre. *The Champion*, October 19, 1817, p. 333.

Covent Garden Theatre, "The Siege of Belgrade," *The Champion*, October 26, 1817, p. 341.

Drury Lane Theatre, "The Beggar's Opera. Miss Byrne." Drury Lane Theatre, "Othello." Covent Garden Theatre, "The New Melodrames and The Beehive— Mr. Denning." *The Champion*, November 2, 1817, pp. 349–350.

Covent Garden Theatre, "A Friend Indeed." Drury Lane Theatre. *The Champion*, November 9, 1817, p. 357.

"Zapolya. A Christmas Tale. By S. T. Coleridge," *The Champion*, November 16, 1817, p. 365. For evidence of Reynolds' authorship, see the first note to the reprint of the article in this book.

Covent Garden Theatre, "Miss O'Neill." Covent Garden Theatre, "Love, Law, and Physic.—Mr. Denning." *The Champion*, November 30, 1817, p. 381.

Drury Lane Theatre, "King Richard. Mr. Fisher," *The Champion*, December 7, 1817, p. 389.

Drury Lane Theatre, "Hamlet. Mr. D. Fisher." Drury Lane Theatre, "Lilliput." *The Champion*, December 14, 1817, p. 397.

Drury Lane Theatre, "Richard Duke of York." "Outwitted at Last." *The Champion*, December 28, 1817, p. 413.

"Pulpit Oratory, Nos. I, II, and III," *The Yellow Dwarf*, February 7, 14, 28, 1818, pp. 46–48, 51–53, and 67–68. Signed "Caius." William H. Marshall has demonstrated that Hazlitt wrote the fourth unsigned article of the series in "An Addition to the Hazlitt Canon: Arguments from External and Internal Evidence," *Papers of the Bibliographical Society of America*, 55 (1961): 347–370.

"Sonnets on Robin Hood" (two), *The Yellow Dwarf*, February 21, 1818, p. 64.

"To E——, With the Foregoing Sonnets" (on Robin Hood), *The Yellow Dwarf*, February, 21, 1818, p. 64.

"To F—— B——, Aged Three Years," *The Examiner*, June 14, 1818, p. 377. Signed "J.H.R."

"The Quarterly Review—Mr. Keats," *The Alfred, West of England Journal and General Advertiser* (published at Exeter), October 6, 1818. Reprinted in *The Examiner*, October 11, 1818.

"Mr Hazlitt's Lectures on the Comic Genius of England," *The Scots Magazine*, December 1818, January and February 1819, pp. 540–548, 12–14, and 143–148.

Peter Bell, A Lyrical Ballad. London, 1819.

One, Two, Three, Four, Five: By Advertisement. In *Cumberland's British Theatre.* London, no date. First acted at the English Opera House, July 17, 1819.

"Boswell Redivivus, A Dream," *The Scots Magazine*, October 1819, pp. 304–310. Signed "S.D."

Prologue to James Sheridan Knowles' *Virginius*. First acted at Covent Garden, May 17, 1820.

The Fancy, a Selection from the Poetical Remains of the Late Peter Corcoran, of Gray's Inn, Student at Law. With a brief memoir of his life. London, 1820.

"Living Authors, A Dream," *The Scots Magazine*, August 1820, pp. 133–140.

"The Jewels of the Book, Nos. I and II," *The London Magazine*, 2 (August and September 1820): 155–161 and 268–276.

"Exmouth Wrestling," *The London Magazine*, 2 (December 1820): 608–618.

The Garden of Florence and Other Poems. London, 1821.

"Warwick Castle," *The London Magazine*, 4 (July 1821): 5–13.

"The Drama," *The London Magazine*, 4 (July 1821): 81–85.

"Lamb's Translation of Catullus," *The London Magazine*, 4 (July 1821): 86–90.

"The Coronation, Letter from a Gentleman in Town, to a Lady in the Country," *The London Magazine*, 4 (August 1821): 184–196. Signed "Edward Herbert."

"The Drama," *The London Magazine*, 4 (August 1821): 196–202.

A letter signed "Edward Herbert" in "The Lion's Head," *The London Magazine*, 4 (September 1821): 235.

"The Champion's Farewell" (verse), *The London Magazine*, 4 (September 1821): 236.

"The Drama," *The London Magazine*, 4 (September 1821): 319–323.

"A New Hymn-Book," *The London Magazine*, 4 (September 1821): 323–325.

"The Cook's Oracle," *The London Magazine*, 4 (October 1821): 432–439.

"Warner's Church of England Theology. Mock Manuscript Sermons," *The London Magazine*, 4 (November 1821): 516–517.

"Edward Herbert's Letters to the Family of the Powells. No. II. Greenwich Hospital," *The London Magazine*, 4 (November 1821): 527–538.

"The Drama," *The London Magazine*, 4 (November 1821): 549–555.

"The Drama," *The London Magazine*, 4 (December 1821): 666–672.

"The Drama," *The London Magazine*, 5 (January 1822): 90–95.

"Bradgate Park, the Residence of Lady Jane Grey," *The London Magazine*, 5 (February 1822): 166–174.

"The Drama," *The London Magazine*, 5 (February 1822): 179–184.

"The Green-Room. The Letters of Edward Herbert, No. III," *The London Magazine*, 5 (March 1822): 236–243.

"Faithless Sally Brown" (verse), *The London Magazine*, 5 (March 1822): 202–204. In collaboration with Hood. See Peter F. Morgan, "John Hamilton Reynolds and Thomas Hood," *Keats-Shelley Journal*, 11 (Winter 1962): 88.

"The Drama," *The London Magazine*, 5 (March 1822): 290–294.

"The Youthful Days of Mr. Mathews." A theatrical production for Charles Mathews, first acted on March 11, 1822. It was written by Reynolds and R. B. Peake, according to "The Manager's Note-Book," *The New Monthly Magazine*, 52 (January 1838): 73.

"The Drama," *The London Magazine*, 5 (April 1822): 395–397.

"The Drama," *The London Magazine*, 5 (May 1822): 481–484.

"Some Passages in the Life of Mr. Adam Blair," *The London Magazine*, 5 (May 1822): 485–490.

"Ode to a Sparrow Alighting before the Judge's Chambers, in Serjeant's Inn, Fleet-Street," *The London Magazine*, 6 (August 1822): 148.

"The Inside of a Stage Coach. Letters of Edward Herbert. No. IV," *The London Magazine*, 6 (August 1822): 163–166.

"Gil Blas! At 17, 25, 52." An operatic drama by Reynolds and Hood (?), first performed at the English Opera House on August 15, 1822. No printed version of the play has been discovered. Alvin Whitley questions Hood's share in "Thomas Hood as a Dramatist," *University of Texas Studies in English*, 30 (1951): 187–188.

"At Evening's Close," a song from "Gil Blas," printed in "The Drama," *The London Magazine*, 6 (August 1822): 187. That the poem is by Reynolds rather than some collaborator is proved by the fact that a clipping of the printed poem appears in the Reynolds Commonplace Book at the Bristol Central Library with "J.H.R." written in ink beneath it. An addition to the bibliographical articles cited in the headnote.

Another song from "Gil Blas," *The Literary Gazette*, August 17, 1822. An addition to the bibliographical articles cited in the headnote.

Another song from "Gil Blas," *The Drama; or Theatrical Magazine*, August 1822, p. 137. An addition to the bibliographical articles cited in the headnote.

"The Cockpit Royal. Edward Herbert's Letters to the Family of the Powells. No. V," *The London Magazine*, 6 (November 1822): 389–402.

"The Drama," *The London Magazine*, 6 (November 1822): 466–473.

"The Drama," *The London Magazine*, 6 (December 1822): 570–573.

"The Drama," *The London Magazine*, 7 (January 1823): 99–103.

"The Literary Police Office, Bow-Street. Edward Herbert's Letters to the Family of the Powells. No. VIII," *The London Magazine*, 7 (February 1823): 157–161.

"The Drama," *The London Magazine*, 7 (February 1823): 195–199.

"The Loves of the Angels. By Thomas Moore," *The London Magazine*, 7 (February 1823): 212–215.

"Abridgement of Paradise Lost for the Use of Young Persons. By Sarah Siddons," *The London Magazine*, 7 (February 1823): 216.

"The Drama," *The London Magazine*, 7 (March 1823): 354–358.

"Mr. Kemble," *The London Magazine*, 7 (April 1823): 449–460.

Extracts from B. W. Procter's *The Flood of Thessaly*, with a few sentences of introduction, in "The Miscellany," *The London Magazine*, 7 (April 1823): 460–462.

"The Drama," *The London Magazine*, 7 (April 1823): 473–476.

Reply to a letter from William C. Macready in "The Lion's Head," *The London Magazine*, 7 (May 1823): 489–491. Overlooked by Marsh and Jones in earlier bibliographical accounts.

"A Parthian Peep at Life, An Epistle to R——d A——n," *The London Magazine*, 7 (May 1823): 525–526. Signed "Ned Ward, Jun."

"Spring Song," *The London Magazine*, 7 (May 1823): 533. Signed "E.W."

"The Drama," *The London Magazine*, 7 (May 1823): 558–562.

"Angling and Izaak Walton," *The London Magazine*, 7 (June 1823): 633–636. Signed "E.W."

"Ode to the Printer's Devil," *The London Magazine*, 7 (June 1823): 644–645. Signed "Ned Ward, Jun."

"The Flood of Thessaly, the Girl of Provence, and Other Poems. By Barry Cornwall," *The London Magazine*, 7 (June 1823): 669–672.

"The Drama," *The London Magazine*, 8 (July 1823): 101–102.

"The Drama," *The London Magazine*, 8 (August 1823): 212–215.

"The Drama," *The London Magazine*, 8 (September 1823): 321–324.
"A Chit Chat Letter on Men and Other Things" (verse), *The London Magazine*, 8 (October 1823): 361–364. Signed "Ned Ward, Jun."
"The Drama," *The London Magazine*, 8 (December 1823): 637–643.
"Stanzas to the Memory of Richard Allen," *The London Magazine*, 9 (January 1824): 35–36. Signed "Ned Ward, Jun."
"The Drama," *The London Magazine*, 9 (January 1824): 92–96.
"A Pen and Ink Sketch of a Late Trial for Murder, in a Letter from Hertford. By Edward Herbert, Esq.," *The London Magazine*, 9 (February 1824): 165–185.
"The Drama," *The London Magazine*, 9 (February 1824): 197–202.
"The Drama," *The London Magazine*, 9 (March 1824): 311–315.
"The Drama," *The London Magazine*, 9 (April 1824): 429–431.
"A Trip to America." Another dramatic piece for Charles Mathews, written by Reynolds and James Smith according to "The Manager's Note-Book," *The New Monthly Magazine*, 52 (January 1838): 78. That the sketch was performed shortly before April 1824 is indicated by Reynolds' comment on it in *The London Magazine*, 9 (April 1824): 430.
"The Drama," *The London Magazine*, 9 (May 1824): 567.
"The Drama," *The London Magazine*, 9 (June 1824): 671.
"The Drama," *The London Magazine*, 10 (July 1824): 89–91.
"Professor Wilson's Danciad," *The Westminster Review*, 2 (July 1824), 213–224.
"The Drama," *The London Magazine*, 10 (August 1824): 197–201.
"Vauxhall Meminiscences [*sic*]," *The London Magazine*, 10 (September 1824): 289–291 Signed "Ned Ward, Jun."
Odes and Addresses to Great People. London, 1825. Written in collaboration with Hood. Seven different divisions of the poems between the two have come to light with a multitude of conflicting claims. The vexing problem will doubtless never be solved beyond dispute. But of this much we can be certain: none of the records disagrees with the assigning of the following four poems to Reynolds alone: "Ode to Mr. M'Adam," "Address to Mr. Dymoke," "Ode to R. W. Elliston," and "Ode to the Dean and Chapter of Westminster." If John Payne Collier's report be dismissed as a faulty record of a conversation, "Ode to Sylvanus Urban" can be added to the four: both Hood and Reynolds agree on Reynolds' authorship in all other accounts. For the morass of claims on disputed poems and poems of joint composition, see Walter Jerrold, *Thomas Hood: His Life and Times* (London, 1907), pp. 163–165; M. Buxton Forman, ed., *The Letters of John Keats*, 4th ed. (London, 1952), p. xxxix; George L. Marsh, *John Hamilton Reynolds: Poetry and Prose* (London, 1928), p. 31; Alvin Whitley, "Keats and Hood," *Keats–Shelley Journal*, 5 (Winter 1956): 36; and Peter F. Morgan, "John Hamilton Reynolds and Thomas Hood," *Keats–Shelley Journal*, 11 (Winter 1962): 86–87.
"Sir Thomas Parkyns' Progymnasmata," *The Retrospective Review*, 11 (1825): 160–173.
"Memorandum Book." Another entertainment for Mathews by R. B. Peake and Reynolds, first performed on March 10, 1825.
"Remonstratory Ode from the Elephant at Exeter Change, to Mr. Mathews," *The London Magazine*, 11 (June 1825): 189.
"Four Sonnets, Composed during Ascot Race Week, By a Person of Sentiment," *The London Magazine*, 12 (July 1825): 443–445.

"A Free and Friendly Address to the Author of 'Odes and Addresses to Great People,' &c.," *The Literary Gazette*, March 15, 1828, p. 171. Signed "Sam Wildfun."

"Sonnet Copied from the Album of a Wholesale House in the City. By Edward Herbert, Esq.," Hood's *The Gem*, 1829, p. 24.

"The Pillory," Hood's *Comic Annual*, 1830, pp. 27–32.

"Sonnet to Vauxhall. By Edward Herbert, Esq.," *Comic Annual*, 1830, p. 38.

"To Fanny" (verse), *Comic Annual*, 1830, p. 85.

"The Royal Academy Exhibition," *The Athenaeum*, June 5, 12, 1830, pp. 347–348 and 363–364.

"The Oxonians; a Glance at Society," *The Athenaeum*, June 19, 1830, pp. 374–376.

"Various Subjects of Landscape from Pictures by John Constable, R.A.," *The Athenaeum*, June 26, 1830, p. 396.

"Water-Colour Exhibition," *The Athenaeum*, July 3, 1830, p. 412.

"The Juvenile Library. Lives of Remarkable Youth, of both Sexes," *The Athenaeum*, July 17, 1830, pp. 440–441.

"Mr. Kean's Benefit," *The Athenaeum*, July 24, 1830, p. 461.

"The Juvenile Library, Vol. II," *The Athenaeum*, August 14, 1830, pp. 497–498.

"Lines Written in a Lady's Album," *The Athenaeum*, August 21, 1830, p. 522. This poem appears in the manuscript "Poems by Two Friends" in the Leigh Browne Collection.

"Lines Written under the Foregoing," *The Athenaeum*, August 21, 1830, p. 522.

"National Library, No. I.—The Life of Lord Byron. By John Galt," *The Athenaeum*, September 4, 11, 1830, pp. 552–555 and 568–569.

"Conversations of James Northcote . . . by William Hazlitt," *The Athenaeum*, October 2, 23, 1830, pp. 611–612 and 662.

"Galt's Life of Byron," *The Athenaeum*, October 2, 1830, pp. 616–618. Editorial defense of the review of September 4, 11, 1830.

"Juvenile Library, No. III.—The History of Africa," *The Athenaeum*, October 23, 1830, pp. 657–659.

"The Gardens and Menagerie of the Zoological Society Delineated," *The Athenaeum*, October 23, 1830, p. 662.

"Maxwell: a Story of the Middle Ranks. By Hook," *The Athenaeum*, November 13, 1830, pp. 712–714.

"Twelve Sketches, Illustrative of Sir Walter Scott's Demonology and Witchcraft. By George Cruikshank," *The Athenaeum*, November 27, 1830, p. 749.

"The Comic Annual. By Thomas Hood," *The Athenaeum*, December 18, 1830, pp. 792–794.

"Letters and Journals of Lord Byron. By Thomas Moore," *The Athenaeum*, December 25, 1830 and January 1, 1831, pp. 801–804 and 1–6. In the marked file of *The Athenaeum*, no name is attached to the third notice of the same book on January 8, 1831, pp. 22–24.

"Miss Inverarity" (two poems with an introduction in prose), *The Athenaeum*, January 1, 1831, p. 10.

"On Ellar's Excellent Performance of Harlequin" (verse), *The Athenaeum*, January 1, 1831, p. 14.

"Military Memoirs of Field Marshal the Duke of Wellington. By Captain Moyle Sherer," *The Athenaeum*, January 8, 15, 22, 1831, pp. 17–18, 33–36, and 57. The second notice is marked "Swane and Reynolds" in the file.

"Children in the Wood (illustrated)," *The Athenaeum*, January 8, 1831, pp. 24–25.

Prologue to *Olympic Revels*, in *The Athenaeum*, January 8, 1831, pp. 28–29.

"Olympic Theatre.—Notice of Mis-Apprehension," *The Athenaeum*, February 5, 1831, p. 93.

"Attempts in Verse, by John Jones," *The Athenaeum*, February 26, 1831, pp. 130–132.

"Exhibition at the Suffolk St. Gallery," *The Athenaeum*, March 26, 1831, pp. 204–205.

"Royal Academy," *The Athenaeum*, May 14, 1831, pp. 315–316. The article is marked "Reynolds and Self" in Dilke's file. Two more articles on the same subject are not marked: May 21 and June 11, pp. 331 and 380.

"Matrimonial Advertisements," *The Athenaeum*, June 18, 1831, p. 395.

Accounts of the Newmarket, Epsom, and Ascot races, *The New Sporting Magazine*, I (May, June, and July 1831): 17, 113, and 198. Reynolds' authorship is established by Peter F. Morgan, "John Hamilton Reynolds and Thomas Hood," *Keats–Shelley Journal*, 11 (Winter 1962): 89–90.

"Lord Byron's 'English Bards and Scotch Reviewers,'" *The Athenaeum*, September 10, 1831, pp. 585–586.

"Journal of Richard Gossip, Esq., Manager, Dentist, Author, etc., etc.," *The Athenaeum*, October 1, 1831, p. 635.

"The Horseman's Manual," *The Athenaeum*, November 5, 1831, p. 720.

"Hood's Comic Annual for 1832," *The Athenaeum*, December 10, 1831, p. 799. A continuation of the review is not marked, December 17, p. 813.

"Byron's Letter to a Young Author," *The Athenaeum*, December 31, 1831, p. 841.

"The New Sporting Magazine," *The Athenaeum*, December 31, 1831, p. 847.

"Letters of Edward Herbert, New Series. No. I," *The Athenaeum*, January 7, 1832, pp. 5–6.

"Sonnet to Retirement," *The Athenaeum*, January 7, 1832, p. 8. Signed "J. H. Reynolds." It is a revised version of a sonnet first published in *The Fancy*.

"Lines to Clarkson Stanfield, on His Sketch of a Merchant in Venice," *The Athenaeum*, May 26, 1832, p. 336. Signed "J.H.R."

"Milton and Spenser. Sonnet to a Friend," *The Athenaeum*, July 7, 1832, p. 432. The poem appears in the Leigh Browne Collection. Reynolds finally published the poem which he had written seventeen years earlier. The friend was Benjamin Bailey.

"Lines to Miss F. Kemble on the Flower Scuffle at Covent Garden Theatre. By Curlpated Hugh," *The Athenaeum*, July 7, 1832, p. 436.

"Twenty-five Years in the Rifle Brigade," *The Athenaeum*, January 12, 1833, pp. 23–25.

"The Catechism of Whist," *The Athenaeum*, January 19, 1833, p. 40.

"A Right Conceyted Verse toe Master Hoode," *The Athenaeum*, January 19, 1833, p. 43. Signed "Thomas Brown."

The actress Frances Kelly's "Recollections." London, 1833. Attributed to Reynolds in Edith J. Morley, *Henry Crabb Robinson on Books and Their Writers*, 3 vols. (London, 1938), I, 424.

"Death of Edmund Kean," *The Athenaeum*, May 18, 1833, pp. 313–315.

"The Parson's Daughter. By Hook," *The Athenaeum*, June 1, 1833, pp. 339–341.

"Correspondence of Horace Walpole with Sir Horace Mann," *The Athenaeum*, June 8, 1833, pp. 354–357.

"A History and Description of Modern Wines," *The Athenaeum*, October 5, 1833, pp. 657–658.

"Love and Pride. By Hook," *The Athenaeum*, November 23, 30, 1833, pp. 785–786 and 804–805.

"Turfiana, No. I," *The New Sporting Magazine*, 6 (January 1834): 153–160. For the basis of the attribution of this article and of the subsequent articles in the Turfiana series, see the first note to the selection from *The New Sporting Magazine* in this book.

"Lives and Exploits of English Highwaymen, Pirates and Robbers," *The Athenaeum*, January 4, 1834, p. 6.

"Lines Written in a Lady's Album," *The Athenaeum*, May 31, 1834, p. 414.

"Unpublished Letters of Coleridge," *The Athenaeum*, October 18, 1834, p. 771.

"Ode to the Author of 'Bubbles from the Brunnens,'" *The New Monthly Magazine*, 42 (October 1834): 221–223.

"A Garland for Grisi," *The Athenaeum*, April 25, 1835, p. 322.

"The Life of Edmund Kean. By Barry Cornwall," *The Athenaeum*, May 30, June 6, 1835, pp. 401–403 and 428–430.

"The Comic Annual for 1836," *The Athenaeum*, December 12, 19, 1835, pp. 928–929 and 942–944. For this attribution, see Peter F. Morgan, "John Hamilton Reynolds and Thomas Hood," *Keats-Shelley Journal*, 11 (Winter 1962): 89, footnote 45.

"Attic Philosophy for 1836–37. By a Wealthy Pauper" (verse), *The Athenaeum*, December 31, 1836, pp. 918–919. Signed "R."

"Farewell to Charles Kemble" (verse), *The Athenaeum*, January 14, 1837, p. 33. Reprinted with slight variations in *Notes and Queries*, 4th series, 8: 408; and also in J. R. Planché, *Recollections and Reflections* (1901), p. 253.

"The Letters and Works of Lady Mary Wortley Montagu," *The Athenaeum*, January 21, 28, 1837, pp. 48–50 and 61–63.

Confounded Foreigners. A Farce in One Act. Vol. III of *The Acting National Drama*, ed. Benjamin Webster. London, no date. The play was first performed at the Haymarket on January 6, 1838.

A letter from Reynolds about his authorship of *Confounded Foreigners*, in *The Athenaeum*, January 20, 1838, p. 52.

"Trade-itional Confessions. No. I, The Pawnbroker," *The New Monthly Magazine*, 52 (February 1838): 199–212. Signed "H.R."

"Monosania. Mr. Klünchünbrüch," *Bentley's Miscellany*, 3 (March 1838): 267. Signed "J.H.R."

"A Legend of a Committee of Paviours" (verse), *The New Monthly Magazine*, 52 (April 1838): 562–565. Signed "J.H.R."

"Lamb and Pitman's Racquet Match.—Van Amburgh the Lion Tamer," *The New Sporting Magazine*, 15 (October 1838): 245–256. For the basis of this attribution, see the first note to the selection from *The New Sporting Magazine* in this book.

"Epsom Races" in *Sporting*, edited by "Nimrod" (Charles J. Apperley). London, 1838. Pages 75–83.

"Stanzas on Two Fox-hounds" in *Sporting*. Pages 105–107.

"Turfiana, No. II," *The New Sporting Magazine*, 16 (February 1839): 132–140.

"Turfiana, No. III," *The New Sporting Magazine*, 16 (April 1839): 253–265.

"Turfiana, No. IV," *The New Sporting Magazine*, 17 (September 1839): 196–200.

"Sonnet Written on the 21st of October, 1839, the Anniversary of the Battle of Trafalgar. By Edward Herbert," *Bentley's Miscellany*, 6 (November 1839): 542.

"Greenwich and Greenwich Men, with the Song of Trafalgar and Nelson," *Bentley's Miscellany*, 7 (February 1840): 279–289. Signed "J. H. Reynolds."

"Turfiana, No. V," *The New Sporting Magazine*, 18 (February 1840): 127–130.

"Oriana and Vesperella; or, The City of Pearls," *Ainsworth's Magazine*, 5 (January, February, March, and April 1844), 130–135, 242–247, 357–361, and 432–436. By "John Hamilton," Reynolds' pseudonym for *The Garden of Florence* (1821).

"An Ode-let, to Master Izaak Walton," *Ainsworth's Magazine*, 5 (June 1844): 403. Signed "John Hamilton."

"The Mouser Monarchy" (verse), *The New Monthly Magazine*, 75 (September 1845): 17–23. Signed "John Hamilton Reynolds."

"The Wall" (verse), *The New Monthly Magazine*, 78 (December 1846): 469. By "John Hamilton."

"On the Opening of the Ports of St. Paul's Cathedral and Westminster Abbey," *The New Monthly Magazine*, 79 (February 1847): 162–172. By "John Hamilton."

"Have You Heard a Lute? A Song," *The New Monthly Magazine*, 79 (February 1847): 248. By "John Hamilton."

"The Two Enthusiasts. No. I, The Enthusiast Dead. No. II, The Living Enthusiast" (verse), *Bentley's Miscellany*, 21 (February 1847): 209. By "John Hamilton Reynolds."

"The Dead Bird" (verse), *The Athenaeum*, January 29, 1848, p. 211. Signed "J.H.R."

"Written in a Lady's Album" ("An artist when he draws from nature"). This poem and the two following were printed without dates of composition by Dorothea M. R., Lady Charnwood from manuscripts in her possession in *An Autograph Collection and the Making of It* (London, 1930) and *Call Back Yesterday* (London, 1937). Signed "J.H.R."

"To Selima" ("Peace to thy bosom, Selima, my dove"). Signed "J.H.R."

"Imitation of Martial" ("Oh! Selima, why send the flower"). Signed "R."

"To T. Hood on Hearing of His Sickness." Undated and unsigned in the Reynolds Commonplace Book in the Bristol Central Library. Attributed to Reynolds and printed by Paul Kaufman in "The Reynolds-Hood Commonplace Book: A Fresh Appraisal," *Keats–Shelley Journal*, 10 (Winter 1961): 50–51.

SELECTED BIBLIOGRAPHY ON

THE BIOGRAPHY OF REYNOLDS

Byron, George Gordon, Lord. *The Works of Lord Byron, Letters and Journals*, ed. Rowland E. Prothero, Lord Ernle. 6 vols. London, 1898–1901. Contains Byron's letter praising *Safie* and Lord Ernle's account of Reynolds' deterioration in his last years.

Clare, John. *The Prose of John Clare*, edd. J. W. and Anne Tibble. London, 1951.

[Dilke, Charles W.] Obituary of Reynolds, *The Athenaeum*, November 27, 1852, p. 1296.

Dilke, Charles W. *The Papers of a Critic*, ed. Sir Charles W. Dilke. 2 vols. London, 1875.

[Dilke, Charles W.] "'Think of Me,' 'The Garden of Florence,' and John Hamilton Reynolds," *Notes and Queries*, second series, no. 40 (October 4, 1856), pp. 274–275.

Hood, Thomas. *The Works of Thomas Hood*, ed. Thomas Hood, Jr. 7 vols. London, 1862–1863. Memoir contains references to Reynolds. Works contain false ascription of "The Cook's Oracle" to Hood and correction of the error in the Appendix.

Howe, P. P. *The Life of William Hazlitt*. Third edition, London, 1947.

Jones, Leonidas M. "The Essays and Critical Writing of John Hamilton Reynolds." Unpublished dissertation, Harvard, 1952.

———— "New Letters, Articles, and Poems by John Hamilton Reynolds," *Keats–Shelley Journal*, 6 (Winter 1957): 97–108.

———— "Reynolds and Keats," *Keats–Shelley Journal*, 7 (Winter 1958): 47–59.

Marchand, Leslie A. *The Athenaeum, A Mirror of Victorian Culture*. Chapel Hill, North Carolina, 1941.

Marsh, George L. "A Bibliography of the Writings of Keats's Friend Reynolds," *Studies in Philology*, 25 (October 1928): 491–510.

———— ed. *John Hamilton Reynolds, Poetry and Prose*. London, 1928.

———— "New Data on Keats's Friend Reynolds," *Modern Philology*, 25 (February 1928): 319–329.

———— "Newly Identified Writings by John Hamilton Reynolds," *Keats–Shelley Journal*, 1 (January 1952): 47–55.

Morgan, Peter F. "John Hamilton Reynolds and Thomas Hood," *Keats–Shelley Journal*, 11 (Winter 1962): 83–95.

Pope, Willard B. "John Hamilton Reynolds, the Friend of Keats," *Wessex*, 3 (1935): 3–15.

———— "Studies in the Keats Circle; Critical and Biographical Estimates of Benjamin Robert Haydon and John Hamilton Reynolds." Unpublished dissertation, Harvard, 1932.

Rollins, Hyder E., ed. *The Keats Circle*. 2 vols. Cambridge, Massachusetts, 1948.

———— ed. *The Letters of John Keats*. 2 vols. Cambridge, Massachusetts, 1958.

———— ed. *More Letters and Poems of the Keats Circle*. Cambridge, Massachusetts, 1955.

Whitley, Alvin. "Keats and Hood," *Keats–Shelley Journal*, 5 (Winter 1956): 33–47.

Wordsworth, William. *The Letters of William and Dorothy Wordsworth, the Middle Years*, ed. Ernest de Selincourt. 2 vols. Oxford, 1937. Contains Wordsworth's letter to Reynolds criticizing *The Naiad*.

EDITOR'S NOTES

Essays and Literary Reviews from *The Champion*

1. Lines 369–372.
2. "Essay Supplementary to the Preface" of *Poems* of 1815, *The Poetical Works of William Wordsworth*, ed. Ernest De Selincourt (Oxford, 1944), II, 426, hereafter cited as *Works of Wordsworth*.
3. II, ii, 19–20. The line numbering is my own. In this and later cases of plays in verse where lines are not numbered, I have counted the lines to facilitate location of quotations.
4. II, ii, 29–49.
5. V, iii, 52–66.
6. II, ii, 61–70.
7. II, i, 345–362.
8. III, ii. 36–44.
9. II viii, 15–34.
10. I, vi, 84–94.
11. II, ii, 72–87.
12. I, i, 277–288.
13. II, i, 52–54.
14. *The Bondman*, IV, ii, 87–98.
15. V, ii, 68–77.
16. Reynolds never wrote, or at least never published, a third essay.
17. IV, iii, 16–23.
18. III, i, 1–2.
19. I, i, 104–106.
20. V, i, 205–218. There are variants from the 1613 text.
21. Like Hazlitt and Lamb, Reynolds accepted Marlowe's authorship of this play, which is now generally excluded from his works.
22. *Doctor Faustus*, ed. John D. Jump (Cambridge, Massachusetts, 1962), pp. 102–103, scene xix, ll. 176–190. Several words and phrases in Reynolds' quotation differ from this text.
23. II, ii, 200–205, 209–213. Reynolds omits without indication ll. 206–208.
24. III, i, 63–79.
25. In *'Tis Pity She's a Whore*. Reynolds' squeamishness in withholding the title anticipates amusingly the Victorian abbreviation of the title.
26. V, iii, 83–86.
27. *'Tis Pity She's a Whore*, V, v, 53–74.
28. "Of Nature in Men," *Essays* in *The Works of Francis Bacon*, edd. James Spedding, Robert L. Ellis, and Douglas D. Heath (New York, 1864), XII, 211.
29. Reynolds later incorporated this essay in a thoroughly rewritten form in "Living Authors, A Dream," *The Scots Magazine*, August 1820, reprinted in part below
30. Stanza 1, ll. 1—2.

31. A thrust at what Reynolds regarded as Southey's apostasy from the democratic principles of his early poetry.

32. William T. Fitzgerald (?1759–1829). Attacks on him in *Rejected Addresses* and *English Bards and Scotch Reviewers* had made him something close to a standing joke. Reynolds' "for his own use" refers to his practice of reciting his own verse at public dinners. The "small beer" probably derived from Byron's remark in a note to *English Bards and Scotch Reviewers*, l. 1, that William Cobbett had called him the "Small-Beer Poet."

33. A reference to the hymns of James Montgomery (1771–1854).

34. *The Pleasures of Hope* was published in 1799.

35. Campbell served both as lecturer on poetry and as critic for periodicals. Reynolds attended his lectures and described them later in "Living Authors, A Dream," *The Scots Magazine*, August 1820, reprinted below.

36. *The Story of Rimini* was published in 1816. Like Keats, Reynolds wrote a sonnet in praise of it.

37. Percy C. M. Smythe, Lord Strangford, translated *Poems from the Portuguese of Camoens* in 1803.

38. Lamb contributed four sonnets to Coleridge's *Poems* of 1796; Lamb and Charles Lloyd collaborated on *Blank Verse* in 1798.

39. William R. Spencer (1769–1834), writer of society verses, moved freely in aristocratic London circles.

40. William Hayley (1745–1820) was a fashionable versifier who is now best known as Blake's temporary patron.

41. John Wilson (1785–1854), later to be coeditor of *Blackwood's*, published *Isle of Palms* in 1812 and *The City of the Plague* in 1816.

42. William Lisle Bowles's (1762–1850) *Fourteen Sonnets* (1789) won the favor of a number of the Romantics, especially of Coleridge, who praised them lavishly and repeatedly. Bowles's indignant reply to Reynolds' satire is printed immediately after this essay.

43. Joseph Cottle (1770–1853) was a Bristol versifier, bookseller, and friend of Southey, Coleridge, and Wordsworth.

44. This letter is not reprinted in *A Wiltshire Parson and His Friends, the Correspondence of William Lisle Bowles*, ed. Garland Greever (London, 1926).

45. Lamb and Lloyd.

46. Bowles was probably thinking chiefly of Coleridge's extravagantly laudatory note to the sonnet "To the Rev. W. L. Bowles" in *Poems* of 1796. In the year after Bowles's letter to *The Champion*, Coleridge was to reaffirm the same extremely favorable judgment of Bowles's sonnets in *Biographia Literaria*.

47. *Il Penseroso*, ll. 109–110. Reynolds misquotes "untold" for "half-told," as he always does.

48. The mistaken attribution of the poem to Chaucer was common at the time. Cf. Keats's sonnet "On the *Flower and the Leaf.*"

49. Line 100.

50. Lines 109–112.

51. Line 109. Reynolds' mistaking of "not" (closely cropped) as "nut" makes him misinterpret the line.

52. Lines 97–98.

53. Lines 23–24.

54. Another non-Chaucerian piece commonly ascribed to Chaucer in Reynolds' day.

55. This is not Chaucer's statement of the argument. I have been unable to locate the source of this crisp summary.

56. Lines 63–64.

57. Lines 82–88.

58. Lines 393–394.

59. Lines 643–646.

60. Line 287.

61. Lines 1491–1496.

62. Lines 1987–1988.

63. Lines 1999–2007. Either Reynolds or the printer omitted l. 2006, probably inadvertently.

64. Line 2019.

65. Lines 2163–2164.

66. General Prologue, ll. 72, 822–823; Knight's Tale, l. 1451.

67. General Prologue, l. 746; Squire's Tale, ll. 34, 41; *Legend of Good Women*, l. 1557.

68. It is interesting to compare Reynolds' view on the subject with the related views of Keats, as expressed in the discussions of "negative capability," "the egotistical sublime," and the poet's identity. See *The Letters of John Keats*, ed. Hyder E. Rollins (Cambridge, Massachusetts, 1958), I, 193–194, 223–224, 386–388, hereafter cited as *Letters of Keats*.

69. After an attack on Wordsworth's egotism, Keats selects Jaques to set in contrast with the eccentrically private egotism of Wordsworth's Matthew "with a bough of wilding in his hand" (*Letters of Keats*, I, 224).

70. "Moods of My Own Mind" was a heading which Wordsworth gave to one of his groups of poems.

71. Misquoted from "those bright blue eggs" of "The Sparrow's Nest."

72. Probably William Hazlitt, whom Reynolds admired as much as Keats did. See Reynolds' review of *The Characters of Shakespeare's Plays* in *The Champion*, July 20, 27, 1817, reprinted below; "Mr Hazlitt's Lectures on the English Comic Writers," *The Scots Magazine*, December 1818 and January, February 1819, reprinted below; and "Living Authors, A Dream," *The Scots Magazine*, August 1820, reprinted below. Except in the review of *Characters of Shakespeare's Plays*, Reynolds seldom mentions Hazlitt by name in *The Champion*; in a theatrical notice, for example, he speaks of "the critic of the Times" (December 14, 1817).

73. *Ode: Intimations*, l. 178.

74. Obviously a printer's error for "J.H.R." Reynolds' handwritten capital "I's" and "J's" are often very difficult to distinguish.

75. Though this essay is not initialed, Reynolds' authorship is clearly indicated by the link between its first paragraph and the earlier initialed essay on Chaucer, May 26, 1816. See Reynolds' second note to his essay on Chaucer, reprinted above.

76. *Paradise Lost*, I, 535–551.

77. IV, 76.

78. *Paradise Lost*, V, 544–548.

79. III, 337–343.

80. *Paradise Lost*, V, 285–297.

81. *Ibid.*, IV, 236–240.

82. *Ibid.*, IV, 252–260.

83. Lines 391–395.

84. Reynolds quotes ll. 85–102. The passage is too long and too familiar to warrant reprinting here.

85. Lines 23–24.

86. Reynolds quotes *Paradise Regained*, III, 203–210; *Paradise Lost*, IV, 641–656; and I, 591–604. Again length and familiarity prevent reprinting.

87. Though this essay is not initialed, Reynolds' authorship is indicated by a reference in the second paragraph ("personal circumstances of interruption") to a long vacation he had recently spent at Exeter.

88. *Personal Talk*, ll. 27–28.

89. Wordsworth, "Essay Supplementary to the Preface" of *Poems* of 1815, *Works of Wordsworth*, II, 429.

90. Wordsworth, *Thanksgiving Ode* (1816).

91. *The Faerie Queene*, I, i, 1.

92. *Hamlet*, I, v, 34.

93. Cf. *The Tempest*, II, i, 173.

94. Still unidentified. Perhaps the editor, William Gifford, wrote the attack in 14 (January 1816): 473–481.

95. *The Faerie Queene*, I, v, 1–2.

96. Wordsworth, "Essay Supplementary to the Preface" of *Poems* of 1815, *Works of Wordsworth*, II, 428.

97. Reynolds is remarkably generous, if not fanciful, in attributing to Francis Jeffrey a basic admiration of Wordsworth, after Jeffrey's vigorous attacks on Wordsworth over a long period of years.

98. The poem was *Christabel*.

99. *A Midsummer Night's Dream*, V, i, 5–6.

100. *Ibid.*, V, i, 17–18.

101. Wordsworth, "Essay Supplementary to the Preface" of *Poems* of 1815, *Works of Wordsworth*, II, 426.

102. *Ibid.*, II, 428.

103. *Ibid.*, II, 425.

104. *Ibid.*, II, 428.

105. The date of publication is given: "January 18th, 1816." I relegate it to a note to avoid confusion with the date of the weekly *Champion*.

106. In this famous passage from the Preface to *Lyrical Ballads*, Reynolds of course misquotes "remembered" for "recollected."

107. "Preface to Lyrical Ballads," *Works of Wordsworth*, II, 396.

108. *Thanksgiving Ode*, ll. 1–35.

109. Milton. Of course much of Reynolds' critical case is based on the result of this jocular mystification.

110. *Samson Agonistes*, ll. 652–681.

111. John Scott, who was in Paris and would not see the article until it was already in print.

112. By Thomas Campbell (1799).

113. See *Goody Blake and Harry Gill*. Later Reynolds himself mocked the poem mercilessly in his parody of *Peter Bell*.

114. Byron wrote several poems entitled *Farewell*, but Reynolds probably means *Fare Thee Well*, the highly emotional poem to Bell after the separation, which had been first published openly in *The Champion* six months earlier.

115. First published in *The Examiner* earlier in the year, and sharply attacked by John Scott in his controversy with Hunt over the Byron separation.

116. "Essay Supplementary to the Preface" of *Poems* of 1815, *Works of Wordsworth*, II, 411.

117. *Ibid.*, II, 426.

118. *Laodamia*, l. 75.

119. *Thanksgiving Ode*, ll. 35–41.

120. *The Works of John Milton*, edd. Frank A. Patterson *et al.*, the Columbia edition (New York, 1932), X, 3.

121. *Thanksgiving Ode*, ll. 139–146.

122. These passages in the 1816 edition were excised in 1845 and revised as a separate poem. The revised versions appear in *Ode: 1815*, ll. 8–15 and 19–36.

123. In the enthusiasm of his admiration for Wordsworth at this time, this cautious reservation is as close as Reynolds could come to showing the political difference between Wordsworth's conservatism and his own liberalism. Later, after both he and Keats became disenchanted with certain aspects of Wordsworth, he spoke more forthrightly. For example, see the Preface to *Peter Bell*, reprinted below.

124. *Thanksgiving Ode*, ll. 137–144.

125. The first line serves as the title for this sonnet, written in 1803.

126. This essay was later republished in a revised and somewhat more diffuse form as "Boswell Redivivus, A Dream," *The Scots Magazine*, October 1819. Though the matter is debatable, I judge the earlier version the better one and therefore reprint it. I have taken the liberty of reparagraphing this essay. Reynolds' compression of all the conversation into one mammoth paragraph obscures the changes in speakers.

127. I, v, 125–126.

128. *Carmen*, XXXI, l. 10. Reynolds has just approached a translation, "And we repose in the wished-for bed." Catullus was Reynolds' favorite Latin poet. He had translated him loosely in "A Paraphrase of Catullus's Address to his Vessel," *The Inquirer, or Literary Miscellany*, May 1814, p. 17. Later he reviewed George Lamb's translation of Catullus, *The London Magazine*, 4 (July 1821): 86–90, where he again quoted this line.

129. V, iii, 40–42.

130. *Catalogue Raisonée of the Pictures Now Exhibiting at the British Institution* (1815) and *Catalogue Raisonée of the Pictures Now Exhibiting in Pall Mall* (1816) were anonymous attacks on the directors of the British Institution. The *Dictionary of National Biography* assigns both to the painter Robert Smirke (1752–1845). Reynolds' satire of the latter pamphlet was doubtless encouraged by Hazlitt's attacks in *The Examiner*, November 3, 10, 17, 1816, and by Haydon's disapproval (See *The Diary of Benjamin R. Haydon*, ed. Willard B. Pope, Cambridge, Massachusetts, 1960, II, 48, 65).

131. A narrative poem in the Spenserian stanza (1809).

132. Horace Twiss (1787–1849) published *Melodies of Scotland* (1814). After Reynolds and Keats met Twiss socially (*Letters of Keats*, I, 225n and II, 15), Reynolds eliminated this passage from the later version of the essay, "Boswell Redivivus."

133. *The Poetical Works of the Late Thomas Little, Esq.* (1802).

134. Moore's translation of the *Odes of Anacreon* (1800).

135. Byron's comment on *Christabel*, which was used to advertise the first edition of the poem. Reynolds also mocked the remark in "Popular Poetry—Periodical Criticism," October 13, 1816, reprinted above.

136. *The Quarterly Review.*

137. In 1802.

138. In John Gay's *The Beggar's Opera.*

139. The protagonist of Charles R. Maturin's tragedy of that title, which Reynolds had reviewed on May 12, 1816 See the dramatic review below.

140. Amos S. Cottle (1768?–1800) was the brother of Wordsworth's and Coleridge's friend Joseph, and the translator of the *Edda* of Saemund.

141. V, v, 17–18.

142. Joanna Southcott (1750–1814) was a religious fanatic, who prophesied that she would give birth to a new Messiah.

143. *Kubla Khan* and *The Pains of Sleep*, which were published along with *Christabel* in 1816.

144. After political service in both England and India, Sir Nathaniel W. Wraxall published *Historical Memoirs of My Own Time* in 1815.

145. *The Edinburgh* blistered Sir Nathaniel in 49 (June 1815): 178–220, of which this is a fair sample: "He is so perfectly regardless of the truth that we are convinced there is not a single anecdote in the book which can be safely believed on his testimony." In *An Answer to the Calumnious Misrepresentations of the Quarterly Review, the British Critic and the Edinburgh Review* (1815), Wraxall included the "questionable answer," "Is not a single anecdote to be believed?" *The Edinburgh* replied in 50 (October 1815): 527–541, with spirited raillery that it could not "on his testimony" alone.

146. Though this essay is not initialed, internal evidence suggests Reynolds' authorship strongly. It was published in the "Poetry" section, which Reynolds managed, and for which he wrote most of the material. The satire on Southey, Coleridge, and Byron is quite consistent with the treatment given them in "The Pilgrimage of Living Poets to the Stream of Castaly" and "Boswell's Visit." And the jesting about Cocker resembles that in "The Cock-Pit Royal," *The London Magazine*, 6 (November 1822): 395n.

147. *Epistle to Dr. Arbuthnot*, l. 128.

148. From Edward Cocker (1631–1675), author of numerous works on arithmetic.

149. *Othello*, I, i, 19.

150. 1693–1770? A clever rogue, who ran away from school and joined the gypsies.

151. *We Are Seven*, ll. 17–21. In the last line "dwell" is misquoted for "lie."

152. *The Thorn*, ll. 27–33. Reynolds quotes the last two lines inaccurately from the original version in *Lyrical Ballads*, "I've measured it from side to side;/ 'Tis three feet long and two feet wide." Wordsworth later changed those two lines, but probably because of Coleridge's criticism of them in *Biographia Literaria*, Chapter XVII, rather than because of Reynolds' ridicule.

153. *Christabel*, ll. 93–94.

154. *Ibid.*, ll. 9–12, misquoted in l. 11, "moonshine" for "by shine."

155. Lines 17–21.

156. Line 27.

157. *The Battle of the Baltic*, l. 14.

158. *The Lay of the Last Minstrel*, canto I, stanza III.

159. *Ibid.*, canto I, stanza V.

160. Though this article is not initialed, Reynolds' authorship is established by Keats's letter to him expressing gratitude of March 9, 1817, *Letters of Keats*, I, 123.

161. *Sleep and Poetry*, ll. 33–34.

162. Coleridge and Byron. Coleridge is attacked sharply for mystification in the review of *Christabel*, May 26, 1816, and for infecting poetry with metaphysics in "Boswell's Visit." The review of *The Prisoner of Chillon* for December 1, 1816, charged Byron with imitating Coleridge's mystification in *Darkness* and *A Dream*.

163. *I Stood Tip-toe*, ll. 36–37.

164. *Ibid.*, ll. 125–126.

165. *Ibid.*, ll. 141–142.

166. *Ibid.*, ll. 163–180. The last word, "Vale," is misquoted from "bale."

167. Evidently Reynolds knew from his close association with Keats that Keats's original intention had been to entitle this poem *Endymion* instead of using as a title the first few words, *I Stood Tip-toe* (*Letters of Keats*, I, 121).

168. *I Stood Tip-toe*, ll. 113–124.

169. *Calidore*, ll. 34–37.

170. *To Some Ladies, On Receiving a Curious Shell*, and *To ****￭* ("Hadst thou liv'd in days of old"). Reynolds' deprecation of these early poems undoubtedly contributed to the sharpness of George Felton Mathew's defense of them in *The European Magazine*, May 1816. See Walter Jackson Bate, *John Keats* (Cambridge, Massachusetts, 1963), pp. 221–222.

171. *To George Felton Mathew*, ll. 31–52.

172. *To Charles Cowden Clarke*, ll. 1–20.

173. *Keen, Fitful Gusts Are Whisp'ring Here and There*, ll. 11–14.

174. Leigh Hunt's.

175. *Sleep and Poetry*, ll. 71–84.

176. *Ibid.*, ll. 125–137.

177. *Ibid.*, ll. 185–187.

178. *Ibid.*, ll. 381–395.

179. Reynolds was only one year older than Keats, but he may have misunderstood Keats's age. In 1820 he wrote Francis Jeffrey that Keats was two years younger than he actually was. See my "Reynolds and Keats," *Keats–Shelley Journal*, 7 (Winter 1958): 52.

180. Although this essay is not initialed, Reynolds' authorship is established clearly by the reference in the first paragraph to his earlier deprecation of popularity as a standard for measuring poetic merit in "Popular Poetry—Periodical Criticism," October 13, 1816, reprinted above. If any corroboration be needed, Reynolds' misquotation (or perhaps unusual quotation from a faulty text) of *Her Triumph* can serve. After offering the poem as an example of Jonson's lyric ability in this article, Reynolds later included the same poem in "Mr Hazlitt's Lectures," *The Scots Magazine*, December 1818, p. 548. Two lines are misquoted slightly in both articles: "*Have* you *mark'd* but the fall *o'* the snow," and "*Have* you felt the wool of *the bever*?" (Italics supplied). Cf. ll. 23 and 25 of Jonson's poem: "*Ha'* you *marked* but the fall *of* the snow," and "*Ha'* you felt the wool of *beaver*?"

181. John Aikin's (1747–1822) *Essays on Song-Writing* (1774) was reissued with revisions and additions in 1810.

182. Reynolds had earlier argued that popularity or public opinion counted for absolutely nothing in the judging of literature. Now unfortunately he must admit

that it does count for something (though it is dangerously erroneous), since so great an authority on composing songs as Dr. Aikin has echoed the popular cliché that Jonson's successful lyrics were rarities. Of course Reynolds' "recantation" is ironic.

183. William Cartwright, "In the memory of the most Worthy Beniamin Iohnson," *Works* (London, 1651), l. 104, reprinted in *The Plays and Poems of William Cartwright*, ed. G. B. Evans (Madison, Wisconsin, 1951), p. 514.

184. According to the late George L. Marsh, this review is initialed R in the 1817 volume of *The Champion* at the British Museum. Curiously, it is not initialed in the 1817 volumes at the University of California and the New York Public Library. One can only speculate as to how the initial was dropped from two copies; there seem to be no such discrepancies between the volumes elsewhere.

185. August Wilhelm Schlegel, *A Course of Lectures on Dramatic Art and Literature*, trans. John Black, 2 vols. (London, 1815).

186. Almost certainly Keats, who had been reading Shakespeare intensely, and who had requested Reynolds on April 17, 1817, "Whenever you write say a Word or two on some Passage in Shakespeare that may have come rather new to you; which must be continually happening, notwithstandg that we read the same Play forty times" (*Letters of Keats*, I, 133). If the friend was Keats, possibly Reynolds' tribute helped to give him confidence to claim nine months later, "thank God I can read and perhaps understand Shakespeare to his depths" (*ibid.*, I, 239). See also the next note.

187. Although Reynolds does not quite say that a young poet should hang a picture of Shakespeare above his books, he seems clearly to be thinking of Keats's letter to him from Carisbrooke of April 17, "In the passage I found a head of Shakespeare which I had not before seen—It is most likely the same that George spoke so well of; for I like it extremely—Well—this head I have hung over my Books" (*Letters of Keats*, I, 130). On the significance of the incident to Keats, see Bate, *John Keats*, pp. 159 and 698–699.

188. Reynolds' enthusiasm for Hazlitt led him to include very long extracts, almost one half of the lengthy review. Only the first and last sentences of each passage are reprinted to permit location in Hazlitt's works, P. P. Howe, ed., *The Complete Works of William Hazlitt* (London and Toronto, 1930), IV, 180–181.

189. II, i, 14–23.

190. *Works of Hazlitt*, IV, 191, 187–188.

191. *Ibid.*, IV, 200.

192. *Ibid.*, IV, 225.

193. *Ibid.*, IV, 228, 229.

194. II, v, 28–29.

195. V, ii, 310–311, 313–314.

196. III, ii, 37–38.

197. *Works of Hazlitt*, IV, 232–233.

198. *Ibid.*, IV, 249.

199. Although this article is not initialed (none of the reviews are except that of Hazlitt's *Characters of Shakespeare's Plays*), Reynolds' authorship is indicated by the similarity between the attack on Bowles and the earlier attack in "Pilgrimage of the Living Poets to the Stream of Castaly." Also noteworthy is the similarity of attitude toward Coleridge's delight in the mysterious in this review and in "Boswell's Visit," December 15, 1816.

200. Wordsworth, *A Narrow Girdle of Rough Stones*, l. 38.

201. The opening stanza of *Gamelyn*. But Reynolds quotes a variant which I have not located.

202. *Romeo and Juliet*, II, ii, 160–161.

203. An adaptation of *Lycidas*, ll. 8–9.

204. By Henry H. Milman, performed in 1815.

205. Lamb's play (1802).

206. Reynolds quotes at length, II, ii, from "In the name of the boy-god" through "And all things on earth, how fair they be."

207. II, iv, 72–81.

208. *Christabel*, *Kubla Khan*, and *The Pains of Sleep* were published together in 1816. *Sibylline Leaves* followed in 1817.

209. Wordsworth, *The Solitary Reaper*, ll. 15–16. Wordsworth has "among."

210. This contrast between Milton's conscious striving and Shakespeare's concentration on the object to be developed poetically vaguely anticipates Keats's discussion of "negative capability" six weeks later (*Letters of Keats*, I, 193–194).

211. *Zapolya*, I, i, 488.

212. II, i, 536–540.

213. II, i, 213–216.

214. I, i, 433–450.

215. I, i, 375–378.

216. II, i, 430–435.

217. II, i, 47–50.

218. II, i, 168–170.

219. I, i, 503–509.

220. II, i, 379–382.

221. *The Tempest*, IV, i, 128–129. The lines doubtless appealed to Reynolds because of his own strong interest in naiads, as evidenced by his long poem *The Naiad*, published a year earlier in 1816.

222. *To the Small Celandine*, ll. 37–39. Wordsworth has "spy," instead of "see."

223. Lines 180–182.

224. II, iii, 192–195.

Dramatic Reviews from *The Champion*

1. Reynolds' service as regular theatrical critic for *The Champion* has long been known from George L. Marsh's "A Bibliography of the Writings of Keats's Friend Reynolds," *Studies in Philology*, 25 (October 1928): 491–510. For an account of the evidence, see below, pp. 429–431.

2. By Thomas Otway (1680).

3. *The Faerie Queene*, III, ii, 23.

4. Robert Tailor (fl. 1614); the play was published in 1614.

5. Eliza O'Neill (1791–1872), later Lady Becher, the most celebrated English actress from 1814 through 1819.

6. By John Tobin (1770–1804), first performed in 1805.

7. Edmund Kean (1789–1833). Reynolds' great admiration for this celebrated actor was shared by virtually all the Romantics.

8. In Nicholas Rowe's *Tamerlane* (1702).

9. *Remorse* (1813).

10. *Lalla Rookh* (1817).

11. III, ii, 207–208.

12. IV, ii, 122–128.

13. V, i, 270–271.

14. III, ii, 399.

15. III, i, 167–177.

16. IV, i, 12–13.

17. III, ii, 100–101.

18. II, i, 175–176. Reynolds' citation of scene 2 is erroneous.

19. Wordsworth, *To H. C., Six Years Old*, l. 33.

20. II, i, 132–135.

21. II, i, 162.

22. Thomas Harris, manager of Covent Garden.

23. A musical comedy (1815) by Charles Brown, later to be a friend of both Reynolds and Keats. Presumably Reynolds had met him by August 18, 1816, when he published Brown's article on *Two Gentlemen of Verona* in *The Champion*.

24. Residence of the Prince Regent, therefore signifying modern regal splendor.

25. I, iii, 181.

26. I, iii, 394–399.

27. V, iii, 96–99. The last five words are not in Massinger.

28. V, iii, 150.

29. By Nicholas Rowe (1703).

30. In Edward Moore's (1712–1757) *The Gamester* (1753).

31. By Charles R. Maturin (1782–1824).

32. II, iii, 92. Maturin has, "A blighted lily on an icy bed." Reynolds quoted from his memory at the theater.

33. III, ii, 193–194. Maturin has, "Imogine's tear doth linger on my cheek,/ But ne'er must dew my grave."

34. *Well! Thou Art Happy*, ll. 9–16.

35. Slang for sporting rogues. An anticipation of Reynolds' successful comic book of that title in 1820.

36. Act II, scene xiii, air xx, ll. 7–8.

37. Character in Sheridan's play of that title (1775).

38. Reynolds vacationed in Devonshire from about August 25 to about October 6, 1816. In 1815 he had spent an extended period there with James Rice and Benjamin Bailey, writing verses and associating with the Leigh sisters. After his engagement to the Leighs' friend, Eliza Powell Drewe, his attachment to the area became even stronger.

39. *Hamlet*, II, ii, 582–583.

40. George Crabbe, *The Borough* (1810), Letter XII: Players, ll. 66–71.

41. Probably the three Leigh sisters, Mary, Sarah, and Thomasine, of Salcombe Regis, near Sidmouth, with whom he had spent much leisure time during his vacation in Devonshire.

42. Maurice Morgann, *Essay on the Dramatic Character of Sir John Falstaff* (1777).

43. The capital letter is to prevent the reader from missing Reynolds' ironic allusion to the Prince Regent.

44. *Coriolanus*, IV, vi, 73–74.

45. By William Dimond (fl. 1800–1830). First acted October 7, 1816.

46. Thomas Amory's novel (1756–1766). Married seven times, Buncle turns after brief mourning for each death to a search for a new wife.

47. Reynolds' view of Othello is based on August Schlegel's, from whose lectures he draws a long quotation as a preface for this article.

48. *Paradise Regained*, IV, 76.

49. Henry Mackenzie's best-known work was *The Man of Feeling* (1771).

50. In *The Beggar's Opera*.

51. Dryden, *Alexander's Feast*, ll. 80–81.

52. IV, iii, 259–266.

53. IV, iii, 378–380.

54. V, i, 217–221.

55 Wordsworth, *Ode to Duty*, l. 46.

56. Cf. *Childe Harold*, III, 913, "With a most voiceless thought, sheathing it as a sword."

57. Charles Dibdin (1745–1814).

58. Frederic Reynolds (1764–1841).

59. Isaac Pocock (1782–1835).

60. George Lamb (1784–1834).

61. Andrew Cherry (1762–1812).

62. Thomas Morton (?1764–1838), author of *Speed the Plough* (1798), from which the phrase about Mrs. Grundy is quoted above.

63. Note the title of the play reviewed. The ravens reveal the guilt of the criminals.

64. Bill Soames and Nimming Ned were well-known underworld characters. This passage is another anticipation of Reynolds' *The Fancy* (1820). He came close to following his own tongue-in-cheek suggestion; though he did not write a play on the subject, he wrote a mock autobiography.

65. James Kenney (1780–1849).

66. Reynolds had butchered Macready's performance of Othello in the issue of October 20, 1816.

67. *Ode to Duty*, ll. 45–46.

68. This passage offers a clue to Reynolds' later dislike of Fanny Brawne, who had "a penchant . . . for acting stylishly" (*Letters of Keats*, II, 13).

69. I am no expert on rooks' nests, but I suggest that the arrangement of Fanny Brawne's hair as it is shown in the Augustin Edouart silhouette might fit that description. Though the silhouette was cut when Fanny was twenty-nine, it "was thought by her children to have caught her in a very characteristic pose" (Bate, *John Keats*, p. 425). It would seem that Reynolds just did not like Fanny Brawne's kind of woman.

70. It is significant that Reynolds was already at war with the Tory John Wilson Croker a year and a half before his slashing attack on Keats's *Endymion* in *The Quarterly Review*. One of the "brother critics" mentioned by Reynolds was Hazlitt, who shared Reynolds' high regard for the Dennett sisters. Rather curiously, Keats disliked one of them when he saw her in a pantomime (*Letters of Keats*, I, 199).

71. Robert Southey.

72. Charles Phillips (?1787–1859), well known at the time for the florid nature of his speeches. Though effective with juries, his extravagance was generally condemned by the bar.

73. William Wycherley's *The Country Wife* (1675) was adapted by David Garrick as *The Country Girl* (1766).

74. By August F. F. von Kotzebue, translated by Benjamin Thompson (1798). Cf. this review with Keats's strictures (*Letters of Keats*, I, 336–337).

75. Matthew G. Lewis (1775–1818), William Dimond, and Sir Lumley St. George Skeffington (1771–1850). Lewis wrote numerous dramas as well as the novels for which he is now best known.

76. Adapted by Mrs. Elizabeth Inchbald (1753–1821) from Kotzebue's *Das Kind der Liebe* in 1798.

77. By Richard L. Sheil (1791–1851), first performed in 1814.

78. A pun on the contemporary slang meaning of spectators in the balcony.

79. Before Charles R. Maturin's authorship was revealed, Keats reported a rumor that a young lady had written it (*Letters of Keats*, I, 123).

80. IV, i, 154–157.

81. IV, i, 158–163.

82. This and the following two are characters from Schiller's *The Robbers*.

83. II, ii, 14–15.

84. By Colley Cibber (1707).

85. Of course this is Wordsworthian orthodoxy. Cf. "Preface to Lyrical Ballads," *Works of Wordsworth*, II, 389, where Wordsworth lists "great national events" as the first cause of "this degrading thirst after outrageous stimulation."

86. Reynolds is joking about Southey's troubles in attempting to suppress his earlier revolutionary play (1794), which had been published piratically in 1817 much to the discomfiture of the converted Tory.

87. See below, May 25, 1817.

88. It is perhaps worth remarking that this passage, which resembles in tone a part of Lamb's *Old China*, preceded that great Romantic essay by six years.

89. In Edward Young's *The Revenge* (1721).

90. Hazlitt noted this argument, agreed about the Roman characters in general, but argued that Brutus was an exception (*Works of Hazlitt*, V, 379).

91. Drury Lane.

92. A subordinate actor.

93. Since the word is misspelled so three times within a dozen lines, it seems unlikely that the error is a printer's slip.

94. I, vii, 41–43.

95. François Joseph Talma (1763–1826). Reynolds was more fortunate than Hazlitt, who received an invitation to meet him, but was unable to accept. See *Works of Hazlitt*, XII, 86, and XVIII, 454n.

96. V, v, 19–28. Reynolds' "way of delivering the passage" was even newer (and certainly weirder) than Kemble's could possibly have been. Evidently the jarring misquotations resulted from his quoting from memory.

97. Frederic Reynolds (1764–1841), author of many plays. But at the same time Reynolds was probably joking about his own ability for the benefit of those who knew his authorship of the review. In connection with this and the subsequent passage on fame, it is well to remember Reynolds' profound humility in the presence of great genius, as seen in his letter to Keats of October 14, 1818: "Do *you* get Fame,—and I shall have it in being your affectionate and steady friend." (*The Keats Circle*, ed. Hyder E. Rollins, Cambridge, Massachusetts, 1948, I, 44).

98. *Sic*. Probably Reynolds wrote, or intended to write, "which are at the same distances."

99. Reynolds quotes himself, perhaps unconsciously. He had given the same sentence to the imaginary Dr. Johnson in "Boswell's Visit."

100. *Lycidas*, ll. 70–71. In the review of June 29, 1817 (not included in this selection), Reynolds wrote, "We never met with more than three or four who knew any thing of Shakespeare, who did not at heart think Milton as great a genius."

101. The farewell dinner for John Philip Kemble on his retirement.

102. II, i, 123–124. As the last word, Shakespeare has "otherwise" not "so."

103. The combination of serenity and strength in the last stanza does suggest Desdemona. Reynolds did not know that the poem described Mary Hutchinson Wordsworth.

104. By Richard L. Sheil (1791–1851), reviewed unfavorably by Reynolds on May 11, 1817.

105. Thomas Campbell's farewell ode to Kemble recited by Young at the retirement dinner.

106. The printer garbled this passage badly. I have rearranged the lines to restore them as Reynolds intended. Keats's attack on bluestockings in the recent letter of September 21, 1817 (*Letters of Keats*, I, 163), perhaps stimulated him to write the account.

107. Reynolds was so fascinated by this minor character that later he used the name as a pseudonym for a poem, "Lines to Miss F. Kemble," in *The Athenaeum*, July 7, 1832.

108. A place in Surrey where prizefights were held. For example, Tom Oliver fought George Cooper there on May 15, 1813.

109. Here Reynolds echoes Hazlitt's *Characters of Shakespeare's Plays*, "Hamlet is a name; his speeches and sayings but the idle coinage of the poet's brain" (*Works of Hazlitt*, IV, 232).

110. *Characters of Shakespeare's Plays* in *Works of Hazlitt*, IV, 254.

111. Reynolds had earlier distinguished between Mrs. Siddons as the character of the mind and Miss O'Neill as the character of the heart in the review of June 8, 1817

112. Thomas Morton (?1764–1838), playwright.

113. Hazlitt. I do not find the remark in *Works of Hazlitt*. Probably Reynolds meant precisely what he wrote, that Hazlitt *said* it.

114. For many years this review was mistakenly attributed to Keats. See my "Keats's Theatrical Reviews in the *Champion*," *Keats-Shelley Journal*, 3 (Winter 1954): 55–65. Amy Lowell, who supposed Keats the author, judged it to be an improvement over the review which Keats wrote for the issue of December 21, 1817 (*John Keats*, Boston and New York, 1925, I, 539).

115. The abridgement of the three parts of *Henry VI* into one play was done by J. H. Merivale.

116. Probably a printer's error. Apparently he wrote, or meant to write, "retract."

117. 2 *Henry VI*, III, ii, 161–176. Lines 161–162 have been changed considerably from Shakespeare's text. The last six lines (after l. 176) are not in Shakespeare.

118. Reynolds is playing with the tradition that Shakespeare acted the part of the Ghost in *Hamlet*.

119. Evidently Reynolds did not know of Merivale's preparation of the script.

120. This is not Shakespeare's, but apparently an addition of the compiler, J. H. Merivale.

121. Benjamin West's painting, which had recently been exhibited. Keats also damned it (*Letters of Keats*, I, 192).

Essays from *The Yellow Dwarf*

1. *The Yellow Dwarf* was a weekly journal published every Saturday by John Hunt from January 3 through May 23, 1818. The leading contributor was Reynolds' idol, Hazlitt. For the most detailed accounts of *The Yellow Dwarf*, see William H. Marshall, "An Addition to the Hazlitt Canon: Arguments from External and Internal Evidence," *Papers of the Bibliographical Society of America*, 55 (Fourth Quarter 1961): 347–370, and Marshall, "'Pulpit Oratory,' I–III: Essays by John Hamilton Reynolds in Imitation of William Hazlitt," University of Pennsylvania *Library Chronicle*, 28 (Spring 1962): 88–105. I am grateful to Professor Marshall and the Pennsylvania *Library Chronicle* for permitting me to include in this edition most of the notes to the text of Reynolds' essays in the latter article; these are identified below by the author's name appended in parentheses.

2. *The Faerie Queene*, II, xii, 3. Hazlitt had discussed the poem in "On Chaucer and Spenser," the second of his *Lectures on the English Poets* (*Works of Hazlitt*, V, 19–44), which was delivered in January, shortly before Reynolds began writing this essay. (Marshall.)

3. The speech was delivered on January 27 ("Parliamentary Intelligence," *The Times*, January 28, 1818). (Marshall.)

4. "Their principles ... 'a harbour and ultimate repose.'" Cf. Hazlitt: "*Principle* is a word that is not to be found in the Young Clergyman's Best Companion" ("On the Clerical Character," *The Yellow Dwarf*, January 31, 1818 [*Works of Hazlitt*, VII, 251]). (Marshall.)

5. "Their temporal wealth ... sleeping and feeding life away." Cf. Hazlitt: "They indulge in all the sensuality that is not prohibited in the Decalogue" ("On the Clerical Character," *The Yellow Dwarf*, January 31, 1818 [*Works of Hazlitt*, VII, 248]). (Marshall.)

6. "Hymn to Adversity," l. 20. (Marshall.)

7. Gray, "The Bard," l. 51. Cf. Hazlitt: "if the labyrinth of metaphysics did not afford him 'ample scope and verge enough,' he would resort to necromancy and the cabbala" ("Mr. Coleridge's Lay Sermon," *The Examiner*, September 8, 1816 [*Works of Hazlitt*, VII, 116–117]). (Marshall.)

8. "He calls us his brethren ... and see how he will act." Cf. Hazlitt: "we hate much more to meet a three-cornered well-pinched clerical hat on a prim expectant pair of shoulders, that seems to announce to half a street ... 'Stand off, for I am holier than you'" ("On the Clerical Character," *The Yellow Dwarf*, January 24, 1818 [*Works of Hazlitt*, VII, 243]). (Marshall.)

9. *The Merry Wives of Windsor*, III, ii, 69: "he smells of April and May." (Marshall.)

10. Delivered annually at Oxford since the foundation of a trust by the bequest of the Reverend John Bampton in 1751.

11. *As You Like It*, II, vii, 164. (Marshall.)

12. Cf. Hazlitt, "On the Causes of Methodism," *The Examiner*, October 22, 1815 (*Works of Hazlitt*, IV, 57–61). (Marshall.)

13. *Hamlet*, III, iv, 47–48. Cf. Hazlitt, "On the Causes of Methodism," *The Examiner*, October 22, 1815 (*Works of Hazlitt*, IV, 60). (Marshall.)

14. Cf. *All's Well That Ends Well*, V, iii, 17–19. (Marshall.)

15. Gray, "Elegy Written in a Country Churchyard," l. 76. Cf. Hazlitt: "Among those few persons who 'have kept the even tenor of their way,' the author of *Evelina*,

Cecilia, and Camilla, holds a distinguished place" ("Standard Novels and Romances," *The Edinburgh Review*, February 1815 [*Works of Hazlitt*, XVI, 21]). (Marshall.)

16. Benjamin Bailey (1791–1853), whom Keats praised just as lavishly (*Letters of Keats*, I, 160). A year later Reynolds had to revise his judgment when Bailey abruptly married a bishop's daughter, Hamilton Gleig, after having courted Reynolds' sister Mariane ardently for two years.

17. Cf. Pope, *An Essay on Man*, II, 136. (Marshall.)

18. William Wilberforce (1759–1833).

19. Nicholas Vansittart (1766–1851), chancellor of the exchequer. Cf. Hazlitt: "A well-meaning man is one who often does a great deal of mischief without any kind of malice ... Mr. Vansittart is a well-meaning man" ("On Good Nature," *The Examiner*, June 9, 1816 [*Works of Hazlitt*, IV, 104]). (Marshall.)

20. Joseph Butterworth (1770–1826).

21. Henry Addington, Viscount Sidmouth (1757–1844), Home Secretary.

22. Cowper, *The Task*, VI, 906–914. Hazlitt had used *The Task*, V, 177–179 and 187–188, as an epigraph for his essay, "On the Effects of War and Taxes," *The Champion*, August 31, 1817 (*Works of Hazlitt*, VII, 219), and more recently he had delivered his lecture "On Thomson and Cowper" at the Surrey Institution (*Works of Hazlitt*, V, 85–104). (Marshall.)

23. Daniel Wilson (1778–1858) received the M.A. from Oxford in 1804. He was made Assistant Curate of St. John's Chapel, Bedford Row, Bloomsbury, in 1808, and was sole minister there from 1812 to 1824. He was named Bishop of Calcutta in 1832. (Marshall.) It seems pertinent to add that his home at the time was generally recognized as the headquarters of the Tory Evangelical party in London. Reynolds' hostility toward the Evangelicals attacked in these articles was to a considerable degree political.

24. Cf. *Othello*, I, iii, 149–150. (Marshall.)

25. Cf. Hazlitt, "On the Causes of Methodism," *The Examiner*, October 22, 1815 (*Works of Hazlitt*, IV, 57–61). (Marshall.)

26. Goldsmith, *Retaliation*, ll. 29–42. Cf. Hazlitt: "The best character of him [Burke], and perhaps the finest that ever was drawn of any man, is that by Goldsmith, in his poem of Retaliation" (*The Eloquence of the British Senate*, 1807 [*Works of Hazlitt*, I, 171]); "The finest things he has left behind him in verse are his character of a country school-master, and that prophetic description of Burke in the Retaliation" ("On Swift, Young, Gray, Collins, etc.," the sixth of *The Lectures on the English Poets*, which Hazlitt had at least prepared at the time of Reynolds's composition [*Works of Hazlitt*, V, 120]). (Marshall.)

27. *Hamlet*, II, ii, 197: "I mean, the matter you [read] my lord." Cf. Hazlitt: "What do you read, my lord?—Words, words, words./ What is the matter?—*Nothing*" (Epigraph for the fifth part of "Illustrations of Vetus," *The Morning Chronicle*, January 5, 1814 [*Works of Hazlitt*, VII, 66]). (Marshall.)

28. Cowper, *Truth*, ll. 327–328. In his lecture "On Thomson and Cowper," delivered at the Surrey Institution, Hazlitt had quoted *Truth*, ll. 317–336 (*Works of Hazlitt*, V, 94). (Marshall.)

29. Another account of the same incident is quoted from Thomas Noon Talfourd's *Final Memorials of Charles Lamb* by P. P. Howe in *The Life of William Hazlitt*, third edition (London, 1947), p. 223.

30. *1 Peter*, ii, 17: "Fear God. Honour the King." Cf. Hazlitt: "*Fear God and honour*

the King, is the motto of priestcraft" ("On the Clerical Character," *The Yellow Dwarf*, February 7, 1818 [*Works of Hazlitt*, VII, 258]). (Marshall.)

31. *A Midsummer Night's Dream*, I, ii, 83–85: "but I will aggravate my voice so that I will roar you as gently as any sucking dove." Cf. Hazlitt: "With Bottom in the play, he may be said to 'aggravate his voice so, that he roars you an 'twere any sucking dove'" ("Illustrations of Vetus," *The Morning Chronicle*, December 2, 1813 [*Works of Hazlitt*, VII, 61]); "Can he not, upon occasion, 'aggravate his voice' like Bottom in the play?" ("Cobbett and Shakespear: A Postscript," *The Examiner*, November 26, 1815 [*Works of Hazlitt*, XX, 59]); "He [Kemble] 'aggravated the part so, that he would seem like any sucking dove'" ("Mr. Kemble's Sir Giles Overreach," *The Examiner*, May 5, 1816 [*Works of Hazlitt*, V, 303–304]). (Marshall.)

32. *1 Timothy*, vi, 6. (Marshall.)

33. *Joseph Andrews*, Bk. II, ch. xvii. (Marshall.)

34. Henry Gostling White (b. 1769) was ordained in 1793 and came to London in 1801. He was elected Alternate Morning and Evening Preacher at the Asylum for Female Orphans, St. George's-fields, in 1813. (Marshall.)

35. Cf. Hazlitt: "Perhaps, after all, Parson Adams is his finest character ... Its unsuspecting simplicity makes it not only more amiable, but doubly amusing, by gratifying the sense of superior sagacity in the reader" ("Standard Novels and Romances," *The Edinburgh Review*, February 1815 [*Works of Hazlitt*, XVI, 16]); "Parson Adams could not dispose of his manuscript sermons to the booksellers; and he ruined his hopes of preferment with Lady Booby, by refusing to turn pimp" ("On the Clerical Character," *The Yellow Dwarf*, February 7, 1818 [*Works of Hazlitt*, VII, 258]). (Marshall.)

36. *Joseph Andrews*, Bk. I, ch. iii. (Marshall.)

37. Possibly Reynolds' reference is to "The Day of Tears," *The Gentleman's Magazine*, LXXXVII (Part II, 1817), 609. However, this review, though extremely brief, was favorable to White. (Marshall.)

38. James Asperne was publisher of *The European Magazine and London Review*. A portrait of White, engraved by T. Blood from a painting by George Hayter, faces "A Brief Memoir of the Rev. Henry G. White, A. M.," with which the number for January 1816 opens (LXIX, 3–5). (Marshall.) *The European* was a conservative journal with a strong religious inclination. Keats's former friend George Felton Mathew had reviewed *Poems* of 1817 in it, disagreeing so completely with Reynolds' praise and blame in the earlier *Champion* review that recent biographers have viewed it as a rebuttal of Reynolds (See Bate, *John Keats*, pp. 221–222). Reynolds' contempt for the magazine, revealed by this sneer, suggests that Mathew's rebuttal had not gone unnoticed.

39. Reynolds's description of the picture must be regarded, in all fairness to White, as at best an exaggeration. (Marshall.)

40. John Mitchel, Curate of Isleworth, wrote a letter dated February 23, 1818, protesting that he had been falsely listed in *The Times* of February 21 for a donation of £1 in support of the fight against "Arbitrary Imprisonments": "Those who know me will not, I trust, for a moment believe that statement; and it is for the information of those who do not, that I feel myself called upon thus publicly to disclaim all knowledge of the subscription in question" (*The Times*, February 25, 1818). (Marshall.)

41. Richard Watson (1737–1816) was Bishop of Llandaff from 1782 until his death.

His successor, Herbert Marsh, was the object of Hazlitt's attack in the fourth essay of this series. (Marshall.)

42. That is, he might have become Archbishop of Canterbury if he had been willing to sacrifice his liberal principles.

43. Princess Charlotte, only child of the Prince Regent and Princess Caroline, died November 6, 1817, at the age of twenty-one. (Marshall.)

44. *Julius Caesar*, III, ii, 221–223: "I am no orator, as Brutus is;/ But, as you know me all, a plain, blunt man/ That love my friend." (Marshall.)

45. Henry G. White, *The Day of Tears: A Sermon preached at the Church of Allhallows, Barking, Great Tower-street, November 19, 1817* (London: Asperne, 1817). This had passed through a seventh edition by the time Reynolds composed his essays. (Marshall.)

Review from *The Alfred*

1. Reynolds' authorship was revealed by Keats (*Letters of Keats*, I, *393*). The article was reprinted in *The Examiner* of October 11, 1818, where it was introduced by the following note: "A manly and judicious letter, signed J. S. appeared in The Morning Chronicle the other day, respecting the article in The Quarterly Review on the Endymion of the young poet Mr. Keats. It is one of several public animadversions, which that half-witted, half-hearted Review has called indignantly forth on the occasion. 'This is the hastily-written tribute,' says the writer, 'of a stranger, who ventures to predict that Mr. K. is capable of producing a poem that shall challenge the admiration of every reader of true taste and feeling; nay, if he will give up his acquaintance with Mr. Leigh Hunt, and apostasise in his friendships, his principles, and his politics (if he have any), he may even command the approbation of *The Quarterly Review*.'—We really believe so; but Mr. Keats is of a spirit which can afford to dispense with such approbation, and stand by his friend. We should have given the whole of this letter, but we have since met with another in the Alfred Exeter paper, which is more elaborate on the subject; and we have not room for both." It has usually been assumed that "J. S." was John Scott.

2. Government spies, who were the subject of heated Parliamentary debates in 1817. See Hazlitt, "On the Spy System, I and II," *The Morning Chronicle*, June 30 and July 15, 1817 (*Works of Hazlitt*, VII, 208–214).

3. Reynolds begins here, and continues throughout the article, the pretense that he is a stranger to Keats, a rural resident of Devonshire who has been attracted to *Endymion* by the very passages quoted by *The Quarterly* in condemnation, and whose subsequent reading of the entire poem has left him appalled at the unfairness of *The Quarterly's* treatment.

4. Henry Kirke White's (1785–1806) *Clifton Grove* (1803) was judged undistinguished by *The Monthly Review* of February 1804. Southey, who rushed to White's defense and championed his reputation after his death, exaggerated the reviewer's adverse judgment, and Reynolds repeats that exaggeration, which was the generally accepted view of his day.

5. Sydney Owenson, Lady Morgan (?1783–1859), who was savagely attacked in "France. By Lady Morgan," *The Quarterly Review*, 17 (April 1817): 260–286. Because she was supported by influential Whigs, and because her liberal political principles

caused her to view the French Revolutionists with some sympathy, she had been subjected to vicious treatment by *The Quarterly* since its very first number.

6. Samples of the fiercest passages are as follows: "What manner of woman she must be that revives and displays such false and detestable grossness of which even a modern jest book would be ashamed " (*Quarterly*, 17: 281). "But the climax of Lady Morgan's laxity will be found in nine pages of eulogy upon a Madame D'Houdetot, an avowed adulteress, and, if we are to believe Lady Morgan's friendly account, a prostitute ... however blameable the countenance given in this passage to vice may be, it would be uncandid and unjust to take her *au pied de la lettre*, and suppose that she would *really have found delight in tracing* the *steps* of Madame D'Houdetot" (17: 283).

7. In "Young Poets," *The Examiner*, December 1, 1816.

8. See above, p. 447, n. 68. Probably the danger of egotism in literature had been a subject of conversation with Keats and Reynolds.

9. Thomas Campbell, *The Pleasures of Hope* (1799).

10. Samuel Rogers, *The Pleasures of Memory* (1792).

11. John Wilson Croker (1780–1857). Though Reynolds was guessing, as his listing the other three names indicates, his first guess was correct. Croker did indeed write the attack on *Endymion* in *The Quarterly*. Reynolds chose reasonably for his subsequent guesses from heavy contributors to *The Quarterly*: George Canning (1770–1827), John Barrow (1764–1848), and of course its editor William Gifford (1756–1826). The first three were high in the Tory Ministry (thus automatically enemies for Hazlitt and Reynolds), and, as Reynolds remarks at the beginning of this article, even Gifford held the minor but lucrative posts of Commissioner of the Lottery (£100 a year) and Paymaster of the Gentlemen-pensioners (£1,000 a year).

12. The most obvious fiction in the pose described in note 3 above. Reynolds corresponded with Keats about the poem during its composition, echoed it while it was still in manuscript in the theatrical review for *The Champion* of December 7, 1817, requested from James Hessey a copy of the proof before publication (*Letters of Keats*, I, 247n), and persuaded Keats to substitute for his first brash preface the temperate one which was printed (*Letters of Keats*, I, 266–267).

13. *Endymion*, I, 453–460.

14. I, 817–831.

15. II, 195–198.

16. II, 441–449.

17. II, 827–839.

Essays and Reviews from *The Scots Magazine*

1. *The Scots Magazine; or Edinburgh Magazine and Literary Miscellany*, a venerable monthly periodical which had been running since its inception in 1740, was published by Archibald Constable and coedited at this time by Thomas Pringle and James Cleghorn, who had taken their posts only a year earlier after their dissatisfaction with six months' service as the first joint editors of the newly founded *Blackwood's*. On January 24, 1818, Keats wrote: "Constable the Bookseller has offered Reynolds ten gineas a sheet to write for his magazine. it is an Edinburgh one which, Blackwoods started up in opposition to" (*Letters of Keats*, I, 216–217). In the month in which the first installment of the review of Hazlitt's *Lectures on the English Comic Writers* appeared,

Keats wrote that Reynolds "has become an edinburgh Reviewer" (*Letters of Keats*, II, 7). The review can be attributed confidently to Reynolds because in the third install-ment he included a long passage from an essay which he had initialed earlier in *The Champion*. Practically the entire essay, "On the Spectator," *The Champion*, June 16, 1816, p. 190, is included in *The Scots Magazine*, February 1819, pp. 148–149. See my "New Letters, Articles, and Poems by John Hamilton Reynolds," *Keats–Shelley Journal*, 6 (Winter 1957): 102.

2. They were delivered at the Surrey Institution in November and December 1818 and January 1819 (*Works of Hazlitt*, VI, 367).

3. Misprint for "forgetive." Cf. *2 Henry IV*, IV, iii, 107, and the quotation of it in *Works of Hazlitt*, VI, 35.

4. *Works of Hazlitt*, VI, 8. Since Reynolds' quotations show a host of verbal differ-ences from the printed text, which was not published until April 1819 (P. P. Howe, *The Life of William Hazlitt*, third edition, London, 1947, p. 252), he was undoubtedly quoting from a manuscript which Hazlitt lent him before making the final revision for the press. Keats probably quoted from the same manuscript.

5. *Works of Hazlitt*, VI, 8. This and subsequent long quotations are omitted except for the first and last passages to permit location in Howe's standard edition of Hazlitt.

6. *Works of Hazlitt*, VI, 11.

7. *Ibid.*, VI, 12.

8. Reynolds' birthplace, where he lived his first ten years. He entered Shrewsbury School in 1803.

9. *Works of Hazlitt*, VI, 15

10. *Ibid.*, VI, 22.

11. *Ibid.*, VI, 31–32.

12. The metaphor doubtless came to Reynolds' mind because he was very much aware that Keats was writing one of the versions of *Hyperion* at this time (*Letters of Keats*, II, 12, 14, 18, 21). It is now generally accepted that the version was *Hyperion* rather than *The Fall*.

13. *Works of Hazlitt*, VI, 33.

14. *Ibid.*, VI, 36.

15. *Ibid.*

16. *Ibid.*, VI, 38–39.

17. *Ibid.*, VI, 40.

18. Reynolds quotes the three stanzas of *Her Triumph*, from which he had already quoted the last two stanzas in "Ben Jonson," *The Champion*, May 4, 1817, reprinted above.

19. Reynolds quotes *The Alchemist*, II, ii, 72–87, exactly as he had earlier in "On the Early Dramatic Poets, I," *The Champion*, January 7, 1816, reprinted above. In the last paragraph Reynolds also repeats many phrases from the earlier essay.

20. *The Blossom*. Quoted in *Works of Hazlitt*, VI, 51.

21. Lines 1–4. Quoted in *Works of Hazlitt*, VI, 52.

22. *Ibid.*

23. *Musick's Duel* is praised in *Works of Hazlitt*, VI, 53. But Reynolds had earlier praised the same poem independently in a footnote to his essay on Chaucer, *The Champion*, May 26, 1816, reprinted above.

24. *Works of Hazlitt*, VI, 55.

25. *Ibid.*, VI, 56.

26. He read *Drinking* and *To the Grasshopper, Works of Hazlitt*, VI, 59–60.

27. *Ibid.*, VI, 62.

28. *Hudibras*, II, ii, 831–832. Quoted in *Works of Hazlitt*, VI, 64.

29. *The Man of Mode*, I, i. Not quoted by Hazlitt.

30. *Works of Hazlitt*, VI, 71.

31. *Ibid.*, VI, 72–73.

32. *Ibid.*, VI, 74.

33. Like Hazlitt, Reynolds knew Wycherly's *The Country Wife* (1672) largely through Garrick's adaptation of it to *The Country Girl* (1766), the version which was regularly performed on the stage in his day.

34. *Works of Hazlitt*, VI, 79.

35. *Ibid.*, VI, 84–85.

36. *Ibid.*, VI, 95–96.

37. Reynolds here inserts the entire essay on *The Spectator* from *The Champion*, June 16, 1816, reprinted above, with only a very few changes in words and phrases. The ethics of Reynolds' conduct is debatable: he probably intended to deceive both the editors and his readers, for he wove the old essay into the new article very skilfully. The trick was by no means without precedent, since Hazlitt, himself, as is well known, had frequently transferred long passages from earlier essays to later ones. I have stumbled on another example which has hitherto gone unnoticed by Hazlitt scholars: Hazlitt's essay "On the Opera" for *The Yellow Dwarf*, January 3, 1818, was not an original article, but merely a reprint from *The Champion* of August 24, 1817 (where it contains a few lines of introduction later excised as inappropriate for *The Yellow Dwarf*). Just as Hazlitt presumably collected twice for the same essay, so Reynolds received his ten guineas a sheet under false pretenses. Although Reynolds had reviewed only five of Hazlitt's eight lectures by the end of this article, no final installment appeared. We might suspect that Reynolds' deception had been detected if it were not for the fact that he repeated the same trick in two later articles for the magazine, "Boswell Redivivus" of October 1819 and "Living Authors, A Dream" of August 1820 (both include reprints from *The Champion*).

38. *Mr. Francis Beaumont's Letter to Ben Jonson*, ll. 45–46. The article was first attributed to Reynolds by George L. Marsh in "A Bibliography of the Writings of Keats's Friend Reynolds," *Studies in Philology*, 25 (October 1928): 491–510.

39. "Boswell Redivivus," *The Scots Magazine*, October 1819, not included in this collection because it is an altered, and I think thinner, version of "Boswell's Visit" of *The Champion*, December 1 and 15, 1816, reprinted above.

40. The usual claim of pamphlets supposed to be written by condemned criminals before execution. The subsequent passage expands the comparison.

41. Samuel Rogers, *The Pleasures of Memory* (1792).

42. Wordsworth, *The Pet Lamb* (1800).

43. *Christ's Entry into Jerusalem*. Haydon depicted Wordsworth as standing reverently with head slightly bowed. Reynolds ironically suggests that such humility is hardly appropriate for a man as proud and egotistical as Wordsworth.

44. Lamb.

45. On May 22, 1817. Not having attended to the performance, he wrote generally about Kemble for *The Champion*, May 25, 1817.

46. Five lectures, beginning in April 1812.

47. Unfortunately only one of these commonplace books has been preserved. Now

in the Bristol Central Library, the best account of it is Paul Kaufman, "The Reynolds-Hood Commonplace Book: A Fresh Appraisal," *Keats–Shelley Journal*, 10 (Winter 1961): 43–52.

48. "Le Rameau d'Or" by Madame Marie-Catherine D'Aulnoy (?1650–1705).

49. The simile suggests *The Eve of St. Mark*. Although there is nothing in the fragment to indicate that Bertha was looking for her "love-fate" in the legend book, there is also nothing that would have prevented its introduction later if the poem had been completed. Perhaps Reynolds simply guessed after reading the fragment.

50. The reference is to *Fare Thee Well*, addressed to Bell in 1816 at the time of the separation, and *A Sketch* written at the same time to satirize Bell's companion, Mrs. Clermont. The poems were first printed openly by John Scott in *The Champion*; this passage reveals that Reynolds sided with Scott in the heated argument between *The Champion* and *The Examiner* which followed publication of the poems.

51. Amelia Alderson (Mrs. John) Opie (1769–1853), novelist and versifier whom Keats probably met (*Letters of Keats*, I, 227). She was a cousin of Richard Woodhouse.

52. Sydney, Lady Morgan, whom Reynolds had earlier defended against the attacks of *The Quarterly Review* in "The Quarterly Review—Mr. Keats," *The Alfred*, October 6, 1818, reprinted above.

53. The allusion is to Charles Perrault's "Blue Beard" (1697), probably read by Reynolds in the translation of Robert Samber (?1729). Fatima is the last wife who disobediently enters the locked chamber to discover the bodies of the earlier wives.

54. Henry Luttrell (?1765–1851) published *Advice to Julia* in 1820.

55. Hazlitt.

56. Hunt's article was "On Shaking Hands," *The Indicator*, July 12, 1820.

57. After a long and elaborate introduction (including a very bad poem), Reynolds then inserts in a thoroughly rewritten form "The Pilgrimage of Living Poets to the Stream of Castaly" from *The Champion*, April 7, 1816, reprinted above. The most significant changes, which can be seen by comparing what follows with the earlier essay, are the increased sympathy for Coleridge and the sharp objection to faults in Wordsworth.

58. "At length I hailed him, seeing that his hat/ Was moist with water-drops, as if the brim/ Had newly scooped a running stream." I, 444–446.

Prefaces

1. The date of publication is established by Keats: "Reynolds hearing that said Peter Bell was coming out, took it into his head to write a skit upon it call'd Peter Bell. He did it as soon as thought on it is to be published this morning, and comes out before the real Peter Bell" (*Letters of Keats*, II, 83–84). The parody was so successful that it went through two more editions. It was widely reviewed; George L. Marsh lists thirteen journals on the microfilm *Poetical Works of John Hamilton Reynolds* (University of Chicago). Keats wrote the review for *The Examiner*, April 25, 1819. Shelley followed Reynolds' lead with *Peter Bell the Third*. Byron praised it in a letter to Moore: "Did you write the lively quiz on Peter Bell? It has wit enough to be yours, and almost too much to be any body else's now going" (*The Works of Lord Byron: Letters and Journals*, ed. Rowland E. Prothero, Baron Ernle, London, 1901, V, 71).

2. Susannah Centilivre (?1667–1723), *Bold Stroke for a Wife* (1718), V, i. Colonel

Fainwell impersonates Simon Pure, a Quaker preacher, only to have the real Simon Pure appear on the scene to expose him.

3. *To the Same Flower*, l. 25.
4. *King Lear*, III, iv, 144.
5. The reference is to Wordsworth's *The Sparrow's Nest*.
6. Wordsworth had been Distributor of Stamps for Westmorland since March 1813.
7. *The Thorn*.
8. Francis Jeffrey.
9. *The Edinburgh Review*.
10. See "Essay Supplementary to the Preface," *Works of Wordsworth*, II, 423–424.
11. Either Reynolds was present during a meeting between Wordsworth and Keats, or he had heard of Wordsworth's vanity on that occasion, described by Charles Cowden Clarke: "Someone having observed that the next Waverly novel was to be 'Rob Roy,' Wordsworth took down his volume of Ballads, and read to the Company 'Rob Roy's Grave;' then, returning it to the shelf, observed, 'I do not know what more Mr. Scott can have to say upon the subject'" (*Recollections of Writers*, London, 1878, pp. 149–150).
12. The heading mocks Wordsworth's "Essay Supplementary to the Preface" of *Poems* of 1815.
13. Reynolds' citation of source is misleading for modern readers. By *Lyrical Ballads*, he means the *Poems* in two volumes of 1815 (*Works of Wordsworth*, II, 426). An indication of the change in Reynolds' judgment of Wordsworth can be seen from the fact that he had quoted nearly all the same passage with firm approval three years earlier in "Mr. Wordsworth's Poetry," *The Champion*, December 9, 1815, reprinted above. That the change was a modification rather than a reversal, however, is revealed by John Taylor's explanation to Coleridge that the parody "was written by a sincere admirer of Mr. Wordsworth's Poetry, by a person who has been his advocate in every place where he found an opportunity of expressing an opinion on the subject" (quoted in *The Letters of Samuel Taylor Coleridge*, ed. Earl L. Griggs, Oxford, 1959, IV, 1191).
14. The book was published anonymously by Taylor and Hessey with the explanatory subtitle: "a Selection from the Poetical Remains of the late Peter Corcoran, of Gray's Inn, student at law." Of course Peter Corcoran was a fiction, and the entire book was based upon the elaborate hoax, though Reynolds did draw upon his own experience in a number of ways: for Corcoran's birthplace, his date of birth, his profession, and his interest in sports. Marsh lists eight reviews in the microfilm *Poetical Works of John Hamilton Reynolds*, and most of them were favorable, but the book did not go beyond the one edition.
15. Note to *Childe Harold*, IV, lxxv, 8, in praise of Dr. Joseph Drury, headmaster of Harrow. Reynolds changes the pronouns from first to third person, and alters the verb tenses to make the passage applicable to Peter Corcoran.
16. By the most popular sporting writer of the period, Pierce Egan (1772–1849), *Boxiana* was a monthly serial which ran from 1818 to 1824.
17. The inclusion of this letter was a hoax, perpetrated by Reynolds and Richard Woodhouse on the latter's sister, Nan. She had written the letter to her brother, protesting against his extravagant praise of a prize fight. Reynolds quoted closely from the letter, changing only words and phrases here and there. Reynolds, Woodhouse, and Reynolds' fiancée, Eliza Powell Drewe, were all delighted with Nan's amazement when she read the passage from her letter in *The Fancy*. Eliza and Wood-

house enjoyed the joke so much that they sought to prolong it by keeping Nan in the dark for a time. See Rollins, *The Keats Circle*, I, 106–107, 116–117.

18. Moulsey Hurst in Surrey, site of many boxing matches.

19. Dr. John J. Gall (1758–1828) and Dr. Johann G. Spurzheim (1776–1832) were phrenologists whose system was outlined in *The Physiognomical System of Drs. Gall and Spurzheim* in 1815.

20. Mario de Calasio (1550–1620) published a Hebrew dictionary, a copy of which I have been unable to locate. I am grateful to Rabbi Max B. Wall of Ohavi Zedek Synagogue in Burlington, Vermont, for informing me that the word, which may be transliterated as "corcornam," is not classical Hebrew, but very probably an obscure Aramaic term. The first root of the word means a circling movement. Although Reynolds' mock pedantry was evidently concerned for the most part with the resemblance of the sound to "Corcoran," it may also have involved a parallel between the meaning and the circling head or flailing fists of a boxer.

21. Spenser, *Colin Clout's Come Home Again*, ll. 446–447.

22. Octavius G. Gilchrist (1779–1823) was a literary scholar who contributed occasionally to *The Champion* and *The London Magazine*; Reynolds refers to him as an expert in biography who could be very severe on the errors of others.

23. Published as by John Hamilton, possibly to avoid the anti-Cockney attacks of the Tory critics. But the inclination to write anonymously or under a pseudonym was deep-seated in Reynolds, often with no apparent motive other than delight in mystification. Clare wrote, "There is a good deal of Reynolds manner of expression about the poetry as I think & some things are as good as his" (*The Letters of John Clare*, edd. J. W. and Anne Tibble, London, 1951, p. 92). No doubt Reynolds enjoyed Clare's confusion as much as he had that of Nan Woodhouse.

24. Keats.

25. *Isabella, or the Pot of Basil.*

Essays and Reviews from *The London Magazine*

1. During the first five years of its publication, *The London* was one of the finest of all the English literary periodicals; a list of its contributors would approach a roll call of significant Romantic authors. Initiated by John Scott in January 1820 for the publishers Baldwin, Cradock, and Joy, it continued under Scott's editorship until his death in the duel with J. H. Christie in February 1821, whereupon it was sold to Taylor and Hessey, who edited the magazine with extensive assistance from Reynolds and Thomas Hood until it was sold once again to Henry Southern in 1824. The most comprehensive account of the magazine is Josephine Bauer, *The London Magazine, 1820–1829* (Copenhagen, 1953). The best records of Reynolds' work for the magazine are the correspondence included in *The Keats Circle* and George L. Marsh, "Newly Identified Writings by John Hamilton Reynolds," *Keats–Shelley Journal*, 1 (1952): 47–55.

Reynolds' authorship of "Exmouth Wrestling" was suggested by Marsh in "Newly Identified Writings," p. 50. The attribution can be confirmed beyond any reasonable doubt. The writer reports that he visited Exmouth in September; in that month Reynolds wrote John Taylor a letter from Exmouth, describing the scenery and sunsets in the same manner as in the article (see *The Keats Circle*, I, 157). The writer of the article quoted a phrase, "an untumultuous fringe of silver foam" (l. 91), from

Keats's unpublished verse letter to Reynolds. Finally, "A Cornish Wrestling Match," etched by George Cruikshank for the book of essays that Reynolds planned to publish in 1824, was clearly designed to illustrate this article.

2. I, ii, 151–153.

3. Since Reynolds' letters to Haydon reveal that he took a long September vacation in Devonshire in 1816, and Keats's letters (especially I, 166) show that he vacationed during the same month in the same section in 1819, there is no reason to suspect fiction in the assertion here that a long September vacation in the country was his annual practice.

4. Later Reynolds described such an experience in "The Inside of a Stage Coach. Letters of Edward Herbert, No. IV," *The London Magazine*, 6 (August 1822), reprinted below.

5. As Reynolds had been since November 4, 1817.

6. Richard Carew (1555–1620), *The Survey of Cornwall* (1602), ed. F. E. Halliday (London, 1953), p. 150.

7. Joseph Strutt (1749–1802), *The Sports and Pastimes of the People of England* (London, 1834), p. 81.

8. John Stowe (?1525–1605), *A Survey of London* (1598), reprinted in *London under Elizabeth*, ed. Henry Morley (London, 1890), p. 120.

9. Strutt, *Sports and Pastimes*, p. 82.

10. *Ibid.*, p. 83.

11. Carew, *Survey of Cornwall*, pp. 150–151. But Reynolds' variants show that he quoted from the quotation in Strutt, *Sports and Pastimes*, pp. 83–84. *Circumferanci* is evidently Strutt's error for *circumforanei*, vagrants.

12. Strutt, p. 84.

13. Sir Thomas Parkyns, *Progymnasmata, The Inn-Play* (London, 1714).

14. 1664–1741.

15. Sit here, traveler, if you are tired of walking.

16. From here Justice Dormer was accustomed to mount his horse.

17. It is not to live, but to be strongly alive [that matters]. The entire quoted passage is from Parkyns, *Progymnasmata*, pp. 9–10. Reynolds evidently modernized the eighteenth century capitalization, spelling, and punctuation in all quotations, but see the next note.

18. The illustration and poem do not appear in the first edition of 1714. Reynolds used a later edition, which I have not located.

19. Parkyns, pp. 12–13.

20. *Ibid.*, p. 15.

21. *Ibid.*, p. 20.

22. *Ibid.*, p. 40.

23. *Ibid.*, p. 43.

24. *Ibid.*, p. 44.

25. *Ibid.*, p. 59.

26. Reynolds' pun on "Plague-Poet" is based on John Wilson's *The City of the Plague* (1816). The scathing pun on "Moral Professor" derives from Wilson's appointment to the chair of Moral Philosophy at the University of Edinburgh. Despite all the scandalous abuse in *Blackwood's*, for which he shared the responsibility as coeditor, he had been elected by the Tory majority of the town council over the rival candidate, Sir William Hamilton. Earlier John Scott had encouraged this satire by remarking

in "Lion's Head" that Reynolds "regards the joke of electing one of Blackwood's Editors to be professor of moral Philosophy, as infinitely more laughable than anything that has ever appeared in the pages of that work"—2 (August 1820): 123.

27. *The Spectator*, no. 161 (London, 1720), 2: 284.

28. Reynolds' authorship of this anonymous essay is revealed by his handwritten initials in his file of *The London Magazine*, now in the Keats Memorial House at Hampstead. Dr. Kitchiner's book quickly became a favorite joke with Reynolds and Hood. Hood wrote an "Ode to Dr. Kitchener" for the "Lion's Head" of *The London* in November, and he later included a longer ode to the same author in *Odes and Addresses to Great People*, published jointly with Reynolds in 1825. Probably because of Hood's many references to Dr. Kitchiner, Thomas Hood, Jr. assumed that the essay in *The London* was his father's and included it in *The Works of Thomas Hood* (London, 1862–63), I, 7–25. Since he published the set over a period of two years, however, he was able to correct the error by the time he reached the last volume, where he wrote in an appendix that someone had informed him of Reynolds' authorship (VII, 379).

29. Dugald Stewart (1753–1828) discusses the vogue of the picturesque and analyzes the conception in Chapter Fifth of "On the Beautiful," *Philosophical Essays, Part II* (first published 1810), *The Works of Dugald Stewart* (Cambridge, Massachusetts, 1829), IV, 220–232.

30. Thomas Thornton (1757–1823), colonel of the West Riding militia, was a well-known sportsman.

31. This line does not appear in the standard quarto version of Massinger's *A New Way to Pay Old Debts* (1633). For my convenience, I cite a careful reprint in *English Drama, 1580–1642*, edd. C. F. Tucker Brooke and Nathaniel B. Paradise (Boston, 1933), pp. 875–910. That version omits an eight-line speech at III, ii, 3, containing Reynolds' line almost exactly, "the substantials—O, Sir Giles, the substantials," which was included in the acting copy, *The British Theatre*, ed. Mrs. Elizabeth Inchbald (London, 1808), VI, 42–43.

32. Reynolds' quotation does not appear exactly in *The Rehearsal* (1672) by George Villiers, Duke of Buckingham (1628–1687). Probably Reynolds had in mind Smith's question to Bayes as to how he adapted wit from other men's books for his own use: "what d'ye do with it then?" (I, i).

33. Charles Mathews (1776–1835), comic actor for whom Reynolds subsequently wrote with R. B. Peake "The Youthful Days of Mr. Mathews," first acted on March 11, 1822, and with James Smith "A Trip to America," which was puffed by Reynolds himself in "The Drama," *The London Magazine*, 9 (April 1824): 430. There is a copy of "A Trip to America" in the Widener Library at Harvard.

34. I cite an American reprint, the only edition which I have found, William Kitchiner, M.D., *The Cook's Oracle* (New York, 1831), p. xii.

35. *Ibid.*, p. 15.

36. Desirous of the strange, extravagant of himself.

37. Greed for things.

38. Hannah Glasse was the author of *The Art of Cookery Made Plain and Easy* (1747).

39. Richard Bradley (died 1732), a professor at Cambridge, wrote several works on gardening.

40. Anna Seward (1747–1809), poetess.

41. Kitchiner, *The Cook's Oracle*, p. 24.

42. *Ibid.*, p. 33.

43. *Ibid.*, p. 36.
44. *Ibid.*, p. 37.
45. *Ibid.*, p. 41.
46. *Ibid.*, p. 42.
47. *Ibid.*, p. 45.
48. *Ibid.*, p. 53. Kitchiner cites Trusler, *Domestic Management*, p. 11, for the subsequent quotation.
49. Kitchiner, p. 54.
50. *Ibid.*
51. *Ibid.*
52. *Ibid.*, p. 61.
53. Jockeys.
54. Kitchiner, p. 72, has "poor joint of meat." Of course the parenthesis is Reynolds'.
55. *Ibid.*, p. 74. The later American text deletes "in the open air, to ventilate the meat from its own fumes." The italics are Reynolds'. Of course Kitchiner had not meant that the meat should be roasted out-of-doors; probably Reynolds' jesting at the ambiguity caused the deletion.
56. *Ibid.*, p. 75.
57. *Ibid.*, p. 77.
58. *Ibid.*, p. 80.
59. *Ibid.*, p. 84. Italics are Reynolds'.
60. *Ibid.*, p. 85.
61. *Ibid.*, p. 90.
62. *Ibid.*, pp. 102–103. As the first word of the last paragraph, the American edition has "I" instead of "We," consistently with the "me" that follows.
63. *Ibid.*, p. 104.
64. *Ibid.* Reynolds omits numerous italics.
65. *Ibid.*, p. 105. The italics are Reynolds'.
66. *Ibid.*, p. 114.
67. *Ibid.*, p. 115. The italics are Reynolds'.
68. *Ibid.*, p. 134.
69. *Ibid.* The italics are Reynolds'. For Sir Thomas Parkyns, see "Exmouth Wrestling," reprinted above.
70. Kitchiner, p. 133.
71. *Ibid.* Except for the cod's skull on p. 177, the quotations in the paragraph are drawn from pp. 180–182.
72. *Ibid.*, salmon on p. 181; lobster on p. 188.
73. *Ibid.*, p. 190.
74. *Ibid.*, p. 217.
75. *Ibid.*, pp. 220–221.
76. *Ibid.*, p. 222.
77. *Ibid.*, p. 244.
78. *Ibid.*, p. 281.
79. Sheridan's play (1779).
80. Kitchiner, p. 296. But the American edition omits the puffs for the dealers.
81. *Ibid.*, p. 301. The italics are Reynolds'.
82. *Ibid.*, p. 308n. Reynolds strains a little for his joke by dropping Kitchiner's italics in "*Of all the fowls of the air.*"

83. *Ibid.*, p. 332. But the later American edition deletes "*buttery-caseous* relish."

84. *Ibid.*, p. 337.

85. *Love for Love*, I, i. It is Valentine's remark, not Jeremy's.

86. "The Coronation, Letter from a Gentleman in Town, to a Lady in the Country," *The London Magazine*, 4 (August 1821), not reprinted in this selection. In that first essay Reynolds gave no clear indication that he planned to continue his pose as Edward Herbert in a series of letters. Presumably a favorable response to his account of the very timely subject of the coronation, lengthy and minutely detailed though it was, persuaded him to devise the plan for the series suggested in this essay. Of the seven letters published in *The London* (No. VIII is misnumbered, and "Bradgate Park," though signed "E.H.," is not a letter), five are reprinted in this selection.

87. Friedrich A. M. Retzsch (1779–1857). Reynolds doubtless saw one of the two early English editions of Retzsch's illustrations to Goethe's *Faust, Part I: Retzsch's Series of Twenty-six Outlines Illustrative of Goethe's Tragedy of Faust*, engraved by H. Moses (London, 1820), or *Extracts from Goethe's Tragedy of Faustus, Explanatory of the Plates by Retzsch*, trans. George Soane (London, 1820).

88. While editor of *The New Monthly Magazine* from 1820 to 1830, Thomas Campbell published a number of his poems there.

89. *Marino Faliero* and *The Prophecy of Dante* were published together on April 21, 1821.

90. Addison, *Cato*, I, i, 147.

91. Nicholas Vansittart, first Baron Bexley (1766–1851), as chancellor of the exchequer is held responsible for the heavy taxation. More specifically, Reynolds seems to refer to the fact that in 1820 an earlier reduction in taxes "was disallowed for gold rings and gold articles not exceeding 2 oz. in weight" (Stephen Dowell, *A History of Taxation and Taxes in England*, London, 1888, IV, 371).

92. Latimer declared the devil to be the most diligent bishop: "ye shal neuer fynde hym idle" (*Sermon on the Ploughers*, ed. Edward Arber, English Reprints, nos. 1–7, London, 1868, p. 30).

93. Lancelot Andrewes (1555–1626), *Ninety-six Sermons* (1628).

94. In Goldsmith's *Vicar of Wakefield* (1766).

95. Sir James Thornhill (1676–1734). The paintings at Greenwich Hospital, on which he worked for twenty years, are his best-known productions.

96. Peter Grimes in George Crabbe's *The Borough*, Letter XXII (1810), *The Poetical Works of George Crabbe*, edd. A. J. and R. M. Carlyle (London, 1914), pp. 196–200, is a fisherman and thief who drives three orphan apprentices to their deaths and then, ostracized by the villagers, sits gazing out over the water hour after hour.

97. Sheridan, *The Critic* (1779), III, i.

98. Reynolds had described this in "Warwick Castle," *The London Magazine*, 4 (July 1821), not reprinted in this selection.

99. *The Lover*, no. 33, May 11, 1714, reprinted in *The Lover and Other Papers of Steele and Addison*, ed. Walter Lewin, in the Camelot Series (New York, 1887), pp. 155, 157–158. Reynolds quoted from an edition different from the one on which this text was based. In addition to modernization of capitalization and spelling, Reynolds' quotation shows verbal differences. For example, Reynolds' "the great eclipse of the sun that *happened* in April, 1715" differs from the cited text's "the great Eclipse of the Sun that *will happen* on April 1715" (italics supplied). That change in tense sent the present editor on a long and fruitless search of Steele's publications *after* 1715.

100. Edward Dorrington, *The Adventures of Philip Quarll* (1727), a story of a pseudo–Robinson Crusoe.

101. George Spearing, *A Wonderful Account of Mr. G. Spearing a Lieutenant in the Navy, Who Fell into a Coal Pit in Northwoodside, Near Glasgow* (?1810).

102. This unsigned article is attributed to Reynolds because of his own handwritten initials after it in the marked file in the Keats Memorial House at Hampstead. This one *London* dramatic review reprinted in this selection should not be regarded as typical of the dozens of theatrical articles which Reynolds wrote for the magazine; it has been chosen because it is clearly the best of the lot. Unlike his inclination in *The Champion* to stress literary criticism of the earlier drama, his inclination in *The London* was usually to stress the acting and the affairs of the theaters or to criticize ephemeral contemporary plays.

103. *Il Penseroso*, ll. 83–84.

104. The passages are from *A Midsummer Night's Dream*, II, i, 89–92, 96–111.

105. The actor was probably William Dowton (1764–1861). At the time some of the most successful performers were receiving as much as twenty pounds a week.

106. Evidently an error for "taut-strung." Possibly Reynolds draws on his legal profession for a pun on "tort"; if so, it is a tortured one.

107. Adriaen van Ostade (?1610–1685) and Adriaen Brouwer (1605–1638).

108. Janus Weathercock was a pseudonym of Thomas Griffiths Wainewright (1794–1852), a regular contributor to *The London* who was later convicted of forgery and accused of poisoning his wife's sister. For Hazlitt's attack on Wainewright's vulgarity, see *Works of Hazlitt*, VIII, 160–161.

109. Junius Brutus Booth (1796–1852), whom Reynolds had accused of imitating Kean in 1817.

110. Amandus Gottfried Adolph Müllner (1774–1829). Reynolds has in mind the one play by Müllner translated into English at this time: *Guilt or the Gipsey's Prophecy*, trans. W. E. Frye (London, 1819).

111. In Nicholas Rowe's *Jane Shore* (1714).

112. August W. Schlegel, *A Course of Lectures on Dramatic Art and Literature*, trans. John Black (Philadelphia, 1833), p. 401.

113. Rowe adapted *The Fair Penitent* (1703) from *The Fatal Dowry* (1632), a joint production of Massinger and Nathaniel Field (1587–1633). Reynolds forgot that six years earlier he had reviewed a performance of it for *The Champion* of March 10, 1816.

114. Eleazer in *Lust's Dominion* (first printed in 1657), which in Reynolds' day was ascribed to Marlowe; Oedipus in the play of that title by Dryden and Nathaniel Lee (?1653–1692); and Alexander in Lee's *The Rival Queens* (1677).

115. *A Woman Killed with Kindness*, V, v. In Lamb's *Specimens of English Dramatic Poets Who Lived about the Time of Shakespeare* (London, 1854; first published 1808), pp. 93–100. Reynolds took the epithet "prose Shakespeare" from Lamb.

116. *Jane Shore*, V, i, 329–333, 336–347. The indication of ellipsis is misplaced; the omission of three lines is from "friend" to "look up."

117. Robert Dodsley, *A Select Collection of Old Plays* (1744). Isaac Reed later published an edition of Dodsley's *A Select Collection* with notes (1780).

118. Gifford edited *The Plays of Philip Massinger* (1805) and *The Works of Ben Jonson* (1816). Henry W. Weber (1783–1818) edited *Dramatic Works of John Ford* (1811) and *Works of Beaumont and Fletcher* (1812).

119. Frederic Reynolds (1764–1841).

472

120. Sir Epicure Mammon in Jonson's *The Alchemist*. The phrase does not appear exactly in the play. Reynolds' memory seems to have fused two lines: "We will be braue, *Puffe*, now we ha' the med'cine" (II, ii, 71) and "I am the lord of the *Philosophers stone*" (IV, i, 120).

121. *Antony and Cleopatra*, II, ii, 196–197.

122. *Ibid.*, II, ii, 206–210.

123. Sir Henry R. Bishop (1786–1855) composed the music.

124. *Two Gentlemen of Verona*, IV, ii, 54–62.

125. Although the concluding initials "E.H." stand for Edward Herbert, this article departs from the usual Edward Herbert pattern in that it is not epistolary and in the degree to which it is autobiographical. Drawing heavily upon his visit to Bradgate Park in the autumn of 1815, Reynolds writes anonymously of his own experiences and feelings. The final initials are the only suggestion of Edward Herbert.

126. The writer was Reynolds himself. He quotes from "Warwick Castle," *The London Magazine*, 4 (July 1821): 5, not reprinted in this selection.

127. Roger Ascham, *The Scholemaster*, English Reprints, no. 23, ed. Edward Arber (London, 1870), pp. 46–48. Later in the essay Reynolds quotes the entire passage from which this information is drawn.

128. Daniel Paterson (1738–1825), author of numerous travelers' guides, such as *A New and Accurate Description of All the Direct and Principal Cross Roads in England and Wales*, 13th ed. (London, 1803), *Paterson's Roads in Pocket Size* (London, 1804), and *A Travelling Dictionary* (London, 1797).

129. Shrewsbury.

130. Under one of these trees he wrote "Stanzas Composed under an Oak That Grows over a Brook in Bradgate Forest," *The Champion*, February 18, 1816.

131. John Nichols (1745–1826), *The History and Antiquities of the County of Leicester* (London, 1795–1815), vol. III, pt. 2, p. 680.

132. Dante, *Inferno*, XXIII, 61–63.

133. Usually spelled "poitrel," the breastplate of a horse.

134. Cf. *The Rime of the Ancient Mariner*, ll. 371–372: "That to the sleeping woods all night/ Singeth a quiet tune."

135. *Roderick, the Last of the Goths* (1814).

136. Scott's novel (1819).

137. Charles Fearne (1742–1794), *An Essay on the Learning of Contingent Remainders and Executory Devises* (1772).

138. In George Colman, the younger, *The Mountaineers* (1795).

139. In Otway's *Venice Preserved* (1682), as is Belvidera.

140. Sir Clowdisley Shovell (1650–1707). The *Dictionary of National Biography* says that the monument to him in Westminster Abbey is "in very questionable taste."

141. In "The History of the Young King of the Black Isles," the unfaithful queen bewitches her irate husband thus: "I command thee from this moment to become half marble and half man" (*The Arabian Nights Entertainments*, London, 1890, p. 44).

142. In the play (1803) by George Colman, the younger, Dan is a servant who dons attractive boots for a journey (IV, i).

143. Characters in Fielding's *Tom Thumb* (1730).

144. Monimia in Otway's *The Orphan* (1680), and Isabella in Thomas Southerne's (1659–1746) *The Fatal Marriage* (1694).

145. Title character in the play by James S. Knowles (1784–1862), for which Reynolds wrote the prologue.

146. In Scott's *The Lay of the Last Minstrel* (1805).

147. Title character in the opera (1730; first performed in England in 1782) by Metastasio or Pietro B. Trepassi (1698–1782).

148. Character in Isaac Bickerstaffe's *The Hypocrite* (1769).

149. Also in *The Hypocrite*.

150. In *Artaxerxes*.

151. Also in *Artaxerxes*.

152. In *The Hypocrite*.

153. Almost certainly the statement that the verses were received from the comic actor Harley is a fiction, and this poem, as well as the earlier sonnet "A Dream," is by Reynolds himself. After he met Hood, Reynolds wrote a large volume of comic doggerel in the same vein as "The Exhibition."

154. Exeter, where Reynolds married Eliza Powell Drewe on August 31, 1822.

155. Cf. *Romeo and Juliet*, II, ii, 12: "She speaks, yet she says nothing."

156. Title character in Benjamin Thompson's translation of Kotzebue's play (1798).

157. Cf. Coleridge, *Christabel*, l. 253: "A sight to dream of, not to tell!"

158. Cf. *Tristram Shandy*, bk. III, chap. 32: "you have little or no nose, Sir."

159. Amelia Alderson (Mrs. John) Opie (1769–1853) wrote *Tales of Real Life* (1813).

160. *Don Juan*, canto IV, stanza LXI, ll. 1–2.

161. Keats, "On the Sea," l. 10. Keats had included the poem in a letter to Reynolds, who was doubtless responsible for its publication in *The Champion*, August 17, 1817. It had not been published elsewhere when Reynolds wrote this article.

162. Cf. *Coriolanus*, IV, vi, 73–74: "He and Aufidius can no more atone,/ Than violentest contrariety."

163. Tate Wilkinson (1739–1803) was actor, manager of the York theater, and mimic, who was in turn mimicked by Charles Mathews in a performance co-authored by Reynolds, "The Youthful Days of Mr. Mathews" (first acted on March 11, 1822). The *Dictionary of National Biography* reports that Wilkinson had "a curious method of speech, jolting out, as from a bag, disconnected phrases."

164. Richard Preston (1768–1850), *An Essay in a Course of Lectures on Abstracts of Title* (1818).

165. A reference to Thomas Hood, whose pseudonym in *The London* was "Theodore M." Hood had been apprenticed to an engraver before he began work on *The London*, and he later exploited his talent with woodcuts in the *Comic Annual* and *Hood's Own*. Reynolds was properly modest about his own limited ability at sketching, which he later called "a very remote uneducated turn for sketching"—"Greenwich and Greenwich Men," *Bentley's Miscellany*, 7 (March 1840): 282.

166. Expounded in Joseph Lancaster's (1778–1838) *Improvements in Education* (1803). Reynolds indicates the basic principle of the system in the next sentence.

167. Edward Cocker (1631–1675) wrote *Tutor to Arithmetic* (1664) and other arithmetical works.

168. "Rare" indeed, the title is not listed in the *British Museum Catalogue*. But the volume included Charles Cotton's *Compleat Gamester* (1674), from which Reynolds' subsequent quotation and the poem by Wild were taken, and perhaps additional material—the game of brag mentioned by Reynolds is not included in *The Compleat Gamester*, though all the other games are.

169. Charles Cotton, *The Compleat Gamester* (1674), reprinted in *Games and Gamesters of the Restoration*, ed. Cyril H. Hartmann (London, 1930), pp. 101–102. Reynolds omits "secondly," "thirdly," and "fourthly" as the first words of his second, fourth, and fifth paragraphs.

170. Reynolds' extract is printed in *Games and Gamesters of the Restoration*, pp. 112–113.

171. Joys of contest.

172. A curious adaptation of a phrase from Keats's then unpublished *The Cap and Bells*, XXVIII, 1: "By thy ungallant bearing and sad mien."

173. This letter was misnumbered; the last one had been No. V. James Hessey was so uncertain about the advisability of printing in full the names of the authors satirized that he took a poll of a number of the contributors and reached his decision only after he found that the majority agreed with Reynolds that the names should be printed (Rollins, *The Keats Circle*, II, 431).

174. III, v. 49–56, 62–66.

175. See "To the Spade of a Friend" (1807). The friend was Thomas Wilkinson (fl. 1800–1825), a Quaker of Yanwath, near Penrith.

176. Bowles began his attacks in his edition of Pope in 1806.

177. The last sentence mocks the ridiculous vanity Bowles displayed in praising his own works, which is revealed most clearly in his letter to *The Champion* in 1816, reprinted above.

178. Mistakenly supposing Octavius G. Gilchrist (1779–1823) to be the author of an attack on him in a review of Spence's *Anecdotes* in *The Quarterly Review* of October 1820, Bowles replied in *The Pamphleteer*, vol. XVII. Gilchrist then attacked Bowles vigorously in *A Letter to the Rev. William Lisle Bowles* (Stamford, 1820), and the controversy was on in earnest. Perhaps the "ruffian" was Isaac D'Israeli (1766–1848), the real author of the review in *The Quarterly*.

179. Though "sixpence a day" is of course an exaggeration, it is not so ridiculously far off the mark as might be supposed. At this time Clare had received contributions which secured him forty-five pounds a year. The "ten little children all under the age of four" may be a questionable jest at the birth of Clare's first child one month after his marriage on March 16, 1820. Clare had only two children at the time.

180. His publishers, Longman, Hurst, Rees, Orme, and Brown. The book was *The Loves of the Angels*, which Reynolds reviewed unfavorably in the same issue of *The London*. For Reynolds' authorship of that review, see Rollins, *The Keats Circle*, II, 429.

181. Like Byron and others, Reynolds frequently charged Moore's amorous lyrics in *The Poetical Works of Thomas Little* (1801) with an immoral tendency.

182. Reynolds' chief argument in condemning *The Loves of the Angels* was that Moore had debased religious subject matter by mingling physical love with spiritual; he made much of the fact that one of Moore's female angels was "a fallen angel."

183. Moore translated *Odes of Anacreon* (1800).

184. Most of the joking turns upon Rogers' occupation, banking. He was best known for *The Pleasures of Memory*, but Reynolds may have known his authorship of the first section of his anonymous *Italy*, a collection of tales in verse which had been published recently (1822).

185. George Crabbe was parodied in James Smith's "The Theatre," *Rejected Addresses* (1812), reprinted in *A Century of Parody and Imitation*, edd. Walter Jerrold and R. M. Leonard (London, 1913), pp. 64–69. Crabbe's inability to swear to his hand-

writing refers to an anecdote recounted by Horace Smith in a footnote, according to which Crabbe failed to recognize a passage from his own poetry recited to him by Horace Smith (*ibid.*, p. 64).

186. Dead authors satirized in *Rejected Addresses* were "Anna Matilda" or Hannah Cowley (1743–1809), Dr. Samuel Johnson, and George Lillo (1693–1739).

187. William T. Fitzgerald (?1759–1829) was parodied in Horace Smith's "Loyal Effusion," *A Century of Parody*, pp. 1–7.

188. In 1822 Horace Smith set out to join Shelley in Italy, but when he heard of the poet's death, he remained at Paris for three years.

189. Unless it had some meaning which time has now obscured, the play on "confined" illustrates the kind of merely decorative pun which Lamb condemned as distracting. James Smith had no wife; he died a bachelor in 1839.

190. The playwright Thomas J. Dibdin (1771–1841) adapted several plays from novels and poems. His most recent adaptation had been *The Ruffian Boy* (1820) from a tale by Amelia Opie.

191. The Whig colors, buff and blue, are appropriately associated with Jeffrey and *The Edinburgh*.

192. The comparison with David alludes to Gifford's small stature; the sling to his lifelong poor health, which had become especially bad in 1822.

193. Undaunted by Byron's attack in the opening couplet of *English Bards and Scotch Reviewers*, Fitzgerald was ever ready to recite his own poetry on public occasions.

194. Pierre Bayle (1647–1706), author of *Dictionnaire Historique et Critique* (1697–1702). There were several English editions dating from 1710.

195. Byron's collection of pets at times made his quarters resemble a zoo.

196. Byron's *Heaven and Earth* had recently been published in *The Liberal* (1822).

197. Byron was nineteen when he wrote *English Bards and Scotch Reviewers*.

198. The modest items of the first sentence refer especially to the stark realism of *The Village* (1783), *The Parish Register* (1807), and *The Borough* (1810). The jokes of the last sentence allude to Crabbe's slight shift to grim comedy in parts of *Tales* (1812) and *Tales of the Hall* (1819).

199. Although Scott's authorship of the novels was generally known by this time, he had not yet acknowledged them publicly.

200. The most profitable of Longman's publications of Scott's poetry was *The Lay of the Last Minstrel* (1805). Reynolds also refers to Longman's publication of Moore's *The Loves of the Angels* (see note 180 above).

201. In the same February issue of *The London* containing "The Literary Police Office," Reynolds also reviewed unfavorably Sarah Siddons' *Abridgement of Paradise Lost for the Use of Young Persons*. For Reynolds' authorship of that review, see Rollins, *The Keats Circle*, II, 429.

202. Southey's most recent departure from conventional meter had been his attempt at classical hexameters in *A Vision of Judgment* (1821).

203. Southey wrote *Life of Nelson* (1813) and *Life of Wesley* (1820).

204. See Southey's apologia for the morality of his own works preceding the diatribe against the Satanic School in the Preface to *A Vision of Judgment* (1821).

205. When Reynolds wrote this article, he thought that Lamb had discontinued the Elia series. On the publication of *Elia—Essays That Have Appeared under That Signature in The London Magazine* at the opening of the year 1823, Lamb planned to cease contributing to *The London*. By March he had changed his mind (*The Life and*

FROM *THE LONDON MAGAZINE*

Works of Charles Lamb, ed. Alfred Ainger, London and Boston, 1888, I, 177–178). Both "Lion's Head" and "Janus Weathercock" had joked about Elia's death in the *London* of the preceding month.

206. Allan Cunningham (1784–1842), who was over six feet tall, fabricated much of the material which he submitted to R. H. Cromek for *Remains of Nithsdale and Galloway Song* (1810). Tom Cribb (1781–1848), a champion boxer, had retired in 1821. His first "act of kindness" was service as a guard at Westminster Hall during the coronation of George IV.

207. Barry Cornwall was the pseudonym of Bryan W. Procter (1787–1874), whose *Mirandola* was produced in 1821.

208. The Little-go, a private illegal lottery, was Campbell's *Specimens of the British Poets* (1819), which included some very obscure versifiers.

209. William R. Spencer (1769–1834) wrote numerous society verses.

210. Lord John Russell, first Earl Russell (1792–1878), published *Don Carlos, a Tragedy* (1822). The connection between Russell's play and Carlos, a minor character in Sheridan's *The Duenna* (1775) who is deceived along with his master Isaac, goes no further than the name.

211. Charles J. Gardiner, first Viscount Mountjoy and first Earl of Blessington (1783–1829), was no author; he appears only because of his wife's literary and social activities. In Maria Edgeworth's *The Absentee* (1812), Lord Colambre objects to the extravagance of his Irish parents who live in London. Reynolds' allusion to Lord Colambre in satirizing the lavish expenditure of Lady Blessington is not perfectly appropriate, since the Earl was as extravagant as his wife.

212. Marguerite, Countess of Blessington (1789–1849), had written *The Magic Lantern, or Sketches of Scenes in the Metropolis* (1822) and *Sketches and Fragments* (1822) by the time of this article. Eric Partridge, *A Dictionary of Slang and Unconventional English* (New York, 1961), explains "ready rhino" as money. On August 22, 1822, the Blessingtons started a continental tour which included the Rhine.

213. John Henry Manners, fifth Duke of Rutland (1778–1857), had by this time written four travel books, the most recent of which was *A Tour through Part of Belgium and the Rhenish Provinces* (1822). Of course his English and European travels were a far cry from the African explorations of Mungo Park (1771–1806).

214. Edward Thurlow, second Baron Thurlow (1781–1829), edited Sir Philip Sidney's *Defence of Poesy* (1812) and published numerous volumes of his own verse.

215. George Colman, the younger (1762–1836), wrote *The Law of Java*, performed at Covent Garden on April 11, 1822, which turns upon the fictitious custom that any condemned criminal who could survive the experience of fetching poison from the deadly Upas-Tree would be pardoned. Having long supposed that Colman had real dramatic talent, Reynolds thought that he was committing literary suicide with such trash.

216. Isaac D'Israeli (1766–1848), since young Benjamin had not yet published. But I have failed to discover what the "burglary" represents, unless it is somehow connected with D'Israeli's authorship of the review of Spence's *Anecdotes* in *The Quarterly Review* of October 1820, which initiated the Bowles controversy (see note 178 above).

217. Amelia A. (Mrs. John) Opie (1769–1853). I have not succeeded in identifying Mrs. Donatty, who does not seem to be a character in Mrs. Opie's fiction.

Essay from *The Westminster Review*

1. George L. Marsh proved Reynolds' authorship of this anonymous article in "Newly Identified Writings by John Hamilton Reynolds," *Keats–Shelley Journal*, 1 (January 1952): 54. Founded in 1824 and edited by John Bowring (whom Reynolds had doubtless known as a fellow contributor to *The London*), *The Westminster Review* was the organ of the Benthamites. Although Reynolds was always liberal in politics, and hence not unsympathetic to the general direction of the views expressed in the magazine, there is no evidence that he was ever a doctrinaire Utilitarian. For background on this one article which has been identified as Reynolds', see above, pages 17–18.

2. Wordsworth, *The Excursion*, IX, 151. Very probably Wordsworth adapted the phrase independently, rather than following Blake, from *Paradise Lost*, III, 44: "human face divine." It seems certain that Reynolds quoted Wordsworth rather than Blake, since he knew *The Excursion* well, and there is no other evidence that he ever read Blake.

3. Tom Crib (1781–1848), boxing champion.

4. For William Kitchiner (?1775–1827), see "The Cook's Oracle," reprinted above.

5. Richard Porson (1759–1808). Probably the patron was Samuel Rogers, who was proud of having entertained Porson, and whom we know Reynolds visited. See "Living Authors, A Dream," reprinted above.

6. The butterfly dances lazily on the banks of a brook. Then it darts and hovers over the water. The fish below the flowery banks, the lambs in the meadows, the shepherds, and the flocks, and even the little dogs dance. *The Dance.*

7. In Isaac Bickerstaffe's *The Hypocrite* (1769).

8. Edinburgh, 1812.

9. *The City of the Plague* (Edinburgh, 1816) included in addition to the title play, the shorter poem "The Children's Dance."

10. *The Children's Dance*, stanza 32.

11. Astley's Amphitheatre presented spectacles including numerous animals.

12. See the epigraph to *Peter Bell*, reprinted above.

13. Pages i–ii. Here and in later quotations Reynolds has altered the punctuation slightly and supplied the italics (a few exceptions where Thomas Wilson italicized will be noted specifically). The doggerel here, as well as that sprinkled through the later prose quotations, is by Thomas Wilson.

14. Pages vi–vii.

15. Thomas Wilson italicized only the words in the second line of the verse.

16. Page xix.

17. George Colman, the younger (1762–1836), *Sylvester Daggerwood* (1795), scene i, *The Dramatic Works of George Colman the Younger* (Paris, 1823), I, 221.

18. Pages 1–2. The italics are Thomas Wilson's.

19. Page 7.

20. Page 8. These italics are Thomas Wilson's, who explains that the italicized words are quoted from false advertisements.

21. Pages 10–11. The italics are Thomas Wilson's.

22. Pages 13–14.

23. Virgil, *Aeneid*, VII, 312: "If I am unable to change the minds of the gods above, I shall arouse the infernal region." Mrs. Olivia Serres (1772–1834) claimed to be the

daughter of Henry Frederick, Duke of Cumberland, brother of George III; placed the royal arms on her carriage; and dressed her servants in the royal livery. Although every court that ever examined her evidence denied her claim, she was able to persuade Sir Gerald Noel to petition the House of Commons in her behalf in March 1823.

24. Page 17.

25. Pages 42–43.

26. Stanzas 5, 8, and 9.

27. James Hogg (1770–1835), contributor to *Blackwood's* who figured prominently as a character in "Noctes Ambrosianae."

28. Cf. Molière, *Le Bourgeois Gentilhomme*, I, ii: "*Le Maître de Musique*—La philosophie est quelque chose; mais la musique, monsieur, la musique. *Le Maître a Danser*—La musique et la danse. La musique et la danse, c'est là tout ce qu'il faut."

29. Page 53.

30. Thomas Wilson explains in a footnote, which Reynolds omits for the sake of the joke on James Hogg, that Hogg and Co. was a cheap publisher who announced trashy books in a pompous fashion.

31. Pages 57–58. The italics in the stage directions are Thomas Wilson's.

32. Pages 61–62.

33. John Wilson, "The Children's Dance," stanza 33.

Essays and Reviews from *The Athenaeum*

1. Reynolds owned a part of *The Athenaeum* from 1828 until June 8, 1831, when he was unlucky enough to sell his share because of apprehensiveness at the drastic reduction in price effected by the editor, his old friend Charles Dilke. As the magazine prospered, undoubtedly much to Reynolds' dismay since his financial affairs were desperate at the time, he continued to contribute regularly. Many of his contributions, including this review, were marked in a special file kept by Dilke to record authorship. For a thorough study of the magazine, see Leslie A. Marchand, *The Athenaeum, a Mirror of Victorian Culture* (Chapel Hill, N.C. 1941).

2. Hazlitt had died three weeks earlier, on September 18, 1830. Northcote died in 1831.

3. As he did frequently throughout most of his work. Howe indexes a full page of references to Titian and a half page to Poussin.

4. Chiefly in "On Court Influence" (*Works of Hazlitt*, VII, 241), "My First Acquaintance with Poets" (XVII, 109–111), and "On a Sun-Dial" (XVII, 245).

5. Keats, *Endymion*, I, 239. Keats wrote "dreary."

6. Coleridge, *The Rime of the Ancient Mariner*, l. 624.

7. Hazlitt divorced Sarah Stoddart Hazlitt on July 17, 1822, married Mrs. Isabella Bridgwater probably in April 1824, and separated from his second wife in 1827.

8. The unhappy relationship with Sarah Walker from 1820 to 1822, the subject of *Liber Amoris* (1823).

9. The rest of the first installment of the review consists largely of extracts, with very meager commentary by Reynolds.

10. This limited defense of Haydon shows some impartiality on Reynolds' part, since the two had quarreled bitterly in December 1817, Reynolds had written Haydon

"one of the most cutting letters" that Keats had ever seen (*Letters of Keats*, I, 205), and Reynolds had not associated with him during the intervening twelve years (Haydon never mentions Reynolds in his journal after the quarrel).

11. These passages are taken from the second of three notices of the book, the first two of which are assigned to Reynolds in Dilke's marked copy. The other two installments consist almost entirely of extracts.

12. The *New English Dictionary* explains "Swing" as "Used . . . to designate a system of intimidation practised in agricultural districts of the South of England in 1830–1, consisting in sending to farmers and landowners threatening letters over the signature of a fictitious Captain Swing, followed by the incendiary destruction of their ricks and other property."

13. Byron's mother-in-law, Lady Judith Noel (1752–1822), who had earlier been Lady Milbanke.

14. This refers to Byron's praise of Reynolds' *Safie* (1814) in a letter which he later published in *The Athenaeum*, December 31, 1831, p. 841.

15. This passage clarifies Reynolds' earlier statement in *The Garden of Florence*, which might otherwise be easily misunderstood, that Keats "was of too sensitive a nature—and thus he was destroyed!" In accord with medical opinion of the time, Reynolds believed that Keats's sensitivity made him especially susceptible to consumption, but he did not say that Keats crumpled under the blows of the reviewers. Thus Reynolds disagrees with Shelley's and Brown's firm conviction that the reviews caused Keats's death and joins the large group of his friends who agreed that the reviews were not an important cause: Clarke, Severn, Bailey, Dilke, Stephens, and Mathew (see Rollins, *The Keats Circle*, II, 95–96).

16. Henry H. Milman (1791–1868) and George Croly (1780–1860).

17. Thomas Davison of Whitefriars, the printer.

18. Unfortunately Reynolds dropped the plan to continue with a second series of Edward Herbert letters after publishing this one article.

19. Cf. Keats, "Addressed to the Same [Haydon]," ll. 9–10: "standing apart/ Upon the forehead of the age to come." Reynolds might also have used quotation marks for "Great spirits," the words with which the sonnet begins.

20. *Comus*, ll. 477–480.

21. Ignorance of all the circumstances caused Reynolds, along with most of his contemporaries, to blame Moore unfairly for the burning of Byron's memoirs on May 17, 1824 (Leslie A. Marchand, *Byron, a Biography*, New York, 1957, III, 1249–1250).

22. To perpetuate his name, Herostratos burned the temple to Diana at Ephesus, one of the Seven Wonders of the World.

23. Scott left Portsmouth on October 25, 1831, and arrived at Naples a week before Christmas. He worked a little on *The Siege of Malta* while in Italy, but more to keep himself occupied than because of pressure from others.

24. Letitia Elizabeth Landon (1802–1838) had published five books of poems and abundant magazine verse by this time.

25. Thomas Percy, *Reliques of Ancient English Poetry* (Philadelphia, 1823), III, 226, l. 128.

26. Cf. Richard Cumberland, *Wheel of Fortune* (1779), III, iii: "Heaven grant it may be the last."

27. John Martin's (1789–1854) *Belshazzar's Feast* (1821) is generally considered his finest work.

28. John Debrett (d. 1822) published so many editions of *Peerage of England, Scotland, and Wales* that his name came to represent that type of work.

29. Bob Booty is an alias of Robin O'Bagshot in *The Beggar's Opera*, scenes iii and iv.

30. An eighteenth century criminal.

31. Clause Patch (d. 1730), king of the beggars, was succeeded by Bamfylde Moore Carew.

32. He succeeded Thomas Campbell as editor in 1831.

33. Caroline E. S. Norton (1808–1877), daughter of Thomas Sheridan and grand-daughter of Richard B. Sheridan, was best known at this time for *The Sorrows of Rosalie, a Tale, with Other Poems* (1829), though she also contributed frequently to periodicals. Colburn's publishing firm was located in Burlington Street.

34. Felicia D. Browne Hemans' (1793–1835) *Forest Sanctuary* (1825) achieved a second edition in 1829. Another recent volume was *Songs of the Affections* (1830).

35. Cf. Smollett, *Humphry Clinker*, letter of Tabitha Bramble dated April 2: "I hope you'll have a watchful eye over the maids."

36. Richard Cumberland, *Wheel of Fortune* (1779), III, iii.

37. *The Athenaeum*. On June 8, 1831, Reynolds had sold his share of the magazine in protest at Charles Dilke's reduction of the price from eightpence to fourpence (see Charles Wentworth Dilke, *The Papers of a Critic*, selected by his grandson, Sir Charles Wentworth Dilke, London, 1875, I, 25–26).

Essay from *The New Sporting Magazine*

1. This anonymous essay is here attributed to Reynolds for the first time by a combination of external and internal evidence. He edited the magazine at the time; his service as editor lasted from about August 1838 to December 1840—Peter F. Morgan, "John Hamilton Reynolds and Thomas Hood," *Keats–Shelley Journal*, 11 (Winter 1962): 92–93. As editor, he contributed considerable anonymous material: "Turfiana, No. II," *New Sporting*, 16 (February 1839): 132–140; "Turfiana, No. III," 16 (April 1839): 253–265; "Turfiana, No. IV," 17 (September 1839): 196–200; and "Turfiana, No. V," 18 (February 1840): 127–130. The entire series is clearly by the same hand; No. I was published several years before he became editor, in 6 (January 1834): 153–160. Such limited external evidence merely offers the strong possibility that an editor who is known to have written much of the other anonymous material may have written the article in question. But that possibility can be confirmed by the appearance in the article of a very unusual quotation, a phrase which, to the best of my knowledge, no one besides Reynolds has ever quoted (as checks, I have consulted Howe's index of Hazlitt's quotations, and I have recently given myself the pleasure of rereading Lamb). The quotation, which appears in the passage printed in this book, is "violentest contrarieties." Cf. *Coriolanus*, IV, vi, 73–74: "He and Aufidius can no more atone,/ Than violentest contrariety." In "The First Part of Henry the Fourth.— Mr. Stephen Kemble as Falstaff," *The Champion*, October 13, 1816, p. 325, Reynolds had included the adapted quotation: "They can no more atone,/ Than violentest contrariety." In "The Cockpit Royal," *The London Magazine*, 6 (November 1822): 392, he had adapted it to "in violentest contrarieties." It is significant that in both *The London* and *New Sporting* the nouns are adapted from singular to plural to suit the

author's purpose. The quotation is so brief and so unusual as to allow the conclusion that it was eccentrically Reynolds', and Reynolds' alone.

2. *A Midsummer Night's Dream*, III, i, 30–34.

3. Cf. Thomas Holcroft, *The Road to Ruin* (1792), II, ii: "He would not leave the court for a thousand pounds."

4. Reynolds alludes to the many amazing pedestrian feats of Robert Barclay Allardice (1779–1854), generally known as Captain Barclay. His father had taken his wife's name, Allardice, as a condition of the marriage.

5. Andrew Ducrow (1793–1842), equestrian performer at Astley's Amphitheatre, where Van Amburgh's lion-taming act was performed.

6. The "other" gentleman was clearly Charles Cowden Clarke, whose advancement of "valuable literature" was the publication of *Tales from Chaucer* (1833) and *Riches of Chaucer* (1835), as well as his lectures on literature beginning in 1834, and whose advancement of "cheap" literature was the publication of *Adam the Gardener* (1834) and his editing of Nyren's *Young Cricketer's Tutor* (1833). If Reynolds means precisely what he says, the "intimately" known gentleman was Charles Dilke, the only one of Keats's personal friends with whom Reynolds was still intimate in 1838. Because of a peculiar twist at the end of the anecdote, however, I suspect that "We intimately know a gentleman" was simply a disguise and that the first gentleman was Reynolds himself. The rambling correction of himself involved in "for on reaching the farm-house, or a man from it" suggests a man's relating a story which he recalls distantly from firsthand experience.

The incident could not have occurred before the autumn of 1816, when Reynolds first met Keats (Dilke first met Keats through Reynolds at some time in 1817). And it probably did not occur later than December 1818, after which time Clarke saw Keats rarely, if ever.

INDEX

484